*Grand Opera*

*The publisher gratefully acknowledges the generous support of the Ahmanson Foundation Humanities Endowment Fund of the University of California Press Foundation.*

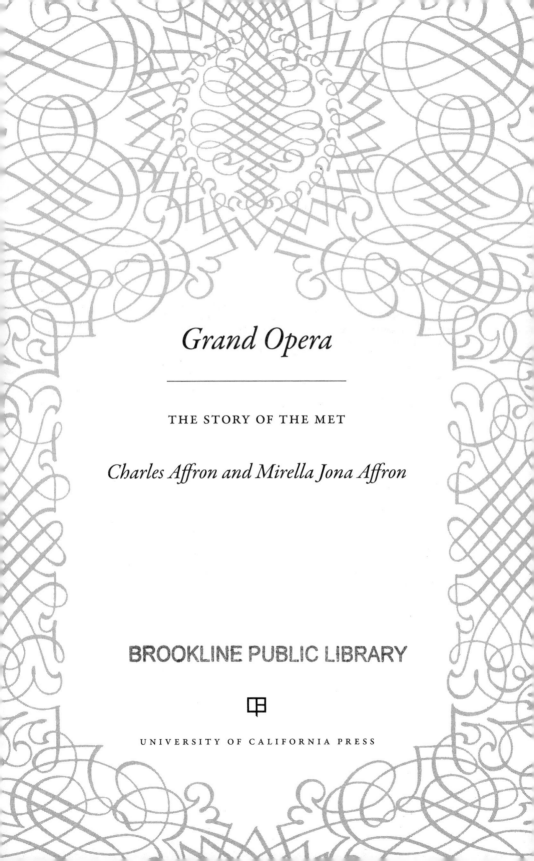

# Grand Opera

## THE STORY OF THE MET

*Charles Affron and Mirella Jona Affron*

UNIVERSITY OF CALIFORNIA PRESS

University of California Press, one of the most distinguished university presses in the United States, enriches lives around the world by advancing scholarship in the humanities, social sciences, and natural sciences. Its activities are supported by the UC Press Foundation and by philanthropic contributions from individuals and institutions. For more information, visit www.ucpress.edu.

University of California Press
Oakland, California

Library of Congress Cataloging-in-Publication Data

Affron, Charles, author.
   Grand opera : the story of the Met / Charles Affron and Mirella Jona Affron.
      pages   cm
   Includes bibliographical references and index.
   ISBN 978-0-520-25033-8 (cloth : alk. paper) — ISBN 978-0-520-95897-5 (ebook)
   1. Metropolitan Opera (New York, N.Y.)—History. I. Affron, Mirella Jona, 1937– author. II. Title.
   ML1711.8.N3M384   2014
   792.509747'1—dc23

                                        2014015091

Manufactured in the United States of America

23  22  21  20  19  18  17  16  15
10  9  8  7  6  5  4  3

In keeping with a commitment to support environmentally responsible and sustainable printing practices, UC Press has printed this book on Natures Natural, a fiber that contains 30% post-consumer waste and meets the minimum requirements of ANSI/NISO Z39.48–1992 (R 1997) (Permanence of Paper).

In memoriam
George Custen, Elliot Rubinstein, and Gloria Vilardell,
*fedeli amici nostri*

# CONTENTS

# ILLUSTRATIONS

## FIGURES

TABLES

# PREFACE

Three decades have passed since Martin Mayer recalled the response of Oscar Hammerstein I to a casual, "How's business?" "Opera's no business," Hammerstein shot back. "It's a disease." His quip resonated with Mayer, as it does with us and, we suspect, with many of our readers. Mayer's *The Met* (1983) is the most recent comprehensive history of the company prior to this volume. And like *Grand Opera: The Story of the Met,* it is both an institutional and performance history of the premier opera company in the United States, one of the world's most prestigious and influential cultural organizations. Thirty years and a changed universe later, an updated reconsideration is due.

Each of our eleven chronologically sequenced chapters focuses on an area of the repertoire: a national canon (French opera, for example, as in chapter 2) or a composer, (for example, Giacomo Puccini, the central figure of chapter 4). The history of the company is in large part the history of the fortunes of bel canto and verismo, of Verdi and Wagner, and eventually of Adams and Glass. We trace the evolving profile of the repertoire as it responds to the push of reinvention and the pull of tradition, as it conforms to the talents of the stars, the interests of the board and of the management, the will of conductors, the taste of the critics, the predilections of the public. Through 1949–50, we are concerned primarily with premieres; to that point, new productions of revivals were generally staged as they had always been, simple refittings with fresh scenery and costumes. Beginning in 1950 with the advent of Rudolf Bing, and the attention he gave to direction and design, we take note of many revivals as well.

And each chapter engages numerous remarkable performances in the context of the issues that informed the times. The inaugural 1883 *Faust* affirmed the compatibility of an aristocratic European entertainment with the temper of the still young New World republic. In 1907, the Met's first performance of *Salome* erupted into a scandal that pitted the board of directors against the management; Richard Strauss's opera spent the next twenty-seven years in exile from the Met. The 1910 world premiere of Puccini's *La Fanciulla del West* was a vehicle for Enrico Caruso whose fame in live performance ballooned through the diffusion of opera via the phonograph at the dawn of sound reproduction. The very survival of the Metropolitan during the Great Depression depended in large measure on the Tristan and Isolde of Lauritz Melchior and Kirsten Flagstad, the two mighty pillars of a brilliant Wagnerian epoch. Bruno Walter's Met conducting debut in *Fidelio,* less than a year before the US entry into World War II, speaks to the myriad positive and negative consequences of international conflict on an international company. In 1966, the choice of Leontyne Price to head the cast of Samuel Barber's *Antony and Cleopatra* as it opened the new house at Lincoln Center joined the politics of labor and race relations to the politics of opera as an American idiom. With John Dexter's mise-en-scène for Francis Poulenc's *Dialogues des Carmélites* in 1977, the Met sought to address its straitened budget while embracing cutting-edge stage practice. The 2002 company premiere of Sergei Prokofiev's *War and Peace* kept the promise that perestroika would bring a notable expansion of the Slavic wing of the repertoire together with an influx of East European artists. The clamorous success of Peter Gelb's ongoing initiative that between 2006–07 and 2012–13 beamed Robert Lepage's contested "Ring" and more than sixty other Metropolitan productions onto screens that now number nearly two thousand drew millions of global spectators into animated debates over opera and its performance, staging in particular. However different the issues that pertained to the first *Faust* from those that surrounded the Barber premiere or the Wagner tetralogy, these extraordinary occasions, and so many others memorable and not, and invariably their reception, are products of multiple factors: the status of the work in the repertoire, the musical and dramatic values of the performance, the weight of institutional pressures, the broader political, social, and economic context. They call for the layered approach that underpins this history.

A word about our sources. The Metropolitan Opera Archives house a rich lode of primary documents that shed light on the 290 different operas that the company has presented in nearly twenty-eight thousand performances between 1883 and spring 2013. The decisions that shape seasons and careers emerge in the day-to-day memoranda and correspondence of the board and its committees, of the general managers and their assistants, of artists and agents, in minutes of meetings, in contracts and paybooks, in box-office records, in audition notes. We have made extensive use of the archives through the 2005–06 season, Joseph Volpe's last, and the last for which documents have been accessible to us. All primary sources we cite without attribution are holdings of the Met Archives.

Along with Mayer's *The Met,* we draw upon Henry Krehbiel's two-volume chronicle, *Chapters of Opera* (1908) and *More Chapters of Opera* (1919), erudite and eloquent firsthand recitals of Met premieres and of the singers of the Golden Age. Irving Kolodin's *The Metropolitan Opera, 1883–1966* (1966) is the last of the author's several editions (1936, 1940, 1953). Kolodin takes into account shifts in the relationship of the company to its patrons and organizational restructurings. He also makes note of every premiere, revival, new production, debut, and cast change. We have chosen instead to provide tables that constitute an inventory of all the operas produced by the company. These tables record the name of the composer, the date of the company premiere, the date of the most recent performance as of this writing, the number of seasons in the repertoire, the number of productions and performances, the date and place of the world premiere, and the names of the director and designer. Titles that made negligible impressions may be referenced only in these tables. Two other histories timed to coincide with the close of the Old Met, Quaintance Eaton's *The Miracle of the Met* (1968) and John Briggs's *Requiem for a Yellow Brick Brewery* (1969), are less systematic, more anecdotal than Kolodin's. John Dizikes's *Opera in America* (1993) locates the Met within the orbit defined in its title. Johanna Fiedler's *Molto Agitato* (2001) is a spirited survey centered on the 1980s and 1990s, when the author was the company's general press representative. *Saturday Afternoons at the Old Met* (1992), *Sign-Off for the Old Met* (1997), and *Start-Up at the New Met* (2006), Paul Jackson's three-volume history and analysis of Metropolitan broadcasts, have been a valued companion to our own listening.

Well before 1883, New York's music journalism was a going concern. The city's numerous dailies, the *Times,* the *Tribune,* the *Herald,* along with the *World,* the *Sun,* the *Evening Post,* the *Morning Journal,* the *Commercial Advertiser,* the *Mail and Express,* the *Evening Telegram,* and the German-language *Staats-Zeitung,* routinely devoted many inches to opera. New works earned the lengthiest columns: the 1883 *La Gioconda* racked up an astonishing three thousand words in the *New York Times.* Such extensive coverage continued through the 1930s. Singing, acting, playing, and dramaturgy came under expert, detailed scrutiny, not infrequently laced with vitriol. Today, for a Met premiere, the *Times* rations its music critics to half the ink allotted to their predecessors seventy-five years ago. Many dailies and weeklies have ceased publication altogether, and of those that remain, pitifully few have a regular opera beat. We have turned principally to the *Times,* the *New Yorker,* the *Wall Street Journal,* and to the out-of-town press, the *Washington Post, Christian Science Monitor,* and *Philadelphia Inquirer.* Until the 1950s, reviews appeared on the day following the performance, since then on the day after that; we date only the exceptions to this rule. After 1950, we add our voices to published accounts of live performances. Mindful of the balance between the register of the historian and that of the critic, we lodge our views, whenever possible, among those of a sampling of the musical press.

*Grand Opera* is the first history of the Metropolitan to exploit the audio, visual, and Internet technologies that have lengthened the reach of opera studies. We are especially indebted to the Metopera database at www .metoperafamily.org, the company's online portal that opens onto the casts of all Met performances, the careers of artists, a wealth of photographs, reviews, essays, and other materials. We have also relied on audio resources, commercial recordings of singers from the early periods, transcriptions of Met broadcasts from the mid-1930s on, and videos of Met performances since 1977. Unattributed evaluations of recordings, broadcasts, and videos are ours. We urge readers to make their own judgments by tuning into "Met on Demand" and SiriusXM. "Met on Demand" is a vast online subscription library of audio and video transcriptions of performances from the late 1930s to the present; SiriusXM is a satellite radio station that broadcasts historic performances along with live transmissions. Artists active since the beginning of the twentieth century, and a handful even before, can also be heard on "Sounds of the Met," accessed through the Metopera database, as well as on www.archive.org and www.youtube.com. "National Jukebox," on the Library of Congress website www.loc.gov, makes available recordings that predate 1926. The "Un bel dì" of Farrar and Destinn, Rethberg and Albanese, de los Angeles, Tebaldi, and Racette are just a few clicks away.

# ACKNOWLEDGMENTS

We acknowledge with gratitude our debt to Mary C. Francis, executive editor at University of California Press, for taking on our project and providing informed counsel and friendly support all along the way. We are also grateful to our agent, Ellen Geiger, vice-president at the Frances Goldin Literary Agency, who arranged the happy encounter between us and Mary.

A special thank you is due the Metropolitan Opera Archives. Its resources were indispensable to our research. That the Archives are a model repository of print and visual documents is, in large measure, a testament to the stewardship of Robert Tuggle. Bob has been a remarkable fount of knowledge and encouragement. Archivist John Pennino's deep acquaintance with the company's history has been critical to the search for pertinent documents. We also thank Met archivists Jeff McMillan and John Tomasicchio. Other archivists and librarians have facilitated our work: Alexa B. Antopol, Reference and Research Librarian, *Opera America;* Wilma Jones, Chief Librarian, College of Staten Island-CUNY; Devin Nix, Academic Technology Specialist, NYU Digital Studio; Jane L. Poole, Metropolitan Opera Guild.

We are especially beholden to friends who gave so generously of their time to read our manuscript and offered invaluable suggestions for its improvement: Rachel Brownstein, Phebe Chao, Miguel Lerin, Bridget Lyons, Robert Lyons, Stephen J. Mudge, Daniel Schlosky, Roger Sorkin. Beatrice Jona Affron lent her expertise in matters of musicology. Si Affron, Zoë Affron, and Miranda Scripp assisted in the preparation of the manuscript. Ralph Tarica and Suzanne Tarica supplied translations from German. Elaine Bowden, David Dik, Russell Frost, Bob Madison, and David Podell were forthcoming with aid and advice. The Metropolitan Opera Press Office made press passes available; Brent Ness of the Press Office cleared permissions for the illustrations of chapter 11.

Finally, we wish to remember here those who have been part of our opera-going over the years. They have shared our enthusiasm and engaged with us in debates that often continued long into the night: John Albert, Cecilia Bartoli, Jacqueline Carter, Olivier Ferrer, John Haskell, Claudia Lindsey, Allan Novick, Tamar Schneider, François Scott, Michel Slama, Elizabeth Seder, Gilles Venhard.

*Cragsmoor and New York City, November 12, 2013*

# A Matter of Boxes, 1883–1884

## BEL CANTO

### FIRST NIGHT

THE CONFUSION OUTSIDE THE NEW OPERA HOUSE on opening night October 22, 1883, and the commotion within, delayed the prelude to Charles Gounod's *Faust*. As one wag put it, no one seemed to mind except "a few ultra musical people in the gallery." On the sidewalk out front, scalpers hawked parquet seats at $12 and $15 each and places in the balcony at $8. Overeager takers apparently failed to notice that as late as 7:30, $5 balcony tickets were still on sale at the box office. "It comes high but we must have it," read the caption under *Puck*'s lampoon of the rush for pricey tickets. Ushers in evening dress escorted patrons to their seats. The three tiers of boxes and the parquet were filled, the balcony nearly sold out. Only the $3-a-pop uppermost section, the "family circle," so renamed to repel roués accustomed to calling it their turf, showed empty seats. When the prelude was over and the curtain rose on the old philosopher's study, the audience finally fell silent.[1]

Before the show was over, the most affluent, the least, and all those in between had cause for complaint. The carriage trade had had to cope with long lines at the three entrances, north on 40th Street, east on Broadway, south on 39th. Many of their seats, despite prime locations, had poor sight lines and equally dismal acoustics. Nonetheless, seventy boxes offered what a set of prominent New Yorkers had demanded and ultimately resorted to buying for themselves: a house that would accommodate the spectacle of their power and riches. The press paid particular attention to the movements of William Henry Vanderbilt, whose two boxes held, among other distinguished guests, the Lord Chief Justice of England. In the course of the evening, Vanderbilt sat by turn in each of his boxes and was seen stopping in at those of friends and relations. His valet was posted at the door to pass on the calling cards of visitors—unfailingly male, women rarely left their seats—who sought an audience with the son of the Commodore. The cumulative wealth of the several Vanderbilts and of the others of their crowd was estimated at upward of $500 million.[2]

The building's design guarded class distinctions most jealously through a feature modeled on European examples: a staircase at street level that segregated the upper galleries from the select precincts of the house, barring holders of cheap tickets from mingling with their betters below. In the family circle, the stage was visible only to those willing to crane their necks. And to these least privileged patrons, the high notes alone were audible. From the overheated rear of the balcony, one tier closer to the stage, the single "animated thing visible to the occupants of a seat was the expanse of [conductor] Signor [Auguste] Vianesi's cranium. At first the audience knit their brows and cocked their heads, and there was a disposition to lay the blame upon their own ears, which many imagined had suddenly become defective, but during the entr'acte, on comparing notes, it was discovered that persons in each of the various tiers and in all parts of the house—near as well as at a distance from the stage—experienced the same inability to catch the notes of the artists clearly" *(Times)*.[3]

Vanderbilt made show of his satisfaction with the occasion: "[He] loomed up against a pallid background and appeared to enjoy the music, though his soul, probably, was filled with a different sort of harmony." Savvy subscribers would have picked up *Life*'s wink at the widely circulating story of the birth of the Metropolitan. They would have translated "a different sort of harmony" as the particular gratification the glittering evening promised Vanderbilt, erasing as it did the slight to his name suffered three years earlier when his wife was denied a box at the Academy of Music, since 1854 the dominant venue for opera in New York. His offer of $30,000 had been turned down; there were no suitable boxes to be had. Overflowing the already full Vanderbilt cup may have also been the memory of the ball seven months earlier at which Knickerbocker society, "the Nobs" or "the Old Families," turned out in numbers at the invitation of his daughter-in-law, Alva. That night had trumpeted the acceptance by the Colonial and Revolutionary gentry of the far wealthier parvenus, "the Tens" (the upper ten thousand fashionable nouveaux riches) or "the Newcomers," moneyed during and after the Civil War. The process had taken four decades.[4]

The Academy of Music at 14th Street between Third Avenue and Irving Place was a sufficient home for opera. Its resident impresario, James H. Mapleson, or better, Colonel Mapleson, as he liked to be called, delivered the stars his patrons considered their due. But as the city's upper crust grew in size and, more to the point, in financial clout, it became apparent that the Academy was saddled with a fatal flaw: its too few boxes could not accommodate New York's growing elites. And further, on those rare occasions on which a box became available, it went to a member of the tight Knickerbocker circle and not to one of "the Newcomers." Approached by George Henry Warren, a Vanderbilt lawyer, for a way out of the impasse, leading Academy stockholders offered to increase the number of boxes from eighteen to forty-four, a supply still substantially short of the demand. Worse, the twenty-six additions would not necessarily be in the coveted proscenium. The occupants would be less advantageously exhibited than they thought befit their station. And so the proposed remodeling was rejected and the campaign for a new opera house was on. Within days, Warren had secured the required capital through sixty-two subscriptions. The central committee of the infant Metropolitan Opera Company met on April 10, 1880, and agreed to move forward with the project, later recapitalized by the Vanderbilts, the Morgans, the Roosevelts, and others. There were bumps in the road: negotiations for a site on 43rd Street and Madison Avenue fell through; at a later point, the anticipated costs had so escalated that there was pressure to abandon the undertaking altogether. In the end, will and fortune prevailed and, amazingly, in just two and a half years, between the March 1881 acquisition of the 39th Street block and the October 1883 opening, construction was completed, the boxes (ultimately tagged at $15,000 each) were assigned by lot, an impresario was hired, and the inaugural season launched.

## HOUSE

As they stepped out of their carriages, some among the box holders may have had buyer's remorse. The new edifice looked nothing like the stupendous Paris theater dedicated just eight years earlier, an obligatory stop on the grand tour. The Opéra, standing proudly on a pedestal above the pavement, its broad staircase leading to the seven portals of the sumptuously adorned neo-Baroque

FIGURE 1. Exterior of Metropolitan Opera House, Broadway and 39th Street, 1883 (courtesy Metropolitan Opera Archives)

façade crowned with gilded statues, was the focal point of the principal thoroughfare that bore its name. The exterior of the Metropolitan, in the moderate Renaissance style, aspired to no such magnificence. J. Cleveland Cady and his colleagues, architects of the still extant Romanesque revival southern wing of New York's American Museum of Natural History, avoided flights of fancy for this, their first theater commission. Their chief concern was that the most capacious auditorium for opera in the world meet the expectations for display, comfort, and safety of its prosperous patrons. And to these desiderata, they bent whatever largesse the budget allowed. The snide sobriquet of "yellow brick brewery" attributed to Mapleson stuck. Others disagreed, finding the "elegance" of the new building admirable: "Architecturally it is a fine creation, imposing not alone by its size but by its dignity, simplicity, and intelligent adaptation to its ends. And if on the exterior we miss the grandeur and beauty which must belong to a building ere it can be called truly monumental, we have a scholarly, quiet, eminently respectable piece of work."[5]

The five-hour-long *Faust* allowed first-nighters a leisurely look at the theater's interior. They found not the traditional stage frame capped by an arch but

FIGURE 2. Interior of Metropolitan Opera House, 1895. This is the oldest extant photograph of the auditorium. (courtesy Metropolitan Opera Archives)

a nearly square opening, likely inspired by Wagner's dictates for his 1876 opera house in Bayreuth. The decision to forgo proscenium boxes obviated the difficulty that had precipitated the break with the Academy. The stockholders occupied the first and second of the three tiers, grouped as "a republic of oligarchs with no precedence among themselves, nodding on equal terms all round Olympus." With the parquet orchestra floor and the two upper galleries, the capacity of the Met exceeded three thousand. Critics grumbled that the cramped staircases, corridors, and lobbies were inadequate to assembly, let alone parade, during the long intermissions. Public spaces had been sacrificed to the volume of the hall. The color scheme that provided the "pallid background" for Mr. Vanderbilt's posturing met with scorn. The *Times,* ever attentive to the interests of ostentation, railed against what it judged an unbecoming contrast to "full dress"; the *Herald* lamented that the diamonds were deprived of "that flashing and blazing of rays that come from a darker setting." More generally, appreciations of the new Metropolitan ranged from the *Mirror*'s (Oct. 27) quip that "if Oscar Wilde had a nightmare in which an opera house played a conspicuous part we imagine it would appear to him as the Metropolitan did," to the encomium of the *Critic* (Oct. 27, 435): "one of the best-arranged places of amusement in the world." For the more than eight decades of the building's life, through the devastating fire of 1892 to the major reconstruction that followed, and subsequent modifications to the seating and décor, sight and sound at the Met continued to be hit or miss.[6]

*FAUST:* OCTOBER 22

The lease of the house to theatrical manager Henry E. Abbey came with the board's charge that he assemble a company for the Met's first season. Abbey's enviable client list included the actors Sarah Bernhardt, Edwin Booth, Henry Irving, and Lily Langtree. The "Italian" of his "Grand Italian Opera" meant that French and German works would be sung in Italian. That was no surprise. Years later, in evoking an 1870s *Faust* with Christine Nilsson at the Academy of Music, Edith Wharton took a jab at this practice: "An unalterable and unquestioned law of the musical world required that the German text of French operas sung by Swedish artists should be translated into Italian for the clearer understanding of English-speaking audiences." Abbey chose that same *Faust* and that same Marguerite for his opening fare. He had his conservative patrons in mind. No sooner had Gounod's original version of the work as an opéra comique, that is, with spoken dialogue, premiered in Paris in 1859 than it was on its way to the top of the operatic charts. At its 1863 landing in New York, *Faust* "leaped . . . into popularity. . . . All the leading *morceaux* were encored" (*Times,* Nov. 30). But unlike the performance retrieved in Wharton's *The Age of Innocence,* at the lackluster Met premiere, the principals were off their form: "Mme. Nilsson and Signor Campanini sang positively badly."[7]

New Yorkers had reason to expect better from stars they knew well. Nilsson and Campanini had been Mapleson singers; both had been seduced by Abbey's lucrative offers. Nilsson had made her US debut in 1870, soon after her Paris creation of Gounod's heroine in the grand opera version of *Faust,* through-composed, that is, without spoken dialogue, and with lengthy ballet. The high point of the Met opening was the interruption of the garden scene to mark Nilsson's proprietary relationship to the role. Presented with a sash of golden leaves in a velvet case, "first holding the box down so that the audience obtained a view of its contents, she placed it upon the chair in front of the casket, and kneeling repeated the [aria]" *(Times).* But for the reviewer, who took note of the soprano's wonted acting and musical expressivity, the

FIGURE 3. Christine Nilsson as Marguerite in *Faust,* 1883 (courtesy Photofest)

"Jewel Song" "was scarcely rendered with the requisite buoyancy and brilliancy." Campanini, arguably the world's leading tenor, had been Italy's first Lohengrin, London's first Don José, and New York's first Radamès. As Faust that night, his "old-time sweetness" was intermittent and his "old-time manly ring" suffered "the evidences of labor" *(Tribune).* In their subsequent appearances that season, separately and together, in *Lucia di Lammermoor, Lohengrin, Mignon, Don Giovanni,* and *Mefistofele,* reservations about Nilsson and Campanini vanished. Their initial reception might have been more sympathetic had the architects gotten their way in situating the orchestra. Borrowing again from Bayreuth, they had sunk the pit below the level of the parquet, though less deeply than the covered "mystic gulf" of the Festspielhaus. But Vianesi and his band objected to the near invisibility to which they had been relegated. The pit was raised, putting maestro and orchestra in full view, obstructing the stage picture for many seated in the parquet, and, of greater import still, undoing the balance of voices and instruments. The orchestra descended to the intended plane two weeks later, and there, with sporadic minor adjustments, it stayed.[8]

## *LUCIA DI LAMMERMOOR:* OCTOBER 24

When Gaetano Donizetti's *Lucia di Lammermoor,* as comfortably old-shoe as *Faust,* had its turn two days later, disquiet about the acoustics had subsided. The *Evening Post*'s Henry Finck conjectured that on the previous Monday the sound had been dampened by the mass of the near-capacity audience. The far smaller Wednesday crowd compensated for its poor size by its vociferous response to the twenty-five-year-old Polish soprano Marcella Sembrich in her New York debut. Notices pointed to her perfectly placed tone, to her "refinement of expression," and to a voice of great compass capable of both bel canto brilliance and "velvety softness" *(Tribune)*. Sembrich had learned from the disappointing *Faust* "to sing her arias as near the footlights as possible" *(Evening Post)*. The scenery was "admirable, the chorus resplendent in voice and real satin" *(Sun),* the "Sextet" and the "Mad Scene" were encored, and Campanini convinced his critics that "the greatest of living tenors retain[ed] his position at the front" *(Times)*. A mile or so south at the Academy, Sembrich's formidable competitor, Etelka Gerster, was cast as Gilda in *Rigoletto.* For the second time in three days, New Yorkers took up sides for either Mapleson or Abbey. They had had to choose between Gerster's Amina or Nilsson's Marguerite. Adelina Patti, the Academy's headliner, would enter the fray two weeks later. But for the *Times,* Sembrich had "nothing to fear from the few popular rivals she now has." One reviewer went so far as, "[her Violetta] surpasses [Patti's] in sympathy." In the age of Patti, there could be no higher praise. Soon after her debut, the company's first new diva remarked cheerfully, "I have sung never before such an empty house in my life. . . . Naturally, I am not known yet, or rather I was not known until last Wednesday" *(Times,* Oct. 28).[9]

Sembrich was the product of the pedagogy of bel canto, itself derived from the technique of seventeenth- and eighteenth-century virtuosi. Briefly put, bel canto is founded on the most rigorous command of the breath, indispensable to the accuracy of intonation and to the emission of equalized, linked tones from the bottom of the range to the top, whether singing piano (softly), singing forte (loudly), or executing the *messa di voce* (the swelling and diminishing of a note). The perfection of breath control is also essential to the free and even use of *fioritura* (embellishment): melismatic trills, turns, *appoggiature* (grace notes), scales, arpeggios, and other figures of the bel canto rhetoric. Well into the nineteenth century, all students of singing were expected to master the technique and its battery of florid ornaments. Later, the ornaments became the nearly exclusive property of the high soprano.

Following Lucia, Sembrich went on to play the other bel canto heroines of the 1883–84 season: Vincenzo Bellini's Elvira *(I Puritani)* and Amina *(La Sonnambula)*, and Giaochino Rossini's Rosina *(Il Barbiere di Siviglia)*. *Tribune* critic Henry Krehbiel leveled his sarcasm at the "lugubrious" *I Puritani,* charging it with "a simplicity that is almost amusing"; W. H. Henderson (of the *Times* from 1887 to 1902, then of the *Sun* until 1937) thought the soprano irreproachable and the orchestra and chorus in better form. The *Evening Post* extoled the principals of *La Sonnambula,* Campanini, who, in the space of a few days, sang a lyric Elvino and a heroic Lohengrin, and Sembrich, who lent the sleepwalker the "warm, emotional quality" of her voice, her bravura, her "artistic discrimination and taste." As for *Il Barbiere di Siviglia,* the *Times* opined that "without a great Rosina" it would be "simply unbearable," to us a startling appraisal. But then, the Met had a great Rosina. During the inaugural season, Sembrich applied her refined art to many other roles: Violetta, Gilda, Zerlina, Martha, Ophélie, Marguerite de Valois, and Juliette.

Sembrich returned to the company in 1898 after a hiatus of fifteen years. Some time later, thanks to the Met's librarian, Lionel Mapleson, her voice was captured live from the stage. Between January 1901 and March 1903, Mapleson, the Colonel's nephew, first placed his recording device, replete with horn, in the prompter's box, and then in the flies above the stage, an aerie that produced better results. His primitive equipment and makeshift conditions yielded transcriptions rich in the vibrancy of the event. The dim and scratchy sounds emitted by modern transfers of the Mapleson cylinders are the only echoes of "golden age" voices accompanied by full orchestra caught in the ambience of a large auditorium. In the case of two historic artists, Jean de Reszke and Milka Ternina, they are all we have. With Sembrich, we are more fortunate. Her very late commercial "Mad Scene" (1906) and "Sextet" (1908) bear traces of the impression she must have made in 1883. These acoustic records, though superior to Mapleson's, suffer the shortcomings of attempts to reproduce sound prior to the introduction of electrical processes in 1925. The limited range of frequency cuts the

FIGURE 4. Lionel Mapleson with recording horn and cylinders, c. 1901 (courtesy Metropolitan Opera Archives)

harmonics, impacting negatively on the body and resonance of the tone. Particularly affected were sopranos. But if the quality of Sembrich's timbre is compromised by crude technologies, her agility, range, and phrasing survive, and they are prodigious.[10]

Before making her farewell in 1909, Marcella Sembrich had appeared nearly five hundred times on 39th Street and on tour. Her final Met performance was a splashy exhibition of the range of her artistry: she topped off three acts from her favorite operas by interpolating two show pieces into the "Lesson Scene" of *Il Barbiere di Siviglia* and then accompanying herself at the piano in Chopin's "A Maiden's Wish." At her retirement banquet, Enrico Caruso, Geraldine Farrar, Antonio Scotti, Louise Homer, and others of the company sang the titles of many of the twenty-seven operas in her New York repertoire to the tune of "The Merry Widow" waltz, beginning, "Ri-go-le-to, Pu-ri-ta-ni, Hu-gue-nots." Henderson, who at the time of Sembrich's death in 1935 had heard everyone from Adelina Patti and Christine Nilsson to Rosa Ponselle and Kirsten Flagstad, wrote in memoriam, "this famous soprano was not only one of the greatest singers of her period, but of all lyric history."[11]

With the docking of Manuel Garcia's troupe on November 7, 1825, well over a half-century before the 1883 *Lucia,* Italian opera alighted in New York on the wings of Rossini. It was a time of high civic pride and optimism. Three days earlier, the arrival of the *Seneca Chief,* the first packet boat to make the trip from Buffalo to Albany through the newly completed Erie Canal and then down the Hudson, had been the occasion for a demonstration one hundred thousand strong, the largest yet seen in North America. The canal, waterway to the West, guaranteed the city's position as the country's manufacturing, commercial, and financial center. Ambitions to be its cultural capital too had begun to stir. Garcia, a Spanish tenor, composer, and impresario, launched his New World venture on November 29 in Park Row's Park Theatre with Rossini's *Il Barbiere di Siviglia.* His Rosina was his seventeen-year-old daughter, mezzo-soprano Maria Garcia, soon to be the legendary Maria Malibran. In attendance on that evening were personalities as disparate as Mozart's librettist Lorenzo Da Ponte, instrumental in bringing Garcia to New York; Napoleon's brother Joseph Bonaparte, for a time King of Naples and then of Spain, now a resident of New Jersey; and novelist James Fenimore Cooper, whose *The Last of the Mohicans* was soon to be published. Garcia himself sang Count Almaviva, the role he had created in Rome in 1816. During his one New York season, Garcia introduced the city to nine works, among them *Don Giovanni* and four more by Rossini.[12]

It would be another seven years before New York built a venue expressly for opera, and it would be twenty-two more and three tries before one such effort, the Academy of Music, would become firmly embedded on the city's cultural map. However different the three failed enterprises, they had in common the near monopoly of bel canto on their stages. The first, the Italian Opera House, owned and administered by a group of business and civic leaders, was another effort on Da Ponte's part to bring opera to his adopted country. From the time of Garcia's visit, Da Ponte had been a vigorous proponent of Italian music and letters, and professor of Italian literature at Columbia College, the first such position in the United States. The Italian Opera House (1833–1835), a small theater located at Leonard and Church streets, opened with Rossini's *La Gazza ladra.* Nine years later, Palmo's Opera House (1844–1847), also small, seating only eight hundred, opened on nearby Chambers Street. For a single season it was owned and operated by Ferdinand Palmo, a former restaurateur, who raised his first curtain on Bellini's *I*

*Puritani*. Bellini shared the season's bill evenly with his two bel canto competitors, Rossini, of course, and Donizetti. In contrast to the Italian Opera House and to its immediate successor, the Astor Place Opera House, Palmo's mission was to bring opera to the people at prices families could afford. But his target audience of immigrants had not swelled to numbers sufficient to support his intentions. For the next two years, a series of directors and companies made doomed attempts to rescue the project. As with the Italian Opera House, Palmo's small capacity and mediocre casts were the undoing of the balance sheet. On the heels of Palmo's demise came the Astor Place Opera House (1847–1852), administered, like the Italian Opera House, by wealthy patrons.

New York had taken sharp financial, social, and demographic turns between the passing of the Italian Opera House in 1835 and the christening of the opera house on Astor Place in 1847. The accompanying cultural turn was animated by the inauguration of steamship service between Bristol and New York in 1837; it had increased and quickened transatlantic itineraries for goods and persons, including singers and instrumentalists. The establishment of the Philharmonic Symphony Society of New York in 1842, still the oldest orchestra in the United States, had begun to shape the musical taste of the city's population. The new opera house had pursued the affluent to 8th Street and Broadway, a neighborhood undergoing upscale development. And although bel canto continued to hold sway over the repertoire, the opening night *Ernani* bore witness to the advance of Giuseppe Verdi. The problems of the eighteen-hundred-seat house were obvious from the beginning: disappointing subscription rolls and ticket sales, unexceptional casts. The fatal blow was the Astor Place riot of 1849, the bloodiest episode in New York theater history. On May 10, armed with stones, nativists in support of the American actor Edwin Forrest, who was playing Macbeth at the Bowery Theatre, laid siege to the theater on Astor Place, where the English actor Charles Macready was performing, he too as Macbeth. The militia, called to reinforce the police, fired into the crowd. Before it was over, the dead numbered around twenty-five—no one could say for sure. Tangential to opera, at least on the surface, the riot raged in front of the opulent edifice built by the establishment largely for its own gratification. More importantly for our discussion, the issues that provoked the carnage were also central to debates about the place of opera, if any, in the American democratic order. On one side stood the old guard, determined to defend the patrician signs of their European origins. On the other stood the nativists, joined by fiercely anti-English Irish immigrants for whom opera represented a foreign, aristocratic tradition incompatible with their republican slogans.[13]

It took three decades for Italian opera to plant lasting roots in New York, the span that separated Garcia's visit from the 1854 inception of the Academy of Music, the last of the Metropolitan's antecedents. In the interim, various incongruous factions were on the attack: "populists who disdained aristocratic pretense in Americans, intellectuals who mistrusted music's power over people, moralists for whom a foreign-language genre could not contribute to theatrical reform, romantic conservatives who wanted to hold onto the 'palmy days' of the legitimate stage, and self-proclaimed outsiders who disparaged the wealth and social prestige that attendance at the opera was seen to represent."[14]

Led by German-born banker August Belmont, the subscribers of the Academy of Music made an appeasing gesture in the direction of "populists" and "self-proclaimed outsiders" by attaching "academy" to the name of the impressive new building six blocks north of Astor Place, thereby underscoring the institution's didactic mission: the promotion of American composers, the training of American performers, and the musical education of the people. Moreover, the enormous initial capacity of the hall, pegged by the press at four thousand and greater (rebuilt after an 1866 fire, it shrank by more than half), was cited as prima facie evidence of the will to accommodate the vast spectatorship of the polis. But high-minded social purposes went largely ignored. Critics focused instead on the miserable sight lines, lighting, and ventilation; while the rich were framed to flattering effect by the extreme pitch of the tiers and the elegance of the setting, fully half the seats, primarily those at prices as low as $.25, offered scant, if any, visibility of the stage.[15]

On the Academy's first night, October 2, 1854, the New York debuts of two undisputed international stars, Giulia Grisi and Giovanni Mario, crowned what was already an event of significance to New York's standing. The three-month-long inaugural Grisi-Mario season began with *Norma* and continued with works by the bel canto composers exclusively. Grisi had created the role of Adalgisa in Bellini's opera, as well as those of Elvira in *I Puritani* and Norina in Donizetti's *Don Pasquale;* Mario was widely touted as the greatest tenor of his generation. The magical resonance of their names is captured by Henry James who, as a boy, lived with his family a stone's throw from the nascent Academy: "when our air thrilled, in the sense that our attentive parents reechoed, with the visit of the great Grisi and the great Mario, and I seemed, though the art of advertisement [James refers to the theater's billboard] was then comparatively so young and so chaste, to see our personal acquaintance, as he could almost be called [Monsieur Dubreuil, a *comprimario,* a singer of secondary roles], thickly sandwiched between them. Such was one's strange sense for the connections of things that they drew out the halls of Ferrero [a nearby dancing school] till these too seemed fairly to resound with Norma and Lucrezia Borgia, as if opening straight upon the stage, and Europe, by the stroke, had come to us in such force that we had but to enjoy it on the spot."[16]

Grisi and Mario had sailed in the wake of the fabled Jenny Lind and Marietta Alboni, lured to New York by generous fees. In the years to come, the Academy's sponsors leased the theater to a series of managers, some for only a season, others returning to try again. Bel canto programs were peppered with the first American performances, soon after their European premieres, of Verdi's *Rigoletto, La Traviata,* and *Il Trovatore,* Meyerbeer's *L'Africaine,* and Gounod's *Roméo et Juliette.* On February 20, 1861, on his way to his inauguration, Abraham Lincoln's stop in New York included an Academy performance of Verdi's *Un Ballo in maschera;* the President-elect left before act 3 and was thereby spared the onstage spectacle of a ruler's assassination. Less than two months later, on April 12, Fort Sumter would be attacked and the American Civil War would begin. New York would soon enjoy the boom that led to its recognition as a magnet for capital. By the 1880s, the city was no longer a cultural backwater where fading singers could succeed on the strength of a European reputation. A discerning and exigent musical press was ready and able to point out in expert detail a performer's technical weaknesses, faulty intonation, and stylistic vulgarities. The public had evolved as well. In 1850, P. T. Barnum had created frenzy for Jenny Lind with concerts largely devoted to timeworn melodies; thirty years later, Adelina Patti, the acknowledged "Queen of Song," undisputed star of Europe's opera stages, returned to the United States after a two-decade absence, prepared to feed her public a diet of ballads. "But it was another America to which Patti came. It was an America which had half outgrown the Italian opera, and which listened with delight to the music of the future ... [a] cultivated, intelligent, musically developed America." On November 8, 1880, to take one spectacular but by no means unique example, Gerster sang *La Traviata* at the Academy, Campanini was at Steinway Hall, a block or so away on 14th Street, and, at Booth's Theatre on 23rd Street, Sarah Bernhardt was making her US debut in the Scribe-Legouvé melodrama *Adrienne Lecouvreur.*[17]

By 1878, the year Colonel Mapleson took over at the Academy, society had again moved northward. Fourteenth Street was no longer the fanciest address in town. Millionaires had marched their mansions up Fifth Avenue, the Astors to 34th Street, the Vanderbilts to 52nd, the Roosevelts to the corner of 57th. The Metropolitan had followed in the footsteps of its stockholders. If the opening round of the opera war was a dustup between the "Old Families" and the "Newcomers," as soon as the Nobs and the Swells were amicably ensconced in their fauteuils (some had boxes in both houses), a second battle was engaged, on another ground, the stage, and with other contestants, the stars. Sopranos, in particular, would vie night after night on boards little more than a mile apart. The managements had no choice but to compete in ways they knew would perforce end in the ruin of one or the other of their companies. In fact, it ruined both. Mapleson was at an initial disadvantage. He had lost some of his best-known artists to offers from Abbey that could not be refused. But, he held two trump cards, Gerster and Patti. Early on, the *[Dramatic] Mirror* (Oct. 27) predicted, adopting the inescapable military metaphor, that the Academy would emerge victorious as long as Mapleson would keep "on giving such eminently satisfactory performances as that which opened his campaign." But sometimes even Patti could not fill more than two-thirds of the auditorium; on Gerster nights, the theater was two-thirds empty. Patti's fee, the highest of any singer in the world, could simply not be amortized. And what is more, her grip on the company, not to mention on the public's attention, rankled Gerster and put the mediocrity of other colleagues in unflattering relief. The quality of the Met's ensemble was decidedly higher and its new sets and costumes beyond the Academy's reach. Still, Abbey was faced with his own problems. Best estimates put the cost of the Met's principal singers, comprimarios, orchestra, chorus, and the rest just shy of $7,000 per performance; revenues fell far short of expenses. If Mapleson's season closed deeply in the red, it also closed in glory: Patti trilled in duet with Sofia Scalchi, who had wandered downtown at the expiration of her Met contract. They, and Rossini, and *Semiramide* filled every seat and "all available standing room" (*Herald,* April 25).[18]

Each company had presented a fall and spring season of nineteen operas (Abbey added a twentieth for Philadelphia alone); nearly half the titles were identical, for the most part bel canto and early Verdi works. The titles exclusive to Mapleson were Rossini's *La Gazza ladra* and *Semiramide,* Donizetti's

*Linda di Chamounix* and *L'Elisir d'amore*, Bellini's *Norma*, the Ricci broth-ers' *Crispino e la comare*, and Verdi's *Ernani*. With the exception of *Aïda* and *Roméo et Juliette*, none of the Academy's offerings was thought of as modern. The contrasting profile of the Met emerged from relatively recent French works, along with *Lohengrin*, Arrigo Boito's 1868 *Mefistofele*, and the first US performance of Amilcare Ponchielli's *La Gioconda*, premiered at La Scala in 1876. Abbey, unlike Mapleson, was bent on demonstrating that his "Grand Italian Opera" was alert to the public's predilection for Wagner and for con-temporary fare.

*Lohengrin* showed off the company to marked advantage, and although sung in Italian, of course, this edition of Wagner prompted Krehbiel to make the case for Abbey's more inclusive policy. A passionate Wagnerite, he cited the audience's patience as proof "that the patrons of the opera in New York are ripe for something better and nobler than the sweetmeats of the hurdy-gurdy repertory, and that a winning card to play in the game now going on between the rival managers would be a list, not necessarily large, of the best works of the German and French schools" *(Tribune)*. *Mefistofele* and *La Gioconda* were, for the most part, well performed. By all accounts, Campanini and Nilsson sang Boito's Faust and Margherita to far better effect than they had when impersonating the same characters in Gounod's version on open-ing night. Krehbiel chose to take issue with the opera itself, "the novelty of Boito's conception having worn off"; he now found it "bizarre ... inane, insipid, when it is not positively vulgar in style" *(Tribune)*. Despite the misfire of its act 2 explosion, the premiere of Ponchielli's sumptuously staged *La Gioconda* elicited lengthy and mostly positive reactions. Henderson, who thought it "among the most important art occurrences of the season," placed the composer in "a sort of half-way ground between Verdi's latest manner and the moderate productions of Wagner," his score, though unoriginal, contain-ing "much that is beautiful and impressive." While Henderson judged Nilsson ill cast in a role intended for dramatic soprano, Krehbiel reported that she "kept the audience in a state of almost painful excitement by the vivid manner to which she depicted the sufferings of the street singer" *(Tribune)*. He was harsher on Ponchielli than his colleague, charging the composer with resorting to "the old style." The two magisterial critics agreed that the enterprise did credit to the fledgling company by offering "grand opera in a style worthy of the metropolis" *(Tribune)*.

Performed in Abbey's new raiments, some of the "old style" operas made strong impressions. On the third night of the season, *Il Trovatore* introduced

TABLE 1  The Metropolitan's Inaugural Season, 1883–84

(all operas given in Italian)

| Composer and Title | Met Premiere | Most Recent Met Performance | No. of Seasons in Met Repertoire | No. of Met Productions | No. of Met Performances, 1883–2013 | World Premiere | Director/Designer |
|---|---|---|---|---|---|---|---|
| Charles Gounod, Faust | Oct. 22 | Apr. 5, 2013 | 77 | 9 | 752 | Mar. 19, 1859, Paris, Lyrique; grand opera version: Mar. 3, 1869, Paris, Opéra | Corani, Abbiati / Fox, Jr., Schaeffer, Maeder, Thompson |
| Gaetano Donizetti, Lucia di Lammermoor | Oct. 24 | Mar. 19, 2011 | 79 | 8 | 591 | Sept. 26, 1835, Naples, San Carlo | Corani, Abbiati / Fox, Jr., Schaeffer, Maeder, Thompson |
| Giuseppe Verdi, Il Trovatore | Oct. 26 | Jan. 24, 2013 | 78 | 9 | 637 | Jan. 19, 1853, Rome, Apollo | Unknown / Fox, Jr., Schaeffer, Maeder, Thompson |
| Vincenzo Bellini, I Puritani | Oct. 29 | Feb. 15, 2007 | 8 | 3 | 50 | Jan. 24, 1835, Paris, Italien | Unknown / Fox, Jr., Schaeffer, Maeder, Thompson |
| Ambroise Thomas, Mignon | Oct. 31 | May 18, 1949 | 22 | 4 | 110 | Nov. 17, 1866, Paris, Opéra-Comique | Corani, Abbiati / Fox, Jr., Schaeffer, Maeder, Thompson |
| Giuseppe Verdi, La Traviata | Nov. 5 | Apr. 6, 2013 | 106 | 10 | 984 | Mar. 6, 1853, Venice, La Fenice | Corani, Abbiati / Fox, Jr., Schaeffer, Maeder, Thompson |
| Richard Wagner, Lohengrin | Nov. 7 | May 6, 2006 | 71 | 7 | 618 | Aug. 28, 1850, Weimar, Court Theatre | Corani, Abbiati / Fox, Jr., Schaeffer, Maeder, Thompson |
| Vincenzo Bellini, La Sonnambula | Nov. 14 | Apr. 3, 2009 | 13 | 5 | 75 | Mar. 6, 1831, Milan, Carcano | Corani, Abbiati / Fox, Jr., Schaeffer, Maeder, Thompson |
| Giuseppe Verdi, Rigoletto | Nov. 16 | Apr. 27, 2013 | 95 | 9 | 854 | Mar. 11, 1851, Venice, La Fenice | Corani, Abbiati / Fox, Jr., Schaeffer, Maeder, Thompson |
| Giacomo Meyerbeer, Robert le Diable | Nov. 19 | Apr. 15, 1884 | 1 | 1 | 7 | Nov. 21, 1831, Paris, Opéra | Corani, Abbiati / Fox, Jr., Schaeffer, Maeder, Thompson |

(continued)

**TABLE 1** (continued)

| Composer and Title | Met Premiere | Most Recent Met Performance | No. of Seasons in Met Repertoire | No. of Met Productions | No. of Met Performances, 1883–2013 | World Premiere | Director/Designer |
|---|---|---|---|---|---|---|---|
| Giacchino Rossini, Il Barbiere di Siviglia | Nov. 23 | Jan. 5, 2013 | 74 | 7 | 607 | Feb. 20, 1816, Rome, Argentina | Corani, Abbiati/Fox, Jr., Schaeffer, Maeder, Thompson |
| Wolfgang Amadeus Mozart, Don Giovanni | Nov. 28 | Dec. 20, 2012 | 64 | 8 | 538 | Oct. 29, 1787, Prague, National | Corani, Abbiati/Fox, Jr., Schaeffer, Maeder, Thompson |
| Arrigo Boito, Mefistofele | Dec. 5 | Feb. 26, 2000 | 11 | 5 | 67 | Mar. 5, 1868, Milan, La Scala | Corani, Abbiati/Fox, Jr., Schaeffer, Maeder, Thompson |
| Amilcare Ponchielli, La Gioconda | Dec. 20 | Oct. 9, 2008 | 40 | 5 | 287 | Apr. 8, 1876, Milan, La Scala | Corani, Abbiati/Fox, Jr., Schaeffer, Maeder, Thompson |
| Friedrich von Flotow, Martha | Jan. 4, Boston; Mar. 14, New York | Feb. 3, 1968 | 20 | 5 | 116 | Nov. 25, 1847, Vienna, Kärntnertor | Corani, Abbiati/Unknown |
| Georges Bizet, Carmen | Jan. 5, Boston; Jan. 19, New York | Mar. 1, 2013 | 88 | 10 | 984 | Mar. 3, 1875, Paris, Opéra-Comique | Corani, Abbiati/Fox, Jr., Schaeffer, Maeder, Thompson |
| Giacomo Meyerbeer, Le Prophète | Feb. 12, Cincinnati; Mar. 21, New York | Oct. 26, 1979 | 18 | 4 | 99 | Apr. 16, 1849, Paris, Opéra | Corani, Abbiati/Fox, Jr., Schaeffer, Maeder, Thompson |
| Ambroise Thomas, Hamlet | Feb. 21, Cincinnati; Mar. 10, New York | Apr. 9, 2010 | 6 | 3 | 17 | Mar. 9, 1868, Paris, Opéra | Corani, Abbiati/Unknown |
| Giacomo Meyerbeer, Les Huguenots | Mar. 19 | Apr. 26, 1915 | 18 | 3 | 129 | Feb. 29, 1836, Paris, Opéra | Corani, Abbiati/Unknown |
| Charles Gounod, Roméo et Juliette[a] | Apr. 16 | Mar. 26, 2011 | 38 | 7 | 329 | Apr. 27, 1867, Paris, Lyrique | Unknown/Unknown |

[a] The season's sole performance of Roméo et Juliette took place at Philadelphia's Academy of Music.

Roberto Stagno. The tenor thrilled the audience with his long-held high B at the end of "Di quella pira." The Azucena of Zelia Trebelli "was a triumph of high vocal art worthy of being ranked with Madame Sembrich's brilliant performance on Wednesday" *(Tribune)*. On hearing the Leonora of Alwina Valleria, the Met's first American-born diva, the *Tribune* declared, "there can be no 'off night' at the Metropolitan so long as she relieves either Madame Nilsson or Madame Sembrich" *(Tribune)*. Soprano Emmy Fursch-Madi had glowing notices for her Alice in Meyerbeer's *Robert le diable*. Fursch-Madi was also compelling as Ortrud to Nilsson's Elsa and as Donna Anna in a *Don Giovanni* that flaunted Nilsson as Donna Elvira and Sembrich as Zerlina. Abbey's Met had its fair share of disappointing evenings as well, many occasioned by the weak contingent of male singers. Stagno soon found that his reliable high notes did not suffice to trigger favorable reviews for his Don Ottavio *(Don Giovanni)*, Jean de Leyde *(Le Prophète)*, Lionel *(Martha)*, and Enzo *(La Gioconda)*. Italian baritone Luigi Guadagnini was trounced as Rigoletto: "It is a thousand pities that the poor man came so far to do so little" *(Times)*. In an underprepared *Mignon*, Nilsson was judged to have fallen short of her own more youthful and graceful performance of thirteen years earlier, when she had introduced Ambroise Thomas's portrait of Goethe's touching waif to America. Trebelli's Carmen compared unfavorably to Minnie Hauk's, New York's first, in 1878. Thomas's take on *Hamlet* was denounced as lèse-Shakespeare in its solitary New York hearing. With the exception of Nilsson, Campanini, and Scalchi, the principals of *Les Huguenots* were "simply earnest, correct, and lifeless" and the orchestra "almost continuously irresponsive to Signor Vianesi's baton" *(Times)*.

### FALL AND RISE OF BEL CANTO

The lesson of the Met's first season was that Thomas, Bizet, and Meyerbeer, not to mention Wagner, Gounod, Boito, and Ponchielli, had eclipsed "old" Italian opera. Verdi's *Rigoletto, Il Trovatore,* and *La Traviata* and the bel canto works fell well below the 1883–84 box-office average, trailing far behind *Faust, Lohengrin, Mignon, La Gioconda, Les Huguenots,* and *Don Giovanni*. No one, not even Marcella Sembrich, could stem the tide. In the interest of protecting their investment, the pro–bel canto box holders took a grudging back seat to the ticket-buying public. The influential coterie of Wagnerite critics that had railed often and loudly against the dramatic implausibilities and musical shallowness of Italian opera, together with the "ultra musical people in the gallery," had won the day. In a moment of particular hauteur, Krehbiel dismissed Rossini, Bellini, and Donizetti, throwing in Verdi for good measure, for clinging to "the petty world of feelings," the "skeleton" for their abiding and exclusive interest in melody (*Tribune,* Nov. 6, 1883). For the next seven years, the war would be waged not between two houses and two companies, but as a latter-day "quarrel of the ancients and the moderns." Lucia, Elvira, and their sisters lived on at the Academy for the remaining season-and-a-half of Mapleson's tenure. At the Metropolitan from 1884 until 1891, its German years, Donizetti was absent, Rossini was represented only by his French grand opera, *Guillaume Tell,* and Bellini was confined to just three performances of *Norma.* When *Lucia di Lammermoor* was revived for the formidable Nellie Melba in 1893, Henderson, unmoved, pronounced the opera "dead to the world" (*Times,* Dec. 5). And so it went for decades. Caruso himself was unable to shield the 1904 premiere of Donizetti's *Lucrezia Borgia* from the vituperations of Krehbiel ("a mouldering corpse") and Henderson ("empty formulas . . . without a trace of dramatic characterization"). In fact, bel canto programming continued to be so spotty that partisan critical attacks were largely moot.

The beginning of the turnabout came with the February 18, 1918, revival of *I Puritani.* Without explanation, the Bellini that Krehbiel had once pilloried was suddenly a model to be emulated: "If only the composers of *Francesca da Rimini* or *Mârouf* could exchange three-quarters of their orchestral mastery for a tithe of the lyric ecstasy which floods the operas of Bellini, the world of modern opera would take on a more hopeful aspect" *(Tribune).* Krehbiel's conversion aside, *I Puritani* served the critic's present purpose: to bludgeon Riccardo Zandonai and Henri Rabaud, whose operas had had recent Met premieres. A week later, Krehbiel devoted an entire column to a summary of *I Puritani* notices, nearly all glowing (*Tribune,* Feb. 24). When Olin Downes became principal music reviewer for the *Times* in 1924, bel canto found a true champion. He took the occasion of the January 18, 1926, production of *Il Barbiere di Siviglia* to celebrate Rossini. The next year, it was Bellini's turn. *Norma* retained "a surprising amount of its formal strength, its beauty and eloquence" (Nov. 17, 1927). And he loved *La Sonnambula:* "The music unfolds one faultless melody after another, always appropriate in warmth or pathos or tenderness to the emotion of the text, yet never violating the shape of the formal musical speech" (March 16, 1932). By the mid-1930s, the bel canto operas most frequently revived at the Met, *Lucia di Lammermoor, Il Barbiere di Siviglia, L'Elisir d'amore, Norma,* and *Don Pasquale,* were no longer wanting for rehabilitation by the critical establishment. They had stood the test of time and belonged to the ages.

It took another couple of decades for the neglected operas of Rossini, Donizetti, and Bellini to emerge from near oblivion. Their rediscovery turned on the confluence of two phenomena, a soprano, Maria Callas, and a technology, the long-playing record. In January 1949, soon after the start of her career, Callas stunned the Venetian public by following a run of *Walküre* Brünnhildes with her first *Puritani* Elviras. During these performances at La Fenice, a role unquestionably the property of the *soprano leggero* (a light, flexible soprano voice) was triumphantly reinvented by a *soprano drammatico d'agilità* (a soprano voice of both power and agility). Her recording of Bellini's then unfamiliar opera was released on the heels of the familiar *Lucia.* Callas went on to breathe new musical and dramatic life into other works long in limbo as Italian theaters mounted rarities specifically for her, Rossini's *Il Turco in Italia* and *Armida,* Donizetti's *Anna Bolena* and *Poliuto,* and Bellini's *Il Pirata,* all captured live or in the studio. The conservative Met trod more timorously than did venues abroad. During her all-too-brief string of twenty-three performances with the company, the only bel canto roles Callas sang were Norma, her calling card, and Lucia. The December 8, 1956, broadcast finds her in less than optimal form. Still, the poignancy of Lucia's predicament explodes at the intersection of bel canto ornamentation and Callas's incisive accents and diction. She brings the plangency of a "Lacrimosa" to the "Soffriva nel pianto" duet; for the "Mad Scene," she summons despair and ecstasy at will. Many sopranos, mostly *leggero* like her predecessors, have followed Callas as Lucia at the Met; few have been deaf to her lessons.[19]

Least of all Joan Sutherland. And she had none of Callas's instability in the upper register, none of the weakness of most *coloraturas* in the lower. Her 1961 Met debut as Lucia was front-page news (*Herald Tribune,* Nov. 27). Twelve minutes of curtain calls saluted the "Mad Scene." Alas, cameras and microphones were absent. Two months later, television's Bell Telephone Hour documented her star turn live, preserving not only the voice of "la Stupenda," but the impact of her interpretation. As her career progressed, Sutherland was often perceived as an indifferent actress. In this telecast, she makes vivid the young woman's hallucination, the encounter with her beloved by the fountain, her joy at hearing the wedding music, the tender evocation of love, the febrile search for the invisible flute. For the nearly four-

FIGURE 5. *Lucia di Lammermoor* "Mad Scene," Joan Sutherland as Lucia, 1961 (courtesy Photofest)

teen minutes of scrutiny by the cameras, the singer's virtuosity serves the drama. Sutherland's complete Lucia was captured in a Met telecast on November 13, 1982. At fifty-six, less nimble of foot and, naturally, less fresh of voice, hers remained the standard to be met.

It was the drive to find vehicles for Sutherland that called back works not heard at the Met for at least three decades: *La Sonnambula* (1962–63), Donizetti's *La Fille du régiment* (1971–72), *I Puritani* (1975–76), and new productions of *Lucia di Lammermoor* (1964–65) and *Norma* (1969–70). She had become one of the company's most potent and ultimately most durable attractions. Marilyn Horne was the raison d'être for Rossini's *L'Italiana in Algeri* (1973–74) and *Semiramide* (1990–91), both long absent. The newsworthy debut of Beverly Sills at La Scala in *The Siege of Corinth* propelled the soprano and Rossini's opera onto the Met stage for the first time (1974–75). Cecilia Bartoli secured a place for Rossini's *La Cenerentola* (1997–98). For Renée Fleming, keen to add bel canto credentials to her title of Mozart-Strauss specialist, the management scheduled Bellini's *Il Pirata* (2002–03) and Rossini's *Armida* (2009–10). Juan Diego Flórez, the sole *tenore di grazia* (a light, flexible tenor voice) in Met history to spearhead a bel canto premiere, was matched by Joyce DiDonato and Diana Damrau in the pyrotechnics of Rossini's *Le Comte Ory* (2010–11). Donizetti's *Anna Bolena* (2011–12) provided another opportunity for Anna Netrebko to extend her lyric voice into the domain of the *coloratura*. And DiDonato shone in the title role of Donizetti's *Maria Stuarda* (2012–13). Callas had worked her magic. The appetite for unfamiliar bel canto she reawakened has continued to be satisfied by ensuing generations of artists trained to negotiate the most difficult embellishments with amazing virtuosity. The feast continues.[20]

# TWO

## *Cultural Capital, 1884–1903*

### THE GERMAN SEASONS AND FRENCH OPERA

### THE GERMAN SEASONS: 1884–1891

AS THE 1883–84 SEASON CAME TO AN END, there was no clear decision as to which impresario, Mapleson or Abbey, or which house, the veteran Academy or the rookie Metropolitan, would emerge the victor in what was in retrospect the city's first opera war. The outcome would have little to do with the tiff between the Nobs and the Swells that had set it off. Nor would the endgame be other than marginally affected by the much publicized face-off between sparring divas. It would, instead, have everything to do with the economics of producing opera on an internationally competitive scale in New York.

When the smoke cleared, Mapleson was left weakened but standing, if only until Christmas 1885. Abbey was gone. His Grand Italian Opera had run up a heavy deficit for which he was personally responsible. Not that he was extravagant; he was actually quite frugal. But by neglecting to factor into his equation that the upper tiers held half the seats of the house, and that they accounted for one-third of the receipts of sold-out performances, he had made a costly miscalculation: at $2–$3 each, tickets were beyond the grasp of the popular, largely immigrant audience. Sales fell sharply as curiosity surrounding the new house dwindled. By the time Abbey adjusted prices downward it was too late. He offered to return for a second season with the proviso that the stockholders shoulder his losses; the directors refused to levy the requisite assessments. The board received bids from two managers based in England, and another from Leopold Damrosch, founder and conductor of the Oratorio Society of New York and of the New York Symphony Society, rival of the Philharmonic-Symphony Society led by Theodore Thomas. German-born like Thomas, Damrosch had been a musical force in the city since his arrival in 1871. His proposition departed radically from conventional arrangements between owners and leasing impresarios. For an annual salary and a percentage of the profits, Damrosch agreed to put on a season of fourteen operas at ticket prices cut by half and more, and at an anticipated average cost per performance less than half that incurred by Abbey—all the while balancing the books. Risks and rewards would accrue to the stockholders in their new capacity as producers.[1]

## German New York

Damrosch had in mind a season of opera not in Italian, but in German, its repertoire principally consigned to works composed on German texts, with casts recruited in Germany at fees far lower than Abbey's stars had commanded. The orchestra would be drawn from the German players of his New York Symphony Society, by all accounts superior to the Italian instrumentalists Abbey had hired. Damrosch would do all the conducting. In making his case, he contended that the German speakers of New York, the population he was confident of luring to the half-empty upper tiers, were interested neither in Italian opera nor in German opera sung in Italian. Ultimately, and despite resistance from influential box holders, the bottom line won out. On and off the stage for the next seven years, German was in every way the lingua franca of the Metropolitan.

Damrosch had come to New York to direct the by then well-established Arion Society, one of the many singing groups active in the United States in the second half of the century. The influx of German intellectuals and cultural workers, musicians in particular, had begun with their flight from Europe following the aborted 1848 revolutions. In 1855, the Philharmonic was 79 percent German; by 1892, 97 percent of its players were of German descent. German music dominated programming; until World War I, 70 percent of the repertory of US orchestras was German or Austrian. The 1880 federal census recorded 360,000 persons of German origin in Manhattan alone, roughly 30 percent of the population. Had their Lower East Side Kleindeutschland (Little Germany) been an independent municipality, it would have been the fourth largest in the United States. New York had become the third German-speaking metropolis in the world, outstripped only by Berlin and Vienna. The immigrant audience that was still too small to support Palmo in 1844 and that, in spite of its greater numbers, had eluded Abbey in 1883 would become Damrosch's target market. By that time, the

German community had established cultural institutions of all sorts. The Atlantic Garden on the Bowery was a favored destination where "German families sang songs of the fatherland and listened to orchestras perform Strauss, Wagner, and Beethoven." The Stadt Theater, founded in 1854, and later the Germania, the Thalia, and the Irving Place Theatre brought distinguished German actors to New York for seasons of classical drama: Schiller's *Don Carlos,* Hauptmann's *Die Weber,* Shakespeare's *Hamlet,* Dumas's *La Dame aux camélias,* Ibsen's *A Doll's House.* Two, three, and sometimes more professional repertory companies were active in Manhattan from mid-century to 1918 or so, when anti-German sentiment put them out of business. The most prominent and durable of the twenty-eight German-language papers that could be found on New York newsstands in the early 1850s was the *Staats-Zeitung;* it carried extensive reviews of Met performances well into the twentieth century.[2]

The trans-Atlantic exportation of its musical culture as a matter of Germany's national interest began in the last decades of the nineteenth century with maneuvers to draw the United States to its side—and away from England and France. The implications of this policy "were vast, political, and universal, and extended far beyond the development of American musical life." The calling of German musicians to spread their native canon from coast to coast intersected with the Kaiser's imperial agenda. Through their engagement with German music, audiences advanced the conflicting intentions of liberal German musicians and nationalist German expansionists. In the end, "while the efforts of Theodore Thomas and Walter Damrosch [Leopold's conductor-composer son] may not have represented a diplomatic act, they clearly had a diplomatic effect. For the art of the three Bs or Wagner evoked precisely the respect for German greatness, *Heimat* [homeland] and emotionalism that Reich officials wanted to convey, and their legacy lasted much longer than the German *Kaiserreich* [empire]."[3]

## Culture Wars

Leopold Damrosch signaled his intention to promote the cause of Wagner by scheduling *Tannhäuser* for opening night 1884 and lavishing his best effort on the preparation of *Die Walküre.* Although neither was new to New York, never before had either been heard to such advantage. The early, Italianate *Tannhäuser* was a safe choice; *Walküre,* the most accessible component of the "Ring," represented the more mature Wagner. Henderson pointed to *Lohengrin,* the season's third Wagner opera, as proof of his axiom: that the "sincere and realistic" interpretation of German artists was in all ways superior to the Italian practice of privileging "a few tuneful numbers" (*Times,* Dec. 4). It was *Walküre,* reportedly up to the Bayreuth production standard, marvelously cast with Bayreuth regulars Amalie Materna and Marianne Brandt, that made the deepest impression. In the spirit of ensemble that divided Damrosch's German troupe from Abbey's assembly of stars, Brandt, who had already sung leading soprano roles in *Fidelio* and *Don Giovanni* and the principal contralto and mezzo-soprano parts in *Le Prophète* and *Lohengrin,* and had done comprimario duty to boot in *Rigoletto* and *William Tell,* impersonated both the powerful goddess Fricka and one of Wotan's well-nigh anonymous daughters in *Walküre.*

Don Giovanni, Le Prophète, Les Huguenots, and Rigoletto were holdovers from the inaugural season. Apart from the Wagner firsts, there were two other German novelties, *Fidelio* and *Der Freischütz.* The premieres of three French operas, a response to the preference of the public, confirmed that the Met had become home to a serious company, devoted to serious music. Reviewers underscored the historical interest of Auber's *Masaniello* (usually titled *La Muette de Portici*) and Rossini's *William Tell* (born *Guillaume Tell*), formative influences on the development of *le grand opéra français,* and Halévy's *La Juive,* a telling example of the genre's maturity. Henry Finck went so far as to shower Auber with reflected glory; the composer was credited with leaving his "mark on a much greater master, Richard Wagner, whose enthusiasm for *Masaniello* was unbounded" (*Evening Post*). The scenic and dramatic effects of French grand opera productions, in particular the eruption of Vesuvius in the Auber and the transformation from moonlit night to Alpine "rosy morn" (*Tribune*) in the Rossini, impressed critics and public. Damrosch had delivered more than he had promised. Not only had he kept to his budget, but he had presented, in opulent settings and compelling stagings, a talented ensemble of singing actors in a challenging repertoire. New York had never before experienced so rich an operatic season.[4]

On February 15, an exhausted Leopold Damrosch died suddenly of pneumonia. True to his word, he had conducted every performance, fifty-two in three months, including in a last burst of nine days five *Die Walküres,* a *Le Prophète,* and a *Lohengrin.* Shocked and disconcerted, the board turned to its secretary, Edmund C. Stanton, who had come to opera—and to Wagner—only lately and almost by chance. Stanton was named executive director and general manager. But as novelist Louis Auchincloss, his great-nephew, put it years later,

"Something in the haunting strains of *Tristan und Isolde* ... or in the stirring motifs of the 'Ring' ... must have penetrated the polished surface of this well-mannered and obliging young man to turn him into the ardent champion of operas detested by the frivolous but powerful society of which he had once been so compliant and affable a member." Walter Damrosch, twenty-three years old, was made assistant manager and assistant conductor. It was Walter who had led most of the remaining performances of the season, and it was he who was dispatched to Europe to find a successor to his father. For the upcoming season, 1885–86, he conscripted the Hungarian-born Anton Seidl, assistant to Wagner in the years just prior to the composer's death in February 1883.[5]

By the time he landed in New York with his wife, soprano Auguste Seidl-Kraus, Seidl, who had been central to the preparation of the first "Ring" cycle in 1876, was an accomplished conductor, poised to fulfill Wagner's prophecy: that he would become the master's American apostle. In the German seasons to come, he would be responsible for the momentous US premieres of *Die Meistersinger* (1886), *Tristan und Isolde* (1886), *Siegfried* (1887), *Götterdämmerung* (1888), and *Das Rheingold* (1889). Critics were unfailingly dithyrambic: Seidl's "impulse dominated reflection, emotion shamed logic.... As for the rest, professional and layman, dilettante and ignorant, their souls were his to play with." The company's leading soprano, the acknowledged *prima donna assoluta* Lilli Lehmann, incomparable in her exploration of the entire repertoire, was a surpassing Isolde and Brünnhilde. The other Seidl/Stanton novelties, and as often their execution, evoked a mixed response. *Aïda* was admired for its modernity and for its sumptuous décor, but only Brandt, the Amneris, emerged unscathed, and Seidl was chastised for his "dragging" tempos *(Times)*. Another Verdi masterpiece, *Un Ballo in maschera,* headed by the always exceptional Lehmann, was buried in scorn, its "more than familiar music wedded to a plot almost comic in its lack of ideas" *(Herald)*. To add insult to injury, the act 3 festivities were "beefed up" by the interpolation of Massenet dance tunes. *Norma* was dismissed as a relic. The two French premieres—Spontini's *Fernand Cortez* ("a good deal like an attempt to resuscitate a mummy" *[Tribune]*) and *L'Africaine* ("There are plenty of good musical judges who think it was a pity Meyerbeer lived to complete this opera" *[Herald]*)—provided opportunities to applaud the scenery, if little else. German pieces, Wagner and Weber's *Euryanthe* aside, were chosen for their spectacle or their *gemütlichkeit,* their amiability. Among the offerings intended to leaven the heavy dose of Wagnerian music-drama, *Die Königin von Saba* was the only hit, its exotic melodies and décors creating

TABLE 2  Metropolitan Opera Premieres, 1884–85 to 1890–91

*(Italian and French operas given in German)*

| Composer and Title | Met Premiere | Most Recent Met Performance | No. of Seasons in Met Repertoire | No. of Met Productions | No. of Met Performances, 1883–2013 | World Premiere | Director/Designer |
|---|---|---|---|---|---|---|---|
| Richard Wagner, *Tannhäuser* | Nov. 17, 1884 | Dec. 18, 2004 | 62 | 6 | 470 | Oct. 19, 1845, Dresden, Hoftheater | Wilhelm Hock / Charles Fox, Jr., William Schaeffer |
| Ludwig van Beethoven, *Fidelio* | Nov. 19, 1884 | Apr. 13, 2006 | 43 | 7 | 230 | *1st version:* Nov. 20, 1805, Vienna, an der Wien; *2nd version:* Mar. 29, 1806, Vienna, an der Wien; *3rd version:* May 23, 1814, Vienna, Kärtnertor | Wilhelm Hock / Charles Fox, Jr., William Schaeffer |
| Carl Maria von Weber, *Der Freischütz* | Nov. 24, 1884 | Apr. 19, 1972 | 7 | 4 | 30 | June 18, 1821, Berlin, Schauspielhaus | Wilhelm Hock / Unknown |
| Giacchino Rossini, *William Tell* | Nov. 28, 1884 | Dec. 5, 1931 | 8 | 2 | 31 | Aug. 3, 1829, Paris, Opéra | Wilhelm Hock / F. Baptiste Ceruti |
| Daniel Auber, *Masaniello (La Muette de Portici)* | Dec. 29, 1884 | Feb. 19, 1887 | 2 | 1 | 6 | Feb. 29, 1828; Paris, Opéra | Wilhelm Hock / F. Baptiste Ceruti |
| Richard Wagner, *Die Walküre* | Jan. 30, 1885 | May 6, 2013 | 85 | 9 | 536 | June 26, 1870, Munich, Königliches Hof- und Nationaltheater | Wilhelm Hock / Josef Hoffmann, William Schaeffer, Gaspar Maeder |
| François-Adrien Boieldieu, *La Dame blanche* | Mar. 12, 1885 | Feb. 13, 1904 | 2 | 1 | 3 | Dec. 10, 1825, Paris, Opéra-Comique | Wilhelm Hock / Unknown |
| Fromental Halévy, *La Juive* | Jan. 16, 1885 | Dec. 19, 2003 | 16 | 3 | 70 | Feb. 23, 1835, Paris, Opéra | Wilhelm Hock / Unknown |

*(continued)*

TABLE 2 (continued)

| Composer and Title | Met Premiere | Most Recent Met Performance | No. of Seasons in Met Repertoire | No. of Met Productions | No. of Met Performances, 1883–2013 | World Premiere | Director/Designer |
|---|---|---|---|---|---|---|---|
| Christoph Willibald Gluck, Orfeo ed Euridice | Apr. 11, 1885 | May 14, 2011 | 20 | 7 | 98 | Oct. 5, 1762, Vienna, Burgtheater | Wilhelm Hock / Unknown |
| Karl Goldmark, Die Königin von Saba | Dec. 2, 1885 | Apr. 16, 1906 | 4 | 2 | 46 | Mar. 10, 1875, Vienna, Hofoper | Van Hell / Henry E. Hoyt |
| Richard Wagner, Die Meistersinger von Nürnberg | Jan. 4, 1886 | Mar. 13, 2007 | 68 | 7 | 408 | June 21, 1868, Munich, Hoftheater | Van Hell / Henry E. Hoyt |
| Richard Wagner, Rienzi | Feb. 5, 1886 | Feb. 26, 1890 | 3 | 1 | 21 | Oct. 20, 1842, Dresden, Königliches Sächsisches Hoftheater | Van Hell / Unknown |
| Giuseppe Verdi, Aida | Nov. 12, 1886 | Dec. 28, 2012 | 104 | 9 | 1,132 | Dec. 24, 1871, Cairo, Opera House | Van Hell / Henry E. Hoyt |
| Ignaz Brüll, Das Goldene Kreuz | Nov. 19, 1886 | Dec. 22, 1886 | 1 | 1 | 4 | Dec. 22, 1875, Berlin, Königliches Opernhaus | Van Hell / Unknown |
| Richard Wagner, Tristan und Isolde | Dec. 1, 1886 | Dec. 20, 2008 | 70 | 8 | 455 | June 10, 1865, Munich, Königliches Hof- und Nationaltheater | Van Hell / Unknown |
| Karl Goldmark, Merlin | Jan. 3, 1887 | Feb. 11, 1887 | 1 | 1 | 5 | Nov. 19, 1886, Vienna, Hoftheater | Van Hell / Henry E. Hoyt |
| Richard Wagner, Siegfried | Nov. 9, 1887 | May 8, 2013 | 65 | 8 | 270 | Aug. 16, 1876, Bayreuth, Festspielhaus | Theodore Habelmann / Johann Kautsky |
| Viktor Nessler, Der Trompeter von Säkkingen | Nov. 23, 1887 | Feb. 24, 1890 | 2 | 1 | 11 | May 4, 1884, Leipzig, Stadttheater | Theodore Habelmann / Unknown |

| Work | | | | | | | |
|---|---|---|---|---|---|---|---|
| Carl Maria von Weber, *Euryanthe* | Dec. 23, 1887 | 2 | Feb. 26, 1915 | 2 | 10 | Oct. 25, 1823, Vienna, Kärntnertor | Theodore Habelmann / Unknown |
| Gaspare Spontini, *Fernand Cortez* | Jan. 6, 1888 | 1 | Jan. 14, 1888 | 1 | 4 | Nov. 28, 1809, Paris, Opéra | Theodore Habelmann / Henry E. Hoyt |
| Richard Wagner, *Götterdämmerung* | Jan. 25, 1888 | 62 | May 11, 2013 | 8 | 235 | Aug. 17, 1876, Bayreuth, Festspielhaus | Theodore Habelmann / Unknown |
| Giacomo Meyerbeer, *L'Africaine* | Dec. 7, 1888 | 21 | Feb. 24, 1934 | 4 | 71 | Apr. 28, 1865, Paris, Opéra | Theodore Habelmann / Henry E. Hoyt |
| Richard Wagner, *Das Rheingold* | Jan. 4, 1889 | 59 | May 4, 2013 | 8 | 167 | Sept. 22, 1869, Munich, Königliches Hof- und Nationaltheater | Theodore Habelmann / Johann Kautsky |
| Richard Wagner, *Der Fliegende Holländer* | Nov. 27, 1889 | 22 | May 14, 2010 | 7 | 154 | Jan. 2, 1843, Dresden, Königliches Sächsisches Hoftheater | Theodore Habelmann / Unknown |
| Giuseppe Verdi, *Un Ballo in maschera* | Dec. 11, 1889 | 34 | Dec. 14, 2012 | 8 | 297 | Feb. 17, 1859, Rome, Apollo | Theodore Habelmann / Unknown |
| Peter Cornelius, *Der Barbier von Bagdad* | Jan. 3, 1890 | 3 | Jan. 18, 1926 | 2 | 18 | Dec. 15, 1858, Weimar, Hoftheater | Theodore Habelmann / Unknown |
| Vincenzo Bellini, *Norma* | Feb. 27, 1890 | 20 | Dec. 7, 2007 | 4 | 147 | Dec. 26, 1831, Milan, La Scala | Theodore Habelmann / Unknown |
| Alberto Franchetti, *Asrael* | Nov. 26, 1890 | 1 | Jan. 2, 1891 | 1 | 5 | Feb. 11, 1888, Reggio Emilia, Municipale | Theodore Habelmann / Henry E. Hoyt |
| Antonio Smareglia, *Il Vassalo di Szigeth* | Dec. 12, 1890 | 1 | Dec. 27, 1890 | 1 | 4 | Oct. 4, 1889 (in German), Vienna, Hoftheater | Theodore Habelmann / Henry E. Hoyt |
| Ernst II of Saxe Coburg-Gotha, *Diana von Solange* | Jan. 9, 1891 | 1 | Jan. 12, 1891 | 1 | 2 | Dec. 5, 1858, Coburg | Theodore Habelmann / Unknown |

sufficient demand to justify a whopping twenty-five performances in its first season. Reviewers who showed indulgence toward Goldmark's Biblical extravaganza were merciless toward his Arthurian *Merlin*. The lighter pieces, Ignaz Brüll's *Das Goldene Kreuz,* Viktor Nessler's *Der Trompeter von Säkkingen,* and Peter Cornelius's *Der Barbier von Bagdad,* pleased only the Germanophile press corps.[6]

In 1892, looking back, Stanton rehearsed his apology for German opera one last time. He began by opposing "old favorite operas" (namely, bel canto) to the "new," the "modern" (namely, Wagner above all). He aimed his sharpest barbs at the star system; in its place, he had advocated repertory casting and the thorough preparation of chorus and orchestra. He was persuaded that New York operagoers, who had come to expect the high musical and dramatic standards of the German ensemble, "could no more sink back into the enthusiasms that satisfied the audiences of a quarter of a century ago than could our modern theatregoers applaud the mouthing and strutting of the dead histrionic heroes of melodramatic fame." The public's affinity for "modern orchestration," that is, for more contemporary music, had been cultivated by exposure to the symphony. The point of no return was long passed. In conclusion, he taxed the Abbey prescription of stars singing an "old favorite" repertory with "prohibiting the production of opera as an Art-Work."[7]

In Stanton's first season, and for the next two, 50 percent of the repertoire was given over to Wagner, 70 percent to German works. The German share dipped to over 50 percent in 1888–89, about 60 percent in 1889–90 and 1890–91. In the period 1886–1891, Wagner receipts were higher by 21 percent than the average take of the non-Wagner repertoire, German or not. By the end of the seven years, all the operas of Wagner had been produced by the Met with the exception of two early works, *Die Feen* and *Das Liebesverbot,* and *Parsifal,* until 1903 staged only at Bayreuth's Festspielhaus. Four years into Stanton's regime, Henderson gave a rhapsodic assessment of what he considered the ennobling effect of German opera: "Musical amateurs are beginning to understand that this is a serious art form, capable of mighty purposes and almost fathomless meanings. . . . It is beginning to stand in the estimation of thinking men and women beside the most elevated drama and poetry" (*Times,* Jan. 19, 1888).[8]

## Class Strife

Throughout the German seasons and after, box holders waged a tug-of-war with yet another segment of the operagoing public, "culturist" habitués of the parquet. The two classes squared off on the code of conduct appropriate to the opera house, a front related to the ongoing culture war over musical taste. Early on, *Musical Courier* (Dec. 10, 1884) threatened to publish the names of those who, like the occupants of prominent boxes at the season's first *Lohengrin,* chatted and laughed during performances. Two years later, nothing had changed. A satirical piece in *Harper's* (April 1886) turned the volume up a notch, urging that the philistines who treated the opera house as their private salon repair to "the congenial circles of miners and Indian reservations upon the frontier," an allusion to the West, where so many recent fortunes had been made. In a reversal of class typology, it was the ill-behaved, well-born, well-heeled, and stubbornly middlebrow box holders who were shown up by the well-behaved, modestly born, middle-class, and highbrow ticket holders. The reviewer goes on to pity those "whom an unkind fate dooms to sit near [the noisemakers]." More circumspect observers, such as Henderson, attempted to mediate what had become "continual warfare" by noting that "like most questions in this world, this has two sides. The stockholders built and maintain the opera house and they have undeniably the right to derive as much pleasure as possible from the fruits of their enterprise." And after all, compared with the prestige that the presence of high society lent the cause of German opera, "a matter [not] to be lightly considered," turning the house into a "social resort" was "by no means so heinous a procedure" as some irate opera lovers protested. He proposed a middle ground: "No one objects to talk which is not too loud. If the occupants of the boxes will bear that in mind, neither they nor their valuable friends in the other parts of the house will be annoyed" (*Times,* Dec. 29, 1887). The compromise fell flat. And three years later, the board was obliged to issue the following notice: "Many complaints having been made to the directors of the Opera House of the annoyance produced by the talking in the boxes during the performances, the board requests that it be discontinued."[9]

The stockholders remained disinclined to moderate their deportment. They demanded long intermissions timed not to scene changes, but to leisurely social intercourse, complete with refreshments delivered from a nearby restaurant. Their power was such that the lights in the auditorium were turned up when they complained about the dark, the effect on theatrical illusion be damned. Here Henderson drew the line: "This last fact is a sufficient commentary on any professions of devotion to the laws of art" (*Times,* Jan. 22, 1889). But despite the outrage of much of the public, the lights stayed on. Sightings of those who mattered would have otherwise been foiled, above all the entrance of Mrs. Astor into box 9 (box 7 after 1892) at precisely 9:00 P.M. on Monday nights. "What she did was copied slavishly by the rest of society," commented soprano Frances Alda. As a result, more often than not, the first act was sung to a half-empty auditorium; occasionally, the curtain would be held until she arrived. Alda described the moment thus: "As nine o'clock drew near, there would be the swish and rustle of silk trains, the tramp of feet coming down the orchestra aisles, the scrape of chairs being moved to better positions in the boxes. Interest in happenings on the stage dwindled. Opera glasses were raised and focused on the curtains of Box Seven. . . . Mrs. Astor came in and took her seat. An audible sigh of satisfaction passed through the house. The prestige of Monday Night was secure. Only, then, was the attention of all but the ardent music-lovers in the audience turned to the singers and orchestra." With the same regularity that marked her entrance, at the close of the second intermission, Mrs. Astor made her exit—in time for the competing Monday night Patriarch or Assembly balls.[10]

## The Waning German Hegemony

As early as spring 1885, the Wagnerites declared the campaign won. German opera was no longer an "occasional and curious experiment on off evenings and with a chance-medley company," but a repertoire whose interpretative style had been "approved by and accepted by 'fashion' and 'the town.'" In truth, less than halfway through the German seasons, grumbling among "fashion," audible from the first, grew louder as stockholders became ever more exasperated with "the town" and what they experienced as a surfeit of Wagner. Nostalgia for the Italian operas of the past kept pace with their increasing hostility. Rising costs rubbed salt into the wounds inflicted night after night by the repertoire. Salaries of German artists had mushroomed over time: Lilli Lehmann's fee was $600 per performance, Albert Niemann's $1,000. At the January 21, 1888, meeting of the board, the directors determined that two alternatives be put before the stockholders: to cancel the 1888–89 season, which would have entailed an assessment, or to continue German opera at more than three times the current price per box. The option of an Italian season was judged an extravagance not worth considering. The stockholders agreed to continue German opera. By opening night 1890, Stanton was in still deeper trouble: he had lost his most bankable stars, Lehmann and tenor Max Alvary.[11]

FIGURE 6. The war between the German and the Italian/French wings, *Puck* cartoon, February 11, 1891 (courtesy Metropolitan Opera Archives)

On January 7, 1891, Henry Abbey, this time with Maurice Grau (a lawyer by training, he had managed the American tours of Anton Rubinstein, Henri Wieniawski, and Jacques Offenbach) and John B. Schoeffel (a silent partner), offered to lease the house once again, guaranteeing a season of sixty shows in Italian and French, and promising Jean de Reszke, Édouard de Reszke, and Nellie Melba, all for $2,000 per performance. With the understanding that there would be no additional assessment, the stockholders voted a decisive yes. As Auchincloss described it, the "revolt . . . against . . . the longueurs of Wagner" had succeeded. "Lilli Lehmann [had] tried to warn Edmund of it; she begged him to make some concessions." But he had refused. Stanton submitted his resignation. The German era had come to an end. In a long lament for the seven seasons gone by, Henderson held out this caution to Stanton's successor: "The Italian singer is always a singer, and he conceives it to be his divine right to face the footlights, sing directly to the audience, and dwell on all his high notes. . . . This style of thing, however, is dead in New York" (*Times*, March 22, 1891).[12]

Maybe so. But there was no question that Stanton had presided over a disastrous final German year. In a desperate move to address one of the crushing criticisms leveled at his stewardship, that he had failed to deliver on novelties as stipulated, he staged three New York premieres. The season opened with Alberto Franchetti's Wagnerian *Asrael;* it ran for five performances to feeble box office and to weak and, in at least two instances, overtly anti-Semitic reviews: "The modern Hebrew composer has the faculty of absorbing, assimilating, call it what you will, the dominating influences of his environment.... Look at Meyerbeer and Halévy, consider Mendelssohn and Goldmark, and Franchetti has the advantage over them all—he comes last" (*Musical Courier,* Dec. 3, 1890). Krehbiel, too, was driven to the Meyerbeer analogy: weren't the two composers both Jewish and wealthy? The second novelty was Anton Smareglia's *Il Vassalo di Szigeth,* which had four performances and an uneven reception. And finally, and fatally, Stanton presented the thirty-year-old *Diana von Solange,* the inspiration of Ernest II, Duke of Saxe-Coburg-Gotha. A public outcry forced the cancellation of the run after two performances. Fearing a boycott by the Wagnerites following the announcement of the impending changeover to French and Italian, Stanton scheduled a flurry of twenty-five performances of Wagner out of the season's remaining thirty-five. Audiences came and vented their anger at the board by cheering Seidl and the German casts at every curtain call.[13]

### THE THREE PROPHETS

Meyerbeer's *Il Profeta* (March 21, 1884), *Der Profet* (Dec. 17, 1884), and *Le Prophète* (Jan. 1, 1892) mark the transitions that define the slice of history we cover in the first two chapters of this book: from the Grand Italian Opera to the German seasons to the international house the Metropolitan became in 1891. *Il Profeta* was on Abbey's bill for the inaugural season, *Der Profet* on Damrosch's program for the first German season, and *Le Prophète* on the boards on Abbey's return. Meyerbeer, who in 1815 traded the Jakob he was given at birth for the Italian Giacomo, was arguably the most cosmopolitan of his peers. He composed operas on Italian and German texts (*Il Crociato in Egitto* and *Ein Feldlager in Schlesien,* for example), and most memorably on French librettos. His works range in style from bel canto to the grand opéra he is credited with founding, in the company of Auber and Rossini. *Le Prophète* shared with his *Les Huguenots,* Bizet's *Carmen,* and Gounod's *Faust* the distinction of trilingual hearings in the Met's Italian, German, and early international years.

The positive reception of the March 21, 1884 *Il Profeta* was buried under three distractions. The first was the misguided staging of one of the opera's best-known pages; the second, the misbehavior of the box holders; and the third, a suit brought by the impresario against his star contralto. The *Times* reported affably on the "general merriment" provoked by "the evolution of the [roller] skaters, one of whom fell twice" during what the composer and his librettist, Eugène Scribe, intended as a coup de théâtre, a spectacular ice-skating scene. The reviewer took a less genial tone toward the "indifference or servility of the multifarious management" vis-à-vis arrogant box holders who "considered themselves privileged to indulge in conversations which are heard over half the house." And lastly, the contralto sued by Abbey for damages was Sofia Scalchi; she had refused to replace an ailing colleague. Abbey was forced to cancel. The defense protested that "Mme. Scalchi was and is but human, and had eaten a hearty breakfast. It was impossible for her to appear at so short a notice as Fidès, but she offered to sing in anything else and even two or three acts of *The Prophet*." Delighted to strike a blow for the Academy, Mapleson testified in favor of Scalchi and, more to the point, against Abbey: "His experience, you know, was only obtained in 1883 and 1884. Before that he knew nothing of operatic management" (*Times*, Dec. 18, 1884).

The New York press seized the opportunity to bask in its pro-German biases by contrasting the December 17, 1884, *Der Profet* to the earlier *Il Profeta*. The *Mail and Express* drew out the parallel: "Last year's interpretation of it at the same house sinks into insignificance compared with last night's. Then it seemed merely a show opera. Now it is revealed as a musical and dramatic composition of solid and substantial worth." The German-language performance had disclosed the opera's previously obscured qualities. Putting aside his contempt for the composer in the interest of the larger agenda, Krehbiel proclaimed *Der Profet* "an extraordinary work," a judgment absent from his review of *Il Profeta*. He went on to cite "the great amount of really fine dramatic writing, both vocal and instrumental, with which Meyerbeer has enriched Scribe's poor libretto" (*Tribune*, Dec. 20). For the *Times*, Marianne Brandt, as Fidès, "acted . . . with a mastery of the methods of expression quite foreign to the exponents of Italian art." The press corps's declaration of unconditional German superiority rings hollow: the year before, the same newspaper, and in all likelihood the same reviewer, had lauded the performance of Scalchi in the same role in approximately the same terms. And although one critic asserted that "the *Prophet* was given with a magnificence of ensemble last night at the Metropolitan that made it one of the notable representations of Dr. Damrosch's already notable season" *(World)*, another pointed out that Damrosch conducted from a piano score and failed to cue musicians, to the detriment of the musical product (*Musical Courier*, Dec. 24, 1884). This much is clear: that during the inaugural and German seasons, *Il Profeta/Der Profet* ran a close second to the thirty-three performances chalked up by *Faust*, the period's leading title, excepting the Wagner entries, of course.[14]

Meyerbeer's opera is set in sixteenth-century Holland and Germany during the uprising of the fanatical Anabaptists. The spectacle devised by the composer and his librettist includes not only the skating ballet derided by reviewers in 1884, but a Bacchic orgy, a cataclysmic explosion, and Jean de Leyde's coronation in the Münster cathedral. Here, the private drama is enacted in the public arena: Fidès, begging alms of the assembled, recognizes her lost son in the newly crowned king; fearing for their lives, Jean denies that Fidès is his mother; and grasping the danger, she denies him in return. Critics extoled this scene and, in particular, Scalchi's Italian rendition and, some months later, Brandt's in German. On New Year's Day 1892 *Le Prophète* finally made it to 39th Street in the original French. The cast was led by Polish tenor Jean de Reszke as Jean, the reluctant false prophet, by German soprano Lilli Lehmann, who had often sung the role of Berthe in German at the Met, and by Giulia Ravogli, an Italian contralto, as Fidès, the selfless mother.

### INTERNATIONAL SEASONS, 1891–1903

On opening night 1891, a fortnight prior to *Le Prophète,* de Reszke, his brother Édouard, and Emma Eames made their New York debuts in Gounod's *Roméo et Juliette*—and French was heard at the Metropolitan for the first time. But through the end of the season, *Les Huguenots, Faust, Mignon, L'Africaine,* and *Hamlet,* all French, were sung in Italian, the language to which *Lohengrin, Der Fliegende Holländer, Die Meistersinger,* and *Fidelio* reverted in the early international years. The reinstatement of Italian opera in Italian was immediate. But only in 1893–94 were *Faust* and *Carmen* given wholly in French; *Mignon* and *Les Huguenots* continued in Italian. It was not until 1898–99 that the reconversion of Wagner into German was complete. In the intervening years, circumstances called for hybrid solutions, polyglot performances in which one or more of the principals sang in the original language while lesser members of the cast, and more often the chorus, sang in another, or indeed others. But whatever the fits and starts, the Metropolitan was ahead of the world's great houses by fifty years and more in the practice of setting scores to the texts to which they had first been wed.

In the initial international season, audiences clamoring for *Il Barbiere di Siviglia, Lucia di Lammermoor, Norma,* and *Rigoletto* were placated by fourteen Italian titles, half the program. German opera fell away to a mere sixteen performances of four works, all given in Italian. Between 1891 and 1903, the company mounted sixteen French premieres, exceeding even the quotient of Italian novelties. For these firsts, the managers engaged a cadre of French specialists: Emma Eames, Nellie Melba, and Jean and Édouard de Reszke, whose reputations were cemented in Paris; Jean Lassalle, Pol Plançon, and Emma Calvé, who had created major roles in works by Massenet; Marie Van Zandt, the first Lakmé; and Sybil Sanderson, the first Thaïs. In all, twenty-five French operas were staged. Abbey, Schoeffel, and Grau could count on *Faust, Carmen, Roméo et Juliette,* and *Les Huguenots*—assuming, of course, that they paraded stellar casts. *Werther, Hamlet, L'Africaine,* and others languished even when sung by these same artists. Still, the frequency of performance, the new works, the number and glamour of French and Francophone stars, and the generous receipts of the beloved chestnuts conspired to assure pride of place for French opera in the early international years.

## 1891–1892

First-night notices were condescending for the most part, if not out and out inimical. But underlying disdain for *Roméo et Juliette* as the vanguard of the Met's new era and the mixed reception of Eames and Jean de Reszke was the invidious comparison of the international chapter just opened with the German chapter just closed. As usual, the *Musical Courier* reviewer went further than his more judicious colleagues. He let fly with the prognostication that the Gounod performance was the harbinger of what would prove a disastrous regime. His devastating critique of opening night concluded, "Let us hope that the two managers [Abbey and Grau] will not live to rue the day. But we are under the impression that a public which has had seven years of education in a school of opera in which artistic ensemble and dramatic vraisemblance are not sacrificed to the glorification of two or three high salaried stars will not hail the new dispensation with hymns of abiding joy" (Dec. 16, 1891). The *Musical Courier*'s most venomous diatribes were reserved for the *Herald*'s francophilic editor and founder of the Paris edition, James Gordon Bennett, whose paper had spoken for the anti-Wagner forces during the German seasons. In its rave of *Roméo et Juliette,* distilled as "a general impression of beauty, grace and pleasure; a grateful freedom from the fatigue which has almost invariably accompanied even the best performances at the Metropolitan by German singers," the *Herald* gave the Wagnerites as good, and with far better humor, as it got: "Dark haired, romantic sons of the South in sky blue hose and doublet, pointed of shoe and plumed of cap, held the stage so lately occupied by stern, blond knights in silver armor; clinging girlhood trembled and thrilled where stalwart demi-goddesses lately strode the boards." The French repertoire claimed the lion's share of that season's New York performances. Nine *Faust*s, with the de Reszkes and Eames, headed the pack. The two French novelties, neither new to the city, were as lightweight as the voice of Van Zandt, for whom they were staged. Meyerbeer's opéra comique *Dinorah,* with its demented heroine and her pet goat, was "too small and unattractive for so vast a house as the Metropolitan" *(Herald).* Reviewers indulged Léo Delibes's *Lakmé* as "exceedingly pleasant" *(Tribune),* an "exquisite little romantic opera, with the charming little American prima donna" *(Herald).*

Two of the three Italian entries got off to disappointing starts in the winter of 1891. That September, a touring company had presented a rough-and-ready edition of *Cavalleria rusticana* in Philadelphia; Pietro Mascagni was seen as pumping new energy into the spent traditions of Italian opera. At the Met in December, Eames's patrician Santuzza and the "stridulous" Turiddu of Fernando Valero *(Tribune)* earned only tepid receipts for the Sicilian melodrama. Just two years later, Calvé, "a woman with hot blood in her veins" *(Tribune,* Nov. 30, 1893), set *Cavalleria* on the palmy road it has since enjoyed. As for *Otello,* first performed at the Academy of Music in 1888 by an Italian ensemble assembled for the purpose, it was immediately acknowledged as the crowning work of Verdi's immense oeuvre. *(Falstaff* was yet to come.) But de Reszke himself, as the Moor, could not rescue *Otello* from the ignominy of the poorest box office of the Met's 1891–92 season. The opera's enduring appeal would be realized only many decades later. The third novelty, *Semiramide,* given only in Boston and never to become a fixture, was an ephemeral showcase for Adelina Patti. Later that year, she would bid yet another of her many "farewells" to her devoted New York public. The "Lesson Scene" of *Il Barbiere di Siviglia* was an anthology of old favorites, capped by "The Last Rose of Summer." That was not all: Patti stood before the final curtain and regaled her fans with "Comin' through the Rye."[15]

In August, a catastrophe befell the house. Fire destroyed the stage, the floors below, and those above all the way to the roof, and damaged parts of the auditorium. The Met's year-old management had no recourse but to cancel the 1892–93 season. Security measures had been so mindlessly circumvented that it took no more than one vagrant match to ignite the conflagration. The vaunted sprinkler system had been turned off in the cold of winter and remained inactive; in the heat of summer, the asbestos curtain had been raised to better ventilate the stage; iron girders had been replaced by more flexible, and flammable, lumber supports. The estimated cost of rebuilding was far higher than the amount for which the house had been insured; it was precisely the state-of-the-art fireproofing, cavalierly disabled, that had justified the low valuation.

The board seized the opportunity of the crisis to restructure the Metropolitan Opera House Company as the Metropolitan Opera and Real Estate Company. The number of stockholders was reduced from a cumbersome seventy to a more manageable thirty-five, all of whom had exclusive rights to their boxes. A couple of negative ballots would suffice to block the transfer of shares. And the directors of the reorganized company reserved for themselves unprecedented control over artistic decisions: during the Abbey-Schoeffel-Grau years, and later, they cleaved to the prerogative of endorsing six of the principal singers each season, two of whom were to appear in every subscription performance. The new architects replaced the boxes at the parquet level with an orchestra circle and additional standing room. Seating capacity grew from 3,045 to 3,400; with standees, the theater held 4,000. Following Cady's lead, the firm of Carrere and Hastings slighted theatrical red—not for the original yellow and ivory, but for cream. This time there was no carping. The new electric lights accented the parures sparkling in the thirty-five coveted boxes to such dazzling effect that the "golden" of the 1883 "horseshoe" appreciated to the more precious "diamond." And as important as the reinvention of the company and the house that the year off allowed was the time for planning afforded to Abbey and Grau by the calamitous event of summer 1892.[16]

## 1893–1897

*Faust* opened the rebuilt theater in 1893 as it had the Met a decade earlier. For the first five of the Abbey-Schoeffel-Grau years, it, together with *Roméo et Juliette,* held a monopoly on opening night, a sign of the preeminence of French opera under the new administration. *Faust,* in particular, was performed with such numbing frequency that Henderson famously dubbed the

FIGURE 7. Emma Calvé as Carmen (courtesy Metropolitan Opera Archives)

Metropolitan the "Faustspielhaus." On February 14, 1896, de Reszke and Melba so incited the audience that a piano had to be rolled onto the stage so that Jean might accompany Nellie in her melodious urging that the crowd wend its way "Home, Sweet Home." *Carmen,* at last in French, came into its own when the management brought together a cast—Calvé, de Reszke, Eames, and Lassalle—that the *Times* (Dec. 21, 1893) described as "near to justifying the epithet 'ideal.'" In 1893–94, Calvé appeared in all but one of the thirty performances of Bizet's opera, half in New York, half on tour; she set what still stands as the single-season record for a singer in a major role. Abandoning all restraint, Krehbiel called hers "the most sensational triumph ever achieved by any opera or singer." If, in the course of the hundreds of Carmens she sang all over the world during her long career, Calvé became capricious, even ridiculous, in 1896 Henderson thought her perfect: "Her performance last night was that of a genius" (*Times,* Dec. 12). Iterations of the 1894–95 *Les Huguenots* with Melba, the two de Reszkes, Lillian Nordica, Plançon, Scalchi, and Victor Maurel were promoted as "The Night of the Seven Stars." The price for orchestra seats was raised from $5 to $7 and hyped at $1 a luminary.[17]

Throughout this period, as before and since, critics petitioned loudly for new music that they then found wanting for one reason or another. It was the rare house premiere that won over the press, or indeed the audience. The nine French novelties introduced between 1893 and 1897 were all box-office failures. To Gounod's sweetened versions of Goethe and Shakespeare, the company added the composer's *Philémon et Baucis,* based on Ovid by way of La Fontaine; it found a tenuous place in the repertoire through the end of the Grau regime. Far more surprising was that Massenet's sorrowful *Werther,* with de Reszke and Eames, eked out but one solitary performance on 39th Street. The francophilic *Herald,* no longer obliged to defend the underdog as it had during the Stanton years, reckoned *Werther* "a trifle tiresome for all classes of operagoers." Herman Bemberg's *Elaine,* dedicated to Melba and de Reszke, its original interpreters in London, soon disappeared, despite favorable reviews and good box office. *Manon* (Jan. 16, 1895) was a vehicle for Sibyl Sanderson, a California-born soprano, the darling of Paris and, more particularly, of the opera's composer, Massenet, incidentally one of Bemberg's teachers. "A much-advertised woman" *(Tribune),* with a small voice and "thin and strident" high notes *(Times),* Sanderson was cited for her charm and beauty, and her costumes, to which the *Herald* consecrated four detailed paragraphs. De Reszke's Chevalier des Grieux made off with the few honors there were. The work itself was found ill suited to the cavernous Met. Camille Saint-Saëns's *Samson et Dalila* was even more poorly received, attacked as an oratorio passing as an opera. The *Herald* would have preferred "a little more love in the libretto and not so much Hebrew lamentation!" And during what ought to have been the spectacular finale, "in the midst of wild hilarity" malfunctioning stage machinery hoisted a column that the Samson, Francesco Tamagno, had valorously toppled. Donizetti's *La Favorite,* sung in its more familiar Italian translation, was dismissed as beneath contempt by Krehbiel and Henderson. Calvé appeared as Anita, a role written for her, in *La Navarraise.* The *Herald* wondered at the good London press for the one-acter: "To be perfectly blunt, Massenet's opera is no opera at all. . . . Imagine a series of living pictures, with speech and music thrown in." An abbreviated *Les Pêcheurs de perles,* also with Calvé, made its debut the same evening as *La Navarraise.* Bizet's exotic piece bred rare discord between the *Times* ("it abounds in lyric beauties") and the *Tribune* ("the opera is insufferably stupid"). *Le Cid* was an occasion for de Reszke to reprise the role he had originated in Paris in 1885; the brickbats for Massenet's music, his fourth Met flop in successive years, and poor receipts for the second performance foretold the opera's early demise.[18]

Only one of the four new Italian works did any better than the French novelties. *Pagliacci* was initially programmed with the neoclassical *Orfeo,* a coupling as odd as that of the Gluck opera with *Cavalleria rusticana* two years earlier. Ruggero Leoncavallo's trenchant depiction of a crime of passion within an itinerant commedia dell'arte troupe rang up average receipts until it found its niche that very season as half of *Cav/Pag,* the most indissoluble of all operatic double bills. The ever prodigal Grau again presented his two top sopranos for the price of one, Calvé, who as Santuzza "fairly outdid herself" (*Herald,* Dec. 23, 1893), and an indisposed Melba as Nedda. The response of the *Times,* "the effect of bringing the two operas together in one night was good," is surely among operatic criticism's rare understatements. *Falstaff,* starring Maurel, Verdi's first "Fat John," fell far below the season's average. The modest take of *Le Nozze di Figaro* was a faulty predictor of its brilliant future. Even the magnetic Fernando de Lucia and Emma Calvé, in the roles they had created in Rome in 1891, were unable to generate enthusiasm for *L'Amico Fritz.* Mascagni's romantic comedy had but one complete hearing. Its second act was drafted as a curtain-raiser for, what else, his own inevitable *Cavalleria rusticana,* Calvé as the sweet-tempered Suzel in the former and the impassioned Santuzza in the latter.

How to explain the management's persistence in mounting new works, given the dismal grades racked up by one premiere after another? If pressure came from the might of reviewers, it also came from within. Like all major companies, the Met guarded its prestige jealously and its standing depended, in significant part, on the propagation of opera as a living art. Equally compelling, perhaps more, was the imperative to keep its stars happy by obliging them with the novel and flattering roles they craved. And after all, if Calvé failed to put over *La Navarraise* or *L'Amico Fritz,* there was always *Carmen;* de Reszke could rely on the trusty *Faust* and *Les Huguenots* to offset *Werther* and *Le Cid.* Then there was the Wagner he demanded to sing in German,

FIGURE 8. Jean de Reszke as Siegfried in *Götterdämmerung* (courtesy Metropolitan Opera Archives)

seconded by two thousand starved Wagnerites who had lobbied the management for German performances. Abbey and Grau made their case to the board, and a lucrative fifth slot, Thursday evening, was added to accommodate the German repertoire, with Seidl conducting. Of the many resplendent moments of this period, none is remembered as more electrifying than November 27, 1895, when de Reszke sang Tristan in the original for the first time, brother Édouard King Marke, Nordica Isolde. Before the season ended, the tenor had added Lohengrin in the original. The following year, de Reszke continued to grow his Wagnerian laurels with the young hero of *Siegfried* (for which he shaved his famous moustache), seemingly unperturbed by the drama that surrounded the production. When Melba was announced for Brünnhilde, Nordica, having reason to presume the role to be hers, took understandable umbrage. She held the tenor responsible for the offense and canceled her season. But Melba came to grief in this, her first and only attempt to rise to the warrior maiden (Dec. 30, 1896). She too dropped out of 1896–97, or what was left of it. In the end, it was de Reszke who counted: his assumption of the heroic roles of the "Ring" guaranteed Wagner stage time comparable, if not to the French wing, certainly to the Italian. That he sang only eight performances of Italian opera out of his more than three hundred in seven years with the company attests not only to the primacy of French and German opera at the end of the century, but to the low estate to which the bel canto composers and Verdi had fallen.[19]

Well before Henry Abbey's death on October 17, 1896, it was evident that the managing triumvirate was close to bankruptcy. The opera company had held its own, and more; Abbey's other theatrical ventures were to blame. The board designated William Steinway, principal of the piano firm, to restructure the enterprise as Abbey, Schoeffel, and Grau Ltd., and to rebalance the books. The situation continued to deteriorate nonetheless. Following Abbey's death and Schoeffel's withdrawal, Grau found himself alone in charge. He refused to lease the house for 1897–98, when the de Reszkes, Calvé, and Melba chose to sing elsewhere, and repaired instead to Covent Garden, where he was also managing director. For the second time in six years, the Met had no resident company. Those who argued for the primacy of music in the German manner over that of the star system endemic to French and Italian practice were, in some perverse way, vindicated by Grau's desertion of New York for an entire operatic year.[20]

## 1898–1903

On Grau's return in 1898, the star system ruled as aggressively as ever. The five-year tenancy of the Maurice Grau Opera Company is often cited as the apogee of the Met's "golden age." And as if to silence the opposing camp, for the first time in seventy-three years of intrepid entrepreneurship, it was Grau who proved opera fiscally viable in New York. The company showed a profit in each of his years. His winning strategy was this: to engage the most celebrated artists of the time for the entire season, and to pay them extravagantly, to the despair of competing houses and on the backs of supporting singers, of the orchestra, and of the chorus; to assemble so large a roster of international singers that he could field casts capable of performing in all styles and operatic languages then current; and to make frequent cast changes so as to oblige reviewers to attend again and again. The public, he knew, would put up with scenery hung interchangeably for Verdi, Wagner, and Meyerbeer as long as it framed the Melbas, the Calvés, and the de Reszkes. As to conductors, he quipped that "no one has ever paid a nickel to see a man's back."[21]

In 1898–99, audiences at last heard an uncut "Ring" cycle, under Franz Schalk, with de Reszke, Lehmann, and Nordica reconciled with the company and her tenor. Sembrich made an emotional return after fifteen years. Melba was absent in 1899–1900 but resurfaced the next year, when, for the first time, the board exercised its right to choose the lead singers, by voting her a contract. She, in turn, cast a ballot of her own: the veto of Sembrich. The following year, with Melba's defection, Sembrich was again on the roster. Most eagerly awaited was Jean de Reszke as Lohengrin on New Year's Eve 1900, after a season's hiatus. Admiration for de Reszke, his style, his acting, his musicality, and his sincerity bordered on delirium. The story of the Met's golden age is largely his story. It was he who defined the Met primarily as home to the French repertoire and who soon thereafter rehabilitated Wagner. The turn of the first year of the new century would coincide with de Reszke's adieu. The Gay Nineties were over. So was an extraordinary operatic era. At the April 29, 1901, gala, during which a reported sixteen women were revived by the ammonia providentially dispensed by ushers posted at every door, an astonishing two thousand standees were jammed behind the orchestra seats. The program featured de Reszke, Melba, and Nordica, of course. Ovations for the Polish tenor oscillated from "frantic" to "frenzied" (Times). The gala also blandished two French guests, the actors Sarah Bernhardt and Coquelin, in a one-act comedy.[22]

La Bohème and Tosca were new to the Met in the 1900–01 season. Henderson and Krehbiel had snubbed Puccini's bohemians when an Italian troupe of no particular distinction introduced them to New York at Wallach's Theatre in 1898. And when Melba, in search of suitable new roles, and Albert Saléza sang the doomed seamstress and the impoverished poet on 39th Street, the fractious critics saw no reason to change their minds. Tosca had by far the stronger cast, particularly in the Roman diva of Milka Ternina and the lecherous police chief of Antonio Scotti, who would go on to sing more than two hundred Scarpias with the company. The Tribune decried the opera's "repulsive" subject; Krehbiel was particularly hard on Puccini's score, "much of it like shreds and patches of many things with which the operatic stage has long been familiar." Audience response through the end of the Grau years was unexceptional. It was not until Heinrich Conried took over from Grau in 1903 and Enrico Caruso assumed the tenor leads that these Puccini masterworks would take their undying place in the public's affections.

TABLE 3 Metropolitan Opera Premieres, 1891–92 to 1902–03

| Composer and Title | Met Premiere | Most Recent Met Performance | No. of Seasons in Met Repertoire | No. of Met Productions | No. of Met Performances, 1883–2013 | World Premiere | Director/Designer |
|---|---|---|---|---|---|---|---|
| Pietro Mascagni, *Cavalleria rusticana* | Dec. 4, 1891 | Apr. 10, 2009 | 75 | 7 | 667 | May 17, 1890, Rome, Costanzi | Theodore Habelmann / Unknown |
| Giuseppe Verdi, *Otello* | Jan. 23, 1892 | Mar. 30, 2013 | 39 | 7 | 325 | Feb. 5, 1887, Milan, La Scala | Theodore Habelmann / Unknown |
| Giacomo Meyerbeer, *Dinorah* (in Italian) | Jan. 18, 1891 | Feb. 3, 1925 | 2 | 2 | 5 | Apr. 4, 1859, Paris, Opéra-Comique | Theodore Habelmann / Unknown |
| Léo Delibes, *Lakmé* | Feb. 22, 1892 | May 1, 1947 | 14 | 4 | 63 | Apr. 14, 1883, Paris, Opéra-Comique | Theodore Habelmann / Unknown |
| Gioachino Rossini, *Semiramide* | Mar. 22, 1892 | Jan. 16, 1993 | 5 | 3 | 28 | Feb. 3, 1823, Venice, La Fenice | Unknown / Unknown |
| Charles Gounod, *Philémon et Baucis* | Nov. 29, 1893 | Jan. 27, 1903 | 5 | 1 | 13 | Feb. 18, 1860, Paris, Lyrique | Armand Castelmary / Unknown |
| Ruggero Leoncavallo, *Pagliacci* | Dec. 11, 1893 | Apr. 10, 2009 | 77 | 5 | 712 | May 21, 1892, Milan, dal Verme | Armand Castelmary / Unknown |
| Pietro Mascagni, *L'Amico Fritz* | Jan. 10, 1894 | Dec. 22, 1923 | 2 | 2 | 6 | Oct. 31, 1891, Rome, Costanzi | Armand Castelmary / Unknown |
| Wolfgang Amadeus Mozart, *Le Nozze di Figaro* | Jan. 31, 1894 | Nov. 17, 2012 | 54 | 7 | 458 | May 1, 1786, Vienna, Burgtheater | Armand Castelmary / Unknown |
| Jules Massenet, *Werther* | Mar. 29, 1894 | Jan. 22, 2004 | 11 | 3 | 73 | Feb. 16, 1892, Vienna, Hofoper | William Parry / Unknown |
| Herman Bemberg, *Elaine* | Dec. 17, 1894 | Jan. 5, 1895 | 1 | 1 | 2 | July 5, 1892, London, Covent Garden | William Parry / Unknown |
| Jules Massenet, *Manon* | Jan. 16, 1895 | Apr. 23, 2012 | 41 | 6 | 266 | Jan. 19, 1884, Paris, Opéra-Comique | William Parry / Unknown |

| | | | | | | | |
|---|---|---|---|---|---|---|---|
| Giuseppe Verdi, *Falstaff* | Feb. 4, 1895 | Oct. 22, 2005 | 21 | 4 | 175 | Feb. 9, 1893, Milan, La Scala | William Parry/Unknown |
| Camille Saint-Saëns, *Samson et Dalila* | Feb. 8, 1895 | Mar. 2, 2006 | 33 | 5 | 226 | Dec. 2, 1877, Weimar, Grossherzogliches (in German) | William Parry/Unknown |
| Gaetano Donizetti, *La Favorita* (in Italian) | Nov. 29, 1895 | June 9, 1978 | 5 | 2 | 25 | Dec. 21, 1840, Paris, Opéra | William Parry/Unknown |
| Jules Massenet, *La Navarraise* | Dec. 11, 1895 | Jan. 9, 1922 | 2 | 2 | 12 | June 20, 1894, London, Covent Garden | William Parry/Unknown |
| Georges Bizet, *Les Pêcheurs de perles*[a] | Jan. 11, 1896 | Dec. 13, 1916 | 2 | 2 | 4 | Sept. 30, 1863, Paris, Lyrique | William Parry/Unknown |
| Hector Berlioz, *La Damnation de Faust*[b] | Feb. 2, 1896 | Nov. 17, 2009 | 5 | 2 | 26 | *In concert:* Dec. 6, 1846, Paris, Opéra-Comique; *staged:* Feb. 18, 1893, Monte Carlo, Opéra | In concert |
| Jules Massenet, *Le Cid* | Feb. 12, 1897 | Apr. 4, 1902 | 2 | 1 | 11 | Nov. 30, 1885, Paris, Opéra | William Parry/Unknown |
| Luigi Mancinelli, *Ero e Leandro* | Mar. 10, 1899 | Mar. 14, 1903 | 1 | 1 | 5 | Nov. 30, 1897, Madrid, Reale | Pierre Baudu/Unknown |
| Gaetano Donizetti, *Don Pasquale* | Dec. 23, 1899 | Feb. 19, 2011 | 22 | 5 | 135 | Jan. 3, 1843, Paris, Italien | Unknown/Unknown |
| Otto Nicolai, *Die Lustigen Weiber von Windsor* | Mar. 9, 1900 | Mar. 9, 1900 | 1 | 1 | 1 | Mar. 9, 1849, Berlin, Königliches Opernhaus | Pierre Baudu/Unknown |
| Wolfgang Amadeus Mozart, *Die Zauberflöte* (in Italian) | Mar. 30, 1900 | Jan. 6, 2011 | 44 | 8 | 408 | Sept. 30, 1791, Vienna, auf der Wieder | Pierre Baudu/Unknown |

*(continued)*

TABLE 3 (continued)

| Composer and Title | Met Premiere | Most Recent Met Performance | No. of Seasons in Met Repertoire | No. of Met Productions | No. of Met Performances, 1883–2013 | World Premiere | Director/Designer |
|---|---|---|---|---|---|---|---|
| Giacomo Puccini, La Bohème | Nov. 9, 1900 | Dec. 8, 2011 | 104 | 4 | 1,245 | Feb. 1, 1896, Turin, Regio | William Parry/Unknown |
| Giacomo Puccini, Tosca | Feb. 4, 1901 | Jan. 28, 2012 | 90 | 5 | 925 | Jan. 14, 1900, Rome, Costanzi | William Parry/Unknown |
| Ernest Reyer, Salammbô | Mar. 20, 1901 | Mar. 26, 1901 | 1 | 1 | 3 | Feb. 10, 1890, Brussels, La Monnaie | William Parry/Unknown |
| Gaetano Donizetti, La Fille du régiment | Jan. 6, 1902 | Jan. 6, 2012 | 15 | 5 | 109 | Feb. 11, 1840, Paris, Opéra-Comique | Unknown/Unknown |
| Isidore de Lara, Messaline | Jan. 22, 1902 | Feb. 7, 1902 | 1 | 1 | 4 | Mar. 21, 1899, Monte Carlo, Casino Municipal | Unknown/Unknown |
| Ignacy Paderewski, Manru | Feb. 14, 1902 | Apr. 19, 1902 | 1 | 1 | 9 | May 29, 1901, Dresden | Unknown/Unknown |
| Daniel Auber, Fra Diavolo | In concert: Dec. 24, 1902; staged: Jan. 11, 1910 | Apr. 23, 1910 | 2 | 2 | 9 | Jan. 28, 1830, Paris, Opéra-Comique | In concert at the Freundschaft Club |
| Giuseppe Verdi, Ernani | Jan. 28, 1903 | Feb. 25, 2012 | 13 | 4 | 94 | Mar. 9, 1844, Venice, La Fenice | Fernand Almanz/Unknown |
| Ethel Smyth, Der Wald | Mar. 11, 1903 | Mar. 20, 1903 | 1 | 1 | 2 | Apr. 9, 1902, Berlin, Opernhaus | Unknown/Unknown |

[a] Only acts 1 and 2 of Les Pêcheurs de perles were performed.
[b] La Damnation de Faust was given in concert form.

Reviewers heaped abuse on Ernest Reyer's *Salammbô* and Isidore De Lara's *Messaline,* the first served up on a scale that vied with the grandiosity of Flaubert's orientalist novel, the second a personal triumph for Calvé as the Roman empress, a "foul-minded, utterly carnal, and debased woman" *(Times).* Two German-language works, *Manru,* Ignacy Paderewski's sole opera, and Ethel Smyth's *Der Wald,* were fresh from their European premieres. Critics faulted the libretto of *Manru,* "awkward in construction, and at times amazingly silly in language" *(Tribune);* Paderewski's score was coddled as "an amazing first opera" *(Tribune),* "the conception of a genuine composer" *(Times).* The beloved pianist was called to take repeated bows as early as the second-act curtain. And Sembrich was indebted to her Polish compatriot for a congenial vehicle. *Manru* failed to survive its initial season. Grau's final premiere was also attended by the composer, in this case the composer-librettist, a British feminist largely trained in Leipzig. *Der Wald* was the first and remains the only opera by a woman to be staged at the Met. The one-act piece was given two performances. The *Telegraph* couched its favorable notice in blatantly sexist terms: "In fact, this little woman writes music with a masculine hand and has a sound and logical brain, such as is supposed to be the especial gift of the rougher sex. There is not a weak or effeminate note in *Der Wald,* nor an unstable sentiment." The *World* bridled at "an hour of ultra-modern music, strident, formless." The *Times* regretted that "Mr. Grau's long and distinguished career as an impresario should be marked by a production of so little importance." By then, in declining health, Grau had announced his retirement for the end of the 1902–03 season. The board named Conried to replace him. Five years later, the exasperated directors bought Conried out. High on the list of complaints was that he had strayed from the French path Grau had charted so profitably.

## THE PARABOLIC FORTUNES OF THE FRENCH REPERTOIRE

In the Met's inaugural year, France provided approximately one-third of the operas and performances given by the Grand Italian Opera. The French repertoire claimed an even higher quotient under Leopold Damrosch the following season, when *Le Prophète* and *La Juive* gave *Tannhäuser* and *Lohengrin* a run for their money. From 1885 to 1891, the six remaining seasons under the leadership and aesthetic bias of Stanton and Seidl, the German juggernaut drove the French roster to a distant second place at 15 percent of the program. The era of French dominance came under the directorships of Abbey-Schoeffel-Grau, as we have seen, and then of Grau alone. Between 1891 and 1903, the Gallic repertoire accounted for one-third of the total performances; it led the box office in all but three seasons, in four exceeding 50 percent of the gross, and in 1893–94 reaching the top of the parabola with a stupefying 70 percent share. The institutional and performance history of the period exhibits the degree to which French opera shaped the Metropolitan's *âge d'or.* Through the Conried, Gatti-Casazza, and Johnson years, French works would average around 15 percent of the performances, falling between 10 percent and 13 percent since then.

The inventory of Metropolitan titles from 1883 to 2013 includes sixty-one French works, a number far short of the ninety-eight Italian and slightly greater than the German forty-seven. But by the measure of titles that have tallied more than one hundred performances, only eight are French, while nineteen are German and twenty-nine Italian. *Carmen* and *Faust* have been presented regularly, which is to say, like *Lucia di Lammermoor* and *Il Barbiere di Siviglia,* for example, in half or more of 128 Met seasons. Six other works have persisted through good times and bad: *Manon, Roméo et Juliette, Les Contes d'Hoffmann, Samson et Dalila, Pelléas et Mélisande,* and *La Fille du régiment. Werther,* long dormant, has taken on new life in recent decades. Then there are those operas, once popular, that have been absent since the 1940s, some longer: *Mignon, L'Africaine, Les Huguenots, Lakmé, Louise, Guillaume Tell.* Neglected at the Met, they have been exhumed elsewhere, occasionally with considerable success. And finally, there are those such as *Salammbô* and *Messaline* that lapsed into virtual oblivion after their first exposures.

# THREE

# Opera Wars, 1903–1908

## PARSIFAL, SALOME, AND THE MANHATTAN OPERA COMPANY

### HEINRICH CONRIED

THE YEARS 1880 AND 1910 bracket a dazzling chapter in the cultural history of New York City. At one end, the three-decade span is anchored by the opening of the Metropolitan Museum of Art on the eastern edge of Central Park and, at the other, by the completion of the New York Public Library on Fifth Avenue. The period saw the founding and, in cases such as that of the Museum, the expansion into grand permanent quarters of many of the arts and science institutions that catapulted New York into the orbit of world cultural capitals: the Metropolitan Opera (1883), the New York Music Hall (1891, later Carnegie Hall), the New York Botanical Garden (1891), the New York Zoological Park (1899, later the Bronx Zoo), the Institute of Musical Art of the City of New York (1904, later the Juilliard School of Music), the Jewish Museum (1904), the Rockefeller Institute for Medical Research (1906, later Rockefeller University), the Pierpont Library (1906, later the Morgan Library and Museum), the Brooklyn Academy of Music (1908), and the New-York Historical Society (1908). In 1910, the books from the Astor and Lenox libraries were transferred to the new edifice on 42nd Street. Instrumental in the birth and burgeoning of these institutions were the men who served also on the executive committee of the first Metropolitan Opera board of directors: James A. Roosevelt (an uncle of Theodore Roosevelt), William C. Whitney, George G. Haven, William K. Vanderbilt, and Adrian Iselin.[1]

Whitney, Haven, and Iselin were still on the board in 1903 when its executive committee met to choose a successor to Maurice Grau. On the lists, along with Heinrich Conried, were Walter Damrosch and Andrew Carnegie's choice, Pittsburgh music manager George W. Wilson. Carnegie's backing of Wilson carried with it the support of seventy-six other million-aires and the pledge to raise $150,000 for the company in a matter of weeks. But not unexpectedly, "New York plutocrats had no intention whatsoever of allowing Pittsburgh to encroach on their playground." Passing over Damrosch by the narrowest margin, seven to six, the executive committee settled on Conried, opting for a theater rather than a music professional, just as they had twenty years earlier in selecting Henry Abbey. With Conried's ascendency, the Metropolitan name was joined to that of an impresario for the first and last time, and for the first time the impresario was accorded a seat on the board of what was now the Conried Metropolitan Opera Company. Born in Silesia, Conried had emigrated to the United States in 1878, as had the very young Maurice Grau from Moravian Austria in 1854 and Leopold Damrosch from Germany in 1871. Only twenty-three at his arrival, Conried nevertheless had sufficient credits as a stage manager and actor in Austria and Germany to have attracted the interest of the director of the Germania Theatre, at whose invitation he came to New York. He would soon be named artistic manager of the Thalia, then of the Casino Theatre, which specialized in operetta, and, in 1893, of the German Theatre in Irving Place, where he developed an exceptional resident stock company. The artistic and financial success of his promotion of German culture on Irving Place, a model of the ensemble repertory adopted by other theater reformers, won him the Metropolitan plum. He brought with him no experience and precious little knowledge of grand opera. His compensation was guaranteed at $20,000 annually and 50 percent of the presumed profits; his expenses included the purchase of Grau's assets, among these, contracts with Enrico Caruso and Olive Fremstad.[2]

Conried's five-year term would be neither the shortest nor the longest in the early history of the Metropolitan. Abbey's first stint lasted just one year, Leopold Damrosch's, tragically, even less. Edmond Stanton was in charge for six years, Abbey-Schoeffel-Grau for five, and then Grau alone for five more. But of all the regimes to that point, and arguably since, Conried's was the most flamboyant and, year for year, the most turbulent. His reign began lav-ishly with the renovation of the auditorium, its décor finally acceding to the traditional deep red and gold it would preserve for the remaining sixty-three years of the theater's life. The former stagehand insisted on the revamping of the stage and the upgrading of its machinery to the most modern standard. Newly framing the stage was a proscenium arch inscribed with the names of Gluck, Mozart, Verdi, Wagner, Gounod, and Beethoven. Public rooms

FIGURE 9. Metropolitan stage rebuilt for *Parsifal, Scientific American*, February 6, 1904 (courtesy Metropolitan Opera Archives)

reserved for pampered patrons were fitted with luxurious new appointments. So was the general manager's extravagant office. Ushers and other employees were dressed in evening clothes, complete with tails, as they had been in 1883. These changes took place in an atmosphere of relative peace. It was the repertoire, though not the repertoire alone, that became the site of conflict.[3]

No sooner had the choice of Conried been made public in February 1903 than the general manager–elect began dropping hints of an exploit he had been plotting for a while: the first staging of *Parsifal* outside of Bayreuth. And so by the time the curtain rose on *Rigoletto,* the 1903–04 season opener and Caruso's debut, the board found itself caught up in a battle waged against its new lessee from pulpits, courts, and press rooms. In Conried's second year, a stage bridge collapsed during a performance of *Carmen;* ten choristers were injured in the nine-foot fall. That same year, the unhappy chorus, demanding a raise in pay from $15 to $25 weekly, shorter hours, and sleeping car instead of coach accommodations on overnight travel, walked out for three days in what was to be the first of the several strikes in Metropolitan history. Eames, Caruso, and other principals filled in for the many choruses of *Faust.* Engelbert Humperdinck made his initial visit to New York to supervise the November 1905 unveiling of *Hänsel und Gretel.* Six months later, and throughout the breathless 1906–07 season, one crisis after another, musical and paramusical, made the goings-on at the opera house riveting copy. A less intrepid impresario might have found just one of these happenings more than enough excitement for little more than a single operatic year.[4]

On April 18, 1906, not long after a performance of *Carmen* (again!) with Caruso and Fremstad, the company on tour in San Francisco felt the first tremors of the historic earthquake. Contralto Louise Homer suffered a miscarriage. The scenery and costumes for thirteen productions were destroyed, a staggering blow for an already compromised budget. In a characteristic gesture of noblesse oblige he could ill afford, the general manager ordered that the $12,000 advance take of the aborted San Francisco engagement be refunded to whoever claimed to have bought a ticket. Musicians, too, took a devastating hit; many of their instruments were lost in the fire. To make matters worse, that fall, Oscar Hammerstein and his Manhattan Opera Company unleashed a competition so ferocious that the opera war with Mapleson and the Academy paled by comparison. In November, as further bad luck would have it, Caruso was arrested for allegedly accosting a woman in the monkey house of the Central Park Zoo. His sensational trial (the charge was disturbing the peace, a misdemeanor) ended in a guilty verdict and a fine of $10. Protestations that it had all been a misunderstanding stemming from the tenor's awful English, coupled with multiple challenges to the prosecution's contradictory evidence and to the deeply flawed judicial proceedings, failed to persuade the judge or, indeed, the tribunal that heard the subsequent appeal. Geraldine Farrar, Conried's other superstar, debuted on opening night. On January 18, 1907, Giacomo Puccini, an international celebrity, made a delayed entrance into the theater (the liner on which he was traveling had met heavy seas and docked later than scheduled) while the Metropolitan premiere of his *Manon Lescaut* was underway. Spotted by the audience at the first act intermission, he was saluted with a fanfare and then an ovation insistent to the point that he was obliged to leave his box so that the performance could continue. Four days later at another premiere (with Puccini present), that of Richard Strauss's *Salome,* another scandal erupted, and with it the revolt of the Metropolitan Opera and Real Estate Company directors, by now at the end of their rope. February 11 brought the company premiere of *Madama Butterfly,* prepared under Puccini's stern glance. Gustav Mahler made his debut in the pit on January 1, 1908.[5]

## BLASPHEMY AND DEPRAVITY

### *Parsifal,* December 24, 1903

Conried was ready for the firestorm he knew would be ignited by the special prospectus announcing the premiere of *Parsifal* for, of all provocative dates, Christmas Eve 1903. This and all subsequent performances of the great work would be outside the subscription schedule, with the best seats at raised prices. Cries of foul and shame originated from legal and religious quarters on both sides of the Atlantic. As the flippant *Brooklyn Eagle* put it, "The area of low pressure was seen first over the roof of Wahnfried [the home of Cosima, Wagner's widow], its most natural starting point. Thence it went to Munich and Berlin; thence all over Teutonic Europe, skirting the Latins and the Slavs, and it finally has settled down for real business here in New York" (Nov. 12, 1903). Cosima's imprecations, befitting her vocation as keeper of the flame, were fueled by the contention that the Metropolitan's proposed staging was tantamount to piracy committed in violation of copyright law. Following an informal and ultimately futile appeal to the Kaiser, her lawyers went to work, arguing that the Met should be enjoined from producing the opera. Conried's European colleagues, his fellow *intendants,* whined that playing Wagner's *Bühnenfestspiel* (stage-consecrating festival drama) on an ordinary operatic platform was an act of artistic heresy.

From the New York Protestant establishment, through its spokesperson, the Rev. Dr. George L. Shearer, Secretary of the American Tract Society, came the charge that the work itself was sacrilegious. Shearer's slippery case for censorship took the form of a loaded question: "If Christianity is the law of the land, and is protected by that law, because its morality is the foundation of the government, would not this proposed travesty of the most sacred things of our worship be indictable under the statute which authorizes the suppression of whatever is an offense to public decency?" His "Anti-*Parsifal* Crusade" was launched in defense of the "most sacred things of our worship." Shearer's brief held that the flower maidens were nothing other than a "red light legion"; Parsifal he likened somewhat more credibly to Jesus, Gurnemanz to John the Baptist, Kundry to the Magdalen. He railed against the representation of the "Lord's Supper" as an "amusement . . . for the sake of gain"; the washing of Parsifal's feet he decried as an impious reference to an episode in the life of Christ (*Tribune,* Nov. 11, 1903). The *Eagle* had its own take on Shearer's screed: "They [Shearer and a second New York minister] . . . say that if anybody is allowed to produce it *[Parsifal]* he should be a Christian and not a Jew. . . . As for denouncing Mr. Conried because he is a Jew, that is an unworthy business for a Christian clergyman. . . . We can conceive no earthly or celestial difference in the effect to be produced on the spectator by the nationality or belief of the man who hires the singers and pays the rent" (Nov. 11, 1903). The Metropolitan counsel, the same attorney who failed to exonerate Caruso, argued that *Parsifal* had already been presented in concert form in Brooklyn in 1890, with Anton Seidl conducting, and again in concert in Boston; the Wagners, he noted, had voiced no objection on these occasions. The case was ultimately thrown out on a simple finding: the *Parsifal* copyright did not extend to the United States. The city's mayor, petitioned to uphold Shearer, refused to revoke the license issued to the Met.[6]

By the time Judge Lacombe rendered his decision, November 24, 1903, preparations for *Parsifal* were well along. Most astounding had been the advance ticket sales, reputedly the greatest ever seen in New York. Weeks before the opening, the *American Journal* reported melodramatically, "Women Faint amid Crush for Seats to *Parsifal.* Many of Them Took Places in Line before Daylight and Were Too Weak to Reach the Window When It Was Opened" (Nov. 11, 1903). Mail orders were delivered so thick and fast that their processing required a room of its own. The paymaster was sequestered for the three days it took to address the refund envelopes. A special police guard was called to be on hand for the opening performance. The *Evening Telegram* published a special edition, the "Parsifal Extra" (Dec. 24, 1903), that included a front-page story, "Great Crush to See *Parsifal*," and a series of drawings of scenes from the opera.

The premiere began at the unlikely hour of five o'clock in the afternoon. The doors were shut at the start of the prelude and, again exceptionally, no one arrived late. A hush was reported to envelop the auditorium at the end of the almost two-hour-long act 1, in imitation of Bayreuth's reverent response to the consecration of the Holy Grail. The audience filed out for the dinner intermission, a concession to the more than five-hour-long score. Many returned in evening clothes (one answer to the question of what to wear to a performance that begins in late afternoon and ends just before midnight) for the second act flower maidens, for Kundry's attempted seduction of Parsifal, for the spectacle of a deadly spear arrested in midair, and for the collapse of the castle of Klingsor, the reprobate knight. It was here that soprano Milka Ternina disclosed Kundry's contrasting identities most artfully: "the strange fascination of a Greek maenad . . . a soul racked and torn with an anguish that freezes the blood . . . a figure of wondrous charm" (*Times*, Jan. 1, 1904). Seven minutes of applause and shouts for the cast and production staff were followed by calls for Conried himself, who obliged with an uncharacteristically modest bow before the curtain. At the end of act 3, the impresario came forward again to congratulate "American operagoers" for the discerning enthusiasm they had displayed for "a great, solemn, beautiful work like this" (*Tribune*). Critics acquainted with the Festspielhaus production pronounced the Met's superior. Devout Wagnerite Henry Finck consigned much of his notice to the décor—which, as he put it, "at every moment dovetailed with the orchestral score, and [was] an essential part of the total effect, arousing deep emotions, and constituting a succession of real works of art." He marveled in particular at the transformation from forest to temple as Parsifal and Gurnemanz traversed the stage (*Evening Post*, Dec. 26, 1903). The engagement of leading contralto Louise Homer for an off-stage, six-word phrase was one more sign of the impresario's profligate showmanship. Against odds of all sorts, Conried had brought off an operatic coup as memorable as any to be found in the annals of the Metropolitan before or since. Barely a month into his first season, he had reached what in retrospect would be thought the high point of his tenure. Met stockholders had eleven *Parsifal* performances to thank for their dividend. The twelfth filled the general manager's purse.[7]

## Salome, January 22, 1907

Ever ready to stir the pot, Conried announced on his return from his summer 1906 European rounds that the coming Metropolitan season would see the premiere of Richard Strauss's *Salome,* the first of the composer's operas to be staged in the United States. Conried had attended a Dresden performance and had been struck by its effect on the audience. Soon after, he began haggling in correspondence with Strauss over royalties for prospective Metropolitan dates and terms that might induce the composer to make a second trip to New York. In winter and spring 1904, Strauss had led several local orchestras at venues as disparate as Carnegie Hall and Wanamaker's department store. The negotiations concluded with an agreement for ten shows without Strauss, at what Conried protested were unheard-of, "ridiculously high" fees. In October, the general manager advertised the first performance, at double the usual prices, of the one-act opera that had, "for more than a year, been the storm center of the musical world." *Salome* would be presented as the second half of his annual benefit, the first part a starry concert. Conried expected another personally lucrative succès de scandale. What he got was more than even he bargained for. Based on Oscar Wilde's notorious 1894 French play, *Salome* had been first performed in Dresden in 1905 to an extraordinary number of curtain calls. While Conried could claim without dissembling, and did, that the opera had been produced in twenty houses throughout Europe, including decorous German court theaters, it was also the case that it had been censored by the Kaiser, if briefly, and banned in Vienna and London. The impresario himself had qualms about the work's New York reception. He wrote to Strauss, "I ... don't know how the American people will take to the subject, and I have simply said that, even at the risk of my audiences not liking the material, I, as Director of the Metropolitan Opera House, would be bound to produce your opera before my audiences—an opera which I, personally, and unendingly, admire."[8]

Preparations for the premiere began in fall 1906. To add to the drama, the general manager had been taken ill, seriously so; at his insistence, some rehearsals were conducted at his bedside. On a Sunday morning, two days before the January 22, 1907, premiere and little more than three years after the cheeky Christmas Eve *Parsifal,* Conried scheduled a semipublic dress rehearsal of *Salome,* a repetition of his earlier scheduling gaffe. Many of the one thousand invited guests—Met stockholders, subscribers, friends and relations of the management and cast, journalists, and music critics—had come to the opera house directly from their devotions. This misstep would haunt discussions of the propriety of staging *Salome* for decades to come. Two days later, on January 22, a capacity audience was treated to the much ballyhooed preopera concert starring, among others, Caruso, Farrar, and Scotti; Sembrich sang two Strauss songs. The last selection was the redemptive climax of *Faust,* "as though to make the maximum contrast with what would follow," Salome's erotic encounter with saintliness and death.[9]

Those who went to the trouble and expense of buying tickets surely knew what they were in for. The Gospel tale of the depraved daughter of Herodias was very much in circulation. There had been persistent press coverage of Strauss's controversial work; there was also the more immediate buzz surrounding the dress rehearsal. And, to gild the lily, on January 21, the day that separated the rehearsal from the gala, the Sothern-Marlowe Company had opened at the Lyric Theatre up the street with Julia Marlowe as Salome in *John the Baptist*. Many operagoers would have read the review of Hermann Sudermann's play in the *Tribune:* "This is a repulsive drama ... in which a wanton woman can perform a lascivious dance, in the presence of a lewd despot, in order to inflame his passions and so entirely to enslave him that he will become a rabid monster of lust and cruelty" (January 22). Two days earlier, the same newspaper had carried a large photo of Fremstad costumed as Salome, holding a silver platter on which sat the papier-mâché head of John the Baptist, the spitting image of Anton van Rooy's, the baritone of the occasion. All this, and notices of the "Dance of the Seven Veils" as a *danse du ventre* (belly dance) to be executed not by the soprano but by a company ballerina, and of yet many "other sensational features, brought a throng of men and women such as no previous opera [had] drawn to the Metropolitan" *(Times)*. Librettos sold at quadruple the usual price *(Times,* Jan. 28, 1907). And once again, police reinforcements were called in to control the crowd *(Times,* Jan. 23, 1907).

The audience recoiled in revulsion, we are told, when Fremstad "presse[d] her teeth into the gelid flesh" of the severed head with only somewhat less ardor than she had exhibited at the dress rehearsal, although still at the very front of the stage. The Swedish-American dramatic soprano had leapt at the chance to play the Judaean princess once Farrar refused the role. Searing as Isolde and Kundry, she was known to be fiercely dedicated to her art. Her studies for *Salome* had included a much publicized trip to the city morgue to gauge the weight of a human head, far heavier, she learned, than the prop she was to fondle. Moments before Salome demanded "den Kopf des Jochanaan [the head of John]," women en masse had averted their eyes from the other famously outré scene, the iconic dance. As for the men, "very few . . . seemed comfortable. They twisted in their chairs, and before it was over there were numbers of them who decided to go to the corridors and smoke." But when Fremstad began to address the Baptist's head, "the horror of the thing" sent occupants of the front rows and boxes from the auditorium to call for their carriages. The galleries responded with greater equanimity. No one walked out. "Men and women left their seats to stand so that they might look down upon the prima donna as she kissed the dead lips. . . . Then they sank back in their chairs and shuddered" (*Times*). Still, many accounts conceded, the company had recorded "one of the most remarkable achievements in the way of a lyric production ever accomplished in this country" (*Times*). Among *Salome*'s partisans was Henderson, now writing for the *Sun*. He held the work up as a "perfect adaptation of the musical expression to the scene" (Jan. 27, 1907). But surprisingly, his reading of audience reaction ran counter to the majority report: "On Tuesday [Fremstad] moderated her transports so that even little girls . . . were not shocked. As for the society women, they viewed the spectacle with perfect calmness." With the passing days, Henderson changed his tune. On February 3, he called *Salome* a "fester on the body operatic" and, adopting Krehbiel's language, "a stench [in] the nostrils of society." The events that followed Conried's benefit no doubt persuaded Henderson to this awkward reversal.[10]

The Metropolitan board had sidestepped the *Parsifal* controversy, remaining largely silent in the face of accusations of illegality and blasphemy brought against its lessee. *Salome*'s degeneracy was another matter. While Conried had worried about the response of his public, he had failed to reckon with the puritanical sensibilities of his patrons. Not only did the Metropolitan directors weigh in, they intervened quickly and decisively. Three days after the premiere, on January 25, they effectively demanded that Conried cancel the three non-subscription performances he had announced at the conclusion of the benefit. Their resolution read: "The directors of the Metropolitan Opera and Real Estate Company consider that the performance of *Salome* is objectionable and detrimental to the best interests of the Metropolitan Opera House. They therefore protest against any repetition of this opera." It was one thing to take on Cosima Wagner and a handful of New York ministers, however vociferous. It was another to resist the orders of financier J. Pierpont Morgan, called by one commentator the "moving spirit and virtual dictator of the Metropolitan Opera and Real Estate Company," and his powerful cronies. Led by Morgan, whose daughter, Louisa Satterlee, had been deeply offended by *Salome* and prodded her father to take action, the executive com-

FIGURE 10. Olive Fremstad as Salome, 1907 (courtesy Metropolitan Opera Archives)

mittee was unanimous in its condemnation. One member, D. Ogden Mills, threatened more than termination of contract: "I understand that if Mr. Conried attempts to put the opera on in spite of the objections which have been made the board is quite likely to use force to prevent his doing so" (*Times,* Jan. 28, 1907). Several pastors took advantage of Sunday sermons to vent their outrage. Methodist Episcopal Rev. Dr. Charles Edward Locke, for one, came to the dubious conclusion that "such productions were responsible for such tragedies as the Stanford White case" (*Tribune,* Jan. 28, 1907).[11]

The "protest" of the board of the Metropolitan Opera and Real Estate Company was, in essence, an interdiction that the board of the Conried Metropolitan Opera Company, principally Otto H. Kahn and Robert Goelet, attempted in vain to have rescinded. In a letter of January 30, 1907, Conried's board argued that *Salome* was "recognized by the consensus of the

# HARPER'S WEEKLY

## JOURNAL OF CIVILIZATION

VOL. LI.　　　　New York, Saturday, February 9, 1907　　　　NO. 2616

## DISCHARGED WITHOUT HONOR

FIGURE 11. Salome banished, *Harper's Weekly,* February 9, 1907

most competent critics of modern music as a monumental work, probably the greatest which musical genius has produced in this generation." They argued further that in opera, as everyone knew, it was the music that counted, that the text was inconsequential and, in any case, "sung here in a foreign language." Strauss himself was known to consider the libretto "so subordinate to the orchestral composition that, when told that the orchestra augmented to over 100 men would drown the voices on the stage, he said: 'I don't care if it does, never mind the voices or the words, bring out the music of the orchestra regardless of the singers.'" As to the opera's source, the letter to Morgan and his allies made clear that Conried had no interest in defending Wilde, now several years dead. Strauss was the issue. In the future, Conried promised, the head of John the Baptist would be all but hidden from view. Besides, early sales predicted brisk business. Fremstad threw herself into the debate. She confessed that she too had been appalled when she first encountered the work in Cologne but had come to appreciate the grandeur of the score. In her evocation of the final scene, as Salome "sees his severed head she feels the only love of which she is capable, and her feeling is partly passionate and partly ideal. Strauss tells me this. Wilde tells me nothing" (*Times,* Jan. 27, 1907).

At one point, there was talk that if the opera could not be performed on 39th Street, the contract with the composer would be honored on tour in Chicago, Philadelphia, and Boston (*Times,* Jan. 28, 1907). That fell through. Conried spoke of moving *Salome* to another house; the New Amsterdam Theatre was mentioned (*Tribune,* Jan. 30, 1907). That too failed to materialize; Conried's own board was opposed. More than once, the Metropolitan directors offered to share in losses estimated at $30,000 in production costs and $50,000 in missed box-office receipts. Morgan declared himself ready to make Conried whole on his own. The Conried Metropolitan Opera Company would not be co-opted. To the credit of the *Times,* its editorial of January 29, 1907, sided with Conried and Kahn in protesting the censorship: "We tremble to think what the result may be if the newly aroused conscience of the Directors of the Opera House and Realty Company, seeking what it may devour, should be turned in this direction. Not only *Salome,* but a good many other musical masterpieces would be put upon the Index."[12]

In 1907, Salome danced but a single night at the Metropolitan. Here are three footnotes to that story. On February 17, the *Sun* kept the polemic going with a page-wide spread, "Salomes of Many Lands," featuring photographs of singers and actresses who had taken on the role and extensive notes on their costumes and interpretations; the next month, Conried exacted some small revenge on Morgan and the others by producing the Wilde play in German at his old hunting grounds, the Irving Place Theatre; and soon after, France decorated Fremstad as an Officer of Public Instruction for her service to art in the recent Paris production of Strauss's *Musikdrama* (*Tribune,* July 19, 1907).

Two years after its Metropolitan premiere, *Salome* returned to New York, this time in an opulent French-language edition at the Manhattan Opera House. News of the run must have been a bitter pill for Conried to swallow. Although much had changed in the intervening seasons, the 1909 reviews of Strauss's score and libretto varied little from the notices of 1907. Observers described the responses of the overflowing opening night audiences in strikingly similar terms. Prominent clergy dusted off their thundering sermons. Nonetheless, the Manhattan put on ten performances of *Salome* in 1909 and four the next year. In the end it came to this: Hammerstein owned his own theater, answered to no executive committee, was beholden to no investors, and the show went on. There was another important difference, and that was Mary Garden. In the obligatory pairing with Fremstad, critics agreed that Garden came up impossibly short. The "plain truth," as Henderson condensed it, was "that Miss Garden [could not] sing a phrase of Strauss' music" (*Sun,* Jan. 10). But her magnetism, her extraordinary acting, and her own unabashed interpretation of the erotic dance carried the day.[13]

Well before Mary Garden's *Salome,* Hammerstein offered the composer generous terms for *Elektra,* his still-to-be-produced next opera. On May 29, 1908, Kahn wrote to Strauss acknowledging the Met's disastrous handling of *Salome,* placing the blame largely on the broad shoulders of J. P. Morgan. He hoped to divert Strauss's "lust for revenge" by appealing to the composer's famed cupidity: "Since you aim your wrath at us you affect Mr. Morgan not at all; instead you harm *us* first of all and second, yourself, financially at least . . . your works will be done only by Hammerstein and not in both houses." Kahn's entreaties went unheeded; in January 1910, Hammerstein staged the American premiere of *Elektra.*[14]

Fifteen years after the *Salome* debacle, Kahn pleaded with the Metropolitan Opera and Real Estate Company for a reprieve. The opera was a specialty of his new favorite, Maria Jeritza, "an artist of the highest attainments and of dignity and refinement." His request came with the pious assurance that he would "be unwilling to sanction any performance which could give just offence to the moral or religious sentiments of the community." Kahn was again rebuffed, and this time there was no question of not being co-opted. On the contrary, the matter was considered settled when Kahn put his name to a joint communiqué upholding the continued proscription. On January 13, 1934, twenty-seven years after her stand-in had shed the seventh veil, Fremstad was in the audience to witness the famous dance, at last reprised at the Met. Soprano Göta Ljungberg executed the number herself, as have all Salomes since, scandalizing no one, with the exception of Terpsichore; she did little more than drop the scarves she had tucked into her costume moments before. Conductor Artur Bodanzky was "the most refulgent star of the evening." Strauss's opera had finally entered the company's repertoire. But Fremstad aside, it was not until the debut in 1949 of Ljuba Welitsch that Salome was rendered in full, both histrionically and vocally. *Variety* came up with one of its irreverent headlines: "Met's Sensational New Soprano, Welitsch, Puts 52d St. [New York's burlesque district] Shimmy to Shame" (Feb. 9). Unlike Fremstad and most of her Met successors, Wagnerians with instruments weighted for the midrange heroic perorations of Isolde and Brünnhilde and often taxed by the high-lying moments of their jubilation or fury, Welitsch was a finely focused *spinto* (a lyric soprano with incisive potential), firm throughout her range, free and incandescent in an upper register that cut through Strauss's orchestral mass without apparent effort. Here was the youthful sound Strauss had wanted for the spoiled and murderous teenager. The fifteen-minute ovation was followed by the print hosannas of the morning-after reviews. Fritz Reiner's precise baton shared in the triumph, repeated in the air check of the March 12 broadcast and the commercial recording of the final scene made at that time. For those of us in the audience on January 19, 1952, the force of the conductor-singer collaboration was overwhelming—although, if truth be told, the soprano's voice was a shade less vivid than her flaming red hair. The Reiner-Welitsch *Salome* is the opera's touchstone.[15]

## SECOND OPERA WAR: 1906–1908

The four-year second opera war pitted the by now entrenched Metropolitan against the upstart company lodged in the more recent of the two venues that Oscar Hammerstein named the Manhattan Opera House. His headquarters stood on 34th Street between Eighth and Ninth Avenues, just a short walk south and west of Conried's. The campaign would be waged half by the Met's current intendant and half by his successor, Giulio Gatti-Casazza. On one of many of the period's extraordinary nights, January 2, 1907, 6,720 persons were reported to have made their way to 34th Street to hear Nellie Melba,

Alessandro Bonci, and Maurice Renaud in *La Traviata* or to 39th Street to hear Emma Eames, Enrico Caruso, and Antonio Scotti in *Tosca*. On occasion, and no doubt on purpose, the two managers scheduled the same work at the same hour, for instance, January 26, 1910, when the operaphile was presented with a wrenching choice: whether to cheer Caruso's Rodolfo at the Met or John McCormack's at the Manhattan. For four stunning seasons, New York witnessed hundreds of performances at very high standards as once again two major companies sought to outdo and, above all, to outlast each other. If in this contest and the one with Mapleson the Met was the last house standing, its survival was due not so much to its facilities, its roster, or its repertoire as to the backing it enjoyed from the New York families that called it their own.[16]

The no-holds-barred feud of 1906 was fed by the bad blood between the men in charge. Their rivalry dated back several decades to the first stage assignment of the freshly emigrated Conried, when fate willed that Hammerstein bankroll his show. The dueling impresarios may have had both too little and too much in common. Like Conried, Hammerstein was an immigrant and Jewish. He had landed as a teenager in 1863, fourteen years before Conried's arrival. German, not Austrian, he had had training in music rather than in drama. Once in the United States, he went to work making cigars and eventually turned his trade into a fortune by inventing machines for their manufacture. In the 1870s, he began to back shows of all sorts. By the late 1880s, he had become obsessed with building theaters. The first of his astounding series was the Harlem Opera House, completed in 1889. It was followed by the Columbus Theatre in 1890, also in Harlem. In 1892 came the original Manhattan Opera House, located on 34th Street between Broadway and Seventh Avenue, home to opera for only two weeks. The most profitable of the several legitimate and vaudeville houses whose construction Hammerstein financed was the 1899 Victoria, at Seventh Avenue and 42nd Street. There would be others, in New York and elsewhere, most particularly the second Manhattan Opera House, of course, and the Philadelphia Opera House, a thumb in the Metropolitan's eye. Hammerstein rushed it to completion in record time in 1908, the midpoint of the four-year contest. The Met had been performing regularly down Broad Street at the Academy of Music, then as now as beautiful a theater as any in the country.[17]

Whether Hammerstein's first season ended in the black or not, which is a matter of dispute, the Manhattan was judged to have gained the upper hand thanks to the illustrious and colorful troupe the impresario assembled, to the musical leadership of conductor Cleofonte Campanini (brother of Italo, the

Met's leading tenor in 1883–84), and particularly to the defection of Melba from the Metropolitan. But Hammerstein labored under two crippling disadvantages. The company had been unable to attract the cohort of German singers necessary to Wagner. And, at least as enfeebling, Puccini was strictly off-limits. The composer's publisher, Casa Ricordi, had ceded exclusive American rights to Puccini's works to the Metropolitan, and this time legality was not in question, as it had been in Bayreuth's claims against Conried's *Parsifal* three years earlier. Hammerstein's strategy to circumvent the prohibition so as to mount *La Bohème* for Melba was both cumbersome and chancy, cumbersome because the score had to be reconstructed from a mutilated copy (with help from Campanini's prodigious memory), and chancy because to provoke Ricordi invited a lawsuit, which was indeed filed and ultimately ended in the predictable injunction.[18]

In his second year Hammerstein took a bold turn. With Wagner and Puccini off the table, he opted for recent French works never before performed in the city and engaged artists who could do them justice, Mary Garden in particular, in her first New York appearances. In short order, the Manhattan took on the cachet of a "Parisian" theater. Claude Debussy's *Pelléas et Mélisande,* refused by Conried "with a contemptuous wave of his hand," was premiered with nearly the very cast that had introduced the work at the Opéra-Comique in 1902. Garden gave New York not only its first Mélisande, but its first Thaïs and its first Louise. Jacques Offenbach's *Les Contes d'Hoffmann,* not yet heard at the Met, sold out its eleven Manhattan performances. The public embraced these novelties as firmly as it had resisted Grau's French premieres not five years earlier. Was it the glamorous and compelling Garden that accounted for the difference? Or was it the quality of the works? By any measure, *La Navarraise, Salammbô,* and *Messaline* paled before *Pelléas et Mélisande, Thaïs,* and *Louise.* In his first year, Hammerstein scheduled French opera for 25 percent of the Manhattan's performances; in 1907–08, he went to 48 percent, in 1908–09 39 percent, in 1909–10 54 percent. The corresponding percentages at the Met were substantially lower: 16 percent, 9 percent, 9 percent, 12 percent. Hammerstein found yet another way to outmaneuver his antagonist: he stole Luisa Tetrazzini from Conried. Two years earlier, the Met's general manager had negotiated a contract with the coloratura that he carelessly left unsigned. From the moment of her debut as Violetta, Tetrazzini had New York at her feet as she had had London the year before.[19]

The two *indendants* fought over everything: over repertoire, over casts, and over the always thorny issue of the audience that opera was duty bound to serve. Hammerstein's seating plan spoke volumes for his position. He wanted nothing like the Diamond Horseshoe or, for that matter, any horseshoe at all. What he hatched was a comfortable auditorium holding thirty-one hundred, three hundred fewer than the Met, with increased proximity to the well-equipped stage, good sight lines, and acoustics that many preferred to those of the older house. His refusal to bend to the frivolous demands of the gentry proved risky; so was the proposition that the growing immigrant population would fill the void. By 1910, the Manhattan's last season, the number of Italian-born New Yorkers, roughly 340,000, up dramatically from 145,000 ten years earlier, was approximately equal to the number of German-born New Yorkers at the time of the Met's German seasons, 1884–1891. Assuming affection for opera by many transplanted Europeans and their first-generation offspring, an enormous pool was theoretically available to Hammerstein for what he fervently believed to be a popular art form. Still, that New York would sustain two such high-rolling competitors as the Manhattan and the Metropolitan remained a long shot.[20]

### PREMIERES: 1903–1908

Seven of eleven premieres of Conried's half-decade tenure, excluding *Parsifal* and *Salome*, were Italian. Of these, two looked to bel canto, and the five remaining to the contemporary generation of composers. Old or new, all seven were sung by Caruso. He had been an overnight sensation, the darling of audiences of all social and economic strata.

### Bel Canto

The bel canto novelties were Gaetano Donizetti's *L'Elisir d'amore* and his *Lucrezia Borgia*. None of Caruso's thirty-seven Met roles better suited the tenor's chunky physique and legendary sense of fun than the endearing bumpkin of the comic *Elisir*. His Nemorino and Sembrich's Adina filled the Met's coffers; they succeeded in the daunting enterprise of softening the hearts of the Wagnerites, so long hardened in contempt of bel canto. Reverting to form, critics shot the poisoned arrows they reserved for bel canto tragedy at *Lucrezia Borgia,* "a repetition of empty formulas and passages ... absolutely without a trace of dramatic characterization" (*Tribune*).

# Verismo

Composed by the masters of *la giovane scuola* (the young school, a group of late-nineteenth- to early-twentieth-century post-Verdi Italian composers) during the Belle Époque, *Manon Lescaut* and *Madama Butterfly, Iris, Fedora,* and *Adriana Lecouvreur,* all Conried premieres, belonged to a manner that continues to carry the problematic brand of "verismo." They have in common the signature feature of the "hidden" aria. To be sure, and to the relief of singers and record companies, verismo admits excerptable pieces designed to invite applause and timed to the capacity of early disks. But the two-part structure of the bel canto aria, the slow cavatina capped by the fast cabaletta embellished with intricate fioritura and stratospheric high notes, gave way to a shorter-breathed and shorter-ranged arioso embedded in an ongoing fabric of dramatic recitative accompanied by orchestral comment. Sung phrases often approached the rhythms of spoken dialogue. At the same time, the subjects of Conried's five verismo premieres fit uncomfortably under a single umbrella. An Italian outgrowth of French literary naturalism, verismo applies accurately to the plebeian characters and locales of *Cavalleria rusticana* and *Pagliacci,* but much less well to the exotic *Iris* and *Madama Butterfly,* to the ancien régime of *Manon Lescaut*'s young lovers, to *Adriana Lecouvreur*'s aristocrats, or to *Fedora*'s contemporary European nobility.[21]

*Manon Lescaut* and *Madama Butterfly* reaped the lion's share of press attention and its most fulsome praise. Puccini's stock had risen rapidly in the wake of the 1900–01 first nights of *La Bohème* and *Tosca.* For the *Times, Manon Lescaut,* which predated *La Bohème* by three years, was the title that had lifted Puccini above his *giovane scuola* cohort. Even Krehbiel was willing to succumb to its allure: "fresher, more spontaneous, more unaffected and more passionate in its climaxes" *(Tribune).* Caruso's Des Grieux met the usual high expectations. Manon exposed the vocal and dramatic limits of Lina Cavalieri, better known for her looks than for her art. Another great beauty, Geraldine Farrar, made a phenomenal impression as Cio-Cio-San, the most important assignment of her debut season. Winning "the tribute of tears from many eyes . . . her triumph was complete" *(Tribune).* The extended excerpts recorded by Victor a couple of years later capture the commitment of the inaugural cast. Puccini had been happy with the production of *Manon Lescaut* and with Cavalieri's performance; he was disappointed in *Madama Butterfly.* He complained about the inadequately prepared orchestra and its conductor, Arturo Vigna, but most especially about Farrar, who sang out of tune and failed, in his view, to make the desired impact in the large auditorium. For sixteen consecutive seasons, Met audiences disagreed; Farrar portrayed Puccini's tragic geisha a record 139 times.[22]

The role of yet another Japanese woman abused by a callous lover, the unfortunate Iris, fell to Emma Eames. She had more success than the work bearing the victim's name. Caruso in kimono (much to the amusement of the spectators) made the most of limited opportunities. And the pioneering Mascagni, who had blazed the trail of verismo with *Cavalleria rusticana,* suffered in the inevitable comparison with Puccini. *Iris* was generally dismissed as a collection of Eastern effects with a few lyric effusions, an excess of tired symbolism, and an unsavory subject. The Met's décor and lighting received special mention; admired particularly was the metamorphosis of a trash heap, the site of the heroine's death, into a field in bloom. It was not the first time *Iris* had been heard in New York or, for that matter, the first time it had been staged at the Met. Mascagni had brought his opera to the city and to the house with his own touring company in October 1902 during a three-month-long visit that Krehbiel called the "most sensational fiasco ever made by an artist of great distinction in the United States." The composer had contracted to prepare and conduct "not more than eight operas or concerts a week," including productions of *Cavalleria rusticana, Zanetto, Iris,* and *Guglielmo Ratcliff.* The last never saw American footlights. "It was foolishly reckless in the composer to think that with such material as he had raked together in his native land and recruited here he could produce four of his operas within a week of his arrival." When Mascagni moved on to Boston, he was arrested for breach of contract. He countersued for damages. "The scandal grew until it threatened to become a subject of international diplomacy, but in the end compromises were made and the composer departed to his own country in bodily if not spiritual peace."[23]

Giordano and Cilea fared more poorly still than Mascagni. Reviewers noted uncharitably that their music detracted from the plays on which *Fedora* and *Adriana Lecouvreur* were based, both previously staged in New York with Sarah Bernhardt. Cavalieri was unequal to the challenge of the eponymous roles. But Farrar herself could not have saved either title from its excruciating reception. Caruso, who had appeared in their world premieres, did his superlative best, as evinced in his recordings of *Fedora*'s "Amor ti vieta" and in an excerpt from act 4 of *Adriana.*

# German Operetta and Opera

Conried produced five German novelties, two of which, *Parsifal* and *Salome,* set off the mayhem we recall above. *Die Fledermaus* and *Der Zigeunerbaron* came in for attack. Only *Hänsel und Gretel* emerged unscathed.

The controversy over Johann Strauss's operettas was two-pronged. Reviewers took up their old refrain: operettas, no matter how charming, even brilliant, had no place at the Met. Their dialogue was lost in its vast reaches; their scores befit only intimate theaters. And as he had been for *Parsifal* and would be again for *Salome,* Conried was chided for pocketing the first-night receipts of *Die Fledermaus,* designated, like the others, "director's benefit," an annual event at which the artists were called upon to make a gift of their services to the boss. The prospect of hearing the Met's stars during the act 2 ball all but guaranteed a rich haul. The soloists joined the chorus in the "Brüderlein" finale and then, led by Caruso and Eames on one side of the stage, Fremstad and Plançon on the other, proceeded to dance a raucous cancan. But the critics, even as they acknowledged the *Fledermaus* precedent at some European opera houses, and the luster and merriment of the occasion, were prepared to forgive neither the musical trespass nor Conried's greed. He repeated the stunt the next season with *Der Zigeunerbaron.* Humperdinck's *Hänsel und Gretel* needed no star wattage to galvanize success. The critics were predisposed to the score's Wagnerian sonorities. And they agreed that "it did not seem as if there could be anybody in the house to whom [it] did not appeal as something beautiful, something delightful and enjoyable" *(Times). Hänsel und Gretel* remained in the repertoire until German was banned in 1917; it has returned regularly since 1927–28.

With the exception of *Lucrezia Borgia,* all of Conried's novelties have had subsequent productions and more than half have become staples of the repertoire. However vexed *Parsifal* was in New York in 1903, it had been blessed at Bayreuth, and the two Puccini operas and Humperdinck's had been applauded throughout Europe. In that sense, they were sure bets just as *Salome* would have been but for Mr. Morgan and his pew. *Adriana Lecouvreur* and *Fedora* have languished, but have refused to die. Nearly five decades after its company premiere, Rudolf Bing found the winning formula for *Die Fledermaus.* The survival rate of novelties under Conried's much maligned leadership far exceeded that recorded by the premieres of Stanton and Abbey-Grau.

TABLE 4  Metropolitan Opera Premieres, 1903–04 to 1907–08

| Composer and Title | Met Premiere | Most Recent Met Performance | No. of Seasons in Met Repertoire | No. of Met Productions | No. of Met Performances, 1883–2013 | World Premiere | Director/Designer |
|---|---|---|---|---|---|---|---|
| Richard Wagner, *Parsifal* | Dec. 24, 1903 | Mar. 8, 2013 | 70 | 6 | 295 | July 26, 1882, Bayreuth, Festspielhaus | Anton Fuchs / Leopold Rothaug, Burghart & Co. |
| Gaetano Donizetti, *L'Elisir d'amore* | Jan. 23, 1904 | Feb. 9, 2013 | 37 | 5 | 277 | May 12, 1832, Milan, Cannobiana | Karl Schroeder / James Fox |
| Gaetano Donizetti, *Lucrezia Borgia* | Dec. 5, 1904 | Dec. 5, 1904 | 1 | 1 | 1 | Dec. 26, 1833, Milan, La Scala | Eugène Dufriche / Unknown |
| Johann Strauss II, *Die Fledermaus* | Feb. 16, 1905 | Jan. 7, 2006 | 23 | 3 | 209 | Apr. 5, 1874, Vienna, an der Wien | Emil Greder / Unknown |
| Engelbert Humperdinck, *Hänsel und Gretel* | Nov. 25, 1905 | Jan. 7, 2012 | 40 | 4 | 264 | Dec. 23, 1893, Weimar, Hoftheater | Jacques Goldberg / Burghart & Co. |
| Johann Strauss II, *Der Zigeunerbaron* | Feb. 15, 1906 | May 31, 1960 | 2 | 2 | 18 | Oct. 24, 1885, Vienna, an der Wien | Unknown / Unknown |
| Umberto Giordano, *Fedora* | Dec. 5, 1906 | May 1, 1997 | 6 | 3 | 35 | Nov. 17, 1898, Milan, Lirico | Eugène Dufriche / Unknown |
| Giacomo Puccini, *Manon Lescaut* | Jan. 18, 1907 | Feb. 23, 2008 | 33 | 5 | 216 | Feb. 1, 1893, Turin, Regio | Eugène Dufriche / Unknown |
| Richard Strauss, *Salome* | Jan. 22, 1907 | Oct. 16, 2008 | 24 | 5 | 157 | Sept. 9, 1905, Dresden, Hofoper | Anton Schertel / Max Brückner |
| Giacomo Puccini, *Madama Butterfly* | Feb. 11, 1907 | Mar. 8, 2012 | 81 | 5 | 842 | Feb. 17, 1904, Milan, La Scala | Eugène Dufriche / Burghart & Co. |
| Francesco Cilea, *Adriana Lecouvreur* | Nov. 18, 1907 | Feb. 28, 2009 | 7 | 2 | 73 | Nov. 6, 1902, Milan, Lirico | Eugène Dufriche / Unknown |
| Pietro Mascagni, *Iris* | Dec. 6, 1907 | Apr. 9, 1931 | 3 | 2 | 16 | Nov. 22, 1898; Rome, Costanzi | Eugène Dufriche / Kautsky & Rottonara Brothers |

By the end of Conried's first season, 1903–04, the directors of the Metropolitan Opera and Real Estate Company were already displeased: numerous subscription performances had dodged the required inclusion of two of the six approved artists, some of whom had decamped before the season was over; and above all, there had been "unsatisfactory performances, notably of the French operas *Faust* and *Roméo*" (board minutes, March 2, 1904). Another set of minutes tells us that two years later similar complaints were aired, namely, "that performances of opera lately produced have been below the standard called for under [the] lease" (Jan. 24, 1906). At the end of two rounds in the mano a mano between Conried and Hammerstein, 1906–07 and 1907–08, the board of the Conried Metropolitan Opera Company, separately and distinctly from the equally distressed board of the Metropolitan Opera and Real Estate Company, had had enough. A letter from Otto Kahn to the general manager itemized his "grievous and irreparable faults": the failure to sew up the Tetrazzini contract, to bring conductor Campanini to the Met, to produce successful novelties (an unfair charge), to secure the rights to the Puccini operas at less than exorbitant cost, to secure the rights to modern French works, leaving those prizes to Hammerstein, "and many other acts of omission and commission . . . of great advantage to the competing house—so much so that it is within bounds to say that the very existence today of the Manhattan Opera House is, in considerable part, attributable to what you [Conried] did and failed to do." Besides, only in the first three years of Conried's regime had the company showed a profit; in the last two it racked up significant losses. Conried's poor health, greed, ignorance of grand opera, and imperious vulgarity did the rest. The board bought out his contract; he resigned in February 1908. And so the early period in the Metropolitan's history came to a close.[24]

One year after the exhausted impresario retired to Europe, the banner above his obituary in the April 27, 1909, *Times* ran: "Former Metropolitan Opera Director Succumbs at 2:30 This Morning to Apoplectic Stroke. Health Undermined by Worries Growing Out of the Management of the Opera House." The policy taken out on Conried's life was still in effect. A sizable payment to his widow left the Met with $150,000 with which to offset the losses he had incurred. Friends and enemies alike recognized that if at his appointment Conried had found a "public [that] was opera-mad," as Krehbiel put it, five years later, when he was gone for good, he left behind a city more opera crazed than ever.[25]

FOUR

# Modernity, 1908–1929

PUCCINI

## REGIME CHANGE

HERE IS THE STORY as Giulio Gatti-Casazza tells it in his memoirs: The first intimation that he was being spoken of as a successor to Heinrich Conried came in a letter of June 1907 from an unnamed woman writing on behalf of an unidentified "very important person" not known to him. Was he disposed to enter into negotiations with the Metropolitan, she asked? That evening, Gatti, general director of La Scala for almost a decade, happened to be at dinner with Arturo Toscanini, La Scala's music director. Gatti showed his host the letter. He was, of course, well aware that some years earlier Toscanini had declined an invitation from the Met. Toscanini urged Gatti to test the American waters: should Gatti take the position, this time the conductor would be prepared to leave Milan; they would go to New York as a team. At the mysterious woman's subsequent suggestion, Gatti met in Rome that same month with Count di San Martino di Valperga, president of Santa Cecilia, the Royal Conservatory, who was to be named to the board of the Metropolitan Opera Company later that year. San Martino advised Gatti to meet with Otto Kahn, which he did in July in Paris.[1]

Back in New York in late summer, Conried was issued an ultimatum: things would have to change. Above all, he would have to provide a steady presence, whether in good or ill health (*Sun,* Aug. 1, 1907). Rumors began to fly, as did names of replacements: Gustav Mahler (said to have refused the offer), Jean de Reszke, Cleofonte Campanini, André Messager (lately head of Covent Garden), Italian music publisher Tito Ricordi, and Met tenor Andreas Dippel. On January 4, 1908, the *Times* carried Conried's resignation, although no official announcement had been made. Negotiations between Gatti and the Met continued in trans-Atlantic secrecy. On January 25, Gatti denied reports that he would be coming to the Met. On that same day, Campanini, who had worked under Gatti at La Scala before moving to Hammerstein's Manhattan Opera Company, had this to say of his competitor: "He is not a musician and depends entirely on his chef d'orchestra. At La Scala only eight operas are given in a season of five months. What a man of this sort would be capable of doing in New York I cannot imagine" *(Times)*. Krehbiel went further in an opinion piece of February 11: "From the point of view which is likely to be shared by all who have been hoping for years to see New York's foremost operatic establishment put upon a permanent footing and raised to the plane of a truly artistic institution above the reach of managerial greed, the personal caprices and ambitions of individuals and the whimsies of fad and fashion, the influence of Milan in the American metropolis will be deplored" *(Tribune)*. But by then, despite the opposition of board members and critics who feared the Italianization of the institution, the die was cast. The next day, February 12, Conried's retirement for medical reasons was announced together with the appointment of Gatti-Casazza as general manager. The surprise was the simultaneous appointment of Andreas Dippel as administrative manager, an awkward and ultimately misguided move to pacify the anti-Gatti forces, whether xenophobic, or Germanophilic, or paradoxically both. Dippel was placed in charge of the German repertoire and the separate German chorus and orchestra. The announcement also named both Toscanini and Mahler music director, a title neither would ever hold. Krehbiel was certain that "Mr. Dippel's appointment and Mr. Mahler's retention were obviously made, no doubt in good faith, to allay the fears of a large contingent of the opera's patrons that the German branch of the repertory, already in the shadow as I have said, was to suffer a total eclipse."[2]

On May 1, the 1907–08 season well over, Gatti arrived in New York on the *Lusitania,* exhibiting energy, optimism, and very little English. In excellent French he declared to the press that the theater was wonderfully suited to opera; yes indeed, he was a staunch Wagnerian; in fact, he admired all modern music, Strauss, Debussy, Charpentier. In response to a reporter who hoped "there [would] be no more *Adriana Lecouvreur*s," he replied agreeably, "I hope so, too" *(Times,* May 2, 1908). Whatever else, after five years of the impolitic Conried, the Met had hired itself a diplomat. But it would not be long before Gatti made two distressing discoveries: that the stage, back and front, and scenery were in deplorable shape; and worse still, that Dippel had been named administrative manager two months earlier, news that had somehow not reached him. Kahn promised to address the deficiencies highest on Gatti's list: an enlarged pit was fitted with a movable floor, the stage machinery was upgraded, some of the many shabby sets were replaced. The issue of dual management was far more troublesome. Dippel's contract, drawn up when Conried was bought out, named him unambiguously "codirector" (*Times*, Dec. 10, 1908).

Gatti left New York on May 28 for a summer of maneuvers. To begin with, there was the imminent danger of a conspiracy among Italian and South American theaters ready to offer Italian singers full-time contracts so as to block their engagement in the United States and Great Britain. The "trust" had to be foiled, and quickly (*Times*, Aug. 9, 1908). Then there was the untenable Dippel compromise. The crisis came to a head with a letter dated November 25 (the season had begun at the newly completed Brooklyn Academy of Music ten days earlier), engineered by Dippel himself and signed by half the contingent of approved artists of the preceding season: Enrico Caruso, Emma Eames, Geraldine Farrar, Marcella Sembrich, and Antonio Scotti. The text read: "We, the undersigned artists of the Metropolitan Opera Company, hearing of a movement to grant Mr. Gatti-Casazza, the general manager, and Mr. Toscanini, conductor, a three years' binding contract, do hereby express our desire, in the protection of our artistic interests and the welfare of the Metropolitan Opera House, that Mr. Dippel be granted the same privileges under contract that may be accorded to the above-named gentlemen. Our confidence in the managerial and artistic capabilities of Mr. Dippel gives us sufficient reason to associate ourselves firmly with his ideas, which have been, always will be, and are for the best of the Metropolitan Opera House. Therefore, we heartily endorse Mr. Dippel in whatever measures he may be obliged to take." What led the five signees to threaten support for Dippel in an eventual legal action against the company? Dippel had been at the Met since 1890 and was a good colleague; he would have made an indulgent manager. By contrast, in the first couple of weeks of the season, Toscanini, surely with Gatti's backing, had made his demands brutally clear: everyone, stars included, would show up for rehearsal, and on time, and everyone, on stage and in the pit, would be expected to toe the conductor's line. During several stormy sessions, Toscanini had dared question Eames's Tosca, an injury now added to the insult of her imminent forced retirement. For her part, Sembrich had often sung with Dippel and was, in any case, herself on the way out. Neither had much to lose. Kahn and others on the executive committee responded tactfully that they were grateful for the "service and renown" of the petitioners and had every confidence that they would under-stand that it was "not possible to administer an organization like the Metropolitan Opera House under two heads" (*Times,* Dec. 6). Gatti alone was renewed through 1910–11. A chastened Scotti pleaded that he had signed reluctantly; both he and Caruso had been swayed by Farrar. And Farrar, although smarting from Toscanini's criticism of her Butterfly, had the good grace to take responsibility. She soon made up with the conductor: their affair became an open secret. The outfoxed Dippel would not go gently into the night. After the meeting in which he was "taken to task for attempting to stir up dissension in the Metropolitan," he "went to Gatti and asked for assurances on the renewal of his contract. A heated argument is said to have followed, in which the general manager flatly declined to accede to the proposition" (*Tribune,* Dec. 11).[3]

The sweeping changes of 1908 had been ratified by the Metropolitan Opera and Real Estate Company at a meeting held in J. P. Morgan's library. Kahn's announcement at the session's close signaled not only the transfer of power from one general manager to another, opposed by training, experi-ence, temperament, and nationality, but a consequential restructuring of the opera company in its relationship to both the Real Estate Company and the manager himself. The freshly incorporated Metropolitan Opera Company was awarded a five-year lease, replacing the impresario-led model of the past. From here on out, the general manager would be a salaried employee, without financial stake in the enterprise. This decision was sealed with the embarrass-ing discovery that not $130,000, as Conried had averred, but only $30,000 remained in the coffers. Gone would be the gala evenings on behalf of man-agers or, for that matter, of stars. Whatever such performances there might be would benefit the company itself. Other measures to limit star power were swiftly introduced. No longer would leading singers congregate around the intendant's desk to grab as many performances as they could. Gatti would decide who would be assigned which role and for which performance. The clout that leeched from the stars and, more significantly, from the Real Estate Company passed to the Metropolitan Opera Company; it would ultimately reside with the general manager and the three executive directors, Kahn, W. K. Vanderbilt (also on the Real Estate Company board), and Bayard Cutting. The new leadership quashed the proviso that two approved artists appear in every subscription performance. More profound was the novel concept that as a matter of policy the opera would be managed not on a profit but on a not-for-profit basis and that any gains realized would "be used for the establishment of an endowment or pension fund or for some similar purpose for the advancement of the Metropolitan Opera House as an art institution." Punctual as always, Mrs. Astor died on October 30, a fortnight before the opening of Gatti's inaugural season, leaving Box 7 dark for a time.[4]

## Kahn, Gatti, Toscanini

With the revisions in governance, the great New York families relinquished much of their prerogative, and the Metropolitan's modern era was launched. Much, but not all. They succeeded, for example, under Morgan's heavy hand, in enforcing the unwritten ordinance that no Jew could acquire a box at the opera house, whatever his qualities, wealth, or even his standing within the organization. That included Kahn, who joined the opera company board in 1903, Conried's first year, and became its chair in 1911 and its president in 1918, a position he held until 1931. When he stepped down, he owned well over 80 percent of the company's stock. John Kobler, one of his biographers, ventures this answer to why Kahn swallowed so much humiliation: "Perhaps his love of opera, the opportunity to take an active hand in its production, stifled any impulse he may have had to resign. (His initials, O.H.K., it was suggested, stood for 'Opera House Kahn.') Perhaps, too, he welcomed the prospect of fraternizing with the grandees of New York society. Some seasons he would rent a parterre box from the owner. At times he subscribed to two orchestra seats, one for his hat and coat. Seventeen years after his election to the board, Kahn was allowed to buy Box 14."[5]

Otto Kahn was born into a Mannheim family in 1867. To this extent, he would be familiar, years later, in the administrative corridors of the Metropolitan; like Leopold Damrosch, Austrian-Moravian born Maurice Grau, and Heinrich Conried, he was natively a German speaker and Jewish. At an early age, he was tapped to walk in his father's shoes as a banker and a friend to artists and literati. In his twenties, he went to work for Deutsche Bank in London and became a British subject. In 1893, he moved to New York at the invitation of Kuhn, Loeb, & Co., was taken under the wing of Jacob Schiff (the firm's head), married the daughter of a former senior partner, and made his fortune as financier of railway expansion. He became a US citizen in 1917. On his March 29, 1934, demise, the *Times* carried no fewer than three pieces on his life and accomplishments: a front-page article announcing his sudden death in the private dining room of the private bank of which he had been so long a principal, an editorial in homage to the man and his work, and a full-page obituary titled "Life as a Boy Made Kahn Arts Patron." Kahn's philanthropy supported Diaghilev's Ballets Russes, the Habima Players, the Moscow Art Theatre, the Provincetown Players, and the Washington Square Players, later the Theatre Guild; his patronage extended to the composers Georges Enesco, Deems Taylor, and Ernst Krenek. Kahn spoke English perfectly and was at consummate ease in business, political, civic, and charitable circles. The restricted diamond semicircle of thirty-five boxes was a different matter.

Giulio Gatti-Casazza, on the other hand, remained adamantly a foreigner. Although the Met quickly became his home, the United States never became his country; he did not see himself as an American, nor did anyone else. Throughout his unprecedented and unequalled twenty-seven-year tenure, he transacted business in Italian or, if need be, in French, officially because his English was halting, which it was not. More probably, his refusal of English was intended to keep others on the defensive and to distance an uncongenial culture and a tiresome ruling class. In truth, Gatti spoke little in any language. This extract from a *New Yorker* profile published in the very first issue of the magazine is typical of impressions left by the austere general manager: "Six and three-quarter days out of every week he preserves the fiction of a courteous, imperturbable, quite inscrutable Jove. Silence is a great aid to him, there. It is the apron he puts on while kneading, over and over, the personnel and property of his company. It preserves his air, not only of efficiency, but of mystery. He will sit for hours among vivid talkers—even at some dinner in his honor—without spilling more than an occasional monosyllable down upon his embonpoint." Frances Alda, the New Zealander soprano he married in 1910, recalls their first meeting: "I wondered at the temperament of this grave, middle-aged man with the heavily bearded face in which the dark melancholy eyes seemed to brood on unfathomable things."[6]

Born in Udine in 1869, two years after Kahn and Toscanini, Gatti belonged to an old and distinguished family. He studied mathematics and naval engineering. At the age of twenty-four, he replaced his father as director of the opera house in Ferrara. Five years later, he was drafted to rescue La Scala from fiscal, physical, and artistic disarray. And with him was appointed music director Arturo Toscanini, born in Parma. While Gatti was studying music as an amateur, Toscanini was embarked on a career as a professional cellist. In 1886, at the age of nineteen, he made his podium debut in Rio de Janeiro in *Aïda* when the scheduled conductor walked out on a jeering crowd and a second was booed out of the pit. It was on that occasion that Toscanini first cast aside the score, working from what would become a legendary memory. On his return to Italy, he led the world premieres of *Pagliacci* (1892) and *La Bohème* (1896). Toscanini's path crossed with Gatti's as they prepared for their first season at La Scala in 1898. Gatti opened the year with Wagner's *I Maestri Cantori di Norimberga* and was called a "madman" and "disloyal to Italy" for his pains (*Herald Tribune*, Sept. 3, 1940). Nevertheless, he persisted in renewing the repertoire with Wagner's "Ring," sung in Italian, of course, and other modern works, *Louise, Salome*, and *Pelléas et Mélisande*, all led by Toscanini. His ten years at La Scala were marked by intelligence, probity, and ultimately widely recognized success. He had taken to heart the caution that the aged Verdi had offered him: "The theatre is intended to be full and not empty. That's something you must always remember."[7]

### MOSTLY TOSCANINI: 1908–1910

Toscanini conducted not the inaugural performance of Gatti's first season, the Brooklyn Academy of Music *Faust*, but the much anticipated second, the 39th Street opening night *Aïda*, in which Emmy Destinn also made her debut, and Caruso, Louise Homer, and Scotti joined her in a spectacular new investiture replete with Radamès's triumphal entrance on a chariot drawn by two white horses. Here was a thrilling first example of what the *Evening Post* dubbed the grand "Milanese" style (Nov. 17, 1908). One reviewer observed that, mirabile dictu, the singers followed the conductor, and not the conductor the singers, as had been the rule for the Italian repertoire *(Sun)*. A single performance was all it took to convince critics and public that the star in the pit was at least as captivating as those on the stage. Seats at the extreme sides of the theater were suddenly hot; they afforded a full view of the dramatic maestro. As to the orchestra, its members bore stupefied witness early on to Toscanini's prodigious talent when he rehearsed the six-hour *Götterdämmerung* without a score, singing along at will note for note, word for word. Farrar gives the following account of the effect Toscanini first made on singers and instrumentalists: "The Maestro ... was a bundle of concentrated quicksilver. Neatly compressed into his black jacket, he wore a broad-brimmed fedora crammed over deep-set burning eyes. Portentous silence was broken by an occasional and solemn raven's croak. This was the result of long assault upon protesting vocal cords. We were to experience—later and often—the amazing crescendi to screams and expletives that rose to unparalleled dynamics in rehearsals. However, these tempests became less terrifying by reason of their frequency. We recognized the lightning's play, sure to be followed by disarming—if unstable—serenity."[8]

For one brilliant season, Toscanini and Mahler, formerly of Milan and Vienna, were on the program in ninety-four of the Met's 224 performances. In the space of five extraordinary days in February 1909, the public heard Toscanini conduct the Verdi Requiem and *Götterdämmerung,* and Mahler *Fidelio* and *The Bartered Bride.* That year, Toscanini led the Met premieres of Puccini's early *Le Villi* and Alfredo Catalani's *La Wally,* Mahler those of Eugen d'Albert's *Tiefland* and Smetana's comic opera, the only popular novelty of the season. The inevitable clash between the two star conductors was sparked by Toscanini's move to have *Tristan und Isolde* assigned to him. He had made it clear that he was a committed Wagnerian in the stupendous performance of *Götterdämmerung,* with Fremstad as Brünnhilde for the first time. Mahler prevailed, nonetheless. In his letter to Dippel of fall 1908, he argued, "I have . . . expressly retained *Tristan* for myself. I lavished a great deal of effort on the *Tristan* last season and may reasonably assert that the form in which the work now appears in New York is my intellectual property." The following season, 1909–10, *Tristan* was Toscanini's, and Wagnerites got to debate whether Mahler's version was too pale, Toscanini's too Italianate. Mahler's adieu came in spring 1910 when he returned briefly for the US premiere of Tchaikovsky's *The Queen of Spades,* sung in German, the first staged performance of a Russian opera in New York. Krehbiel thought it a triumph, but the public disagreed, and the opera was absent from the Met until 1965.[9]

In fall 1909, not content to compete with Oscar Hammerstein, the Metropolitan went into competition with itself at the recently completed New Theatre. The project began in an atmosphere of optimism: sparing no expense, the fabulous edifice would offer all the amenities the performing arts could dream of, along with the educational programs the citizenry had repeatedly been promised. But what New York worthies trumpeted as "the people's theatre" was soon attacked as "a hobby for millionaires" and "a gilded incubator." Again, the perceived betrayal of a theater for the common man— and woman—threatened an embryonic cultural institution, as it had the Academy of Music on 14th Street in 1854. The anger of the press and activist theatrical personalities was directed in particular at the thirty founders, who were, to a man, affiliated with the Metropolitan. The early financing was identified with the familiar names of Kahn, Belmont, Vanderbilt, Huntington, and Mackay. In its relationship to the Metropolitan, the New

Theatre was modeled on that of the Opéra-Comique to the Paris Opéra. It opened on November 16, 1909, with *Werther*, starring Farrar and Edmond Clément in his American début, soon followed by the premiere of Alfred Bruneau's *L'Attaque du moulin*. A mixed repertoire ranged from the intended "light" operas, *Zar und Zimmermann, La Fille de Madame Angot, Fra Diavolo*, to works also regularly presented in the larger house, *Manon, La Bohème*, and *Tosca*. The Met persevered at the New Theatre through only forty performances in the single season, 1909–10. The sight lines were wonderful, the acoustics awful. The elegance and comfort of the 2,318-seat auditorium, sized to opera somewhat less than grand, could not offset the hostility of the left, inept management, and a location considered hopelessly inconvenient, Central Park West at 62nd Street. Sadly, the splendid building was demolished in 1931.[10]

When American composer-critic Reginald De Koven lashed out at the corporate "ambition to make the Metropolitan a central depot for supplying opera in large and small doses to the world at large" (*World*, Nov. 14, 1910), he was thinking not only of the New Theatre but also of the company's first international tour, scheduled for the following May and June. The Met brought to Paris's Théâtre du Châtelet its best: Caruso's Canio, Leo Slezak's Otello, Fremstad's Santuzza, Destinn's Aïda, Scotti's Falstaff, and a new production of *Manon Lescaut,* never before heard in France, in deference to Massenet and his own *Manon*. Adding to the heated coverage of this controversial premiere was the news that the indisposed Lina Cavalieri would be replaced by a young Spanish soprano, Lucrezia Bori, destined to become a pillar of the Met. De Koven's paper carried glowing news of opening night. It was generally agreed that the heroes of the occasion were Gatti and Toscanini. The first had pulled off the logistical miracle of mounting the opera in two days on a stage inadequate to the grandiosity of the company's ancient Egypt; Toscanini had conducted incomparably despite only one week of rehearsal with the initially resistant Colonne Orchestra and acoustics inadequate to Verdi's sonorities (May 28). But that was not the whole story. Rowdies in the gallery had booed Toscanini at the beginning of the second act, ostensibly to protest the absence of even one French principal in the whole of what was tagged the "Italian," never the "Metropolitan," visit. When the curtain rose, the cool Louise Homer began to sing over the tumult; her ovation was such that the catcalls were lost in the applause. *Musical America* carried the headline "Our Opera Hissed by Paris Claque, Brilliant Success Achieved Despite Short Violent Anti-Italian Outbreak" (May 28).

The next day, Gatti was pilloried in the literary periodical *Gil Blas* for refusing to reengage a leading French mezzo-soprano, Marie Delna. The writer contended that behind this decision was the powerful Toscanini, Italian to the core, who had pressed his bias against French artists. It was well known too that Edmond Clément had complained bitterly that only those who would sing Italian parts would be retained at the Met, implying what the numbers did not show, that French opera was unfairly slighted in New York (*Times*, March 20, 1910). While Gatti declared, perhaps indelicately, that he had brought the company to France to demonstrate the high standard demanded every day on Broadway, *Gil Blas* alleged that what had actually motivated the impresario and the conductor was the lure of the Légion d'honneur. And while the French, wounded in their national pride, railed against an offending cultural invasion from the south, the far-off American press was busy claiming as its own the altogether Italian triumvirate of Gatti, Toscanini, and Caruso.[11]

The defining event of 1909–10, the buyout of Hammerstein at the end of a season of ruinous rivalry, served to cement the power of the Kahn/Gatti directorate. (Kahn himself made up the $500,000 debt incurred in the first two years of the new administration, accruing to himself enormous control over the company in the bargain.) The last straw was Hammerstein's provocative incursion into Philadelphia, a Met outpost since the year of the company's founding. On most Tuesdays, the Met held forth at the Academy of Music on South Broad Street; Hammerstein was positioned defiantly at his new opera house on North Broad. Not content with the Philadelphia power play, Hammerstein boasted that he would acquire yet another house, this time in Baltimore, and spoke of extending his empire even further. Meanwhile, the Metropolitan made no secret of its own imperial agenda, starting with Boston and Chicago. Between November 1909 and April 1910, the company put on 135 shows of thirty-eight works on 39th Street, in addition to those mounted at two other New York venues, the New Theatre and the Brooklyn Academy of Music, and on tour in the United States and abroad, for the unbelievable total of 360 performances of forty-two works.

Debilitated by the four-year contest, at the end of his financial rope, and having ripped out the grand tier boxes of his theater to spite his already alienated society supporters, Hammerstein capitulated. In April 1910, the Metropolitan Opera Company forked over the $1.25 million it took to cover Hammerstein's obligations and to acquire the sets, the costumes, the Philadelphia opera house—in effect his entire operation, excluding only the

34th Street Manhattan. The Hammerstein deal was contingent on his agreement to desist from operatic activity in New York, Boston, Philadelphia, and Chicago for the ensuing ten years. The Manhattan Opera Company went out in glory on tour in Boston: Garden sang four of her roles, including Mélisande, Tetrazzini and John McCormack starred in *La Fille du régiment* and *La Traviata*. The indefatigable impresario turned to London, where he went ahead and built himself, yes, another opera house. The British chapter lasted only two years. In 1913, Hammerstein attempted to circumvent the American injunction with a popularly priced season of opera in English at New York's Century Theatre, the renamed New Theatre. When the Met stopped him from going forward with his plans, he built yet another opera house, the Lexington, home to moving pictures and vaudeville until 1917, when it was leased by the Chicago Opera. Hammerstein lost the Lexington too. He died in 1919, just six months before the end of his exile, but not before he had announced the imminent resumption of his battle with the Met. Hammerstein represents the only serious challenge the Met faced in New York from the days of Mapleson to the bright years of the New York City Opera at Lincoln Center in the 1960s and 1970s.[12]

### *La Fanciulla del West,* December 10, 1910

Gatti had presided over the fiasco of the world premiere of *Madama Butterfly* at La Scala in 1904. But within a few months, Cio-Cio-San had endeared herself to Europe's audiences and solidified Puccini's claim to the title of the most popular of living opera composers. At the front of the verismo wave, he had "staged a coup d'état and seized control of opera's commanding heights." It was to Gatti again, now at the Metropolitan, that Puccini entrusted his next work, *La Fanciulla del West*. As early as 1907, in New York to oversee *Butterfly,* he was on the lookout for a wholly American subject. A performance of Belasco's *The Girl of the Golden West* left him hesitant. Often accused of repeating himself, and most painfully during the catcalls that greeted the La Scala *Butterfly,* Puccini was bent on avoiding the humiliating charge. As the plot would have it, the act 2 struggle between Minnie, the saloon keeper, and Jack Rance, the sheriff, over Dick Johnson, the bandit, bore a marked similarity to the act 2 confrontation between Tosca, the singer, and Scarpia, the police chief, over Mario, the painter. Moreover, *The Girl* was an old-fashioned melodrama, and Puccini, alert to cutting-edge contemporaries such as Claude Debussy and Richard Strauss, was eager to be judged

FIGURE 12. From left to right, Giulio Gatti-Casazza, David Belasco, Arturo Toscanini, Giacomo Puccini (courtesy Metropolitan Opera Archives)

modern. It was only when an Italian translation of the Belasco play became available that he was convinced he had found his story. He embarked on the project with enthusiasm: "The *Girl* may become a second *Bohème,* but stronger, more daring, with greater scope." Set in the requisite American locale, the play was alive with action and spectacle animated by a powerful female protagonist. The modernity absent from the plot would be invested in the score. Puccini signed his agreement with Gatti on June 9, 1910, during his visit to Paris for the Metropolitan performances of *Manon Lescaut.*[13]

The dailies devoted lengthy articles to Puccini's visit to New York for the premiere, to dinner at the Vanderbilt mansion, to the score, to Belasco's staging of the opera. Skeptical reporters doubted that the colloquial English of Minnie and the brawling miners and the pigeon English of the Amerindian couple Billy Jack Rabbit and Wowkle would survive translation into Italian. Or, in fact, that Puccini could infuse his score with the local color of the Wild West. The *Sun* recorded Toscanini's gravelly instructions during rehearsal, Belasco's volcanic imprecations, Puccini's air of calm, "an unlighted cigarette between his lips." When Caruso had to leave for an evening performance, Toscanini barked Dick Johnson's lines from the pit. The conductor declared, "The opera is flooded with melody. And the melody is of the kind with which Puccini has already won us. But there are new things above all, exquisite new timbres, tones and colors in the instrumentation. It has more vigor, more variety, and more masculinity, than the orchestration of the composer's earlier operas. It is more complex. In one word, it is more modern" (*American,* Oct. 18, 1910). Puccini appeared to have gotten it right.[14]

Opening night of *La Fanciulla del West,* the Met's first world premiere, was the perfect fit for a company poised to leverage its international reputation. The public assembled not only for the inaugural of a major work but for a happening "that could not be equaled, nor even approached by any of the great opera houses in Europe" (*Morning Telegraph,* Dec. 11, 1910). New York alone could bring together on one glittering stage Enrico Caruso, Emmy Destinn, Pasquale Amato, Arturo Toscanini, and David Belasco. *Musical America* predicted that "the great composers will learn to make their first appeal for a verdict here, and so show the world that we have taken the lead in presenting the works of the masters, as other great cities of the old world have done hitherto." Less than three weeks later, the Met would stage the world premiere of Engelbert Humperdinck's *Königskinder* with Geraldine Farrar. To top it all off, the composer of the lovable *Hänsel und Gretel,* like Puccini, would come to New York for his new work. This double coup, unmatched in modern operatic history, was worthy of the cultural Mecca the city had become.[15]

A stouthearted crowd gathered to catch sight of the rich and famous as they made their way into the opera house on the bitterly cold December night. Snow covered the frozen sidewalks. Ticket-holders braved both the weather and the prices, which management had doubled for the occasion. The police were on hand to control the crush, while in the lobby, in an effort to discourage intrepid scalpers, ushers checked the signed and countersigned tickets. Kahn, unrecognized, was denied admission until his identity could be confirmed. Chaos delayed the curtain for twenty-five minutes. A profusion of US and Italian flags flew over the heteroclite Italian-American event. After the short prelude, the curtain rose on the Polka, the saloon familiar to the many who had seen the play when it was a hit of the 1905–06 Broadway season. The set had been pumped up to conform to the Met proscenium, three times the size of that of the 42nd Street Belasco, today the New Victory. The playwright/director had worked his magic: he had shaken the secondary singers and chorus from their stock gestures. There they stood, authentically garbed, muddy miners at the bar. On a stage accustomed to the likes of Aïda's ancient tomb, Brünnhilde's mythic mountaintop, and Marguerite's medieval garden, Belasco had simulated Minnie's 1849 Gold Rush California, filled with cigar smoke, flush with rounds of whiskey and poker. And most amazing, he had persuaded Destinn, dressed in a shirtwaist and a cardinal-red skirt, to sing from upstage while serving drinks, and the holstered Caruso to deliver his opening phrases with his back to the audience.[16]

Puccini sat through act 1 in agony, as he would confess. Without a conventional aria conventionally greeted by applause, he had no way of gauging the response of the audience before the first curtain had fallen. He need not have worried. The act 1 bravos demanded bow after bow, fourteen curtain calls in all. And that was just the beginning. The act 2 blizzard was Belasco's chance to prove that his brand of realism could cross over from the legitimate to the operatic platform. Thirty-two stagehands were there to assure that the moment Minnie and Dick Johnson embraced, the cabin door would fly open, snow would drift in, the walls would tremble, the curtains would flutter, and ice would form on the window panes. The act's dramatic climax—Johnson's blood dripping from the attic, Minnie cheating at cards for his life—met with nineteen curtain calls. For act 3, Puccini had urged his librettists, Guelfo Civinini and Carlo Zanganari, to depart from Belasco's script and add a scene in which Johnson is captured in the redwood forest. The bandit escapes death by hanging thanks only to Minnie's impassioned plea to her adoring miners. For the first time in Metropolitan history, trees were built in the semiround, with leaves cut from leather. A posse of eight galloped their horses across the stage. According to the libretto, Minnie was to make an equestrian entrance, "her hair flying in the wind, a pistol clenched in her teeth." That particular coup de théâtre went by the wayside; having taken a spill during rehearsal, and having been saved only by the quick reflexes of baritone Dinh Gilly (her real-life partner), Destinn opted for caution and walked her pony onto the stage. Whether the audience missed this additional thrill we cannot say; it had just roared its approval for Caruso's big number, "Ch'ella mi creda" (Telegram). Minnie and Dick bid farewell to their beloved California against a background of snow-capped Sierras, pink with dawn's first light. During the many final curtain calls, Caruso, ever the cowboy, drew his revolver and rubbed his neck, recently delivered from the noose. Puccini was summoned to the stage, where Gatti, breaking his rule by appearing before the public, presented him with a laurel wreath. Belasco received one too. Floral tributes hid the composer from view. The *World*

FIGURE 13. *La Fanciulla del West,* act 3, Enrico Caruso as Dick Johnson in center, and on the right, Emmy Destinn as Minnie, and Pasquale Amato as Jack Rance, 1910 (White Studio; courtesy Metropolitan Opera Archives)

predicted, far too optimistically as it turned out, that Belasco's daring would mark a turning point in operatic stagecraft.

Puccini was delighted with Caruso ("grande"), Destinn ("benissimo"), Amato ("ottimo" [very good]), and Toscanini ("un vero angelo" [a real angel]). The New York critics concurred. They had only praise for the artists and the mise-en-scène. Many did, however, fault the music. Krehbiel sniped, "nine-tenths of the time his [Puccini's] vocal melody is nothing" *(Tribune).* For Aldrich, who noted Puccini's embrace of Debussian harmonies, the loss of sustained lyricism was regrettable: the "scraps of melody . . . are commonplace, impotent to express what they are associated with and frankly dull . . . there is little that is characteristic of the Puccini of earlier years" *(Times).* The composer was taken to task for the irritating contrast between his musical idiom and the familiar "Western" ditties sprinkled throughout the score. But to judge by the consistently high box-office returns, the public remained faithful through the initial four-season run. Since then, *Fanciulla* has had sporadic revivals. The work, a milestone in the composer's steady evolution toward a more modern lyricism through the expansion of his harmonic palette, has secured a permanent place in the repertoire.[17]

## Other Premieres

In December 1910, odds would have favored the Met's other world premiere. For the Wagnerite critics, there was no contest: *Königskinder* was "the work of a master of his art and of his material, a melodist of the first water," and Humperdinck was congratulated on having "been able to . . . attain results of such pure beauty" *(Times)*. Finck pronounced *Königskinder* nothing less than "the greatest operatic work that has come from Germany in three decades—since the production of *Parsifal*" *(Evening Post)*. Humperdinck, who had demonstrated the viability of the fairytale opera with *Hänsel und Gretel*, here added dimensions of interest to an adult audience: a love story and a social message that decried the defeat of idealism at the hands of materialism. If Puccini asked for galloping horses, Humperdinck wanted a gaggle of waddling geese, "which last night did what was required of it with exemplary fidelity" *(Times)*. By all accounts, Farrar's Goose Girl was exquisite. In their four-year runs, *Königskinder* far surpassed the number of performances racked up by *Fanciulla,* but after 1910–11 it dropped below the season's box-office average. Never revived at the Met, it has turned up infrequently elsewhere.

In his first seven years, in addition to *La Fanciulla del West* and *Königskinder,* Gatti bet on fully thirty company premieres, of which only five had significant life spans. Franco Leoni's one-act melodrama, *L'Oracolo,* was retired with Scotti in 1933. Italo Montemezzi's *L'Amore dei tre re* was given regularly until 1949. The durable legacies of this period are Jacques Offenbach's *Les Contes d'Hoffmann,* Richard Strauss's *Der Rosenkavalier,* and Modest Mussorgsky's *Boris Godunov.*

### THE POLITICS OF LANGUAGE

Toscanini left New York suddenly in spring 1915. Farrar had pushed him to choose between his mistress and his family. And since divorce, from his point of view, was unthinkable, he was left with no choice at all. The diva's ultimatum was not the only consideration. There was also the escalating conflict with Gatti, the conductor unmovable in matters of quality, never mind the cost; the intendant fixated on the balance sheet to the last penny. One of their many rows had erupted during the preparation for the 1913 *Un Ballo in maschera,* tied to the centennial celebration of Verdi's birth. Toscanini insisted on a stage band for the act 3 masked ball. Gatti maintained that the music could just as well emanate from the pit. There were endless conflicts over rehearsal time. The camel's back was broken, the story goes, by a mediocre *Carmen*. The infuriated Toscanini announced that he was canceling his six remaining performances. Besides, he was eager to return to Italy, by now at war with Austria-Hungary. Thus it was that the great man and his wife and daughters were not, as had been planned, on the *Lusitania* sailing from New York on May 1 and sunk by a German U-boat on May 7. Kahn and Gatti did their best to lure the irreplaceable conductor back to the Met, even at the price of naming him "General Musik Director" with increased power over repertoire, casts, and schedule. Toscanini refused to rejoin the company. In fact, he would never again conduct an opera at the Metropolitan.[18]

Two years after Toscanini's departure, during the third intermission of the April 2, 1917, performance of De Koven's *The Canterbury Pilgrims,* the audience was thunderstruck by the news that Woodrow Wilson had appeared before Congress to call for a declaration of war against Germany. Late editions of New York papers circulated from hand to hand in the Diamond Horseshoe. The recently recalled ambassador to Berlin James Gerard, a guest in one of the boxes, exhorted the crowd to cheer the president; from another box came a shout for cheers for the Allies and the US Army and Navy. The orchestra struck up "The Star-Spangled Banner." As act 4 began, the mezzo-soprano Margarete Ober, "one of a dozen German stars [more accurately, two stars and a handful of comprimarios] on the stage at the time, had the leading part with Mr. [Johannes] Sembach in the final scene. She was singing a phrase of the Wife of Bath when she stopped and fell full length upon her back, striking heavily on the floor. Sembach and [tenor] Max Bloch lifted her, but she sank again, and the two men carried her out through the stage crowd, considerably to the detriment of the Wife of Bath's bridal gown" (*Times,* April 3, 1917). The cast sang on without her or her character to the opera's end. In the years of America's neutrality, 1914–1917, Ober and her compatriots had had no problem singing with French and British colleagues, nationals of countries with which Germany was at war. Nor was there any serious threat of anti-German feeling affecting the repertoire. Among the premieres of the period were two works performed in German, Hermann Goetz's *Der Widerspenstigen Zähmung (The Taming of the Shrew)* and Gluck's *Iphigénie en Tauride,* in a version arranged by Richard Strauss.

The challenge to the customary multinational casting lay principally in the perils of transporting European artists to the United States and back again; passports and safe-conducts were precious commodities. By 1916, the dangers of ocean travel had been brought home to the extended Met family by the tragic death of Spanish composer/piano virtuoso Enrique Granados. On his return from New York following the world premiere of his opera *Goyescas,* the ship on which Granados and his wife were crossing the English Channel was torpedoed by a German submarine. Still, the Met carried on its programming very much as usual. As late as October 16, 1917, six months after the disrupted performance of *The Canterbury Pilgrims,* Olive Fremstad had signed to sing Isolde. A week before opening night and only nine days before her homecoming after a three-year absence, Fremstad was told that all opera in German was canceled for the season and so, therefore, was her engagement. The long-awaited *Tristan und Isolde* turned into *Boris Godunov.* The action was taken, according to the official explanation, "lest Germany should make capital of their [operas in German] continued appearance to convince the German people that this nation was not heart and soul in the war." Though no one could have guessed it at the time, the last performance in German from the Met stage for the duration and beyond had taken place on April 13, 1917. On that occasion, Isolde was sung by Fremstad's archrival, Johanna Gadski, a fixture at the Met from 1900 to 1917.[19]

In May 1915, a day after the attack on the *Lusitania,* a gala for the benefit of the German Red Cross, a performance of *Die Fledermaus* not sponsored by the company, was scheduled for the house. Gadski, who had lately made no secret of her ill will toward the United States, was to sing "Deutschland über Alles." But in light of the immediacy of the outrageous act of German aggression, she thought better of it. In the same year, the soprano's husband, Captain Hans Tauscher, was charged with conspiracy to blow up the canal between Lake Erie and Lake Ontario; he was acquitted. Gadski herself was alleged to have said publicly that, given half a chance, she would happily blow up New Jersey's munitions plants. In an editorial titled "Overriding Tolerance," the *Globe* urged Gadski's ouster from the company for hosting a 1915 New Year's Eve party at which her colleague, German baritone Otto Goritz, was reputed to have sung a parody in celebration of the sinking of the *Lusitania.* At war's end, Gadski sued the *Tribune,* claiming that Krehbiel, in response to protests over her impending Carnegie Hall concert, had made libelous statements. Krehbiel had simply repeated what had been previously reported and Gadski lost at trial.[20]

The press was, of course, correct in separating the denunciation of Gadski and her fellow revelers from the defense of German opera in time of war. The newspapers had engaged the issue for months. A *Tribune* headline read, "German Opera Is Still Welcome at the Metropolitan" (Sept. 23, 1917). The *Sun* was confident that the public did not "think of Bach, Beethoven, Brahms and Wagner as exclusively representing the Teutonic people." The *Mail* declared, "Art knows no frontiers." A ban on German opera would, for the *Times,* be analogous to "excluding the great classics of German literature from the public libraries." Signed contracts and the views of influential music critics notwithstanding, in a charged climate the board bowed to war hysteria, voting to exile the German language from its auditorium and Fremstad and other leading Wagner specialists from its roster.[21]

Subscribers who objected to the new policy and demanded refunds were refused on the grounds that the company had "made no definite promise as to the complete and precise repertoire of its present season." They were informed that "the decision of the Board of Directors to withdraw opera sung in the German language was dictated not only by a sense of patriotic duty but also by a desire to safeguard the interests of our patrons and to prevent possible disorder." The German-language repertoire tentatively announced for 1917–18, *Fidelio, Lohengrin, Tannhäuser, Tristan und Isolde, Meistersinger, Parsifal, Rheingold, Walküre, Siegfried,* and *Götterdämmerung,* was scratched. The company premiere of *Saint Elisabeth,* a Liszt oratorio staged as an opera, was done in English, not in the anticipated German; *Martha* was given in Italian as usual. In 1916–17, forty-six performances had been sung in German. To compensate for the boycott, in 1917–18 the Italian total rose from eighty-eight to 122, the French from thirty-three to forty-eight. The premieres represented Great War allies Italy, France, Russia, and the United States: Mascagni's *Lodoletta,* Henri Rabaud's *Mârouf,* Nikolai Rimsky-Korsakov's *Le Coq d'or,* and *The Robin Woman: Shanewis* by Charles Wakefield Cadman, a specialist in Native-American music.[22]

The November 11, 1918, armistice converged with the opening of the season; the company celebrated offstage and on. In the afternoon, a procession to Times Square of Met administrators (Gatti-Casazza included), instrumentalists, and singers followed a "dummy" Siegfried, hung in effigy from a gibbet and helmeted to resemble Kaiser Wilhelm. Between acts of the evening's opera, *Samson et Dalila,* national anthems rang through the house, "The Star-Spangled Banner" capped by Caruso's high B flat.

The reintegration of Wagner began in 1919–20 with *Parsifal,* in English; in 1920–21, *Lohengrin* and *Tristan* were on the program, also in English; all did well at the box office. In 1921–22, with the lifting of the linguistic ban,

TABLE 5  Metropolitan Opera Premieres, 1908–09 to 1917–18

| Composer and Title | Met Premiere (*World Premiere) | Most Recent Met Performance | No. of Seasons in Met Repertoire | No. of Met Productions | No. of Met Performances, 1883–2013 | World Premiere | Director/Designer |
|---|---|---|---|---|---|---|---|
| Eugen d'Albert, Tiefland | Nov. 23, 1908 | Jan. 9, 1909 | 1 | 1 | 6 | Nov. 15, 1903, Prague, Neues Deutsches | Anton Schertel / Anton Brioschi |
| Giacomo Puccini, Le Villi | Dec. 17, 1908 | Mar. 3, 1909 | 1 | 1 | 6 | May 31, 1884, Milan, dal Verme | Jules Speck / Mario Sala, Angelo Parravicini |
| Alfredo Catalani, La Wally | Jan. 6, 1909 | Feb. 4, 1909 | 1 | 1 | 4 | Jan. 20, 1892, Milan, La Scala | Jules Speck / Mario Sala, Angelo Parravicini |
| Bedřich Smetana, The Bartered Bride | Feb. 19, 1909 | Feb. 20, 2011 | 15 | 3 | 86 | May 30, 1866, Prague, Provisional | Anton Schertel / Kautsky & Rottonara Brothers |
| Albert Lortzing, Zar und Zimmermann | Nov. 30, 1909 | Apr. 6, 1910 | 1 | 1 | 6 | Dec. 22, 1837, Leipzig, Stadttheater | Anton Schertel / Burghart & Co. |
| Ferdinando Païr, Il Maestro di Cappella | Dec. 9, 1909 | Apr. 20, 1910 | 1 | 1 | 8 | Mar. 29, 1821, Paris, Feydeau | Unknown / Unknown |
| Charles Lecocq, La Fille de Madame Angot | Dec. 14, 1909 | Feb. 23, 1910 | 1 | 1 | 5 | Dec. 4, 1872, Brussels, Fantaisies Parisiennes | Jules Speck / Antonio Rovescalli |
| Alberto Franchetti, Germania | Jan. 22, 1910 | Feb. 6, 1911 | 2 | 1 | 9 | Mar. 11, 1902, Milan, La Scala | Jules Speck / Antonio Rovescalli, Mario Sala |
| Friedrich von Flotow, Alessandro Stradella | Feb. 4, 1910 | Feb. 25, 1910 | 1 | 1 | 6 | Dec. 30, 1844, Hamburg, Stadtheater | Anton Schertel / Unknown |
| Alfred Bruneau, L'Attaque du moulin | Feb. 8, 1910 | Mar. 9, 1910 | 1 | 1 | 6 | Nov. 23, 1893, Paris, Opéra-Comique | Jules Speck / Burghart & Co. |

(continued)

**TABLE 5** *(continued)*

| Composer and Title | Met Premiere (*World Premiere) | Most Recent Met Performance | No. of Seasons in Met Repertoire | No. of Met Productions | No. of Met Performances, 1883–2013 | World Premiere | Director/Designer |
|---|---|---|---|---|---|---|---|
| Peter Ilyich Tchaikovsky, *The Queen of Spades* | Mar. 5, 1910 | Mar. 26, 2011 | 9 | 3 | 71 | Dec. 19, 1890, St. Petersburg, Mariinsky | Anton Schertel / Burghart & Co. |
| Frederick Converse, *The Pipe of Desire* | Mar. 18, 1910 | Mar. 31, 1910 | 1 | 1 | 3 | Jan. 31, 1906, Boston, Jordan Hall | Unknown / Unknown |
| Christoph Willibald Gluck, *Armide* | Nov. 14, 1910 | Feb. 11, 1912 | 2 | 1 | 9 | Sept. 23, 1777, Paris, Opéra | Jules Speck / Paul Paquereau |
| Giacomo Puccini, *La Fanciulla del West* | Dec. 10, 1910* | Jan. 8, 2011 | 13 | 4 | 104 | | David Belasco, Edward Siedle / James Fox |
| Engelbert Humperdinck, *Königskinder* | Dec. 28, 1910* | Apr. 18, 1914 | 4 | 1 | 39 | | Anton Schertel / Burghart & Co., James Fox |
| Paul Dukas, *Ariane et Barbe-bleue* | Mar. 29, 1911 | Mar. 2, 1912 | 2 | 1 | 7 | Mar. 10, 1907, Paris, Opéra-Comique | Jules Speck / Antonio Rovescalli |
| Ludwig Thuille, *Lobetanz* | Nov. 18, 1911 | Feb. 9, 1912 | 1 | 1 | 7 | Feb. 6, 1898, Karlsruhe | Anton Schertel / Hans Kautsky |
| Ermanno Wolf-Ferrari, *Le Donne curiose* | Jan. 3, 1912 | Mar. 20, 1913 | 2 | 1 | 8 | Nov. 27, 1903, Munich, Residenz (in German) | Anton Schertel / Antonio Rovescalli |
| Leo Blech, *Versiegelt* | Jan. 20, 1912 | Apr. 12, 1912 | 1 | 1 | 5 | Nov. 4, 1908, Hamburg | Anton Schertel / James Fox |
| Horatio Parker, *Mona* | Mar. 14, 1912* | Apr. 1, 1912 | 1 | 1 | 4 | | Loomis Taylor / Paul Paquereau |
| Ermanno Wolf-Ferrari, *Il Segreto di Susanna* | Dec. 13, 1912 | Apr. 27, 1922 | 4 | 1 | 14 | Dec. 4, 1909, Munich, Hoftheater (in German) | Jules Speck / Unknown |

| Jacques Offenbach, *Les Contes d'Hoffmann* | Jan. 11, 1913 | Oct. 19, 2010 | 30 | 6 | 256 | Feb. 10, 1881, Paris, Opéra-Comique | Jules Speck / Burghart & Co. |
|---|---|---|---|---|---|---|---|
| Walter Damrosch, *Cyrano* | Feb. 27, 1913* | Apr. 23, 1913 | 1 | 1 | 6 | | Jules Speck / Antonio Rovescalli |
| Modest Mussorgsky, *Boris Godunov* | Mar. 19, 1913 | Mar. 17, 2011 | 36 | 3 | 273 | Feb. 8, 1874, St. Petersburg, Mariinsky | Jules Speck / Alexander Golovine, Alexander Benois |
| Richard Strauss, *Der Rosenkavalier* | Dec. 9, 1913 | Jan. 15, 2010 | 48 | 2 | 377 | Jan. 26, 1911, Dresden, Königliches Opernhaus | Franz Hörth / Hans Kautsky |
| Italo Montemezzi, *L'Amore dei tre re* | Jan. 2, 1914 | Jan. 15, 1949 | 16 | 1 | 66 | Apr. 10, 1913, Milan, La Scala | Jules Speck / Mario Sala |
| Victor Herbert, *Madeleine* | Jan. 24, 1914* | Mar. 25, 1914 | 1 | 1 | 6 | | Jules Speck / Joseph Novak |
| Gustave Charpentier, *Julien* | Feb. 26, 1914 | Apr. 8, 1914 | 1 | 1 | 5 | June 4, 1913, Paris, Opéra-Comique | Jules Speck / Paul Paquereau |
| Ermanno Wolf-Ferrari, *L'Amore medico* | Mar. 25, 1914 | Apr. 17, 1914 | 1 | 1 | 4 | Dec. 4, 1913, Dresden, Hoftheater (in German) | Jules Speck / Hans Kautsky, James Fox |
| Umberto Giordano, *Madame Sans-Gêne* | Jan. 25, 1915* | Apr. 8, 1918 | 4 | 1 | 19 | | Jules Speck / Antonio Rovescalli |
| Franco Leoni, *L'Oracolo* | Feb. 4, 1915 | Jan. 20, 1933 | 13 | 1 | 55 | July 3, 1905, London, Covent Garden | Jules Speck / James Fox |
| Alexander Borodin, *Prince Igor* | Dec. 30, 1915 | Dec. 15, 1917 | 3 | 1 | 10 | Nov. 4, 1890, St. Petersburg, Mariinsky | Jules Speck / Attilio Comelli |
| Enrique Granados, *Goyescas* | Jan. 28, 1916* | Mar. 6, 1916 | 1 | 1 | 5 | | Jules Speck / Antonio Rovescalli |
| Hermann Goetz, *The Taming of the Shrew (Die Widerspenstigen Zähmung)* | Mar. 15, 1916 | Apr. 13, 1916 | 1 | 1 | 3 | Oct. 11, 1874, Mannheim | Jan Heythekker / Ludwig Sievert |

*(continued)*

**TABLE 5** *(continued)*

| Composer and Title | Met Premiere (*World Premiere) | Most Recent Met Performance | No. of Seasons in Met Repertoire | No. of Met Productions | No. of Met Performances, 1883–2013 | World Premiere | Director/Designer |
|---|---|---|---|---|---|---|---|
| Christoph Willibald Gluck, *Iphigénie en Tauride* | Nov. 25, 1916 | Mar. 5, 2011 | 3 | 2 | 19 | May 18, 1779, Paris, Opéra | Jan Heythekker / J. Monroe Hewlett, Charles Basing, A. T. Hewlett |
| Riccardo Zandonai, *Francesca da Rimini* | Dec. 22, 1916 | Mar. 22, 2013 | 5 | 2 | 43 | Feb. 19, 1914, Turin, Regio | Jules Speck/Mario Sala, Pieretto Bianco |
| Jules Massenet, *Thaïs* | Feb. 16, 1917 | Jan. 8, 2009 | 10 | 4 | 73 | Mar. 16, 1894, Paris, Opéra | Jules Speck/Pieretto Bianco |
| Reginald De Koven, *The Canterbury Pilgrims* | Mar. 8, 1917* | Apr. 21, 1917 | 1 | 1 | 7 | | Richard Ordynski / Homer F. Emens, James Fox |
| Henri Rabaud, *Mârouf* | Dec. 19, 1917 | Apr. 27, 1937 | 4 | 1 | 15 | May 14, 1914, Paris, Opéra-Comique | Richard Ordynski / Ernest M. Gros |
| Franz Liszt, *Saint Elisabeth* | Jan. 3, 1918 | Mar. 13, 1918 | 1 | 1 | 6 | Aug. 15, 1865, Budapest | Richard Ordynski/Joseph Urban |
| Pietro Mascagni, *Lodoletta* | Jan. 12, 1918 | Feb. 15, 1919 | 2 | 1 | 9 | Apr. 30, 1917, Rome, Costanzi | Richard Ordynski / Pieretto Bianco |
| Nikolai Rimsky-Korsakov, *Le Coq d'or* | Mar. 6, 1918 | May 3, 1945 | 11 | 1 | 68 | Oct. 7, 1909, Moscow, Solodovnikov | Adolph Bolm/Willy Pogany |
| Charles Wakefield Cadman, *The Robin Woman: Shanewis* | Mar. 23, 1918* | Apr. 4, 1919 | 2 | 1 | 8 | | Richard Ordynski/James Fox, Norman Bel Geddes |

Italian maintained its plurality, although performances in German increased gradually through the 1920s. In the mid-1930s, with the coming of Kirsten Flagstad, German reclaimed its prewar share of approximately 30 percent.

## CARUSO AND FARRAR: CELEBRITIES
## FOR MODERN TIMES

At the very top of the operatic pyramid stood those few whose fame eclipsed the genre itself. The adventures of these artists/personalities made juicy copy for gossip columns and other channels of extramusical discourse. In Caruso's case, most clamorous were stories surrounding the monkey-house episode and his daring defiance of racketeers of the Black Hand; in Farrar's, her reputed affair with Crown Prince Friedrich Wilhelm, son of the Kaiser. That Farrar was the only diva to command her own dressing room and that she traveled in a private railroad car when the company was on the road were details to pique the public's curiosity. Spaghetti Chaliapin, Chicken Tetrazzini, Lattuga alla Caruso, Coupe Patti, and Peach Melba showed up on the menus of sophisticates. In a handful of years at the end of the 1920s, likenesses of Melba, Farrar, Jeritza, and Bori appeared on the covers of *Time*.[23]

Caruso's name all but ensured a sold-out house and, in 1913–14, for example, that meant a take of $12,000; Farrar, without Caruso, raked in the next highest receipts. They could salvage even as coolly received a novelty as *Julien*. From 1906–07 to their last joint appearance, opening night 1919, Caruso and Farrar sang together at the Met and on tour more than ninety times, despite the fact that the bottom line argued against the extravagance of casting the star couple. On the other hand, the pairing of the two could be counted on to turn performance into mega-event, notice into feature article, delight into delirium. In answer to the frequently asked question of which performance in Met history unleashed the greatest number of curtain calls and the longest ovation, the Metropolitan Opera online archive researchers award the palm to the April 22, 1914, Caruso/Farrar *Tosca*. The *Times* carried a long account of the show's reception: "OVATION FOR CARUSO AND MISS FARRAR. Opera Stars Recalled 40 Times after Last Appearance of Season in *Tosca*. TENOR DANCES JIG STEPS. Audience Refuses to Leave and Miss Farrar Drags in Caruso in Dressing Gown and Makes Speech." The *Tribune* put the number of curtain calls at forty-five. Twenty-one minutes elapsed before Farrar consented to address the public: "When we had to make a speech last year, Mr. Caruso ran away and left me in the lurch. So now I will just say, 'I thank you.' Thereupon she poked Caruso rather violently in the ribs; making every word count, he said in full, 'And-I-say-Thank-you.'"

Keeping pace with his mounting popularity was Caruso's fee. It shot up from $960 per performance in 1906–07 to $2,500 in 1914–15, and there it stayed to the end. Wary of the onerous expectations that came with an exorbitant cachet, Caruso turned down further increases. By way of comparison, in 1920–21, Giovanni Martinelli, with whom he shared many roles, made less than half his wage; arriving on the scene in that season, Caruso's last, Beniamino Gigli negotiated for $1,600. Amelita Galli-Curci, the highest-paid female star of the time, exacted $2,000 per performance. By 1920, outside the purview of the Metropolitan, the tenor was happy to accept as much as $10,000 a night. But all of this—fame far beyond the operatic sphere, impassioned fans, enormous box-office draw, glamour, power—had been the perquisites of previous generations of operatic luminaries: Lind and Patti, De Reske and Melba. For Caruso and Farrar, the reach of fame would be exponentially greater. As the march of technology would have it, it fell to them to be the first Metropolitan stars of the dawning age of mechanical reproduction.[24]

Caruso's Met career spanned seventeen years, from 1903 to 1920, Farrar's from 1906 to 1922, decades in which the then new media leapt into maturity. Before he had set foot in New York, the voice of the Italian tenor had been introduced to journalists by Conried. The recorded arias the impresario played for the New York press were likely among the ten Caruso cut in spring 1902 at the Grand Hotel in Milan, where, coincidentally, Verdi had died the year before. Caruso could not have dreamed that these wax transcriptions would be the first of 498 (245 are extant) that would net him more than $1 million and the industry twice that amount. A Victor Talking Machine Company advertisement in *Theater Magazine* (Dec. 1919) depicts Caruso leading a parade of twenty or so Metropolitan—and Victor—singers. Farrar, who made 160 recordings with the company, including duets from *Butterfly, Bohème, Faust, Tosca,* and *Manon* with Caruso, is pictured, fittingly, just behind him. The caption reads: "Will Caruso thrill you?" And for each of these recordings, the Metropolitan Opera Company stood to pocket royalties that would go some way toward recovering the salaries of their phonogenic artists.[25]

Farrar's disks document a voice of ample power, with a warm, solid middle. Others of her generation, Gadski and Destinn, for example, were more

FIGURE 14. Geraldine Farrar (Hartsook; courtesy Photofest)

polished vocalists, with more brilliant techniques. But Farrar was the more remarkable singer-actress; she had to be heard *and* seen. Or even only seen, as some in the (silent) motion picture industry were willing to gamble. Between 1915 and 1920, she made fifteen movies of diverse genres: costume dramas, contemporary melodramas, mysteries, westerns. *Carmen,* her first released film and her best known, premiered at Boston's Symphony Hall, a departure for this staid sanctuary of classical music. A telephone hookup was arranged between the auditorium and the Lasky Studio, where producer Jesse Lasky and director Cecil B. DeMille tracked the film's reception as they watched the movie simultaneously with the east coast audience. In her debut on the big screen, Farrar exhibits the flashing dark eyes, the alluring smile, the supple body, and the singularly uninhibited presence that defined her. And

*Carmen* allows us to assess the crossover lessons from opera to film back to opera that Hollywood taught her. Frances Alda brings to life a 1916 performance of Bizet's opera: "During the scene with the cigarette girls, Farrar suddenly shook one of them so realistically that the rest of the chorus gasped. 'Hollywood tricks' Caruso snorted to me. 'What does she think this is? A cinema?'" During the act 3 tussle between Carmen and Don José "she turned in [Caruso's] grasp, bent her head swiftly, and bit the hand that held her. Furious and bleeding, [he] flung her from him. She went down, smack on her btm *[sic]*! I stood staring, my mouth open, entirely forgetting my cue, until called to my senses by a sharp rap of the conductor's baton. Then curtain. Immediately the heavy velvet folds hid the stage from the audience, Farrar was up on her feet, and she and Caruso were having it out between them, whilst I tried to soothe them both." The next day, the headline ran: "Caruso Tells Farrar He'll Quit If She's Rough in *Carmen*" (*Tribune,* Feb. 19).[26]

Caruso, too, was seduced by the movies, although he first contemplated with some anxiety the potential loss of prestige should he, as Farrar put it, follow her "towards the concentrated vicinity of the lens." Ultimately, his foray onto the silent screen was both brief and forgettable. Between July 15 and September 30, 1918, Caruso made two films, *My Cousin* and *A Splendid Romance,* for which he was paid the astronomical sum of $100,000 by Lasky's Famous Players. Only *My Cousin* was released in the United States. It opens with a series of shots of Caruso as a celebrated tenor in mufti, and then in costume as Rodolfo, Canio, Samson, and the Duke of Mantua. He also plays the part of an impoverished Little Italy sculptor who has made a plaster bust of his cousin, the singer. The sculptor is portly and mustachioed, his face deeply lined, and immensely likable. He smokes a pipe and accompanies himself on the obligatory guitar. As the famous tenor, Caruso resembles his photographs, clean-shaven, sporting a cigarette holder. Throughout the opera sequences there are views of the Met's family circle, the boxes, the orchestra, the stage, and moments from *Pagliacci* itself. Caruso manages the pantomime of "Vesti la giubba" without excessive expression or gesticulation, not an easy task. In a subsequent scene, as if to underscore his own onstage restraint, he parodies the caricatural Italian tenor, grimaces and all.[27]

Barely two years later, Caruso's *L'Elisir d'amore* of December 11, 1920, at Brooklyn's Academy of Music made the front pages of both the *Times* and the *Tribune,* but not, alas, for the wonder of his artistry. During the first act, the tenor began to cough up blood. From the wings, his wife and physician implored him to leave the stage. He refused and continued to pass red-stained

FIGURE 15. Enrico Caruso as Nemorino in *L'Elisir d'amore,* 1904
(White Studio; courtesy Metropolitan Opera Archives)

handkerchiefs to choristers who passed him fresh handkerchiefs in return. At the end of the act, the theater manager stepped in front of the curtain: "'He assures me that he is willing, in spite of the accident, to finish the performance, and if you wish he will go on with it. It is for you to decide.' Hundreds of persons rose to their feet, crying 'No! No!'" *(Tribune).* Caruso would make just three more appearances with the company, his last in *La Juive* on Christmas Eve 1920. The Brooklyn *Elisir* foreshadowed his death the following August from complications of lung disease. During the critical phase of Caruso's illness, as hopes of recovery faded, the Metropolitan management was faced with the frightening prospect of a post-Caruso season. On March 5, 1921, Edward Ziegler, assistant general manager and right hand to Gatti, recommended the engagement of the coloratura soprano Galli-Curci and of the baritone Titta Ruffo, both with the Chicago Opera. "Whatever happens to Caruso," he wrote to Kahn, "we shall be in a position to offer to those of our subscribers whose first thought is of the 'stars,' if not an absolute substitute at least a relative substitute."

By August 2, 1921, the date of Caruso's death, the time for signing credible replacements for the coming season was at an end. Gatti wrote to Kahn on August 7, "The loss of poor Caruso is indeed great: we may have now and later tenors possessing some of his qualities, i.e., who may have a beautiful voice, who may be good singers or artists, etc., but I think it will be impossible to have the fortune to find again another personality who possesses in himself all the artistic and moral gifts that distinguished our poor and illustrious friend!" Once the long funeral cortege had followed the crystal coffin from the Royal Basilica of Naples, a replica of Rome's Pantheon, to the cemetery, Gatti was ready to float the names of tenors who might fill the void: Gigli and Martinelli, already at the Met, and Aureliano Pertile and Giacomo Lauri-Volpi, whom he had auditioned during the summer and would subsequently sign. Gigli took over from Caruso in the Met premiere of *Andrea Chénier*. Pertile made his debut as Cavaradossi on December 1, 1921, the night Maria Jeritza sang her historic first Met Floria Tosca, after which the role was essentially hers for the next decade. The Moravian diva stole the show by redefining the title role that had been created by Ternina, had been favored by Eames and Fremstad, and had lately been jealously guarded by Farrar. The composer, effusive in his praise of Jeritza ("perhaps the most original artiste that I have ever known," "sublime"), had sanctioned her blonde Tosca despite the "bruna" Floria inscribed in the libretto. The fair-haired soprano invented new inflections and gestures, all of which elicited glorious notices. Her most vivid coup de théâtre, a "Vissi d'arte" sung prone on the floor, was not to the taste of at least one in the audience. Farrar wrote caustically in her autobiography, "From my seat . . . I obtained no view of any expressive pantomime on her pretty face, while I was surprised by the questionable flaunting of a well-cushioned and obvious posterior."[28]

Farrar sang *Tosca* only twice more after that. She had turned forty, the age at which she had pledged to leave the company. Despite her explicit preference and the vociferations of her most ardent fans, the Gerryflappers, Gatti refused to allow *Tosca* for her farewell, some said in retribution for her zeal in the insurrection that had met his appointment fourteen years earlier. He scheduled Leoncavallo's *Zazà* instead. Nonetheless, Farrar's April 22, 1922, adieu remains among the most emotional in the history of the company, the house festooned with banners, its stage covered with flowers, the star, queen of the event, wearing a tiara and bearing a scepter, her car surrounded by noisy admirers, traffic halted as it carried her away. We are left to wonder what a Caruso farewell would have been.

## MOSTLY PUCCINI: 1918–1929

During World War I and after, Gatti held fast to the policy of repertoire expansion set at the beginning of his regime. Each season, he introduced two or three operas, more often four or five, once seven, and in 1918–19 as many as ten, including five one-acters. From 1918–19 to 1928–29, Gatti presented forty-eight novelties, proportionally as many as in his prewar period. New York's music critics were generally happy with older scores new to the Met, such as Verdi's *La Forza del destino* ("a vital opera still" [*Times,* Nov. 16, 1918]) and Mozart's *Così fan tutte* ("some of the most delightful music ever written" [*Tribune,* March 25, 1922]). As always, they were hard on contemporary European compositions and inclined to condescend to the American pieces. Gatti's repertoire continued to show commitment both to opera's past and to its vitality as a contemporary art form.

Of the seven world premieres listed in table 6, the three that made up *Il Trittico* aroused far and away the most excitement. For one thing, they were creations of Maestro Puccini. For another, his triptych was the first world premiere to be staged in New York, or indeed anywhere, after the armistice. *Il Tabarro,* Puccini's slice of squalid proletarian life, his sole excursion into the heart of verismo, was attacked for its naked realism, for the perceived paucity of lyric passages, and for the ostensible monotony of the river motif that threads through the narrative. No one liked *Suor Angelica* ("over an hour of almost unrelieved female chatter" [*Tribune]*) despite Farrar's moving portrayal of the hapless nun, deprived of her illegitimate child and ultimately driven to madness and suicide. *Gianni Schicchi,* a hilarious demonstration of the composer's farcical vein, mustered all the acclaim. Florence Easton's "O mio babbino caro," "the most exquisite bit of melody and singing of the evening" *(Tribune),* was encored. Puccini's first and, as it turned out, only comic opera had entered the repertoire to stay. The negative view of the other panels endured for half a century, shattering the conception as a whole until the trio was reunited in 1975. By then, *Il Trittico* was seen as yet another successful turn in the composer's inspired journey. Leaving aside

TABLE 6  Metropolitan Opera Premieres, 1918–19 to 1921–22

| Composer and Title | Met Premiere (*World Premiere) | Most Recent Met Performance | No. of Seasons in Met Repertoire | No. of Met Productions | No. of Met Performances, 1883–2013 | World Premiere | Director/Designer |
| --- | --- | --- | --- | --- | --- | --- | --- |
| Giuseppe Verdi, La Forza del destino | Nov. 15, 1918 | Mar. 23, 2006 | 27 | 3 | 230 | Oct. 29, 1862, St. Petersburg, Bolshoi Kamenny | Samuel Thewman / Joseph Urban |
| Giacomo Puccini, Il Tabarro (Il Trittico) | Dec. 14, 1918* | Dec. 12, 2009 | 10 | 4 | 80 | | Richard Ordynski / Pietro Stroppa |
| Giacomo Puccini, Suor Angelica (Il Trittico) | Dec. 14, 1918* | Dec. 12, 2009 | 8 | 3 | 74 | | Richard Ordynski / Pietro Stroppa |
| Giacomo Puccini, Gianni Schicchi (Il Trittico) | Dec. 14, 1918* | Dec. 12, 2009 | 21 | 4 | 138 | | Richard Ordynski / Galileo Chini |
| Carl Maria von Weber, Oberon | Dec. 28, 1918 | Jan. 6, 1921 | 3 | 1 | 13 | Apr. 12, 1826, London, Covent Garden | Richard Ordynski / Joseph Urban |
| Federico and Luigi Ricci, Crispino e la comare | Jan. 18, 1919 | Feb. 10, 1919 | 1 | 1 | 4 | Feb. 28, 1850, Venice, San Benedetto | Richard Ordynski / Pieretto Bianco |
| Xavier Le Roux, La Reine Fiammette | Jan. 24, 1919 | Mar. 18, 1919 | 1 | 1 | 5 | Dec. 23, 1903, Paris, Opéra-Comique | Richard Ordynski / Boris Anisfeld |
| Charles Gounod, Mireille | Feb. 28, 1919 | Apr. 16, 1919 | 1 | 1 | 4 | Mar. 19, 1864, Paris, Lyrique | Richard Ordynski / Victor Maurel |
| Joseph Breil, The Legend | Mar. 12, 1919* | Apr. 4, 1919 | 1 | 1 | 3 | | Richard Ordynski / Norman Bel Geddes |
| John Adam Hugo, The Temple Dancer | Mar. 12, 1919* | Apr. 4, 1919 | 1 | 1 | 3 | | Richard Ordynski / Joseph Novak |
| Gioachino Rossini, L'Italiana in Algeri | Dec. 5, 1919 | Mar. 17, 2004 | 7 | 2 | 71 | May 22, 1813, Venice, San Benedetto | Richard Ordynski / Willy Pogany |
| Albert Wolff, The Blue Bird (L'Oiseau bleu) | Dec. 27, 1919* | Apr. 2, 1921 | 2 | 1 | 12 | | Richard Ordynski / Boris Anisfeld |

| Composer, Work | | | | | | Premiere | Director / Designer |
|---|---|---|---|---|---|---|---|
| Ruggero Leoncavallo, *Zazà* | Jan. 16, 1920 | 3 | Apr. 22, 1922 | 1 | 23 | Nov. 10, 1900, Milan, Lirico | Richard Ordynski / James Fox |
| Henry Hadley, *Cleopatra's Night* | Jan. 31, 1920* | 2 | Feb. 23, 1921 | 1 | 9 | | Richard Ordynski / Norman Bel Geddes |
| Peter Ilyich Tchaikovsky, *Eugene Onegin* | Mar. 24, 1920 | 15 | Feb. 21, 2009 | 3 | 135 | Mar. 29, 1879, Moscow, Maly | Richard Ordynski / Joseph Urban |
| Giuseppe Verdi, *Don Carlo* | Dec. 23, 1920 | 28 | Mar. 16, 2013 | 4 | 209 | Mar. 11, 1867, Paris, Opéra | Samuel Thewman / Joseph Urban |
| Gustave Charpentier, *Louise* | Jan. 15, 1921 | 9 | Feb. 5, 1949 | 2 | 52 | Feb. 2, 1900, Paris, Opéra-Comique | Samuel Thewman / James Fox, Triangle Studio |
| Umberto Giordano, *Andrea Chénier* | Mar. 1, 1921 (Philadelphia), Mar. 7, 1921 (New York) | 27 | Apr. 18, 2007 | 4 | 179 | Mar. 28, 1896, Milan, La Scala | Samuel Thewman / James Fox, Triangle Studio |
| Karel Weis, *The Polish Jew* | Mar. 9, 1921 | 1 | Mar. 25, 1921 | 1 | 3 | Mar. 3, 1901, Prague, Neuen | Samuel Thewman / Willy Pogany |
| Erich Korngold, *Die Tote Stadt* | Nov. 19, 1921 | 2 | Feb. 26, 1923 | 1 | 12 | Dec. 4, 1920, Hamburg and Cologne | Samuel Thewman / Hans Kautsky |
| Édouard Lalo, *Le Roi d'Ys* | Jan. 5, 1922 | 1 | Mar. 6, 1922 | 1 | 6 | May 7, 1888, Paris, Opéra-Comique | Samuel Thewman / Joseph Urban |
| Nikolay Rimsky-Korsakov, *Snegurochka* | Jan. 23, 1922 | 2 | Apr. 16, 1923 | 1 | 11 | Jan. 29, 1882, St. Petersburg, Mariinsky | Samuel Thewman / Boris Anisfeld |
| Alfredo Catalani, *Loreley* | Mar. 4, 1922 | 2 | Jan. 8, 1923 | 1 | 10 | Feb. 16, 1890, Turin, Regio | Samuel Thewman / Antonio Rovescalli |
| Wolfgang Amadeus Mozart, *Cosi fan tutte* | Mar. 24, 1922 | 23 | Dec. 2, 2010 | 4 | 178 | Jan. 26, 1790, Vienna, Burgtheater | Samuel Thewman / Joseph Urban |

the non-subscription premiere in 1918 at raised prices, the initial two-season run missed even the box-office mean. Leoncavallo's *Zazà,* which soon disappeared, did better.

Gatti would produce twenty-four new works between 1922–23 and 1928–29, all but two (Gaspare Spontini's *La Vestale,* Massenet's *Le Roi de Lahore*) born in the twentieth century. The 1928–29 season alone registered four modernist novelties, fresh from their European réclame. Ottorino Respighi's fantasy *La Campana sommersa,* Ildebrando Pizzetti's declamatory *Fra Gherardo,* and Ernst Krenek's jazz-inflected *Jonny spielt auf* disappointed the critics and the public. So did *Die Ägyptische Helena,* further evidence, insisted the reviewers, of Richard Strauss's waning invention. Igor Stravinsky's *Le Rossignol* would return after a protracted absence; it has yet to prove its staying power. Debussy's *Pelléas et Mélisande* found its way into the repertoire without delay. Leoš Janáček's *Jenufa* was made to wait even longer than the thirty years it took Puccini's *Turandot* to break through.[29]

The posthumous *Turandot* (unfinished at the composer's death in November 1924, with the final scene completed by Franco Alfano) was an event of national moment at its La Scala world premiere in April 1926. Prior to reaching the Met in November of that year, it had been the subject of copious attention. Gatti filled the stage with stars, comprimarios, choristers, dancers, and supers reported to number between six hundred and seven hundred. Joseph Urban's spectacular orientalist design, a pinnacle of art direction under Gatti, was just one of his fifty or so Met commissions, an oeuvre never to be equaled. Jeritza had the heroic upper register, the charisma, and the fabled beauty of the eponymous Chinese princess. The reviews marveled at her imperious manner and prodigal tone. For Olin Downes, Lauri-Volpi had the "leather lungs" and "good stage presence" *(Times)* demanded by Calaf. Conductor Tullio Serafin marshaled the multitudes with his wonted authority. Fifteen curtain calls spoke eloquently of the public's approbation. But most critics disagreed, some vehemently. Downes, for one, embarked on the mission of striking the opera from the boards. He fulminated whenever it was revived: "a whole resplendent operatic edifice, destined sooner or later to collapse like a house of cards, has been made of virtually nothing" *(Times,* Nov. 21, 1926); "Puccini had stopped creating when he wrote it, but had mastered the art of saying nothing exceedingly well" *(Times,* Nov. 1, 1927); and in a final insult, "there is only one work by a great composer of modern times that we think as bad, and that is the *Egyptian Helen* by Richard Strauss" *(Times,* Nov. 17, 1928). *Turandot* led the box office in 1926–27 and rang up

TABLE 7 Metropolitan Opera Premieres, 1922–23 to 1928–29

| Composer and Title | Met Premiere (*World Premiere) | Most Recent Met Performance | No. of Seasons in Met Repertoire | No. of Met Productions | No. of Met Performances, 1883–2013 | World Premiere | Director/Designer |
|---|---|---|---|---|---|---|---|
| Franco Vittadini, *Anima allegra* | Feb. 14, 1923 | Mar. 28, 1924 | 2 | 1 | 10 | Apr. 15, 1921, Rome, Costanzi | Wilhelm von Wymetal / Antonio Rovescalli |
| Max von Schillings, *Mona Lisa* | Mar. 1, 1923 | Feb. 18, 1924 | 2 | 1 | 7 | Sept. 26, 1915, Stuttgart, Kleines Haus | Samuel Thewman / Hans Kautsky |
| Primo Riccitelli, *I Compagnacci* | Jan. 2, 1924 | Feb. 16, 1924 | 1 | 1 | 3 | Apr. 10, 1923, Rome, Costanzi | Wilhelm von Wymetal / Augusto Carelli |
| Raoul Laparra, *La Habanera* | Jan. 2, 1924 | Mar. 4, 1924 | 1 | 1 | 4 | Feb. 26, 1908, Paris, Opéra-Comique | Samuel Thewman / Antonio Rovescalli |
| Jules Massenet, *Le Roi de Lahore* | Feb. 29, 1924 | Apr. 19, 1924 | 1 | 1 | 6 | Apr. 27, 1887, Paris, Opéra | Wilhelm von Wymetal / Boris Anisfeld |
| Leoš Janáček, *Jenůfa* | Dec. 6, 1924 | Feb. 17, 2007 | 6 | 3 | 45 | Jan. 21, 1904, Brno, National | Wilhelm von Wymetal / Hans Pühringer |
| Italo Montemezzi, *Giovanni Gallurese* | Feb. 19, 1925 | Mar. 24, 1925 | 1 | 1 | 5 | Jan. 28, 1905, Turin, Vittorio Emmanuele | Samuel Thewman / Giovanni Grandi |
| Claude Debussy, *Pelléas et Mélisande* | Mar. 21, 1925 | Jan. 1, 2011 | 28 | 3 | 114 | Apr. 30, 1902, Paris, Opéra-Comique | Wilhelm von Wymetal / Joseph Urban |
| Maurice Ravel, *L'Heure espagnole* | Nov. 7, 1925 | Jan. 8, 1926 | 1 | 1 | 7 | May 19, 1911, Paris, Opéra-Comique | Samuel Thewman / Joseph Urban |
| Gaspare Spontini, *La Vestale* | Nov. 12, 1925 | Jan. 4, 1927 | 2 | 1 | 9 | Dec. 15, 1807, Paris, Opéra | Wilhelm von Wymetal / Joseph Urban |
| Ermanno Wolf-Ferrari, *I Gioielli della Madonna* | Dec. 12, 1925 | Feb. 12, 1927 | 2 | 1 | 13 | Dec. 23, 1911, Berlin, Kurfürstenoper (in German) | Wilhelm von Wymetal / Antonio Rovescalli |
| Umberto Giordano, *La Cena delle beffe* | Jan. 2, 1926 | Jan. 11, 1927 | 2 | 1 | 12 | Dec. 20, 1924, Milan, La Scala | Samuel Thewman / Joseph Urban |

(continued)

TABLE 7 (continued)

| Composer and Title | Met Premiere (*World Premiere) | Most Recent Met Performance | No. of Seasons in Met Repertoire | No. of Met Productions | No. of Met Performances, 1883–2013 | World Premiere | Director/Designer |
|---|---|---|---|---|---|---|---|
| Manuel de Falla, La Vida breve | Mar. 6, 1926 | Apr. 5, 1926 | 1 | 1 | 5 | Apr. 1, 1913, Nice, Municipal Casino (in French) | Wilhelm von Wymetal / Joseph Urban |
| Igor Stravinsky, Le Rossignol | Mar. 6, 1926 | Feb. 21, 2004 | 5 | 2 | 31 | May 26, 1914, Paris, Opéra | Samuel Thewman / Serge Soudeikine |
| Jules Massenet, Don Quichotte | Apr. 3, 1926 | Dec. 21, 1926 | 2 | 1 | 9 | Feb. 19, 1910, Monte Carlo, Opéra | Samuel Thewman / Joseph Urban |
| Giacomo Puccini, Turandot | Nov. 16, 1926 | Jan. 28, 2010 | 27 | 3 | 296 | Apr. 25, 1926, Milan, La Scala | Wilhelm von Wymetal / Joseph Urban |
| Deems Taylor, The King's Henchman | Feb. 17, 1927* | Mar. 28, 1929 | 3 | 1 | 17 | | Wilhelm von Wymetal / Joseph Urban |
| Erich Korngold, Violanta | Nov. 5, 1927 | Dec. 22, 1927 | 1 | 1 | 5 | Mar. 28, 1916, Munich, Staatsoper | Wilhelm von Wymetal / Joseph Urban |
| Franco Alfano, Madonna Imperia | Feb. 8, 1928 | Apr. 7, 1928 | 1 | 1 | 6 | May 5, 1927, Turin | Wilhelm von Wymetal / Joseph Novak |
| Giacomo Puccini, La Rondine | Mar. 10, 1928 | Feb. 26, 2009 | 6 | 2 | 28 | Mar. 27, 1917, Monte Carlo, Opéra | Wilhelm von Wymetal / Joseph Urban |
| Richard Strauss, Die Ägyptische Helena | Nov. 6, 1928 | Apr. 7, 2007 | 2 | 2 | 14 | June 6, 1928, Dresden, Semperoper | Wilhelm von Wymetal / Joseph Urban |
| Otorino Respighi, La Campana sommersa | Nov. 24, 1928 | Dec. 20, 1929 | 2 | 1 | 8 | Nov. 18, 1927, Hamburg, Stadttheater (in German) | Wilhelm von Wymetal / Joseph Urban |
| Ernst Krenek, Jonny spielt auf | Jan. 19, 1929 | Apr. 4, 1929 | 1 | 1 | 7 | Feb. 10, 1927, Leipzig, Neues | Wilhelm von Wymetal / Joseph Urban |
| Ildebrando Pizzetti, Fra Gherardo | Mar. 21, 1929 | Apr. 12, 1929 | 1 | 1 | 5 | May 16, 1928, Milan, La Scala | Armando Agnini / Joseph Urban |

receipts far above average the following season. After a run of twenty-seven performances between 1926 and 1930, it was dropped, no doubt the victim of high production costs, hefty royalties, and the departure of Jeritza in 1932. In 1961, the clarion voices of Birgit Nilsson and Franco Corelli would secure *Turandot*'s place in the Met's canon.[30]

Gatti presented one last Puccini premiere. Commissioned as an operetta for Vienna in 1913, reconceived as an opera first heard in Monte Carlo in 1917, *La Rondine* came to New York only in 1928. Critics were generally well disposed to Urban's sets and the stellar cast. Lucrezia Bori had, they avowed, imbued Magda with exceptional charm and pellucid diction, qualities we discern in a 1934 broadcast of a live Chicago performance and in a recording of the aria "Ore dolci e divine" made a year after her retirement in 1936. Gigli compensated for his unprepossessing appearance and rudimentary stagecraft with honeyed timbre. Although reviewers granted the work its due in terms of craft and melody, and some even admitted to liking it, almost to a man they dismissed the composition as "the afternoon off of a genius." *La Rondine* failed to take flight in its initial Met run and in its 1935–36 revival. Box-office receipts came up short. But then, in the late 1920s and into the 1930s, even *La Bohème* and *Madama Butterfly* languished. That would, of course, change.[31]

# FIVE

## Hard Times, 1929–1940

### WAGNER

### DEPRESSION

THE LAST SIX YEARS of Gatti's regime saw difficulty depreciate into misery. In 1929–30, the company coasted on the momentum of the cushy 1920s and on fortuitous new revenue streams. For the next two seasons, it survived on the $1 million the tightfisted administration had squirreled away. The final three years were, in the words of the famously unflappable general manager, his "Calvary."[1]

### Business as Usual: 1929–1930

The season opened with Puccini's *Manon Lescaut,* Lucrezia Bori as the flighty Manon and Beniamino Gigli as the besotted Chevalier Des Grieux. Bori and Gigli, on-stage lovers in so many of the 129 performances they sang together, were soon to find themselves on opposite sides of an internecine divide. Opening night was October 28, 1929, a Monday, as had been and continues to be the almost unbroken tradition. "Black Monday," a day in which the Dow Jones lost almost 13 percent, followed on the "Black Thursday" of the week before. The next day, the front-page headline in the *Times* ran, "STOCK PRICES SLUMP 14 billion dollars in nation-wide stampede." The customary opening-night feature article, oblivious to the crisis that shook the wealthy regions of the auditorium, devoted its considerable length to the glamour of the occasion. The following day was "Black Tuesday," October 29; the market fell another 12 percent, and the Great Depression was on. The only reference to the likelihood of less glittering future openings was linked not to the financial bust, but to a prospective new house at Rockefeller Center: "These events need the half antiquated setting, the absurd plush and gold manner which they have at Broadway and Thirty-ninth Street, and cannot have when that locality has given place to something a little less pompous and splendid, and a little more comfortable, practical and contemporaneous, uptown" (*Times*, Oct. 29, 1929). In his balancing act, Olin Downes betrays the ambivalence that had plagued plans for a new house in the preceding decades and would prove to be an insurmountable hurdle for decades to come.[2]

The most persistent and passionate advocate for a state-of-the-art home was Otto Kahn. He had made it his personal crusade beginning in 1903 with his appointment to the board, had promised Gatti new quarters in 1908, and from 1925 to 1927 had played his last and strongest hand. He put together a nearly $2.7 million deal for a plot bounded by 56th and 57th Streets and Eighth and Ninth Avenues. What he lacked was the backing of the "fogeys," the directors of the Real Estate Company. In an effort to stare them down, Kahn embarked on a campaign to draw the city's music constituencies to his side. His "Statement" of October 5, 1925, titled *The Metropolitan Opera*, could only have irritated his socially prominent opposition: "It is a solemn obligation of a semi-public institution, such as the Metropolitan Opera, to provide amply and generously for music lovers of small or modest means. I have had frequent occasion to observe how much music means to such devotees of the art. Indeed, I venture the assertion that it means a good deal more to the denizens of, say, Third Avenue than to those of Fifth Avenue." In a letter of early 1926 in which he rehearsed the deficits of the present house— too many seats with poor visibility, a hopelessly outmoded stage, minimal storage, inadequate rehearsal space—Kahn informed the Real Estate Company of his acquisition. He went on to rub the noses of the directors in their classism: "A considerable number of the lower priced seats are so bad that it is really an act of unfairness to take money for them—especially from people of small means." On January 25, 1927, he detailed his plan: increased seating to at least four thousand, improved sight lines, and, most distasteful to the old guard, the reduction of the number of boxes to thirty, which would be leased, not owned. However the matter was decided, the company would not produce opera on 39th Street beyond the next five years. Expenses had proved too great, the facilities too decrepit. On February 2, its back to the wall, the Real Estate Company board recommended Kahn's proposal to the stockholders. On April 12, the stockholders, led by Mrs. Cornelius Vanderbilt and Robert Goelet, turned their board down. They objected to the 57th Street location: as the directors put it, the site was simply not "monumental enough." Monumentality was not what Kahn was after: "Our conception is that [the theater] should be plain and dignified, on good but simple lines, seeking its distinction in being perfectly adapted to its purpose, both on the stage and in the accommodation to the public, rather than in outward impressiveness." But Kahn knew he had lost. He put the property up for sale. In the months and years that followed, he kept his counsel in debates on the Rockefeller Center solution that was assumed imminent by Downes on opening night 1929.[3]

Despite the crash and ensuing crisis, 1929–30 recorded the highest revenues in company history. Attendance was off, although not dramatically. For the most part, subscriptions had been nailed down before the start of the season. By great, if temporary, good fortune, non-box-office income had risen to a dazzling $350,000 from rights to engage Metropolitan artists for recordings and broadcasts, rights to publish Met programs and to advertise in their pages, rentals to outside producing agents, commercial endorsements, and food and drink concessions. Gatti's stash remained untouched. The general manager's contract was renewed through 1934–35.[4]

## Signs of the Times: 1930–1931

The ever so delicate balance that obtained through 1929–30 was undone by the more than 10 percent decline in 1930–31 subscriptions. Income dropped by $308,000; another $100,000 was lost with the cancellation of tours to Atlanta and Richmond when local operators balked at the required guarantees.

Opening night belonged once again to *Aïda*. Mediocre reviews kicked off what was sure to be a troubled season. The companion feature article in the *Times* was peculiarly upbeat. The message? All was well at the Metropolitan— and beyond: "Regarded always as the acme of luxury by the man in the street, the opening of the opera was watched with especial interest this year. It was felt to be an index to prosperity. And Broadway hailed with satisfaction its solidly maintained subscriptions, backed by leaders in world finance, as an indication of better times to come in the theatres and trade of the metropolis." The front page of the *Telegram* carried the headline "The Opera Opening Is Still the Opera Opening, Depression or No Depression, and Kahn or No Kahn." That may have been the case for this particular night. But otherwise, the conversation was all about a break with the past, about a new and modern theater within the perimeter of the projected "Rockefeller City" between

Fifth and Sixth Avenues, 48th and 51st Streets. John D. Rockefeller Jr. brought his voice to bear in acquiring the site from Columbia University in early 1929. His intention was to have as the centerpiece of this ambitious development a "Place de l'Opéra for New York City." The clinching argument for the "uptown" location was its contiguity to Radio City, a proximity that would further Rockefeller's grand communications design while freeing the Met from its physical confines, allowing it to reach millions across the nation, indeed across the world. The prospect was dizzying: "It [radio] has captured the opera stars and brought them to the microphone so that the people of the land might hear their wondrous voices. . . . The broadcasters look forward to the day when the Metropolitan will cast away from the Victorian environs at Fortieth Street and Broadway and smile on the microphone." The future for opera was not only rosy, it was transcendent. But by December 6, 1929, little more than a month after the stock market crash, prospects for an alliance between the Metropolitan and Rockefeller were dead. Ironically, no sooner had Kahn sold his 57th Street plot in September 1930 than the Real Estate Company came around to the view that a new house was artistically and fiscally imperative.[5]

Broadcasting would not wait. It took on a life of its own, impervious to the sparring over the pros and cons of a new house. In spring 1931, NBC agreed to transmit twenty-four complete or partial performances from the 39th Street stage each season for the two upcoming, at the substantial fee of $120,000 per year. It was Kahn who closed the deal. Up to that point, Gatti had vetoed broadcasts, blaming poor sound quality, and no doubt harboring the fear that attendance would suffer. NBC paid $30,000 annually for the exclusive right to negotiate with Met stars for other programing.[6]

### "The Deluge": 1931–1932

As summer and early fall wore on, omens for the coming season grew darker. Subscriptions would shrink by another 10 percent, and despite swelling non-box-office income, revenues would drop by another $506,000. With expenses projected to outpace receipts by nearly 23 percent, the last dregs of the $1 million reserve would be gone by the end of the season. On October 26, Kahn resigned as president and chairman, keeping his seat on the opera board. The weight of the Depression, a widely publicized suit brought by a Swedish soprano with whom he had had an affair, and surely bitterness at the quashing of his ambitions for a house on 57th Street had contributed to his decision. He was also painfully aware that the leadership of a Jew (he had joined the Fifth Avenue Episcopal parish church of St. Thomas in the vain hope that greater acceptance would follow) had been tolerated only as long as the company was profitable. He bequeathed the presidency and chairmanship to his lawyer, Paul D. Cravath. Son of a minister, the Ohio-born Cravath was an early architect of corporate structures retained as attorney and consultant by Westinghouse, RCA, and Kahn's own firm. His long record of public and international service had begun with the Armistice. At the time of the transition, he was seventy years old. Knowing little of opera, he "charmingly ... undertook music appreciation lessons." He quickly made organizational and policy changes aimed, he said, at preserving 'our last Victorian tradition'" (*Times*, Nov. 3, 1931).

The *Times* gave its usual airbrushed account of opening night, November 2. The headline, echoing that of the previous year, proclaimed in fanciful denial that there was "No Sign of Depression in Brilliant Opening," and suggested that subscriptions had held up. It was at this point precisely, as Gatti wrote in his memoirs, that "the deluge" was upon the house. "The gossip that broke loose did not help us," he continued. "Rumor and tales concerning the Metropolitan were rife on every hand.... There were tales of rivalry and dissension in the company. There was talk of Radio City, Roxy, bankruptcy, and I don't know what other far-fetched ideas." In fact, not so far-fetched. Minutes of a November 18, 1931, meeting read, "It was ... proposed that Mr. Gatti-Casazza ... be authorized to accept the cooperation of all artists, musicians and other employees of the Company who might volunteer to accept reductions in their respective salaries, and to enter into such arrangements ... as he might think expedient to assure completion of the season." Only days later, the general manager "voluntarily" reduced his own salary by 10 percent "and the administrative and executive staff, together with the principal singers and conductors, 'spontaneously followed his example'" (*Times*, Nov. 22, 1931). Not all the principal singers, it soon turned out.[7]

There was one bright note: the Christmas Day broadcast of *Hänsel und Gretel*, the first nationwide transmission of the Metropolitan Opera. It was carried by more than one hundred stations on both the Red and Blue (later ABC) networks of NBC and by shortwave around the world. The announcer of the occasion, and for the next forty years, was Milton Cross. Deems Taylor narrated the action over the score, to the distress of many listeners. All but one of the twenty-three subsequent broadcasts that season were limited to one hour. The only available recordings of the first two broadcast years are

FIGURE 16. Backstage after the first matinee broadcast, *Hänsel und Gretel,* Deems Taylor, the announcer, second from left, and Giulio Gatti-Casazza, far right, December 25, 1931 (Carlo Edwards; courtesy Metropolitan Opera Archives)

extracts of *Manon* with Grace Moore and Gigli and of *Tristan und Isolde* with Frida Leider and Lauritz Melchior.[8]

In the frenetic spring of 1932, events followed furiously one after the other. In March, the Rockefeller alternative was back on the table, revived by the astonishing success of the radio programs. But again there was a snag, an apparent deal breaker: Rockefeller insisted that every component of his development be self-sustaining. The market rate he would exact would far exceed the meager rent charged by the Real Estate Company. For a time, arguments in favor of the move seemed to prevail: that broadcast fees would take up the slack, and that "as soon as opera [became] a common radio experience, especially with television, the native American composers and their librettists [would] begin to use it as their medium of expression and truly modern opera [would] result" (*Times,* March 16, 1932), a variation on the perennial, deluded refrain. The outcome of years of negotiation, of rising and falling hopes, was again in the hands of the old moneyed crowd, keenly aware that it would be left holding the bag, the white elephant of an opera house on Broadway, should the company relocate (*Times,* March 25, 1932). By April 18, Cravath was said to be ready to vote "yes"; he was not, however, in a position to speak for the stockholders of the Real Estate Company. Meanwhile, Mr. and Mrs. Rockefeller were seen more frequently in their box at the Met.

Also in March came the game-changing announcement that the Metropolitan Opera Company would be replaced by the Metropolitan Opera Association, Inc. The nascent venture would follow not the old shareholder plan, but a membership model. Everyone was welcome to join by contributing either to the operating fund or to the endowment, or simply by volunteering services. What had been since Gatti's appointment in 1908 an enterprise unhitched from the profit motive as a matter of policy would become a not-for-profit corporation, "organized for educational purposes" as a matter of law. Tickets would no longer be subject to federal entertainment taxes; their prices could be lowered without strain on an already constrained budget. The purpose of the conversion, it was explained somewhat disingenuously, was to streamline operations. In effect, the new producing entity would be freed from many of the obligations of its predecessor. By June, the Association was official. Each member of the board would have one vote; no longer would power be weighted in favor of those owning the larger block of shares, in the case of Kahn, now 84 percent. And no longer would the Real Estate Company be responsible for shortfalls. The financial crisis and the reluctance of the old families to foot bill after bill had opened the door to the public. The larger middle class, through its support, would take ownership: "It is this new public now forming, and assuming more and more power, which must, and undoubtedly will, determine the future of opera in America. The days of the Maecenases and of gifts of millions to opera companies are flown. . . . The men of finance who 'could,' to say nothing of 'would,' come to the rescue are growing fewer every day. Our suffering millionaires! They are no longer to be waited upon which on the whole is a good thing." But for the moment, the elites, "the bankers and the backers," who conductor Artur Bodanzky disparaged as quitters, had won. Free of liability for production debts, they still sat pretty in their very own boxes in the theater that showed them off to best effect.[9]

The day after the restructuring was announced, March 25, Gatti outlined the austerity measures anticipated for the 1932–33 season. He called for shared sacrifice so that the Metropolitan might "continue to live." "In such a critical and decisive moment," he wrote, "it would be petty and without a realization of this grave situation, to raise questions of contracts and rights. When a house is on fire one does not send for lawyers or notaries." If necessary, he himself would serve without pay; others, whether American-born or foreign, would be subject to lowered compensation. By mid-April, as 1932–33 began to take shape, and more than one-tenth of the city's population was on public or private assistance, it was understood that the season would be shortened from twenty-four to sixteen weeks, and that subscription costs would be halved and individual ticket prices reduced in order to generate more robust sales (*Times,* April 16, 1932). Twenty-eight singers were let go, most for reasons of financial exigency. All those retained, together with their administrative colleagues, accepted the news of a salary cut with resignation. All, that is, except Beniamino Gigli, who had previously rejected the reduction of fall 1931. In spring 1932, he stuck to his guns, to the disgust of many of his colleagues, thirty-two of whom were willing, some said encouraged or even coerced by the management, to sign an open letter of condemnation dated April 12 and published on May 2. Among the signatories were conductors Artur Bodanzky and Tullio Serafin, and singers Lucrezia Bori, Grace Moore, Lily Pons, Rosa Ponselle, Elisabeth Rethberg, Giovanni Martinelli, Lauritz Melchior, and Ezio Pinza. Aware that the letter was about to be released, on May 1 Gigli took the offensive: "My sincere offers were met with conditions and impositions which would have diminished my dignity as a man and as an artist" *(Times)*. In any case, it had already been announced that he would not return for the 1932–33 season. Nor would Maria Jeritza. The press hinted that she too had refused the salary cut. Correspondence between the soprano, Gatti, and Ziegler leads to a different conclusion: that her departure was their choice, not hers. Their excuse was the reduced length of the season to come and the too great number of guaranteed performances in her contract. In July, Ziegler wrote to Gatti that, moved by the desire to bid farewell to her fans, Jeritza was willing "to sing guest performances for little or no money." Just the month before, on June 8, the Dow had bottomed out at 41.82; on September 3, 1929, it had stood at 381.17.[10]

## Repertoire: 1929–1932

In each of the first three Depression years, Gatti introduced six new productions, divided between premieres and familiar operas. The same quotient had prevailed in the three prosperous seasons prior. The complexion of the repertoire remained similarly constant. The general manager's policy held steady:

to present Met premieres of works of popular composers and to revive those long neglected, to add Russian and Czech titles, to import the latest European successes, to showcase the specific talents of box-office stars, and to introduce American works. This last was underscored by Kahn in his 1925 "Statement" in defense of Gatti against the charge of Italian bias: "Under the management of the Italian Gatti-Casazza, the Metropolitan Opera has produced thus far nine operas and one ballet by American composers, whilst not a single work composed by an American was produced at the Metropolitan Opera House under any of the preceding managements." Renewed interest in Verdi brought the long overdue *Luisa Miller* and *Simon Boccanegra. Don Giovanni,* absent since 1908, returned in 1929 to stay. *Der Fliegende Holländer* made port once again after a like hiatus. The new Russian entries produced a short-lived hit, Rimsky-Korsakov's opulent *Sadko,* and a miss, Mussorgsky's *The Fair at Sorochintzy.* Weinberger's *Schwanda the Bagpiper,* despite its success in Prague and elsewhere and good press in New York, ran for only one season. Montemezzi's *La Notte di Zoraima* and Lattuada's *Le Preziose ridicole* suffered the same fate. Of only passing interest, two of Franz von Suppé's operettas, *Boccaccio* and *Donna Juanita,* were there to indulge Jeritza's comic bent.[11]

Gatti's ongoing American wager had paid off with the seventeen performances in three consecutive seasons of *The King's Henchman* (1927) of Deems Taylor, music critic for the *World* and editor of *Musical America.* The libretto of Edna St. Vincent Millay on a comfortably familiar Tristanesque subject, the leadership of the Met's preeminent conductor Tullio Serafin, and a cast of principals equipped to project the text intelligibly had impressed reviewers and attracted the public. The world premiere of Taylor's *Peter Ibbetson* brought *le tout* New York-Hollywood out in force: novelist Edna Ferber, columnist Alexander Woollcott, conductors Walter Damrosch (to whom the score was dedicated) and Leopold Stokowski, Irving Berlin, Ruth Chatterton, Charlie Chaplin, and Harpo Marx. The composer was on hand to acknowledge the applause that elicited thirty-six curtain calls. Enthusiasm for *Peter Ibbetson* persisted through twenty-two performances in four seasons, records for an American premiere that stand to this day. Edward Johnson later boasted, "*Peter Ibbetson* made more money than any other single opera during the past twenty years." Its subject is the thwarted love of childhood soul mates who meet again as adults, are once more parted by tragic circumstance, and finally achieve perfect understanding in shared dreams and then in the afterlife. Reviewers were taken with Taylor's expert setting of the text: "a tremendous argument for opera in English, as all the essential parts of the

TABLE 8 Metropolitan Opera Premieres, 1929–30 to 1931–32

| Composer and Title | Met Premiere (*World Premiere) | Most Recent Met Performance | No. of Seasons in Met Repertoire | No. of Met Productions | No. of Met Performances, 1883–2013 | World Premiere | Director/Designer |
|---|---|---|---|---|---|---|---|
| Giuseppe Verdi, *Luisa Miller* | Dec. 21, 1929 | Apr. 1, 2006 | 10 | 3 | 86 | Dec. 8, 1849, Naples, San Carlo | Ernst Lert / Joseph Urban |
| Nikolay Rimsky-Korsakov, *Sadko* (in French) | Jan. 25, 1930 | Apr. 16, 1932 | 3 | 1 | 20 | Jan. 7, 1898, Moscow, Mamontov Private Opera | Ernst Lert / Joseph Urban |
| Modest Mussorgsky, *The Fair at Sorochintzy* (in Italian) | Nov. 29, 1930 | Jan. 15, 1931 | 1 | 1 | 5 | Dec. 30, 1911, St. Petersburg, Comedy | Ernst Lert / Serge Soudeikine |
| Felice Lattuada, *Le Preziose ridicole* | Dec. 10, 1930 | Jan. 15, 1931 | 1 | 1 | 4 | Feb. 9, 1929, Milan, La Scala | Ernst Lert / Robert Edmond Jones |
| Franz von Suppé, *Boccaccio* | Jan. 2, 1931 | Apr. 6, 1931 | 1 | 1 | 10 | Feb. 1, 1879, Vienna, Carltheater | Wilhelm von Wymetal / Joseph Urban |
| Deems Taylor, *Peter Ibbetson* | Feb. 7, 1931* | Apr. 4, 1935 | 4 | 1 | 22 | | Wilhelm von Wymetal / Joseph Urban |
| Jaromir Weinberger, *Schwanda the Bagpiper* (in German) | Nov. 7, 1931 | Dec. 30, 1931 | 1 | 1 | 7 | Apr. 27, 1927, Prague, National | Hanns Niedecken-Gebhard / Joseph Urban |
| Italo Montemezzi, *La Notte di Zoraima* | Dec. 2, 1931 | Jan. 12, 1932 | 1 | 1 | 5 | Jan. 31, 1931, Milan, La Scala | Alexander Sanine / Joseph Novak |
| Franz von Suppé, *Donna Juanita* | Jan. 2, 1932 | Feb. 10, 1932 | 1 | 1 | 8 | Feb. 21, 1880, Vienna, Carltheater | Hanns Niedecken-Gebhard / Joseph Urban |
| Giuseppe Verdi, *Simon Boccanegra* | Jan. 28, 1932 | Feb. 5, 2011 | 19 | 4 | 139 | Mar. 12, 1857, Venice, La Fenice; *revision,* Mar. 24, 1881, Milan, La Scala | Alexander Sanine / Camillo Parravicini |

story could be clearly understood." At the same time, they found the score "rather negligible," "oddly featureless." The plot ("Strong men [were said to have] actually wept") and the quality of the performances carried the piece to the top of the season's box office. Through the execrable sonics of the March 17, 1934, broadcast, we hear the original principals. As Peter, the soon-to-retire Johnson is still comfortable on high, still capable of translucent diction. Tibbett luxuriates in Colonel Ibbetson's act 1 love song, as close as the opera comes to a hummable aria. Bori sings Mary, her English accented but thoroughly intelligible, her voice fresh, her manner unaffected. The transcription is both a precious document of the Spanish soprano's refined art and a bridge to early Met history. Bori had made her company debut opposite Caruso during the 1910 Paris tour.[12]

The previous month, January 1931, had seen the nick-of-time debut of Lily Pons. Galli-Curci had recently retired, her final seasons plagued by a long-standing goiter condition that compromised her intonation and, as serious, the brilliant upper register required by her repertoire. The company was desperate for a star coloratura, a virtuoso singer whose name would sell out the house. Pons filled the bill. Chic, petite, vivacious, she was ubiquitous in concerts, on records, on the radio, in the movies. And she managed her career shrewdly, marketing her persona through a handful of showcase arias. The staccati of her "Bell Song" triggered a long run for Delibes's *Lakmé;* she sang the Hindu priestess fifty times over a fifteen-year span. She owned Lucia in particular, assuming the character for a role-record ninety-three performances, an astounding fourteen of which were broadcast between 1932 and 1956, the year of her retirement. The French soprano's stunning high notes, often sweet tone, and glamour held the audience hostage for nearly three decades.

## "Save the Met": 1932–1933

The choice of Franklin Roosevelt as the Democratic nominee for president in summer 1932 deepened the gloom that hung over the company's management. For one thing, a Roosevelt victory would strengthen the cause of labor, to the benefit of the Metropolitan's unionized workers; they alone had rejected pay cuts in 1931–32. For another, a Roosevelt win would threaten the interests of the patrons of the opera, the class to which, ironically, the candidate belonged. Together with the Vanderbilts and the Morgans, James A. Roosevelt, Theodore's uncle and Franklin's distant Oyster Bay cousin, was a contributor to the capitalization of the Metropolitan in the early 1880s; at the opening of the house, he was president of the board and owner of a second-tier box. On July 8, Ziegler wrote to Gatti bemoaning the prospect of an FDR White House, and then went on: "Our present form of government has proven a failure at this time and I believe what we need here is what you have in Italy, namely a dictator." Eleanor Roosevelt's December 10 appeal on behalf of the Emergency Unemployment Relief Committee during the first intermission of *Simon Boccanegra* could only have stoked Ziegler's fears. It was not the fact of her appeal; others, including a former secretary of state and Kahn himself, had taken a turn at what had become a routine part of the proceedings. It was her tone: "When you come face to face with people in need, you simply have to try to do something about it" (*Times,* Dec. 11, 1932). Most urgent from Ziegler's point of view was that drastically reduced prices had done little to spur subscriptions.[13]

It was *Simon Boccanegra* that had inaugurated the 1932–33 season. This time, the feature article on opening night hailed not the brilliance of the occasion or the illustrious history of the institution, but the ways in which the Met had confronted the crisis in order to "carry on": the sacrifices of so many employees, the legal and fiscal restructuring of the organization, and, above all, the shortening of the season by a third, from twenty-four to sixteen weeks. That winter, the by now tired proposition of a new home for the Met in Rockefeller Center resurfaced. This time, the word that came down from the Real Estate Company was unrelated to the elegance of the neighborhood or the scale of the property. In the present economic circumstance, a move was simply out of the question. The stockholders were clear: they would not be left in the lurch on 39th Street (*Times,* Feb. 1).

The wider Metropolitan community began to mobilize, stepping into the breach left by ever more stingy millionaires. Mrs. August Belmont Jr., the former Eleanor Robson, who had retired from the stage on marrying a son of the banker August Belmont, an early supporter of opera in New York, is credited with the idea for public fund-raising. Belmont was soon to be the first woman director of a Metropolitan board. The radio campaign was launched during an intermission of *Tannhäuser* on February 22, 1933, with an appeal by Lucrezia Bori. Eleanor Roosevelt, apparently listening in, was among the first to send a check. Operagoers found an insert in their librettos addressed "To the Subscribers and Friends of Opera at the Metropolitan." The flyer announcing a "CAMPAIGN TO SAVE METROPOLITAN OPERA" was signed by Bori (the chair), Johnson, Tibbett, and two members of the Real

Estate Company board, Cornelius N. Bliss and Robert S. Brewster, identified as a committee to raise a "substantial guaranty fund," without which the company would be unable to undertake another season: "The closing of the Metropolitan Opera House next year would be nothing short of a national misfortune. Not only would thousands of operagoers and millions of listeners to opera over radio suffer a serious loss in their cultural life, but it would be a catastrophe to throw out of employment at this time of acute depression, the 770 employees of the Opera Company, most of whom, because of their highly specialized training, would be unable to find any other employment."[14]

The "Grand Operatic Surprise Party" of February 26 celebrated Gatti's twenty-fifth anniversary as general manager. Its $16,000 take was directed to the Metropolitan Opera Emergency Fund. Marcella Sembrich, who had sung Lucia a half-century earlier on the second night of the Met's first season and, again, a quarter of a century later in Gatti's first season, was on hand for the festivities. In the audience was Maestro Toscanini. Among the many comic spoofs of popular operas was an Apache dance that partnered the petite Lily Pons and the corpulent Lauritz Melchior. Gatti sat in the director's box. He acknowledged the ovation at the end of the evening with standard bows and twice with the Fascist salute.

In early March, NBC transmitted a half-hour program during which Cravath owned that it was no longer possible to "rely . . . upon a small group of rich men"; the Metropolitan was turning for help to its faithful clientele and "to the vast radio audience that listens to opera through the National Broadcasting Company." Bori sang a short recital, and then made her pitch: "Are you, my dear radio listeners, going to forsake this national institution, the Metropolitan Opera, in its present crisis, or are you coming to the rescue? I can almost hear you shout: To the rescue! Because I know you want the Metropolitan to carry on—just as we do." Other solicitations over the airways originated from the stage during the remaining Saturday matinees. Geraldine Farrar returned to add her voice to those of current stars. Within two months, the $300,000 goal was reached. One-third of the total came from radio listeners, $50,000 from the Juilliard Foundation, and $45,000 from benefit performances and charity events. A meager $39,000 was contributed by the Real Estate Company and the Association, the very folks that Cornelius IV, an iconoclastic member of the Vanderbilt clan, had excoriated for extracting pennies from Macy's employees while continuing to flaunt the luxury to which they were accustomed. This relatively young Cornelius, much to the dismay of his parents a working journalist, was the great-nephew of the W. H. Vanderbilt who had made so proud a display in his two boxes at the opening of the house in 1883. His mother was the Mrs. Cornelius Vanderbilt who had led the opposition to Kahn's cherished 57th Street plans.[15]

By January 1933, it was clear that if the Met was to make it through 1933–34, there would have to be additional immediate, that is, midyear budgetary, adjustments. Among other stringent measures, Gatti ordered that singers be denied the number of performances guaranteed by their contracts. He cloaked his actions in the premise that the transfer of functions to the Metropolitan Opera Association had nullified the terms agreed to in the name of the Metropolitan Opera Company. Unions that had rejected cuts the year before now had no alternative but to accede to an even more dire threat: that the Met might go the way of the bankrupt Chicago Civic Opera, which had shut its doors in 1932. The first of the years that Gatti had described to Bruno Zirato, Caruso's old secretary, as an unimaginable Calvary was finally over.

### Jubilee: 1933–1934

Salary negotiations between Gatti and those tapped for the 1933–34 and 1934–35 rosters were particularly grueling. For most, 1933–34 would represent a second round of cuts, and 1934–35 a painful third. Ponselle, who had commanded $1,900 per performance, dropped to $1,500 and then to $1,000, the top fee. Pinza was paid by the season; he was promised $20,000 for 1932–33 and saw only $17,000. Among the principals who were talked down by relatively small amounts was Friedrich Schorr, who went from $562.50 per show to $500. The Met was watching its pennies—literally. Perhaps the most telling figure is this: that the aggregate expense for female soloists in 1928–29 was $407,000; in 1933–34, it was $147,000. The shortening of the season by two weeks more to fourteen accounted for approximately one-half of the savings. Even so, 1933–34 would end with a deficit of $317,000.[16]

All told, this would be a sorry jubilee year for the company. With disgruntled stars contracted for only part of the season and lucrative concert, radio, and recording dates trumping operatic commitments, casting was subject to the vagaries of availability as never before. In the fall of 1933, Rockefeller came back with a variant on his recurrent proposal: that the company share the Centre Theatre, already erected on his property, until a house designed for the

Metropolitan could be built. The Centre was not suited to opera, and if for that reason alone, the offer was rejected. By spring, the management was confronted with another pressing issue; an inspection had revealed violations that rendered the 39th Street facility unsafe. Without major renovation, the theater's license would be revoked. Work on the stage and backstage, on the lighting bridges, on a new broadcasting booth, and on the much-needed face-lift of the auditorium could only be financed through a mortgage. The dreaded Roosevelt regime began on March 4; on March 5, the newly inaugurated president ordered a four-day bank holiday. The New Deal would soon be underway. For the Met as for the nation, it was a time of firsts and lasts. The year 1933–34 was the first in which citizen contributions offset company costs and the first in which the Saturday matinees had a radio sponsor, Lucky Strike cigarettes. For the first time, the public and publicly traded firms played a significant role in keeping the company afloat, indeed in safeguarding the Met's prestige. And if donors, individual and corporate, had no say in artistic matters, their clout had nonetheless ground down that of the stockholders, as the return of *Salome* in January 1934 signaled. Gatti's penultimate season was the first to open with an American work, *Peter Ibbetson,* and the first in ten to see liquor served in the foyer ("Magnums Pop and Cocktail Shakers Rattle" [*Herald Tribune,* Dec. 27, 1933]). As to lasts, in March 1934, Otto Kahn died, and by the end of the operatic year, Giulio Gatti-Casazza had told Paul Cravath that he would not serve beyond spring 1935.

To avoid a Christmas start, opening night was set for Tuesday, December 26. The feature article in the *Times* of the next day was full of praise for the *Peter Ibbetson* principals, Bori (the Met's "Joan of Arc"), Johnson, and Tibbett, who, "through their public appeals spread country-wide on the upper air, had saved" the day. Yet the campaign that season was predominantly an in-house affair: fund-raising through Metropolitan contacts, another "surprise party," and another Juilliard Foundation subvention brought in $250,000. The ball was a Louis XV extravaganza for which the stage was dressed as the Forest of Fontainebleau and visiting monarchs celebrated the birthday of the Dauphine of France. During the pageant, New York's upper crust took on the roles and garb of the vanished aristocracy: Mrs. Vincent Astor was Maria Theresa, Queen of Hungary and Bohemia, Theodore Steinway the King of Prussia. Walter Damrosch came as Bach. Music of the ancien régime gave way to Joe Moss and his Band as the assembly proceeded to the dance floor laid over the pit and orchestra level. Meanwhile, Mrs. Belmont was at work. In early December, she announced the founding of the Women's Metropolitan Opera

Club, whose members would have use of the quarters and Grand Tier omni-box of the Metropolitan Opera Club on popularly priced, generally second-string Saturday nights (*Times,* Dec. 3, 1933). An exclusive and well-to-do fraternity, the Metropolitan Opera Club was by then an institution. It had been established in 1899 for the "cultivation of vocal and instrumental music, the encouragement and support of operatic and musical performances, and the promotion of social intercourse among its members." Eleanor Belmont's initiative, on the other hand, was directed toward women who could not afford subscriptions and were, in any case, reluctant to attend unaccompanied. The next month, January 1934, on joining the board of the Association, she declared "that the people should look upon [opera] as an integral essential part of the life of the city." The next year, she would launch the Metropolitan Opera Guild with herself as chair, firm in her contention that "the democratization of opera had begun."[17]

## *Addio* Gatti: 1934–1935

Gatti left for Europe at the end of the 1933–34 season to attend performances, audition singers, and have his vacation. Back in New York, the seven-month May to November recess provided the space for confabulations over the company's future. The power to determine the direction and director of the post-Gatti era had careened uptown to the Juilliard School of Music and to the conference room of its president, John Erskine. Erskine's candidate for the position of general manager was Herbert Witherspoon, known to old-timers as a Metropolitan Wagnerian bass between 1908 and 1916. In 1931–32, he had been artistic director of the Chicago Civic Opera Company. In that capacity, on May 25, 1932, he had written to Ziegler seeking advice on the threat of closure facing his troupe. Ziegler responded two days later, laying out the steps the Met had taken to meet its own emergency: lowering prices so as to compete with the Philharmonic and shaving the season at beginning and end, periods in which box holders were mostly out of town. Despite Ziegler's good counsel, the Civic Opera would not live to see another season, and its artistic director was on his way to Cincinnati to head up its conservatory.

Witherspoon began angling in earnest for the Metropolitan job in 1933 when rumors of Gatti's retirement began to circulate. He asked his colleague on the board of the American Academy of Teachers of Singing, Percy Rector Stephens, to intercede on his behalf, boasting that he "could assemble a company in thirty days which would make New York sit up." Stephens wrote to

Cravath, insisting that, "if an appeal is to be made to the general public for support, the opera must take on the complexion of an American institution.... An American as manager of our Opera House would do much, at the present time, to stimulate interest." He then put forward Witherspoon's name. Cravath was unwilling to take the issue head on: "Shifting the Opera Company to American management and a more American personnel than it has today is a very complicated problem." Stephens then advised Witherspoon to pin his hopes on Erskine: "The Juilliard backing will have to be given consideration to a great extent." It was in fact Erskine who would be the deal maker. Witherspoon wrote to Erskine offering a blueprint for Metropolitan policy and practice in the coming years. His letter had the desired effect.[18]

In September 1934, Witherspoon moved back to New York and was promptly appointed to the Juilliard faculty. The next month, the story goes, Erskine walked into a room in which Mrs. Witherspoon was lunching with Mrs. Tibbett and said, "I've just dumped the Metropolitan Opera in Herbert's lap." For the length of the season, Witherspoon would be a presence at the opera house, privy to the detail of operations, scribbling proposals for reform. His involvement, however unofficial in 1934–35, was a condition of what would later be announced as a Juilliard grant of $150,000 for the next year and $100,000 for the year after. Other provisos recorded in the March 7, 1935, minutes of the Metropolitan Opera Association include increased subscriptions, a balanced budget, and the appointment of three members of the Juilliard Musical Foundation, Erskine among them, to the Association board. A last stipulation was that the Met introduce a popularly priced supplementary spring season featuring young Americans, possibly Juilliard trained. By the time Gatti returned to New York in November, and his resignation effective April 1935 was made public, the Met's future had been charted.[19]

Gatti's final season lasted again only fourteen weeks. And again he opened with *Aïda* and not on a Monday, but on a Saturday, December 22, this time to avoid Christmas Eve. The audience was cheered by the more comfortable seating, the new lobby chandeliers, and ice water in the just installed drinking fountains. (Hot water flowed for the first time in the dressing rooms.) Nearly a third of the names attached to the boxes were preceded by "The Estate of..." Harriman, for example, or Mills, Whitney, or Kahn. One critic attributed the more subdued atmosphere to a sense that an era was coming to an end and that "somewhere and somehow, [the opera's] own New Deal is taking form" *(Times)*. Contrary as usual, Henderson thought the audience "unacquainted with the sinister word 'depression'" *(Sun,* Dec. 24). Another reviewer wrote under the caution "Metropolitan Opera and Its Musical Prestige Now in Danger. Support Is Needed. Future of Lyrical Art in This City Is Problem That Must Be Met" *(American)*. The hopeful news was once again the number of radio listeners, estimated at fifty million for the season. During intermissions, Geraldine Farrar was at her miniature piano in Box 40 to illustrate passages from the afternoon's opera and sing the words she herself had translated into English *(Times,* Jan 13, 1935).

On March 6, the press reported Witherspoon's appointment. The previous November, the *Daily Mirror* had quoted odds on Gatti's replacement: Johnson 10 to 1, Sir Thomas Beecham 15 to 1, Cornelius Bliss 20 to 1, Bori 25 to 1, Ziegler 35 to 1, Erskine 40 to 1; bringing up the rear was Witherspoon at 50 to 1 (Nov. 19). The *Mirror's* musical bookie notwithstanding, Witherspoon had had no real competition. Ziegler was named assistant manager for business administration and Johnson assistant manager in charge of the supplementary spring season. Also announced were drives to increase subscription rolls and opportunities for young American talent. Juilliard's fingerprints were everywhere. *Time* gave this version of the nearly year-long maneuvers: "In a desperate attempt to save its life, the Metropolitan sold its independence. . . . To further their aims the Juilliards demanded greater representation on the Metropolitan board. It was not a suggestion but a command when they named as their candidates Lawyer John M. Perry, who drew up Augustus Juilliard's will, Dean Ernest Hutchison of the Juilliard School of Music, President John . . . Erskine who has long been ambitious to dictate Metropolitan policies" (March 18, 1935).[20]

The company staged a gala on behalf of the "Save the Met" campaign, the only farewell Gatti would countenance. And during the whole of the evening in his honor, he listened to the proceedings from the privacy of his office. Rosa Ponselle and Gladys Swarthout sang act 3 of *Norma,* Lucrezia Bori and Richard Crooks act 4 of *Manon,* Kirsten Flagstad and Friedrich Schorr the act 3 finale of *Walküre.* But the pièce de résistance was act 4 of *Otello* with Rethberg and Melchior. Verdi's opera had been last heard in 1912. Melchior's sensational interpretation put into relief Gatti's failure to mount the Verdi masterwork in the last two decades and more of his tenure, and especially since the ascent of the Danish heldentenor. Four days later, during the intermission of the final broadcast of his final season, on March 23, 1935, Gatti spoke three sentences: "I have often expressed my faith in American talent and operatic ideals. I am sure they will continue. I thank all who have enjoyed the performances." He sailed for Italy on the *Rex* on April 27. When he said good-bye, he did it in eight words: "Viva America, viva Italia, viva Roosevelt, viva Mussolini." The band struck up the Fascist anthem "Giovinezza" and Ponselle sang "The Star-Spangled Banner."[21]

Repertoire: 1932–1935

By the time the Metropolitan had exhausted its reserves in fall 1931, the 1931–32 schedule was set. It was not until 1932–33 that the repertoire felt the effects of the Crash. That season, and for the next two, the number of new productions was cut by half, from six to three. But even with straitened budgets the company managed to stage important premieres and revivals. *Elektra* finally made it to 39th Street, more than two decades after its thunderous New York debut at Hammerstein's theater on 34th. A more permissive climate and the waning influence of the Real Estate Company moguls repaved the way for *Salome,* banished since the night of its notorious 1907 premiere. Tibbett's success in indigenous works, along with his exposure in radio, movies, and concerts, encouraged the management to introduce three American pieces in three successive seasons. As Brutus Jones in Louis Gruenberg's adaptation of Eugene O'Neill's *The Emperor Jones,* Tibbett held nothing back. Even more explosive was his Wrestling Bradford, the tormented protagonist of Howard Hanson's *Merry Mount.* Gruenberg and Hanson drew lukewarm notices at best. John Lawrence Seymour's one-act *In the Pasha's Garden* drowned in audience indifference and critical opprobrium. The company premiere of Donizetti's *Linda di Chamounix* and a new production of Bellini's *La Sonnambula* were vehicles for Lily Pons. The Met's first hearing of Giovanni Pergolesi's *La Serva padrona* and its revival of Donizetti's *Don Pasquale* shared a décor, a concession to frugality.

The standard titles of the French and Italian repertoire, some given just once or twice a season, suffered from obsolete sets and little, if any, rehearsal. Ernst Lert, in charge of staging from 1929 to 1931, could only pity the director "responsible for the production, even though he [Gatti] has not granted him a single rehearsal for nineteen out of twenty such productions." The run-of-the-mill opera was often cast with run-of-the-mill singers. By 1934–35, the defections of Gigli and Lauri-Volpi had left the tenor roster so depleted that utility singer Frederick Jagel was scheduled, with Ponselle and Tibbett, for the high-profile broadcast of *La Traviata. Cavalleria rusticana, Pagliacci,* and *Madama Butterfly* were also his; their second-rank casts relegated even their first performances of the season to the popularly priced Saturday night slot.[22]

Herbert Witherspoon, the new broom, was quick to sweep Gatti's last seasons into the dustbin: "The plain truth is that the opera has been dead for years." However graceless his pronouncement, Witherspoon had a point. Much of the standard repertoire had fallen into disrepair. Of late, no new star had captivated the public—none, that is, until Kirsten Flagstad made her debut on February 2, 1935, two months before Gatti quit the scene. Flagstad was an overnight sensation—some twenty-two years into a career almost exclusively confined to the operatic hinterlands of Scandinavia. She had sung everything from operetta to Micaela and Marguerite, Aïda and Minnie, all in Norwegian or Swedish. Kahn had heard her *Tosca* in Oslo in 1929. He had urged a Met agent to test the waters; the soprano had not responded. Her 1932 Oslo Isolde led to small roles at the 1933 Bayreuth Festival and success as Sieglinde the following year. Her engagement in New York came about almost by accident. In fact, but for the withdrawal of one dramatic soprano and the limited dates of another, Flagstad might not have come to the Met at all. Frida Leider had decided to forgo her contract after two seasons, citing the poor exchange rate. Anny Konetzni, in the limelight in Berlin and Vienna and a flop in New York, could commit only to the first half of 1934–35. Flagstad was hired for the remainder of the season.[23]

Both Gatti and Bodanzky had underestimated their amazing acquisition. They had auditioned Flagstad in a St. Moritz hotel room where heavy drapes dampened the impact of her voice. Only when he heard her in rehearsal in the vast auditorium did Bodanzky realize what the Met had in this remarkable artist. Fortuitously for us, her debut in *Die Walküre* coincided with a Saturday matinee broadcast. Act 1 conveys the wonder of her Sieglinde. Her voice is perfect over its full range, caressing at pianissimo, thrilling at fortissimo. If her Sieglinde lacks the febrile intensity of Lotte Lehmann's interpretation, the refulgence of Flagstad's instrument and her warm timbre, crystalline diction, precise intonation, sensitive phrasing, and dignified and disarming manner pulverize all quibbles. Farrar put aside her script and announced to the radio audience, "Today we are witnessing one of the greatest events that can happen during an opera performance.... A new star is born!" In little more than two months, Flagstad took on six more Wagnerian roles, including three she had never sung before: Kundry, learned in just three weeks, and the *Walküre* and *Götterdämmerung* Brünnhildes. The post-

TABLE 9  Metropolitan Opera Premieres, 1932–33 to 1934–35

| Composer and Title | Met Premiere (*World Premiere) | Most Recent Met Performance | No. of Seasons in Met Repertoire | No. of Met Productions | No. of Met Performances, 1883–2013 | World Premiere | Director/Designer |
|---|---|---|---|---|---|---|---|
| Richard Strauss, Elektra | Dec. 3, 1932 | Dec. 29, 2009 | 18 | 3 | 101 | Jan. 25, 1909, Dresden, Semperoper | Alexander Sanine/Joseph Urban |
| Giacchino Rossini, Il Signor Bruschino | Dec. 9, 1932 | Jan. 24, 1933 | 1 | 1 | 5 | Jan. 1813, Venice, San Moisè | Armando Agnini/Joseph Urban, Joseph Novak |
| Louis Gruenberg, The Emperor Jones | Jan. 7, 1933* | Apr. 5, 1934 | 2 | 1 | 15 | | Alexander Sanine/Jo Mielziner |
| Howard Hanson, Merry Mount | Feb. 10, 1934 (staged form)* | Apr. 12, 1934 | 1 | 1 | 9 | In concert: May 20, 1933, Hill Auditorium, Ann Arbor, Michigan | Wilhelm von Wymetal/Jo Mielziner |
| Gaetano Donizetti, Linda di Chamounix | Mar. 1, 1934 | Mar. 25, 1935 | 1 | 1 | 8 | May 19, 1842, Vienna, Kärntnertor | Armando Agnini/Unknown |
| John Lawrence Seymour, In the Pasha's Garden | Jan. 24, 1935* | Feb. 13, 1935 | 1 | 1 | 3 | | Wilhelm von Wymetal/Frederick J. Kiesler |
| Giovanni Battista Pergolesi, La Serva padrona | Feb. 23, 1935 | Jan. 14, 1943 | 2 | 2 | 6 | Aug. 28, 1733, Naples, San Bartolomeo | Désiré Defrère/Unknown |

ers imprinted with Flagstad's name were inevitably stamped "Sold Out." She was by far Gatti's most precious bequest.[24]

## AMERICANIZATION

### Witherspoon's Legacy

In late spring 1935, in the wake of Gatti's retirement to Italy, and in defiance of best-laid plans, events took a turn no one could have foreseen. On May 1, Witherspoon gave a speech to the National Music League calling on the public to take up the cause of the arts. On May 2, at a meeting of the Advertising Club, he promoted opera grandiloquently as a force "to train the spiritual emotions and inner values of the people." And then suddenly, on May 10, in the executive offices of the Metropolitan, after receiving better news about ticket sales for the coming season and stepping into the hallway to tell his wife he would not be long, Witherspoon collapsed to the floor. His death from a coronary at sixty-one came without warning. He had served as the Met's general manager for all of two weeks. And he was, by all accounts, exuberant, looking forward to leaving for Europe on the new French liner *Paris* the following day. The appointment of a successor could not wait. The names of Erskine, Ziegler, and Johnson were again bruited about, along with that of Bodanzky. Much to Ziegler's relief, on May 15 Johnson got the nod, and much to the relief of a very green Johnson, Ziegler was willing to continue as assistant general manager. A month later, on June 13, still shaken, Ziegler wrote to Gatti that he was not yet up to recounting Witherspoon's death "at the threshold of my office." He added confidentially that had Witherspoon lived, "I am perfectly certain that we would have found ourselves in the most tragic state imaginable."

No sooner had Johnson been appointed than he set about reassuring nervous stakeholders that a smooth transition was already in progress and that the season would proceed as extensively planned by his predecessor. Witherspoon had mapped out operational reforms in a series of undated and unaddressed communications drafted in his preparatory year. Budgetary strictures (the last five years of Gatti's regime showed a loss of more than $1.7 million), Juilliard demands, and his own biases converged around a set of interlocking measures: to engage new, less costly artists, present fewer operas, winnow the chorus and orchestra, renegotiate union contracts, and reduce the administrative staff. In response to the "Americanization" mandate, he would seek to rely more heavily on native talent, thereby also circumventing the travel expenses incurred by Europeans. Some costs would rise: he favored investing in stagings, publicity, and a friendlier, more efficient box office. As to the season's program, as late as May 7, Witherspoon's repertoire list included *Le Jongleur de Notre Dame* for Helen Jepson and *Adriana Lecouvreur,* presumably for Ponselle. On the list released on May 16, these titles had disappeared, and without the two rarities, Johnson was left with Witherspoon's conservative repertoire, devoid of even a single novelty.[25]

As to the roster, although Witherspoon thought Rethberg, Bori, and Martinelli "shaky," he had put them under contract and was still haggling with Ponselle. He had been slow to reengage several others of the Met's most highly paid stars, including the enormously popular Lily Pons, who, he asserted, "has lost a great deal in the last two years." He was "confident we can get somebody who is better." Cravath pointed out that "the outstanding success [of the tour to Boston] was not Mme. Flagstad, but Lily Pons in *Lucia.*" Essential to Witherspoon's lineup were Melchior, Tibbett, and Pinza. Johnson went ahead and secured agreements from Ponselle and Pons. He filled three slots identified by Witherspoon as critical, that of an Italian dramatic soprano with Philadelphia-born Dusolina Giannini, that of an Italian dramatic mezzo with Bari-born Bruna Castagna, and that of a dramatic tenor with Belgian René Maison. Johnson's magic bullet was Flagstad. Flights of fancy—casting her in a revival of *Rienzi,* as the Countess in *Le Nozze di Figaro,* as Tosca—were forgotten, leaving the Wagner roles and her first *Fidelio.*[26]

## Edward Johnson

From the very start, Johnson wrestled with a question that resonated deeply in his own career: how to reconcile the necessity to present major international artists with the obligation to give Americans the chance they deserved. In 1897, the nineteen-year-old Canadian arrived in New York. He met early success as a concert and church singer, thanks in part to an exceptionally secure high C. At one point he toured with Herbert Witherspoon through whose good offices he found work in operetta two blocks from the Metropolitan. In 1908, as Edoardo di Giovanni, he made his way to Paris, and then to Florence for serious opera study. In time, he was engaged by La Scala; there, in 1914, he was Italy's first Parsifal, Toscanini conducting. On June 17 of that year, Johnson heard from an agent that Kahn had been approached on his behalf, but that, alas, there was little hope of an affirmative response. As the agent put it, "Beneath the surface I know positively that Gatti-Casazza is not favorable to Americans." In 1920, Johnson returned to the United States to sing in Chicago. In 1922, as one of several tenors contracted to fill the void left by Caruso, he debuted at the Met in *L'Amore dei tre re*. Twelve seasons later, soon after his appointment as assistant general manager under Witherspoon, he made his farewell as Pelléas, the role he had created at the Metropolitan and for which he was best known. By the middle of May, Johnson was installed as general manager, a seat he would occupy for the next fifteen years. It was now up to him to champion the American cause. At hand were three examples of the construction of homegrown fame in contrast to the European-born celebrity of Eames, Nordica, Fremstad, and Farrar: Rosa Ponselle, whose electrifying entrance in 1918 opened the path to the top; Marion Talley, whose fleeting and problematic renown had been fabricated by publicists; and Lawrence Tibbett, propelled from secondary roles to instant stardom by audience acclaim.[27]

## Rosa Ponselle

Opposite Caruso at the Met's first performance of Verdi's *La Forza del destino* was a twenty-one year old who had never had a voice lesson, let alone sung on an operatic stage. Ponselle had begun as a song plugger, had played piano at the nickelodeon, and, most recently, had been one of Those Tailored Italian Girls, a sister act on the vaudeville circuit. Caruso heard her in her manager's office and brought her to the attention of the Met. Verdi roles had recently fallen to Claudia Muzio, a spinto even younger than Ponselle. But for the dramatic soprano role of the *Forza* Leonora, Gatti took a chance on the untested Ponselle. Reviewers acknowledged both her inexperience and her "vocal gold." In 1918–19, Ponselle was entrusted with two more premieres, Carl Maria von Weber's *Oberon* and Joseph Breil's *The Legend*. In subsequent seasons, there followed numerous *Gioconda*s and *Cavalleria*s and a fair share of rarities. "Caruso in petticoats" would be the Met's first Elisabetta *(Don Carlo)*, its first Luisa Miller. In 1927, Gatti revived *Norma* for her; Bellini's opera had not been heard for more than three decades. The title role calls for creamy legato (sung without separation between successive notes), emphatic recitative, and lyric and dramatic coloratura, all executed within the refined parameters of bel canto. Ponselle's rendition of "Casta diva" was caught in the studio of the Victor Talking Machine Company. The forceful resolve of the

FIGURE 17. Rosa Ponselle as Norma, 1927 (Herman Mishkin;
courtesy Metropolitan Opera Archives)

recitative, the rapture of the prayer, and the agitation of the cabaletta are
plied without apparent effort. Through a broad dynamic range, the characteristically dark Ponselle voice remains ideally equalized here and in the duet
"Mira, o Norma," the other excerpt she recorded with her stage Adalgisa,
Marion Telva. At its revival in 1928 with the identical cast, Downes proclaimed that this edition of *Norma* "would make history in any opera house"
(*Times,* Nov. 8). Ponselle had brought a work of bel canto genius into the
repertoire at last and for good. The kid from Meriden, Connecticut, set the
bar for all future Normas.[28]

# Marion Talley

The *Times* first mentioned Talley ("Singer of 16 a Prodigy") on November 9, 1922, three years and more before her Metropolitan debut. She had auditioned for Kahn, Gatti, and Bodanzky. They encouraged her to continue her studies—and the construction of a star, born and raised in Missouri and American as apple pie, had begun. Two years later, Kahn, voicing his "high expectations," confirmed that Talley had been asked to prepare two roles (*Times,* April 2, 1924). She was just seventeen. By July, she was off for coaching in Italy. In October 1925, her debut was featured in the prospectus of the upcoming season: "She will be heard for the first time by the public as a prima donna, though it was as a child in short dresses that she sang an audition just three years ago." Gatti wrote to Kahn in uncharacteristically effusive terms: "I would be very much surprised if this young singer who possesses all the qualities to succeed brilliantly should not make a deep impression. . . . I hope that this time we have found a good ace who will make happy also all the nationalistic elements." The press, meanwhile, had seized on the story of the shy teenager whose father had worked seven days a week for eighteen years as a telegraph operator with the Missouri Pacific Railroad.

As the debut approached, the hype grew more intense. Two hundred Missourians had hired a train to carry them to New York for Talley's Gilda in *Rigoletto;* there would be a reception on the Metropolitan stage; all unsubscribed seats for the February 17, 1926, performance had been snatched up; all of America would be hearing her over the radio on February 19. A *Kansas City Star* editor wrote to the Met that "the Talley debut is, so far as Kansas City is concerned, an event comparable with the inauguration of a President or the sinking of the Lusitania" (*Times,* Feb. 10, 1926). Photographs depict a chubby young woman of no particular distinction. The debut itself made the front page: "Father Telegraphs Story Home from the Wings." Ten curtain calls followed "Caro nome," and double that number the final scene as hundreds stayed on after the asbestos curtain was lowered. "The story of the girl's progress, a household word at home, has in the last week been told to thousands of children practicing their scales in New York's schools" *(Times).* But when it came to the notices, the ballyhoo was largely irrelevant; reviews sank from mixed to devastating. On February 28, looking on the bright side, Kahn wrote to Ziegler, "Even if Marion Talley should turn out, as the majority of the critics and some other benevolent people are good enough to forecast, a lemon, in due course of time, at least she has brought us a few full houses and the opportunity to squelch for some time to come the absurd talk about the Metropolitan not being willing to give a fair chance to American artists." And on March 4, Ziegler responded: "Her vogue and drawing power continues and the public for the greater part range itself on her side, and is angry at the critics, which attitude of course is of advantage to us."

The promotion of Talley, and through her the philo-American posturing of the Met, continued, deaf to critical reception. She made the cover of *Time* on March 1, 1926. In August, a Vitaphone short that memorialized her immature "Caro nome" was on the program at the gala premiere of the Warner Bros. *Don Juan,* the first feature-length movie with synchronized sound. On October 7, Talley's Des Moines recital grossed $9,000; the gate for Gertrude Ederle's aquatic exhibition (she had just swum the English Channel), scheduled against Talley's concert, was only $400. On December 21, Gatti and Talley agreed to a new contract consonant with her value to the company. By that time, her concert fee had reached $3,000–$3,500. A year and a half later, there were reports that in the coming season she would appear at the Met only sporadically. Earnings from her recitals were estimated at $335,000 over a period of just two years. Talley had exploited her bargain with the Metropolitan as deftly as the wily management itself. On April 12, 1929, the *Times* headline ran, "Marion Talley, Prima Donna Four Seasons, Quits to Buy Farm and Live on Earnings." Talley was blunt: "I'm just through with it—that's all." She had sung seven roles; soon after her burst of success, her appeal had declined. Amelita Galli-Curci, long past her prime, was still the company's star coloratura. On New Year's Eve 1933, Talley sang one more Gilda, with the Chicago Opera Company, to good reviews. A few days later, she decamped over a salary dispute.[29]

### Lawrence Tibbett

Tibbett's Metropolitan career began inauspiciously. His knees shaking during the whole of the audition, as he recounted it, he cracked on the high F-sharp of "Eri tu" from *Un Ballo in maschera.* In the dark, cavernous theater sat the hulking general manager; the baritone was dismissed with a curt "thank you." Three weeks went by before Gatti, at the insistence of his wife, soprano Frances Alda, agreed to a second hearing. A far less agitated Tibbett sang the "Credo" from *Otello.* This time, Gatti was impressed enough to hire the twenty-seven-year-old Californian who had never sung in opera, not in New York, not anywhere. Tibbett's elation turned to dismay when Gatti offered a paltry $50 a week. At Alda's urging, the salary was upped to $60.

That was not all. His boilerplate contract stipulated that whereas the company was responsible for costumes, "gloves, feathers, wigs, tights, boots, shoes, and other similar articles shall be furnished by the Artist himself." And what is more, Tibbett was expected to master twenty-seven roles, mostly comprimario and secondary parts, two leads (Amonasro and Escamillo), and one role for bass (King Dodon in *Le Coq d'or*). For the next year and a half, he was little noticed by public or press.[30]

In fall 1924, Tibbett got his big break. Gatti cabled Alda, on a concert tour with Tibbett, to ask if her protégé was up to Ford, the second baritone role in *Falstaff*. She replied yes, definitely, and did her best to help her young colleague. But rehearsals went poorly for the inexperienced singer, who was challenged by a weak musical memory and a difficult score. The formidable, almost all-Italian cast included Antonio Scotti, as Falstaff, and Gigli; the venerated Serafin was the conductor. To top it all off, the revival had been staged expressly for Scotti's twenty-fifth anniversary with the company. During rehearsal, annoyed that Tibbett's on-the-job training was slowing things down, Scotti and Gigli engaged in mocking exchanges over the novice's histrionic and vocal difficulties. Although he had never set foot in Italy and did not know Italian, Tibbett got the drift. He was furious. Then came the night of the first performance, January 2, 1925. Tibbett sang the bitter aria that concludes the first scene of the second act ("È sogno? o realtà'?") with an extra dose of passion. During the ovation that followed, the scene's principals took their bows. Then Scotti came out alone. But the audience kept up the clapping, stamping, whistling, and, finally, to make its will perfectly clear, began shouting, "Tibbett, Tibbett." For once, the claque was not the instigator of the commotion. Meanwhile, assuming the tribute was for Scotti, Tibbett had repaired to his dressing room two floors above. Serafin did his best to carry on with the performance, but the audience, presuming that Tibbett had somehow been kept from appearing before the curtain alone, would not let up. A member of the orchestra was dispatched to plead that he be allowed to acknowledge the applause. Gatti acceded reluctantly; attention had shifted from the veteran Italian baritone, the honoree of the evening, to the humble newcomer: "An American audience had decided that one of its own nationality should be properly recognized for his talent" *(Times)*. The sixteen-and-a-half-minute demonstration subsided at last and the curtain rose on the interior of Ford's house. From then on, Tibbett was given increasingly important assignments. He became the cornerstone of Gatti's American opera initiative, and with his assumption of the title role in the Met's first

FIGURE 18. Lawrence Tibbett as Ford in *Falstaff*, 1925 (Herman Mishkin; courtesy Metropolitan Opera Archives)

*Simon Boccanegra,* he was uncontested as the company's leading baritone in the Italian and French repertoires. He sang the last of his 603 Met performances on March 24, 1950.

## Metropolitan Opera Auditions of the Air

Kahn's 1925 rejoinder of "absurd" to charges that the Met had been unfair to Americans was understandable. That very year, there were forty native singers on a roster of ninety-five. The eccentric examples of Ponselle, Talley, and Tibbett offered little guidance for the company's further Americanization: Talley was an experiment that did not bear repeating, Ponselle and Tibbett phenomena that defied repetition. What was needed was a broadly based and systematic process for the discovery of talent. The answer was the "Metropolitan Opera Auditions of the Air." The opening broadcast of the competition took place on December 22, 1935, the first week of the season. Hosted by Johnson himself and sponsored by Sherwin-Williams, the paint company, the fifteen-week-long series (expanded to twenty-six the next year) featured "the hit tunes of opera brought down to the level of Mr. Average John Q. Public." However condescending, the copy was intended to reassure diffident audiences that opera was no longer the exclusive domain of the highborn or the highbrow. The "tunes" would be rendered by "finely trained singers who are at the threshold of stardom." Beyond publishing the company's brand, and increasing familiarity with already familiar music, the program would help satisfy the Juilliard prescription that the Met provide opportunities to young American singers. As winning soprano Eleanor Steber later pointed out, Americans "had as yet no regional opera companies or, for the most part, conservatory opera schools." For many, Europe was out of bounds for reasons of budget and, for all starting in 1939, for reasons of security. The Auditions promised Americans a foot in the door of the country's major opera company.[31]

The Auditions fielded roughly seventy contestants each year. First place carried with it a prize of $1,000, a plaque, and a contract; runners-up were often asked to join the company as well. The untried aspirants were thrust onto the stage, occasionally for as little as a Sunday night concert, but more often in a role that led to a Met career in the cadre of comprimarios, where the company had particular need of local talent. One of the 1936 finalists was Risë Stevens, who turned down the Met's offer, opting instead for training in Europe; she came back as a principal artist in 1938–39. Stevens, Steber, Leonard Warren, Patrice Munsel, Regina Resnik, and Richard Tucker all became stars of the 1940s. Merrill Miller failed to place in 1939; in 1945, as Robert Merrill, he won. On the radio, and briefly on television, the Auditions chalked up a twenty-three-year run. The banner year of 1958 produced Martina Arroyo and Grace Bumbry. Since then, although gone from the air, the Auditions have continued to thrive under the auspices of the National Council of the Metropolitan Opera, founded like the Metropolitan Opera Guild by Mrs. August Belmont. In the last many generations it would be the rare American member of the company who missed this rite of passage.[32]

## Anti-Americanization

If Gatti's exit in 1935 accelerated the Americanization of the Met's roster, his departure also prompted a wave of *italianità* within a swath of the Italian-

American community. Nostalgia for the old management and hostility toward the new served the right wing of the Italian-language press as a rallying point for the chauvinism of its editorial policies and its colony of subscribers. The relentless comparison between Italy and the United States devolved into the affirmation of Italian cultural superiority. Gatti had been gone two years when *La Settimana* (March 14–21, 1937) published a piece titled "Naufragio al Metropolitan" (Shipwreck at the Metropolitan); *La Sentinella* (March 1, 1940) varied the metaphor three years later with "Il Tramonto del 'Met'" (The Sunset of the Met). Their authors lamented the "golden age" of Gatti-Casazza and decried the present Johnson era, in which the "great Italian musical tradition [has] been suffocated little by little." Italians who thought themselves "citizens of the Metropolitan" were now again "foreigners" in the "magno teatro," as they had been in the years of German and French dominance. The strain of ethnic journalism sympathetic to the Italian regime accused the "Juilliard dictatorship" of annihilating Italian opera in New York and, with it, Italian casts.

The injudicious Gigli took aim at the United States and then at the Metropolitan before zeroing in on several of its most prominent American stars. He had left the Met in 1932 only to return under Johnson for a handful of performances in early 1939. If his colleagues had somehow forgotten his refusal of salary cuts in the darkest days of the Depression, they must have found it impossible to forgive the vicious statements he made on his Italian reentry: "There are those who foresee in the not far distance something like civil war" in the United States; the unions "in the hands of Jews" were to blame; as for the Metropolitan, hard times had obliged the company to engage singers who "cost less and substitute notoriety created by publicity for intrinsic value, namely Moore, Tibbett, and Crooks" (*Times*, Feb. 26, 1939). Moore diagnosed Gigli as having "a case of sour grapes." Tibbett parried, "Gigli is a great tenor. High notes must go to the head." And Crooks responded, "Mr. Gigli should have learned by now to use his mouth for singing only. It sounds better" (*Times*, Feb. 27, 1939).

## DEMOCRATIZATION

For one reason or another—often to loosen purse strings—operatic discourse during the Depression inclined toward the perennial question of the place of opera in the American order. The arguments made in the 1930s found their way into the March 5, 1941, issue of *Variety,* whose headline, "Urge Not So Grand Opera," said it all. Those "urging" were Johnson, Gaetano Merola (head of the San Francisco Opera), Walter Damrosch, and Metropolitan singers Melchior, Pons, Moore, Pinza, and Tibbett. Asked to speak to the future of opera in America, their statements coalesced around the fond hope that an American city of any size have "a municipally-owned, subsidy-encouraged, tax-free opera house" dedicated to serving as a training ground for "embryonic" singers. The cities named were Atlanta, Dallas, Miami, Seattle, Des Moines, St. Paul, Omaha, Detroit, Cleveland, Newark, and Hartford. *Variety* argued that Americans had been "initiated into the idea of government subsidy for cultural undertakings through the Federal Theatre and Music and Radio Projects and more recently the National Youth Administration." That same spring of 1941, the Texaco Corporation, which had taken on the sponsorship of the radio broadcasts the previous December, wrote to Johnson that it had received "30,000 letters of which 3,884 contained expressions of preference for certain operas." The astonishing response attested to the Metropolitan's conquest of a truly national audience. Less surprising were the titles of favored works: *Carmen* was first, then came *Aïda, La Traviata, Faust, Rigoletto, La Bohème, Tristan und Isolde, Madama Butterfly, Lucia di Lammermoor,* and, tied for tenth, *Lohengrin* and *Manon.* Although *Tristan* registered seventh in the rankings, the number of letters fell off by half after the Wagner broadcast. Texaco wondered whether the decline might not be taken "to mean it is a little long and hard going for the radio audience."[33]

## Metropolitan Opera Guild

Among the transformative events of spring and summer 1935—the Juilliardization of the Met, the imposition of Witherspoon and his agenda, his death, the naming of Johnson to the post—was the inception of the Metropolitan Opera Guild, the brainchild of Eleanor Belmont. With the onset of the Depression, she had chaired the Women's Division of the Emergency Unemployment Relief Committee on whose behalf Eleanor Roosevelt, Otto Kahn, and others solicited contributions from the Met stage. And she became one of the pillars of the "Save the Met" campaign. In 1933, she joined the Association board with the intent to help "to avert unemployment [among Opera House workers], with which I was all too familiar, rather than any lofty idea of preserving art." Her signal contribution, the founding of the Metropolitan Opera Guild, was seeded with a $5,000 Association grant. The Guild's formal mission read, "to develop and cultivate public interest in opera and its allied arts, and to contribute to their support; to further musical education and appreciation; and to sponsor and give assistance to operatic, musical and cultural programs and activities of an educational character."[34]

The Guild's first annual report, dated April 7, 1936, pointed to impressive achievements: a dress rehearsal of Flagstad's *Fidelio* open to members; a ticket service, again a member benefit; a fund to provide needy music students discounted tickets; a costume exhibition; and its first publication, *The Metropolitan Opera Guild Primer,* a slim volume of one-sentence plot summaries. A Guild-sponsored poll uncovered that, unlike the wider radio audience that would voice its partialities in 1941, its membership of aficionados appreciated *La Traviata* and *Rigoletto* least and *Lohengrin* and *Tristan und Isolde* most. The organization's accomplishments of the following year, 1936–37, were a balanced budget, the doubling of its rolls from two thousand to four thousand, and an increase in out-of-town adherence. The introduction of junior memberships via schools was synchronous with the first Met performance offered expressly to students, an *Aïda* with Rethberg and Bruna Castagna underwritten by a $2,000 Guild donation. There were fund-raising luncheons, public lectures, *Operagrams,* pamphlets devoted to single titles, and "Operalogues" (later "The Metropolitan Opera Guild on the Air"), short radio programs designed to prepare listeners for the upcoming Saturday afternoon broadcast. In gratitude for the Guild's gift of a cyclorama, the company treated members to an evening of arias and skits.[35]

Between 1935 and 1940, activities increased further in number while remaining essentially constant in kind. Publications of the late 1930s included *Opera Cavalcade,* a brief history of the Met, and *The Metropolitan Opera Guide,* synopses intended for the radio audience. Student performances thrived for decades. They surrendered to censorship at least once when several schools objected to *Carmen* "on the basis of an immoral libretto"; the less raw, equally licentious *Il Barbiere di Siviglia* took its place. Student performances slackened in the 1980s, and ended altogether in 1996; school groups continue to attend open rehearsals. Boosted by a $3.00 "National" category, membership exceeded twelve thousand by 1940, the year the Guild was rewarded with a room of its own on the Grand Tier level. Membership reached twenty-four thousand in 1945 and upward of one hundred thousand in 2010.[36]

The face of the Guild, almost from the start, has been *Opera News*. Its progenitor, the "Bulletin," was first distributed on December 7, 1936, as a modest broadsheet folded into four pages; it grew into a twelve-page magazine two months later. In 1940, the editors of what was by now *Opera News* settled on a template that would take it through the next quarter of a century: thirty-two pages published twenty-four times annually, with a focus, during the season, on the week's broadcast. A representative example, the February 5, 1941, issue devoted to *Tristan und Isolde* depicts a smiling Kirsten Flagstad on the cover. In "Names, Dates and Places" we find a plug for Risë Stevens's new movie, *The Chocolate Soldier,* and the note that the war in Europe has prevented Joel Berglund and Germaine Lubin from joining the company. One feature article, on the *Alceste* dress rehearsal, is the submission of the winner of a letter-writing contest. Another recounts the sometimes conflicting memories of the Misses Wetmore, boxholders since 1883. The new coloratura Josephine Tuminia traces her itinerary from St. Louis to 39th Street. The issue also carries book reviews, squibs on a chorister and on the state of American opera. "Arias on the Air" is a detailed schedule of radio programs, both live and transcribed. The Saturday broadcast is documented by photographs and descriptions of the artists in costume, the text of the "Liebestod" in German and English, a guide to related readings and recordings, a cast list replete with transliterations ("E-soul'-duh," "Keer'-shten Flag'shtat," actually the Germanized pronunciation of her name), and an essay by the recently deceased critic Lawrence Gilman on the beauties of the score. The Met schedule for that and the coming week reflects the prominence of Wagner, Flagstad, and Melchior. If, at the time, *Opera News* was a self-congratulatory house organ, it was also, and continues to be, the often literate and informative agent for the initiation and instruction of budding operaphiles.

## Spring Seasons

The first of what would turn out to be just two popularly priced spring seasons had a promising start on May 11, 1936. The house was full. Admission to the family circle set its occupants back only $.25; the parterre and the boxes, pegged at $3.00, had drawn those eager to sit in desirable and, for once, affordable seats. Gilman noted the heterogeneous, "unmistakably democratic" audience: "a lady of African ancestry, wearing a sailor hat was seated a few rows in front of a white-haired grande dame in low neck and pearls. The parquet was sprinkled with business suits" *(Herald Tribune)*. But for the moment, and for the sake of a smashing opening night, a basic Juilliard tenet was put aside. Castagna, a stunning Carmen, was the beneficiary of flattering comparisons with Rosa Ponselle, who had had her capricious way with the role during the regular season. Castagna was known to New York from popular-priced performances at the Hippodrome and at the yet more capacious Lewisohn Stadium; she had made her tremendously successful Met debut as Amneris just two months earlier. But Castagna was neither American nor a neophyte. In fact, only one of the principals, the Micaela, Natalie Bodanya, could be counted as a young American singer.

With few exceptions, the tyros thrust into leading roles in the big theater for the spring seasons were wanting in voice, in technique, in experience, and in presence. The bargain-basement budget that yielded most principals the munificent sum of $50 per week got the company what it paid for. When it came to the familiar operas, economies plagued the stage direction (nonexistent), the lighting (erratic), and, most conspicuously, the scenery, much of which had been retired early in Gatti's regime. The "Triumphal Scene" of *Aïda* sported a backdrop "which was so peppered with rents and holes that it looked as if the royal palace had suffered a long siege before the entry of the victorious army of Radamès" *(Times,* May 28, 1936). Only the novelties enjoyed a measure of care. *The Bartered Bride,* in a colloquial translation, was a big hit; *Mârouf* and *Il Matrimonio segreto,* also in English, were not. A modernist *Orfeo ed Euridice,* mimed and danced by George Balanchine's American Ballet, the resident troupe, relegated the singers to the pit, a conceit reviewers trounced mercilessly. The best that could be said for the single world premiere, Walter Damrosch's *The Man without a Country,* was that it launched Helen Traubel, a dramatic soprano who would become an indispensable member of the company in the 1940s.

The flaws of the spring seasons emerged in an informal survey. Regular patrons, who declared themselves in favor of the program's ideals, would not attend, absent "big stars" in "superb performances." Precious few votes were cast for the novelties. To make matters worse, the recently installed system of air circulation failed to render the auditorium bearable in the often hot and humid days of May. Attendance was sparse. On July 7, 1937, Ziegler wrote to Johnson, "I have whipped Mr. Cravath up to a point of realization that unless the Juilliard assumes some of the loss, that they are not helping us but crucifying us." The high-minded, ill-conceived, and poorly executed experiment was quietly terminated on January 5, 1938. The one requisite of the Juilliard

Foundation grants that might have expanded opportunities for operagoing and opera training in New York had been a dud.[37]

## Opera in English

Pushback against opera in English translation kept this requirement out of the Juilliard decree. Otto Kahn, for one, had been a staunch defender of the nexus between the original language and the music. He had argued, half seriously, that the absurdities of many librettos were better left untranslated, and had boasted that the "best informed artistic leaders" of Europe envied the Met's policy of linguistic authenticity, at least as it applied to works originally in Italian, German, and French. Not only did the United States lack a state-sanctioned official language, but it was a country of immigrants, and these very same immigrants were counted on to fill the top tiers of the opera house. They would cringe at hearing Aïda invoked as "Heavenly" rather than "Celeste" or Lohengrin's "Lieber" swan addressed as "Beloved." Russian and Czech operas had long been given in translation, but still not in English. Boris Godunov vented his sorrows in Italian, Jenufa transgressed in German, Zolotoy Pyetushok (The Golden Cockerel) crowed in French. The early 1930s board was divided on the question of English translation: Bliss was in favor and Cravath opposed. Skirting the question, Ziegler foresaw (mistakenly, as it happened) that, in any case, patriotic fervor would soon sound the call for English. He suggested that *Gianni Schicchi,* both short and comic, would be a good fit for an English version. Gatti could not be budged: Giuseppe De Luca was his choice for the title role, and De Luca would sing it only in Italian. Gatti would reconsider if "nationalistic demand" persisted. But with Gatti gone, so was the impediment, and Johnson was free to schedule *Gianni Schicchi* in English for Tibbett in 1935–36 and in 1937–38. Through the end of the decade, the Met mounted only four other translated productions, Gian Carlo Menotti's *Amelia Goes to the Ball* (*Amelia al ballo* done in English even at its 1937 Philadelphia world premiere), *The Bartered Bride, Mârouf,* and *Il Matrimonio segreto.* Prospects for opera in English would improve in the coming decade.[38]

## Buying the House

The Met's fiscal crisis set off in October 1929 was resolved a decade later through the remarkable coalition formed to buy the house and its assets. The system that favored the original seventy box holders had unraveled bit by bit. By 1932, with the reorganization that gave rise to the Association, its edges were badly worn; by 1935, it was clear that the Real Estate Company was coming apart. The founders had died, their estates were immune to assessments, and descendants could not be made to assume the obligations of deceased shareholders. The Real Estate Company was at risk of defaulting on its taxes and on the mortgage it had incurred for facility upgrades imposed by the building code. By spring 1939, the Real Estate Company board concluded that it was no longer in a position to lease the theater to the Association. The building would have to be sold. On March 29 of that year, Cornelius Bliss, who had taken Paul Cravath's seat as head of the board in 1938, received a letter from the Real Estate Company advising that "the only recourse of the company is the sale of . . . shares, for which at present, there appears to be no market." The whole of the truth was that many a new Nob was unwilling to swallow the presence of a nouveau Swell in the neighboring box. And besides, boxes had lost much of their mystique. On May 5, 1939, Bliss drafted a response. He could contemplate only one solution: the purchase of the house and its warehouse on West 40th Street either by the Association "or by a group it would enlist for the sake of the future of opera in New York." He requested a one-year option. The amount proposed was $1.5 million, subject to $500,000 in cash and the assumption of a first mortgage of $470,000. The balance would be covered by a second mortgage. There was bound to be dissension among the stockholders. A vocal group, indifferent to the public purposes of the institution, pressed for the better return that could be had on the open market. The dissenters sued and lost. In November 1939, the Association approved the deal; two months later, 68 percent of the outstanding shares were voted yes, barely more than the two-thirds majority needed.

Now it was a question of raising roughly $1 million before the option expired, half to cover the cash payment due the Real Estate Company and half as a cushion against expenses, the most immediate and telling of which was the replacement of the grand tier boxes with conventional seats. Foundations, banks, and corporations were dunned for contributions, as were subscribers, directors of the Association, Met artists, the managers and other company employees, members of the Metropolitan Opera Club, and labor and theatrical organizations. The Metropolitan Opera Guild coordinated the efforts of its affiliates. Fiorello LaGuardia, long a subscriber and since 1936 mayor of New York City, chaired a fund-raising committee of 175 civic and educational leaders. But it was the radio audience that would constitute the largest single source of funds, $327,000. Olin Downes wrote, "This is the development due in large part to the epochal effect upon our culture of radio and records, which have democratized and disseminated upon a previously unheard of scale great music" (*Times,* May 19, 1940).[39]

On June 28, 1942, the title to the 39th Street property was transferred to the Metropolitan Opera Association. After fifty-seven years, the company was at home in its own house.

<br>

REPERTOIRE: 1935–1940

The repertoire of Johnson's first half-decade, sung mostly by the Met's veteran stars, had the ring of Gatti's final years. The 1935–36 season opened with *La Traviata* in a new investiture, a gift to Bori, who had announced her retirement. Pons spiced her usual diet of *Lakmé, Lucia di Lammermoor, Rigoletto,* and *Il Barbiere di Siviglia* with *Le Coq d'or;* Pinza was King Dodon to her Queen of Shemakha. Ponselle took on *Carmen* and little else. To his warhorses, Tibbett added the four villains of *Les Contes d'Hoffmann,* as well as the vainglorious Falstaff. Fearful that an exciting new Ford might repeat his own 1925 upstaging of the principal baritone, he nixed the young Leonard Warren. Sopranos Gina Cigna, Maria Caniglia, Zinka Milanov, and Licia Albanese made their debuts, enlivening the Italian side of the repertoire, the latter two for decades to come. European tenors came and went. The truly memorable of these, Jussi Björling, returned at war's end, and then sporadically until his death in 1960.[40]

Between 1935 and 1940, Johnson hazarded a skimpy total of four novelties; taken together, they eked out only fifteen performances of the nearly nine hundred presented by the company. Richard Hageman's *Caponsacchi* was roundly ignored. It had made the news during rehearsal when Tibbett accidentally stabbed a chorister in the hand: the wound was slight, but within five hours, the victim died of cardiac complications. *Il Matrimonio segreto,* imported in Juilliard's English-language version, was lost in the vast house. *Amelia Goes to the Ball* played cleverly with the conventions of opera buffa, Italian comic opera, but it too was undersized for the theater. *The Man without a Country* was dismissed out of hand as uninspired, retrograde. Among the six new productions of revivals, two corrected errors of omission. On December 22, 1937, *Otello,* wonderfully served by Martinelli, Tibbett,

TABLE 10  Metropolitan Opera Premieres, 1935–36 to 1939–40

| Composer and Title | Met Premiere (*World Premiere) | Most Recent Met Performance | No. of Seasons in Met Repertoire | No. of Met Productions | No. of Met Performances, 1883–2013 | World Premiere | Director/Designer |
|---|---|---|---|---|---|---|---|
| Richard Hageman, Caponsacchi | Feb. 3, 1937 | Feb. 10, 1937 | 1 | 1 | 2 | Feb. 18, 1932, Freiburg (in German) | Désiré Defrère / Unknown |
| Domenico Cimarosa, Il Matrimonio segreto | Feb. 25, 1937 | Mar. 5, 1937 | 1 | 1 | 2 | Feb. 7, 1792, Vienna, Burgtheater | Leopold Sachse / Jonel Jorgulesco |
| Walter Damrosch, The Man without a Country | May 12, 1937* | Feb. 17, 1938 | 2 | 1 | 5 | | Désiré Defrère / David Twachtman |
| Gian Carlo Menotti, Amelia Goes to the Ball (in English) | Mar. 3, 1938 | Jan. 30, 1939 | 2 | 1 | 7 | Apr. 1, 1937, Philadelphia, Academy of Music | Leopold Sachse / Donald Oenslager |

Rethberg, and Panizza, reclaimed its place of privilege after twenty-four years. Following a similar interval, *Le Nozze di Figaro* made its comeback on February 20, 1940, again conducted by Panizza. Pinza in the title role and Bidú Sayão as Susanna, his bride, were the nucleus of an ensemble that sparked the Mozart revival of the 1940s.

Johnson had hoped to crown his initial season with Kirsten Flagstad as Norma. A past Met Wagnerian had already had a go at Bellini's heroine. Lilli Lehmann, the company's first *Siegfried* and *Götterdämmerung* Brünnhilde, had also been the first to sing "Casta diva" on its stage. And Flagstad had heard the only other Norma, Ponselle, in act 3 of the opera during Gatti's farewell gala. In fact, much of act 3—the legato of the recitative "Teneri figli," the andante section of the duet "Mira, o Norma"—was well suited to Flagstad. But there was reason for caution: she had never undertaken a bel canto role or a role that demanded dramatic coloratura. Besides, she had never sung a role in Italian. Ziegler urged the soprano on, predicting "a great triumph," and Flagstad was game to give it a try. In fall 1935, after an encouraging run-through with Panizza, a coach was enlisted to infuse her delivery with the apposite style. But Flagstad soon determined that Norma was not for her and asked to be released from the commitment; Johnson consented. He scheduled Dusolina Giannini in her place. Following Giannini's dress rehearsal, for reasons still not clear, the February 26, 1936, *Norma* morphed into *La Bohème* and Martinelli exchanged Pollione's helmet for Rodolfo's beret. The next season, he sang the Roman proconsul to Cigna's Druid priestess. As for Flagstad, she never again strayed from the Wagnerian manor to which she was born, except, like so many Brünnhildes, for incursions into the dank prison of *Fidelio,* and in 1952, the temples of Gluck's *Alceste.*[41]

### WAGNER: 1929–1940

Once the ban on opera in German was lifted in 1921, Artur Bodanzky had a magnificent crew of Wagnerians at his command. Maria Jeritza, Elisabeth Rethberg, and Maria Müller were all expert interpreters of the lighter lyric roles, the *jugendlich dramatischer* Elsa, Elisabeth, and Eva. Friedrich Schorr, the world's leading *heldenbariton* (heroic baritone) was there for Hans Sachs, Wotan, Wolfram, Amfortas, Kurwenal, and the Dutchman, and dramatic mezzo Karin Branzell for Ortrud, Fricka, and Brangäne. Among the heldentenors was Lauritz Melchior, just coming into his own. There was weakness in one crucial rank: the *hochdramatischer.* The foremost Wagnerian dramatic soprano of the time, Frida Leider, was under contract to Chicago. Brünnhilde and Isolde were left to the able Gertrude Kappel and to the disappointing Elisabeth Ohms. Thanks to the demise of the Chicago Civic Opera in 1932, the Met's Wagner goblet ran over. Lotte Lehmann came to New York for the *jugendlich* roles, Leider for the *hochdramatisch.* The air check of March 11, 1933, preserves Leider's Isolde, her warm, finely centered voice alert to the character's shifting moods. On the March 24, 1934, broadcast, Melchior, Leider's Tristan, is Lohengrin to Rethberg's ethereal Elsa. Maria Olszewska—she, too, lately from Chicago—although squally in Ortrud's highest notes, exudes terrifying authority. As for Lehmann's *Meistersinger* Eva, having exhausted his reservoir of superlatives, Gilman could only exclaim, "But this is the real thing!" (*Herald Tribune,* March 16, 1934). Less than a year later, Gilman was present for Flagstad's first New York Isolde. His notice, he said, was not as much a review of the performance as it was the exercise of what Swinburne called "the noble pleasure of praising" (*Herald Tribune,* Feb. 7, 1935).

Other critics, too, spent themselves in panegyrics over Flagstad's Isolde—over her voice, of course, but also over her acting. The youthful sound she adopts as "Irlands Maid" at the beginning of act 1 comes through in the broadcast of March 9, 1935. Minutes later, she captures all of Isolde's confusion and despair, rising to the wrath of the "Narrative and Curse" without resorting to the shrieks so often emitted in the execution of these trying pages. The long lines of the act 2 love duet hover on her phenomenal column of breath; the "Liebestod" builds gradually to its two climaxes as Flagstad rides the great orchestral wave, and then climbs to the ecstatic, pianissimo transport of the final note. On this spectacular afternoon, she was supported by Branzell, who delivers a rock-solid act 2 "Warnung" (Warning). Although stretched by the highest notes, Schorr's Kurwenal is heartbreaking in the act 3 tending of his master. And the master, Tristan, takes the measure of his Isolde, tireless as he bends his pliant voice to the character's inner conflicts. He ascends with ease from a baritonal lower register to luminous high notes and, perhaps most remarkable, given his enormous instrument, summons a dulcet pianissimo legato for Tristan's yearnings. If Flagstad is one of the very greatest dramatic sopranos of the twentieth century, Melchior's gifts defy comparison. No other tenor has come close.

The historic Flagstad-Melchior partnership and their collaboration, individually and as an operatic couple, with other artists are preserved in many transcriptions of early broadcasts. We consider a sampling here. Flagstad's

Elisabeth of January 18, 1936, is striking most particularly for the purity of tone at fortissimo on high. Paul Jackson points to this performance, and specifically to Tannhäuser's "Rome Narrative," as demonstration of "the enormous range of expression of [Melchior's] splendid instrument." Also in this *Tannhäuser,* Tibbett, in his sole broadcast of a Wagnerian role, negotiates the lyric stanzas of the minnesinger Wolfram as convincingly as he had the outbursts of Scarpia. *Siegfried* is, of course, the tenor's show. On the afternoon of January 30, 1937, Melchior, after hours of singing at full tilt, remains primed for the act 3 duel with Flagstad, who had spent those hours resting in her dressing room. She strikes the treacherous high C of "Ewig war ich" as she would a giant bell, although she opts for the lower octave at the end of the duet. Lotte Lehmann, in the *Lohengrin* of December 21, 1935, invests the virginal Elsa with desire for the mysterious knight. Marjorie Lawrence, as Ortrud, is her worthy antagonist. In the January 11, 1938, *Götterdämmerung* with Melchior, the Australian soprano made news with an athletic coup de théâtre at the end of the "Immolation Scene." The first Brünnhilde in Met history to obey Wagner's stage directions almost to the letter, this valkyrie leapt onto her faithful steed and galloped offstage.[42]

That audiences were mad for Wagner is the story of the 1935–1940 box office; receipts came in consistently and significantly above average. In 1937–38, the predominantly Wagnerian German repertoire claimed approximately the same percentage of the total subscription gross as the Italian, in the lead since the days of Conried. And *Tristan und Isolde* was the most popular draw of all five seasons. In fifty-six performances, Flagstad was the sole Isolde, Melchior her Tristan in all but three. In the course of its seven Met seasons, the team of Flagstad and Melchior racked up 202 performances, a company record: they outdistanced Nordica and de Reszke, more than doubled the output of Farrar and Caruso. The coincidence of the Norwegian soprano and the Danish tenor was as serendipitous for the Met's balance sheet as it was for the history of Wagner performance.[43]

The 1930s closed with a power struggle over a Wagner conductor, Erich Leinsdorf. Assistant to Toscanini in Salzburg and Bruno Walter in Florence, the well-credentialed Leinsdorf came to the Met in the same capacity under Bodanzky. His January 21, 1938, *Die Walküre* debut was a success; there were no significant caveats. During the remainder of this season and the whole of the next, Leinsdorf conducted six more operas, of which thirty or so performances featured Flagstad or Melchior or both. Bodanzky's death on November 23, 1939, just four days before opening night, thrust upon the

FIGURE 19. Kirsten Flagstad as Isolde and Lauritz Melchior as Tristan, c. 1940 (Morton; courtesy Metropolitan Opera Archives)

young conductor substantial responsibility for the German wing. And suddenly, Leinsdorf was no longer acceptable to the famous pair he had led without incident, and apparently without complaint, for nearly two years. It all revolved around *Tristan und Isolde*. Flagstad incited the revolt. She insisted that her accompanist, Edwin McArthur, be assigned the podium. She took the poorly timed occasion of a condolence cable on the very day of Bodanzky's death to pitch the case for her protégé to Ziegler: "I know that Melchior will join me in requesting that you give Edwin McArthur the opportunity to conduct our Tristan performances which he did so brilliantly in California [at the San Francisco Opera] and in which opera we both feel so perfectly at ease with him in the pit."

The feud made the front page on January 25, 1940: "Wagnerian Rift at Opera over Leinsdorf Revealed" *(Herald Tribune)*. In support of Flagstad, Melchior mounted his own attack, alleging that Leinsdorf was "not yet ready to be senior conductor of the finest department of the greatest opera house in the world." Flagstad threatened to walk out if Leinsdorf was not replaced, claiming first that his conducting "made her ill" (*Mirror,* Jan. 26, 1940), later expatiating on her malaise: "Since Mr. Leinsdorf is inexperienced in playing Wagner, he watches the music. I see his arms moving, but I can't tell where the music is." The normally compliant Johnson would not be budged by "some old boats in the company." Four days after the affair became public, during the first intermission of *Die Walküre,* board member David Sarnoff arranged a photo-op handshake between Leinsdorf and Melchior, to which he appended jokingly, "Now, ladies and gentlemen, you can see for yourselves this is truly a house of harmony. If we could get Hitler and Stalin, Daladier and Chamberlain to come on this stage and shake hands, the war soon would be over and all would be lovely" *(Times).* The Met mollified Flagstad by engaging McArthur for a total of six performances of *Tristan und Isolde* over this and the next season, during which period she was obliged to submit to Leinsdorf's baton fifty-six times.[44]

In the 1920s and 1930s, between seven and nine of the ten Wagner titles in the repertoire were programmed each season, a bounty greater than that offered pilgrims to Bayreuth. A Wagnerite could count on at least one "Ring" cycle and an Easter *Parsifal.* By way of comparison, the opening decade of the twenty-first century saw an average of fewer than three works by Wagner per season.[45]

# Strains of War, 1940–1950

## THE CONDUCTOR'S OPERA

### OPENING NIGHT, DECEMBER 2, 1940

THE 1940–41 SEASON OPENED with *Un Ballo in maschera,* absent from the Metropolitan for a quarter of a century. Curiosity was directed at both the stage and the Diamond Horseshoe, occupied for the first time not by owners but by subscribers. In fact, the "hereditary holders," now more democratically holders of season tickets, were largely one and the same. And for the most part, they were settled in the same seats they or their kin had filled since 1883. Family circle standees who had waited from dawn to dusk to buy their tickets looked down on a ring essentially identical to that of the past. On the surface, little had changed. The year's first performance set an opening night record; receipts exceeded $18,000, nearly $6,000 above the usual capacity gross.

By fall 1940, it was evident that the Met's day-to-day operations would be more and more affected by the European conflict. The same front page that carried Edward Johnson's comment that the war presented the company with both "opportunity and challenge" and Howard Taubman's review of opening night led with the story that Germany had attacked Greece. Taubman pronounced the season's opening a shining example of peaceful coexistence: "Last night's cast was, in its makeup, the Metropolitan's answer to the nationalist passions that are rampant in Europe. Following its tradition of bringing together the best artists of the world, whatever their race, nation, or politics, the Metropolitan had singers last night who were an international assemblage." Unlike the houses of Europe, where largely native performers sang in the vernacular of the audience, the Met's roster was diverse in language and culture. The management had opposed the 1937 Alien Artists Exclusion Bill, citing limited opportunities for opera training in the United States and the intolerable price the operagoing public would pay for restrictions on foreign artists. Though section 2 of the bill allowed for a quid pro quo, the provision would be of little use if there were no American seeking engagement in, say, Norway, in exchange for Kirsten Flagstad. As to "whatever their race," Taubman was probably referring to the Jews on the Met payroll. He could not have foreseen that, fifteen years later, in the very opera that opened 1940–41, Marian Anderson would be the first African-American to be cast in a major role.

Despite the historic transfer of ownership of the house, the novelty and brilliance of Verdi's opera, and the voices of Zinka Milanov and Jussi Björling, the most noteworthy event of the season was not opening night but the US operatic debut of conductor Bruno Walter.

### FIDELIO: FEBRUARY 14, 1941

Walter made his way to a podium that sat high on the raised floor of the pit. Conductor and players were visible throughout the performance. While February 14 is lost to us, an off-the-air recording of the following week's Saturday matinée is a precious approximation of the extraordinary evening of music and of its impassioned reception. The Leonore Overture No. 3 provoked an outburst that lasted more than a minute; at the opera's conclusion, the ovation for the cast was punctuated by shouts of "Walter." European audiences knew him as a conductor of opera as well as symphony; America had known him only in concert, never in the opera house. He first appeared in the United States in 1923 with the New York Symphony Orchestra. He returned frequently as guest from coast to coast. No conductor, with the exception of Arturo Toscanini, had more cachet. According to stage director Herbert Graf, Johnson "was practically trembling before their first meeting."[1]

Walter's Fidelio belongs to that rarified theatrical category in which history, work, composer, and performer come together to inscribe a single narrative. Here was a moment in which the grave issues confronting the nation converged with those engaged by the masterwork. These same issues intersected with the biographies of the lionized artists. Uncompromising, defiant, Beethoven and Walter were conflated in a common profile whose prominent feature was the massive cranium of genius. The deteriorating situation overseas—an all-too-present story of oppression and persecution—reverberated in the ardent

FIGURE 20. Bruno Walter (courtesy Metropolitan Opera Archives)

libretto and score. As the conductor put it some years later, "In the first act of *Fidelio* . . . we witness the hand of the tyrant. In the second, we observe the victim, bent but unbroken. In the finale, we see the Minister of State, representative of goodness, and share in the glorious apotheosis of brotherhood."[2]

The media blitz surrounding Walter's debut imbricated the *Fidelio* scenario and the exemplary life told and retold in the national press, in newsreels, and on the radio: an illustrious musician of German-Jewish origin, having escaped religious and political persecution by fleeing first Germany, and then Austria, and finally France, takes refuge in the United States, and for the first time in his long career conducts an American performance of a magisterial work by one of nineteenth-century Europe's titanic composers, a fierce champion of freedom. *Fidelio*'s place in the Walter mythology was further privileged by the fact that the first work he conducted at the Met was also the last he chose to perform in Munich and then in Berlin. Had Walter not left, like so many who shared his liberal views and/or Jewish heritage, he might have suffered a fate much like that of Florestan, the idealistic hero of *Fidelio,* imprisoned by order of a tyrant. There the parallel ends. Leonore, Florestan's loving wife, disguised as the eponymous youth, rescues her husband from the political prison of the villainous Don Pizarro. During the opera's final scene, a paean to liberty and justice, Leonore removes Florestan's shackles. A grateful populace salutes her.

### TRIBULATIONS

### Artists

The cast of Walter's 1941 *Fidelio* would never again be assembled. The quandary into which reports from Europe threw many of the company's inner circle is conveyed in the memoirs of the Swedish-Hungarian-American soprano Astrid Varnay: "At the end of her penultimate prewar season, Kirsten [Flagstad] was on the train to Cleveland to join the Metropolitan tour, already in progress. There, Lauritz and Kleinchen Melchior told her that the Germans were about to attack and occupy both Norway and Melchior's native Denmark. The Melchiors had decided to wait out the war in America and urged Flagstad to do the same. At the next station, Melchior hopped off to buy a newspaper. When he returned, his expression was grim: Norway and Denmark were now in a state of war with Germany. Arriving in Cleveland, they saw Kerstin Thorborg and her husband, Gustav Bergman, on the platform, weeping uncontrollably. Although their own native Sweden had been allowed to remain neutral, their feelings for their fellow Scandinavians were so strong they were both reduced to tears." Melchior's advice went unheeded and in 1941 the Met lost its star soprano.[3]

As early as 1933, the routine of Metropolitan affairs had been perturbed by the advance of fascism. The year in which Adolf Hitler was elected Chancellor of Germany was also the year Luigi Villa, Giulio Gatti-Casazza's secretary, received a distraught letter from Erich Simon, agent to many leading singers. Simon, a German Jew, had fled to Paris to escape the Nazis "after terrible times and undescribable days." He had been summarily dismissed, as had all of his Jewish colleagues. He wanted Gatti to know that the Berlin agency to which he had been attached was "absolutely a national-socialistic institution which declines to make any engagements for artists who are not of real German and Christian origin." Within five years of Simon's anguished account, the religious affiliation of the Met's correspondents would be at issue in Italy as well. On May 7, 1938, Milanese agent Attilio Lamponi complained to Villa that he had had no response to his solicitation of Metropolitan business. He explained frankly that the recent growth of his influence had situated him to be of invaluable service. As things stood, he pointed out, his Jewish competitors would soon find it difficult to work in Europe; artists would be looking elsewhere for the negotiation of their contracts. Not that he, Lamponi, held any animus toward Jews. It was just that as a businessman it was his responsibility to report on conditions objectively. Besides, he had been called to Rome and would soon have official charge of all international theatrical arrangements.[4]

By mid-decade, the major German singers who had been at the Met in the early 1930s—Frida Leider, Maria Müller, and Max Lorenz, for example—were gone. And numerous stars of the leading German houses, among them Tiana Lemnitz, Margarete Klose, Helge Roswaenge, and Heinrich Schlusnuss, would miss their chance to sing opera in New York. In return, Jewish and anti-Nazi artists such as Jan Kiepura, Alexander Kipnis, Lotte Lehmann, Jarmila Novotna, and Friedrich Schorr, forced out of European theaters, were available to the Met. In 1939, Italian artists would be barred by their government from traveling to the United States; the question of whether Lamponi or someone else would handle their contracts would be moot. A flurry of telegrams documents the negotiations between the Metropolitan and the State Department, the Italian Embassy in Washington, and the pertinent Italian bureau. On September 28, 1939, a cable from the Federazione Fascista Lavoratori Spettacolo (Fascist Federation of Theater Workers) informed the Met that ten contracted singers would not be honoring their commitments, among them Maria Caniglia, Mafalda Favero, and Carlo Tagliabue, who had already made successful Met debuts, and the much anticipated Ebe Stignani. As the *Times* (Oct. 7, 1939) explained it, several of those forbidden to travel were contracted to Italian theaters following their projected stints at the Met; there was concern that increasing international tensions might preclude their timely repatriation. Of more diplomatic consequence was the eventuality that Italian artists caught in the United States would be marooned on enemy shores should America enter the war. There was a good deal of back and forth on the matter over the course of many months. The authorities were sensitive to the propaganda value of *italianità* at the Metropolitan and were, therefore, reluctant to offend the management; they were also loath to forgo the hard currency their nationals would deposit in Italian banks. The Met applied what pressure it could, both at home and in Italy, through numerous intermediaries. One such go-between, the retired Lucrezia Bori, long a US resident and great friend of the company, agreed to bring the Metropolitan's position to the attention of the Italian Ambassador in Washington: if the ten contracted singers did not come, the management would have no recourse but to redraw the season's repertoire, with serious consequences for the company and for Italian opera itself. On the other hand, should Johnson receive assurances that the restrictions imposed in 1939–40 would be lifted for 1940–41, he would be favorable to scheduling a greater number of operas by Italian composers than had originally been planned. In May 1940, Johnson received the guarantees he sought from the consul general. In the end, Licia Albanese, who was not one of the ten, was allowed to make her debut. But of the detainees in 1939, only Alessio De Paolis and Salvatore Baccaloni were on the roster in 1940–41. In addition, star tenor Tito Schipa would not return. Well known for his fascist sympathies, Schipa canceled just a month before the United States declared war on Germany and Italy.[5]

Ezio Pinza's tribulations unfolded entirely stateside. He was diligently fulfilling his Met contract for the 1941–42 season when FBI agents showed up at his suburban New York door and placed him under arrest on the accusation of a fellow bass, Norman Cordon. Pinza had been a Met star since 1926 and one of its most popular draws. Furthermore, he had been a permanent resident since 1939 and lately married to an American. Among the charges he faced were that he was a personal friend of Il Duce (they had never met), that his nickname was Mussolini (an invention), that by changing tempos during Met broadcasts he had sent coded messages abroad (too absurd to contest), that he had transmitted radio communications from his boat (he had sold the boat soon after Pearl Harbor), that he had a tortoise-shell ring in the shape of a swastika (it was an antique ring that bore an archaic symbol), that in 1935 he had organized a collection of gold and silver for the benefit of the war in Ethiopia (he had not organized the collection but had contributed a gold ring to the war effort that year). While columnist Walter Winchell went on the attack with his signature malice (Winchell appeared to be particularly seized by what he considered the damning evidence of the ring), many others came to Pinza's defense, including Mayor Fiorello LaGuardia and Carlo Tresca, editor of the antifascist New York paper *Il Martello*. So did Bruno Walter. Johnson deposed in Pinza's favor: "I should indeed be remiss in my duties as an American and as General Manager of the greatest American Opera House, should I tolerate enemies of our country on our staff, no matter how exquisite their talents." Far from undermining the American cause, Pinza's gifts, Johnson attested, would fortify the nation in the difficult times ahead. At Pinza's successful second hearing, colleagues testified that Cordon had bragged about informing on his celebrated competitor. After three month's detention, Pinza was released. His return to the Met in 1942–43 came in Philadelphia, where, as Don Giovanni, he had the pleasure of murdering Cordon's Commendatore in a performance conducted by Walter. In his first New York appearance of that season, he sang the message of brotherhood of the wise Sarastro in Mozart's *Die Zauberflöte,* again under Walter.[6]

The first major European singer to make his debut after the war was the Swedish tenor Torsten Ralf, a target in 1945 of one of Winchell's many insidious attacks: "A singer at the Met is said to have entertained the Nazis in Berlin and Vienna until three years ago. And didn't he make recordings for Goebbels?" According to an official of the US Legation in Stockholm, Ralf had served the Allied cause both in Berlin and in Sweden before and after 1941. He was cleared of all charges. So too in 1947, by authority of the Military Government in Germany, were the bass-baritone Hans Hotter and the coloratura Erna Berger. Berger ran into trouble three years later with the adoption of the McCarran Act of 1950, passed by a dangerously zealous Congress over the veto of President Harry Truman. Among other provisions, the McCarran Act barred entry into the United States to "aliens who are members of or affiliated with . . . the Communist or other totalitarian party . . . of any foreign state." Berger had not been a member of the Nazi party; she had enrolled in the *Reichstheaterkammer,* a requirement for working musicians. When Berger first appeared at the Met in 1949, the *Reichstheaterkammer* was classified a union; the next year it was reclassified a "subsidy" of the Nazi party. For a time, Berger was denied a visa.[7]

But no case aroused more consternation than that of Flagstad, who had spent the war years in Norway with her husband, Henry Johansen. At the close of hostilities, Johansen was indicted on charges of collaboration with the Nazi occupiers and the Quisling government; he died in June 1946 awaiting trial for treason. Flagstad had sung rarely during the war, and only in neutral Switzerland and Sweden. Nonetheless, rumors were rife that she had performed for German soldiers, made pro-Nazi statements, and called Erich Leinsdorf a "damned Jew." There were those who lobbied that her reengagement not be delayed; Mrs. Belmont was certain, and said so publicly, that

FIGURE 21. Protest against Kirsten Flagstad's Carnegie Hall appearance, April 21, 1947 (courtesy Metropolitan Opera Archives)

once the State Department granted Flagstad a visa, there would be a place for her on the roster. In 1947, Flagstad was issued the requisite document, and in spring of that year she embarked on an American tour. There was some question of a stop at the Metropolitan. But many of her appearances around the country sparked protests, even angry demonstrations, precisely the reaction that Johnson and his board were determined to avoid. Despite earlier vague overtures, it was not until the January 27, 1950, meeting of the executive committee of the Association that she was approved for the coming season. By then, Johnson would have relinquished the Metropolitan reins.[8]

## Money and Labor

In spring 1942, the *Frankfurter Zeitung* spread the word that the remainder of the Metropolitan season had been canceled: "Money alone does not suffice to maintain grand opera on a sound and artistic basis. The closing of the Metropolitan four months after the declaration of war symbolizes something more than the bankruptcy of a leading private establishment. It exposes to all the world the cultural weakness of a country which is now proclaiming itself the guardian and defender of traditional cultural values" (*Times,* April 26, 1942). Johnson picked up the gauntlet. In his report to the board on the fiscal year ending May 31, 1942, under the heading "Metropolitan Opera in War Time," he declared that, yes, "the center of grand opera had shifted from Europe to this side of the Atlantic." And looking ahead to 1943–44, he answered the Nazi broadside with the rebuttal that the season would be extended to twenty weeks, "not as a retort to you, but because our attendance of more than 405,623 people last year warranted it! And 400,000 Americans can't be wrong.... And you will learn to your destruction that it is by the drums and the trumpets that men march to victory, whether it be to the music of the War March by Felix Mendelssohn or the Radetzky March by Johann Strauss or 'The Star Spangled Banner' by Francis Scott Key. America has come into its musical heritage. Let the drums roll. Let the trumpets blow. On with the show!" (*Mirror,* Aug. 29, 1943).

The triumphalism of Johnson's public pronouncements notwithstanding, the Met's daily administration continued to be dogged by one crisis after another, even as the Depression was overtaken by the conversion to a wartime economy and even after the buying of the house had brought an end to dependency on the Real Estate Company. Particularly irksome were the taxes that had burdened the Association's landlord and now weighed heavily on the Association itself. The exemption the Met requested was opposed by LaGuardia and approved only in April 1943 over the mayor's objections by Governor Thomas E. Dewey, he too a committed operaphile. But by then, the Met had registered losses of $200,000 in each of the two previous years. The deficits of 1941–42 and 1942–43 were attributed by some to the embargo on European voices and by others to trepidations of all sorts following the Japanese attack on Pearl Harbor. The management was justified in worrying that in 1942–43 the house would be dark. Although ticket prices for the top seats were lowered from $7.70 to $6.05, single sales dropped by 11 percent. Unsold tickets were distributed to service men and women. In the end, the season went on as planned, as did the tour. In 1943–44, the season was extended, as Johnson had boasted, to twenty weeks, not because of demand, as he implied in his riposte to the German attack on America, but in anticipation that the spring tour would be canceled. The company lost $110,000 that year. Again the Guild came to the rescue; a successful appeal narrowed the shortfall.

With the approaching end of the war, the Metropolitan was subject to the labor unrest that rocked so many sectors of the economy. The increasing strength of the American Guild of Musical Artists (AGMA) in its negotiations with the Metropolitan management, in part the result of the dramatic rise in the number of Americans on the roster, produced a contract with this protectionist clause: that for every alien engaged, three Americans would be hired. For reasons having everything to do with the European conflagration and only marginally with Johnson's Americanization policy or his labor accords, in 1944–45 no foreign-born singer joined the company; fourteen Americans made their debuts. The 1944–45 season ended in profit. Travel restrictions had been lifted and the tour was lengthened. Attendance in 1946–47 reached 97 percent of capacity and the tour that season was the longest ever. In the same year, the Met tapped a fresh income stream. On February 19, the company announced that it had entered into a five-year contract with the Columbia Recording Corporation for two operas annually. The first recording from the Met stage, that March, was the "Liebesnacht" from *Tristan und Isolde,* with Helen Traubel and Torsten Ralf, and the first complete opera, recorded that June, was *Hansel and Gretel,* in English, with Risë Stevens and Nadine Conner. The second was *La Bohème* with Bidú Sayão and Richard Tucker. In late summer 1947, a dispute with AGMA over the size of the chorus was finally settled. The management won a reduction in the number of choristers: those who were let go after twenty years or more received a year's severance, and those that remained a substantial boost in salary. That was by no means the end of labor-management strife. Despite an income of $3 million in 1947–48, the upcoming season was repeatedly declared in doubt. In fact, ploy or not, on August 4, 1948, the Met announced its cancellation. Three weeks later, a compromise was reached: the Association agreed to fund unemployment insurance and the unions conceded on salary hikes.[9]

### REPERTOIRE: 1940–1950

The company made good on Olin Downes's 1939 prediction, "If ever we enter the conflict [it is hard to believe that] it will be necessary to take Wagner off the lists. This kind of thing can be left to Germany" (*Times,* Oct. 15). The Association directors accepted what their Great War predecessors had rejected: to program works in the language of the enemy. This time it would have meant banning opera in Italian as well. Between 1940 and 1945, there was little deviation in the number of scores based on German and Italian texts. *Madama Butterfly* was alone interdicted. At issue was the libretto that, as Virgil Thomson put it, "shows Japanese behaving more or less properly and a United States naval officer behaving (with consular benediction) improperly" (*Herald Tribune,* Jan. 20, 1946). *Butterfly* was performed for the last time on November 29, 1941, a week before Pearl Harbor, and then not again until January 14, 1946, six months after V-J Day.[10]

For the rest, the Met lived, if nervously, with the threat of the injection of international politics into performance. During the numerous iterations of *Aïda* in the late 1930s, the general manager and his staff held their breath at the chorus' exultant "Ritorna vincitor" ("Return a conqueror"), fearing that "somebody might yell, 'Down with Mussolini!' Somebody, 'Evviva Mussolini.' The first thing you'd know, the Metropolitan would have a riot on its hands." As the operatic army of ancient Egyptians set off to vanquish the Ethiopians, those on opposite sides of Italy's aggression toward that same African kingdom might well have found reason to cheer or to boo. The management took every opportunity to put patriotism on display, occasionally to stirring effect. The 1942–43 season opened with Donizetti's *La Fille du régiment.* Newspapers all over the country carried the story and a photograph of the opera's finale, in which, in place of the traditional French Tricolor, the Cross of Lorraine of General Charles De Gaulle's Free French was waved by French-born Lily Pons. After the closing "Salut à la France," the Met orchestra played first "La Marseillaise" and then, as the Stars and Stripes were brought to the front of the stage and the Cross of Lorraine was dipped in tribute, "The Star Spangled Banner." In 1943, opening night went to Modest Mussorgsky's *Boris Godunov,* a nod to the recent alliance between the United States and the Soviet Union. On the other hand, the Met declined the suggestion made by Rabbi Steven S. Wise, President of the American Jewish Congress, that it "associate itself with many other groups throughout the country and indeed throughout the world who wish to give expression to their sympathy to the Jewish people in this hour of agony" by reviving an opera that depicts the persecution of Jews, Halévy's *La Juive.* Johnson replied regretfully that a new production of the work would not be feasible. In February 1944, the director general of the Pan American Union urged Johnson to consider Darius Milhaud's *Bolivar.* Johnson answered that although he knew and liked the score, the cost of the production was simply prohibitive.[11]

Fettered by a war economy and a conservative management, the 1940s registered the fewest novelties and new productions of any decade in Met

FIGURE 22. The conclusion of *La Fille du régiment,* Lily Pons as Marie waving the tricolor, 1942 (courtesy Metropolitan Opera Archives)

history, none at all between 1943 and 1945 or in 1948–49. Among the seven novelties were two world premieres, one-acters presented on double bills. Gian-Carlo Menotti's *The Island God,* Pucciniesque in musical idiom, not in dramatic punch, got unsympathetic notices; the composer expunged it from his catalogue. Bernard Rogers's *The Warrior* began life as a radio play. The composer's modernist, dissonant orchestration, the staging, its projected scenery, and the performers were admired by some reviewers; the austere *sprechstimme* (halfway between speech and song) of this retelling of Samson and Delilah fell into the tuneless "modern music" category detested by Met patrons. Sir Thomas Beecham made his conducting debut in *Phoebus and Pan,* his own adaptation of a Bach secular cantata, also programmed on a double bill. The slight piece was out of place in a large opera house. The four remaining Met premieres fared poorly; they would find success in the future. We discuss *Alceste* and *The Abduction from the Seraglio (Die Entführung aus dem Serail)* further on in this chapter. In 1948, three years after its world premiere at London's Sadler's Wells, Benjamin Britten's *Peter Grimes* split the New York critics. What Thomson dismissed as adding "nothing to the history of the stage or the history of music" *(Herald Tribune)* would soon be counted among the landmarks of twentieth-century opera. *Khovanshchina* was doomed to a four-performance run even before it opened; Rudolf Bing, the incoming manager, announced that he had no intention of reprising Mussorgsky's fresco of seventeenth-century Russia. With this balance sheet, Johnson's regime was faulted for timidity, and rightly so.

Save for *Alceste,* the 1940s novelties were sung in English, in two instances the language of composition. The opera-in-English agenda of the Americanization project was beginning to take hold. The popular Ruth and Thomas Martin *Magic Flute* was the harbinger of English for operas with spoken dialogue, *Fidelio* and *The Abduction from the Seraglio,* both singspiels. *Falstaff* reverted to the language of Shakespeare. *Hänsel und Gretel* lost its umlaut and its "und." Unheard at the Met in their original Czech and Russian even to this day, *The Bartered Bride,* which had been given in German, and *Le Coq d'or,* previously in French, were anglicized along with *Khovanshchina.* English translation was in play when the music was suspended for stretches of speech, when the opera drew a children's audience, and when the work was composed in Czech or Russian, neither in use at the Met. For purposes of accessibility, English had become one of the company's languages. Whether the words, uttered either by foreigners or by native speakers, could be understood was up for grabs.[12]

By 1940, most productions of repertory standards had seen roughly twenty years of service. The editions of *Aïda* and *Carmen,* for example, went back to 1923–24. *Lucia di Lammermoor, Rigoletto,* and *Il Barbiere di Siviglia* had been mounted for Amelita Galli-Curci and *Lohengrin* and *Tristan und Isolde* for Wagner's return from his World War I exile. Of still older vintage were *Il Trovatore* and *Faust.* As for the sets of *La Bohème,* no one could remember who designed them. Some productions, particularly those of Joseph Urban, deserved their long life. But with longevity came depredations particular to the New York opera house. Space was at a premium on 39th Street. Drops, flats, and platforms had to be stored in a nearby warehouse, trucked to the Met, covered with tarpaulins, and stacked on the Seventh Avenue sidewalk against the exterior back wall of the theater to wait their turn in the daily change of program. Exposure to harsh winters took its toll on the painted scenery, too soon drab, slack, and worn.

In the course of the 1940s, only a handful of the most popular operas strutted new trappings. The outlines of Richard Rychtarik's castle, garden,

TABLE 11 Metropolitan Opera Premieres, 1940–41 to 1949–50

| Composer and Title | Met Premiere (*World Premiere) | Most Recent Met Performance | No. of Seasons in Met Repertoire | No. of Met Productions | No. of Met Performances, 1883–2013 | World Premiere | Director/Designer |
|---|---|---|---|---|---|---|---|
| Christoph Willibald Gluck, Alceste | Jan. 24, 1941 | Feb. 11, 1961 | 3 | 2 | 18 | Dec. 26, 1767, Vienna, Burgtheater | Herbert Graf / Richard Rychtarik |
| Johann Sebastian Bach, Phoebus and Pan (Der Streit zwischen Phoebus und Pan) | Jan. 15, 1942 | Mar. 4, 1942 | 1 | 1 | 5 | Circa 1729, Leipzig, Collegium Musicum | Herbert Graf / Richard Rychtarik |
| Gian Carlo Menotti, The Island God | Feb. 20, 1942* | Mar. 12, 1942 | 1 | 1 | 4 | | Lothar Wallerstein / Richard Rychtarik |
| Wolfgang Amadeus Mozart, Die Entführung aus dem Serail (The Abduction from the Seraglio) in English | Nov. 29, 1946 | May 7, 2008 | 9 | 2 | 68 | July 16, 1782, Vienna, Burgtheater | Herbert Graf / Donald Oenslager |
| Bernard Rogers, The Warrior | Jan. 11, 1947* | Jan. 31, 1947 | 1 | 1 | 2 | | Herbert Graf / Samuel Leve |
| Benjamin Britten, Peter Grimes | Feb. 12, 1948 | Mar. 24, 2008 | 10 | 3 | 71 | June 7, 1945, London, Sadler's Wells | Dino Yannopoulos / Joseph Novak |
| Modest Mussorgsky, Khovanshchina (in English) | Feb. 16, 1950 | Mar. 17, 2012 | 5 | 2 | 38 | Feb. 21, 1886, St. Petersburg, Kononov | Dino Yannopoulos / Mstislav Dobujinsky |

and crypt for *Lucia di Lammermoor* held no surprise. Harry Horner's towers framed and unified the narrative of *Il Trovatore,* all the while serving the action rapidly unfolding in the melodrama's many separate locations, the castles, the garden, the gypsy camp, the dungeon. Lee Simonson was drubbed for a "Ring" dressed with geometric rocks and a Rhine landscape inspired by the New World vistas of the Hudson and the Palisades. Then there was the reprise of five neglected works. Mstislav Dobujinsky's sets restored *Un Ballo in maschera* to its original Sweden, precincts more luxurious than the colonial Boston of the previous production. Puccini's Manon and Des Grieux enacted their fatal attraction in the appealing, unremarkable eighteenth-century sites that M. Krehan-Crayon conceived for *Manon Lescaut.* Jonel Jorgulesco's *La Fille du régiment* played well as a cartoon. Joseph Novak's dockside for *Il Tabarro* was no more than utilitarian. Rychtarik supplied modest digs for *La Serva padrona.*

## CONDUCTORS

It was the phalanx of masterful conductors that made the difference. Bruno Walter was as demanding as any prima donna: "I cannot accept to function as a 'vieux Routinier' [old hack] again and again appearing in the same well-established works. I must wish to see that the management is interested to make use of my artistic capacities and there is only one way to show this interest: by inviting me to conduct, to revive operas of importance." He took offense at the suggestion of *Hänsel und Gretel,* rejected the company's version of *Carmen,* shrank from *Norma,* and turned down *Die Entführung aus dem Serail,* which was unsuited in his view to the Met's auditorium. His rebuff of "Mozart specialist" was undercut by the sixty-four performances of *Le Nozze di Figaro, Don Giovanni,* and *Die Zauberflöte* he conducted between 1941 and 1959. In the end, aside from *Fidelio,* which he led not only in 1941 but in 1945, 1946, and 1951, and the three Mozart works, the titles Walter directed were *Orfeo ed Euridice, Un Ballo in maschera, La Forza del destino,* and *The Bartered Bride.* The *Pelléas et Mélisande* he requested was assigned to Emil Cooper, the *Falstaff* to Beecham. Walter could dispose of what the Met proposed. But the reverse also obtained: Walter could propose the works he favored, but the power to dispose lay with the management.[13]

Beecham followed Walter in early 1942 as the second of the generation of star European conductors to debut at the Metropolitan during the roiling

FIGURE 23. George Szell rehearsing *Tannhäuser*, 1953 (Sedge Leblang; courtesy Metropolitan Opera Archives)

1940s. His brief American interlude came in the wake of the darkening of Covent Garden for the duration. The dominant force for opera in England throughout an already long career, Beecham had introduced London to *Salome, Elektra, Der Rosenkavalier,* and *Boris Godunov.* During his three Metropolitan seasons, he took primary responsibility for the French repertoire. George Szell arrived barely a year later and stayed through the 1945–46 season, when he was named music director of the Cleveland Orchestra. He had been a principal conductor at the Berlin Staatsoper and music director of the German opera company in Prague from 1929 to 1937. At the outbreak of the war, Szell, of Jewish background and antifascist, found himself stranded in New York. At the Met, he was charged chiefly with the German repertoire and with rebuilding the orchestra. Cooper was Russian by birth. His pedigree included Diaghilev's seasons in Paris and the 1909 first night of Rimsky-Korsakov's *Le Coq d'or.* Johnson would assign Cooper the Met premieres of *Die Entführung aus dem Serail, Peter Grimes,* and *Khovanshchina.* Fritz Busch came in 1945 and Fritz Reiner in 1949. Busch, who had conducted premieres of Strauss, Hindemith, and Weill in Germany, had been removed from his Dresden post as punishment for his outspoken opposition to Nazism. As the first music director of Glyndebourne, he had spearheaded the Mozart revival of the 1930s; when Glyndebourne too suspended operations, he moved to podiums in North and South America. Famed as a Mozartean, Busch, at the Met, was heard primarily in Wagner. Reiner, who had conducted meticulously prepared, staged performances of operas with the Philadelphia Orchestra in the mid-1930s, made his Met debut in *Salome*. Walter, Beecham, Szell, Cooper, Busch, and Reiner molded the 1940s into a conductor's decade. Their engagements, one after the other, can be seen as a contingency of war. They cannot be seen as accidental. In his 1942 report, Johnson announced that the practice of inviting conductors of international repute as guests, begun the previous season with Walter, would continue. At the peak of their Metropolitan activity, the 1943–44 season, Walter, Beecham, and Szell conducted more than half the performances on 39th Street.[14]

## MONUMENTS

The jubilant critics predicted that the conductor's decade would lead to the triumph of the esteemed "conductor's opera" over the deprecated "singer's opera." "Monuments of operatic art," as Edward Johnson called them, would at last take their rightful and regular place at the Met. In Johnson's taxonomy, "monuments" are those works of the literature "which do not enjoy (and may never have enjoyed) the following they deserve but which have been a source of inspiration to operatic composers and a delight to students of the art." They are canonical pieces whose presence in the repertoire rests on prestige and not popularity. Revivals of the monuments, Johnson hoped, would so captivate the general public that these rarely performed works would, in time, join such favorites as *Carmen* and *Tristan und Isolde* in the second of his four categories, "perennial classics." (Johnson's remaining classes were "operas revived for a distinguished personality" and "contemporary opera.") Olin Downes, for one, claiming that the future was already here, asserted that the plaudits of the public were, in this new age, dependent not on the singer but on the conductor (*Times,* Nov. 23, 1941).[15]

Johnson defines monuments without naming them. In a similar reflection, Walter exhibits no such reticence: "Men and events stand in the glaring light of historic glory today and disappear tomorrow, and we may ask: What has remained of all this danse macabre? What has proved durable in those dust storms of history? A question of problematic meaning. Certain is one thing: Survival of Mozart's *Nozze di Figaro,* of Beethoven's *Fidelio,* Gluck's *Orfeo.*" To Walter's list, and through the lens of the repertoire of the 1940s, we add Gluck's *Alceste,* Mozart's *Don Giovanni, Die Zauberflöte,* and *Die*

*Entführung aus dem Serail,* Verdi's *Otello* and *Falstaff,* and Debussy's *Pelléas et Mélisande.*[16]

## *Orfeo ed Euridice:* January 20, 1940

Along with the German repertoire, Erich Leinsdorf inherited Artur Bodanzky's *Orfeo ed Euridice.* Young Leinsdorf's Gluck of January 1940 is markedly faster than Bodanzky's in the November 26, 1938, broadcast. Where Bodanzky's tempos are elegiac, Leinsdorf's, often driven and metronomic, harden the music's serene figures. As a result, under Leinsdorf, the sky over the Elysian Fields is less clear than the composer desired, the sun less bright. New in 1938, the production was admired for Harry Horner's sets, Herbert Graf's direction, and especially the Orfeo of Kerstin Thorborg, who, according to Downes, "achieved the grand simplicity, and by this simplicity and grandeur deeply moved her listeners" (*Times,* Nov. 27, 1938). As we hear it, the same can be said of her in 1940. Thorborg's is the ideal voice for Orfeo, solid yet not heavy through the middle of the range where so much of the role lies, deep but not cavernous, reaching the low notes of the character's noble lamentations without resorting to an emphatic chest register. Walter conducted *Orfeo ed Euridice* in 1941, again with Thorborg. Oscar Thompson summed up the critical consensus: "this was the most noteworthy performance of the score at the opera house since the Toscanini performances [1909–1914]" (*Sun,* Nov. 27). We have no record of Walter's way with Gluck's work. And like Toscanini before him, not even the Met's most prestigious and popular conductor could attract large audiences to this monument.

## *Otello:* February 24, 1940

When it returned at last on December 22, 1937, *Otello* had been out of the repertoire since 1913. The production was the capstone of Giovanni Martinelli's long career. Lawrence Tibbett was the Iago. Elisabeth Rethberg substituted for the scheduled Desdemona, Eidé Norena. Reviewers targeted Tibbett's tendency to oversing and overact and the aging voices of Martinelli and Rethberg. The Met released the third of its transmissions of the opera, the 1940 *Otello,* in its series "Historic Broadcast Recordings." Martinelli, even less plush than he had been in the first in 1938, manages nonetheless to reach the full stature of the tragic hero through phrasing and intensity. Here, Tibbett recalibrates his tone to keep pace with Iago's shifting machinations.

And Rethberg sounds fresher and more engaged than she had in the earlier broadcast. Panizza's orchestra is, as always, sensitive to the smallest variations of rhythm and dynamics. The opera was revived in 1945–46, 1946–47, and 1948–49, conducted by Szell and Busch. The first Otello of this later run, Wagnerian Torsten Ralf, was insufficiently Italianate, and the second, converted baritone Ramon Vinay (he had recently been in Toscanini's historic broadcast with the NBC Symphony), was strained by the tessitura. Stella Roman enchanted listeners with her high pianissimos, only to exasperate them with her clunky phrasing; as the other Desdemona, the overparted Licia Albanese dropped the role after one season. Leonard Warren, sumptuous yet nimble, went on to sing more Iagos than anyone in Met history. The opera slumped at the box office. *Otello* would finally be anchored in the public's affections in January 1955 when Mario Del Monaco was the Moor of Venice and Renata Tebaldi his unfortunate wife.[17]

### *Le Nozze di Figaro:* March 9, 1940

Like *Otello, Le Nozze di Figaro* had been missing for more than two decades when it reentered the repertoire on February 20, 1940. During the long span, Mozart had been present only in *Don Giovanni,* with some regularity, and *Die Zauberflöte* and *Così fan tutte,* rarely. Reviewers of the February *Le Nozze di Figaro* took issue with Graf's broad direction, with an interior stage both difficult to negotiate and acoustically inimical, with Rethberg, the Countess, her best years behind her and garishly costumed, and with an ensemble only at dress rehearsal level. But the importance of the occasion was uncontested. Best of all, the audience had a wonderful time at what was still thought of as fare for the cognoscenti. With this production, *Le Nozze di Figaro* became a fixture at the Met. In the 1940s, led first by Panizza, and then most notably by Walter, Busch, and Reiner, it was scheduled in all but two seasons. The principals remained largely unchanged: John Brownlee sang fifty-five Counts out of a possible sixty-two, Pinza and Sayão had a near monopoly on Figaro and Susanna, Jarmila Novotna and Risë Stevens alternated as the lovesick Cherubino, and Eleanor Steber soon became the Countess of choice. Evident in the March 9, 1940, broadcast is the degree to which Panizza's brisk tempos sustain the hilarity. In contrast, in the broadcast of January 29, 1944, Walter infuses the score with the warmth of his expansive phrasing, both guiding and cosseting the singers. In 1944, Steber, through seamless legato, even articulation of fioritura, and the silvery sound that identify her as an exemplary practitioner of Mozart, fills the music with the sadness of the wronged wife. Under Walter, Pinza dispenses with buffoonery, Sayão has the time to put a smile in her voice, Novotna to tease out the threads of Cherubino's adolescent ardor. Only Brownlee, careless in passagework, labored at the top, insufficient in resonance, and deficient in Italian pronunciation, disappoints in both broadcasts.

### *Fidelio:* February 22, 1941

Kirsten Flagstad was the Leonore both of Bruno Walter's debut and of the broadcast of the following week. If the soprano is ill at ease with rapidly articulated notes and her high Bs lack her familiar resonance, the beauty and size of her voice and the fullness of her commitment to the heroine's plight compensate for these shortcomings. René Maison makes palpable the anguish of Florestan, traversing the arduous course of "Gott! Welch Dunkel hier!" with precise and piercing tone. The luxury casting of Alexander Kipnis as Rocco ensures the broad bass line of the ensembles as it does the geniality of the character. In its revival in 1945, *Fidelio* again belonged to Walter, this time in English. The star conductor led a starless and largely inadequate cast. The exception was the Leonore of Regina Resnik. Her performance, as documented in the broadcast, is difficult to reconcile with reviews that find her, in her debut season, unready for so demanding a part. To be sure, she does not possess Flagstad's tonal mass; on the other hand, her slimmer voice is more responsive to the technical difficulties and dramatic requirements of the role.

### *Alceste:* March 8, 1941

For the Met's very first *Alceste* (Jan. 24, 1941), Rychtarik designed an impressive neoclassical décor, tiers of stairs and imposing Greek columns. Graf's staging was too often punctuated by tableaus in imitation of temple friezes. The production was to mark the debut of Germaine Lubin, a French dramatic soprano, a Wagnerian, and a great favorite of Hitler's. Before the war she sang frequently in Germany; during the occupation she maintained close contacts with the Reich. There is ample reason to doubt the candor of her apology, received by Johnson just two months before the premiere of *Alceste*: "I am heartbroken that it is impossible for me for the moment to leave occupied France. Let me hope I will be able to sing at the Metropolitan Opera next season" (*Times*, Jan. 4, 1941). That opportunity lost, there would not be another. Marjorie

Lawrence was the obvious replacement. Lawrence's early career had been based in Paris, where she and Lubin had often shared roles. In Virgil Thomson's view, the Australian singer made a decidedly inferior Alceste *(Herald Tribune)*. Rose Bampton stepped in for the indisposed Lawrence in the Saturday broadcast. Bampton makes a strong effect when her beautiful middle register is allowed to shine. But her soprano voice, rebuilt from its contralto origins, has deficits at both ends of the scale, particularly glaring in the score's best-known aria, "Divinités du Styx." And lacking sufficient breath to fill out the long phrases with composure, Bampton often comes under stress. Panizza's direction propels the many scenes of sorrow with welcome energy, and sets bracing tempos for the extended dance sequences. Below average box-office receipts and tepid critical reaction dashed hopes for the rapid return of *Alceste*. Gluck's demand for a true dramatic soprano was satisfied at the opera's revival in 1952, in English, for Flagstad's farewell and, again in English, for the long-overdue debut of Eileen Farrell in 1960.

### *Don Giovanni:* March 7, 1942

In 1929, after a lapse of two decades, Don Giovanni resumed his amorous pursuits along Broadway. From then on, Mozart's *dramma giocoso* would stray no more. In the March 1942 broadcast, Kipnis's Leporello, inflected by his dark Russian bass, is maddeningly faulty in diction and rhythm; Charles Kullman, the Ottavio, takes extra breaths in key phrases; Novotna's Elvira is stretched to the limit of her agility and range. Bampton is a secure and incisive Anna, Sayão a refreshingly brazen Zerlina. Pinza's Giovanni is a memorable match of artist and role, and undoubtedly the enduring foundation for the opera's popularity at the Met. In fourteen seasons over the span of twenty years, he sang virtually all of the many performances of the work. Under Walter's direction, the crackling recitatives, passionate arias, and propulsive ensembles of the 1942 broadcast cohere to mark a theatrical event far greater than the sum of its not always perfect parts.

### *Die Zauberflöte (The Magic Flute):* December 26, 1942

Revived for the first time since 1926, this English-language *Die Zauberflöte* captured the audience once and for all. Rychtarik's sets combined "the baroque atmosphere of Mozart's period, the fantastic Egyptian locale of the action and the significance of the drama as a progress from darkness to light."

Taubman viewed the concept as "sensitive and tasteful" (*Times,* Dec. 12, 1941), Thomson as "dignified, fanciful, and tasty" *(Herald Tribune);* Douglas Watts carped at the "endless changes of scenes" *(News).* The principals of the broadcast of the following December are an inconsistent lot. Josephine Antoine is a Queen of the Night without an F above high C. Kullman, the Tamino, produces a weak and bleaty top. At times, Novotna's affecting Pamina finds herself short of breath and obliged to strain for her highest notes; still, she delivers the dialogue not as an opera singer forced to speak, but as an accomplished actress. Brownlee puts over Papageno's antics in diction so crisp that, for once, the audience gets the jokes. In a heavy Italian accent, and sometimes not quite in the center of the pitch, Pinza floods the listener with the depth and breadth of his voice. In the end, it is Walter who lifts the proceedings to their lofty plane. Without loss to the singspiel's humor, the themes of virtue and love emerge transcendent.[18]

### *Pelléas et Mélisande:* January 13, 1945

On January 26, 1944, after a brief hiatus, *Pelléas et Mélisande* returned to the repertoire with the debut of conductor Emil Cooper. Cooper's unorthodox treatment, where overpowering emotions were given their due, prompted Thomson to declare, "The whole musical fabric, vocal as well as instrumental, becomes . . . as straightforward and sincere an expression as anyone can well imagine, and far more so than we are accustomed to hear in the theater" (*Herald Tribune,* Jan. 4, 1945). The broadcast of January 13 bears out Thomson's judgment. Cooper frees the work from the mist in which it had been shrouded. And although Sayão dwells, of necessity, in her weak lower octave, and Tibbett struggles against high notes and dull tone, and Kipnis drenches the French text in Russian phonemes, all three extract vivid characters from Maeterlinck's murky symbolism. Martial Singher, having wrested the role for the first time in Met history from the tenors for whom it was scored, is largely successful in negotiating passages outside his range. He makes a compelling case for a baritone Pelléas. But Debussy's opera remained a difficult sell.

### *Die Entführung aus dem Serail (The Abduction from the Seraglio):* January 18, 1947

With the success of *Don Giovanni, Le Nozze di Figaro,* and *Die Zauberflöte,* Johnson set about increasing Mozart's share of the repertoire even further.

He next programmed *Die Entführung aus dem Serail,* again in a Ruth and Thomas Martin translation. Cooper was the conductor of the November 29, 1946, premiere. Designer Donald Oenslager and director Herbert Graf sought to shore up the opera's appeal by adding "variety and movement" to the spectacle with scene changes of their own invention. Inspired by Persian miniatures, Oenslager filled the stage with intricately decorated structural elements in flattened perspective. Most reviewers were well disposed to the décor and far less to the singing and acting. Five poorly attended shows following on mixed notices would banish the title for more than thirty years. Eleanor Steber, the Constanze, may well have been underpowered in the house, as first-night critics commented. As heard in the January 1947 broadcast, she invests "Deepest sorrow [Traurigkeit]" and "Tortures unabating [Martern aller Arten]"—tests of legato singing and coloratura dexterity, often at the extremes of the range—with delicacy, accuracy, and, when needed, thrust.[19]

### *Falstaff:* February 26, 1949

All split-second changes of rhythm and dynamics and intricate ensembles, *Falstaff* cries out for a virtuoso conductor. It found one in Beecham, who led the 1944 revival. Reviewers were critical of the English translation, cited both Tibbett's impoverished vocal resources and his theatrical savvy, and above all cheered the "brilliantly paced" leadership of Beecham (Thomson, *Herald Tribune,* Jan. 15) and "the playing of the orchestra, which was crisp, full of color, or jocular allusion and lyrical warmth" (Downes, *Times*). Three years later, there was serious, ultimately futile talk of inveigling Toscanini back to the Met for Verdi's comic masterpiece. But in 1949, it was Reiner's turn. Leonard Warren in the title role is only one of the treasures of the broadcast. Cloe Elmo thunders Dame Quickly's hilarious repetitions of "reverenza," Giuseppe Valdengo plumbs the depth of Ford's bitter jealousy, Giuseppe Di Stefano lends his freshest tenor to Fenton's puppy love, and Regina Resnik animates the proceedings with her fleet, funny, and luminous Alice. Only Licia Albanese, unable to float high pianissimos at less than mezzo forte, is mismatched as Nannetta. Reiner's baton forges a precise yet playful *Falstaff.* Referring back to the conductor's triumphant Met debut just weeks before in *Salome,* Cecil Smith wrote that "his transfiguration of the *Falstaff* music demonstrated almost more strikingly how much we miss when we do not hear great operatic music conducted by a great craftsman." Still reluctant to succumb to the mercurial Verdi of his final opera, audiences hovered just

below the box-office average for the three-performance run of this exceptional edition, confirming again that the operatic monuments superlatively
conducted do not necessarily make for capacity houses.[20]

In 1945, Johnson signed a two-year renewal of his contract; at its expiration,
he was continued for two more seasons and then for another. The last extension was accompanied by the announcement that the general manager would
be leaving at the end of 1949–50. He may have talked of resigning once too
often. The board had been distressed at the red ink on the 1947–48 ledger and
had grown increasingly weary of his labor troubles and bad humor. Fifteen
years was decidedly enough. Johnson's gala farewell, February 28, 1950, featured two of the company's biggest postwar stars, Ljuba Welitsch as a tempes-
tuous Tosca and Ferruccio Tagliavini as a lyric Mario. In the pageant that
crowned the evening, a review of the Johnson era, Bori paraded as Violetta
and De Luca as Germont, Martinelli as Otello and Tibbett as Iago, Steber as
the Marschallin, Frederick Jagel as Peter Grimes, Blanche Thebom as Ortrud,
Schorr as Hans Sachs, and Set Svanholm as Lohengrin, decked out in the very
costume Johnson had worn in Italy more than thirty years earlier.[21]

The next month, during an intermission of the final Saturday broadcast of
the season, the outgoing head spoke directly to the audiences sitting in the
hall and by their radios: "You know how often I have told you that my greatest pride in my tenure in office here has been to give the American singer, the
American artist, his chance in opera." If Americanization was axiomatic to
Johnson's regime beginning in 1935, by 1939 it was as much a matter of necessity as of principle. In May 1942, he told his board, "The day is gone for an
operatic manager to have any such surprise [as the withdrawal of so many
performers who had been contracted] in store. His function is undergoing an
inevitable transition from the purveyance of established foreign success to
the discovery and development of native talent." The company's future would
depend on a gifted and well-trained cadre of national singers. Two years later,
with "reconversion . . . in the air," Johnson wrote that the curtain would rise
on "what is predominantly an American opera company," the goal toward
which the Met had tended since his appointment under the Juilliard standard. That fall, "nearly two-thirds of the singing personnel [had] been actually
born in this country." America would soon move from "importer of talent"

to "producer of talent" and ultimately to "exporter of talent" (*Times,* Nov. 26, 1944).[22]

Johnson had gotten ahead of himself. In his Met of the 1940s, new American stars, however lustrous, were insufficiently numerous to compensate for the European deficit. Veterans were kept on when their best days were clearly behind them: Schorr was drafted for Wotans he no longer wished to sing, Rethberg for the *Siegfried* Brünnhilde, a role she should no longer have assumed. Martin Mayer argues another point, that "the frequency with which light-voiced people sang heavy roles—and heavy-voiced people lumbered through light ones—became distressing, quite apart from more subtle questions of whether artists and roles fitted together in temperament or style." Risë Stevens's high mezzo was pressed into service for the contralto pronouncements of Erda. Astrid Varnay's dramatic soprano was mismatched with Eva's lyric lines in *Die Meistersinger.* And then there were those who made debuts with little or no experience. Irving Kolodin, in his epilogue to the Johnson era, questions "the wisdom of allowing young singers with no more than a textbook knowledge of their subject the freedom of a stage traditionally the object of a lifetime's progress. . . . What should have been the tolerable exception became numbingly regular in a flighty, planless, artistically arbitrary shuffling about of personnel." Seventeen years old in 1943, Patrice Munsel was too green for the full battery of coloratura trials to which she was subjected. If Varnay and Regina Resnik, both in their very early twenties, passed their Met initiations with flying colors, there was a price to pay. In her debut season, 1941–42, four Wagnerian roles she had never before sung on any stage drained the bloom from Varnay's voice; she nevertheless prevailed magnificently as Isolde and Brünnhilde through much of her lengthy career. On December 6, 1944, Resnik bowed as the *Trovatore* Leonora, and in less than two weeks added Santuzza and Aïda; the breakneck schedule may have shortened her days as a dramatic soprano but it did not inhibit her subsequent evolution into the dramatic mezzo she would inevitably become.[23]

In his 1949 critique, Virgil Thomson had taken a tack different from the later Kolodin and Mayer analyses. Thomson charged that the Johnson administration had pandered to the low common denominator of audience preference, and that it had tolerated poorly staged and unevenly sung variations of the tried and true. What most galled Thomson was that the management had shunned "experienced musicians and opera lovers" on the one hand, and the critical establishment on the other. His fusillade aimed directly at what he termed "a pure box-office credo," a "renunciation of the education function" for which, he added spitefully, the hard-won tax exemption should be revoked (*Herald Tribune,* Jan. 30, 1949).

If, in this period of intense financial pressures and labor conflicts, the eye of the management was fixed on the bottom line, and too much of the programming was consigned to the chestnuts—Johnson's "perennial favorites"— and too little to new works, it was also an era in which monuments flourished, and Mozart, in particular, took his rightful place. As Johnson had prognosticated in late 1940, the war would present the Metropolitan with both opportunity and challenge. The fundamental challenge was to keep the operation afloat, a precarious feat even with the expert assistance of Edward Ziegler, and more difficult still once Ziegler withdrew for reasons of health in 1946. Kolodin, Mayer, and Thomson focus on the challenges. We have sought to stress the opportunities Johnson seized: the engagement of eminent European conductors and the presentation of neglected masterworks.

# SEVEN

# *Stage Business, 1950–1966*

## VERDI

### RUDOLF BING

### Advent

RUDOLF BING TELLS THE STORY of his appointment as the new general manager in the first of two autobiographies, *5000 Nights at the Opera*. In spring 1949, then head at Glyndebourne, he was in New York to pitch a season for his company at Princeton University's McCarter Theatre. He asked Fritz Stiedry, a Met conductor he had known in Germany in the early 1930s, to introduce him to Edward Johnson, whose retirement at the end of the 1949–50 season had been announced. The conversation with Johnson turned to the running of an opera house in difficult times. As Bing recounts it, Johnson suddenly asked, "How would you like to be my successor?" Bing responded that he would like it very much indeed, upon which Johnson, a supporter of his righthand man Frank St. Leger, Edward Ziegler's replacement, proceeded to mention Bing to George Sloan, chairman of the Metropolitan Opera board. Satisfied that Bing was "socially acceptable," Sloan introduced him to Charles M. Spofford, who certified that Bing was "sufficiently art-minded," and to David Sarnoff, who vouched for his business creds. Meanwhile, visiting in England, Eleanor Belmont made inquiries about Bing's management of Glyndebourne and of the Edinburgh Festival. Her glowing report was read aloud to the executive committee and Bing returned to Europe to await word from New York.[1]

Only weeks after his chat with Johnson, on June 2, 1949, Bing was named general manager at an annual salary of $35,000, raised from $30,000 when the negotiated three-year contract was cut back to a single year in compliance with immigration rules. Bing was asked (it may have been he who asked) to spend the 1949–50 season at the Met as a paid observer. With his wife and dog, he moved into the Essex House on Central Park South, and there took up residence for the twenty-two years he was at the Met, and then until his wife's death in 1983. The fly in the ointment was John Erskine, once again an aggressive advocate for an American at the top. Erskine held Mrs. Belmont responsible for the anointment of the European intendant: "For the first time in Metropolitan history the general manager has now been chosen not by the men of the Opera board but by the ladies of the Opera Guild." He doubted that Mrs. Belmont and Mrs. Otto Kahn "are competent to choose, or are even willing to choose, an American for a general manager if such a person exists." Belmont pushed back. She protested that those charged with the search had done their due diligence with respect to both American and European candidates, and that in any case it was Johnson who had brought Bing to the attention of the directors. She was particularly incensed at the suggestion that the "ladies" had violated the Guild's policy of noninterference in the affairs of the company.[2]

## Vienna to Edinburgh

The new general manager was born Rudolph Franz Joseph Bing in Vienna in 1902 to a prosperous Jewish family. He was not a particularly promising student, and did not go to university. He had had English governesses, had studied voice, and had a year of training in history, the arts, and literature under the guidance of a tutor who introduced him into Vienna's artistic circles. With the collapse of the Austro-Hungarian Empire in 1918, Bing's industrialist father, chairman of the Austro-Hungarian Steel and Iron Trust, lost his position and fortune. Bing took modest jobs in bookstores, one of which had a sideline in concert management; there he organized the opera division. In 1928, he married a Russian ballet dancer, Nina Schelemskaya-Schelesnaya, and moved to Berlin, where he booked singers for provincial theaters. His break came that same year when he was made assistant to Carl Ebert, a stage director then head of opera in Darmstadt. Ebert left much of the programming to Bing. It was in Darmstadt that he met conductors Karl Böhm and Max Rudolf, later his Met artistic administrator. In 1931, Bing moved with Ebert to Berlin's Charlottenburg Opera and was there exposed to avant-garde production.[3]

In 1933, after the expulsion of anti-Nazis from German theaters, Bing left for Vienna and then for Teplitz in the Sudetenland, where the National

Socialists had embarked on the misbegotten promotion of German culture. In a matter of months, the enterprise, bizarrely staffed by numerous Jews and Social Democrats, folded. In 1934, Bing joined Ebert and Fritz Busch at Glyndebourne. By 1935, he was the festival's general manager. Five years later, the war shut Glyndebourne's doors. Bing took a job as sales manager in a London department store; by night, he volunteered as a fire warden. The war over, he returned to Glyndebourne for its 1946 reopening. In the interim, Bing was active in founding the Edinburgh Festival and, from 1946 until 1949, served as artistic director, the first time he held that title.

"You don't need wit to run an opera house, you need style," Bing quipped in *A Knight at the Opera,* the second of his autobiographies. In fact, he had great gobs of both. The "men of the Opera board" were quick to take in his elegance, his worldly manner, his polished speech. But the style that won them over was as much managerial as it was personal. They were seeking a much needed antidote to the Johnson regime. Where Johnson was indulgent, particularly toward singers, Bing would demand discipline; where Johnson had little patience with planning, Bing was unremittingly farsighted; where Johnson oversaw the day-to-day operation of the house from a distance, Bing was an unapologetic micromanager. His words and deeds during the 1949–50 preparatory season seemed to vindicate those who had engineered the unorthodox search. They had hired a character tough enough for what Joe Volpe would later call "the toughest job on Earth." The trains would once again, as not since Gatti-Casazza, run on time.

### Preparatory Season, 1949–1950

From his office at the other end of the building, a sign of the ever widening divide between the sitting general manager and the general manager–elect, Bing was nevertheless able to witness operations at close hand, scrutinize contracts and other documents, and plan obsessively. Johnson's last season barely at midpoint, he insisted on putting his frank analysis of current practice before the board, securing the go-ahead for his agenda, and then making it as public as possible. In his report to the directors of January 27, 1950, Bing proposed the rehabilitation of the house, of course, and nodded vaguely toward the prospect of a new theater. He suggested revised strategies for fundraising and a crusade for the retraction of the 20 percent admissions tax reinstated during the war. He recommended that the Saturday subscription be pegged not at popular but at regular prices and modifications to the

FIGURE 24. Bust of Giulio Gatti-Casazza between Edward Johnson on left, and Rudolf Bing, 1950 (Louis Mélançon; courtesy Metropolitan Opera Archives)

Philadelphia schedule. Most intriguing was the idea of splitting each subscription series into two, doubling their number from six to twelve and thereby attracting a fresh cohort of subscribers. The same opera could be scheduled twice as often, reducing the twenty-six productions on the calendar each season to eighteen or nineteen, effecting considerable savings, and allowing more rehearsal time. He also put on the table the reengagement of Kirsten Flagstad; the motion passed with one dissension.

The press conference of February 1, 1950, was called over Johnson's objections. Bing began by reviewing the actions approved a few days earlier. There would be changes in the upper management. He would be assisted by Reginald Allen, the executive secretary who would handle business matters; by Max Rudolf, who would replace St. Leger, his former boss, and hold the title of artistic administrator; by Francis Robinson, currently tour director, who would reorganize the box office and subscriptions; and by John Gutman, who would join the team as general artistic assistant. Bing knew full well that uppermost in the minds of reporters was word on the artists he was inclined to retain and, of more interest still, on those he would not bring back. He released a list of fifteen singers he had thus far signed. Melchior was not among them. The tenor had had the bad form to demand that the Met decide within forty minutes whether he would be kept on. Bing declared himself "not prepared to submit to ultimatums. I don't care from whom." Melchior did not return. Bing went on to assure the press that he would "go all out to find more American singers" and to further their careers. Of course, he hedged, this "must be a cosmopolitan opera house." Finally, he broke the news of Flagstad's reengagement, adding, "if there is any shooting, shoot at me." He reported further that Helen Traubel, who had threatened to quit when by January she had not been signed, and who had complained loudly that she had been ignored in favor of Flagstad, would share the Wagnerian roles with her Norwegian rival. They would sing one "Ring" each. As for himself, "Apart from murder, there is hardly any crime I am not suspected of. I can assure you I will attempt to run this house—unmoved by promises or threats—on the principle of quality alone."[4]

That was just the beginning. Bing's brushes with singers continued through the winter, spring, and summer of 1950 and well beyond. On February 8, he received a letter from the Brazilian ambassador pleading on behalf of Bidú Sayão; she was granted two performances for the diplomat's trouble. Bing told Lawrence Tibbett that he would not be re-signed, citing the curtailed repertory. In fact, Bing considered Tibbett over the hill, as he did Sayão and Melchior. The problem with Leonard Warren was not his merits as a singer, but Bing's fixation on "loyalty." "We want an ensemble, an ensemble of stars—not of comets." Bing had discovered that Warren was accorded an annual midseason hiatus of several weeks to accommodate lucrative concert gigs. When Warren balked at the repeal of this concession, Bing put out the word that the baritone had been let go. Max Rudolf intervened and Warren capitulated, but too late for opening night. A year or so later, Robert Merrill, Warren's replacement as Rodrigo in the inaugural *Don Carlo,* found himself writing a letter of apology to the general manager for skipping out on the 1951 spring tour; he had decamped for Hollywood to shoot the better-forgotten *Aaron Slick from Punkin Creek.* Bing replied that all was forgiven. Still, the 1951–52 season was essentially lost to Merrill. Where Met stars were concerned, Bing had no more use for cabarets than he had for the movies. He wrote to the irrepressible Traubel on September 25,

1953, that the Met and night clubs "do not really seem to mix very well. Perhaps you would prefer to give the Metropolitan a 'miss' for a single year or so until you may possibly feel that you want again to change back to the more serious aspects of your art." Traubel published Bing's letter and her response, along with a shot across the bow accusing Bing of "rank snobbery" (Sept. 28, 1953). Bing's counterattack no doubt dissuaded others from crossing the line: "Miss Traubel used this affair for cheap and vulgar publicity purposes playing on the chauvinistic instincts of the mob by emphasizing over and over in her letter her admiration for the great American folk music, for the great American composers.... [Miss Traubel's outburst in the press] has everything to do with an artist who is clearly declining in her art and is looking for other and more lucrative fields and, therefore, needs any amount of publicity.... For the last two or three years high parts, both in *Tristan* and *Walküre* had to be transposed and the management of the Metropolitan had difficulty in persuading responsible conductors to accept this arrangement which is unworthy of one of the world's leading opera houses." Traubel never again sang at the Met.[5]

When it came to conductors, Bing set about cleaning house even more thoroughly. Only Reiner and Stiedry were held over from 1949–50. He brought in Kurt Adler, Fausto Cleva, Alberto Erede, and Tibor Kozma, a crew generally thought no stronger than the one he had unloaded. Still, with one key variant, he took up the cause of the illustrious conductor. But where Johnson sought to enlist notable guests for star turns, Bing was intent on a celebrated maestro whose primary commitment of energy—and loyalty, naturally,—would be to the Metropolitan. At the same time, he was opposed to ceding authority to a music director and quick to call on tradition in support of his position. The company had had official and de facto principal conductors—Seidl, Mahler, Toscanini, Bodanzky, Serafin, and Panizza—but never a music director. Bing tried first to recruit Erich Kleiber with assurances that the absence of the coveted title would not prevent his input from counting in all important matters. Kleiber declined and, through his wife, suggested that either Georges Sébastian, Hans Schmidt-Isserstedt, or Robert Denzler be approached, recommendations that Bing dismissed with what was even for him unusual bite. Of Denzler, in particular, he remarked that "he is a mediocre conductor but was an outstanding Nazi. I am only prepared to consider the opposite: a mediocre Nazi who is an outstanding conductor."[6]

The next year, Bing surveyed the field for what he termed a "conductor-personality of an even higher rank than we have now." Bruno Walter was ideal but too old, Erich Kleiber, to whom he returned in spite of the earlier rejection, "personally a highly undesirable gentleman, although a brilliant conductor," and in any case out of the running since he had thrown in his lot with the Soviets. Victor De Sabata was brilliant but difficult and unreliable. "Of the younger set there is Herbert von Karajan who was a real Nazi and whom I, personally, would not propose to invite mainly for that reason." (Bing would relent and invite Karajan for 1967–68.) That left Wilhelm Furtwängler, who had held a high position under the Third Reich as conductor of the Berlin Philharmonic. It may have been he Bing had in mind as the outstanding maestro who had been a mediocre Nazi. "After all we did get away with Flagstad without any real difficulty" was the way Bing phrased it. At an October 25, 1951, confidential meeting of the production committee, Bing proposed Furtwängler for the 1952–53 season. The executive committee turned him down two weeks later. Bing made a second attempt for the 1954–55 season. But Furtwängler eluded Bing; he died in December 1954. That same year, Dimitri Mitropoulos joined the company as the "conductor-personality" for whom Bing had been hoping. With his appointment, the conductor's era inaugurated with Bruno Walter's 1941 *Fidelio* was perpetuated. Before his tenure was over, in addition to Mitropoulos and Karajan, Bing had brought to the Metropolitan, most for short stints to be sure, Pierre Monteux, Georg Solti, Ernest Ansermet, Leonard Bernstein, Colin Davis, Josef Krips, and Claudio Abbado.[7]

## 1950–1951

### *Don Carlo:* November 6

Between 1903 and 1949, Verdi had provided the music for nineteen of forty-seven Metropolitan opening nights. The familiar tunes of *Rigoletto, Aïda,* and *La Traviata* had rung in the regimes of Bing's three immediate predecessors, Conried, Gatti, and Johnson. Bing made the courageous choice of Verdi's *Don Carlo,* somber, uncommon fare for an audience out for a brilliant social occasion and expecting to face only modest musical demands. In its first round at the Met in the early 1920s, the opera had left the public cold. It had had just fourteen performances, despite the best efforts of Rosa Ponselle, Giovanni Martinelli, Giuseppe De Luca, and Adamo Didur. This earlier *Don Carlo* sold out only when the hugely popular Fyodor Chaliapin took on the role of King Philip. In the intervening decades, esteem for the lesser-known

Verdi had risen markedly in Europe, primarily in Germany. The Met itself offered up the stern beauties of *Simon Boccanegra* in seven seasons starting in 1932, including the year Bing had spent as observer.

The new general manager fitted *Don Carlo* with flourishes that signaled a break with the conservative bent of the previous administration. Opening night was detached from its hallowed place at the head of the chic Monday night subscription and sold at raised prices with the upcoming *Fledermaus* and the Flagstad-Walter *Fidelio* as one of a trio of special events. He chose as stage director Margaret Webster, whose revivals of Shakespeare in the 1940s were hits on Broadway: the *Othello* starring Paul Robeson is remembered to this day. Webster was the first woman to stage a Met production, and she had had no experience with opera. The press latched on to the story that the monumental sets were financed by Otto Kahn's children through the sale of a Rembrandt; Rolf Gérard's décor was the tallest ever built for the Metropolitan, designed "to open the proscenium frame vertically, contradicting its usual flat picture-postcard look." And there was more to report: opposition to the current separatist ferment in Belgium was angered by the libretto's sympathy for Flemish independence; Catholic groups objected to the graphic depiction of the Spanish Inquisition. An ongoing dispute between management and stagehands kept Bing's already newsworthy first night in the public eye.[8]

Some reviewers expressed reservations about the opera itself ("not the best work of the Italian master," "singularly powerful if uneven"). Others deplored the edition adopted by the Met, a reduced version of Verdi's 1884 revision of the five-act grand opéra he had composed for Paris in 1867. They were, however, unanimous in praise of the production, Webster's adroit handling of the demanding dramaturgy, and Gérard's moody depiction of sixteenth-century Spain. Bing had made clear that direction and design would distinguish his priorities from those of his predecessors. Virgil Thomson confirmed that with *Don Carlo* Bing had made good on that promise: "Attention to the visual aspect has long been the Met's most pressing need. With this put in order, the musical powers of the company are shown off to advantage. Let us be thankful" *(Herald Tribune)*. Rudolf Bing emerged as the star of the occasion.[9]

A nine-station hookup reached four million television sets and many more viewers, a substantial increase over transmissions of the two previous Met opening nights. Twelve cameras, one in the pit dedicated to close-ups of the singers, enhanced the telecast. The home audience had access to scene changes and intermission interviews, much as telespectators and Live in HD viewers have had since. Although recording technology was available, no kinescope copy of the November 6 telecast is known to exist; the extant audio portions of the evening are of poor quality. Happily, the very same musical forces were on hand for the Saturday, November 11 broadcast; it conveys the strengths and the few weaknesses that likely obtained at the Monday premiere. Communications from Alberto Erede to Bing, friends since their prewar Glyndebourne days, uncover the alternatives weighed in the *Don Carlo* casting. For Elisabetta, Erede preferred Renata Tebaldi to Delia Rigal; but, as bad luck would have it, Tebaldi was busy at the San Francisco Opera. Erede thought Boris Christoff the best King Philip of the day and Cesare Siepi a close second. But the McCarran Act, effective on September 23, 1950, held up permits for both the Bulgarian Christoff and the Italian Siepi. Christoff had been told that his appearance in a 1947 Rome concert sponsored by the Italian-Soviet Society was to blame (*Times,* June 7, 1951). In the end, it was the twenty-seven-year-old Siepi who was allowed entry. The splendid voice and artistry he displays in the broadcast earned him the berth of the Met's principal bass for twenty-two years. For Eboli, Erede rejected Ebe Stignani, the dominant Italian mezzo-soprano of her generation, because of her age and her girth, although he thought her "still *very good*"; he nominated Fedora Barbieri, not attractive either, in his estimation, but younger than Stignani, brimming with "personality," and "really first class." The broadcast preserves Barbieri's plush sound and authoritative manner. Occasionally rough but always ready, she is memorable as Eboli, as she would later be as Verdi's Azucena and Amneris, precarious high As and B-flats notwithstanding. Lucine Amara, as the off-stage Celestial Voice, launched her four-decade-long career. Two stalwarts of Johnson's time, Jussi Björling and Robert Merrill, played Carlo and Rodrigo, the tenor more engaged in the drama than was sometimes his wont, the baritone in gorgeous voice as always in this period, but here also sensitive to the musical line and the libretto's meanings. As for the newly minted general manager, he pronounced unabashedly that he had set "a new standard for operatic productions in America."[10]

Bing waited patiently for the public to catch on to Verdi's magisterial work. It did, and in 1956–57, its fifth reprise, *Don Carlo* finally exceeded the box-office average. Scheduled in more than half of the seasons between 1950 and 1966, and mounted in two new productions since, *Don Carlo* remains one of Bing's enduring legacies.

## Der Fliegende Holländer: November 9

For the second performance of the season, the Met unveiled its new *Der Fliegende Holländer*. The general manager went to the dean of Broadway scenic artists, Robert Edmond Jones, for the décors. Best known for his collaboration with Eugene O'Neill, Jones was credited, by his colleague Mordecai Gorelik, with founding "the whole present-day tradition of scene design in the United States." He fell ill and Charles Elson took over the construction and lighting of the sets. Sea cloth, scrim, and cloud projections conjured the pervasive force of nature so deeply embedded in Wagner's score. "When the curtain rose, the audience burst into applause, for it was clear that the reforms in staging revealed in the [first] night performance of Verdi's *Don Carlo* were being continued in the Wagner opera." Ljuba Welitsch, without whom, as Bing confessed, he would not have revived this "unpopular work," was absent in the end. With his approval, the Bulgarian soprano, in ill health and no longer what she had been just the season before, relinquished all her Sentas to Astrid Varnay. Varnay's concentration and musical probity, as heard in the December 30 broadcast, together with a rich middle register, are a match for Hans Hotter's Dutchman. His dark timbre becomes the vehicle of despair and longing, his attention to text the mark of a great lieder singer. The Met orchestra is as alert to Reiner's light manner for the folk rhythms as it is to his expansive phrasing of the opera's Sturm und Drang. And yet the box-office average for *Der Fliegende Holländer* was the lowest of the season. Downes and Thomson tempered their enthusiasm for the November 9 performance with, "[Hotter's] interpretation was greater than the music that Wagner could give him in this early romantic score" *(Times)*, and "It is an intimate subject and perhaps not properly a grand opera at all" *(Herald Tribune)*. It would be nine years before the Dutchman again dropped anchor at the Met.[11]

## Fledermaus: December 20

Bing made no mystery of the profit motive behind his third new production. He banked on the wide and lasting appeal of Johann Strauss's *Fledermaus*, gussied up with new English lyrics by Hollywood's Howard Dietz and an adapted libretto staged by its author, Broadway's Garson Kanin. *Fledermaus* was the story of the season. It all began in spring 1950 when Johnson, smarting at the preemptive announcements of his successor's grand plans and other offenses, took aim at the scheduling of so many "Fleder-Mice," and more generally, at the decision to present an operetta, particularly one that had recently had a Broadway run. Bing's penchant for publicity raised other eyebrows. How real were the overtures to Danny Kaye for the speaking role of Frosch when it was obvious that the high-priced comedian would not, or could not, commit to twenty or so performances scattered over an opera season? And then there were the well-placed rumors of famous runners-up: Bobby Clark, Fred Allen, and Buster Keaton. The part would go to the lesser-known Jack Gilford.[12]

Of more consequence to the *Fledermaus* saga was the jockeying for position of the foremost classical music labels, Columbia and RCA Victor. No sooner had Columbia agreed to issue complete operas under the Met's imprint, and with its soloists, chorus, and orchestra, than RCA announced that it, too, would produce opera recordings featuring Met artists with whom it had exclusive contracts. The division of the talent pool generated atypical casts: Eleanor Steber, for example, is Columbia's 1949 *Madama Butterfly,* a role she never sang (more's the pity!) on 39th Street; Risë Stevens's Don José in RCA's 1951 *Carmen* is Jan Peerce, who never set foot in the company's dilapidated Seville. Fritz Reiner, the conductor designated for the Met's *Fledermaus,* left Columbia for RCA in summer 1950 and did not see why "Mr. Bing should be unhappy because this [RCA] recording does not concern the Metropolitan." By September, RCA had beaten Columbia to the punch; *Fledermaus* excerpts, led by Reiner, in the Ruth and Thomas Martin translation, were ready for editing. Just after the start of rehearsals late that fall, Eugene Ormandy, music director of the Philadelphia Orchestra, was summoned to replace the rebellious Reiner in the Met's *Fledermaus;* Beecham, Bing's first choice, was unavailable. RCA took out space in the Met's playbills to advertise "Hilarious hit of the 'Met' season … sung (in English) by a cast of great Metropolitan opera voices, Fritz Reiner of the 'Met' conducting." Not to be bested in the corporate tug-of-war, two months later, Columbia emblazoned the names of Lily Pons, the Adele, and Martha Lipton, the Orlofsky, on its album, along with those of "other members of the Original Cast." Neither Pons nor Lipton ever appeared in *Fledermaus* at the Met. Both recordings are hybrids, both feature singers associated with their Met roles, and others recruited for the purpose from the Met roster and elsewhere.[13]

The December 20 first night of *Fledermaus* convinced even jaded observers that all the ado had been about something. Gérard's bright-yellow drawing room for the Eisensteins, a crimson tent for Orlofsky's ballroom, a cheerful blue jail for the final act, and a stageful of bustles, feathers, opera capes, and top hats evoked pleasure-loving Austria in the 1870s. Dietz's lyrics were modern, sometimes clever, and, by 1950 standards, just a tad naughty: "It's nice to have a wife 'round the house, as long as she's not your own"; "the gesture that seems to arouse the ubiquitous male is the swing of my tail." The Met's *Fledermaus* was dubbed a big Broadway hit, just as Bing had intended: "If it could be put on for eight performances a week it would be serious competition for *Guys and Dolls* and *South Pacific*"; "With it Rudolf Bing reestablishes the fact that the Metropolitan Opera has a Broadway address." That first night can be reconstructed by meshing the Columbia recording cut a week later and the January 20 broadcast. Risë Stevens and Richard Tucker sang on both the recording and the broadcast, Ljuba Welitsch on the recording and not the broadcast, and Patrice Munsel on the broadcast and not the recording. The principals are up to the task, Tucker at once plangent and hilarious in his send-up of the vain tenor, Welitsch virtually unintelligible in English yet a glamorous Rosalinde at home in the style of her adopted Vienna. Patrice Munsel deserves the consensus that she stole the show; she transforms the insufferable soubrette into an amiable character.[14]

*Fledermaus* continued to sell out the following season. Bing was eager to capitalize on the craze, once heartlessly by plucking the sixty-three-year-old Maria Jeritza out of semiretirement for Rosalinde in a benefit performance (Feb. 22, 1951). Munsel recalled the discomfiture of the soprano, absent from the Met since 1932 and at sea in the unfamiliar translation and staging. She also recalled the sardonic general manager standing in the wings, "laughing hysterically and eating his usual banana." Confident of the marketability of the Strauss operetta, Bing encouraged the North American tour of a *Fledermaus* troupe. For the first and last time, the Met was on the road with a single work, bankrolled through an interest-free loan from Columbia Records, cast for the most part with singers not on the regular roster. The caravan was scheduled to travel for thirty weeks. Its bumpy trek would come to a premature end. For one thing, a month after its September 1951 Philadelphia opening, a rival troupe, performing the Ruth and Thomas Martin translation, managed by Sol Hurok and the National Concert and Artists Corporation, began its own itinerary in Hartford. Then there was the patriotic wrath of an American Legion post that objected to the presence of alleged Communist sympathizer Jack Gilford. The Met stood up for its

Frosch and the show went on, despite the picketing protesters. Misfortune persisted: tenor Donald Dame, one of the Eisensteins, died suddenly in his Lincoln, Nebraska hotel room just before a performance. The coup de grâce was the box office. The eagerly awaited turnaround in Chicago failed to materialize and the misadventure came to a merciful halt in Minneapolis in February 1952. Columbia Records had overestimated America's appetite for Viennese operetta. The New York public remained loyal to Bing's *Fledermaus* for ten of his sixteen seasons at the old Met.[15]

### *Cavalleria rusticana* and *Pagliacci:* January 17

On December 6, a month after opening night, the company announced that *Don Carlo* and *Der Fliegende Holländer* had come in under budget; the savings would underwrite a new *Cav/Pag* for later that season. Bing tapped Fritz Busch's son Hans, on the faculty of Indiana University, for *Cavalleria rusticana,* Max Leavitt, the director of Greenwich Village's intimate Lemonade Opera, for *Pagliacci,* and Horace Armistead, who had designed the "Broadway operas" of Gian-Carlo Menotti and Marc Blitzstein, for both. Busch set Mascagni's one-acter in the present to, as he put it, strip it of "meaningless routine." For *Pagliacci,* Armistead adopted a more radical scheme. He leeched the surrealism of his oil paintings onto a Calabrian village reduced to a bare central platform and tracings of withered trees flanked by crumbling buildings. In retrospect, *Cavalleria rusticana*'s contemporary southern hill town reflects only a timid departure from tradition. By contrast, *Pagliacci*'s minimalist platform and flats define an authentically experimental playing space. But audiences were accustomed neither to experimental stagings nor to marginal productions, and many agreed with Bruno Walter that these reinterpretations betrayed their penny-pinching allocations. Belatedly, Bing himself called *Cav/Pag* "a bargain-basement, inadequate production." The two together had cost a paltry $22,401. In his near-Brechtian construct, Leavitt sought to "find symbols to express [the opera's] vitality in terms of our own day." As for his principals, Ramon Vinay (Canio), Rigal (Nedda), and Warren (Tonio), the baritone alone delivered Leoncavallo's vocal goods, no surprise to those who owned recordings of Warren's "Prologo." Zinka Milanov, the Santuzza, was, and would always be, imperturbably of the stand-and-sing school of operatic plastique; Tucker responded to the director's cues, projecting a Turiddu variously callous and moving. The March 31, 1951, broadcast of *Cavalleria rusticana* preserves

FIGURE 25. *Cavalleria rusticana,* Zinka Milanov as Santuzza in foreground, 1950 (Sedge Leblang; courtesy Metropolitan Opera Archives)

Milanov and Tucker in peak form, their duet a marvel of technical security, refulgent tone, and passionate expression.[16]

The invectives hurled at the sets and stagings by Olin Downes in the *Times* and Virgil Thomson in the *Herald Tribune* drowned out the raves of the *Journal-American* and *Daily News* and the mixed notices of the *Post* and the *Brooklyn Eagle.* But more significant than the critical response was the controversy that ensued, as alive today as then. The rereadings of *Cavalleria rusticana* and *Pagliacci* called into question for the first time in Met history the legitimacy of altering the temporal, spatial, or cultural framework of pillars of the repertory. Ironically, the counterattacks on Downes and Thomson were invited by the reviewers themselves. In trashing Armistead et al., the two powerful journalists positioned themselves as conservatives, Downes in appropriating the label of "poor old moss-back," and Thomson by moving from the particular of this *Cav/Pag* to the general issue of reinterpretation: "Modernizing operas like these is not a rewarding effort. They are rigid; they have a style of their own; they do not lend themselves to indirection, to added poetry, and intellectual embellishment." To his credit, Downes engaged with those who disagreed with him. He devoted three columns to the question, first countering a young operagoer who complained that "Rudolf Bing's slightest variation from any time-honored methods of dramatizing these operas has been belabored by the traditionalists as heresy" (Jan. 28), then quoting reader responses, pro and con (Feb. 4), and finally quarreling over the distinction between "tradition" and "routine" with playwright Robert E. Sherwood (Feb. 11).

The debate surrounding *Cavalleria rusticana* and *Pagliacci* touched off what would become a perpetual state of war between Bing and the critics. According to Martin Mayer, who worked closely with Bing on *5000 Nights at the Opera*, "The aftermath of this brief squall would plague Bing through the entire twenty-two years of his administration, for the violent defense of the new *Cav* and *Pag* cast doubt both on his taste and on his judgment." That defense took the form of an assault on the critics themselves. One of his more moderate refutations of what one writer called the "critical wrath" aimed at *Cav/Pag* went as follows: "Critics have the right to disapprove of single experiments, and I will not argue with them, since taste and judgment are involved, and these are personal. I will, however, argue vigorously their right to voice blanket disapproval of a general policy which is intended to vitalize opera production in New York." What the reviewers came most to resent was, as Mayer characterized it, Bing's misplaced sense of "cultural superiority to the press . . . shallowly rooted in his own personality and in traditional European attitudes toward America." The polemic on rereadings would pick up steam under Joseph Volpe and come to a head under Peter Gelb. Despite his early principled defense of deviations from past practice, with the possible exception of the *Faust* of 1953, Bing would not again tamper with beloved titles. And under his watch, this particular wrangle with the critics would not recur.[17]

## "VISUAL ASPECTS AND DRAMATIC INTERPRETATIONS"

When the books were closed on 1950–51, the company showed a loss of $462,000; the next year, despite increases in box-office receipts and donations, and the lifting of the admissions tax, the loss was $369,000. Board members vented their irritation at Bing's pricey new productions. The general manager went on the offensive, writing to Lowell Wadmond, the president of the board who had replaced Charles Spofford, "The Metropolitan Opera has had great conductors before my time, it has had great singers before my time, and in spite of all that it had fallen to a level when it ceased to be a theatre of great artistic interest and when, indeed, in the field of visual aspects and dramatic interpretations it had become rather obsolete" (March 24, 1952). In this same letter, Bing complained that he had requested five new productions each year, had been promised four, and was now left with the prospect of only three. He argued that the Metropolitan was in dire scenic disrepair "due to the war and perhaps for other reasons," that it had "now . . . to pay for the sins of the past." If the Met was to return to its former glory as "the world's leading opera house," it would have to operate at an "expensive level," although economically within that parameter. The "cheap level," whether economical or extravagant, was out of the question.[18]

Bing won the round with the support of Wadmond and Mrs. Belmont. He was not the first general manager, nor would he be the last, to champion the theatrical dimensions of opera. In one form or another, his precursors had done the same early in their own tenures. In 1883, Abbey's opulent new décors showed up Mapleson's tired sets. In 1884, Damrosch's German troupe was predicated on the primacy of the dramatic ensemble. In 1903, Conried staked his reputation on a spectacular production of *Parsifal*. Gatti-Casazza hired Broadway designers, Joseph Urban, Norman Bel Geddes, Jo Mielziner, and Robert Edmond Jones. Grau and Johnson were the exceptions. In Johnson's last five years, new productions numbered only ten, six excluding the 1947–48 "Ring," a record that made Bing's case. In his first five years, Bing would mount sixteen new productions.

## COMPETITORS AND CRITICS

By 1952, having stood up to three centers of power—stars, board members, and reviewers—Bing was ready to take on other comers. It was the turn of competitors, starting with the New York City Opera, rumored to be considering *Boris Godunov* (it did not happen) and *Der Rosenkavalier,* both on the Met bill for the season. Since its founding in 1943, City Opera had made its home at the former Shriner-built Mecca Temple a mile or so north of the Met at 55th Street between Sixth and Seventh Avenues. Bing evidently thought this incomparably more modest company dangerous enough to charge it with unfriendly, if not unfair, competition. The next year, City Opera requested that Richard Tucker be released to sing during its fall tour. Bing made this typical response: "It is just wrong in principle that the City Center should go out of New York and suddenly appear with the Metropolitan's leading artist. It does not seem to me dignified for the City Center and it certainly is not good for the Metropolitan." In 1954, Bing had a bone to pick with the equally "unfriendly" and moreover "uncommunicative" Chicago Lyric Opera. Chicago had invited top Met singers without consulting New York. Yet another grievance was voiced to officials as highly placed as the ambassador to Italy, Claire Booth Luce: La Scala's government subsidies, he wrote on April 2, 1953, and its tax-free cachets stacked the deck against the Met. Earlier that spring, he had written to the Italian Ministry of Foreign Affairs: "Not very long ago I had a meeting with Dott. Ghiringhelli [general manager of La Scala] at which I proposed that the leading opera houses of the world should collaborate and that the managements should . . . form a united front against artists who play one management against another." The tables had turned since 1908 when Gatti and Kahn had foiled an Italian–South American plot to keep artists away from New York and London. In 1921, strapped European intendants had pleaded that the Met refrain from luring already contracted singers with its much higher fees. These maneuvers, like Bing's, had come to naught.[19]

Bing found more cause to grumble. On January 21, 1953, he wrote indignantly to Wadmond that broadcast intermission features presented savants hostile to the Met, namely, the quizmaster Robert Lawrence, Deems Taylor, Boris Goldovsky, and George Marek. Marek was an executive at RCA Victor, rival of the Met's partner, Columbia Records, and therefore necessarily biased. Bing enclosed with his letter a clipping of a "stupid and uninformed" interview with Goldovsky (*Herald Tribune*, Jan. 18). In point of fact, the broadcast features were nothing if not benign. Bing was exercised not by on-air antagonism but by negative comments panelists had made elsewhere, the sort of reaction that led observers then and later to evoke "the familiar Bing paranoia." Enmities, eccentricities, and troubled waters notwithstanding, by the spring of 1953, Bing's reputation as a brilliant administrator had brought him the tempting offer to oversee opera in Berlin.[20]

Later that year, his beef was with *Opera News*. In correspondence with Eleanor Belmont (May 15), Bing rehearsed an argument he had brought against the intermission features: that the audience would not know that *Opera News* was independent of the Metropolitan and did not speak for its management. He assured her that no one more than he held dear the freedom of the press. However, a recent article in praise of Fritz Reiner, about to leave for the Chicago Symphony, had fomented discord in the orchestra. Tibor Kozma, Reiner's assistant and author of the piece, had written that the Metropolitan staff included both "professional" conductors, in the tradition of his mentor and, alas, "amateurs" too. Bing also objected to unflattering reviews in *Opera News* of books by Olin Downes and Irving Kolodin. Such critiques, he insisted, damaged the relationship between the management and the two journalists, friction the company could ill afford. The review of Kolodin's *The Story of the Metropolitan Opera, 1883–1950* was especially irksome. It railed in part, "No smallest item that might suggest intrigue, pettiness or personal self-seeking is omitted from the text. It is only necessary for an opera patron to show signs of wealth for Mr. Kolodin to assume that his generosity is either niggardly or bifarious. . . . Even in the accounts of the performances the author seems to relish failures more than successes." True, Kolodin's history is often cranky, and his contempt for wealth and social prominence undisguised. In his accounts of performances, he is prone to dwell on weaknesses. That he would offend some of the Met's oldest and best-heeled benefactors and their progeny was inevitable, and a matter of indifference neither to Bing nor to Belmont—but for different reasons. In her reply to Bing's complaint (May 18, 1953), Belmont asked (and answered) a question to which we will return in the last chapter: "When is *Opera News* a Metropolitan 'house organ' and when is it not a 'house organ'?" She was clear that in intramural matters the magazine should function as a house organ. And, in fact, *Opera News* had, for the most part, avoided "criticism" or "opposition," risking "dullness" and "whitewash." The Kozma article was "an error," she granted. But when it came to "extramural matters," such as book reviews, "more latitude [was] justified." In any case, both Downes and Kolodin understood fully the separation between the Guild, the sponsor of *Opera News,* and the company. They would certainly not, as Bing had asserted, place the blame on him. As to the Kolodin volume, she thought it full of "mistakes in fact, in judgment and in taste." The implication was that, given half a chance, she would have written the scathing review herself.[21]

## STANDEES AND CLAQUES

Of all the rifts of Bing's early years, none ran deeper than that which pitted the general manager against the standees. Bing made a point of confusing

FIGURE 26. The standee line at Maria Callas's Metropolitan debut, October 29, 1956 (authors' collection)

standees and claqueurs. He was, of course, fully aware that although most claqueurs were standees (they were issued free tickets in exchange for cheering on cue), most standees were not claqueurs (they were fans who had paid their way). Their drill consisted of waiting on line for hours, often in the cold of New York winters, before rushing in as the doors opened to grab their favorite spots on the perimeter of the orchestra floor or at the back and sides of the family circle. The standees knew the music, the singers, and when and what to applaud—or not.

The claque was a different matter. Originating in Paris in the early nineteenth century as a concession of managements to their stars, then making its way to other parts of Europe and to the United States, its existence as an unofficial operation had been an open secret at the Met since the 1890s. At the beginning of 1906–07, a season of mishap and scandal, a flurry of references to the claque made its way into the papers. Especially piquant was the item concerning the two hundred tickets Caruso distributed to excellent effect in the wake of his Central Park monkey-house conviction. Three days later, absent a claque, his entrance onto the Met stage was received with little fanfare; from then on, he bought fifty tickets for each of his performances. Four years later, an official claque was engaged by the Met management itself. The story goes that one day Gatti and tenor Alessandro Bonci were bemoaning the New York audience's ignorance of the protocols of applause. Bonci mentioned that he had just the knowledgeable man, his own valet, to initiate clapping at appropriate junctures. And so it was that Max Bennett was hired to organize the claque, and remained steadfastly at his post for decades. He was succeeded by his son, John, who labored noisily until 1935, when the newly appointed Edward Johnson refused to continue to foot the bill for the chief claqueur. Johnson went further, forbidding artists from passing out tickets to fans grateful to repay the debt with well-placed bravos. The *Times* speculated (Dec. 13, 1935) that prior to the interdiction, Bennett had pocketed as much as $100 a week. His fees, higher for Saturday matinees, were based on the number of curtain calls: $25 guaranteed two bows, and for every additional bow another $5 was tacked on to the bill. There was not a set cost for "hissing a rival singer," as was specified on a mid-nineteenth-century Parisian price list: 250 francs, 25 more than for "overwhelming applause." And yet, some believed that "hissing a rival singer" or its equivalent was also for sale at the twentieth-century Met. By the end of 1935, the claque was back. But now, the chief claqueur was paid by the artists. Toward the end of Johnson's tenure, Virgil Thomson weighed in on the matter. In decline during World War II, he said, the claque was reborn with the postwar importation of Italian tenors: Ferruccio Tagliavini's debut "last fall was a brilliant occasion because claques were operating in his favor." Giuseppe Di Stefano's debut, less successful by far, "was defended by a single claque and a very crude one" at that (*Herald Tribune,* March 28, 1948).

On Bing's 1950 opening night, "the activities of a claque were hardly to be noticed" *(Times).* Bing had graciously bought coffee for the first one hundred on the line. But by his fourth year, the standees had become his bête noire, more than an occasional bother. He could not ban the standing room fans, but he did, more aggressively than Johnson, go after the claque, and thus rid the Met of a good part of the "intolerable nuisance" that the singers called "the indispensables." Bing drafted a memorandum to solo artists requesting that they refrain from engaging a claque, and implying, with a wink at Zinka Milanov, that the agreement he had reached with them the previous year had been broken (Feb. 1954). And later that season, when the Milanov fans booed Kurt Baum, frustrated that the detested tenor was her frequent partner, often in *Aida* and almost always in *Il Trovatore,* standing room was cut by half, from two hundred to one hundred.[22]

Bing was again on the warpath on opening night 1954–55. His glance had apparently fallen on one or two standees in the family circle who had hung their coats over the railing. "I think the wearing of a jacket in America's leading opera house can be considered reasonable. Is there any legal aspect to this? Can we force people to wear jackets or request them to leave?" For the second year in a row, the Met hired a detective agency to investigate the "standing room problem." A private eye infiltrated the line on several occasions, including a Tuesday night *La Gioconda* with Milanov and Baum. He reported finding that five or so Milanov fans at the head of the line had let in forty or fifty others just as the doors opened. The sleuth had learned that Milanov cultivated her fans by inviting them backstage after performances and throwing her "children" a party at the end of the year. All this came as no particular surprise; she had long been suspected of encouraging the bad behavior of her fan club. In spring 1955, she and Bing exchanged letters on the Baum affair, Milanov insisting that her conscience was clear (April 8) and Bing responding, with another wink, that he had no doubt she was as distressed as he by the demonstrations against her (unnamed) colleague. Ten years later, there was another eruption, and for the first and last time standing room was shut down, if only for a single matinee. Leonie Rysanek and Lucine Amara had received "inciting presents," anonymous bouquets of garlic (*Times,* Feb. 15, 1964). Although Bing claimed he had proof of the complicity of the standees, he would not call for an inquiry, fearing, he said, that he would embarrass his artists further: "Expressions of disapproval are on a level of vulgarity that cannot be tolerated. The way to express disapproval is to do without applause." He finally prevailed with the opening of the new house. The auditorium was designed so that standees were relegated to the back of the parterre and to the stratospheric heights of the family circle, both distant from the stage. A new policy of advance sales for standing room would guarantee that there would no longer be a rowdy line outside the theater before each performance. And without a line, troops partisan to one singer or another could not be marshaled.[23]


LABOR


The ties that bound the Metropolitan and organized labor were knotted in 1904. Unrest of greater and lesser severity first perturbed the Conried administration and continued through the decades. The year before Bing took up residence, Johnson announced the cancellation of the 1948 season, later restored, citing the prohibitive cost of introducing unemployment and retirement benefits as demanded by musicians and stagehands. Bing got off to a promising start by helping to broker a new contract. He factored into his initial budget unemployment insurance for those laid off the many months each year the house was dark; he also backed the establishment of a retirement fund. But the imperious Bing and the ten or so Met locals, not to mention the American Guild of Musical Artists (AGMA), would soon be at sword's point. In 1953, there was a stagehand wildcat strike, an event that disrupted no performances but raised the frightening specter of the general manager, stationed at the ropes in place of a striker during the dress rehearsal of *Norma,* dropping a heavy curtain on Milanov's head. Threats of season cancellations were issued in 1956, and then in 1961, and again in 1966 as the company was preparing for its Lincoln Center inauguration.

The ultimate bone of contention in 1956 was the status of Robert Herman. Herman was an assistant stage director and, as such, a member of AGMA. He was, at the same time, assistant to Max Rudolf and, in that capacity, had sat on management's side of the negotiating table. In consequence of Herman's conflicting allegiances, AGMA made noises of bringing charges against him. The fundamental question for the Met was whether AGMA had the right to require that holders of certain jobs be members (*Times,* July 19, 1956); the management was determined that AGMA not institute a closed shop in the ranks of directors and stage managers. The matter was debated between July 10 and July 17 when the cancellation was announced; on July 23, following a compromise, in effect a postponement of any resolution, the season was reinstated. Two years later, Herman would succeed Max Rudolf as Bing's artistic advisor and there would no longer be ambiguity about which side of the table was properly his.[24]

Bing and the board again warned repeatedly of cancellation in 1961, and on August 7 made good on their threat. The orchestra had initially asked for a bold increase of 60 percent over three years, the guarantee of year-long employment, and a reduction in workload to six performances a week. As labor moderated its demands, Bing grew more intransigent, claiming that his principal artists had been released, had in fact made other commitments, and that nothing other than an unsatisfactorily "late and patched-up season" could at this point be assured. In light of the company's precarious finances, public opinion was initially opposed to the musicians; it now turned against management. Ostensibly moved by a plea from Risë Stevens, President Kennedy intervened. Speculation went that following a spring and summer of Freedom Riders on bus trips through the South and student sit-ins across the country, Kennedy was eager to save Leontyne Price's opening night *Fanciulla del West*. He ordered Secretary of Labor Arthur Goldberg to mediate the dispute, a step AGMA welcomed and Bing dismissed with a characteristic wave of the pen: "I am deeply appreciative of efforts by Mr. Goldberg and President Kennedy, but the basic issue remains" (*Times*, August 20). The previous day, a *Times* editorial had spoken for the greater good: "Surely, with the musicians continuing to be conciliatory, the management cannot be allowed to flout public wishes so high-handedly." It concluded, pointing directly at Bing, "Better a late and patched-up season than no season at all." Goldberg persisted in his mission, reaching an agreement with Bliss. The musicians acceded to a 14 percent increase over three years, a deal close to that cut with the other unions. But they would not forget what they experienced as Goldberg's betrayal. In 1964, and with even greater vehemence in 1966, the orchestra would leverage its bitterness at what for Bing and Bliss was the worst possible moment. As they struggled to open the new house, the threat of a strike hung over already daunting circumstances.[25]

## COLOR LINE

Some months before taking over the company, Bing made it clear that in the matter of race, as with all facets of the organization, artistic and administrative, it was a new day. He wrote to a subscriber furious at Flagstad's reprieve, "I am determined to run [the Metropolitan] without prejudice of race or politics" (Feb. 6, 1950). To another contentious missive he replied, "I am afraid I cannot agree with you that as a matter of principle, Negro singers should be excluded. This is not what America and her allies have been fighting for" (April 20, 1950). These worthy assertions were accompanied by the more concrete observation that in his first season there would likely be no "Negro singers . . . as there are no suitable parts," leaving "suitable" indeterminate. The *Baltimore Afro* picked up on the ambiguity: "Is Rudolf Bing engaged in a little double-talking in his statement to the press and radio that colored would be welcome as artists at the Met if he could find a 'suitable singer for a suitable part'?"(April 29, 1950). Bing countered that to his knowledge no African-American singer had "ever had operatic experience and I am afraid, in not taking this into account, you are overlooking a most important point." His interlocutor might have reminded him that five years earlier, in 1945, Todd Duncan had made his debut with the New York City Opera, and so had Camilla Williams in 1946, and Lawrence Winters in 1948. Bing's covered meaning of 1950 was revealed in a later statement in which he excluded *Lohengrin*'s Elsa from the roles "suitable" for African-Americans, together with her Germanic sister, the blond Eva of *Meistersinger* (*Times*, Dec. 26, 1954). Looking back on his achievements thirteen years later, Bing prided himself on the fact that in his time Martina Arroyo had sung Elsa von Brabant (*Times*, April 22, 1968).[26]

By opening night of his second season, Bing had taken a step toward the integration of the 39th Street stage: he signed ballerina Janet Collins, the first African-American member of the company, and for the next four years a principal dancer. As Collins told it, Zachary Solov, the Met's new ballet master, seeking a dancer for the triumphal scene of *Aïda*, mentioned Collins to Bing, saying, "She's Black." Bing asked only if she was good before telling Solov to hire her. The press seized upon the comparison of Collins and Jackie Robinson, who four years earlier had broken major league baseball's racial barrier. The African-American *Chicago Defender* thought Collins's engagement significant enough to count Bing among its honorees for outstanding contributions to the "forward march of American democracy" (*Herald Tribune*, Jan. 1, 1952).

As late as 1927, with Ernst Krenek's *Jonny Spielt auf* in the offing, there had been discussion of the wisdom of featuring an African-American, even when impersonated by a white singer in blackface. Gatti wrote to Kahn: "Mr. Ziegler is especially afraid that the fact of the Negro brought on the stage of the Metropolitan might, through some misunderstanding or malignancy, prove a second *Salome* case. Although I tried to reassure him, he persists in his fears." No challenge had ever been made to the representation of Africans, distant from New York in time and place (Aïda, Amonasro, Otello, Sélika), in blackface, of course. A contemporary American "Negro" as the hero of the piece, Ziegler worried, might be a different matter. In the end, Michael Bohnen and then Lawrence Tibbett played Jonny, the Black jazz fiddler. There was no repeat of the *Salome* debacle, in fact no outcry at all. In 1932, with *The Emperor Jones* on the horizon, Walter White, recently named head of the NAACP, suggested that an African-American, either Paul Robeson or Jules Bledsoe, be considered for the part of Brutus Jones in Louis Gruenberg's opera. Tibbett sang the role. There was controversy nevertheless. The Met had commissioned the African-American dancer Oscar Hemsley Winfield to choreograph the work, and his troupe, the New Negro Art Theater Dance Group, to execute his dances. "It almost didn't happen because the Met wanted to blacken the faces of Met . . . dancers rather than use black dancers." When Tibbett threatened to quit the show, the management backed down. The Met omitted the dance company from the playbill credits.[27]

The first insider to advocate for the place of African-Americans on the roster was Paul Cravath, chairman of the board from 1931 to 1940, counsel to the NAACP, and also head of the board of the historically black Fisk University (his father had been its founding president). But even he could not shake his colleagues or the timorous management. He wrote to Ziegler on January 4, 1934, suggesting Catherine Yarborough, who had made a career in Europe as Caterina Jarboro: "I have no special interest in Miss Yarborough beyond the fact that I am interested in colored people generally, and it occurred to me that if she happened to be a first class artist, it might be good policy and result in some publicity if we could give her a chance to sing L'Africaine." Yarborough had been Aïda (Bledsoe was the Amonasro) with Salmaggi's company at the Hippodrome in 1933. Time reported, "Dusky Harlemites, high and low, turned out to cheer her triumph and theirs." Yarborough refused the offer of a Met audition, adamant that her European successes were credential enough. In 1944, the National Urban League approached Ziegler in the hope that the Met would "see itself clear to invite some Negro singers," and in the certainty that "at present there would be no public resentment" (April 14). African-Americans were, in fact, auditioned beginning in the very late 1940s: Muriel Rahn tried out on several occasions, Carol Brice and Lawrence Winters once.[28]

A somewhat less restricted though similarly tacit ban on the integration of the audience was also in effect. We know this not from company records, but from the January 7, 1941, unwitting minutes of the Metropolitan Opera Guild: "Mrs. Tuesdale brought up the question of the colored race in the Guild box. . . . Mr. Lewis [Earle Lewis, assistant manager and head of the box office] had been consulted and he stated it was the practice of the box office to sell seats to them in the family circle. The matter was, therefore, settled in this ruling." Also unwitting was the fleeting desegregation of the chorus. As the Times reported at the death of the pioneering soprano Helen Phillips, "In 1947 Ms. Phillips became the first black singer known to have appeared with the Metropolitan Opera Chorus, in what she recalled as an apparently accidental breaking of an unofficial color barrier." Her agent had been asked by the Met stage manager for his best soprano. When Phillips presented herself, the stage manager looked her over once or twice and then dispatched her backstage. "'I just slipped in,' she would tell friends. 'Then after the performance, I slipped back out again.'" Paul Robeson's name resurfaced when Walter Winchell, who had Robeson in his crosshairs, announced that he would sing Boris Godunov, in Russian no less, in 1949–50. The Met rushed to cable Winchell its correction: Robeson was not a member of the company and "will not be signed for any forthcoming season" (Feb. 4, 1949). At the end of August of that same year, on the day Robeson was to perform in concert, agitators ignited an anti-Communist riot, laced with anti-Black and anti-Semitic vitriol, in the neighboring Peekskill, New York.[29]

In public memory, it is not Janet Collins, and certainly not Helen Phillips, but Marian Anderson who breached the Met's color line at her epochal debut of January 7, 1955. The proposition that Anderson be the first African-American to sing a principal role at the Met had issued from diverse quarters for at least ten years. Before his death in 1940, Cravath had pressed the suggestion on Johnson. At that point, Anderson, born in 1897, was forty-three years old. The matter was later taken up by E. B. Ray of the Afro-American Newspapers, who inquired bluntly "whether or not the Metropolitan Opera Company has a written or unwritten law barring colored artists. If not, what would be your reaction to suggesting an alternate role as Aïda for Miss Anderson?" (March 17, 1944). As usual, it was Ziegler who responded in Johnson's stead, and again he skirted the question of the Metropolitan "law," preferring a high-handed evasion, aggravated by this embarrassing lapsus: "Are you, perhaps, under the impression that the character Aïda in Verdi's opera *Aïda* is of tawny skin. She is the daughter of the King of Egypt. Amneris—a contralto role—is the daughter of the dark-skinned King Amonasro" (March 22). It is, of course, the other way around: Aïda is the daughter of the Ethiopian King and Amneris of Egypt's Pharaoh. This would not be the last of Ziegler's ever more feeble efforts to fend off questions of race. On April 28, 1947, just months before his death, he once again stayed on message: "Only recently have Negro artists shown interest in operatic singing and there is no doubt that eventually one will emerge who is outstanding in the field of opera alone." By this time, Anderson, who in any case did not have the requisite profile, was fifty. Bing's initial response to those promoting Anderson varied little from that of Johnson/Ziegler: "Nobody can admire Marian Anderson more than I do, but I am unaware that she has any operatic experience and it is indeed difficult for a concert singer even of Miss Anderson's high level just to step onto an opera stage."[30]

What finally convinced Bing? It was no doubt in large part the pressure of the times: 1954 was the year of Brown vs. Board of Education, 1955 the year

FIGURE 27. Marian Anderson as Ulrica in *Un Ballo in maschera,* with Rudolf Bing, January 17, 1955 (Sedge Leblang; courtesy Photofest)

Rosa Parks would not relinquish her seat on a Montgomery, Alabama bus. And Anderson was unquestionably the iconic African-American artist. It was also the scheduled revival of *Un Ballo in maschera,* absent since 1947, and the "suitable" role of Ulrica, the fortune teller, alternatively the "sorceress." (By intriguing coincidence, in Verdi's original version set in colonial Boston, Ulrica is an "indovina di razza nera" [clairvoyant of black race]). Crucial also, given the contralto's by then nearly fifty-eight years, was the fact that Ulrica appears in only one scene, and in that scene she is the dominant, mostly static figure. As Anderson recounts it, on running into her at a party in September 1954, Bing asked her to join the Met in the coming season. She was quite rightly apprehensive; the role's high tessitura presented difficulties this late in her career. Although the audition for Dimitri Mitropoulos did not go well (as she said, she had had to "squeeze out" the notes above the staff), the conductor assented. Bing lost no time in calling Sol Hurok, her agent, to close the deal—so long in coming and now suddenly so urgent. Her fee of $1,000 per performance was at the top of the Met scale.[31]

The orchestral introduction to act 1, scene 2 of *Un Ballo in maschera* that Friday evening had to be interrupted when the curtain failed to rise on cue. Mitropoulos reprised the music, the curtain finally rose, and the ovation was such that the characteristically composed Anderson was visibly unsettled. Reviews were respectful, acutely aware of the immense emotional charge of the occasion. Some notices, like that of Olin Downes, tiptoed around Anderson's weaknesses. Perhaps the best summary of an objective consensus is provided by the *New Yorker:* "Miss Anderson's voice ... is far past its prime.... She showed, understandably, considerable nervousness in attacking [the role], and even when this initial nervousness had worn off, she failed to produce the brilliant result that the historic event seemed to demand ... applause was for the principle of the thing, and not for the specific artistic contribution she made. Her voice was unexpectedly small and tremulous, and her stage personality, I regret to say, was timid and lacking in authority."[32]

Anderson was succeeded by a remarkable string of African-American singers: Robert McFerrin, winner of the Met Auditions in 1953 (he received the training but not the contract that ordinarily accompanied the prize), whose debut as Amonasro followed Anderson's by a scarce three weeks; Mattiwilda Dobbs, the first African-American to be cast as a romantic lead (Gilda in *Rigoletto,* Nov. 9, 1956); Gloria Davy (Aïda, Feb. 12, 1958); Leontyne Price (Leonora in *Il Trovatore,* Jan. 12, 1961); Martina Arroyo (the off-stage Celestial Voice in *Don Carlo* in 1959 and then Aïda, Feb. 6, 1965); George Shirley (Ferrando in *Così fan tutte,* Oct. 24, 1961); Grace Bumbry (Eboli in *Don Carlo,* Oct. 7, 1965); Felicia Weathers (Lisa in *The Queen of Spades,* Oct. 21, 1965); and Reri Grist (Rosina in *Il Barbiere di Siviglia,* Feb. 25, 1966). In the southern cities of its spring tour, the Met was caught up in the fight for civil rights that defined the decade. During the 1961 Atlanta run, two African-American holders of orchestra tickets were asked to sit elsewhere. They refused. Protests ensued. The Student Non-Violent Coordinating Committee and the Southern Christian Leadership Conference joined in a telegram to Bing denouncing the company's acceptance of a discriminatory policy: "The SCLC regrets sincerely that the famed Metropolitan Opera Company has allowed itself to be dictated to by the whim and caprice of so-called 'southern custom,' at such a critical moment in history, particularly this community." The text was cosigned by Martin Luther King Jr. Bing's reply was published in the *Times* the next day. The Met, he wrote defensively, "does not allow itself to be dictated to by anyone. ... We have nothing whatsoever to do with the local arrangements." But the following year, officially at least, the Atlanta audience was integrated. Atlanta was again a thorn in Bing's side in 1964. The organizers had balked at the prospect of Price in *Don Giovanni.* Bing dashed off this memorandum to Anthony Bliss, president of the Metropolitan Opera Association: "Leontyne Price at the present time is one of the most valuable properties [an unfortunate choice of words] of the

Metropolitan Opera and there is no doubt that taking her on tour next season, but skipping the whole Atlanta week would terribly upset her, would without question make her refuse the whole tour and might, indeed, jeopardize her whole relationship with the Metropolitan." Price sang Donna Anna in Atlanta that spring.[33]

REPERTOIRE: 1950–1966

## Verdi

Bing ushered in what would be an extraordinary Verdi era with *Don Carlo*. Verdi ruled again on the opening nights in 1951 and 1952 with *Aïda* and then *La Forza del destino*. All this was to be expected. Asked to name his favorite operas, the general manager–designate had ticked off three Verdi titles, and then just one work by each of seven other composers. Between 1950 and 1966, Verdi accounted for 25 percent of Metropolitan performances, significantly more than the 14 percent of Gatti's years and the 19 percent of Johnson's. Under Bing, Verdi pulled far ahead of Wagner, the previous front-runner. He also led the pack in the percentage of new productions, fourteen of fifty-nine. Bing's predilection would have mattered little had the company not had, year after year, a cohort of phenomenal singers capable of doing honor to the master's melos. Casts that included Milanov, Price, Del Monaco, Tucker, Bergonzi, Corelli, Merrill, and Siepi were arguably the best in the world.[34]

Margaret Webster found herself with far less pliable charges for the 1951 *Aïda* (Nov. 13) than she had had for *Don Carlo*. Borrowing from her experience in the theater, she came up with the improbable notion of calling Milanov, Del Monaco, and the other principals together for a reading of the libretto. Neither the Aïda nor the Radamès would play along. Her leading lady in particular could not be persuaded into meaningful movement. "La donn'è immobile," Webster joked. The press appreciated her handling of the Egyptian legions and Ethiopian slaves in Gérard's streamlined Memphis and Thebes. But soon into the run, with new principals and the increasingly shoddy execution of her blueprint for the action, Webster asked that her name be removed from the program. It stayed.[35]

Two days after the *Aïda* opening, the Met put on *Rigoletto* as a frame for the exceptional gifts of Leonard Warren, Bing's Verdi baritone of choice. Warren was cast in seven of the ten new Verdi productions mounted prior to his death in 1960; he had been scheduled for an eighth. In the December 8 broadcast, he navigates this test role with a finesse that bespeaks the practice of the part at the Met since 1943 and the freshness of restudy for the new production that the *Times* called "one of the most interesting and exciting interpretations of this work that we have seen." Tucker's Duke of Mantua is no less seasoned with individual touches and is as stunning in its technical assurance and vocal radiance. The spinning tone of new soprano Hilde Güden comes as a relief after the too often chirpy Gildas, adequate to "Caro nome" but underpowered for the third act duet with the enraged father. Only Erede's uninspired conducting mars the afternoon.[36]

Eugene Berman's striking décor for *La Forza del destino* (Nov. 10, 1952) was so "special" that one critic "found it difficult to wrest [his] attention from the scenery and give it back to the characters." Exceptionally well-matched singers wove the opera's tangled web. The December 6 broadcast catches Milanov in what was her last peak year, solid and centered, soaring at the top, floating her trademark pianissimos. Tucker and Warren fill the arching phrases of their duets. Fritz Stiedry plays the overture after the first scene (as had Bruno Walter before him) so as to accommodate latecomers. Stiedry performed further surgery on the score, boasting that his version "as it now stands is absolutely first class." The conductor excised the inn scene, holding that it "only confuses the audience," when in fact it provides narrative matter essential to the understanding of a complex plot, and he deleted many other pages from one of Verdi's most original compositions. Stiedry might be forgiven these desecrations had he generated a fraction of the frisson of Walter's 1943 *Forza* broadcast.[37]

The two new Verdi productions of 1956–57 were bouquets for Milanov and Tebaldi in the extraordinary season that opened with the debut of Maria Callas. Milanov should not have taken on *Ernani* (Nov. 23) so late in her career. The December 29 broadcast documents her receding range and flexibility. Del Monaco's tenor rings out all too brazenly. The performance is crowned by Warren's legato in his long act 3 scene. Alas, in *Ernani* as in *La Forza del destino,* the composer's intentions were violated. Reviewers praised the energy of Mitropoulos's leadership but failed to mention the numerous cuts that altered the score's proportions, the interpolated act 4 ballet, and the particularly wrongheaded idea of detaching "Infelice" (beautifully sung by Siepi) from its cabaletta and moving it to act 2. The well-received *La Traviata* opened on February 21. In the April 6 broadcast, Fausto Cleva indulges the slow tempos favored by Warren ("magnificent," "stole the show") and Tebaldi ("sends sparks across the footlights," "reached the highest dramatic peaks"). Tebaldi lowers the act 1 aria and cabaletta to the advantage of the florid passages; the highest notes remain hard. The consumptive Violetta, a difficult negotiation for a huge voice with a short top, would be dropped from her repertoire. Still, the soprano sings much of the role with command, and her most dulcet piano lingers in memory. Oliver Smith's enormous staircases in acts 1 and 3 constricted the flow of the action; the tiny terrace of a tiny summerhouse plunked downstage in act 2 was even more confining.[38]

*Macbeth,* again a vehicle for Warren, was one of two Verdi premieres Bing presented at the old Met. In November 1958, the general manager had fired Maria Callas, the Lady Macbeth-to-be, when she demanded that he adjust her schedule to accommodate the arduous role. We retell the oft-told episode later in this chapter. And when in January 1959, Mitropoulos suffered a heart attack, Shakespeare's unlucky "Scottish play" lived up to its reputation once more. Leonie Rysanek, in her debut, took over for Callas, Erich Leinsdorf for Mitropoulos. As the Viennese soprano made her entrance, there came the shout of "Brava Callas." Bing later confessed that it was he who had arranged for the offensive outcry; he had wanted to win sympathy for his substitute. Despite uncertain lower and middle registers, and a frequently ill-tuned though often resplendent top as heard in the February 21 broadcast, the charismatic Rysanek notched a great success. Warren and Bergonzi (in the essentially one-aria role of Macduff) acknowledge the belcantist traces of Verdi's 1847 score. This was the third *Macbeth* with which Bing was intimately involved, all three directed by Carl Ebert and designed by Caspar Neher: the first was produced in Berlin in 1931 while he was Ebert's assistant; the second at Glyndebourne in 1938. The Met's *Macbeth,* hung with the trappings of horror, skulls and the like, was modeled on its two predecessors. But by 1959, the expressionistic concept had had its day.[39]

Warren was the irreplaceable baritone in the new productions of *Il Trovatore* (Oct. 26, 1959) and *Simon Boccanegra* (March 1, 1960). The *Trovatore* cast included Antonietta Stella and Carlo Bergonzi, but it was Giulietta Simionato, in her debut as Azucena, who brought down the house. *Simon Boccanegra* returned that same season after more than a decade. The reviewers admired the neglected masterpiece, Frederick Fox's décor, and Webster for sorting out the convoluted plot. Tebaldi was unavailable for the premiere, utility soprano Mary Curtis-Verna made for a mediocre Amelia, and Warren, as it turned out, sang his last complete performance.

Three days later, during act 2 of *La Forza del destino,* he collapsed at the start of the cabaletta to "Urna fatale [Fatal urn]," a poignant epitaph for this consummate Verdian. Earlier that evening, relevant or not, Warren had been told to brace himself for catcalls from a pro-Italian cabal. Frank Guarrera, Warren's cover, soldiered on for most of the remaining *Boccanegra* performances.[40]

After Warren's death, *Nabucco* went to Cornell MacNeil. In the December 3 broadcast, he thunders majestically as the King of Babylon in defiance of God and unfolds a pure legato as the contrite, fallen ruler. Rysanek, on the other hand, fails in what is surely one of the most difficult roles for soprano. Abigaille's fearsome intervals and coloratura passages demand a technique she simply lacked. Sharing vocal honors with MacNeil are Siepi as Zaccaria and Rosalind Elias as Fenena. Winthrop Sargeant disliked the sets ("fussily arty and completely devoid of atmosphere") and accused Gunther Rennert of resorting to "a repetition of all the formulas for desultory spear-carrying that have beset productions of spectacular opera from time immemorial." Time has vindicated Bing: *Nabucco* vanished at the end of the 1960–61 season only to make a triumphant return in 2001.[41]

Next came reinvestitures of *Un Ballo in maschera* (Jan. 25, 1962), *Otello* (March 10, 1963), and *Aïda* (Oct. 14, 1963). Bergonzi, as *Ballo's* mercurial King of Sweden, juggled playfulness, passion, and benevolent authority with his characteristic finesse; Rysanek was again hollow in Amelia's middle and low registers; Merrill blustered his way through Renato's despair. Sargeant found the intricate sets "rather self-conscious and arty." *Otello* had a better reception. Eugene Berman drew his ornate décors after Carpaccio and Gentile Bellini. Herbert Graf, who had staged a new *Otello* in 1937 and had given James McCracken starring opportunities in Zurich, directed the tenor in his widely acclaimed return to the Met. Gabriella Tucci filled in as Desdemona when Tebaldi left to repair a vocal breakdown. Not since Szell and Busch in the 1940s had the Met seen an *Otello* conductor of Georg Solti's caliber. A few months later, on opening night 1963, Solti presided over *Aïda,* rescuing the score and the orchestra from the routine in which it was mired. Birgit Nilsson's Ethiopian slave dominated the ensemble in the Triumphal Scene. Nathaniel Merrill and Robert O'Hearn, who had demonstrated their talent for mounting big shows with their 1962–63 *Meistersinger,* served up a colossal Egypt. Harold Schonberg thought that "like so many recent Metropolitan productions, it falls between two schools. It is neither conservative nor modern" *(Times).*[42]

FIGURE 28. *Falstaff,* act 1, scene 2, right to left, Luigi Alva as Fenton, Judith Raskin as Nannetta, Regina Resnik as Dame Quickly, Rosalind Elias as Meg Page, Gabriella Tucci as Alice Ford, Paul Franke as Dr. Cajus, Mario Sereni as Ford, Andrea Velis as Bardolfo, Norman Scott as Pistola, 1964 (Louis Mélançon; courtesy Metropolitan Opera Archives)

*Falstaff* (March 21, 1964) was the last new production of Verdi staged at the old Met. And as it must be for this comic final bow of the seventy-nine-year-old composer, it was the ensemble that counted. The principals, among them Anselmo Colzani (Falstaff), Tucci (Alice), Judith Raskin (Nanetta), and Regina Resnik (an incomparable Dame Quickly), played as a community of artists delighted to inhabit the Elizabethan world created for them by director-designer Franco Zeffirelli: the murky Garter Inn, Ford's sunlit garden, the solid half-timbered interior of his house, the moonlit Windsor forest. The integration of music and drama rested with Leonard Bernstein, making his Met debut along with Zeffirelli. With the opening chords, the orchestra's responsiveness fairly leapt at the audience, and so it continued to the great fugue that closes this conductor's opera. *Falstaff* finally escaped from the gilded cage of the succès d'estime to register high among the season's box-office leaders, a fitting capstone to Bing's ongoing celebration of Verdi. For Alan Rich, the production was "a milestone in the history of operatic production in this city, an artistic forward step in the conception of opera, and a challenge that will be met only with the utmost difficulty" *(Herald Tribune).*

# Premieres

Bing proved a cautious gambler. He would bet on novelties only nine times in his first sixteen seasons; with the exception of *La Périchole* and *The Last Savage,* he held the winning hand. Johnson had taken chances more frequently—eleven times in fifteen seasons—and this despite his many fewer new productions. None of the composers of the Bing premieres, from Verdi to Samuel Barber, needed introduction. Nor were the selections particularly adventurous. *Wozzeck* and *Ariadne auf Naxos* were regularly performed in Europe; *The Rake's Progress* had made the rounds following its 1951 Venice first night.[43]

The general manager had promised *Wozzeck* from the start; it was one of the ten titles of his personal hit parade. He finally took the plunge in 1959. Under the banner of the Philadelphia Grand Opera Company, Leopold Stokowski had conducted the first US run of *Wozzeck* in Philadelphia and New York in 1931; since then, concern had persisted that Berg's heavy dose of atonality would alienate Met subscribers. In 1941, Ziegler "deemed it not of the type to warrant its inclusion in our repertoire." The programming of the opera had become an act of courage, a noble cause, as John Gutman saw it: "I would like to start a campaign for *Wozzeck*. . . . I think that it would be well-justified to let artistic reasons for once take precedence over commercial considerations, and do something for the intellectual prestige of this opera house." The Met's product lived up to the high purpose. The company accorded Karl Böhm an unprecedented twenty-four orchestra rehearsals. In excellent English, German baritone Hermann Uhde made palpable Wozzeck's anguish; Steber, whose versatility encompassed the most challenging roles, undertook Marie when Dorothy Kirsten declined. Bing had seen Neher's first designs for the Berg opera in Essen in 1929; Neher had signed five more editions after that. Kolodin thought this seventh "blandly representational and stylistically nondescript." Still, he and his fellow critics shouted unanimous huzzahs for the enterprise. Contrary to dire box-office estimates, *Wozzeck* did reasonably well in 1958–59. Since then, and despite some poorly attended revivals, the Met has kept faith with Berg's masterwork.[44]

The remaining German novelties, *Arabella* and *Ariadne auf Naxos,* filled two Strauss lacunae. Discounting a single season for *Die Ägyptische Helena* in 1928–29, the composer was represented solely by *Der Rosenkavalier* on a regular basis, and intermittently by *Salome* and *Elektra.* Many thought

Strauss's post–World War I scores, however skillfully crafted, largely retreads of the musical gestures that had once seemed so modern. At the time of its US Met premiere, *Arabella* was taken to exemplify the late Strauss, who, "at sixty-nine, was a tired man, largely bereft of original inventiveness, and who had fallen back on a lavender-scented romanticism"; his librettist, Hugo von Hofmannsthal, was tarred with the brush of preciosity and decadence. *Ariadne auf Naxos,* their more familiar, much earlier work, escaped these blanket reproaches; it had had staged performances at the New York City Opera in the 1940s and a 1958 concert reading at Carnegie Hall.[45]

The *Arabella* project nearly foundered on a dispute over its English translation. Strauss's British publisher, Boosey & Hawkes, insisted on a version that Bing, true to Gutman, his friend and advisor, refused to accept. Bing prevailed and New York heard Gutman's text. The February 26, 1955, transmission is a treasurable broadcast. Güden glows in the act 1 duet. Steber's voice, "Immensely supple, . . . retains its delicate sheen but, with mid-career ease, expands to full-throated, tremolo-free *spinto* tone of equal loveliness." George London, just as openhearted as Steber, "projects an almost holy mood." It all comes together under the fine hand of Rudolf Kempe in his debut season. In a revision of the production that Ebert and designer Oliver Messel had devised for Glyndebourne, *Ariadne auf Naxos* was not nearly so well performed. The title role, originally offered to Nilsson, became the property of Rysanek. On the first night, some passages taxed her lower octave and her erratic top. Gianna D'Angelo navigated the coloratura pitfalls of Zerbinetta with excessive care, Jess Thomas stayed Bacchus's ungrateful course without particular élan, and Kerstin Meyer, who never found a tonal center for the Composer, cracked on her aria's high note. Only Böhm, an inveterate Straussian conductor, gave the score its due. But despite critical resistance to *Arabella* and the shaky premiere of *Ariadne auf Naxos,* both titles would prosper. Met audiences would come to cherish the idealistic young woman of the Vienna of the 1860s and the forlorn Cretan princess abandoned on an ancient island, each destined to be united at the final curtain with "der Richtige," the right man.[46]

For material suited to the annual New Year's Eve gala, Bing selected an opéra-bouffe (French comic opera), hoping Offenbach would pull off the box-office miracle wrought by Johann Strauss. He cast *La Périchole* with Patrice Munsel, reneging on the understanding he had with Risë Stevens, whose voice, he decided, was too dark and presence too mature for the Peruvian street singer. Despite the low tessitura of Périchole, Bing opted for the higher, younger voice of Munsel, the irresistible Adele of *Fledermaus*. Paquillo's tenor lines were assigned to the baritone Theodore Uppman. Even more contrary was the engagement of Cyril Ritchard, who sang the Viceroy in a voice barely adequate to musical comedy. Ritchard also staged the piece. Offenbach's frothy confection, with major alterations to the score, revised orchestration, and an interpolated ballet, was pronounced "one of the happiest examples of musical theatre New York has had in our time." Fresh from rapturous reviews, *La Périchole* was included in the subscription series cosponsored by the Met and the Book-of-the-Month Club. Nineteen moderately priced recordings were eventually issued. Many of the casts were led by covers and comprimarios, some of whom had never or hardly ever sung their roles at the Met; others flaunted experienced stars in favored parts, Tucker as Andrea Chénier and Lenski, Kirsten as Tosca and Cio-Cio-San. Jean Morel conducted the abridged *La Périchole*. Gérard's witty sets served four revivals through 1970–71. But unlike the Viennese operetta, the Parisian opéra-bouffe fell well short of miraculous at the box office.[47]

*The Last Savage,* Gian Carlo Menotti's opera buffa vintage 1963, was the third and last of his works to be staged at the Met; it was preceded by the minor success of *Amelia Goes to the Ball* (1938) and the fiasco of *The Island God* (1942). Menotti's popularity in the 1940s and 1950s, unrivaled among contemporary opera composers, had been fueled by Broadway, television, and the movies. He admitted freely that he had "run the risk of sounding unfashionable with *The Last Savage*"; he had hoped to "appeal to open minds and untutored hearts." The Met gave the piece an expert cast: Roberta Peters, George London, Nicolai Gedda, and Teresa Stratas. Beni Montresor's sets mirrored the illustrations of his children's books and received deserved attention. The Met opening on January 23, 1964, was trashed nonetheless, as had been the Paris premiere in October 1963. Alan Rich could not have been more outspoken: "Just about everything that could possibly be wrong with a modern opera—or one of any period, for that matter—is wrong with Mr. Menotti's latest effort. The score is embarrassingly derivative, almost shockingly so. The libretto is a silly piece of fluff, and full of cheap cornball, gag-writing below the level of a backwoods college varsity show" *(Herald Tribune)*. Menotti's "Broadway musical masquerading as an opera" disappeared after a second season.[48]

Horace Armistead designed handsome facsimiles of eighteenth-century London for Stravinsky's *The Rake's Progress,* George Balanchine directed, and Fritz Reiner conducted a cast headed by Hilde Güden (Anne), Blanche

Thebom, (Baba the Turk), Eugene Conley (Tom), and Mack Harrell (Nick). To Stravinsky's request for Elisabeth Schwarzkopf, who had created the role of Anne in Venice, Bing responded, "that for reasons I would rather not discuss in writing [undoubtedly her Third Reich connections], the lady you mention cannot be considered for the Metropolitan Opera." (As with Karajan, Bing relented some years later.) There had been some joking conjecture that Thebom, famous for her floor-length tresses, would conscript her own hair for Baba's beard. The radio audience heard the American premiere on Saturday afternoon, February 14, 1953. Among the standees, the buzz was all about the breathtaking high C that capped Güden's virtuoso act 1 aria. Reviewers were unanimous in lauding the production, performance, and, excepting Downes, the score. There was little enthusiasm for the libretto of W. H. Auden and Chester Kallman. Attendance dwindled rapidly through the short New York run; *The Rake* was scrapped after two undersubscribed repetitions the following season. It took the Met more than four decades to catch up with *The Rake's Progress*.[49]

Samuel Barber's *Vanessa* was the single world premiere the wary general manager sponsored at the old house. That his was a felicitous choice was immediately apparent: "Mr. Barber's mastery of the operatic language is remarkable and second to none now active on the Salzburg-Milan axis"; "American masterpiece"; "capable of holding a respectable place beside the great operatic masterpieces of the past . . . one of the most impressive things of its sort to appear anywhere since Richard Strauss's more vigorous days." A nephew of the legendary contralto Louise Homer and himself a voice student, Barber had already established himself as a composer of vocal music with *Dover Beach* for baritone and string quartet (he sings in its first recording) and *Knoxville: Summer of 1915* for soprano and orchestra. His partner, Gian Carlo Menotti, brought vast experience to the libretto and the staging. Cecil Beaton's affinity for early-twentieth-century style found expression in his elegant sets and costumes. Sena Jurinac was to have created the title role; she suffered a nervous breakdown and canceled just six weeks before the premiere. Eleanor Steber, who had commissioned *Knoxville* and whose recording ensured its popularity, must have felt a twinge of satisfaction when she was called to learn the difficult title role. Gedda as Anatol, Rosalind Elias as the pivotal Erika, Giorgio Tozzi as the Old Doctor, and Regina Resnik as the Old Baroness were the other principals; Mitropoulos conducted. *Vanessa* did little better than most other American novelties—two consecutive seasons and a revival in 1965. Yet Barber's neo-Romantic score lives on, if not at the

TABLE 12  Metropolitan Opera Premieres, 1950–51 to 1965–66

| Composer and Title | Met Premiere (*World Premiere) | Most Recent Met Performance | No. of Seasons in Met Repertoire | No. of Met Productions | No. of Met Performances, 1883–2013 | World Premiere | Director/Designer |
|---|---|---|---|---|---|---|---|
| Igor Stravinsky, *The Rake's Progress* | Feb. 14, 1953 | May 3, 2003 | 4 | 2 | 23 | Sept. 11, 1951, Venice, La Fenice | George Balanchine / Horace Armistead |
| Richard Strauss, *Arabella* (in English) | Feb. 10, 1955 | Dec. 15, 2001 | 8 | 2 | 52 | July 1, 1933, Dresden, Semperoper | Herbert Graf / Rolf Gérard |
| Jacques Offenbach, *La Périchole* (in English) | Dec. 21, 1956 | May 27, 1971 | 5 | 1 | 54 | Oct. 6, 1868, Paris, Variétés | Cyril Ritchard / Rolf Gérard |
| Samuel Barber, *Vanessa* | Jan. 15, 1958* | Apr. 13, 1965 | 3 | 1 | 18 | | Gian Carlo Menotti / Cecil Beaton |
| Giuseppe Verdi, *Macbeth* | Feb. 5, 1959 | Apr. 9, 2012 | 11 | 3 | 98 | Mar. 14, 1847, Florence, La Pergola | Carl Ebert / Caspar Neher |
| Alban Berg, *Wozzeck* (in English) | Mar. 5, 1959 | Apr. 16, 2011 | 13 | 2 | 64 | Dec. 14, 1925, Berlin, Staatsoper | Herbert Graf / Caspar Neher |
| Giuseppe Verdi, *Nabucco* | Oct. 24, 1960 | Nov. 17, 2011 | 6 | 2 | 57 | Mar. 9, 1842, Milan, La Scala | Günther Rennert / Teo Otto, Wolfgang Roth |
| Richard Strauss, *Ariadne auf Naxos* (prologue in English) | Dec. 29, 1962 | Apr. 13, 2011 | 16 | 2 | 91 | Oct. 25, 1912, Stuttgart, Hoftheater; *revised version*, Oct. 4, 1916, Vienna, Hofoper | Carl Ebert / Oliver Messel |
| Gian Carlo Menotti, *The Last Savage* (in English) | Jan. 23, 1964 | May 24, 1965 | 2 | 1 | 16 | Oct. 21, 1962, Paris, Opéra-Comique | Gian Carlo Menotti / Beni Montresor |

Met, in productions elsewhere and in two subsequent complete recordings. And Erika's haunting "Must the winter come so soon?" has become a standard competition aria for generations of mezzo-sopranos.[50]

## Staging the Revivals

At the end of the "yellow brick" epoch, sixteen years into his tenure, the hard question was the degree to which Bing had raised the bar of staging and direction, as he had promised. By 1966, he could certainly claim a far more polished look, consistent blocking from performance to performance, and the retirement of dilapidated shows. If, in 1951, Lily Pons created a mild furor by sneaking into act 4 of *Rigoletto* in see-through tights, the day when artists would wear their own regalia was over. In planning the closing season, Bing did his own accounting. He included those he considered his best productions, he discarded most of his "biggest flops," by which he meant the box-office busts: *Eugene Onegin, Ernani, Don Pasquale,* and *Così fan tutte.* As far back as 1959, Gutman put it on the record that the final 39th Street season, then projected for 1961–62, would be built around "the pearls of the Bing regime." The concept survived the maddening four-year delay, and 1965–66 did indeed feature many of Bing's hits.

How real was the impact of the directors who crossed from the legitimate to the lyric theater? How real could it be? Margaret Webster was reduced to bemoaning the conditions that sabotaged dramatic purpose. In the three weeks prior to the first performance of *Don Carlo,* a sprawling work unfamiliar to the chorus and to many of the soloists, she had to vie for rehearsal space with four other operas in preparation and was allowed only twelve hours on the main stage. She repaired to the "roof" stage high in the building, Sherry's Bar, the lobby, the restrooms, and whatever other nook or cranny she could commandeer. Her hard-won results were compromised as soon as there was a cast change, sometimes by the second or third performance. Not only did directors play second fiddle to the music staff, they were inevitably overwhelmed by the force of tradition. Joseph Mankiewicz, so inventive in the movies, could do little more than freshen *La Bohème* (Dec. 27, 1952). When, early in the run, bits of his staging began to melt away, he asked, as had Webster, that his name be removed from the program. He never returned to the Met. Cyril Ritchard had tightened up *Il Barbiere di Siviglia* (Feb. 19, 1954) and had thrown out its most tired jokes. His subsequent productions, *Les Contes d'Hoffmann* (Nov. 14, 1955), *La Périchole, Le Nozze di Figaro*

(Oct. 30, 1959), and *The Gypsy Baron* (Nov. 25, 1959), were even less intrepid. Those who hoped *Cav/Pag* (Nov. 7, 1958) would be invigorated by José Quintero, renowned for staging Eugene O'Neill, could only have been disappointed.[51]

Only a handful of theater people managed to overcome Bing's attachment to the middle ground, the limitations of the aged plant, foot-dragging stars, and conservative patrons to achieve their ends. Tyrone Guthrie did away with the "romantic trappings" that in his view had disfigured *Carmen* (Jan. 31, 1952). Gérard supplied him with a bare-bones act 1 Seville street corner. For act 4, director and designer, short on budget, came up with the arresting ploy of setting the scene in Escamillo's quarters, where José could convincingly entrap Carmen. The production was a smash. Peter Brook's rereading moved *Faust* (Nov. 16, 1953) from the prescribed Gothic sixteenth century to the Romantic nineteenth, a time trip that now seems unremarkable. Gone were Marguerite's blonde braids and chaste cottage, Faust's doublet and hose, and Méphistophélès's red devil tights. The modishly coiffed heroine retired behind an ample weeping willow, the philosopher turned hedonist was decked out as Lord Byron, and the Prince of Darkness sported evening dress, top hat, and cane. Downes took advantage of this *Faust* to decry the engagement of stage directors who "regard opera as a kind of adulterated theatre, a form to which they must apply the methods of the spoken theatre to redeem it from its ways" *(Times)*. For a new *Madama Butterfly* (Feb. 19, 1958), the company first looked to Japanese cinema. Negotiations with Akira Kurosawa fizzled. Bing was leery of the next candidate, director Yoshio Aoyama, and of the "totally conventional realistic" designs submitted by Motohiro Nagasaka. He need not have been concerned. The "restraint and delicacy" that purged inauthentic representations of Japan yielded a refitting that, for *Time*, "set off the throbbing Puccini score far more effectively than did the old conventional melodramatic breast-beating."[52]

The *Così fan tutte* (Dec. 28, 1951) assigned to Alfred Lunt, Broadway's leading practitioner of the comedy of manners, was a resetting of such refinement that it launched a reappraisal of the work itself. Gérard's sets, as elegant as the movements Lunt taught the principals, brought the action forward onto the apron of an interior proscenium. He limned eighteenth-century Naples from window frames, lattices, chandeliers, and a pastel color scheme accented by the luxuriant taffeta costumes of the fickle sisters. Two other revivals mediated the acceptance of what soon became canonical titles, *Eugene Onegin* (Oct. 28, 1957) and *Turandot* (Feb. 24, 1961). In 1957, in

English, Tchaikovsky filled the prestigious opening-night position. Reviewers were unruffled by the transposition of Onegin and Tatiana's final encounter from the more transgressive interior of the husband's house specified by the libretto to a more picturesque park in the falling snow. They admired Peter Brook's staging and Rolf Gérard's sets, but as for the opera itself, they agreed, as had their confrères in 1920, that *Eugene Onegin* was static, faded, and dated. Thanks to quite frequent revivals, today's critics and audiences are devoted to what Tchaikovsky called not an opera, but "lyrical scenes." And in 1977, Tatiana was at last freed to write her love letter in the original Russian. When Aoyama fell ill, *Turandot* devolved to Nathaniel Merrill. The delicate chinoiserie of Beaton's long-ago Peking, with décor less grandiose than Puccini's grand canvas had known in New York and elsewhere, helped secure a place for an opera not heard at the Met in three decades.

From Europe came Carl Ebert's *Macbeth* and *Ariadne auf Naxos,* sickly transplants from Glyndebourne. His kitschy *Martha* (Jan. 26, 1961) suffered the indignities of an English adaptation disavowed by the translator (in one performance jettisoned by Tucker, who simply sang his big aria in Italian) and of a fractious horse that just missed dumping a wagonload of principals into the pit. *Martha* raised the question of Bing's repertory choices: "One wonders why a great opera house should waste a magnificent cast on such a flimsy period piece when great masterpieces are neglected." Gunther Rennert had piled up a cutting-edge resumé in Germany. After the absurd *Nabucco,* the unobjectionable *Un Ballo in maschera,* and a tepid *Manon* (Oct.17, 1963), Bing could take heart in Rennert's collaboration with Rudolf Heinrich for a suitably decadent *Salome.* Margherita Wallmann's impact on *Lucia di Lammermoor* (Oct. 12, 1964) paled before Sutherland's patented version of Donizetti's demented bride. The last of the European directors to make his debut, Jean-Louis Barrault, staged *Faust* in the clever, Brueghel-inspired designs of Jacques Dupont.[53]

That left the house directors, presumably less dashing and certainly less costly than the guests. It was to these journeymen that Bing turned increasingly as the 1950s drew to an end. The best-known was Herbert Graf, a Met veteran, "an opera man first and last." His blocking and Berman's ingenious decorated two-tiered set combined to smooth the way for the many scene changes of *Don Giovanni* (Oct. 31, 1957). Graf could do little with *Tannhäuser's* flimsy Wartburg valley and Landgrave Hermann's antiseptic castle (Dec. 26, 1953), *Die Zauberflöte's* welter of ugly sets (Feb. 23, 1956, in English), or *Tristan und Isolde's* shriveled proportions (Dec. 18, 1959). Dino Yannopoulos, who had been on the staff since 1946, was handed a lavish *Andrea Chénier* (Dec. 16, 1954), an unsightly *Ernani,* and, for *Don Pasquale* (Dec. 23, 1955), the Met's "first pseudo-revolving stage." The local team of Nathaniel Merrill and Robert O'Hearn delivered the shows Bing was after—modern but not radical, flattering to the stars. Their most spectacular invention for *L'Elisir d'amore* (Nov. 15, 1960) was the balloon landing of the charlatan doctor. *Die Meistersinger* (Oct. 18, 1962) placed Hans Sachs's house at the confluence of steeply raked alleys in a three-dimensional bourgeois Nuremberg. Here was a rare "sample of operatic production that would improve the look of any stage in the world," high praise, indeed, from Irving Kolodin. Merrill and O'Hearn did their best to animate the notoriously static *Samson et Dalila* (Oct. 17, 1964); they devised a progression of shifting spaces for the long choral passages of act 1 and pulled off a spectacular collapse of the Temple of Dagon in act 3.[54]

*Alceste* (Dec. 6, 1960, in English), *La Sonnambula* (Feb. 21, 1963), and *Adriana Lecouvreur* (Jan. 21, 1963) were revived for Eileen Farrell, Joan Sutherland, and Renata Tebaldi, and entrusted to staff directors. Farrell's thrilling debut had been long awaited. As for *Alceste,* Schonberg minced no words: this conductor's opera was "a stately bore, and most of us, if we were honest with ourselves, would admit it." Michael Manuel's bland staging and spare décor were of no help. Given Butler and Gérard's listless production, there could not have been much hope that *La Sonnambula* (Feb. 21, 1963) would survive beyond Sutherland's interest: "To hear her was to appreciate what the art of bel canto must have been when Bellini wrote the opera to show off the leading soprano's voice." Despite a libretto many consider absurd, *La Sonnambula* would be back. More surprising have been the iterations of *Adriana Lecouvreur* since the 1960s. In 1903, Caruso and Cavalieri failed to make a success of Cilea's melodrama. In the late 1930s, Ponselle resigned from the company over Johnson's refusal to program the opera. But Tebaldi's wish was Bing's command. In vocal crisis, she withdrew before the end of the run. A compliant handmaiden for divas more dramatically than vocally secure, and long the object of managerial and critical scorn, *Adriana Lecouvreur* has resurfaced once each decade.[55]

## FAREWELL

The Saturday matinée of *La Bohème* on April 16, 1966, closed out the final subscription season at the Old Met. At eight o'clock that evening, the curtain came up on the farewell concert sponsored by the Metropolitan Opera Guild; it came down at 1:25 A.M. the next day. From the set of *Tannhäuser's* Hall of Song, former baritone and now executive stage manager Osie Hawkins called the roll of retired stars, each of whom took a place on the stage to the cheers of the crowd: in alphabetical order, Marian Anderson, Alexander Kipnis, Marjorie Lawrence (in her wheelchair), Lotte Lehmann, Giovanni Martinelli, Patrice Munsel, Lily Pons, Elisabeth Rethberg, Bidù Sayão, Risë Stevens, and many more, thirty-one in all. The history of the Metropolitan back to Martinelli's 1913 debut paraded before an audience attuned to the emotional pitch of the occasion. And as the honored guests made their entrances, the corresponding section of the chorus seated on the stage rose in tribute: the basses for Kipnis, the sopranos for Lawrence, and so on. When Lotte Lehmann walked in, everyone stood.

A concert of fifty-seven artists, some few of whom had sung under Johnson, opened with the *Lucia di Lammermoor* sextet. Dorothy Kirsten (who sang "Depuis le jour"), Robert Merrill ("Eri tu"), and Regina Resnik (in the *Carmen* quintet) would continue on at Lincoln Center. Especially moving were the turns of those for whom this would be the last hurrah. A long ovation was touched off by Licia Albanese's "Un bel dì"; to shouts of "Save the Met," she kissed her hand and bent to touch the stage floor with her fingers. Another was for Eleanor Steber as Vanessa. This line from Barber's quintet must have been achingly poignant: "Let me look around once more. Who knows when I shall see this house again!" Kurt Baum, too, made his adieu that night. But the most thunderous applause was reserved for Milanov. Near the end of the concert, with Tucker, she sang the final duet from *Andrea Chénier.* Bravos mixed with cries of "We love you, Zinka" lasted a full five minutes.

The gala was also the opportunity to show off the roster that had defined the first sixteen years of Bing's regime, artists who had made their debuts after 1950. Nicolai Gedda (in the final *Faust* trio) was adept in all the languages and nearly all the styles then current at the house. Jon Vickers ("Winterstürme") had become the Siegmund, Florestan, Don José, and Samson of his generation. Régine Crespin (in the Gioconda-Laura duet) had made her mark in Strauss, Wagner, and Verdi. James McCracken (in the "Sì, pel ciel" duet from *Otello*) had served a comprimario apprenticeship with the company before making his name elsewhere and returning to sing major roles. And Teresa Stratas (in the "Soave sia il vento" trio from *Così fan tutte*) had jumped from the ranks of the *Parsifal* Flower maidens to Micaela and

Mimì. Four of the superstars Bing had brought to the Met were also on the gala program: Renata Tebaldi and Franco Corelli (the act 2 *Manon Lescaut* duet), Birgit Nilsson (Brünnhilde's "Immolation"), and Leontyne Price (Leonora's act 4 aria from *Il Trovatore*). Among the dazzling newcomers of 1965–66, Grace Bumbry, Mirella Freni, Nicolai Ghiaurov, James King, Alfredo Kraus, Pilar Lorengar, Sherrill Milnes, Renata Scotto, only Montserrat Caballé was on hand (in the *Rosenkavalier* trio).

There were other, even more notable absences, Lauritz Melchior and Helen Traubel, both of whom had had bitter clashes with Bing. Then there were the stars Bing drew to the Met who had shone brightly and then had disappeared for various reasons in the years before the gala. Joan Sutherland had left in 1964 of her own volition and would return in 1966–67. Antonietta Stella was dismissed after just four seasons, likely because she challenged the general manager's interdiction of the solo bow. Cesare Valletti had been let go for reasons still obscure. Victoria de los Angeles was offended when Bing chose Farrell for Manuel De Falla's *Atlantida*. Farrell herself (not a Bing favorite) sang only forty-seven performances, a total that would have been far greater had she taken on the Wagnerian heroines to which she was so splendidly suited. The most glaring absence at the farewell was that of the most famously difficult of all sopranos, Maria Callas. Callas had sung at the Met for two seasons, 1956–57 and 1957–58. In November of what would have been the third, Bing fired her in as public a manner as he could contrive. She had committed herself in writing to alternating Lady Macbeth with Violetta and, for the first time, to the national tour. But the diva changed her mind, presenting the lame excuse that toggling between the heavier and the lighter Verdi roles, even with a week's rest in between, would invite vocal strain. Bing suggested she replace Violetta with Tosca or Lucia, upon which Callas retorted: "My voice is not an elevator, going up and down." When she failed to comply with her agreement by the deadline Bing set, he sacked her for breach of contract, to the outrage of the press and the public. The story made news the world over. Bing was happy to welcome Callas back in 1965 for two sold-out *Toscas*.[56]

The standard of performance at the Old Met, even in Bing's best years, fluctuated markedly. The disparity was reflected in the gala when Arturo Sergi took the stage as Edgardo, Mary Curtis-Verna as Aïda. That said, in any given week during the last decade and a half on 39th Street, operagoers could hear singers who shook the walls with their mighty voices, others who wafted shimmering pianissimos through the theater, and some capable of both.

There were those who captured audiences with the passion of their song and, more rarely, with the subtlety of their art. Some even had compelling acting skills that enlivened the strategies of the new directors. And a few possessed a personal alchemy of sound, presence, and dramatic instinct that made an irrefutable case for calling Bing's Met a house of stars.

PARIS TOUR

Not long after the gala, in late May-June 1966, the Met made its second trip to Paris. Fifty-five years had passed since Gatti-Casazza, Toscanini, and the New York troupe had played the Théâtre du Châtelet. If in 1910 the French public and critics had been unfairly harsh, even antagonistic toward the American company, the negative reaction this time to the stint at the Odéon was largely justified. The unevenly cast, limp productions of *Le Nozze di Figaro* and *Il Barbiere di Siviglia* were only passable at best. Bing reported to the executive committee on June 3, 1966: "I think it is wise to face up to the fact that the Paris visit was not a success. All sorts of reasons have been advanced—anti-American feelings etc., etc. some of which may or may not be true. The fact remains that our first *Barber* performance was not very good, particularly Roberta Peters was tired and not in good voice. The *Figaro* in my view was an excellent performance but it appears that the majority of the Paris public and press expected the Metropolitan to come with Leontyne Price, Birgit Nilsson, Franco Corelli, etc.... When the invitation for this particular visit in this lovely little theater was made and it became quite clear that we could not possibly do anything but our two smallest works, *Barber* and *Figaro,* I did not have the strength to resist the temptation of a Paris visit."

# EIGHT

# In Transit, 1966–1975

## AMERICAN OPERA

### LINCOLN CENTER

#### The Final Lap

ON SEPTEMBER 29, 1962, more than four years before the farewell to the old house, the Met made its Lincoln Center debut at the newly completed Philharmonic Hall, renamed Avery Fisher Hall in 1973. The Manuel De Falla program opened with *El Amor Brujo,* followed by a badly truncated version of his unfinished dramatic cantata *Atlantida.* The *Times* congratulated the Metropolitan on daring to be represented by the Western hemisphere premiere of Falla's composition, all the while deploring the deep cuts inflicted on his magnum opus: twenty-two soloists were reduced to just three, Eileen Farrell (Leontyne Price had first been asked), George London, and Jean Madeira. Meanwhile, the company's future home next door was nothing more than an immense water hole, dubbed "Lake Bing." And to the general manager's fury, construction had been bumped by the New York State Theater, whose priority was dictated by the opening of the 1964 World's Fair at Flushing Meadows.[1]

The long last lap of the Met's journey northward began in the late 1930s. Otto Kahn's recurrent dream of a new house, born with the promise he made to Giulio Gatti-Casazza in 1908, had died in the late 1920s with the sale of his 57th Street property. The protagonist of the 1929 and early 1930s chapter of the story was John D. Rockefeller Jr. and its setting his pharaonic Depression-era "Radio City" on Fifth Avenue at 50th Street. Both Kahn and Rockefeller came up empty. We pick up the trail we left off in chapter 5 in the late 1930s with talks between board member Charles Spofford and Fiorello La Guardia. New York's mayor wanted to repurpose the Shriners' Mecca

Temple for both the New York Philharmonic and the Metropolitan. Spofford was considering a site in Central Park at Columbus Circle.

Another decade elapsed before two external events finally triggered the realization of the long-deferred ambition. In 1949, Congress voted authorization of Title I, granting subsidies for land costs associated with urban renewal and allowing cultural and educational facilities to be included in the package. The act was destined to mediate the encounter of Robert Moses with the Metropolitan. As chairman of the Triborough Bridge and Tunnel Authority, he was enticed by the prospect of federal funds and the value added the Met would lend neighborhood restoration. Moses first proposed a block south of Washington Square, which was rejected as out of the way and too costly. He then suggested Columbus Circle, just west of Central Park, but thought better of it when a convention center, later the Coliseum, struck him as ideally suited to that particular spot. The majority of Met directors continued to argue for staying put. Late in 1953, Moses attempted yet another overture: he offered a large blighted tract at Lincoln Square, bounded by 61st and 65th Streets and Amsterdam and Columbus Avenues, that could be had for very little. Again, the board stalled; Moses threatened to call off the deal. At this point, the directors grudgingly asked architect Wallace K. Harrison to draft a design with which to initiate a fund-raising campaign. Harrison, married to the daughter of John D. Rockefeller Jr., Abigail, had drawn up the plans for the proposed Rockefeller Center opera house in the early 1930s, and had been a principal architect on such mammoth projects as the United Nations and the Albany State Plaza.

A second event intervened, unrelated to the tangle of Metropolitan and governmental agendas: the purchase of Carnegie Hall by a developer out to demolish the grand old landmark and erect an office tower in its place. The Philharmonic was on notice that in three years it would be homeless. Its board looked to the same Harrison for help. He found himself brokering the partnership of the opera and the symphony. In 1955, the two organizations agreed to approach John D. Rockefeller III. An exploratory committee was formed with Rockefeller as chair. By spring 1956, the committee had morphed into Lincoln Center, Inc., and the game was officially on. It was not until February 21, 1957, that the Met made a formal commitment to Lincoln Center. And it was Rockefeller who added George Balanchine's New York City Ballet, unhappy at City Center, to the mix that would later include a repertory theatre, a library and museum, and finally an educational institution, ultimately the Juilliard School. The many holders of block after block of real estate had to be brought around to the demolition of their buildings. As it happened, Joseph P. Kennedy owned a large warehouse on the site. Hostile to all Rockefellers and indifferent to the arts, Kennedy kept matters tied up in the courts for almost two years. At long last, on May 14, 1959, President Dwight D. Eisenhower, before a crowd of two thousand onlookers, turned over the first shovel of dirt for what would become the Lincoln Center for the Performing Arts. Leonard Bernstein led the New York Philharmonic in Aaron Copland's "Fanfare for the Common Man" and then served as master of ceremonies for a concert in which, representing the Metropolitan, Risë Stevens sang the "Habanera," Leonard Warren the "Prologo" from *Pagliacci*.[2]

In time, it became clear that if Lincoln Center was to receive what amounted to a significant subsidy from the State of New York, the theater meant for ballet alone would have to make room for the New York City Opera, also resident at City Center. The Metropolitan board met on February 11, 1960, to consider the question. The opinion of the Met had not been solicited, but Anthony Bliss, the Association president, thought it politic to make public the board consensus nonetheless. He acknowledged that proximity might affect the box office adversely and create confusion in fund-raising. He preempted Bing's case that City Opera's presence in the complex would "represent a lowering of the standard of perfection which Lincoln Center had set for itself." Bliss recommended all the same that the Association not object to the invitation to City Opera. Mrs. Belmont's conciliatory view was that there was a place for a "moderate size theatre where ballet, intimate operas, and new American works and new American artists may be presented." Spofford drove the decisive point: that funding would be available to Lincoln Center only if the "poor man's opera" were included. Opposition would gain the Met nothing but bad publicity. Bing spoke against what he called a "capitulation to considerations which in the long run have nothing to do with the best interests of the Metropolitan and were, in fact, basically inimical to those interests." He compared City Opera to the "provincial opera houses of Europe rather than those in the first rank such as Vienna, La Scala and Covent Garden in which category the Metropolitan was a peer." He warned that a positive decision might well prove "catastrophic" to the Met and to the standing of Lincoln Center. The Met directors voted unanimously for capitulation.

### "Save the Met"

Sol Hurok sparked the movement to save the theater on 39th Street, hoping to repeat the miracle performed by Isaac Stern in saving Carnegie Hall six years earlier. The "Save the Met" campaign ran counter to the postures of Lincoln Center, of the Met board, and of the company management. The Metropolitan Opera Association had leased its land to Keystone Associates; Keystone was itching to clear the site and begin construction of a commercial skyscraper. The Metropolitan was counting on the desperately needed $200,000 annual income (rising gradually to $600,000) to offset its higher Lincoln Center operating costs. Then there was the gnawing fear of competition. If the theater remained standing, it might well be booked by visiting opera companies. The official line was that as long as the Old Met lived, its magic would deflect allegiance from the New Met (*Post,* Jan. 14, 1967). Lawyers and publicists contested the terrain for nearly a year. The press, and then the courts, and then the New York State legislature, and then the courts again got into the act. So did the politicians when public pressure on the side of preservation mounted: Senators Robert Kennedy and Jacob Javits, Mayor John Lindsay (who waffled in the end), and Governor Nelson Rockefeller (who was caught between his early pro–Old Met stance and the push-back from the family's promotion of Lincoln Center). Even the office of President Lyndon Johnson was heard from. Socialites were joined in last-ditch efforts by Leonard Bernstein, Marian Anderson, Vladimir Horowitz, Agnes De Mille, and Isaac Stern. When it appeared the tide was turning in favor of the old house the unsentimental Bing had no problem playing the heavy: "Stupidity has triumphed. The combination of irresponsible amateurs and frightened politicians has done it again; an old conductor [surely Stokowski] and an aging choreographer [Agnes De Mille] among others can proudly look at the wreck. Now let them save the real Met and then show us how to run the old one. I cannot wait. New Yorkers will thank their distinguished Governor and Mayor when the real Met will face financial ruin and the old one will run its first shoddy movie. Well done." Bing and his troops prevailed. To the chagrin of devotees from all classes, on January 17, 1967, the wrecking ball began its assault on the "Yellow Brick Brewery." The Old Met suffered the fate of the recently demolished Pennsylvania Station.[3]

## The New House

As early as 1955, Bing had instructed his closest advisors to set down their desiderata for the "actual physical plant and building." Max Rudolf responded with an approximation of the number of rehearsal spaces, dressing rooms, and offices, and with reflections on the size of the stage. The pit, he wrote, "must be radically different from our present pit which is too long and not sufficiently deep." He stressed the importance of a hydraulic lift, a television monitor, and a speaker system to connect the stage to the dressing rooms. John Gutman took up the issue of the auditorium. He liked neither the modern squared-off solution with one or two overhanging balconies, nor the traditional horseshoe of the current Met with its awful sight lines. Could there be something in between? Like Bing, he sought four thousand places, no more than the old house and certainly not the forty-five hundred advocated by some. Bing argued that it would be a trial to sell that many tickets, and, besides, that the acoustics would be compromised by the greater volume of the hall. He brought up the matter of boxes, the source of the schism between elitists and populists in the early days of opera in New York; they remained, he knew, dear to status-conscious subscribers: "Personally, I am very much for retaining boxes but how it can be done with the modern shape and without impairing sightlines I would not know." Then there was the question of orchestra floor aisles. In March 1960, the board debated two seating arrangements, one, preferred by Bing, with aisles, the other without. A sense of the meeting registered eight votes for aisles, three against, and five abstaining.[4]

The architects found a middle ground between the traditional horseshoe and the contemporary rectangle. They kept the conventional color scheme: seats and carpeting red, ceiling, proscenium, and balcony faces gold. They specified twenty-nine boxes, six fewer than their seniors had carved out, and eliminated the floor-to-ceiling dividers that impeded visibility. With the exception of those at the extreme sides of the balconies, all spectators would have virtually unobstructed views of the stage, a marked improvement over the one-in-six blighted seats of the Old Met. Final drawings showed an orchestra floor with two aisles. The auditorium had 3,824 seats, with 253 additional standing room spots, for a total of 4,077, very near the 3,625 seats of the old house and its 224 standing spots. Still, the capacity at Lincoln Center would outstrip that of all other opera theaters. Six rapid elevators with stops on each floor would take the place of the creaky lifts that toggled from the street to the family circle and back. Latecomers would no longer be allowed to disturb their neighbors; they would be welcome to view the action on closed-circuit television until the first intermission. There would be not one but three dining facilities. The theater would offer parking under Lincoln Center Plaza. Air conditioning would permit a longer season, thirty-one weeks compared to twenty-five, and 192 subscription performances rather than 146.[5]

The new theater, seven stories above ground and three below, clad in travertine marble and glass, was to have a footprint much greater than the old. The central stage would have the approximate dimensions of its predecessor, as would the proscenium opening, among the smallest of the world's major opera venues, thereby allowing the reuse of the many sets sized to 39th Street. But, and here was the important point, one rear and two side stages would multiply the playing area many fold. While one décor was on the main stage, another could be at the ready on an adjacent platform, permitting far shorter scene changes. The rear and side stages could be rolled to the center; the center stage could be elevated and replaced by another rising from below. Sets would no longer be trucked back and forth to the warehouse or, worse, parked in all weathers on the Seventh Avenue sidewalk. Costumes would no longer be transported off-site or subjected to punishing heat under the roof. The carpenter shop would accommodate the assembly of an entire set; the floor of the scenic studio would be large enough to handle the painting of prodigious drops. And, standing at the privileged focal point of an island of culture, flanked by the New York State Theatre to the south and Philharmonic Hall to the north, the Metropolitan would be the leading partner of a coordinated arts community.

In the months and years of design and construction, tempers flared most heatedly over acoustics. And it was the acoustics consultant working with the architectural firm of Harrison and Abramovitz who bore the brunt of the pervasive anxiety. Wisely, the management refused to pronounce itself on acoustical strategies, never deviating from this mantra: "The new Metropolitan Opera House should have the same acoustics as the old one with a little more brilliance." It was not until April 11, 1966, five months before opening night, that a sound test could be trusted. The terrifying occasion was the final student performance of the season, *La Fanciulla del West,* relocated at the last minute to the new house. The press corps was invited to join thirty-two hundred teenagers as they alighted from a convoy of yellow buses. Sound checks included gunshots and thunderous chords while measurements were taken throughout the theater. Journalists, sworn to secrecy, found ways of letting the cat out of the bag without altogether breaking their word. It was happy news. One reviewer reported that Harrison, who had been seen walking about the theater pale and stern during act 1, a noise meter in hand, had come into the lobby at intermission, "his face wreathed in smiles" (*Times,* April 12, 1966). At that moment, the management might have been grateful to have been last in line behind Philharmonic Hall and the State Theatre. The symphony's new home, drawn by Max Abramovitz, Harrison's partner, and Philip Johnson's digs for the ballet and the City Opera had been panned for their disastrous acoustics. As Harrison recognized, "In an opera house everything has to be designed in terms of sound. Because sound is the main reason to go to the opera. But after the Philharmonic experience the whole science of acoustics was washed away." Among the many lessons learned were these: that the carpeting could be no more than an inch and a quarter deep lest it dampen the sound, and that sheathing the walls with red Congolese wood (all harvested from a single tree!) would cause them to reverberate "just like a violin." In the final reckoning, the invoice for the Metropolitan came to $45 million, startlingly high when contrasted with the $23 million initial estimate and the $55 million projected for the entire Lincoln Center complex. The cost of the whole would be a whopping $190 million.[6]

### OPENING NIGHT

Everyone agreed: the sight lines and especially the acoustics had left the Old Met in the dust. The other shoe, admittedly less weighty, dropped with the art and architecture reviews. Ada Louise Huxtable, the distinguished architecture critic of the *Times,* and John Canaday, its art critic, were in sync. The edifice, outside and in, was in Huxtable's words "a throwback" and in Canaday's "retardatory avant-gardism." Huxtable began her column with a description of what might have been, still not a modern masterpiece, but significantly better than what actually was. The original design had called for "structurally independent stage and seating enclosed within an arcaded shell, the two separated by an insulating cushion of space." Services, administrative offices, and work areas were to have been consigned to a tower west of the stage. The nearly ninety-foot-tall arcaded windows of the façade (an element that recalled the architect's by now yellowed plans for the aborted Rockefeller Center opera house) were to have been continuous north and south. What emerged were essentially unadorned sidewalls. Many services were relocated to the spaces between the outer and inner shells. As to the interior, Harrison had pressed for a more modern design, but his client had insisted on middle-of-the-road solutions at every juncture. Huxtable recorded a "strong temptation to close [her] eyes." Conceding, as all did, that hearing and seeing the opera came first, she concluded, "it is secondary but no less disappointing, to have a monument manqué."

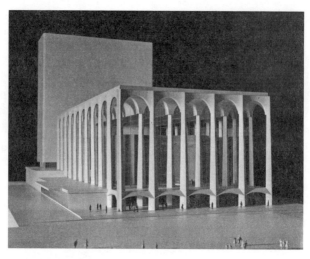

FIGURE 29. Model with side arcades and tower for the new house at Lincoln Center (K. Thomas; courtesy Metropolitan Opera Archives)

In his notice, Canaday checked off the art works chosen to embellish the building's interior: three bronze statues by Aristide Maillol stood in immensely tall lobby niches; a bronze cast of Wilhelm Lehmbruck's "Kneeling Woman" capped the double staircase. On the walls of one of the restaurants, "The Top of the Met" (nicknamed "Dufy's Tavern," or, alternately, "Bing's Bistro"), hung murals by Raoul Dufy. They had belonged to the sets he designed for the New York run of Jean Anouilh's *Ring Round the Moon* in 1951. But what attracted the most attention were the Marc Chagall murals "Les Sources de la Musique" and "Le Triomphe de la Musique," which, incidentally, bore the semblances of Rudolf Bing and ballerina Maya Plisetskaya. These giant murals were an afterthought, a $300,000 attempt to cover the bare walls where the north and south arcades were to have been. Canaday thought them "hardly daring." They might just as easily have been painted "forty years ago, or [by] any person with a nimble wrist and access to a set of color reproductions of Chagall's recent (i.e., since 1930) work." The object that drew the greatest fire was Mary Callery's sculpture above the proscenium. Canaday had this to say: "nominally the most modern work in the place, but its weaknesses are such that only its placement, pinned up like a piece of junk jewelry, atop a proscenium arch that seems to have been built of gilded Nabisco Wafers, could lend it any illusion of weight and strength." He concluded, "The Dufy murals may, in the long run, prove to be the most

FIGURE 30. Interior of Metropolitan Opera House, Lincoln Center, 1966 (courtesy Photofest)

successful decorations in the place, simply because they are the least assuming in a complex that, over-all, suffers from gassy inflation."

Be that as it may, many who entered the opera house for the first time or gaped from the plaza through the glass walls were bowled over by its size, its glitter, and the glamour of the event. Ticket holders had been mailed a large silk-screen program that reproduced the red and gold color scheme of the house. They had contributed $400,000 to the Met coffers on this gala night, twelve times the take of an ordinary sold-out performance. The banquet list included Mrs. Lyndon Johnson, Philippine President Ferdinand Marcos and Mrs. Imelda Marcos, various other foreign dignitaries, Ambassador to the United Nations Arthur Goldberg, Secretary of Defense Robert McNamara, Governor Rockefeller, and Mayor Lindsay. Also present was John D. Rockefeller III, chairman of the Lincoln Center board, as were several Whitney and Vanderbilt descendants of the original founders. In attendance as well was the daughter of Otto Kahn; no one had fought longer or harder than he to see this moment. On the plaza, cheering as the VIPs trod the red carpet, were hundreds of New Yorkers. Twenty-five protestors carried signs that read, "End the War in Vietnam." They were arrested and charged with disorderly conduct.

The joy of the occasion was dampened by worry over the strike called for the day after opening night. That the continuation of the season was in jeopardy had been well publicized. When the 1964 contract was up for renewal, rather than press for a new agreement the orchestra opted for a two-year extension to 1966. The union strategy was to defer the 1964 battle in favor of an all-out offensive timed to coincide with the Lincoln Center opening. Bing would then presumably find it impossible to hold the sword of cancellation over the heads of the musicians. The orchestra would have the upper hand. Its demands included a reduction in obligatory weekly performances from seven to five, improved health insurance and pension benefits, and five weeks of annual vacation. The cloud that hovered over September 16 was lifted during the second intermission of the world premiere of *Antony and Cleopatra* when Bing took the stage to announce that the strike had been averted. This real-life coup de théâtre was met with the longest ovation of the evening.

## AMERICAN OPERA

### *Antony and Cleopatra,* September 16, 1966; *Mourning Becomes Electra,* March 17, 1967

Bing and his artistic team had concocted a stupendous opening season replete with nine new productions, an astounding four in the first eight days. The plan proved to be madness. *Antony and Cleopatra* and *Die Frau ohne Schatten* were company premieres; their novelty was the least of the leaps into the unknown. Each of their designers wanted to put the exciting new stage machinery through its paces. Particularly irresistible was the vaunted turntable, built by an outfit that produced platforms for revolving rooftop restaurants. In *Antony and Cleopatra,* the disk was to carry a huge sphinx surrounded by three hundred marching Egyptians. It was to move forward while rotating. But when the switch was finally thrown during rehearsal, the turntable refused to budge; someone had miscalculated the maximum load by a factor of ten. The overtaxed crew was put to work retrofitting the sphinx so that it could be turned by stagehands hidden within. The repair of the turntable would take nearly four years. Then there was the matter of the schedule, regularly disrupted as one director worked to solve an unanticipated problem and another, along with cast, orchestra, and chorus, waited, sometimes for hours. The principal culprits were the sixteen complex scene changes of *Antony and Cleopatra.* An anxious management piled rehearsal on rehearsal at the expense of the other productions. The company was exhausted, as was Bing's purse, by the unbudgeted overtime. The first week's calendar had to be adjusted, to the great annoyance of ticket holders. *Antony and Cleopatra* opened as promised. *La Gioconda* was delayed by three days, *La Traviata* by two, and *Die Frau ohne Schatten* by more than a week. Bing took the blame: "The fault was mine. I had overplanned the season."[7]

Conductor Thomas Schippers had urged Barber to base his next opera on *Antony and Cleopatra,* the composer's "favorite" play. Franco Zeffirelli agreed to adapt the text and design and stage the production. Bing would assemble a brilliant, (nearly) all-American cast led by Puerto Rican Justino Díaz and Mississippian Leontyne Price. The stage and its machinery would be shown to spectacular advantage. Everything seemed right. Nearly all of it went wrong. There was the glitch of the turntable and, again during rehearsal, the entrapment of Price inside the pyramid, not to mention her imprisonment in grotesquely outsized costumes. Crowds of choristers and supers engulfed her and the other principals. Zeffirelli framed it all—the sphinx, a barge that moved forward from the stage's distant back wall, and his signature menagerie, here a camel, goats, and horses—in shifting patterns defined by metallic rods. The melding of abstraction and realism resulted in a gaudy hybrid that overwhelmed the music and the drama. The critics outdid one another in bashing Zeffirelli's production: "Almost everything about the evening, artistically speaking, failed in total impact . . . a lavish, but completely unoriginal concept that smothered in its own production"; "Appallingly pretentious, appallingly arty, and, in most respects, destructive"; "a disaster." As for the music, one reviewer went so far as to accuse Barber of dealing "a severe blow to the hopes of American opera by denying it the prestige it might have had. *Antony and Cleopatra* is a slick, chic, fashionable opening-night opera, when what was really needed was an opera for all seasons. It could have been both." Little wonder that Barber's composition breathed its last at the Met after only nine performances.[8]

Price was no less an inspiration for the score than Shakespeare for the libretto. The soprano had been Barber's interpreter and friend since the 1950s, when she sang the premiere of his "Hermit Songs." In the words of the composer, "Every vowel was placed with Leontyne's voice in mind. She is all

FIGURE 31. *Antony and Cleopatra,* act 2, scene 4, center left to right Justino Diaz as Antony, Leontyne Price as Cleopatra, Ezio Flagello as Enobarbus, 1966 (Louis Mélançon; courtesy Metropolitan Opera Archives)

impassioned lyricism. I had a problem just keeping her off stage." Far too often, however, he called upon her "'Carmen' voice" (*Times,* Aug. 28, 1966), her harsh low register to express Cleopatra's rage. But when given the chance to carve a soaring line in the upper octave, and then to perch on a high note, Price was at her resplendent best.

*Antony and Cleopatra* had broken the bank and the promise of a triumphant opening night. To add insult to injury, the New York City Opera put on Handel's *Giulio Cesare* a little more than a week after the Barber premiere. The acclaimed production and Beverly Sills's wondrously sung Cleopatra made a mockery of Bing's dismissal of the troupe next door as "provincial." The poor relation on Lincoln Center Plaza had let it be known that it would give the Met a run for its money.

For the final new production of his showcase 1966–67 season, Bing offered the world premiere of another American opera. Agamemnon's family imploded in Martin David Levy's expressionistic *Mourning Becomes Electra* as it had six months earlier in the *Elektra* of Richard Strauss. Henry Butler's skillful adaptation of Eugene O'Neill's gargantuan play, Boris Aronson's remarkable ruin of the Mannon mansion, the entire cast, the staging of film director Michael Cacoyannis, and the conducting of Zubin Mehta gave the work its best shot at success. Reviewers agreed that Levy's suppression of his bent for melody was all too obvious. Thirty years later, when the Lyric Opera of Chicago put on his revised version, the composer confessed that in 1967 he had "felt intimidated" by the fashionable "hard-liners" (*Times,* Oct. 13, 1998). But despite its flaws, *Mourning Becomes Electra* had made great theater even way back then.

## Made in USA

Two weeks before his first night, Giulio Gatti-Casaza announced that the Met would at last present an American opera, Frederick S. Converse's *The Pipe of Desire.* Soon after, the impresario persuaded the board to fund a $10,000 prize for a new work by an American-born composer. "I am convinced," he declared, "that there is enough musical talent in this country to justify a movement in favor of an American grand opera, and I am sure that if the movement is properly organized we shall be able to have operas worthy of the name" (*Times,* Nov. 21, 1908). In his 1925 "Statement," Otto Kahn thought it politic to recognize the Italian intendant's Americanization of the company; Gatti had introduced nine American operas in seventeen years. Kahn neglected to mention the anemic total of thirty-nine performances they had registered; and only two productions had survived into a second season. He elided also the point later made by Frances Alda in her witty account of a rehearsal of Walter Damrosch's *Cyrano:* "I had just finished my first duet with [Pasquale] Amato. The pencil marks on my score were misleading. 'Where do we go from here?' I asked Amato. Before he could reply, [Richard] Hageman, the assistant conductor, who was rehearsing us, spoke up: 'From Gounod to Meyerbeer.'" At its 1937 Met premiere, Hageman's own *Caponsacchi* would be savaged for its borrowings. Gatti let six years elapse between Henry Hadley's 1920 *Cleopatra's Night* (starring Alda) and 1927 when Deems Taylor's *The King's Henchman* became the first American opera to reach double-digit iterations. Before Gatti left in 1935, there were only two more.[9]

As time went by, the stubborn hope that America would find its operatic voice was repeatedly dashed. On October 15, 1935, Edward Johnson informed the board that he had obliged the Juilliard mandate by examining twenty-nine American scores; only Vittorio Giannini's *The Scarlet Letter* and David Tamkin's *The Dybbuk,* one saddled with a poor libretto, the other too costly, got as far as a second look. Like Krehbiel and Henderson before him, Olin Downes was an advocate for American opera in the abstract and a feared critic in the particular. Still, as director of music for the World's Fair, he pitched revivals of *Cyrano, The Emperor Jones,* and *Amelia Goes to the Ball* for the Met's special 1939 spring season. An all-Wagner program won the day. In 1941, the Carnegie Corporation of New York awarded grants-in-aid to composer William Schuman and librettist Christopher LaFarge so that they might learn the workings of the opera house from within. Their residency produced no tangible result. Johnson managed only six indigenous entries. *Newsweek* summed it up: "As far as American opera at the Metropolitan is concerned, the years have shown it to be a case of damned when it does, and damned again when it doesn't" (Jan. 20, 1947).[10]

As for Bing, neglect of American titles (he trotted out a pathetic four in twenty-two seasons) was just one aspect of the hidebound programming of which he was justly accused. When confronted with the choice of *Vanessa* or Louise Talma's twelve-tone score for Thornton Wilder's *The Alcestiad,* he opted for the less-taxing Barber-Menotti collaboration. Bait came in the form of a Ford Foundation grant: Ford pledged to commission three operas of composers selected by the company, any one of which could be rejected by the Met whatever the stage of its development. If chosen for production, the Foundation would cover the difference between the box-office receipts of the new opera and those of a popular title. The financial risk was negligible. But there was a downside, as Gutman noted: "If it finally should turn out that none of them is considered worthy of a Metropolitan production, it would not only be a very bad position in terms of our public relations but would also be an outspoken disservice to the cause of American Opera, which of course we ought to avoid at all cost." The projects of a number of proven composers were considered, among them those of Sergius Kagen, Norman Dello Joio, Nicholas Flagello, William Grant Still, Douglas Moore, Roger Sessions, Marc Blitzstein, and Barber and Levy. Moore gave *The Wings of the Dove* to the New York City Opera in exchange for assurances of production. Sessions's work was "not sufficiently advanced for him to show any part of it." Bliss authorized an additional sum for Blitzstein's *Sacco and Vanzetti;* at the composer's death in 1964, the score was still incomplete. In the end, Ford underwrote *Antony and Cleopatra* and *Mourning Becomes Electra.* Bing never again

TABLE 13 Metropolitan Premieres of American Operas, 1910–11 to 2012–13

| Composer and Title | Met Premiere (* World Premiere) | Most Recent Met Performance | No. of Seasons in Met Repertoire | No. of Met Productions | No. of Met Performances, 1883–2013 | World Premiere |
|---|---|---|---|---|---|---|
| Frederick Converse, The Pipe of Desire | Mar. 18, 1910 | Mar. 31, 1910 | 1 | 1 | 3 | Jan. 31, 1906, Boston, Jordan Hall |
| Horatio Parker, Mona | Mar. 14, 1912* | Apr. 1, 1912 | 1 | 1 | 4 | |
| Walter Damrosch, Cyrano | Feb. 27, 1913* | Apr. 23, 1913 | 1 | 1 | 6 | |
| Victor Herbert, Madeleine | Jan. 24, 1914* | Mar. 25, 1914 | 1 | 1 | 6 | |
| Reginald De Koven, The Canterbury Pilgrims | Mar. 8, 1917* | Apr. 21, 1917 | 1 | 1 | 7 | |
| Charles Wakefield Cadman, The Robin Woman: Shanewis | Mar. 23, 1918* | Apr. 4, 1919 | 2 | 1 | 8 | |
| Joseph Breil, The Legend | Mar. 12, 1919* | Apr. 4, 1919 | 1 | 1 | 3 | |
| John Adam Hugo, The Temple Dancer | Mar. 12, 1919* | Apr. 4, 1919 | 1 | 1 | 3 | |
| Henry Hadley, Cleopatra's Night | Jan. 31, 1920* | Feb. 23, 1921 | 2 | 1 | 9 | |
| Deems Taylor, The King's Henchman | Feb. 17, 1927* | Mar. 28, 1929 | 3 | 1 | 17 | |
| Deems Taylor, Peter Ibbetson | Feb. 7, 1931* | Apr. 4, 1935 | 4 | 1 | 22 | |
| Louis Gruenberg, The Emperor Jones | Jan. 7, 1933* | Apr. 5, 1934 | 2 | 1 | 15 | |
| Howard Hanson, Merry Mount | Feb. 10, 1934 (staged form)* | Apr. 12, 1934 | 1 | 1 | 9 | In concert: May 20, 1933, Hill Auditorium, Ann Arbor, Michigan |
| John Lawrence Seymour, In the Pasha's Garden | Jan. 24, 1935* | Feb. 13, 1935 | 1 | 1 | 3 | |
| Richard Hageman, Caponsacchi | Feb. 3, 1937 | Feb. 10, 1937 | 1 | 1 | 2 | Feb. 18, 1932, Freiburg (in German) |
| Walter Damrosch, The Man without a Country | May 12, 1937* | Feb. 17, 1938 | 2 | 1 | 5 | |
| Gian Carlo Menotti, Amelia Goes to the Ball | Mar. 3, 1938 | Jan. 30, 1939 | 2 | 1 | 7 | Apr. 1, 1937, Philadelphia, Academy of Music |
| Gian Carlo Menotti, The Island God | Feb. 20, 1942* | Mar. 12, 1942 | 1 | 1 | 4 | |

(continued)

TABLE 13 (continued)

| Composer and Title | Met Premiere (*World Premiere) | Most Recent Met Performance | No. of Seasons in Met Repertoire | No. of Met Productions | No. of Met Performances, 1883–2013 | World Premiere |
|---|---|---|---|---|---|---|
| Bernard Rogers, The Warrior | Jan. 11, 1947* | Jan. 31, 1947 | 1 | 1 | 2 | |
| Samuel Barber, Vanessa | Jan. 15, 1958* | Apr. 13, 1965 | 3 | 1 | 18 | |
| Gian Carlo Menotti, The Last Savage (in English)a | Jan. 23, 1964 | May 24, 1965 | 2 | 1 | 16 | Oct. 21, 1962, Paris, Opéra-Comique |
| Samuel Barber, Antony and Cleopatra | Sept. 16, 1966* | Dec. 1, 1966 | 1 | 1 | 8 | |
| Martin David Levy, Mourning Becomes Electra | Mar. 17, 1967* | Dec. 28, 1967 | 2 | 1 | 11 | |
| Virgil Thomson, Four Saints in Three Acts | Feb. 20, 1973 | Mar. 10, 1973 | 1 | 1 | 12 | Feb. 8, 1934, Hartford, Connecticut, Avery Memorial |
| George Gershwin, Porgy and Bess | Feb. 6, 1985 | Dec. 6, 1990 | 4 | 1 | 54 | Sept. 30, 1935, Boston, Colonial |
| John Corigliano, The Ghosts of Versailles | Dec. 19, 1991* | Apr. 21, 1995 | 2 | 1 | 13 | |
| Philip Glass, The Voyage | Oct. 12, 1992* | Apr. 11, 1996 | 2 | 1 | 12 | |
| Carlisle Floyd, Susannah | Mar. 31, 1999 | Apr. 22, 1999 | 1 | 1 | 7 | Feb. 24, 1955, Ruby Diamond Auditorium, Tallahassee, FL |
| John Harbison, The Great Gatsby | Dec. 20, 1999* | May 11, 2002 | 2 | 1 | 12 | |
| Michael Bolcom, A View from the Bridge | Dec. 5, 2002 | Dec. 28, 2002 | 1 | 1 | 7 | Oct. 9, 1999, Chicago, Lyric |
| Tobias Picker, An American Tragedy | Dec. 2, 2005* | Dec. 28, 2005 | 1 | 1 | 8 | |
| Tan Dun, The First Emperor | Dec. 21, 2006* | May 17, 2008 | 2 | 1 | 12 | |
| Philip Glass, Satyagraha | Apr. 11, 2008 | Dec. 1, 2011 | 2 | 1 | 14 | Sept. 5, 1980, Rotterdam, Stadsschouwburg |
| John Adams, Doctor Atomic | Oct. 13, 2008 | Nov. 13, 2008 | 1 | 1 | 9 | Oct. 1, 2005, San Francisco, War Memorial |
| John Adams, Nixon in China | Feb. 2, 2011 | Feb. 19, 2011 | 1 | 1 | 6 | Oct. 22, 1987, Houston, Grand Opera |

a Menotti's three operas presented by the Met were composed to Italian texts and performed in English. The world premiere of The Last Savage (L'Ultimo Selvaggio) was in French. The world premieres of Amelia Goes to the Ball (Amelia al ballo) and The Island God (Ilo e Zeus) were in English.

ventured onto the home field. It was not until December 19, 1991, that the company mounted a new American work, John Corigliano's *The Ghosts of Versailles*. In the new millennium, rising enthusiasm for products "made in the USA" has been generated primarily in other theaters.[11]

POSTMORTEM: 1966–1967

By the end of the first Lincoln Center season, Bing was done with American experimentation. With *Mourning Becomes Electra* he shut the door to native works. And with barely disguised satisfaction, he drove the final nail into the coffin of the Metropolitan's two-year-old National Company, established to bring opera to communities all over North America and opportunities to young American artists. President Kennedy had announced the initiative with some fanfare in October 1963. The enterprise got off to an inauspicious start when the State Department denied a visa to Walter Felsenstein of East Berlin's Komische Oper. Felsenstein had been engaged to do the staging. The recently retired Risë Stevens was drafted to head the operation. The first season opened in Indianapolis in September 1965 with Carlisle Floyd's *Susannah,* one of the few American operas to have gained a measure of acceptance. Occasionally the company played in large urban centers. In New York, it took up residence at the New York State Theatre to the dismay of both the New York City Opera (it had not yet itself christened its new home) and of the Metropolitan's general manager. Both tours were beleaguered by poor attendance, high expenses, and commensurate deficits. Bing resented the diversion of monies and energy to the fledgling troupe and, most particularly, the association of the Met's gilt-edged brand with an undertaking of modest luster. A loan of $1 million, sufficient to keep the project aloft for another year at least, had been promised, but Bing and the board, ignoring Anthony Bliss's remonstrations, refused the gift. Bliss resigned his presidency of eleven years and was replaced by the treasurer, George Moore. The National Company had something of an afterlife. Among the graduates who would go on to careers as Metropolitan leads were bass Paul Plishka, soprano Maralin Niska, and tenors Enrico Di Giuseppe and Harry Theyard.[12]

Looking back on the 1966–67 season in his annual report, Bing acknowledged the failure of *Antony and Cleopatra, Lohengrin,* and *La Traviata,* and boasted of the "outstanding successes," *Die Frau ohne Schatten, Peter Grimes, Mourning Becomes Electra, La Gioconda, Die Zauberflöte,* and *Elektra,* "not too bad an average." Beni Montresor conjured a fantastical Venice for *La Gioconda* (Sept. 22) with Renata Tebaldi as the street-singer. Anna Moffo's Violetta wore Cecil Beaton's extravagant costumes as she traversed his long, winding staircases in Alfred Lunt's staging of *La Traviata* (Sept. 24). It was with the Met premiere of Strauss's *Die Frau ohne Schatten* that the brilliance of the company and of the resources of the new opera house came together. The audience had never seen anything like it. The Merrill-O'Hearn production made smart use of stage elevators, seven in all, to move the action from the netherworld of Keikobad and the Nurse upward to the Earth of Barak and his wife and into the beyond, the ethereal kingdom of the Emperor and Empress. With Straussian Karl Böhm leading Leonie Rysanek, Christa Ludwig, and Walter Berry, the Met made the strongest possible case for the work. Strauss was again well served by the House of Atreus erected by Rudolf Heinrich for the new *Elektra* (Oct. 28), and by the titanic portrayals of Birgit Nilsson, Leonie Rysanek, and Regina Resnik (Oct. 28). Wieland Wagner, the master's grandson, died two months before he was scheduled to stage *Lohengrin* (Dec. 8). Peter Lehmann, his assistant and replacement, based the show on Wieland's prior productions for Bayreuth and Hamburg. Oratorio-like, with the chorus stationed on risers or slowly marching in hypnotic formation, the opera took most of its urgency from Christa Ludwig's Ortrud. "On the whole . . . this is an inoffensive *Lohengrin* . . . not as imaginative (for better or worse) as the best work that comes from Bayreuth." *Peter Grimes* (Jan. 20) returned after a hiatus of nearly two decades; at the center of the gritty production was Jon Vickers, who found a voice to challenge the force of the sea, the community, and the hero's own demons. Although Chagall's décor did little to support the dramatic values of *Die Zauberflöte* (Feb. 19), the painter's iconography delighted most spectators and would continue to do so through eight revivals.[13]

## METROPOLITAN/METROPOLIS IN CRISIS

The cost of inhabiting and maintaining the Met's grand precincts had been grossly underestimated: operating expenses had run over by $796,000; the year's new productions cost $856,000 more than had been budgeted; the settlement reached with the musicians added $280,000 to the burgeoning deficit; and remedying the most pressing defects of the new building added $307,000 more. Ticket prices were raised by 20 percent in November, an unprecedented midseason hike, desperately needed despite near-capacity attendance. At the April 10, 1967, meeting of the Metropolitan Opera Association, chairman Lauder Greenway offered this explanation: "The delay in the delivery of the new house [five months after it was promised], mechanical difficulties with the new equipment, difficult labor negotiations involving work stoppages during the vital rehearsal period, and the problems of launching *nine* new productions in one season (four in the opening two weeks) put unprecedented and almost unmanageable technical and administrative burdens on our staff. We temporarily lost control of our costs, for reasons which we might have partly anticipated, but which, when they arrived, proved beyond our control. We are happy to report that things are now back on track." Greenway's upbeat conclusion notwithstanding, the financial turbulence of 1966–67 would plague the Met for years to come. A sobering caveat was appended to the invitation from Bing to Attilio Colonnello for the design of a new *Luisa Miller:* "I should tell you right now that we cannot again approach anything as heavy and bulky as *Lucia* was. We have neither the money for it, the space for it, nor the manpower to handle these enormous productions any more" (Nov. 9, 1966).[14]

Meanwhile, New York had entered one of the most treacherous periods of its history. On January 25, 1965, after six months of digging by four of its reporters, the *Herald Tribune* published a hard-hitting piece titled "City in Crisis," an indictment of New York under the mayoralties of Democrat Robert Wagner and his Democratic predecessors. The *Tribune*'s jeremiad covered topics from poverty to traffic, business to welfare, housing, hospitals, finances, the elites, the press, the police, and many more. The litany of urban disaster spawned a four-month series that took a deeper look into the most intractable problems of the city. The 1960s saw crime, racial unrest, "Burn, baby, burn," flight to the suburbs by business and the middle class, assassinations, antiwar protests, student takeovers, and strikes. The Metropolitan, like other cultural institutions, suffered the effects of the social and economic turmoil. Of passing consequence was the cancellation of *Il Trovatore* during the blackout of 1965; far more lasting was the drop in ticket sales caused by anxiety over dark streets.

But nowhere was the intersection of the Metropolitan's troubles with those of the city more evident than in the arena of labor relations. In 1966, the year the orchestra threatened to disrupt the Met's first Lincoln Center season, the transit workers took to the picket lines for twelve days. In 1968, the sanitation workers walked off the job; that same year, the firing of white, mostly Jewish teachers and administrators of the Ocean Hill–Brownsville school district led to a three-month strike over decentralization and race. In 1969, the Met musicians made good on their threat. As *New York Magazine* put it, "'They'd Never Strike the Met,' say the same people who said last year that they'd never strike the schools. But opera isn't life." Unlike the teachers, the musicians had not actually struck. As contract talks stalled and opening night approached, Bing was unwilling to schedule costly rehearsals until an uninterrupted season was guaranteed. In effect, he preempted the work stoppage and in doing so gained what he perceived to be a strategic advantage. The standoff lasted three months. Bing was cast as the villain, which was not surprising, given his open hostility toward unions in general and, in particular, his fully reciprocated antipathy for Herman Gray, the musicians' representative. He had no trouble playing hardball: he withheld summer pay and attempted, unsuccessfully, to delay the distribution of unemployment checks. By the time the two sides came to terms on salary and benefits and performances could begin, it was not September 15 (as originally announced), but December 29. The Metropolitan Opera Association had to return $2.3 million of the $2.85 million it had collected in subscriptions; the total box-office take was $7.5 million, down drastically from the $11.2 million of the previous season. Average capacity tumbled from 96 percent to 89 percent.[15]

### BING'S LAST STAND: 1967–1972

Bing was not alone responsible for the failed salary talks of spring and summer 1969. He was under instructions from George Moore, since 1967 president of the Metropolitan Opera Association. The directors had elected Moore, chairman of Citigroup, with the expectation that a banker would succeed in checking the runaway expenditures of the first Lincoln Center season. Bing soon learned to regret the change of the guard, particularly when it came to programming. His infuriating clashes with Moore were reminiscent of early struggles with then board president George Sloan "to get authorization for new productions." Nonetheless, Bing managed to pull off twenty-one restagings, nearly all conferred on the "perennial classics," as Edward Johnson had defined them, or, at the very least, on titles that had enjoyed multiple revivals. Fully nine of the twenty-one were underwritten by Mrs. John D. Rockefeller Jr., the others by a small coterie of Maecenases, foundations, and corporations. Novelties were all but absent. Bing's final half-decade as general manager has the dubious distinction of constituting the longest spell in Met history without a premiere, let alone a world premiere. As for the dramatic and visual dimensions of opera, he came to rely, more and more, on the tried and true. Only five stage directors and three designers made debuts.[16]

Far too many of the new productions were misbegotten. On the second night of the 1967–68 season, austerity was depressingly obvious in the skeletal *Roméo et Juliette* (Sept. 19). Franco Corelli and Mirella Freni were thrilling as the lovers of Verona—and oblivious to the requisite French style. "In terms of linguistic authenticity, it often bordered on the atrocious, especially where the two protagonists were concerned." In fact, the French repertoire was poorly served in the twilight of Bing's regime. There was the ugly *Carmen* (Dec. 15, 1967) that penned the hapless principals in variations on the Plaza de Toros ("ridiculous . . . awkward. . . . It is disheartening to contemplate the fact that the Met will probably be stuck with this conception of *Carmen* for the next decade"); the first *Werther* (Feb. 19, 1971) in sixty years, staged on dreary sets for a miscast Corelli. Appraisals of *Der Freischütz* (Sept. 28, 1971), withdrawn after a single season, ranged from "entirely conventional" to "full of dated notions of movement and groupings" to "hideous." *Luisa Miller* (Feb. 8, 1968), returning to the Met after nearly forty years, was an aural feast in which Montserrat Caballé and Sherrill Milnes honored Verdi and bel canto; Colonnello framed them and the rest of the excellent cast with one of his tired theatrical conceits, onstage spectators in period costume seated in ersatz boxes within the proscenium, a device scratched in later runs of this production. "[The onstage spectators] waved fans, they moved, they stole more scenes than Shirley Temple used to do in her heyday. The trouble was that anyone in the audience with normal peripheral vision picked up their movement and suddenly was watching them rather than the Verdi opera." The unfortunate 1959 *Trovatore* was exchanged for Colonnello's confused and lugubrious 1969 décors (March 6), "a cave-like collection of stalactites and stalagmites" unworthy of Price, Milnes, Grace Bumbry, and Plácido Domingo. The recurrence of Colonnello betrayed the management's flagging vitality. That critics and audiences had hated his 1964 *Lucia* mattered little; he was invited back for the grating *Luisa Miller,* and then awarded the *Trovatore* to boot.[17]

A few shows did the Met proud. O'Hearn and Merrill were in top form in a witty *Hänsel und Gretel* (Nov. 6, 1967), in an opulent *Rosenkavalier* (Jan. 23, 1969) that would flatter fortunate Marschallins, Octavians, and Sophies for decades, and in a *Parsifal* (Nov. 14, 1970) whose serene meadow was an affecting analogue for the mellifluous Gurnemanz of Cesare Siepi. In Gunther Schneider-Siemssen's iconic *Tristan und Isolde* (Nov. 18, 1971), the wizardry of the Met's machinery wrought an ideal stage picture for the "liebesnacht": the act 2 garden faded into darkness as the lovers, singing of ecstasy and death, were borne aloft and then suspended in the night sky. Zeffirelli atoned for *Antony and Cleopatra* with *Cavalleria rusticana* and *Pagliacci* (Jan. 18, 1970). The Beethoven bicentenary *Fidelio* (Dec. 16, 1970), designed by Aronson and directed by Otto Schenk, animated a piece often thought static. In fact, as one reviewer put it, "The sets [were] a drama in themselves" *(Post)*. A rough-hewn, layered, slightly irregular platform focused the action beneath dank prison walls that turned transparent to admit the light of day at the joyous finale. Rysanek and Jon Vickers, arguably the greatest Florestan in modern Met history, led the cast. In this long-lived edition, *Fidelio* earned a currency it had not before enjoyed—over one hundred performances between 1970 and 1994.[18]

The big ticket of the late 1960s was to be Herbert von Karajan's "Ring," courtesy of Eastern Airlines, the first corporate sponsor of a Met production. Karajan began to record the tetralogy in August 1966, and then staged and conducted it, starting in March 1967, at the Salzburg Easter Festival, an annual happening created expressly by and for him. That fall there was no mistaking that the de facto *Generalmusikdirektor* of Europe's major orchestras and lyric theaters had come to town. In a matter of little more than a month, he bracketed his Met debut by marshaling the La Scala forces for the Verdi "Requiem" and those of the Berlin Philharmonic for Bach, both in Carnegie Hall. He had the chutzpah to demand that the New York production be promoted as the "Karajan Ring." He insisted that the pit be raised, the better to release a shimmering transparency from his instrumentalists—and the better himself to be seen. *Die Walküre* (Nov. 21, 1967), the first installment of the "Karajan Ring," was, for some, although not all, a revelation. The Siegmund and Sieglinde, Vickers and Gundula Janowitz, seemed for once to sing to each other. Even so, there was disappointment: Schneider-Siemssen's sets, conceived for the wide stage of the Salzburg Festspielhaus, lost a measure of their impact once rebuilt to fit the proportions of the Manhattan proscenium; the smaller seating capacity of the Salzburg auditorium fostered an intimacy all but impossible at the Met; many key scenes played at the rear of the stage put the singers at an aural and visual disadvantage; the pervasive darkness, a Karajan trademark, and the ever-present front scrim shrouded faces and action. *Das Rheingold* (Nov. 22, 1968) was received with enthusiasm: "ominously magnificent throughout . . . a triumph of subtlety." No one knew that with this run Karajan's days at the Met would be over.[19]

Nilsson was as crucial a factor as Karajan in Bing's Wagner equation. The encounter of the two was sure to set off sparks. Earlier and elsewhere, a Stygian environment had made trouble between the conductor and the soprano. She had responded to his cherished penumbra by donning a miner's helmet during rehearsal, a not-so-friendly prank. Following a series of tortured mediations, Nilsson finally agreed to appear in the 1967 *Walküre*. No one would sing Brünnhilde in 1969–70; *Siegfried* fell victim to the strike. When Karajan announced the cast of the upcoming *Götterdämmerung*, he took the insulting step of replacing the world's leading Wagnerian soprano with his current favorite, Helga Dernesch. The Met paid the price. Nilsson canceled half of her performances for 1970–71, including the Ariadnes she would never sing in New York. When Bing offered to drop Dernesch, it was too late. The resumption of the "Ring" was put off until 1972–73, the *Siegfried* in which Nilsson was conducted by Erich Leinsdorf.[20]

By the time the imperial Karajan departed the Met for good, the die had been cast for the imperious general manager. Bing's future had, in fact, "been in doubt for some time" (*Times*, June 28, 1969). The renewal of his contract for 1969–1972 carried the understanding that the expiration of the agreement would end Bing's incumbency; he would be past seventy and would have served twenty-two years, five short of Gatti-Casazza's record. Some months later, Bing was pilloried for the crippled 1969–70 season. *New York Magazine* had its say in an article titled "The Metropolitan Opera versus the Public." Under a picture of Bing in forbidding profile, the caption read, "Anachronism within an Anachronism?" There had been no public accountability, no disclosure of the balance sheet since he had taken over in 1950. The blame, according to the writer, lay also with the board that had given Bing carte blanche.[21]

The announcement of Bing's impending retirement did nothing to quell the attacks, and Bing, true to his nature and reputation, shot back: "Nine out of ten reviews that we read—if not all ten—are based on ignorance, and on unfair venom of little people who have an axe to grind, and consider themselves important if they can write badly about someone else." And then, the final volley: "Fortunately, the public shares my views and the critics have not the slightest effect on our public or on our boxoffice." Particularly galling to the press corps was that Bing "operated on the principle that he and he alone is in a position to judge how well he has been doing his job." So when Bing cited as one of his achievements the lifting of racial barriers, Alan Rich saw to it that even this permissible bit of self-promotion was debunked: the Met's chief was simply in the right place at the right time. "It would be unthinkable for the Met not to have broken the color line some time during the past twenty years." Rich went about setting the record straight on several other presumptive accomplishments: "It would have been absurd not to assume that the season would be lengthened [from sixteen to thirty-one weeks] and the range of activities broadened. A new house was ordained partly by the magnetism of the Lincoln Center idea-in-the-sky and partly because of the building realities in the Times Square area. You or I, in charge of the Met from 1950 to 1972, could not possibly have acted otherwise." This time, a caricature of Bing getting the hook accompanied the piece.[22]

With respect to another achievement Bing took as a particular point of pride, his restagings of the core repertoire, assessments were mixed at best. The worst were encapsulated in Newsweek's devastating summary: "What the Met has lacked above all is taste. In place of taste it has gotten by on lavishly expensive spectacle and glamor. Its repertory has been top-heavy in cumbersome productions that squandered money on costumes and sets." Critics were willing to concede that a dozen or so of the eighty-eight new productions stood out. There was only partial consensus on the titles of these happy few. The triage seems to us unfairly severe. Our discussions in this and the preceding chapter profess that we would double the number of successes to include many absent from contemporary lists. But we would agree that Bing sanctioned too many clinkers, productions in which misguided décors undercut the score, the libretto, and the artists.[23]

Bing fared no better in the matter of repertoire, where, again, he claimed complete authority: "I am solely responsible for the repertory. Naturally I take advice. I listen to some of my colleagues—on both the musical and artistic staffs. And I have to consider innumerable questions. But the final decision on repertory, as indeed on everything else in this house—including casting— is mine. So all the blame for whatever is blameworthy should come to me." And it did. Conventional programming was laid at the feet of the general manager. If the Metropolitan was called "a museum," as it disparagingly often was, Bing made lemonade out of the lemons tossed in his direction: "I don't see it as an insult at all. I think it is one of the Metropolitan's functions to do the masterpieces of the past as seen through contemporary eyes, and therefore acquaint succeeding generations with these masterpieces." Of course. But another cardinal function, the propagation of new and unfamiliar works, was slighted. His circumspection was all the more conspicuous in contrast to the much applauded and often successful daring of the neighboring New York City Opera. By way of example, in 1971–72 City Opera scheduled eleven rarities, nearly all of which had recently or would soon become titles closely associated with the company: *Roberto Devereux, Maria Stuarda, Giulio Cesare, The Makropoulos Case, Louise, Mefistofele, Le Coq d'or, Susannah,* and *The Turn of the Screw.* That same year, the sole Met offerings outside the core were *Der Freischütz* (a flop) and *La Fille du régiment* (a hit).[24]

Bing also did poorly when it came to conductors. Reviewing the roll of exceptional guest maestros, Martin Bernheimer felt it his "unpleasant duty to point out that most of these admitted giants [Pierre Monteux, Georg Solti, Ernest Ansermet, Bernstein, Colin Davis, Josef Krips, Karajan, and Claudio Abbado] graced the Met podium for only a season or two, some only for a single production." Kurt Adler, Jean Morel, Nino Verchi, Joseph Rosenstock, Silvio Varviso, Nello Santi, Richard Bonynge, Carlo Franci, Leopold Ludwig, Gabor Ötvös, and Michelangelo Veltri were "the far less imposing rule" (*Los Angeles Times,* May 7, 1972). Ubiquitous were the uninspiring Fritz Stiedry, who conducted more than two hundred performances between 1950 and 1958, and the routine Fausto Cleva, who led more than nine hundred between 1950 and 1971. *Stereo Review* distilled the consensus: that the house conducting staff was the weakest link in the general manager's armor, and that the reason for the weakness was his reluctance to suffer the irritant of a competing personality on the podium. "Strong-minded conductors and Mr. Bing do not seem to get along."[25]

Finally, even those who judged Bing's record most harshly acknowledged that he had attracted the illustrious singers of the time to New York. They nevertheless complained about his handling of the stars: he played favorites, snobbishly preferring European artists; he often attributed roles inappropriately; he allowed insufficient rehearsal time. And to top it all off, star salaries had gone through the roof. Although the official ceiling was $4,000 per performance, sweetheart deals were surreptitiously struck with the superstars, Sutherland, Nilsson, Tebaldi, and Corelli: they might be contracted for twenty shows and sing only ten. Perhaps the best deserved of the many grievances was that once the first cast had completed its run, another would be thrown onto the boards with scant if any preparation, subverting the widely touted attention to stagecraft. And there was the other gripe that he had let go some of the most accomplished, if not the most lucrative, artists of the day, Victoria de los Angeles and Cesare Valletti, to name just two.[26]

TABLE 14  Metropolitan Opera Premieres, 1966–67 to 1971–72

| Composer and Title | Met Premiere (*World Premiere) | Most Recent Met Performance | No. of Seasons in Met Repertoire | No. of Met Productions | No. of Met Performances, 1883–2013 | World Premiere | Director/Designer |
|---|---|---|---|---|---|---|---|
| Samuel Barber, Antony and Cleopatra | Sept. 16, 1966* | Dec. 1, 1966 | 1 | 1 | 8 | | Franco Zeffirelli / Franco Zeffirelli |
| Richard Strauss, Die Frau ohne Schatten | Oct. 2, 1966 | Dec. 13, 2003 | 8 | 2 | 59 | Oct. 10, 1919, Vienna, Staatsoper | Nathaniel Merrill / Robert O'Hearn |
| Martin David Levy, Mourning Becomes Electra | Mar. 17, 1967* | Dec. 28, 1967 | 2 | 1 | 11 | | Michael Cacoyannis / Boris Aronson |

By late spring 1972, the gentlemen of the musical press would not have Rudolf Bing to kick around anymore. What they did not know was that Bing would be the last Met general manager to be alone responsible for all administrative and artistic matters. The last, that is, until Peter Gelb.

## "MUSICAL CHAIRS"

The race to define the ideal successor to the lately knighted Sir Rudolf was on, as was the even more intriguing game of identifying who the candidates might be. Should the Met be looking for an administrator, someone who would make ends meet (as George Moore argued)? Or an artistic personality (as recommended by Zubin Mehta)? An American who would take pride in the Met as "an American institution" (Mehta, again)? Or a person "under sixty so that he can give us at least a full decade" (Moore, again)? Or was all this beside the point? For many, the fundamental question was whether the company should at last have a separate and distinct artistic director who would work alongside an administratively and financially astute general manager. Among the names in circulation were Robert Herman (Bing's first choice), Max Rudolf (another longtime member of the inner circle), Herman Krawitz (Bing's aide responsible for business and technical operations), Leonard Bernstein (Moore claimed no offer had been made, while Bernstein insisted he had waved off official and "sub-rosa" overtures), Herbert von Karajan, Rolf Lieberman (head of the Paris Opéra), bass-baritone George London, and board member Anthony Bliss.[27]

### Goeran Gentele

Schuyler Chapin, in charge of programming at Lincoln Center, threw three more names into the hopper: Massimo Bogianckino, director of the Rome Opera; Peter Mennin, president of Juilliard; and Goeran Gentele, intendant of the Royal Swedish Opera. The offer was first made to Mennin, who declined. The selection committee then approached Gentele; he cheerfully accepted. His five-year appointment, beginning in 1972, was announced on December 9, 1970. Like Heinrich Conried, an actor, stage director, and administrator, the fifty-three-year-old Gentele had been a hands-on presence as head of the relatively small Stockholm company since 1963; he had staged more than a score of operas in just seven years, all the while tripling government subsidies. He had been much praised for the premiere of Karl-Birger Blomdahl's science fiction *Aniara* and for an authentically Swedish *Un Ballo in maschera,* in which the love triangle was infused with the bisexuality of Gustav III. The Royal Swedish Opera and its head had attracted international attention when they played Montreal's Expo 67. And most appealing to the media-conscious board president George Moore, Gentele had produced a substantial number of films and several operas for television. Years earlier, Chapin had met with him in Stockholm to request the loan of Ingmar Bergman's production of *The Rake's Progress* for the Hamburg Opera visit to New York. Gentele turned him down with grace and humor, and a friendship was born. A subsequent visit by the John D. Rockefellers cemented Gentele's connections to the Met. All this led to the insertion of his candidacy into what Chapin called "the Metropolitan sweepstakes."[28]

**1971–1972.** Gentele spent 1971–72 as an observer, more than enough time for insiders and outsiders to draw the contrast between the outgoing and incoming general managers. Whereas Bing pressed for formality, Gentele urged one and all to call him by his given name; in an effort to attract a younger audience, he discouraged evening wear. If he announced, just as Bing had at the time of his appointment, that he intended to draw exciting directors to the Met (in Gentele's case Bergman, Jerome Robbins, and Giorgio Strehler), he also expressed this decidedly un-Bing-like sentiment: that he hoped "to bring about close cooperation with other American opera companies" (*Times,* Dec. 11, 1970). As for his relationship to singers, "From my point of view, the best way to get in touch with them—to know how they feel and explain things to them—is by personal contact both with the artist and their agents. . . . I think it impossible to negotiate only by letter because what you accomplish by telephone calls would take months of letter-writing." The chasm between Bing and Gentele opened wide when in June 1971 the general manager–designate declared that, for the first time in its history, the Metropolitan would have an official music director, a position neither Bing nor any of his predecessors had countenanced. His choice was Rafael Kubelik, a self-exiled Czech who had been music director of the Czech Philharmonic, the Brno Opera, the Chicago Symphony, Covent Garden, and Munich's Bayerischer Rundfunk. Gentele followed up with the news that Schuyler Chapin would be the assistant general manager, whereupon a curious John Gutman invited Chapin to lunch, and then hastened to let the vacationing

Bing know that a radically altered organizational model was in the works, a "troika," as he put it, of Gentele, Kubelik, and Chapin.[29]

On his return to the United States that fall, Bing took a swipe at Gentele's break with past practice: "A musical director considers himself responsible for deciding repertory and cast, to say nothing of maintaining the quality of the orchestra and chorus. I was not prepared to abdicate. An opera house must be a total democracy run by one man, and one man only" (London *Times*, Nov. 10, 1971). By the time of this interview, on this point at least, Bing had already been vindicated. The previous month, fully two years before Kubelik was scheduled to take up his duties, the *Times* (Oct. 17, 1971) had published a long profile of the conductor, replete with his overly frank views on the primacy of the music director and his very own plans for the future of the company. Three days later, Gentele chided Kubelik for the "embarrassing" remarks. In reply to Kubelik's assertion that "a general manager must run the administration for the artistic purpose which is set by the music director," Gentele wrote, "You know very well that I was not engaged here as an ordinary administrator but because of my artistic qualifications. I am not going to serve you or anybody but the Met—I hope together with you." And in response to Kubelik's statement that "opera is music and the music director is the conscience of the House," Gentele countered, "Of course opera is music but not only music: it is even theatre. If you don't stick to that, I think we can never get any great director to work here. Neither Bergman nor Robbins—not even myself." Kubelik had also spilled the beans intended for Gentele's forthcoming press briefing: that there would be fewer productions per season, more rehearsal time, and cheaper tickets. He had positioned himself baldly as the lead figure of the troika.

More friction was to come. The demands of advance planning dictated that Bing schedule Gentele's first season and as far into the future as 1973–74. Sir Rudolf was therefore in a position to program his successor's opening night. For that gala occasion he chose Wagner's *Tannhäuser*, to general astonishment and to the counterfeit shock of Birgit Nilsson, Gentele's compatriot: "It's very strange that Mr. Bing who has never opened any season with a German opera, suddenly takes the oldest production he has in the house and gives it to Mr. Gentele. When I did *Tannhäuser* in 1965 the costumes were in terrible condition and some of the scenery was practically transparent" (*Times*, Sept. 12, 1971). Gentele dodged the bullet. The board agreed that Marilyn Horne and James McCracken, signed for the twenty-year-old *Tannhäuser*, be cast instead in a new *Carmen*. When Giorgio Strehler, invited to direct the production, could not be located, Gentele took on the job himself, by now persuaded of the wisdom of putting his own imprint on the house. In the intervening months, the original concept of shared governance among the triumvirate, with the general manager as first among equals, was scrapped for a more distinctly hierarchical organization.[30]

By February 1972, it was clear that the general manager would be in control both administratively and artistically. He would divide responsibility for the stage with the music director, and reporting to the music director would be a principal conductor. Appointed to the latter post on February 15, 1972, was the twenty-eight-year-old James Levine, who had made his Met debut only the summer before. Levine would devote seven months each year to the company and lead four works a season, including one new production. He would be, as he said, "Rafael Kubelik's right-hand man, although not an assistant music director—he feels assistants are useless." He would take on administrative duties when Kubelik was away. The assistant general manager Schuyler Chapin, the artistic administrator Charles Riecker, replacing Herman, and the technical administrator Michael Bronson, replacing Krawitz, would support the artistic team of Gentele, Kubelik, and Levine.

In the end, tragically, it was not to Conried or Bing that Gentele would be compared, but to Herbert Witherspoon, he too freshly appointed Met general manager almost four decades earlier. Both died just months before their opening nights. On July 19, 1972, on holiday in Sardinia, Gentele and two daughters were killed in an automobile accident. His wife and frequent collaborator, Marit, and a third daughter survived. He had been the official company head for only eighteen days. With what little was recorded of his directorial intentions, with the stark designs of Czech scenographer Josef Svoboda, and with Leonard Bernstein in the pit, Gentele had a posthumous debut capable of holding its own against Bing's 1950 *Don Carlo*.

## Schuyler Chapin

The transfer of power to Gentele's successor was necessarily a study in improvisation. There was no time and, understandably, no stomach for dispute about who should take over. Opening night was barely two months away. And the rational solution in the circumstance, bringing back Rudolf Bing, was to all appearances unpalatable. Bing cabled board president Lowell Wadmond, "Deeply shocked tragic disaster. If you feel my temporary help useful naturally at your disposal in this terrible emergency," to which Wadmond replied, "Appreciate greatly your cable and generous offer of assistance. Board appointed Schuyler Chapin acting general manager who is grateful to you and will be in touch in event necessary." Don't call us. The stunned Metropolitan directors had indeed assembled the day after Gentele's death to hear Chapin's detailed report on the accident, and then to vote on what everyone knew to be a fait accompli. Moore made the offer on the spot and Chapin accepted. At the press conference following adjournment, the board's action was made public, together with the implausible assurance that there would be no disruption in the Met's operation: Chapin would carry out Gentele's well-laid plans for the coming season. No immediate search for a permanent general manager was contemplated; the arrangement was to be open-ended. The next day, July 20, as Chapin was in the midst of briefing his staff for the first time, there was, unimaginably, a second fatality: a stage hand fell through a trapdoor to his death. With that, the inexperienced Chapin, forty-nine, was thrust into the crisis-ridden universe of a Metropolitan impresario. As he described it in his memoirs, "Up to this point my entire professional life had been as a second man. . . . Until this moment I had never been in command, never been at the top, never been the one to bear the ultimate responsibility for the decision-making process." Chapin had held a variety of positions in the entertainment industry: at NBC, at Columbia Artists Management, and at Columbia Records. He had come to Lincoln Center as one of its vice presidents, he had helped launch the New York Film Festival, and had brought the Hamburg and Rome operas for summer seasons. But he was neither a musician, nor a theater person, nor ever a CEO.[31]

A wary Wadmond and a diffident, often dismissive Moore made certain that the reins were tight around Chapin's authority. From July 1972 to May 1973, when "acting" was dropped from his title and he was granted a three-year contract, Chapin was in the hapless position of performing the role for which he was auditioning. The vaguely complimentary statement issued in conjunction with his promotion made mention of his successful negotiation of new union contracts (the first peaceful negotiations in more than two decades, for which Gentele had earlier been credited) and an increase in box office for the current year and in subscriptions for the year to come. Few were naïve enough to believe that the Chapin appointment would usher in "a new era of expansion and achievement for the Metropolitan" (*Times,* May 9, 1973). The perilous financial waters in which the Met had foundered for decades were at flood tide. To make matters worse, Kubelik's contract, as negotiated by Gentele, called for his presence in New York only five months out of the year. And those two realities, the ballooning debt and the absent music director, would soon lead to an artistic/administrative meltdown that would end Chapin's regime after just three seasons.

1972–1973. The opening night *Carmen,* September 19, 1972, offered only a glimpse at what might have been. Gentele's discussions with collaborators had been preliminary and general: with Svoboda, agreement on stylized sets; with Bernstein, the return to Bizet's original opéra comique. Assistant director Bodo Igesz, promoted that summer to full responsibility, found no prompt book and just a few annotations in a score. During rehearsals, the principals, Horne in particular, expressed concern over the acoustic effect of the designer's wall-to-wall carpeting. Bernstein could do no wrong. One instrumentalist was quoted, "He makes hard things easy, like Karajan, and he makes old things new. I mean, who else would bother with tambourine dynamics." The result was an invigorated look at one of the beloved warhorses of the repertoire. The uncluttered sets kept the elemental conflicts in focus, sparing the audience yet another picturesque tour of Seville and its environs. The entire production created "a level of musical drama whose attainment is a new chapter in Met history." Horne brought the right voice and an engaging sense of humor to her Carmen; McCracken played José with a riveting mixture of obsession and frustration. Deutsche Grammophon began to record the Met production a few days after the premiere, the first such venture in nineteen years, that is, since union wages dispatched record companies to Europe's more affordable studios.[32]

*Siegfried* (Nov. 17, 1972) was the next new production, a Bing legacy, the third installment of the Salzburg "Ring." Leinsdorf was no Karajan,. Jess Thomas barely adequate in the rigorous title role; Nilsson took heroic charge in the act 3 "Awakening" scene: "the soprano poured waves of golden tone over an audience that had been waiting for some hours for singing of this magnitude." The season's three other new productions were staged at the "Mini-Met." High among Gentele's priorities had been the search for a hospitable venue for chamber opera and contemporary pieces unsuited to the main auditorium. When the ideal alternative of Juilliard was quashed by its president, Peter Mennin, the Mini-Met found a temporary home at Lincoln Center's Forum, later renamed the Mitzi E. Newhouse Theater, which seats around three hundred. Poor acoustics and the lack of a pit (a balcony had to be built above the stage for the orchestra) were flaws that designer Ming Cho Lee could not overcome. Still, Henry Purcell's *Dido and Aeneas* and Virgil Thomson's *Four Saints in Three Acts* found their audience; the microtonality and electronic music of Maurice Ohana's *Syllabaire pour Phèdre* did not. An anonymous donor and grants from the National Endowment for the Arts and the New York State Council on the Arts seemed to ensure a season for 1974–75. Two double bills, a pastiche of Charles Ives with *Miss Donnethrone's Maggot* by Peter Maxwell Davies and Massenet's *Le Portrait de Manon* with Chabrier's *Une Éducation manquée,* were projected, not for the Forum, but for the nearby Harkness Theater. The plan was postponed for a year, and then canceled altogether, on the say-so, it was rumored, of Anthony Bliss. Hopes for an intimate opera theater went uneasily into the night. In 1985, James Levine insisted, "a second, smaller performing space is absolutely critical to the Metropolitan's future" (*Times,* March 3). In 1987, general manager Bruce Crawford contemplated the Victory Theatre on 42nd Street for "smaller productions [that] would offer the Metropolitan Opera the possibility of a thirteen-week season." In 1997, there were discussions of building an annex to serve Lincoln Center's several constituents. The odds against a "little" Met are every bit as high as they have ever been and, alas, likely higher.[33]

In Chapin's first season, planned partly by Bing, and then by Gentele and Kubelik, the Met continued to boast an enviable international roster. *Norma* was sung by Caballé and Fiorenza Cossotto, *Peter Grimes* by Vickers, *Orfeo ed Euridice* by Horne, *Aïda, Der Rosenkavalier, Tosca,* and *La Fille du régiment* by Arroyo, Rysanek, Sutherland, Corelli, Domingo, Pavarotti, Gobbi, and Milnes—and the list went on. Rita Hunter was on hand as a credible backup for Nilsson in Wagner. Gwyneth Jones and Ingvar Wixell made impressive debuts as Sieglinde and Rigoletto. Sixten Ehrling, Charles Mackerras, and Peter Maag strengthened the conducting staff. *The Queen of Spades,* the first opera sung entirely in Russian, had as its principals Raina Kabaivanska and Nicolai Gedda, both of whom possessed not only the language, but the style. True, when evenings featured Marcia Baldwin, a comprimario mezzo, as the lead soprano Lisa, and Robert Nagy, Vickers's overused cover, as Gherman, many wondered who was minding the store. But after all, previous managements had had their share of ho-hum, even dreadful performances. In the main, the casts conscripted by Gentele and Kubelik were up to the standard set by their predecessors.

Chapin weathered his first season, however shakily. He had been obliged to make good on the hefty bill left behind by Gentele while complying with board demands for ever greater fiscal stringency. As early as January 11, 1973, Moore had questioned the number of new productions projected for the year to come, and this despite the private sponsorship already guaranteed for their support. He was apparently looking ahead and "disturbed by the fact that for 1974–75 no such funds were in sight." Levine was scheduled to conduct another monumental Met first, Verdi's *I Vespri Siciliani.* Chapin would have to go to bat for the upcoming double bill of Puccini's *Gianni Schicchi* and Luigi Dallapiccola's *Il Prigioniero,* the latter eventually scuttled in favor of Bartók's *Bluebeard's Castle.* He had to argue for the audience appeal, rehearsal time, and overall expense of the *Les Troyens* scheduled for Kubelik's debut.[34]

In June 1973, with Kubelik's long-anticipated arrival finally imminent, Chapin thought it prudent to warn the music director that a dark horizon had replaced the sunny landscape Gentele had painted all those months earlier in luring him to the Met. The deficit at the end of the 1972–73 season, he wrote, would amount to $4.7 million, which, subtracted from the $15 million in total assets (including the appraised value of the 39th Street site), would leave only $10.3 million. At this rate, the Met would soon be out of business. The boardroom was "close to hysteria"; directors harbored the illusion that issues ignored for years could be quickly resolved: "You and I both must remain flexible because if either of us takes an intransigent point of view, we are in danger of sinking the whole operation." And it went without saying that it would be more difficult to enact the necessary reforms with a music director "who is not here on a daily basis coping with the problems that arise." In his June 28 report to the board, Chapin expatiated on his message to Kubelik. The detail was this: Every production on the calendar for the coming season, bar none, would be scrutinized with an eye to reducing labor costs. That included Gentele's prized *Carmen:* "By removing the [act 1] stairs we free three stage elevators and the labor necessary to build a graduated staircase of ten feet in depth and fifty feet of width. This will not only save on performance crew but also space in storage areas and trucking." There would be fewer orchestra rehearsals, especially for the core repertoire. The number of choristers would be decreased: for *Tristan und Isolde,* for example, thirty would suffice, a third fewer than customary; megaphones would enhance the offstage voices. More use would be made of contract artists. As for star salaries, nothing could be done about the weakening dollar and associated increases in cachets. New revenue streams would have to be explored, perhaps Sunday rentals, or special concerts, or added stops on the tour. And why not hurry the media program advocated by Moore? As always, better-coordinated fund-raising would make a difference. But these measures, even taken together, would be too little, too late.[35]

**1973–1974.** In October, as the 1973–74 season was under way, Chapin announced that the scheduled new *Don Giovanni* was canceled and that there would be no further performances in the city's parks: "The fact is that the Met is broke. If we couldn't borrow money we couldn't mount a season." Three weeks later, Kubelik made his debut in an unusually complete *Les Troyens*. If Berlioz profited little from Peter Wexler's production ("the sets and costumes are excessively busy and rather ugly"), he could hardly have hoped for more stirring interpreters than Vickers, Ludwig, and Shirley Verrett. An additional dose of drama was injected into the first night when Verrett, the Cassandre, was called upon to play Didon as well, in place of the indisposed Ludwig. *L'Italiana in Algeri* (Nov. 10), a congenial vehicle for Horne's high-spirited virtuosity, returned after more than a half-century in Jean-Pierre Ponnelle's first Met staging; the rest of the cast and the conductor, Gabor Ötvös, fell flat. A production of *Les Contes d'Hoffmann* (Nov. 29) was borrowed from Seattle to satisfy Joan Sutherland; predictably stupendous as Olympia, the mechanical doll, she also made hers the dramatic and lyric music of the poet's other loves.[36]

A month later, the revival of *Tristan und Isolde* scheduled for January 11 began to unravel. Chapin had engaged Swedish soprano Catarina Ligendza for the role of Isolde and Vickers for his first Met Tristan. In late December, Ligendza bowed out. Doris Jung, her cover, failed to get the nod, and when Isolde was handed off to Klara Barlow, Vickers, who had exacerbated the situation by arriving late for rehearsals, withdrew. Kubelik, in Europe as usual, was unavailable to manage the crisis. All he could come up with was that Mario and Tosca step in for Tristan and Isolde. Leinsdorf, furious at Kubelik's absence, fanned the discontent. When the dust settled, Barlow was cast opposite Jess Thomas, won praise for her pluck and her acting, and eventually sang the January 26 broadcast with Vickers, who had rethought his earlier stand. Four days later, Nilsson and Vickers sang Wagner's opera together. On an embarrassing evening during Nilsson's debut season, 1959–60, three Tristans pleading illness were needed, one per act, to complete the show. As always, Nilsson had taken all three acts in her confident stride. By 1974, she had sung twenty-nine Met Isoldes opposite seven different leading men, some good, some not, all challenged by the ferocious score. In Vickers,

FIGURE 32. Birgit Nilsson as Isolde, and her three Tristans, left to right Ramon Vinay, Karl Liebl, Albert Da Costa, December 28, 1959 (Louis Mélançon; courtesy Metropolitan Opera Archives)

Nilsson finally met her match. That single smashing evening served to tell Met audiences how otherwise impoverished were the contemporary Wagnerian ranks. "One would have thought the audience as well as the two principals had swallowed that love potion." By comparison, through the 1930s, Flagstad and Melchior had been the tallest in a field of giants. Nilsson and Vickers did justice to the musical and theatrical values of the roles as no one else of their generation could. Regrettably, by reason of schedule, of indisposition, and of the peripatetic life of the opera singer in the 1970s, their voices twined only once in the "Liebesnacht" in New York.[37]

The Nilsson-Vickers *Tristan* was a luminous instant in this dark season. Chapin was obliged to announce that 1974–75 would be shortened from thirty-one weeks to thirty, and 1975–76 to only twenty-seven. The administrative staff would be cut by 20 percent. To add to the adversity, costumes valued at $3 million had gone up in the smoke of a Bronx warehouse fire. Chapin and Kubelik were censured for mediocre casting, inferior conducting, and chaos onstage and off-. Levine, meanwhile, was unsure of the stance he should take vis-à-vis the warring powers. He consulted with his agent, Ronald Wilford, who advised the tactful waiting game the young conductor played to his future advantage. On February 12, in the middle of his first year, Kubelik resigned. His decision, he cabled Moore, had been prompted by three factors: that he had "tried in vain in the past year to get the administration of the Metropolitan Opera House to work as planned," a grievance left ill defined; that the company's "unfortunate financial situation [had changed] the basic conception of my ideals on how to lead musical affairs of the Met"; and "the latest attacks on my person from the New York Times." Only the second of the three found its way into the press release.[38]

Of the original troika, Chapin alone was left standing, although weakened to the point that he learned of Kubelik's resignation only when he read about it in the newspaper. Two weeks later, in an inspired stroke, the general manager appointed John Dexter production supervisor, a new position on a par with the recently vacated slot of music director. Dexter, whose reputation was largely based on landmark stagings of John Osborne, Arnold Wesker, and Peter Shaffer, had come to the Met from England's National Theatre for Verdi's *I Vespri Siciliani* just a couple of months earlier. The dynamic director succeeded in persuading the nearly "immobile" Caballé (shades of Margaret Webster and Zinka Milanov) to negotiate his angular patterns on Svoboda's carpeted steps. With Dexter on board, a reconfigured troika was in the offing.

**1974–1975** The fitting epilogue to the troubles of 1973–74 was the summer double bill of a so-so *Gianni Schicchi* and a wrong-headed *Bluebeard's Castle,* the company premiere of Bartók's opera. The 1974–75 season began no more felicitously. The weeklong Cleveland engagement was a box-office bust, an experiment that would not be repeated. And the aura of the New York opening night was dimmed by the cancellation of its star attraction: Caballé was replaced by Cristina Deutekom in *I Vespri Siciliani*. Anticipation surrounding *Death in Venice* was heightened by the debut of Peter Pears, the original Aschenbach, now in his mid-sixties. Britten's opera, dwarfed by the large house, generated respect, little affection, and average ticket sales. Janáček's *Jenufa* (Nov. 15, in English) was revived a half-century after its Met premiere. The new investiture had many virtues—brooding sets designed by Schneider-

Siemssen, Rennert's staging, the musical leadership of John Nelson, and a strong cast headed by Teresa Kubiak, Vickers, and Astrid Varnay, who had come home after eighteen years. The superb presentation of an unfamiliar masterwork that would eventually find many devotees was hastily moth-balled, not to return until 1986.[39]

On the day of the *Jenufa* premiere, pummeled by the press and the board, and convinced that the only remaining defense was offense, Chapin wrote to the directors: "We are now at a point where there is a developing schism between the general manager and the executive committee as to what steps should be taken." The provocative comment prefaced a review of his accomplishments: receipts had grown by 5 percent in his first season, he had personally secured upward of $1.8 million from private sources, he had negotiated million-dollar federal and state challenge grants, he had brought in John Dexter, and he had engineered the upcoming tour to Japan. And all this in the face of obstacles for which the board was directly responsible. To begin with, he had inherited "staggering building costs"; the trustees had left him hanging as "acting" for almost ten months, causing "enormous problems of uncertainty." Their mistrust of his management had "delayed planning and is continuing to cause us to lose major artists," a state of affairs the press had laid unjustly at his door. The better news was that 1973–74 had ended with a deficit of $532,000, compared with the much greater $2.8 million shortfall of the previous season. Chapin clinched his argument with, "When, for example, you start with a $4 million building liability before creating a season and ask for a deficit limit of $5–6 million, you are really talking about a $1–2 million artistic program. . . . $2 million is the approximate City Opera operating budget." The general manager's brief carried both the ring of truth and the dangers of lèse-majesté.

Within a week, Anthony Bliss was named to the new full-time post of executive director and made chairman of the Association's administration committee, with oversight of the company's day-to-day operation, a move that further rattled Chapin's authority. His father, Cornelius N. Bliss, had been a longtime board member and chair of the Metropolitan Opera Association from 1938 to 1946. Anthony Bliss was elected to the board in 1949 and served as its president in the 1950s and 1960s. William Rockefeller, the current president, made the new chain of command official: "Mr. Bliss as the Metropolitan's chief operating officer will report to me, and Mr. Chapin will report to Mr. Bliss" (*Times*, Nov. 22, 1974). A short three weeks later, the *Times* led off with this question: "Bliss and Chapin: On a Collision Course?"

(Dec. 11). Chapin glossed Bliss's role as liaison between management and board; in Bliss's definition, the job also entailed a large say in artistic policy. The distance between the two understandings could not be bridged.

By February 1975, fiscal exigency had reached a point (the house was at just 86 percent capacity while expenses were still on the rise) that 10 percent across-the-board salary cuts seemed inescapable. Bliss pleaded with the unions to accept a one-month reduction of the hard-won twelve-month provision. He went before the Met employees to explain that these and other steps would ensure the 1976–77 season: "This is distasteful, but I see no alternatives. We must not let the opera house die. If it closes, I question whether it will ever open again" (*Times,* Feb. 27). Joseph Volpe, then a master carpenter, later described Bliss's appearance on that day: "A tall, slender man in a plain gray suit, he didn't make much of an entrance. He introduced himself quietly, without smiling, and when he said his last name, I detected the hint of a lisp. Then he went on to say that his father had helped out the Met in bad times, and that the Met was in bad times again." A headline in *New York Magazine* ran, "Suicidio or Ritorna Vincitor—the Met's Choice" (March 24). Volpe proposed a third way: he demonstrated how equivalent savings could be realized by controlling waste. The salary slashes were not implemented.[40]

The Met's fiscal emergency and that of the city came to a head that month, ten years after the first installment of the *Herald Tribune*'s "City in Crisis." Abe Beame was mayor, succeeding the Republican-turned-Democrat John Lindsay, under whose watch conditions had deteriorated beyond the sorry mess described in the exposé. The short-term debt had climbed to $3.4 billion, three times that of 1971. And by the last day of March, it had reached $6.1 billion. New York was unable to service its debt. The metropolis avoided bankruptcy by the grace of a federal loan and the debt-restructuring plan executed by the Municipal Assistance Corporation. For the next two years, New York was effectively governed by the Emergency Financial Control board. The end of the harrowing decade was punctuated by the speech President Gerald Ford delivered to the National Press Club. It would be long forgotten but for the unforgettable *Daily News* headline: "Ford to City: Drop Dead" (Oct. 30, 1975).

Chapin's last season was crowned by the unconscionably overdue house debut of Beverly Sills in *The Siege of Corinth.* For this company first, Schippers adopted an unsatisfactory edition that patched together several of Rossini's versions; the production was meant "to re-create (not even re-interpret!) the

La Scala settings of the 19th Century premiere. This curious idea is being presented as a widely revolutionary concept. Hardly. The effect created is that of a museum piece." Despite, or better, because of, her years of glory at the New York City Opera, sometimes in roles less brilliantly cast at the Met, Rudolf Bing had boycotted the girl next door. Sills had proudly become the star she was without Bing's help. She was finally appearing at America's foremost opera house and, to top it all off, in a reconstruction of the sumptuous production that had propelled her from La Scala to international celebrity in 1969. New York hailed its Brooklyn-born daughter once again. But when the hoopla had died down, even her most fervent partisans had to acknowledge that the City Opera had enjoyed her best years.[41]

Four days earlier, there had been another long-overdue debut. Among the management's 1974–75 bungles was the scheduling of a mystifying twenty performances of *Tosca*. The last of the seven divas to undertake the title role that season would be a late replacement for Nilsson. At the urging of Marilyn Horne, who had heard her in Dallas, Magda Olivero, age sixty-five, was invited to bow with the company. Her career had begun in Turin in 1932, the year of Jeritza's last Met Tosca; by the late 1950s, Olivero had an international following thanks to mostly pirated recordings. Beginning in 1968, American audiences in Kansas City, in Hartford, in Newark, and even at neighboring Philharmonic Hall had received her rapturously. An unusually committed actress, the Italian soprano transformed her unpromising sound into an expressive and, yes, beautiful instrument that bore little resemblance to conventional voices. On April 18, her third and last Met performance (she sang *Tosca* on tour in 1979), Olivero acknowledged the insistent cheers of the throng pressing forward on the orchestra floor by edging along the narrow lip at the base of the proscenium to touch the outstretched hands of her admirers. A misstep would have plunged her into the pit. With this gesture, Olivero showed what made her unique: she sang and acted as if her life depended on it.[42]

On February 11, Bliss had informed Chapin by memorandum that Levine would, as Chapin himself had proposed, be named music director, and that he would be "the principal voice in the areas of repertoire, casting, and musical decisions." Wilford's waiting game had worked like a charm. He had dragged his feet on Levine's contract and, when finally nudged by Chapin, responded that the matter was now in Bliss's bailiwick. Bliss also let Chapin know that he was on a short leash; he would expect "a written progress report on a bi-weekly basis." On May 27, the handwriting on the wall was there for

TABLE 15  Metropolitan Opera Premieres 1972–73 TO 1974–75

| Composer and Title | Met Premiere | Most Recent Met Performance | No. of Seasons in Met Repertoire | No. of Met Productions | No. of Met Performances, 1883–2013 | World Premiere | Director/Designer |
|---|---|---|---|---|---|---|---|
| Maurice Ohana, *Syllabaire pour Phèdre* | Feb. 17, 1973 | Mar. 9, 1973 | 1 | 1 | 13 | Feb. 5, 1968, Paris, Théâtre de la Musique | Paul-Emile Deiber / Ming Cho Lee |
| Henry Purcell, *Dido and Aeneas* | Feb. 17, 1973 | Mar. 9, 1973 | 1 | 1 | 13 | 1689, London, Josiah Priest's boarding school for girls | Paul-Emile Deiber / Ming Cho Lee |
| Virgil Thomson, *Four Saints in Three Acts* | Feb. 20, 1973 | Mar. 10, 1973 | 1 | 1 | 12 | Feb. 8, 1934, Hartford, Connecticut, Avery Memorial | Alvin Ailey / Ming Cho Lee |
| Hector Berlioz, *Les Troyens* | Oct. 22, 1973 | Mar. 27, 2003 | 5 | 2 | 37 | Nov. 4, 1863, Paris, Lyrique, Part 2, "Les Troyens à Carthage"; Dec. 6–7, 1890, Karlsruhe (complete performance, in German) | Nathaniel Merrill / Peter Wexler |
| Giuseppe Verdi, *I Vespri Siciliani* | Jan. 31, 1974 | Dec. 11, 2004 | 4 | 1 | 45 | June 13, 1855, Paris, Opéra (in French) | John Dexter / Josef Svoboda |
| Béla Bartók, *Bluebeard's Castle* (in English) | June 10, 1974 | Apr. 21, 2000 | 3 | 2 | 24 | May 24, 1918, Budapest, Opera | Bodo Igesz / David Reppa |
| Benjamin Britten, *Death in Venice* | Oct. 18, 1974 | Feb. 26, 1994 | 2 | 2 | 15 | June 16, 1973, Aldeburgh | Colin Graham / John Piper |
| Giacchino Rossini, *The Siege of Corinth* | Apr. 7, 1975 | Jan. 24, 1976 | 2 | 1 | 19 | Oct. 9, 1826, Paris, Opéra (in French) | Sandro Sequi / Nicola Benois |

everyone to read: Levine, age thirty-one, was appointed music director on a five-year contract; he would continue to be at the Met seven months out of the year and would work closely with Dexter. In case of disagreement between the music director and the production supervisor, the music director would have the last word. From May 29 to June 14, Chapin and the Met were in Tokyo, Nagoya, and Osaka for a visit under Japanese sponsorship. Two days after the troupe returned, the press had it on good authority that the June 26 meeting of the board would seal Chapin's fate. And it did. The directors exercised the option of terminating his contract a year before its expiration. Yet another troika would be constituted, now by Bliss, Levine, and Dexter. For the first time in its history, the company would do without a general manager. Rockefeller offered Chapin the consolation of heading up the Metropolitan Opera Foundation, the newly constituted fund-raising arm of the Association. Chapin turned him down.[43]

On February 7, 1976, the *Saturday Review* published a long piece signed by the recently fired general manager, "Musical Chairs at the Met" (39–42). Chapin's apologia began, "Perhaps the story of my experiences there may reveal something of the workings of America's leading opera house and of its responsibilities to the public it serves." He recalled the pique of the Metropolitan board years earlier on learning that, in his capacity as a vice president of Lincoln Center, he had prevailed in bringing the Hamburg and Rome operas to the Met. When Gentele invited him to join his team, he had accepted, but not without reservations. And then, the awful accident, and everything changed. With valid resentment, Chapin quotes Moore at the time of his promotion to general manager in spring 1973: "There wasn't anything better around the ball park." Nothing better apparently once feelers sent to Maria Callas and to Massimo Bongianckino had gone nowhere. In Chapin's second year, relations with the executive committee had decayed further, and by the beginning of the third, plans to remove him were in motion. There was a happy ending—of sorts. On July 1, 1975, as Chapin walked onto the stage to welcome a crowd of seventy-five thousand assembled in Central Park to hear Renata Scotto sing Cio-Cio-San, he was greeted with a tremendous ovation both from the audience and from the cast and crew grouped behind him: "I stood at the microphone in tears, hearing voices chanting, 'Don't go! Don't go!' Suddenly one voice shouted: 'Bring back Tebaldi!' That did it. I was home free. Reality had asserted itself with that cry from an opera nut, without whom none of us could exist. If he could only have known, I thought, of the efforts we had made to persuade that great star to return."[44]

## NINE

# Maestro Assoluto, *1975–1990*

### TWENTIETH-CENTURY EUROPEAN OPERA
### AND THE BAROQUE

## JAMES LEVINE

THE NEW MET POWERHOUSE was born in Cincinnati on June 23, 1943, to a musical and theatrical family, the eldest of three children. His parents recognized his vocation while he was still a toddler. The ten-year-old prodigy made his professional debut with Mendelssohn's Second Piano Concerto in a neighborhood concert of the Cincinnati Symphony. At about the same time, Walter Levin, principal violinist of the LaSalle Quartet, was called to guide the boy's musical training. Levin was said to have designed "a European-style education for Jimmy, an interdisciplinary approach to music that placed it in a cultural, historical and philosophical context." Soon thereafter, Levine began to travel to New York on weekends to study the piano with Rosina Lhévinne. At thirteen, he was at Marlboro working with Rudolf Serkin, where his first conducting assignment was the chorus of *Così fan tutte.* Between the ages of fourteen and twenty-eight, Levine spent his summers at Aspen, graduating from student to performer. It was there at eighteen that he conducted his first opera, Bizet's *Les Pêcheurs de perles.* That same year, 1961, Levine enrolled at Juilliard to work with Lhévinne and, on conducting, with Jean Morel. Three years later, he was heard by George Szell, who brought him to Cleveland, first as apprentice, and then as assistant conductor. "Jim has to brush his own teeth," his mother observed, "but since his Cleveland days he has concentrated on the things that only he can do." On Szell's death in 1970, Levine began conducting elsewhere, with the Philadelphia Orchestra during the summer, with the Welsh National Opera, and then the San Francisco Opera. His Metropolitan debut came during the summer season of 1971, in *Tosca,* with Grace Bumbry, Franco Corelli, and Peter Glossop.

FIGURE 33. James Levine conducting
rehearsal, c. 1980 (Winnie Klotz; courtesy
Metropolitan Opera Archives)

Szell and the other foremost conductors of his generation who "stayed with
their orchestras almost all season long ... [and] supervised everything" set
the pattern of Levine's career. In 2000, Levine was profiled by the *Guardian*.
He had celebrated twenty-five years as the Met's music and, later, artistic
director; he had also chalked up twenty-three summers with the Chicago
Symphony at Ravinia, seventeen at Salzburg, and fifteen at Bayreuth: "I've
always been the opposite of the school of come in and do a program and then
go away." In the crucial matter of artistic management, he landed immediately at the top: his agent, Ronald Wilford, represented Mstislav Rostropovich
and Seiji Ozawa.[1]

## BLISS, LEVINE, AND DEXTER, 1975–1980

The second triumvirate, Chapin-Levine-Dexter, had been met with a rush of
optimism. Dexter wrote in his diary, "The company situation at the Met is
one of the many aspects of the job that appeals. Every opera house should be
run by a triumvirate: a musical director, a theatre director and a general manager or intendant. James Levine, who has taken over the musical side after
Kubelik's resignation, and I will be spending a great deal of next season just

sitting in the theatre, listening and observing. Then we'll be in a position to tell Schuyler Chapin precisely what we think we can achieve over the next few years." For his part, Levine spun this billet-doux: "John and I communicate almost by telepathy. . . . We see eye to eye on almost everything" (*Times,* Feb. 1, 1976). In fact, Levine had signed on as music director with the stipulation that control of the artistic administration would be his alone. On the installation of the third triumvirate, the music director spoke for Bliss in ways that misfired when Chapin tried it. "Mr. Bliss does not plan to have anything to do with artistic decisions, except as they might affect economic matters" (*Times,* June 24, 1975). He would go on to trace the key policies of the regime: "to have every night a performance which is as close as the practicalities allow to what we feel is the composer's intention," to broaden the repertoire, and to adopt a modified *stagione* system (*Times,* Oct. 10, 1976). The first of these ambitions, to keep faith with the score, went without saying. The second, to expand the repertoire, was professed by all incoming general managers, with the exception of Bing. Levine forecast that his diversified repertoire would take these directions: twentieth-century works, "acknowledged masterpieces that haven't been seen at the Met in many years," and "less-played works by important composers" (*Times,* March 2, 1976). As for a *stagione*-leaning calendar—that is, a schedule in which a production is given a first night and numerous subsequent performances within a relatively tight time frame (as contrasted to the repertory system, in which performances of the same production are scattered over much of the season)—Levine's hope was "to work out a balance" between the Metropolitan and, say, the La Scala tradition. The purpose of this modification was to respond to the legitimate complaint that after a handful of performances, the original ensemble moved on, to be replaced by generally lesser and certainly less-well-rehearsed second and then third casts.[2]

The optimism of fresh starts was tempered by the circumstances in which each member of the troika found himself in fall 1975. Bliss was haunted by the fear that the Association would be broke by spring. He knew the company was mired in the deepest hole since the Depression, aside from the ruinous first Lincoln Center season. The infusion of the $2.6 million insurance payment in compensation for the losses suffered in the Bronx warehouse fire, the $5 million legacy of Martha Baird Rockefeller, and the $3.9 million in proceeds from the sale of the 39th Street property would be gone. The operational deficit was chronic and growing. Dexter found an administrative technical staff in which "not a single member . . . could read a blueprint or had practical experience in judging what time, manpower, and space would be needed for any given stage design." Master carpenter Joe Volpe was the exception. As for Levine, he estimated that it would take five to ten years to "bring [the orchestra] up to his standards," a project he was prepared to undertake without firing a single musician.[3]

That fall and winter, one moving event appeared to signal the passing of an era, and another a new beginning. On October 15, 1975, a memorial mass was held at St. Patrick's Cathedral for Richard Tucker, who had died early in the year of a heart attack while on a concert stop in Kalamazoo. Tucker's final Met performance as Canio in the December 3, 1974, *Pagliacci* reminded listeners that three decades after his Met debut, the tenor was still one of the company's treasures. Tucker had been a friend of New York's Cardinal Cooke, had sung at Alfred E. Smith dinners, and had often aided Catholic charities. The mass is believed to be the first such tribute bestowed on a Jew. Before Tucker, only Leopold Damrosch, Anton Seidl, and Heinrich Conried had been honored with a funeral service on the Met stage. In January 1976, Sarah Caldwell was the first woman to conduct an opera at the Met. Her *La Traviata* was received with respect: "She led a sober, carefully paced performance . . . that was free from idiosyncracy, but replete with ideas and spirit"; "Her conducting . . . was brisk but not pell-mell in tempo, it was accurate in rhythm. . . . Above all, Miss Caldwell stressed clarity."[4]

On the labor front, it was more of the same. Management proposed reducing the players' contracted weeks from fifty-one to forty-three a year. Bliss issued the threat the orchestra had heard before: "If we don't open on schedule, we may never open again" (*Times,* Oct. 9, 1975). A strike was deferred until December 31. The two-year agreement was announced during an intermission of the New Year's Eve *Tosca.* The musicians were guaranteed forty-four weeks of work and supplemental unemployment benefits that compensated for half their salary losses. Eighteen months later, it was back to the tired old dance. In summer 1977, management warned that the season would not begin until an agreement was reached. To labor, this was tantamount to a lockout. The union countered with demands for a pay increase, eight weeks of vacation, and a required maximum of four performances a week (just over a decade earlier it had been seven). By early September, the musicians had agreed to a three-year contract that provided for a 7 percent salary increase, without adjusting the number of weekly performances.

While nervous members of the board clamored for downsizing—elimination of the tour, shortening of the season, reversal of contractual guarantees—Bliss was convinced that the way out was through growth, and that growth would require the modernization of structures and protocols. He established a marketing department, where, surprisingly for the mid-1970s, there had been none. He swelled the advertising budget from $30,000 to $400,000 in one year. A full-page ad in the *Times* lead with, "You are cordially invited to strike a blow for civilization. Subscribe to the Metropolitan Opera!" It divulged the season calendar, casts included, information never before available to the public. The company added three thousand subscriptions; attendance rose 10 percent to 95 percent of capacity. The new marketing broom met with opposition. Culture, asserted the detractors, was one thing, commerce another, and the balance was tilting to the commercial side. The development office and its increasingly countrywide donor list grew apace with its marketing counterpart. In time, marketing and development spread to the point that they drove the scene shops across the river to Weehawken. With the help of the Opera Guild, a direct-mail campaign designed to multiply giving was launched. The Met board underwent a profound reorganization, concentrating power in fewer hands and lending the directorship a more national profile.[5]

The policy planning committee met on March 17, 1977, to discuss the "Survival of the Company," as the minutes later put it. Voices of doom predicted bankruptcy down a relatively short road if cutbacks, specifically curtailed seasons, were not immediately factored into artistic decisions and contract talks. In May, Frank E. Taplin, lawyer and accomplished amateur pianist, replaced William Rockefeller as president of the Association. He would soon report that thanks to support amounting to $12.7 million from the National Endowment for the Arts, the New York State Council on the Arts, the Metropolitan Opera Guild, foundations, and individuals—a significant increase over the $8.7 million of the previous year—"operating expenses had been met without invading capital for the first time in eight years" (Aug. 26, 1977).

The stunning innovation of the 1976–77 season, and the one with the longest and most profitable legs, was the March 15 telecast of *La Bohème,* the first of the "Live from the Met" series, and the first such transmission beamed into American homes since Rudolf Bing's 1950 opening night *Don Carlo.* It was not the Met alone that reaped the rewards of the telecast: four million viewers donated nearly $1 million to the Public Broadcasting System. PBS scheduled three "Live from the Met" telecasts for 1977–78, *Rigoletto, Don Giovanni,* and *Cav/Pag,* to be carried by 260 stations. Two years later,

Austria, France, Great Britain, Portugal, Spain, Sweden, Switzerland, and West Germany would receive one live performance per year. As evidence of the impact of the media project, in 1979, subsequent to the opening night telecast, the Guild was swamped with thirty thousand requests for the *Opera News* issue devoted to *Otello*. The magnitude of that number made a deep impression. Bliss observed, "In the long range television will become important to our survival" (*Time,* Oct. 8, 1979). Vastly improved technology enhanced video definition; the availability of FM simulcast bypassed the inadequate audio components of standard television sets and offered listeners a sound image comparable to the one they heard on the Saturday matinee broadcasts. Radio had served the fund-raising needs of the Depression. The Met now had an even more powerful tool with which to penetrate the opera consciousness of a new generation and loosen its purse strings. The viewership of opera telecasts was estimated at eight to nine million, twice that of average PBS programming. And two years later, a spanking new media department, the first of its kind for a performing arts organization, joined the fledgling marketing and older development departments. Levine articulated his stand on "Live from the Met" on the occasion of the RCA release of a concert featuring Leontyne Price and Marilyn Horne: "This recording embodies the entire concert of March 28, 1982, exactly as it occurred on the stage of the Metropolitan Opera House. No material was taken from rehearsals; no remake recording sessions took place. As with all of the 'Live from the Met' presentations, the principle of documenting the truly live performance guided us, and in our view ultimately carried a more sincere and significant artistic statement to our audience."[6]

In 1978, New York was in a position to sell bond notes for the first time since the meltdown of 1975. The Met too was breathing easier. The company would soon be in the black for the third year in a row. Meanwhile, Levine was coming up against the fifth anniversary of his music directorship. To his mind, only 40 percent of 1976–77 could be fairly ascribed to the new triumvirate, and 80 percent of 1977–78. The first season planned entirely by Levine-Dexter under Bliss was 1978–79. By 1980, it was time to gauge how Levine's promise of an expanded repertoire was faring. In the final three years of the Bing administration, operas outside the core accounted for little more than 10 percent of the repertoire; in the three Chapin years, for little more than 20 percent; from 1977 to 1980, for 28 percent. And looking ahead to the whole of the decade, 1975–1985, to 33 percent. As for the modified *stagione* policy, in early 1977, the music director reported to the board that "the management has been successful in getting artists for longer periods of time by putting more performances closer together" (Feb. 17, 1977). By 1983, the Metropolitan was presenting only four to five titles per week. *Stagione* scheduling had become the norm: twenty of the season's twenty-four productions were on the *stagione* plan.

A point of contention dating back to his earliest days as principal conductor, and that would persist long into the future, was Levine's monopoly of the pit, not the quality of his presence, but the quantity that left little room for others. In 1975, Levine explained, "I've offered productions to lots of leading conductors, but everyone is terribly busy, including myself. What I'd like is to get a better level of sound on a night-to-night basis, and hope that periodically a Solti or a Davis or a Mehta will come" (*Times,* July 29). The Met boasted no debut of a top-flight international conductor between 1975 and 1980, not Carlo Maria Giulini's nor Riccardo Muti's. On January 17, 1980, the issue was before the board. Levine's refrain was essentially unchanged. Conductors in high demand were reluctant to commit to a minimum of seven weeks for a new Met production when a lucrative Philharmonic gig had them in and out of New York in five days. Some maestros would come only for a new production, others were exquisitely selective in their choice of repertoire. Whatever the reason, New York missed out not only on a broad spectrum of conductors but on the value added of the star singers they would bring along. As the evenhanded Martin Mayer points out, "There is an argument to be made that other major conductors shun a house where the music director appears to have first choice of artists, works, and rehearsal time." From 1975 to 2010, Levine would preside over all but seven opening nights and three-quarters of the nearly one hundred telecasts. The other side of the coin, to Mayer's thinking, was that "conductors and singers are drawn to work with companies disciplined by a resident leader." Irving Kolodin's acerbic contribution to the debate in "Is James Levine Wrecking the Met?" concludes that Levine "has allowed his ambition to cloud his judgment." Kolodin contends that, in his first five years, Levine used the Met to try out operas he planned to conduct elsewhere, *Parsifal* at Bayreuth, for example. Maybe. But then again, Levine's first *Parsifal,* in 1979, is said to have left Leonard Bernstein in tears.[7]

### Dexter's Stage

By the end of the 1979–80 season, it was no secret that Dexter's authority had been circumvented, if not subverted, by his partners. At a January 1980 meeting of the executive committee, Bliss characterized Dexter as "a trouble-some colleague. . . . His temper tantrums and abuse of colleagues have proved intolerable." Bliss and Levine tried hard to persuade the press that the triumvirate had never been intended to last, that once Dexter had brought the technical operation up to snuff, the position of director of production would have outlived its usefulness (*Times*, July 16, 1980). In a long memorandum to Levine and Bliss dated September 24, 1980, Dexter complained of "being under some kind of attack, more or less day by day," of being ignored, contradicted, undermined. By then, the British director could take satisfaction in having left his imprint on the company. Rarely had the likes of his spare, conceptual schemes been seen in a theater identified with opulent décors and literal stagings. Dexter's aesthetic politics were known to the many New Yorkers who remembered the pantomime he devised for Pizarro's crossing of the Andes in the 1965 Broadway run of Peter Shaffer's *The Royal Hunt of the Sun*. At the Met, his calling card had been the 1974 *I Vespri Siciliani*, stripped of picturesque signs of thirteenth-century Palermo. For a time, the claims of frugality trumped those of tradition, and cost-conscious trustees were happy enough to acquiesce to Dexter's subversive stage. In a 1977 letter to a patron, the director of production decried the grandiosity that the gilded opera house invited, and the clutter: "If there is not too much on the stage you can see any detail, you can see every face and movement. If you concentrate and if you are shown where to look. It's a question of angle, of stage relationship with the audience, and volume. . . . The audience should be looking for faces, not windmills." But Dexter's dazzling originality came at a price: having to put up with the man himself. As Volpe described it, "When Dexter entered a room, he altered the atmosphere. Everything about him was dark—his gaze, his temper, a beard that came and went." With varying degrees of austerity—and success—the twelve new productions he staged through 1979–80, nearly half the total for the period, hewed to his program of reform. He articulated its tenets repeatedly in interviews, and in the letters, memoranda, and diary entries assembled for his posthumous, incomplete autobiography, *The Honourable Beast*. Under Dexter's irascible ways, acid tongue, and relentless quest for excellence, the cash-strapped Met became a cutting-edge theatre.[8]

Dexter first imposed his vision on two of the very grandest operas, *Aïda* and *Le Prophète*. His Spartan credo served neither Verdi nor Meyerbeer. By purging *Aïda* (Feb. 3, 1976) of what he considered gratuitous spectacle, Dexter sought to disclose the racial, political, and cultural chasm that separated the repressive Egyptians (read white) from the subjugated Ethiopians (read black). The languishing princess lost her couch, the victorious hero lost his horse, the large scale ballet of the Triumphal Scene was reduced to a pas de deux to the death between two male dancers, a haughty pharaonic warrior and a defiant Ethiopian captive. Standing sideways, hands pronated, Radamès, Amneris, the King, Ramfis, and the populace of Memphis and Thebes were constricted by the hieratic attitudes of Egyptian iconography, whereas the Ethiopians were free to move naturally. But in banishing the Hollywood colossal, Dexter unleashed the B-movie gestures of *The Mummy*. As for the principals, Leontyne Price, although still glorying in her upper register, was beginning to exert her will over Verdi's rhythms; Marilyn Horne's Amneris was underpowered at those moments that want the punch of an authentic Italian dramatic mezzo. *Le Prophète* (January 18, 1977) had been forgotten by the Met for fifty years. Elsewhere, Meyerbeer was making something of a comeback. Dexter staged the opera on a unit set representing a half-finished Gothic cathedral into which were dragged wagons suggestive of the various locales: a castle, an inn, a war camp, a city square. As the director saw it, "While not explicitly stated, the opera will appear to be acted out by . . . the craftsmen who are building the cathedral, as a kind of morality play that attempts to explain the relationship of man to God" (*Times,* Jan. 16, 1977). The misbegotten stratagem was dressed in Peter Wexler's drab décor. "What Mr. Dexter has dismissed . . . is the scenic power of Meyerbeer's opera, based on carefully planned contrasts of moods, colors, decors, depths and densities of setting. He has achieved the visual monotony the composer sought to avoid." It was left to Meyerbeer and the singers to supply the grandeur of *le grand opéra.* The stentorian James McCracken found an elegant, unearthly falsetto and *voix mixte* (the melding of chest voice and head voice) for the prophet's divine visions. Renata Scotto charged the ungrateful part of Berthe with a manic intensity that compensated for her strident top notes. Marilyn Horne, the astonishing Fidès, had the plangent timbre, the agility, the two-and-a-half-octave range, and the manner for what is arguably the most demanding role written for her voice type. She sang "with the virtuosity that among mezzos is hers alone these days." In fact, no Met contralto/mezzo-soprano in the five decades since Margarete Matzenauer, the previous Fidès, could have risen to her performance.[9]

Dexter was in his element in twentieth-century opera. The Met premiere of Francis Poulenc's *Dialogues des Carmélites,* in English, took place on February 5, 1977. The director came to consider this production the exemplum of his method. By cannibalizing costumes and sets from the warehouse, he kept the cost at an absurdly low $65,000. The décor consisted of a sloping cruciform platform and a few props—a chandelier, a gate, an altar. Dexter's memoirs impart his relief at Callas's refusal of the role of the Old Prioress and his joy at Régine Crespin's acceptance; she had been the New Prioress in the opera's 1957 Paris premiere. The remarkable cast was headed by Maria Ewing as the tormented Blanche and Shirley Verrett as the sublime Madame Lidoine. Jessye Norman and other interpreters have faced the guillotine in Dexter's staging and David Reppa's minimalist bricolage in seven subsequent revivals, the most recent in 2012–13. The director of production was riding high. Later that season, he would again affirm the viability of twentieth-century opera with another house premiere, Alban Berg's *Lulu,* in the unfinished two-act version. The production, "sensitively directed, lovingly conducted, and intelligently and aptly designed," struck a balance between expressionism and naturalism in the fin-de-siècle/art moderne sets of Jocelyn Herbert. Donald Gramm and Tatiana Troyanos were luxury casting in the roles of Dr. Schön and Countess Geschwitz. The title role was intended for Teresa Stratas; she withdrew a month before the first night in a dispute over rehearsal conditions. Her cover, Carole Farley, an experienced Lulu, had little of the magnetism Stratas would radiate when three years later the Met put on the full version of Berg's opera with its third act, edited by Friedrich Cerha. Dexter and his team had made the case for *Lulu:* the box office in 1977 was strong and in the curtailed 1980 season more than respectable. In 2009–10, Fabio Luisi led the work, still fresh in the Dexter-Herbert edition.[10]

Dexter delivered *Rigoletto* (Oct. 31, 1977) and *Don Pasquale* (Dec. 7, 1978) from timeworn practice as he had *Aïda* and *Le Prophète*—with the same disappointing results. The striking central element of the unit set for *Rigoletto* was a tall, decaying tower that revolved from scene to scene and pushed most of the action downstage to the sector Dexter favored. The advantage to voice and gesture, no doubt welcomed by Sherrill Milnes, Ileana Cotrubas, and Plácido Domingo, was offset by the loss of playing space and the profusion of decoration. The mise-en-scène "seemed almost incompetent in the way it tamed what should be a stirring drama." *Don Pasquale,* Beverly Sills's Met swan song, was conceived, said its director, as "a charming offering to her," transposed to the Edwardian era, whose fashion "would suit her well" (*Times,* Dec. 3, 1978). The song this late in the soprano's career rang somewhat brittle. Desmond Heeley confected the outline of a valentine as an inner proscenium;

FIGURE 34. *Dialogues des Carmélites,* act 1, scene 1, 1977 (James Heffernan; courtesy Metropolitan Opera Archives)

Dexter should have had second thoughts about converting the opera buffa into a drawing-room comedy. His *Don Carlo* (Feb. 5, 1979) was enriched by the restoration of the opening scene in the forest of Fontainebleau, whatever Dexter's objections to the flamboyant details forced upon him. Levine led a cast dominated by Nicolai Ghiaurov's Philip. This *Don Carlo* would be the last of Reppa's schematic decors. It would also be the end of the line for Met house designers.[11]

Benjamin Britten's *Billy Budd,* Dexter's return to the twentieth century, was an unqualified hit. The director employed the stage elevators to smashing effect for the *HMS Indomitable,* designed to disclose the harsh life of late-eighteenth-century seamen, on the one hand, and the stacking of the ship's multiple decks as she is prepared for battle, on the other. The choreography of the large ensemble spoke to the class divide between officers and crew, the moral dilemma of Captain Vere (Peter Pears), the seraphic innocence of Billy

(Richard Stilwell), and "the Lucifer-like beauty, sorrow, and passion" of the evil Claggart (James Morris). The production has been revived six times, most recently in 2011–12. Kurt Weill and Bertolt Brecht's *Rise and Fall of the City of Mahagonny* is a political satire rooted in the cabaret tradition. How well it weathered repotting was up for debate. For Manuela Hoelterhoff, "the work [did] not carry in a place the size of the Met. It needs an intimate setting for dramatic effect." Schonberg, who had no problem with the fit of the piece to the big stage, was tough on the text and the score: "It is a pretty dated example of dialectical materialism, and to these ears much of the music is dated." When Stratas sang the lilting "Moon of Alabama," all else was beside the point. Levine and Dexter stuck with Weill and Brecht through twenty-seven performances in two successive seasons; *Mahagonny* came back in 1983–84 to dismal box office, and then in 1995–96, when it did much better.[12]

*The Bartered Bride* (Oct. 25, 1978) and *Die Entführung aus dem Serail* (Oct. 12, 1979) were revivals long overdue. The production of Smetana's comedy, panned by most critics (Andrew Porter called it a "disaster," a "horrid travesty"), beat a hasty retreat. Dexter and Svoboda, ever distrustful of the pretty, had drained the work of its considerable charm. The superb diction of Stratas, Vickers, and Nicolai Gedda exposed a second deadly flaw: the distortions of an English translation hell-bent on matching the stressed syllables of the Czech original. *Entführung* was a down payment on Levine's pledge to bring lesser-known Mozart operas into the active repertoire. *The Abduction from the Seraglio,* as it was known in its English-language introduction, had been dropped after only five performances in 1946–47. Where Donald Oenslager's filigree décors were a riot of color, Jocelyn Herbert insisted on simple lines and a subdued palette. Bass Kurt Moll's Osmin left the strained Belmonte and Constanze of Gedda and Edda Moser in the dust. The production has resurfaced six times; in 2007–08, Matthew Polenzani and Diana Damrau excelled in the difficult principal roles.[13]

Among rarities not signed by Dexter, although staged under his baleful eye as director of production, two succeeded in restoring major works to the repertoire. The three one-act operas of Puccini's *Il Trittico* (Dec. 19, 1975), reunited for the first time since 1920, finally caught on despite uninspiring first casts and Reppa's just serviceable décors. When Scotto took on the three contrasting soprano parts, the house went wild. *I Puritani* (Feb. 25, 1976) was on the bill for the first time in more than half a century. We have not seen as serendipitous a quartet as Sutherland, Pavarotti, Milnes, and Morris in the four revivals of Bellini's opera, the last in 2006–07. Three showcases for reigning stars were borrowed from San Francisco. Massenet provided *Esclarmonde,* in its company premiere, for Sutherland and *Thaïs* (Jan. 18, 1978) for Sills, and Donizetti *La Favorita* (Feb. 21, 1978) for Verrett and Pavarotti. *Esclarmonde* proved the most intriguing of the three, if only for Beni Montresor's handsome décors and the diva's bravura. *Thaïs,* a stronger piece, no longer suited Sills's increasingly fragile instrument; it suffered too from a tacky production. Verrett, whose Leonora had thrilled a Carnegie Hall audience three years earlier, was off form in the disappointing *La Favorita.*[14]

The remaining stagings, all subject to Dexter's oversight, redecorated the familiar. Only Frederica von Stade's Cherubino stood out in a middle-of-the-road *Le Nozze di Figaro* (Nov. 20, 1975), revived just once. *Manon Lescaut* (March 17, 1980) wallowed in naturalism, while its lovers, Scotto and Domingo, disported themselves in erotic play, defying the Met's then prudish standard of decency. More to the point, as Dexter groused, director Gian Carlo Menotti allowed them "to indulge in every acting cliché that has been used since Thespis." Undistinguished sets, borrowed from Chicago as a stopgap for the tattered 1951 *La Bohème,* appeared on home screens across the country in the introductory "Live from the Met" telecast (Feb. 23, 1977). Three new productions took a step or two beyond mere redecoration. *Un Ballo in maschera* (Feb. 4, 1980) was staged by Elijah Moshinsky; he credited Dexter with the idea of setting the action in colonial Boston at the outbreak of the American Revolution, and not in the late seventeenth-century, as specified in the libretto. Peter Wexler designed boxy, minimalist sets; Peter J. Hall modeled costumes on the portraits of John Singleton Copley. The reception of the cast headed by Pavarotti was ecstatic, of the production's historico-political reading mixed. There was much to admire in the new *Lohengrin* (Nov. 14, 1976): the rough river bank, the monumental castle, the acting, and Levine's conducting, which one reviewer called his "finest hour." *Tannhäuser* (Dec. 22, 1977) respected the composer's scenic and narrative markings to a degree rare in contemporary stagings; exacting Wagnerite Andrew Porter called it "a 20th-century landmark." For the stupendous finale of act 2, Schneider-Siemssen's tiered oval set, Schenk's dynamic blocking, and Levine's command of Wagner's arching ensemble joined in a protracted moment of tension that those who were present have not forgotten. Equally memorable, but for the wrong reason, was yet another San Francisco export, *Der Fliegende Holländer* (March 3, 1979), designed and directed by Jean-Pierre Ponnelle. Its premiere set off a volley of jeers and boos from New

TABLE 16  Metropolitan Opera Premieres, 1975–76 to 1979–80

| Composer and Title | Met Premiere | Most Recent Met Performance | No. of Seasons in Met Repertoire | No. of Met Productions | No. of Met Performances, 1883–2013 | World Premiere | Director/Designer |
|---|---|---|---|---|---|---|---|
| Jules Massenet, *Esclarmonde* | Nov. 19, 1976 | Dec. 20, 1976 | 1 | 1 | 10 | May 14, 1889, Paris, Opéra-Comique | Lofti Mansouri / Beni Montresor |
| Francis Poulenc, *Dialogues des Carmélites* | Feb. 5, 1977 | Jan. 4, 2003 | 8 | 1 | 54 | Jan. 26, 1957, Milan, La Scala (in Italian) | John Dexter / David Reppa |
| Alban Berg, *Lulu* | Mar. 18, 1977 | May 15, 2010 | 7 | 1 | 36 | *2-act version:* June 2, 1937, Zurich, Stadttheater; *3-act version:* Feb. 24, 1979, Paris, Opéra (3-act version) | John Dexter / Jocelyn Herbert |
| Benjamin Britten, *Billy Budd* | Sept. 19, 1978 | May 12, 2012 | 7 | 1 | 47 | Dec. 1, 1951, London, Covent Garden; *revised version:* Jan. 9, 1964, London, Covent Garden | John Dexter / William Dudley |
| Kurt Weill, *Rise and Fall of the City of Mahagonny* | Nov. 16, 1979 | Dec. 9, 1995 | 4 | 1 | 39 | Mar. 9, 1930, Leipzig, Neues | John Dexter / Jocelyn Herbert |

York's normally respectful audience. Ponnelle wrapped the action within the dream of a minor character, the Steersman. José Van Dam, the beleaguered protagonist, was alone able to free himself from the convoluted apparatus.[15]

Between 1975 and 1980, the remapping of the repertoire progressed much as Levine had forecast. He added four twentieth-century European masterworks to the company's standard rep. The reintroduction of neglected works succeeded as well, witness the persistence of *I Puritani* and *Il Trittico. Die Entführung auf dem Serail* paved the way for the lesser-known Mozart operas.

### BLISS AND LEVINE, 1980–1985

A tragic augury ushered in the blighted 1980–81 season. On July 23, the young freelance violinist Helen Hagnes disappeared during the intermission of a Berlin Ballet performance. She was found the next morning at the bottom of an air shaft. The trial of the twenty-one-year-old Met stagehand Craig Crimmins, the tabloids' "phantom of the Metropolitan Opera," ended in a guilty verdict on the charge of attempted rape and murder. In September 1981, he was sentenced to twenty years to life in prison. The lurid story kept the Met in the news for the many weeks of the investigation and court proceedings, and the fact that the accused was a company employee drinking on the job made the publicity that much more damaging.

Again in the news that summer were angry talks between the Met and the orchestra. As management increased its offer, the sticking point remained the maximum number of performances to which the musicians were obligated each week. And here neither side would budge. The players asserted that "the demands on their artistry were so heavy that many of them suffered from severe physical and psychological problems," to which Levine, professing "sympathy for the players' feeling," equivocated, "we all would love for some of the pressure to be taken off our schedules. But all work has a certain amount of pressure attached to it" (*Times,* July 20, 1980). Negotiations were declared failed on the September 2 deadline and rehearsals were suspended. Taplin told the board repeatedly that giving in on the four-performance week would mean "a return to 'red ink.'" (Sept. 12, 1980). Opening night was canceled. To the subsequent threat of junking the entire season, the union responded, "It's the classic story of the boy who cried wolf" (*Times,* Sept. 24). This was, after all, the third time in five years that Bliss had issued the same ultimatum. But the Met was not bluffing. On September 30, the season was canceled. The players found themselves caught between wealthy patrons who held that instrumentalists were overpaid as it was for fewer than sixteen hours of work per week and stagehands who considered the musicians spoiled rotten by the cushy terms of their employment, particularly as contrasted with their own. Bliss and company feared that a prolonged delay or, worse, the cancellation of the season would result in the same loss of subscriptions that had followed on the 1969 postponement. Eleven years later, the 16 percent drop had not been fully recovered. Talks resumed in early October at the urging of President Carter. At this point, Volpe, now director of operations, entered the labor fray once again. He later quoted Bliss as saying, "If we don't get this dispute settled in a week or two, we'll just close the place down and start another company from scratch." And himself as responding, "Tony, you can't do that. You don't have that right. . . . The Met doesn't belong to you and the board. It belongs to everyone who works here and the public who loves and pays for opera." Volpe was instrumental in brokering the four-year deal that included hiring subs for the uncovered services, a frugal solution acceptable to both Bliss and Levine, and annual pay hikes of 8 to 9 percent. Players and choristers conceded four free rehearsal hours in exchange for the four-performance week. The two-month delay deprived operaphiles of the pleasure of hearing Caballé's Turandot put the three riddles to Pavarotti's Calaf and of *The Queen of Spades* scheduled for Domingo and Anna Tomowa-Sintow.[16]

The "broken" season opened at last on December 10 with Gustav Mahler's Symphony No. 2, "Resurrection," played and sung by the pacified orchestra and chorus in plain view on the stage, Marilyn Horne and Judith Blegen the soloists. On January 15, the administrative shake-up long in the works was made official: Bliss became general manager in title as well as fact. Dexter's demotion to "production adviser" was sealed. In William Rockefeller's words, he would "continue to stage new productions, oversee the revivals of his old ones, and advise on dramatic matters. He is relieved of administrative duties that will be assumed by the technical department he created." Phoebe Berkowitz was named executive stage director. Three assistant managers were also appointed, Volpe for operations, Marilyn Shapiro for development and public affairs, and Joan Ingpen for artistic administration, a position she had held at Covent Garden and at the Paris Opéra. Levine seemed content: "We have the right structure now. John's [Dexter] work is necessary, but decisions were harder to make. Tony doesn't veto things on artistic grounds. If he and I don't agree on a production, we don't do it" (*Times,* Jan. 17, 1982).

*Parade,* February 20, 1981; *La Bohème,* December 14, 1981

The first of Dexter's stagings as production adviser was *Parade,* a triptych of Eric Satie's ballet, Poulenc's *Les Mamelles de Tirésias,* and Maurice Ravel's *L'Enfant et les sortilèges.* The *Times* waxed hyperbolic over Dexter's program of a modernist ballet and two rare, astringent operas: "Every so often, and sometimes none too soon, something happens at the opera to justify its existence and restore faith in its present and future." The collaboration between painter David Hockney and veteran conductor Manuel Rosenthal (student and friend of Ravel) was a happy one. Dramatic and visual motifs laid bare the World War I origins of the three works: the 1917 premieres of Satie's ballet and of the Apollinaire play on which Poulenc based his opera and the start of Ravel's engagement with *L'Enfant et les sortilèges.* The run sold out. The other new production of the season, originally tagged for Dexter, eventually staged by Colin Graham and designed by Tanya Moiseiwitsch, turned out to be a routine *La Traviata* (March 17, 1981).[17]

*La Bohème* was the splashiest of the five new productions of 1981–82. The 1948 tweaking of the garret aside, in its first half-century at the Met, Puccini's opera had been clothed in the same anonymous, utilitarian décors entrusted to staff directors who were there to remind principals and chorus of the standard blocking. When in 1952, at long last, *La Bohème* earned a new production, it was again on a modest scale. So it came as a surprise when Zeffirelli's *La Bohème* burst forth as one of the biggest spectacles ever mounted at the Met, the touchstone for the megaproductions that were to become the company's norm. The first-night audience roared for close to a minute when the curtain rose on act 2. The street corner occupied by a neighborhood establishment with an awning and a few tables had bulged into a three-level Parisian intersection, jammed with 280 Christmas revelers, a myriad of façades, a wide staircase, a ground-level café, and a terrace above. The toy-seller Parpignol had a pony cart, Musetta and her aged suitor a horse-drawn cab. At the climax, what seemed like all Paris was on parade. Some of Zeffirelli's inventions had strong narrative purpose. The little balcony off the garret was just right for private moments: Rodolfo's longing for Mimì, Colline's "addio" to his overcoat. The upstage area of act 3 provided a plausible vantage from which Mimì could overhear Rodolfo's agonizing forecast of her impending death. But more often, the size and complexity of the designs distanced spectators from the characters. For John Rockwell the sets were made-to-order "for people who come wanting to applaud the

FIGURE 35. *La Bohème,* act 2, 1981 (James Heffernan; courtesy Metropolitan Opera Archives)

scenery." Zeffirelli responded by calling Rockwell a "jerk." He proclaimed his own production "one of the most beautiful, honest, successful" in Met history. The décor was certainly beautiful, and if success is measured by longevity, Zeffirelli's boast was prescient: the lofty garret, the melancholy customs gate, and especially the riotous street scene continue to draw cheers more than thirty years and more than four hundred performances later. As for an honest representation of Puccini's "vie de bohème," that is another matter.[18]

## Other Stagings

With *La Bohème,* Dexter's battle for modern stagings was lost. Two years later, he was still licking his wounds: "Leave it to Franco to celebrate the 19th century—it's easy. The 20th is bloody difficult." Less than a fortnight before the opening of the Puccini sensation, Dexter, once again collaborating with Hockney, had laid down a final challenge to the literal, expensive, overblown style he loathed. *Stravinsky* (Dec. 3, 1981) was another modernist triptych: a ballet, *Le Sacre du printemps,* and two vocal works, the opera-ballet-pantomime *Le Rossignol* (in Russian) and the opera-oratorio *Oedipus Rex* (in Latin). This time, unlike *Parade,* the three components of the omnibus were mismatched. Even Andrew Porter, who thought *Stravinsky* "a big, serious achievement" and "a landmark in New York's operatic history," found it "exhausting." The choreography of Jean-Pierre Bonnefous did little for *Le Sacre du printemps* and Dexter's treatment of *Oedipus Rex* was largely static. Levine's direction of the difficult scores and Hockney's enchanting chinoiserie for *Le Rossignol* garnered what praise there was. Among the remaining new productions of 1981–82, only Hayden Griffin's elegant sliding panels for *Così fan tutte* (Jan. 29) mined the less-is-more Dexter-Hockney vein. John Cox's *Il Barbiere di Siviglia* (Feb. 15) banished comic shtick, losing a good bit of the comic along the way; décor and staging took a backseat to the virtuosity of Horne's Rosina. The new *Les Contes d'Hoffmann* (March 8) gave Zeffirelli a run for his money. Schenk and Schneider-Siemssen's extravagant weave of the realistic and the fantastic attracted the highest average capacity of the season. Spalanzani's laboratory, animated by the body parts of airborne automata, gave the audience entrée into Hoffmann's delusions; the Venetian campo reeked with the decadence of Giulietta and Dappertutto; Antonia's bourgeois sitting room dissolved into the nightmarish realm of Dr. Miracle. Conductor Riccardo Chailly's excellent debut promised a company career more extensive than just eight performances of Offenbach's opera.[19]

In the course of rehearsals for the new, well-appointed *Arabella* (Feb. 10, 1983), finally in German, Kathleen Battle went to war with Kiri Te Kanawa. This would be neither the first nor the last of her run-ins with colleagues. But when the two sopranos wafted the high-lying legato of Strauss's sublime duet for two loving sisters, the public heard nothing but harmony. *Idomeneo,* the sole novelty of 1982–83 and the first of Mozart's neglected operas premiered by Levine, was notable also for the casting of Pavarotti. In this unaccustomed repertoire, the tenor simplified the role's elaborate fioritura, all the while manifesting scrupulous musicianship and exemplary diction. Ponnelle enlivened the stately conventions of eighteenth-century opera seria through a canny pattern of entrances and exits to and from his Piranesi-inspired, multileveled unit set. *Idomeneo* drew large audiences as long as Pavarotti led the cast. *Macbeth* (Nov. 18, 1982) set off one of the most boisterous outbursts in memory. Peter Hall and John Bury had had the ingenious notion of returning *Macbeth* to the theater practice of Verdi's youth, with flying witches and a giant cauldron from which emerged a nearly nude Hecate and effigies of the apparitions. Levine conducted Verdi's complete 1865 Paris revision of his 1847 score; it included a ballet danced by sylphs in tutus as Macbeth lay dying. The public saw it as Gothic gone amok; they responded with laughter, boos, and a few altercations. The *Times* was unequivocal: "The worst new production to struggle onto the Metropolitan Opera's stage in modern history"; Porter's minority report took pains to acknowledge the "serious-minded, ambitious attempt to discover what the composer was about and to present his meanings vividly" without skirting the errors of execution and the miscasting of Scotto as Lady Macbeth. The *Macbeth* fiasco spelled a halt to productions that strayed too far from the beaten path. During the third and last revival of the Hall/Bury show, the Macbeth curse struck again. On January 23, 1988, the Saturday matinée was suspended at the second act intermission by the suicide of Bantcho Bantchevsky, an eighty-two-year-old Bulgarian singing coach and Met habitué, who jumped eighty feet to his death from the family circle.[20]

In early 1983, a year to the day after his sunny "we have the right structure now" comment, Levine pressed ahead once again: "While he never criticizes Bliss," *Time* reported, "it is clear that he wants more control. In renegotiating his contract, which expires in 1986, Levine is demanding complete artistic authority over the Met, including a lump-sum budget to spend as he sees fit" (Jan. 17, 1983). "More control" likely meant freedom from the denial of production overdrafts, and likely also freedom from scrutiny of his expense account. What moved Levine to raise the issue of renewal three years before the expiration of his contract? Bliss's retirement at the end of 1984–85 would be announced on March 21, 1983. Levine wanted to be certain that the terms of his future bargain were widely circulated, particularly to potential candidates, well before the onset of the search. The conditions of his agreement would mark out the limits of the new general manager's purview. As ultimately defined, the position required "knowledge of opera, singing and staging, strong administrative ability, fund-raising, union negotiations, the care and upkeep of the house, working with public and Federal agencies, a knowledge of several languages, a strong personality, close relationship with opera guilds and other opera houses" (*Times,* June 15). Nothing was said of artistic responsibility, let alone vision. For their part, the directors were eager to ensure that Levine, ever more sought after by European orchestras and festivals, would stay close to home. He signed his 1986 contract on September 16, 1983; the centennial season opened three days later.[21]

# Centennial Season, 1983–1984

No one was of a mind to quibble that, in fact, 1983–84 was the Met's ninety-eighth season: 1892–93 was canceled after the fire of the previous summer, 1897–98 erased when Maurice Grau refused to lease the house without his principal stars, Jean and Edouard de Reszke, Emma Calvé, and Nellie Melba. At the dowager age of one hundred, give or take that year or two, the Met was solvent. The 1976–77 season was the first of four consecutive years in the black. The lockout season of 1980–81 had resulted in losses approaching $6 million. Happily, recovery had followed swiftly, and just prior to the centennial there was again a surplus, however small. Capacity was at 90.1 percent. Sybil Harrington, widow of a Texas oilman, cultivated masterfully by Shapiro, had contributed the astounding sum of $20 million in 1980 alone. (Her giving to the Metropolitan over her lifetime is estimated at $30 million.) As its birthday drew near, the Met was 80 percent of the way to the $100 million goal set by the centennial fund, 20 percent of which ultimately sprang from corporate founts. At the start of the campaign, the endowment had been a trifling $2 million.

The season opened with the five-hour marathon of *Les Troyens*. The production, though revised, was no better liked than it had been at its premiere ten years earlier. Domingo had trepidations over the high tessitura of Énée. Only a week or two before showtime, it was still not certain that he would tackle the heroic role. He did, though without his usual confidence, despite some judicious transpositions. He sang only the first four performances, including the telecast. The Cassandre was Jessye Norman, making her long-awaited debut. A star in Europe since 1969, Norman was already well known in the United States through recordings and concert appearances. In the February matinée, she replicated Shirley Verrett's feat by playing both Cassandre and Didon.

The two-part October 22 Centennial Gala was telecast live throughout the United States. When Bliss welcomed the audience that afternoon, he made two upbeat announcements: that the Met had formed a partnership with Pioneer Electronics for laser discs and videocassettes, and that, nine months before the deadline, agreement had been reached with the orchestra and others of the Met's unionized workers. The musicians had won a 6 percent annual increase, improved pensions, and the retraction of the four free rehearsal hours conceded in 1980. Kudos went to Volpe in his now official capacity as labor liaison; he had had the foresight to open talks eighteen months before the old contract expired, and the skill to avoid the bitter wrangles of the past.[22]

In the course of the eight-hour extravaganza, nearly ninety soloists sang arias and joined in duets, trios, and larger ensembles. Levine began the musical proceedings by showing off the high polish of his orchestra in the overture to *The Bartered Bride*. Eva Marton sustained this rush of energy, pulling out all the stops for Turandot's thunderous "In questa reggia." The backdrop to this first segment was Hockney's décor for *Les Mamelles de Tirésias*, oddly mated to the standard rep it framed. Sutherland navigated the fioritura of "Bel raggio," Catherine Malfitano and Alfredo Kraus interlaced their elegant phrasing as Roméo and Juliette, and Anna Tomowa-Sintow gave expansive shape to "Ernani, involami." But unbalanced couplings and haphazard assignments too often compromised the fare. Norman, a formidable Sieglinde, had to put up with the feeble Siegmund of Jess Thomas, pulled out of retirement when Jon Vickers would not participate. Thomas Stewart and Evelyn Lear had neither the style nor the voice for Porgy and Bess. And so it went. Some performances offered irrefutable proof of the company's eminence; far too many ran from good enough to inadequate. The best years of the still-active Crespin, Gedda, and Cornell MacNeil were clearly behind them; those of Moffo and Merrill, no longer with the company, embarrassingly so. The return of sixty-five-year-old Nilsson was a bittersweet reminder that time had marched on even for the seemingly indestructible soprano. After Isolde's "Narrative and Curse," ill-tuned and unfocused, she spun a modest Swedish song with lovely tone and surprising lightness and agility.

For the final segment, a phalanx of former Met stars was seated on the stage. They had been in the audience observing others in roles they themselves had sung with distinction. Erstwhile Otello Ramon Vinay could only have been impressed with McCracken, back after a five-year absence, crushing in the Moor's despair, and Domingo, sweetly lyrical in duet with Mirella Freni. Dorothy Kirsten must have cringed at Leona Mitchell's coarsely phrased Cio-Cio-San. And what could Eleanor Steber have thought as she heard Kiri Te Kanawa's "Dove sono," impeccable until she lost her way toward the end? Steber, Risë Stevens, and Erna Berger, the Marschallin, Octavian, and Sophie of the 1949 opening night telecast, would no doubt have admired the rapturous *Rosenkavalier* trio of von Stade, Battle, and Elisabeth Söderström. Without a doubt, loyal fans of Zinka Milanov would have given their eye teeth to read her mind as she sat just feet away from Price and Pavarotti, at their absolute best in the act 2 duet of *Un Ballo in maschera*. When the curtain rose for the last time, the dozens and dozens of artists cramming the stage struck an emotional tableau of the Met past and present.

FIGURE 36. Centennial Gala, Leontyne Price and Luciano Pavarotti in foreground, seated in first row Risë Stevens fourth from left, Ramon Vinay sixth, Dorothy Kirsten seventh, Zinka Milanov eighth, Erna Berger tenth, Eleanor Steber eleventh, October 22, 1983 (Winnie Klotz; courtesy Metropolitan Opera Archives)

The old-time stars in the chorus of "Happy Birthday" validated the company's reputation, and then some. By contrast, the ranks of the neophytes seemed thin. Complaints about the paucity of great voices would surface with growing frequency in the years to come.

Two of the three new productions of the centennial season subscribed to the grandiloquent Zeffirelli manner. For *Ernani* (Nov. 18), director and designer Pier Luigi Samaritani, a former Zeffirelli assistant, filled the stage with an enormous curving staircase that impeded the movement of the principals. And more importantly, Samaritani's concept suggested that he had not "'seen' the music at all—either its large structures or its action-linked details." In the December 17 performance, preserved on video, Levine allows too few opportunities for expressivity in tempos; Pavarotti is in thrilling form as Ernani, for him a new role; Milnes applies his acumen and formidable experience to Carlo; the bass Ruggero Raimondi lacks the absolute control Silva's great aria demands; and Mitchell is unremarkable as Elvira. *Francesca da Rimini* (March 9), returning to the Met after nearly seven decades, would be the sole installment in Levine's exhumation of Italian verismo and postverismo. Riccardo Zandonai's opera was mounted by Ezio Frigerio and staged by Piero Faggioni in their company debuts. The *Times* ("the evening stretched out end-lessly") and the *New Yorker* ("third-rate music") questioned the effort and money expended on an opera unlikely to enter the repertoire. Harrington had paid for exactly the kind of production she adored. The pitched battle of act 2 unleashed a catapult, crossbows, and "Greek fire." Frigerio's ravishing pre-Raphaelite treatment of the interiors lent Scotto a flattering framework that may have diverted attention from her colorless tone. Domingo's ardent Paolo responded to Levine's love for a score that, he allowed, had fascinated him since the age of sixteen. Despite negative reviews for the opera, the stars drew excel-lent audiences; in 1985–86, with Ermanno Mauro in place of Domingo and Nello Santi in place of Levine, the box office for *Francesca da Rimini* was the season's poorest. The company gave it another chance in 2012–13.[23]

Far more consequential was the premiere of Handel's *Rinaldo,* the first baroque opera ever mounted by the company, a benchmark in the diversifica-tion of the repertoire. In Marilyn Horne, Samuel Ramey, and Benita Valente, the Met had singers unfazed by the challenges of Baroque ornamentation. The trio had combined forces earlier in Ottawa in essentially the same witty pro-duction, conducted by Mario Bernardi. In his Met debut, Ramey made his entrance on an airborne, dragon-shaped chariot and unfurled his mighty voice with an agility unparalleled among his peers. True Handelians decried this impure, heavily rearranged version of the original score. Nonetheless, this pro-duction served to introduce an enthusiastic audience to the Baroque that, in time, and in far more authentic guise, would make the Metropolitan home.[24]

FROM BLISS TO CRAWFORD TO SOUTHERN,
1985–1989

The Artistic Director

The busy centennial was the year of the search for a new general manager, thereby granting the incoming chief a full season, Bliss's last, 1984–85, to learn the ropes and plan the future. Word was out that Levine had tired of Bliss's "reluctance or inability to help effectively with the nitty gritty details of putting together—and holding together—an operatic season" (*Times,*

Sept. 22, 1985). Only one candidate, as far as we know, actually made the pilgrimage to Lincoln Center, the intendant of the Munich Opera and Met stage director August Everding. Two other names found their way into the news, Ardis Krainik, head of the Lyric Opera of Chicago, and Ernest Fleishmann, manager of the Los Angeles Philharmonic. The committee was undoubtedly aware that individuals presenting Everding's credentials, or Krainik's or Fleishmann's for that matter, would expect much of the artistic control that had already been signed away in Levine's 1986 contract. Nonetheless, according to Volpe's later account, the board did offer Everding the position. He declined "because Jimmy Levine's agent, Ronald Wilford, had, in effect, blackmailed the Met into naming Jimmy artistic director. Wilford's threat that Jimmy would walk unless given the title was an empty one, but it worked." By early summer, Bruce Crawford, the new president of the Association replacing Frank Taplin, confided somewhat disingenuously, "All the favorite candidates have disappeared. I still would hope that we can get somebody who is more than an administrative type" (*Times,* June 9, 1984). Crawford himself had been discussed earlier in the process; he had withdrawn from consideration, citing business obligations. Whether or not his vacillation ultimately short-circuited the search, by October Crawford, an advertising executive and the board chair of BBDO Worldwide, a dyed-in-the-wool "administrative type" who knew opera well, was general man-ager–elect. He reported that "the search committee came to the conclusion that what we didn't need was two artistic directors" (*Times,* Oct. 5, 1984). By then, the winds had shifted. In Volpe's words, "the Met was deeper in red ink than at any time in its history, with a deficit of $8 million. . . . The culprits were uncontrolled expenses, a falloff at the box office, and a huge diversion of donations to the endowment drive. . . . The trustees [were] blind to the effect [the drive] would have on the annual giving that was essential to cover oper-ating expenses."[25]

With Crawford in the wings came other changes. To Levine's chagrin, Joan Ingpen retired at the end of 1984–85. Bliss and his successor saw her depart without regret. To their minds, Ingpen's insistence on nailing down casts at a distance of five years had kept the Met from bringing in rising stars at their ascendancy. This intransigence also put the company at risk of field-ing artists past their prime. Her detractors complained that "she'd rather have a mediocre singer than a hole to fill later." Levine was rewarded with the sweeping title of artistic director effective the next year, 1986, blotting out "the separation of musical and dramatic [that had] become to [him] intolerable." He had been candid with the board: "Either engage me as a guest conductor or put me in charge." The new title also celebrated his tenth anniversary with an orchestra that had gone from good to fabulous under his utterly devoted leadership, just as he had promised in 1975. Players and singers loved working with him: "He is one of the few, perhaps the only one, among active big-league opera conductors today, who conducts 'the performance that is actually taking place' [Sherrill Milnes's phrase], responding to the singers instead of leading an ideal performance he hears in his head and leaving the singers to fit into it willy-nilly" (*Times*, Sept. 22, 1985).[26]

Crawford found a sluggish hierarchy "infected" with Levine's penchant for indecision. "My job," he said artfully, "is to keep [Levine] from getting swamped." Stretched by an exhausting schedule of rehearsals and performances, the artistic director–designate was both unwilling to cede control and unable to wield it expeditiously. Crawford's portfolio obviously extended well beyond the modest supporting role he had ascribed to himself for public consumption. Not only would he hold the reins of the complex operation, but he would see to it that Levine himself was reined in. The message he delivered on taking office echoed Bliss's injunction of two years earlier: "We must . . . follow a policy of working much more closely with the marketing department and making certain that the repertoire is chosen with projected box office return to be no less than 90%-91%." In fact, since 1977, essentially the Levine years, capacity had trended downward from 96.3 percent to 85 percent. The revivals of the Dexter productions were partially to blame; once their novelty had worn off, they averaged only 76 percent. Crawford called for a "conservative swing" as the only alternative, with "continued or even increasing reliance on such lavish spectacles as the Franco Zeffirelli *Tosca*" due to open the season. Patrons that evening were treated to a Grand Tier postperformance supper punctuated by a show of Chanel's latest line. That night, the company brought in a total of $1.2 million, of which $750,000 was donated by the celebrity fashion house (*Times*, Sept. 29, 1985). The outrage provoked by the mercantile incursion derailed this particular experiment. Other brainchildren of Crawford appointee Cecile Zilkha, most notably a program of corporate giving, rang up $5 million annually.[27]

### Repertoire and Singers: 1984–1986

Faced with plummeting ticket sales and mounting deficits, Crawford put the brakes on Levine's expansion of the repertoire. Met audiences had been reticent to explore uncharted terrain. The scheduling of *Wozzeck* and *Lulu* in the same season contributed to the depressed 1984–85 average of 84.9 percent. The next year, capacity fell to 82.9 percent, attributable, to some extent, to three hard sells, *Idomeneo, Jenůfa,* and *Khovanshchina.* Then there was the challenge of casting familiar operas with principals worthy of their roles, and the still-higher hurdles of signing those few with unquestioned marquee value and keeping stellar casts intact. Absent Pavarotti, *Ernani* lost its draw; without Domingo, *Francesca da Rimini* flopped. Between 1984 and 1986, audiences too often had no choice but to put up with Ermanno Mauro and Carol Neblett in *Manon Lescaut,* Vasile Moldoveanu in *Simon Boccanegra,* and Franz-Ferdinand Nentwig, Mari-Anne Häggander, and Edward Sooter in *Die Meistersinger,* all of whom were engaged under Ingpen's policy of better safe than sorry. In its roundup of 1985–86, the *Christian Science Monitor* called the season "a shambles." The *Wall Street Journal* found it "so depressing that even long-in the-tooth operagoers can't remember its like." The consensus was that the Met was awash in mediocrity. Adding to the gloom were the defections, some in management's control, some not. Sutherland and McCracken withdrew for several years beginning in 1978, she until 1982 over *The Merry Widow* she had been denied, he until 1983 over a *Tannhäuser* telecast he thought was coming to him. Nilsson ran afoul of the IRS in 1975 and stayed away until 1979. For these and other desertions, and for the too-rare appearances of major artists, the leadership took the heat, "not in most instances because the Met had failed to ask—but sometimes because it did not ask persuasively, insistently, invitingly, imaginatively, or accommodatingly enough."[28]

Like it or not, with or without stars, Zeffirelli's formula, the deluxe investiture of a popular opera, was a winner. In the wake of his *La Bohème,* his *Tosca* (March 11, 1985) would fill the house season after season, indifferent to singers or conductors. The opening of act 3 was by any measure an example of scenic gesture meant principally to astound. Puccini's evocation of dawn breaking over the Castel Sant'Angelo fell victim to the razzle-dazzle of stage machinery as the terrace rose to reveal Cavaradossi's dungeon and then sank back into place for the opera's denouement. The management had attracted a major conductor, Giuseppe Sinopoli; the orchestra was unhappy with him, he with the rate of exchange, and he never again played at the Met. Of the first-night cast, only Domingo had sufficient sweetness and brilliance. Hildegard Behrens, exciting as always, though handicapped by her increasingly weak bottom and thin middle registers, was a curiously unaffecting

Tosca; for Scarpia, MacNeil, his voice nearly drained of vibrato, had to lean heavily on experience.[29]

The Peter Hall/John Bury *Carmen* (March 10, 1986), substantially grown since its birth on the small stage of Glyndebourne, would have been easily forgotten had it not been for Maria Ewing. Her gypsy was pouting, rude, roughly sung, and erotic despite her refusal of the trappings of eroticism. She made Andrew Porter's "short list of those who have left an indelible impression" in the role; she was trounced by many other reviewers ("only a little short of complete travesty," "a manic-depressive urchin who has fits," "an object lesson in how not to do the role"). *Porgy and Bess* had its much belated house premiere at last (Feb. 6, 1985). In the mid-1930s, Otto Kahn had wanted the Met to be the first to mount George Gershwin's opera. The composer rebuffed the company's chintzy guarantee of only two performances and turned to Broadway instead. A world tour of the often revived Broadway format with spoken dialogue, kicked off in 1952, was an early triumph for Leontyne Price. The Met's Bess and Porgy were Grace Bumbry and Simon Estes. Not the "less than convincing" principals, but the large ensemble, Levine in the pit, and Florence Quivar's definitive Serena argued persuasively for Gershwin as grand opera. *Porgy and Bess* played to packed houses through its four-season run.[30]

Among the other new productions of 1984–86, a revival and two premieres added to the company's prestige if not to its profits. *Khovanshchina* (Oct. 14, 1985), sung in Russian, was embraced as a masterpiece. August Everding and Ming-Cho Lee took a spare approach to Mussorgsky's posthumous work, the better to tell the convoluted story as clearly as possible. The final scene made expressive use of the revolving stage as the "Old Believers" advanced from the forest to the interior of the hermitage for their mass immolation. *La Clemenza di Tito* was the last of the three neglected Mozart operas Levine added to the repertoire. Ponnelle's architectonic set, wide steps, porticos, and balconies suited the composer's late masterpiece. As for Handel's *Samson,* Moshinsky and his designer, Timothy O'Brien, attempted to counter the oratorio's endemic stasis by varying the arrangement of chorus and props. Conductor Julius Rudel played fast and loose with the score's length and its Baroque embellishments. Vickers's Miltonic hero, blind at the gate of his Gaza prison, was the lynchpin of the production. *Samson* was a parting gift to the tenor who had touched New York audiences so deeply since 1960. He would make his farewell to the Met the following season as Samson again, this time in Saint-Saëns's opera.

# National Tour, 1883–1986

Bliss was barely out the door when Crawford scuttled the annual national tour, a tradition as old as the Met itself. The growing strength of regional opera, coast-to-coast access to the Metropolitan via television, the increasing difficulty of drafting prominent singers, and, above all, significant losses were reasons to call it quits. In 1883–84, Henry Abbey, an inveterate tour manager, had taken his Grand Italian Opera on the road. At different points in the season, the company visited Boston, where it presented the Met premieres of *Carmen* and *Martha,* Cincinnati for its first *Le Prophète* and *Hamlet,* and Philadelphia for *Roméo et Juliette*. Abbey's troupe traveled as far west as Chicago and St. Louis and south to Washington. The Grand Italian Opera played more performances away that season than on 39th Street. The German ensembles of 1884–1891 were homebound by comparison: for three seasons they did not budge. Under the management of Abbey, Grau, and Schoeffel in 1891, the tour reclaimed its share of the schedule. The De Reszke brothers and Emma Eames made their Met debuts not in New York, but in Chicago during a five-week engagement that featured the premieres of *Otello* and *Cavalleria rusticana*. Just before and after the turn of the century, the company journeyed for long stretches, adding to its itinerary numerous stops, including two in Canada, en route to the Pacific. On November 9, 1900, Los Angeles heard Melba as the Met's first Mimì; on April 17, 1906, Fremstad and Caruso sang *Carmen* in San Francisco only hours before the earthquake. Beginning in 1903, tours were confined to the spring, with rare exception. In the climactic months of the 1910 competition with Hammerstein, not one but two brigades were dispatched from Broadway, the first to Chicago for a month, the second to the midwest and then across the Atlantic to Paris.

With Hammerstein out of the way, Gatti, no friend of long excursions, could afford to keep his stars in his backyard, Brooklyn or Philadelphia. The sole far-flung destination was Atlanta, where opera week was the height of the social season, the occasion for masked balls and lavish parties honoring fun-loving singers wont to reciprocate with musical antics. It was in 1910 that the first citizens' committee was organized to sponsor a Met visit: the Atlanta Festival Association headed by "Colonel" Peel. A prize attraction was the alluring and sometimes shocking Geraldine Farrar; the press took special note of her offstage "peek-a-boo" blouse and her onstage *Zazà* panties. Atlanta knew what it wanted. Mrs. Peel warned Edward Ziegler, Gatti's assistant, that the patrons would not put up with "a bargain counter affair," that the roster had to include "Hell Cats" (if not Farrar, then Frieda Hempel), that Maria Barrientos was "very unpopular here" and Ponselle "an unknown quantity," and that *Il Trittico,* whose New York world premiere she had attended that very evening, was "an awful conglomeration" and "a perfect mess" (Dec. 14, 1918). Although Atlantans did not get their favorite "Hell Cats" and had to suffer the unpopular Barrientos, they had little cause for complaint: the "awful" *Trittico* did not venture below the Mason-Dixon line, the young Ponselle was a hit in Atlanta as she had been in New York, and Caruso was all theirs in three of the seven performances. The circuit grew again in the 1920s with the inclusion of Cleveland, Rochester, Baltimore, and Washington. When one port of call dropped out during the Depression, another close by, Newark, Hartford, or suburban White Plains, took its place. By the end of the 1930s, a truly national tour struck out for New Orleans, Dallas, and points between. Local papers had lots to say about gowns and jewels on display for opening night. And lucky the city favored with Lily Pons or Risë Stevens, who exuded not only the chichi of high culture, but the chic of mass media, radio, movies, and the ubiquitous cigarette advertisement, particularly apt for Stevens's smoldering Carmen.[31]

If the star singers of the 1950s found the American road less appealing than had their elders, from the point of view of management the tour remained a necessity. Bing was categorical: "The tour is the Metropolitan's economic basis for existence: if we have no tour the Metropolitan will close because we will not have the funds to support ourselves. If we continue to tell the important tour cities that they cannot have the distinguished artists who have such outstanding success in New York, they will decline to accept our tours." The particular "distinguished" artist he had in mind was Renata Tebaldi, whose fee he sweetened by a then munificent $500 per performance. Tebaldi's Violetta and Tosca were the drawing cards of the 1957 tour. The following spring, the casts were as good as, and sometimes better than, those in New York: *Aïda* and *Madama Butterfly* with Antonietta Stella and Carlo Bergonzi; *Don Giovanni* with George London, Eleanor Steber, and Cesare Valletti; and *Otello* with Mario Del Monaco, Leonard Warren, and Zinka Milanov. Nonetheless, that very season, the ranks of first-tier traveling artists were perilously thin. The company had had no choice but to announce at the outset two tenor comprimarios in principal roles, Giulio Gari as Turiddu, and Charles Anthony as Almaviva. It was downhill from there.[32]

Twenty years later, the *Times* plumbed the sorry depths to which the tour had descended (June 13, 1976). In many cities, the auditoriums were cavernous civic centers or hockey rinks whose acoustics required amplification, whose tiny pits forced reduced orchestras, and whose pitiful stages were inadequate to the scenery. To avoid paying overtime, scores were hacked: *Carmen* sometimes lost the children's chorus and the orchestral entr'actes, *Meistersinger* a quarter of its music. Too often, management pulled a bait and switch whereby stars listed in the initial announcements were replaced by dimmer lights. Levine himself decried the look and sound of the shows: "The Met used to depend a lot on painted sets. Now our style is so complex that we find it hard to adapt productions to the theatre stages and orchestra pits now available to us. The lack of resonance from concrete floors in the pit, for example . . . changes drastically what we can accomplish" (*Times*, Jan. 17, 1982). From Crawford's perspective, the problem was the repertoire, the *Peter Grimes*, the *Francesca da Rimini*, the *Rinaldo* for which he blamed Levine: "If you had deliberately set out to sabotage the tour [of 1984], you couldn't have done a better job."[33]

Once a cash cow, the tour had become a cash leech, a $1-million-a-year drag on the budget. In 1986, only Boston, Cleveland, Atlanta, and Minneapolis booked the woeful final sampler. If it is unfair to compare Atlanta's Santuzza and Turiddu, Nicole Lorange and Vladimir Popov, to their 1919 counterparts, Ponselle and Caruso, as recently as 1970 the leads of *Cavalleria rusticana* had been the high-powered Fiorenza Cossotto and Plácido Domingo. The national tour went out with a whimper. At its last matinée performance, in Minneapolis on May 31, 1986, neither the Roméo, comprimario Jon Garrison, nor the Juliette, Monique Baudoin, had ever sung their roles at the Met. In fact, Baudoin had never sung any role at all at the Met. Later that June, she came as close as she ever would to Lincoln Center when the company presented Gounod's opera in the Great Meadow of Central Park.

### Repertoire and Singers: 1986–1990

By the end of 1986–87, it was bruited about that Crawford had invaded the artistic realm. Not only had he taken to auditioning singers, but it was he who succeeded in enticing the revered and elusive conductor Carlos Kleiber to the Met. At about that time, Levine had asked to be relieved of some administrative duties so that he might concentrate more fully on the music. He continued to corner new productions. Wagner, Mozart, most of Verdi, and the two modernist works, *Bluebeard's Castle* and *Erwartung,* were his.

Among the guests, only Kleiber enjoyed prestige equal or superior to Levine's. Richard Bonynge was something of a regular as conductor of his wife, Joan Sutherland. Marek Janowski, Manuel Rosenthal, and Charles Dutoit had only brief Met careers. But despite the repeated riff on *Damn Yankees,* "Whatever Jimmy wants, Jimmy gets," with Crawford's growing influence it was plainly no longer "Jimmy's show" alone (*Times,* July 23, 1987; Sept. 22, 1985).

In March 1987, the auditorium was named for Sibyl Harrington. The announcement came during one of Zilkha's onstage corporate dinners. Harrington's generosity had come with the caveat that she would support productions in the grandest manner only. To Dexter's disgust, the horse and wolfhounds on which she insisted had been front and center in the Fontainebleau scene of his *Don Carlo;* and to Zeffirelli's glee, she took a special fancy to his recurrent menageries. Harrington's clout provided another opening for lamentations on the state of opera in New York. "Serious opera fans have received the dedication as a defiant Bronx cheer," griped one critic. Zeffirelli's *La Bohème, Tosca,* and *Turandot,* all underwritten by Harrington, had "turned the Metropolitan from house of art into tourist attraction, a nice conclusion, perhaps, to a bus tour including lunch at Mama Leone's" (*Times,* Nov. 12, 1987).[34]

For four consecutive seasons, in its pursuit of black ink, the Met channeled the Zeffirelli/Harrington aesthetic. From 1982 to 1986, the company had mounted fourteen new productions, seven of them premieres or revivals of operas long absent. Among the eighteen new productions of 1986–90, there were only two premieres, *Giulio Cesare* and *Erwartung,* and no resurrections. Instead, the "Ring," *Aïda, La Traviata,* and other chestnuts acquired the look of luxury. The promise of an expanded repertoire made by Levine and Dexter in the mid-1970s, honored for a decade, was deferred indefinitely. The critics bristled when the company retracted its commission for a new work by Jacob Druckman and canceled a Levine pet project, Schoenberg's *Moses und Aron:* "For box-office reasons, the company has been pulling in its horns ever since James Levine and Bruce Crawford took charge as artistic director and general manager"; "The general manager conceded that it was now company policy to concentrate on popular operas that could fill the Met's 3,800-seat theatre."[35]

For 1986–87, Schenk and Schneider-Siemssen were entrusted with two highly visible projects, the first installment of their "Ring" and *Die Fledermaus* (Dec. 4). Schneider-Siemssen designed a far more naturalistic tetralogy than the one he had contrived for Karajan a decade earlier. Bucking the doctrine of abstraction in vogue since the first postwar Bayreuth festival, 1951, the Met *Die Walküre* (Sept. 22) opted for faithful adherence to Wagner's scenic and dramatic instructions. Levine took command of the Wagnerian marathon for the first time; Behrens was a gripping Brünnhilde; James Morris established himself as the Wotan of his generation. But where were the heldentenors? During the first years of the run, none of the Siegmunds approached the Vickers standard; worse still, none of the Siegfrieds came close to passable. Schenk, who found the Rhine more salubrious than Bad Ischl, the waters of *Fledermaus,* drowned the operetta in age-old Viennese shtick. The lyrics were restored to the original German for the first time since 1905. Although the premiere was an off night for everyone ("about halfway through the first act . . . it became painfully clear that the most generous approach to the remainder of the evening would be to look for bright spots amid the gloom"), the New Year's Eve telecast captures Te Kanawa, the Rosalinde, back in form in a lush "Csárdás." Despite the dwindling box office of subsequent seasons, the Eisensteins and their fellow bon vivants would cavort in their revolving ballroom in nine revivals through 2006.[36]

Zeffirelli's immense *Turandot* (March 12, 1987) was even more overstuffed than his *La Bohème* or *Tosca.* The audience gasped in amazement, and many critics in dismay, during the act 2 riddle scene when the princess's imperial backpack gushed multicolored streamers. *Opera News* raised the specter of the opera itself getting "lost in the shuffle" when "the machinery works better than ever." In the April 4 telecast, Marton's icy princess is frequently strident, Domingo sacrifices the unknown prince's dreamy tenderness to the role's heroic outbursts, and Mitchell is a rich-toned Liù. The intimacy of Verdi's *La Traviata* (Oct. 16, 1989) was smothered under Zeffirelli's hyperbole. The Met's hi-tech stage held out the temptation of re-creating the effects that his 1982 motion picture reduction of the opera owed to camera and editing. He invented action for the two preludes, upstaging as great a conductor as Carlos Kleiber. For *Don Giovanni* (March 22, 1990), with a backward glance at Rococo stagecraft and the canny manipulation of sliding panels and trompe-l'oeil backdrops, Zeffirelli eschewed his customary realism. First-night critics were divided. In the engrossing video, Ramey's forceful Giovanni heads a strong cast; the Elvira, Karita Mattila, in her debut role, displays the bloom and energy audiences would cherish through sixteen seasons and counting. When Zeffirelli's design for *Aïda* was rejected as exorbitant, the commission went to Sonja Frisell and Gianni Quaranta; the management was after Zeffirelli's manner, not his pricetag. Frisell and Quaranta's still-extant spectacle (Dec. 8, 1988)—its monumental statues framing the opening scene, the colossi of act 2 so tall that they exceeded the height of the proscenium—leaves us to wonder at the scale of Zeffirelli's proposal. Ponnelle's "elephantine" *Manon* (Feb. 6, 1987), tested in Vienna and Munich, sported a two-level, four-chamber gambling den, a Cours-la-Reine tightrope walker, and a final scene sited in a garbage dump—a window, said Andrew Porter, into the designer-director's opinion of the work.[37]

In *Il Trovatore* (Nov. 12, 1987), a plethora of wandering columns became the object of hilarity; the staging obliged the cast to fight off an unfriendly acoustical environment, and at least one flight of stairs too many. Designer Rolf Langenfass described his *Faust* (Feb. 1, 1990) as "almost like a *Cabinet of Dr. Caligari* town." German cinematic expressionism may have fit the subject, but it clashed with Gounod's graceful score. This would be the one Met credit of Broadway director Harold Prince. *Giulio Cesare,* the company's third Handel offering, was probably the weakest of all the new productions between 1986 and 1990. The direction and décor, imported from the English National Opera, would have better been embargoed. One critic wrote, "John Pascoe's sets strained for exotic gilded effect, but on the whole reminded one of the lobby décor of a Grand Hyatt hotel." Kathleen Battle, the Cleopatra, exquisite as always, had become overly cautious, and not much voice or temperament crossed the footlights. This *Giulio Cesare* would return with some frequency; with Handelians Stephanie Blythe, David Daniels, and Ruth Ann Swenson, it would make a persuasive argument for the Baroque's place in the Met's repertoire.[38]

Two twentieth-century rarities and one core rereading were beneficiaries of the most intriguing treatments of the Crawford-Levine years. *Bluebeard's Castle* (in English) and *Erwartung* shared not only a heavy dose of pre–World War I angst but the same set. Both would have profited from the direction of Peter Sellars, originally slotted for the productions. For Martin Bernheimer, the result was "all very chic and very silly. The claptrap could even be funny if it weren't such an affront to Bartók's brooding, decaying romanticism and Schoenberg's febrile, ecstatic expressionism." Bartók's tonality and the snatches of melodic contour he fashioned for the mysterious Bluebeard and the inquisitive Judith played to the strengths of Ramey's granitic bass and Norman's deep soprano. The liquid flow of Norman's voice was impeded by the sprechstimme of Schoenberg's monodrama. Low box office may well have dissuaded the management from repeating these seminal works. Jürgen Rose's provocative *Salome* (Feb. 20, 1989) gave Herod a palace all aslant, with much of the staging relegated to a repellent basement floor. The eclectic costumes and décor evoked not Biblical Palestine, but the seamy decadence of Gotham. Eva Marton made no secret of her aversion to Salome's frilly prom dress.[39]

Compounding disappointment over new productions was the decreasing presence of top-flight stars. Second casts were especially weak. Erich Leinsdorf minced no words: "Let's face it, it is today absolutely a fact that even for roles that are not difficult, there are at best two or three first-rate singers in the world" (*Times*, Nov. 12, 1987). Defections persisted: Maria Ewing walked out when the *Carmen* telecast went to Agnes Baltsa, Renato Bruson canceled his Macbeth when the falling dollar cut into his fee, Eva Marton (his Lady Macbeth) found the replacement Thanes of Cawdor beneath her dignity. Already displeased with the *Salome* production and costume, and furious over the assignment of Hildegard Behrens to the telecast "Ring," Marton stayed away for eight seasons. Still, many were happy to be at the Met. Carlo Bergonzi at sixty-three remained a mellifluous Nemorino, and Alfredo Kraus was ever astonishing as an eternally youthful Roméo, Werther, and Hoffmann. Mirella Freni was admired for her brave move to the Russian repertoire. After a seven-season hiatus, Teresa Stratas returned to take on all three heroines of *Il Trittico*. As for newcomers, Dawn Upshaw and Hei-Kyung Hong graduated from Barbarina to Susanna in *Le Nozze di Figaro* (Hong eventually to the Countess), Heidi Grant Murphy from a Servant in *Die Frau ohne Schatten* to the *Rosenkavalier* Sophie, and Dwayne Croft from Fiorello to Figaro in *Il Barbiere di Siviglia*. Among those who debuted as principal artists—June Anderson, Jerry Hadley, Thomas Hampson, Richard Leach, Waltraud Meier, Cheryl Studer, Sharon Sweet, Carol Vaness, Anne Sofie von Otter, and Dolora Zajick—some were infrequent visitors, many came back often, a few to leave their mark on the company. In 2012–13, Hampson added Iago to his long list of roles and Zajick repeated her classic Azucena and Amneris. But the number of estimable singers who joined the Met in the 1980s was inadequate to the demands of the bread-and-butter titles. At the end of the decade, Levine felt impelled to state the obvious: "Our problem is in what used to be mainstream 19th-century repertory. I don't mean to say that you can't get a great performance; you can and you do. But you sometimes don't." Crawford followed suit: "You can sell out *Madama Butterfly* and *Tosca* every single night, but try naming the ladies that can do a good Butterfly—you won't even get to five fingers on your hand" (*Times*, Jan. 22, 1989). Even with its excellent acoustics, the auditorium

TABLE 17 Metropolitan Opera Premieres, 1980–81 to 1989–90

| Composer and Title | Met Premiere | Most Recent Met Performance | No. of Seasons in Met Repertoire | No. of Met Productions | No. of Met Performances, 1883–2013 | World Premiere | Director/Designer |
|---|---|---|---|---|---|---|---|
| Francis Poulenc, *Les Mamelles de Tirésias* | Feb. 20, 1981 | Mar. 28, 2002 | 4 | 1 | 31 | June 3, 1947, Paris, Opéra-Comique | John Dexter / David Hockney |
| Maurice Ravel, *L'Enfant et les sortilèges* | Feb. 20, 1981 | Mar. 28, 2002 | 4 | 1 | 31 | Mar. 21, 1925, Monte Carlo, Opéra | John Dexter / David Hockney |
| Igor Stravinsky, *Oedipus Rex* | Dec. 3, 1981 | Feb. 21, 2004 | 3 | 1 | 23 | *In concert:* May 30, 1927, Paris, Sarah Bernhardt | John Dexter / David Hockney |
| Wolfgang Amadeus Mozart, *Idomeneo* | Oct. 14, 1982 | Dec. 9, 2006 | 8 | 1 | 67 | Jan. 29, 1781, Munich, Residenz | Jean-Pierre Ponnelle / Jean-Pierre Ponnelle |
| George Frideric Handel, *Rinaldo* | Jan. 19, 1984 | June 27, 1984 | 1 | 1 | 21 | Feb. 24, 1711, London, Queen's | Frank Corsaro / Mark Negin |
| Wolfgang Amadeus Mozart, *La Clemenza di Tito* | Oct. 18, 1984 | Dec. 10, 2012 | 7 | 1 | 45 | Sept. 6, 1791, Prague, Estates | Jean-Pierre Ponnelle / Jean-Pierre Ponnelle |
| George Gershwin, *Porgy and Bess* | Feb. 6, 1985 | Dec. 6, 1990 | 4 | 1 | 54 | Sept. 30, 1935, Boston, Colonial | Nathaniel Merrill / Robert O'Hearn |
| George Frideric Handel, *Samson* | Feb. 3, 1986 | Mar. 6, 1986 | 1 | 1 | 8 | Feb. 18, 1743, London, Covent Garden | Elijah Moshinsky / Timothy O'Brien |
| George Frideric Handel, *Giulio Cesare* | Sept. 27, 1988 | Apr. 27, 2007 | 5 | 2 | 23 | Feb. 20, 1724, London, King's | John Copley / John Pascoe |
| Arnold Schoenberg, *Erwartung* | Jan. 16, 1989 | Feb. 21, 1989 | 1 | 1 | 10 | June 6, 1924, Prague, Neues Deutsches | Göran Järvefelt / Hans Schavernoch |

overwhelmed many voices appreciated in European houses, most of them half the size of the Met.

Crawford was right, as far as he went. Big productions yielded big dividends. The *Turandot*s and *Aïda*s helped turn attendance around from the 1985–86 low of 82.9 percent of capacity to 88.6 percent in 1986–87 and to 93 percent in 1989–90. The question for old Met hands was whether the high-caloric Zeffirelli diet, no doubt a tonic for the bottom line, was conducive to the long-term artistic well-being of the company.

### MORE MUSICAL CHAIRS

Levine had built an outstanding ensemble in the decade and a half since his appointment as principal conductor in 1975. The Metropolitan orchestra would soon join four of the big five—the Boston Symphony Orchestra, the Cleveland Orchestra, the New York Philharmonic, and the Philadelphia Orchestra—in the centennial celebration of Carnegie Hall. There was no disagreement either on its remarkable evolution or on the credit due the conductor. If Carlos Kleiber graced New York with so many of his rare appearances, it was because of the quality and responsiveness of the players Levine had cultivated so meticulously. The Vienna Philharmonic had had to make a place for the Metropolitan in the operatic stratosphere that the Austrians had previously had all to themselves. In 1991, Levine began taking his orchestra out on its own, most frequently to Carnegie Hall; seven years later he founded the Met Chamber Ensemble. By 1990, the Metropolitan was three years into a prolific recording schedule following three decades in which only the Leonard Bernstein *Carmen* had been committed to disk. In the course of the next ten years, CBS/SONY, Philips, and Deutsche Grammophon would bring out nearly thirty recordings, mostly complete operas, a few featuring the orchestra alone. In 2000, Levine was still pressing the point: "The Met needs to tour, to record, and to film. These things are essential for the Met's future at every level." Later that year, he articulated what came close to a discourse on his method: "[The orchestra] has to be able to play at the maximum expression and communication in every style, and the only way you can do that is—like Verdi said—working with a file, every day, little by little, until the orchestra's collective qualities emerge. . . . You try on purpose to get players with different qualities which will rub off on one another. . . . [The orchestra] has become like my own voice."[40]

In spring 1988, Levine was on the short list to succeed Karajan at the Berlin Philharmonic; he denied agreeing "even to be thought of." Others mentioned for the Berlin post were Abbado, Barenboim, Haitink, Maazel, Mehta, Muti, and Ozawa. Levine was said to have the inner track: he had no permanent symphonic post, he had conducted often in Berlin, and he had excellent connections with Salzburg, Bayreuth, and Vienna, and with Deutsche Grammophon. But there was "widespread resentment among West Berliners against what they perceive[d] as Mr. Wilford's favoring of his client, Mr. Karajan, over the interests of the Philharmonic" (*Times,* April 26, 1989). And the self-governing musicians did not want to be subject once again to onerous demands made on behalf of another Wilford client. The job went to Claudio Abbado.[41]

On November 4, 1988, Crawford announced that he would be leaving the following April. He gave as his reason an irresistible offer from the Omnicom Group, one of the world's largest advertising conglomerates—at twice his Met salary. The *Wall Street Journal* implied that Crawford was on the losing end of "a tussle over turf" (Nov. 8, 1988) with his artistic director. There was no question of Crawford running the Met as had the general managers of the past, free of the encumbrance of a music director. Volpe later offered a second explanation: "I rarely saw him mixing it up with the singers, the dancers, or the crew." In fact, Crawford had a closed-door policy. Schmoozing bored him, as did squabbles among artists and skirmishes with labor. Whatever the truth, the Crawford regime was over. His evaluation of his time as general manager differed markedly from that of the critics. The minutes of the May 18, 1988, annual Association meeting read, "Mr. Crawford stated that while the box office was a major contributor to our recent successes other important factors played a role. There was the cancellation of the national tour, sound financial decision making, and restructuring the development and marketing departments." Crawford saw the glass as quite full, critics as mostly empty: "During the Crawford administration, the Met has grown increasingly cautious, relying heavily on visual spectacle to sell the audience on its wares." As for Levine, he was no less unhappy at seeing Crawford go than he had been at Chapin's departure thirteen years earlier, at Dexter's soon thereafter, and at Bliss's in 1985. Looking to the future, the question was whether he would be able to face down the fiscally conservative board over his long-standing ambitions for a more recondite repertoire.[42]

The search for a new general manager was on. Louise Ireland Humphrey, a Cleveland heiress, the first woman president of the Association and chair of the search committee, let it be known that this time the directors were of a mind to appoint an opera professional and not one of their own, as Crawford had been and Bliss before him. But that was not to be. Perhaps, as the anonymous head of another major opera company mused, it was because while Levine was in the artistic saddle, "what they [the trustees] want has all the unpleasant aspects of an opera director's job with none of the fun" (*Times*, March 13, 1989). In Hugh Southern, appointed general manager on September 14, 1989, effective November 1, the directors got neither an opera professional nor precisely one of their own. Fifty-seven years old and a Cambridge-educated Brit, Southern came from the National Endowment for the Arts, where he had been acting chair. He had earlier been management associate at the San Francisco Opera and had supervised the tour of the Western Opera Theatre. His chief claim to fame was his stint as executive director of the Theatre Development Fund, a New York operation that supports productions and oversees the discount TKTS booths. Levine had apparently been all but excluded from the selection process; Bliss was so dismayed at the prospect of Southern that he stepped back into Met affairs to warn the directors of their impending mistake. When the announcement of Southern's elevation finally came, it included the assurance that the appointment would in no way impinge upon Levine's prerogatives. Asked about other prospects, Mrs. Humphrey replied, "Of all the candidates, Hugh Southern was the one who everybody said was the most diplomatic and good with people." She would get to know him even better during quail hunts at her Florida plantation. And when asked about his lack of operatic credentials, she answered, "That did concern us. But with all the candidates, we put down the pluses and the minuses in columns, and we felt his attributes outweighed his liabilities—his administrative experience, his way of getting along with people, his relation with the board and his ability to help with fundraising." Besides, Levine's strengths with respect to artistic policy would make up for Southern's deficits.[43]

The straightjacket held taut by Levine on one side and Crawford (as chair of the board's finance committee) on the other left Southern little room to maneuver, although there was scant evidence that he would in any case have been so inclined. Southern did take one action very early on, or rather, he took the fall for the cancellation of a spring 1991 season at the Brooklyn Academy of Music scheduled for John Adams's *The Death of Klinghoffer* and Gluck's *Orfeo ed Euridice*. The company would have had to raise $1.5 million for the project, and Levine and others had come to the conclusion that all in all there was not enough to be gained. By April 1990, the board's inner circle had decided to let the general manager go. On June 22, 1990, Southern submitted his resignation, effective virtually immediately, saying only that the post had left him unfulfilled. Some days later, sources declining to be named reported that he had been dismissed by unanimity; the key players in his firing had been Levine, Humphrey, and Crawford, who, the preceding month, had moved from head of finance to chair of the executive committee, leaving Humphrey very much weakened by the Southern fiasco. Southern was apparently cited for "passivity" and "failure to seize command of the company." Volpe later wrote, "During Southern's seven months in Rudolf Bing's old office, from November of 1989 until June of 1990, I think I laid eyes on the man twice. . . . Jimmy Levine probably saw him even less than that. He apparently had a lot of lunches. If he heard about the Met's daily crises, he didn't hear about them from me, because he never asked." The board promised to act swiftly to find a replacement, by fall if at all possible. The new general manager would be expected to accede to Levine in artistic matters and to Crawford in large policy issues. Nothing much was to change.[44]

# TEN

## Patronage and Perestroika, 1990–2006

### AMERICAN OPERA (REDUX) AND SLAVIC OPERA

JOSEPH VOLPE

THE SEARCH FIRM OF HEIDRICK AND STRUGGLES HAD spent a year rifling through more than four hundred entries. In the end, the board committee "coughed up" (Joseph Volpe's words) Hugh Southern. Volpe himself was passed over; he was presumably undone by a surfeit of minuses in Louise Humphrey's triage. High in the negative column, according to Volpe, was what he later called "the James Levine factor": "Although Jimmy and I had developed a good working relationship, there were times when, as the keeper of the purse and the schedules, I had to tell him that something he wanted, such as extra rehearsal time, wasn't in the cards. Jimmy wouldn't argue with a used-car dealer. He just wanted to be free to be Jimmy." Marilyn Shapiro, whose own candidacy was backed by Humphrey, was also opposed to Volpe. And Humphrey was identified as the anonymous trustee who volunteered blithely that Volpe was "NOCD" (*Times,* June 27, 1990): "I had to ask someone what that meant," confided Volpe later. "The translation—'Not our class, dear'—didn't come as a surprise." Once the ineffectual Southern regime was put out of its misery, there was no question of soliciting scores of nominations or of spending another year on a search. The executive committee, aggressively lobbied by Bruce Crawford, would make the decision. Ultimately NOCD gave way to a compromise. In summer 1990, Crawford informed Volpe that he had been promoted not to general manager—that title was retired for the time being—but to general director. The excuse was that the board wanted to return to "the triumvirate model of management": Volpe would run the house, adding finances, press, and public relations to his current portfolio, and Shapiro, the newly named executive director for external affairs, would continue to head marketing and development. All artistic matters would remain under the control of Levine; Jonathan Friend, the artistic administrator, would report to the artistic director and not to the general director. In this restoration of the troika, each of its members would be responsible to the president of the Association. No sooner had his appointment become official than Volpe made the sort of impolitic comment that must have given pause to even his staunchest supporters; it certainly set the teeth of the musical press on edge: "I am not an opera groupie. I like opera, but I can't say that I love it. But I do love running a theatre" (*Times,* Aug. 2, 1990).[1]

Joe Volpe was born in Brooklyn on July 2, 1940, to an Italian-American family. His father, also born in the United States, was a clothing manufacturer. As the business prospered, the Volpes moved to Bayside, Queens, and then to Glen Cove, Long Island. His formal education ended with a high school diploma, whereupon he started his life's work as a Broadway stagehand. His forty-three-year Metropolitan career began at the age of twenty-three, when he landed the job of apprentice carpenter, having scored first in the city on the union exam. In spring 1966, he was asked to set up the carpenter shop at the new house. Two days after opening night, the master carpenter resigned; Volpe was promoted to the vacated position on Herman Krawitz's say-so. By the time Bing retired in 1972, Volpe, by now thirty-two, saw himself ready to fill Sir Rudolf's shoes. Besides, a Ouija board had prognosticated that one day he would rise all the way to the top. In 1978, this time at John Dexter's insistence, Volpe was appointed technical director. The next year, he became director of operations, with oversight of all but administrative and artistic functions, both backstage and at the front of the house. The climb continued in January 1981 with his appointment as assistant manager for operations, tasked with the coordination of all areas of personnel and budget, excepting fund-raising, repertory, and casting. He also became the company's liaison to the labor unions. In 1986, he took over radio and television broadcasts; in 1987, the tour; in 1988, the summer season. And in 1990, he was named to the new post of general director.[2]

Volpe's first act that August, just days into his tenure, was to cancel the Werner Herzog/Maurizio Balò *Die Zauberflöte* on the calendar for January 1991. His predecessors had led off with similar take-charge gestures: Johnson canceled Witherspoon's plans for *Le Jongleur de Notre Dame* and the Ponselle *Adriana Lecouvreur;* for his opening night, Goeran Gentele swapped Bing's mean-spirited pick, the threadbare *Tannhäuser,* for a new *Carmen* he intended to stage himself; Bruce Crawford put an end to the spring tour. As

Volpe explained it to Levine, and then publicly, it was too late to execute *Die Zauberflöte* properly. Although time was certainly a factor, it was also the case that Volpe found the Egyptian columns and "rugged ship" featured in preliminary sketches fitting perhaps for *Aïda* and *Der Fliegende Holländer,* but not for "Mozart's Masonic fairy tale." How he broke the news to the music director spoke to their relationship, at least at the start: "I knew that Jimmy Levine wouldn't listen to me about Herzog's sketches for *The Magic Flute* unless I kept my artistic opinions to myself." However tactfully broached, the decision signaled that Volpe was boss. The Met eventually borrowed a production from San Francisco. [3]

With Volpe's promotion to general manager in May 1993, the fourth troika folded, again in short order: the Gentele/Kubelik/Chapin triumvirate lasted only days; Chapin/Levine/Dexter for a year or so, Bliss/Levine/Dexter for five years. As Volpe recounts it, he had been in his old assistant manager's office for three years as general director when one day, irritated at finding Aprile Millo asleep on a sofa in Bing's former "elegant domain," lately converted into a conference room, and deciding that enough was enough, he moved lock, stock, and barrel into the space designated for the general manager. A few weeks later, he raised the matter of the change of title with the board, and soon thereafter was named general manager: "Jimmy Levine was the first to congratulate me. I told him that he would retain the title of artistic director, but that I now had final authority over all matters at the Met." The appointment of Sarah Billinghurst, previously the artistic administrator at the San Francisco Opera, as his assistant manager in March 1994 gave legitimacy to his incursion into artistic affairs. Jonathan Friend, since the departure of Joan Ingpen responsible for casting reporting to Levine, would in the future report to Billinghurst, and Billinghurst, of course, to Volpe.[4]


AMERICAN OPERA, 1991–2005

By 1990, Levine had made good on his promise to introduce modern European works, neglected Mozart operas, and the Baroque. American music had been left behind. The omission was glaring, as was another: the music/artistic director had not yet put his stamp on a world premiere. John Corigliano's 1991 *The Ghosts of Versailles* ended the drought unbroken since Martin David Levy's 1967 *Mourning Becomes Electra,* the longest such hiatus in Met history. Levine had reason to be cautious: not one American opera premiered at the Met had secured a place in the company repertoire. Although a few had enjoyed brief currency, most had come up against unreceptive audiences and hostile reviewers.

The first step on the road to *The Ghosts of Versailles* was taken in 1979 when conductor and composer met to discuss a concert scene based on monologues from Seneca's *Medea* for Renata Scotto. Levine asked Corigliano whether he had given any thought to composing an opera; a few months later, the Met made the handsome offer of $150,000 for a work to be premiered in the centennial season. For *The Ghosts of Versailles* (first titled *A Figaro for Antonia*), Corigliano and his librettist, William M. Hoffman, invented a metaoperatic classification, "grand *opera buffa,*" announcing their intention to wed the spectacular and the intimate, the tragic and the comic, the high and the low. Hoffman's libretto is an elaborate riff on the French revolution and the Beaumarchais play *La Mère coupable*. Marie Antoinette, Louis XVI, and characters that step out of *Le Nozze di Figaro* and *Il Barbiere di Siviglia* appear together to echoes of Mozart and Rossini recast in Corigliano's late-twentieth-century neo-Romanticism. If Corigliano and Hoffman missed the deadline for the 1983 celebrations, it was management that stalled production until 1991. Box office far exceeded its 80 percent to 90 percent projections; it did very well for the revival of 1994–95. John Conklin's shifting staircases, interior stages, and fleet of flying objects and characters moved in tandem with Colin Graham's whirlwind staging, all in the service of a narrative at once historical, literary, and fantastic. The Marie Antoinette of Teresa Stratas, her free upper octave sounding the queen's anguish and ultimate resignation, Håkan Hagegård's enraptured Beaumarchais struggling to rewrite "history as it should have been," Gino Quilico's affable Figaro, the slithery, acrobatic villain of Graham Clark, Marilyn Horne's hilarious Egyptian singer, the sweet-toned Rosina of Renée Fleming in her second Met role, in fact the entire, enormous cast (forty-three names are listed in the program) testified that the company was equal to the demands of a complex contemporary work. There were those that first night, December 19, who found the tuneful score and intricate libretto both musically and politically irrelevant. Time has shown that Corigliano's composition, though a homage to his masters, speaks a language of its own, by turn wry, lyric, and grave; Hoffman's libretto comments trenchantly on the excesses of the ancien régime and the *Terreur* that followed.[5]

On October 12, 1992, the world premiere of Philip Glass's *The Voyage* celebrated the cinquecentennial of Christopher Columbus's discovery. Sixteen years before, Robert Wilson's Byrd Hoffmann Watermill Foundation had

FIGURE 37. *The Ghosts of Versailles,* act 1, scene 3, 1991 (Winnie Klotz; courtesy Metropolitan Opera Archives)

rented the Metropolitan for two performances of *Einstein on the Beach,* fruit of Glass's collaboration with Wilson. In the interim, *Satyagraha* (1980) and *Akhnaten* (1984) had further anchored Glass's status as a composer of opera. The Met placed a high-stakes bet, a commission of $325,000, the largest in the company's history, on his continued success. Playwright David Henry Hwang drew his libretto from Glass's own scenario, a meditation on the theme of exploration: Columbus's sailing is bracketed by episodes of previous and future journeys, the first an expedition from a distant planet to Earth during the Ice Age, the last space travel from Earth in 2092. Director David Pountney and designer Robert Israel sent the stage elevators into interplanetary warp; a wheelchair-bound scientist, modeled on Stephen Hawking, floated in the rings of Saturn; Queen Isabella's court dissolved into the deck of Columbus's ship. Conventional narrative and character all but disappear in the wash of Glass's minimalism, the mesmerizing repetition of subtly varied music cells. Generally favorable reviews noted occasional dissonance, even counterpoint, unusual in the composer's idiom. And again, the Met gave its all to the new opera, conducted by Glass specialist Bruce Ferden. The downtown crowd easily compensated for the many Met regulars who stayed away. For the revival of 1994–95, seats went begging. The rapturous critical reception of Glass's *Satyagraha* in 2007–08 and the increasingly wide acceptance of his music theater point to a return trip.

The remaining world premieres of the Volpe/Levine regime, John Harbison's *The Great Gatsby* and Tobias Picker's *An American Tragedy,* were adaptations of two canonical novels published in 1925. Most reviewers held that the musical embodiment of Jay Gatsby lacked the mystery F. Scott Fitzgerald had conjured on the page. The *New Yorker* acknowledged Harbison's "considerable achievement," his "individual and original language," and his deft weave of 1920s pastiches and "music of brittle brilliance and mobile complexity." The unduly harsh conclusion, however, was that *Gatsby* "outstays its welcome and becomes monotonous." Levine led a strong contingent for his twenty-fifth Met anniversary: the production team of Mark Lamos and Robert Israel, Dawn Upshaw as the spoiled, languorous Daisy, Dwayne Croft as the rock-steady, sympathetic Nick, Lorraine Hunt Lieberson as the doomed Myrtle (in her arresting debut), and Jerry Hadley as Gatsby. Despite mixed notices, the house was well filled; attendance fell for the 2001–02 revival, by which time Harbison had effected some judicious pruning. Picker and the librettist Gene Sheer brought off the heavy lift of reducing Theodore Dreiser's nine-hundred-page *An American Tragedy,* fluent in Francesca Zambello's staging on Adrianne Lobel's three-tiered set. Nathan Gunn was Clyde, the weak-willed protagonist; Patricia Racette, Roberta, the poor girl he allows to drown; and Susan Graham, Sondra, the rich girl, his ticket to prosperity. Gunn's musicianship, smooth timbre, and sterling diction helped compensate for a voice not burly enough for the task; Graham put over the opera's most memorable aria, "New York has changed me"; Racette, and Dolora Zajick, as Clyde's Bible-thumping mother, had the gravitas most reviewers found lacking in Picker's score. Eight performances failed to stir the enthusiasm that would have warranted a revival.[6]

Carlisle Floyd's *Susannah* and Michael Bolcom's *A View from the Bridge* had premiered elsewhere. *Susannah,* a staple of conservatories and regional houses, frequently presented by the New York City Opera and once, in 1965, by the Met's own national touring company, is widely recognized as an American classic. The 1999 production was borrowed from Chicago; Renée Fleming and Samuel Ramey reprised the roles they had sung six years earlier at the Lyric Opera. The stars drew large audiences, but Floyd's folksy, small-bored inspiration proved a poor fit for the Met. *A View from the Bridge* was also on loan from Chicago. The fatal passion of Arthur Miller's longshoreman for his niece, often labeled operatic, kindled Bolcom's "modern-day

Mascagni melodrama. Call it Brooklyn verismo." Harbison had composed his own 1920s dance tunes for *The Great Gatsby;* Bolcom, indulging his love of pop music, privileged Johnny Black's "Paper Doll," which was written in 1915 and resurrected by both the Mills Brothers and Frank Sinatra in 1943. Predictably, it was the catchy "Paper Doll" that listeners whistled all the way home. Bolcom's expert score, Frank Galati's taut staging of an ensemble cast, and Santo Loquasto's evocation of working-class Brooklyn attracted skimpy audiences.[7]

## STAR POWER

The Gilded Age belonged to de Reszke and Melba, the first two decades of the twentieth century to Caruso and Farrar, 1935–1941 to Flagstad and Melchior; opening night 1991 shouted that two men, and what is more a pair of tenors, Luciano Pavarotti and Plácido Domingo, had been admitted to the exclusive club. Each sang an act from one of his signature operas; then, together, they closed the gala with the Rodolfo-Marcello duet from *La Bohème.* Two years later, opening night marked the twenty-fifth anniversary of their Met debuts: Domingo strutted his Wagner in act 1 of *Die Walküre,* Pavarotti had a go at a staged *Otello* (act 1) for the first and last time in his career, and the friendly rivals capped the evening with act 3, scene 2, of *Il Trovatore,* Domingo in the first aria, "Ah sì, ben mio," Pavarotti in a rendition of "Di quella pira," whose final high note rang forth with their voices in unison. Opening night 1994 coupled *Il Tabarro* and *Pagliacci,* the first with Domingo, the second with Pavarotti in one of only two Canios he would sing at the Met.

The tenors had made their 1968 debuts two months apart. Almost immediately, Domingo established himself as one of the Met's indispensable assets. The 1969 *Il Trovatore* was followed in the next twenty years by nine more new productions and eight opening nights. Pavarotti began slowly. His bow in *La Bohème* was not especially noteworthy. He made a strong return nearly two years later. And then, on February 17, 1972, when he nailed the nine high Cs of *La Fille du régiment,* the audience belonged to him. By 1990, Pavarotti had notched nine new productions and three opening nights. He owed his cannily constructed celebrity in part to the opera house and in part to concerts of popular arias and songs. His publicist-manager, Herbert Breslin, booked the tenor into arenas and sports palaces where his amplified voice reached

FIGURE 38. Gala celebration of the 25th anniversary of the Metropolitan debuts of Luciano Pavarotti and Plácido Domingo, left to right Pavarotti, Joseph Volpe, Domingo, September 27, 1993 (Winnie Klotz; courtesy Metropolitan Opera Archives)

many thousands of fans. An instantly recognized oversized man who flourished an oversized white handkerchief, he made commercials, rode a horse in New York's Columbus Day parade, and starred in a big-studio movie, *Yes, Giorgio*. In the meantime, Domingo, too, was busy exploring crossover channels—Latin and show tune albums, pop duets with John Denver—all the while maintaining his primary commitment to opera. He appeared on movie screens not in an inane comedy, but in film versions of *La Traviata* and *Otello,* both directed by Franco Zeffirelli, and most memorably in Francesco Rosi's *Carmen*. Domingo was and remains the consummate musician, a master of roles in Italian, French, German, Russian, and English who finds time to pursue a parallel conducting career. Pavarotti read music with difficulty. Nevertheless, through the alchemy of thorough coaching and his own prodigious instincts, he was a remarkably refined singer. And in the end, it was Pavarotti who stood for opera in the public imagination.

In July 1990, the "third" tenor, José Carreras, joined his buddies in a Rome concert scheduled to coincide with the megaevent of the soccer World Cup. Carreras's illness and subsequent recovery provided the catalyst for a fundraiser to benefit leukemia research. The success of the format spawned more than a decade of concerts that united the singers in stadiums around the world. Between 1996 and 2002, from Düsseldorf to Yokohama, they were partnered by Levine on eleven occasions, each of which brought the conductor $500,000. The tenors earned many millions more. However lowbrow the extravaganzas and crass the exhibition, their exploitation raised the profile of opera in the culture at large, jolting attendance at live performances, if only temporarily. In 1997, the president of Opera America declared ebulliently, "Opera's audience is growing, and it is also growing younger." The growth would peak that very year at 4.7 percent of the adult population, up from the 3.3 percent of only five years earlier. These were good times for the Met. The economy was strong, tourists flocked to the city, negotiations with unions were generally civil. The endowment rose from $110 million to $235 million. Looking back, Volpe wrote, "Financially, the Met was in better shape than at any time in its history."[8]

## Luciano Pavarotti

Under Bing, Chapin, Bliss, and Crawford, that is, prior to 1990, Pavarotti had a greater impact on the repertoire than did his Spanish confrere. He participated in the company's bel canto revivals, *La Fille du régiment, I Puritani,* and *La Favorita,* and ventured Mozart's *Idomeneo.* Only *La Favorita* failed to catch on. Under Volpe, two of Pavarotti's three new productions cast him in operas he had often sung with success. Ten years after he played Riccardo, the Boston governor in the 1980 "American revolution" *Un Ballo in maschera,* he donned the royal robes of Gustavo III, Sweden's king, in Verdi's intended setting (Oct. 25, 1990). Piero Faggioni, who was responsible not only for the direction, but also for the sets, costumes, and lighting, mired the elegant score in vulgarity: the fortune-teller's den was a foundry that belched in time to the music; the principals were dwarfed by mountains of scenery and lost in a welter of choristers and supers. As for Pavarotti, if there was a falling off since his earlier *Ballos,* it was barely perceptible. A year later, in the new *L'Elisir d'amore* (Oct. 24, 1991), the Met's record-setting Nemorino had lost his boyish brio. The *Times* and the *New Yorker* (Nov. 18) noted Pavarotti's decline, hailed Kathleen Battle's exquisite Adina, and reviled John Copley's direction and Beni Montresor's triple-decker set, its long flights of steps and cartoonish backdrops "already . . . old," "ugly," and "unhelpful to the singers." In the November 16, 1991, telecast, Pavarotti delivers a perfunctory "Una furtiva lagrima" at nearly uninflected mezzo forte;

the tenor had sung the famous aria once too often. The Met premiere of Verdi's *I Lombardi* was mounted expressly for Pavarotti. At fifty-eight, beset by physical problems that compromised his mobility, he was still capable of sustaining Oronte's long phrases with the sound of youth. Three years later, his success in his first staged *Andrea Chénier* (April 6, 1996) was all the more heartening in that he had failed so miserably that same season in re-creating his breakthrough performance in *La Fille du régiment*. Enjoying a vocal Indian summer, the singer, whose technique was no longer adequate for the high-lying Tonio, gave eloquence and unusual grace to the poet Chénier. But his acting, rarely persuasive in serious roles, was irreparably undermined by age and ailments: "He . . . spent a lot of time leaning on a sword that doubled conveniently as a cane. Contradicting the libretto, he often left the stage when he felt he wasn't needed. He even managed to sip water between arias." Just weeks before the gala that celebrated the thirtieth anniversary of his debut (Nov. 22, 1998), Pavarotti bowed out of an upcoming *La Forza del destino,* pleading inability to learn the new role. He continued to sing at the Met, ever more rarely, until March 2004. The 1996 *Andrea Chénier* preserves the last best example of his artistry.[9]

## Plácido Domingo

At the end of 2012–13, Domingo had set an astonishing company record of forty-seven leading roles in forty-six seasons, including a good number of Met firsts and significant revivals. In the Volpe years, his energy still seemed limitless, his voice indestructible. He starred in solid new productions of *La Fanciulla del West* (Oct. 10, 1991), *Otello* (March 21, 1994), *Simon Boccanegra* (Jan. 19, 1995), and *Parsifal* (March 14, 1991), and in the house premiere of *Stiffelio.* Domingo had won his Wagnerian spurs as a lyric Lohengrin in 1984; the more heroic Siegmund would eventually be one of his specialties. Parsifal, moderate in intensity, range, and length, was the purposeful stepping-stone between the two. The sets lent mood and detail to *Stiffelio,* a neglected work of Verdi's middle period. Particularly striking was the staging of the final scene in which Stiffelio (Domingo), a Protestant minister, forgives his adulterous wife from a pulpit high above the congregation. The opera has been well received in two revivals. More debatable were *La Forza del destino* (Feb. 29, 1996), *Carmen* (Oct. 31, 1996), and *Samson et Dalila* (Feb. 13, 1998). The normally reliable Gian Carlo Del Monaco and Michael Scott came a cropper with *Forza*'s tortured plot, impenetrable in awkward and unsightly sets downgraded to meet Volpe's demands for thrift. Domingo's Leonora, Sharon Sweet, an indifferent actress, sang unevenly. And without a great Leonora, why bother with a new production of one of Verdi's most challenging scores? Domingo's Don José dominated *Carmen:* "Never has a voice so suited a role, or a role a voice" *(Times)*. Waltraud Meier, unconventional, intelligent, and miscast, "found not a single champion among the principal New York reviewers." True to form, and to the disadvantage of the dramaturgy, Zeffirelli lavished his attention on the picturesque two- and four-footed denizens of Seville. Richard Hudson deprived the Biblical lovers of a comfortable divan for their dalliance in the valley of Sorek; seductress (Denyce Graves) and prey (Domingo) had to make do with the hard floor. Samson suffered beneath his physical and spiritual burdens without benefit of millstone.[10]

With Domingo well into the fourth decade of his Met career and going strong, the company subscribed to two vanity projects at his behest, Ermanno Wolf-Ferrari's *Sly* and Franco Alfano's *Cyrano de Bergerac.* Wolf-Ferrari's comic operas deserve a hearing, to be sure; *Sly* is a product of his less satisfying verismo manner. As general director of the Washington National Opera, Domingo had programmed the work in 1999 for his compatriot José Carreras, with staging by Marta Domingo; three years later, he took the role, his wife, and Michael Scott's sets and costumes up the Northeast corridor to Lincoln Center. Nine performances, Domingo or not, made Volpe's point: that unfamiliar operas should be scheduled for few repeats. Given only three times in 2004–05, *Cyrano de Bergerac,* based on Edmond Rostand's evergreen play, sold out. The opera had an age-appropriate role for Domingo and a sympathetic part for the Met's up-and-coming lirico-spinto, Sondra Radvanovsky. The critics thought the score not "especially good," griped that "Mr. Domingo gets what he wants," and argued that as many as "fifty works . . . should have been introduced into the Metropolitan repertory in advance of [this] mediocrity." Domingo was also on hand to add luster to *Fedora* (Oct. 5, 1996) and *The Merry Widow,* farewell productions for Mirella Freni and Frederica von Stade. The rich title role of *Fedora* goes to the soprano; Loris gets to sing the one popular melody, "Amor ti vieta." In the April 26, 1997, telecast, filmed late in the run, Domingo pressures the brief aria unduly. Billed as "the last prima donna," Freni was cheered by adoring fans undeterred by her now too often hollow sound. In the Met's first *The Merry Widow,* Domingo was Danilo to von Stade's Hanna, the role befitting the beloved mezzo whose charm helped redeem a lackluster production. Antony McDonald's "allusions to old cut-out and painted scenery [spoke] . . . of prudence and economy."[11]

## Kathleen Battle and Others

If Volpe was wont to indulge the whim of Pavarotti and the will of Domingo, he stopped short at the caprices of other stars, most famously at those of Kathleen Battle. Her outbursts were legend from New York to San Francisco and beyond. In 1983, Battle had an angry brush with Kiri Te Kanawa as the two prepared for *Arabella*. She incited a messy contretemps during the 1985 *Le Nozze di Figaro:* defying precedent, she was adamant that the principal soprano's dressing room was rightfully Susanna's, not the Contessa's, and threw Carol Vaness's costumes out the door. During rehearsals of the 1993 *Der Rosenkavalier,* she had differences with the conductor, Christian Thielemann. She left the stage demanding that Volpe meet her on the spot. When he failed to appear, Battle walked out of the theater—and out of the production (*Times,* Jan. 30). The curtain finally came down on the erratic soprano in February 1994. She had insisted that rehearsals for *La Fille du régiment* be scheduled at her convenience, arrived late or not at all, left early, and ordered that colleagues divert their gaze when she sang. As the Marquise, Rosalind Elias was called upon to accompany Battle's Marie in the act 2 lesson scene. Battle found Elias's pianistic skills wanting and proceeded to humiliate the veteran mezzo in front of cast and crew. This time, neither the clout that came with aggressive media exposure nor the support of Levine could save her. Volpe's statement to the press read: "Kathleen Battle's unprofessional actions . . . were profoundly detrimental to the artistic collaboration among all the cast members. . . . I have taken this step to insure that everyone involved in the production will be able to rehearse and perform in an atmosphere that makes it possible for them to perform at their best." The cast greeted her firing with applause and Volpe was hailed as a hero by fellow intendants on both sides of the Atlantic (*Times,* Feb. 8, Feb. 21, 1994). Battle never again sang at the Met. Volpe's regret over his handling of the affair came only years later as he looked back on his career. But at the time, or shortly thereafter, his take on the subject fell somewhere between a crack and a boast: "Bing will be remembered for firing Maria Callas; I'll be remembered for firing Battle. Mine will be the bigger funeral."

As to the mercurial couple of Angela Gheorghiu and Roberto Alagna, although Volpe made it clear he was "not banning them from the Met, like Kathleen Battle," when they temporized over signing a joint contract for Zeffirelli's 1998 *La Traviata,* he admonished them sternly, leaving no doubt that their demand for approval of sets and staging was laughable. In the end, the new production was given over to Patricia Racette and Marcelo Álvarez, making his debut. And when Gheorghiu announced in earshot of all that she would absolutely not wear Micaela's blond braids in the *Carmen* of the 1997 Japan tour, Volpe promptly replaced her with her cover. At the next performance, Gheorghiu gave in, letting her dark tresses peek out from under the detested wig.[12]

## MET TITLES

Back again as president of the Association, Bruce Crawford took the occasion of the 1995 annual meeting to review the accomplishments of the past decade. The Met was now a nearly $150 million-a-year operation, and average capacity was projected at 92.5 percent, with revenues covering 60 percent of expenses, leaving $60 million to be raised from private and public sources, a goal no other opera house could begin to contemplate. Crawford cited the years of balanced budgets, a reward for the tight lid kept on expenses. He pointed to the orchestra and its tours, the visits of the company to Japan, Germany, and Spain, the resumption of recordings, and the expansion of telecasts. Then, of course, there were the first commissions in twenty-five years, *The Ghosts of Versailles* and *The Voyage,* fund-raising successes, and fifteen years of labor peace. Finally, Crawford congratulated Volpe and Joseph Clark, technical director, for the design and imminent introduction of Met Titles.

After a decade of indecision, the titles were up and running for the opening night 1995 *Otello.* Volpe was triumphant: "When Plácido Domingo made his entrance ... shouting, 'Esultate!' ... four thousand ... patrons instantly understood that the storm was over, and they got goose bumps." Beginning in 1984, a variety of systems had been considered, including handheld devices and the supertitles already functional at City Opera and elsewhere (*Times,* Sept. 12). Levine had sworn, "Over my dead body will they show those things at this house. I cannot imagine not wanting the audience riveted on the performers at every moment" (*Times,* Sept. 22, 1985). Volpe's objections were more practical: he could not fathom supertitles above a proscenium as high as that of the Met stage. Surely those seated in the orchestra would exit the theater with stiff necks. When in 1992 the Kirov Opera (newly rechristened the Mariinsky, although the company continues to be the Kirov outside of Russia) visited New York and asked to bring along its own supertitles, the answer was no. The turndown was blamed on technical difficulties. But suspicion persisted that the management had wanted to avoid the pressure that was sure to follow on a supertitle success (*Times,* Aug. 20, 1993). In fall 1993, Crawford was finally able to tell prospective donors that the board was committed to individual screens attached to the backs of seats as the least obtrusive option. The solution had been suggested to Clark by an in-flight entertainment system; within six months, his shop had fabricated a viable prototype. Crawford argued that the innovation would build audience capacity, particularly for lesser-known works. By then, major opera houses everywhere had installed titles of some sort. Volpe was conciliatory: "Jimmy and I agreed that if a system could be produced that enhances the experience without distracting those who do not want to use it, we would install it." By and large, the critics were impressed. But as always, there were qualifications. For one thing, the pricetag, originally estimated at $1.25 million, shot up to $2.7 million. Then there was the issue of distraction. While filters prevented light from flowing left and right, screens in the row in front were visible from behind. And as one critic put it, "it is much harder to keep track of these titles than to read ordinary supertitles. Along with large head movements, drastic changes in eye focus are required every few seconds, a wearying ping-pong of the eyes and mind." Levine, it appeared, was satisfied.[13]


ERRANT PATRONAGE

At the end of the 1990s, Volpe was the darling of the hard-to-please press. Tributes to his management emanated from Europe, where reversals in government subsidies had destabilized many of the great houses. La Scala and Covent Garden, for example, were in dire straits. The select committee charged with looking into the Royal Opera published the provocative view that it "would prefer to see the house run by a Philistine with the requisite financial acumen than by the succession of opera and ballet lovers who have brought a great and valuable institution to its knees." The *Telegraph* responded testily to the "false alternative," citing "lucky New York, where the Metropolitan Opera has as general manager Joseph Volpe, a man who not only likes and understands 'the product,' but has worked his way up the institution, over a period of thirty-five years, from humble beginning as a stage carpenter." New York took up the comparison to theaters abroad: "The Met continues a practice of self-sufficiency and free enterprise that is largely unfamiliar to the international opera world. . . . European houses once looked down on the Met as a business operation bent on staying in business. Things have changed. . . . Seven times a week, more than 200 times a year, the Met puts forth seamlessly managed theater. Its backstage is the envy of the world. Things work; people work." But trouble was around the corner, and it came from three directions: the uncertain status of Levine, a clamorous incident of philanthropy gone rogue, and the cataclysm of September 11.[14]

Rumors of Levine's declining health and growing wanderlust began to circulate in 1997. He had long distrusted reporters, wary that his remarks would be taken out of context, and resisted probes into his personal life. The cause of the unmistakable tremor in his left arm and leg had become a matter of widespread conjecture. Levine sought to quash the more drastic hypotheses in a rare interview during which he explained that the problem was caused by a pinched nerve, the result of the habit of holding a towel on his left shoulder. There was no pathology; the condition ran in his family (*Times*, Sept. 15, 1997). That same month, word was out that Levine had been offered the position of music director at the Munich Philharmonic. For five seasons, from 1999–00 through 2003–04, he led both the Metropolitan and the Munich orchestras.

The construction of a narrative of unmatched cultural generosity revolved around the figure of Alberto W. Vilar. It was timed to coincide with the Met's September 1998 announcement of the most ambitious campaign in its history. The goal was to double the $200 million endowment. Half had already been raised—or pledged, and therein would lie the problem. Of especial note was the commitment of the largest gift ever: thanks to the munificence of Mr. Vilar, the Met was slated to receive $20 million over five years, an additional $5 million in challenge grants, and other more modest sums. In recognition of his benefaction, the Grand Tier would henceforth be the Alberto Vilar Grand Tier; its elegant restaurant would likewise bear the patron's name. To that point, Vilar had sponsored three productions valued at $9 million. All told, he had turned over, or pledged, $40 million, surpassing Sybil Harrington, the leader of the philanthropic pack, deceased that very month.

Profiles of Vilar began to appear here and there. The basic biographical elements were these: Born in Newark (later revised to East Orange), New Jersey, in 1940, Vilar was the son of Cuban-Americans (revised to a Cuban-American father and Irish-American mother); he grew up in Cuba and Puerto Rico (revised to Puerto Rico when it was discovered that he had never lived in Cuba, let alone fled Fidel Castro, as he claimed). After college in the United States, he started at Citibank, and then went to Wall Street as a money manager. By that time, he had become his father's worst nightmare, if not exactly a "longhair," "one of those crazy music people" (*Times,* Sept. 29, 1998). In the 1970s, he started his own firm, Amerindo Investment Advisers, and quickly made a fortune in hi-tech growth stocks while toggling between New York and London to attend both to business and to his passion for the opera. His extravagant lifestyle made the news: the thirty-room duplex next door to the United Nations, its fifty-five-hundred-square-foot living room outfitted with three chandeliers simulating those of the Met, they too rising and falling, and an ornate wall that replicated one that had caught his eye at the Mozarteum in Salzburg; the front row seat at the opera, A101, from which he held court at intermission; the one hundred opera performances he attended each year, putting aside the fifty concerts and recitals, a tally even his close associates admitted might be something of an exaggeration. Vilar became fond of crowing, "I think anyone will tell you that I am the largest supporter of classical music, opera and ballet in the world" (*Times,* Oct. 8, 2000). In exchange for his liberality, he demanded unprecedented recognition, both of kind and of degree: his name in the program on a par with that of the composer, curtain calls at the end of first performances. When Volpe balked, Vilar complained, "I don't understand why I should be treated like a second-class citizen. What makes me less important than Plácido Domingo?" Typical of the board was the response of Paul M. Montrone, president of the Association succeeding Bruce Crawford in 1999, "The Met has to do everything it can to make [Vilar] feel appreciated. The donors must be treated as well as possible." But by 2000, the allegation that Vilar deployed his wealth to "manipulate world opera" began to make the rounds in the United States and Europe. Volpe had to tread diplomatically. He drew the comparison of Vilar with Cynthia Wood, on the one hand, and Sybil Harrington, on the other. Wood, an assistant stage director and major contributor, would come into his office, say she wanted to cover the costs of a new production, ask the price, and return the next day check in hand. Vilar emulated neither Wood's unconditional giving nor Harrington's coercive largesse: "Sybil would say I'll give my money if you hire this director or that director. I won't give you my money if you hire so and so" (*Times,* Oct. 8, 2000).[15]

Then came September 11. The Met responded with a benefit that previewed the upcoming opening night Verdi gala, with the addition at the top of the program of *Nabucco*'s stirring chorus "Va pensiero." The performance was transmitted simultaneously to the giant screen of Lincoln Center Plaza, a stone's throw from the flower-covered sidewalk in front of Fire Engine 40/Ladder 35 at Amsterdam Avenue and 66th Street, a company unit that had suffered devastating losses. On September 18, when trading resumed on the New York Stock Exchange with the biggest one-day drop ever, Volpe informed the board that "the box office is soft overall, and given the current situation between the box office and fundraising for the year, we have major budget concerns and must look at many areas to see what we can do in terms of savings." At that same dramatic meeting, Volpe announced that Levine was on the point of accepting an offer from the Boston Symphony Orchestra. The next month, it was official that Levine would take up his duties in Boston beginning with the 2004–05 season. He would quit the Munich Philharmonic and the Three Tenors roadshow, and step down as the Met's artistic director to resume his old rank of music director. That his sights were also fixed on Boston in 2004–05 did not deter him from leading fifty-six, or 23 percent, of the Met's 243 performances.

To add to the tensions of the painful 9/11 season, with the implosion of the dot-com bubble, the Vilar house of cards began to collapse. Vilar had made good on pledges for *Così fan tutte, Le Nozze di Figaro,* and *La Cenerentola* (he was an avid Cecilia Bartoli groupie), and on half the cost of the new *Fidelio.* He was dragging his feet on the second half of the Beethoven bill. Volpe, as he later wrote, was beginning "to get nervous." The Met was also awaiting Vilar's annual contribution of $250,000, an amount expected from each of the thirty-seven managing directors, and the funding stipulated for the Met/Kirov coproduction of *War and Peace,* not to mention the $20 million pledged to the endowment campaign. Eroding confidence turned into the very real fear that Vilar would default on pledges of $225 million to classical music internationally. He had already failed to come up with payments due the New York Philharmonic, the Washington Opera, among other organizations. The Metropolitan executive committee felt it was the better part of wisdom to take down the foot-high metal letters on the Grand Tier wall that spelled his name, and to discard the piles of menu covers that telegraphed his wealth and influence in smaller type. Volpe remarked, "Some board members thought it was a cruel and foolhardy gesture." Where he stood he did not say.[16]

In May 2002, Volpe reported to the board that the season just past was "the most difficult year of my career as general manager." In the face of tightened security and half-empty houses, "it was important [to him] to bring the company together." The 2002–03 season proved equally trying. The Association was confronted with another potential donor debacle. Sybil Harrington had left precise instructions that proceeds from the Harrington trust were "to underwrite traditional productions of standard operatic fare." The suit filed against the Met accused the administration of misusing $5 million in its 2001 telecast of a nontraditional *Tristan und Isolde* and contended that $34 million had gone toward costs unrelated to traditional opera, "the result of a willful and calculated intent to disregard and evade Mrs. Harrington's wishes." The matter was settled in a court-ordered mediation, terms of the settlement undisclosed. Also that year, ChevronTexaco announced it would cease its support for the Saturday broadcasts at the end of 2003–04. Rifts in the historic relationship had opened as early as 1999 when Boston's WCRB-FM dropped the matinees, ostensibly because of the multiple mentions of the sponsor, more probably because of the decline in listenership (*Times* May 21, 2003). In Volpe's report to the board of May 21, 2003, the Met's financial troubles were again front and center: the box office had lost $7.5 million in 2001–02 and $8.2 million in 2002–03. Savings had been effected through the cancellation of telecasts that had had an uninterrupted run of twenty-five years, Carnegie Hall programming that excluded the chorus, the freezing of administrative salaries, and layoffs. Subscriptions had held up reasonably well, but the drop of 50 percent in tourist ticket sales had been disastrous. Prior to September 11, foreign visitors had accounted for 14 percent of box office; in 2001–02, the percentage had decreased by half. In November 2003, Volpe announced a two-week recess for January 2005, a slow period in any case.[17]

The stories that had made headlines at the turn of the millennium had their denouements a few years into the new century. In 2004, it was clear that Levine's time as the Met's artistic czar was over. Volpe had predicted years earlier that Levine's "level of involvement" would change: "By 2005–2006 it might be time to consider younger conductors and focus on strengthening our conducting staff." In March 2004, Beverly Sills, chair of the board since 2002, made a public appeal for $150 million to endow the radio matinees for the next five years. Toll Brothers came to the rescue, guaranteeing a minimum of four years of support for broadcasts that cost $6 million per season. As to Vilar, although disgrace began with the 2002 revelations of his unsavory machinations, in the end the worst of his miseries was only indirectly related to his obsessive philanthropy. In May 2005, a month before his term on the Met board elapsed, he was jailed, accused of defrauding a client of

$5 million. He had apparently spent some of his ill-gotten gains on overdue charitable commitments. Kirov music director Valery Gergiev put up $500,000 toward his friend's $10 million bail, despite the unmet pledge of $14 million to the St. Petersburg company. In November 2008, the compulsive benefactor, on whose sumptuous apartment the IRS by now had a $23 million lien, was convicted on twelve counts related to securities fraud and money laundering. In 2010, he was sentenced to nine years in federal prison for his white-collar crimes, and in 2012 freed on $10 million bail pending appeal. In 2006, the Metropolitan once again announced receipt, this time actual receipt, of the largest individual gift in its history, $25 million. These unrestricted monies would fill the hole left by Vilar. In gratitude, and as if to expunge the past, on September 25, 2006, the Grand Tier was named the Mercedes T. Bass Grand Tier.[18]

## PERESTROIKA

The US/USSR politico/operatic nexus threads through the Metropolitan archives beginning on August 10, 1921, with correspondence from a representative of the English Gramophone Company to Edward Ziegler. The subject was the plight of penniless Gramophone artist Fyodor Chaliapin. The Russian bass had been at the Met in 1907–08, the season before Giulio Gatti-Casazza took over; he had sung Mefistofele, Don Basilio, and Leporello. No Russian roles were available; in fact, no Russian opera had yet found its way to 39th Street. The Gramophone agent informed Ziegler that Chaliapin, hoping he would be granted permission to leave the soon-to-be Soviet Union, pleaded to be met in Riga with cash sufficient for travel to Western Europe. The suspected Bolshevik was unwelcome in Great Britain. Was there a chance he might be welcomed in the United States? Chaliapin did, in fact, sing *Boris Godunov* at the Met that year and remained with the company until 1928–29 as one of its major attractions. Between Chaliapin's 1908 departure and his return in 1921, and for the ensuing decade, Gatti sought to bolster the Slavic wing of the repertoire. From 1909 to 1931, the Metropolitan premiered, in Italian, French, or German, Smetana's *The Bartered Bride* (1909), Tchaikovsky's *The Queen of Spades* (1910), Mussorgsky's *Boris Godunov* (1913), Borodin's *Prince Igor* (1915), Rimsky-Korsakov's *Le Coq d'or* (1918), Tchaikovsky's *Eugene Onegin* (1920), Weis's *The Polish Jew* (1921), Rimsky-Korsakov's *Snegurochka* (1922), Janáček's *Jenufa* (1924), Stravinsky's

*Le Rossignol* (1926), Rimsky's *Sadko* (1930), Mussorgsky's *The Fair at Sorochintzy* (1930), and Weinberger's *Schwanda* (1931), thirteen in all, almost twice as many as the seven that would be premiered under Volpe's second Slavic wave. Nearly 50 percent of the Slavic titles Gatti introduced returned after their initial runs. And of these, three, *Eugene Onegin, The Queen of Spades,* and *Boris Godonov,* would become firmly embedded in the core. Two more, *The Bartered Bride* and *Jenufa,* hover on the edge of the standard rep. His initiative can be counted a lasting success.[19]

In the 1930s and 1940s, Soviet/American relations continued to inject themselves into Metropolitan affairs, and then with increasing intensity at the height of the Cold War, in the 1950s. Mihály Székely, a Hungarian bass at the Met from 1947 to 1950, was barred by Budapest from returning to fulfill his 1950–51 contract. In the same season, Bing's first, the United States refused admittance to the Bulgarian bass residing in Italy Boris Christoff for the opening night *Don Carlo*. Christoff would never sing at the Met. In 1951, Bing felt impelled to write to Eleanor Belmont in defense of director Margaret Webster, who had been accused of Communist sympathies; as far as Bing was concerned, Webster had not been cited as subversive by the government—and that was good enough for him. He would take neither "*Red Channels* nor any other publication as an official guide" (Nov. 7, 1951). On the death of Josef Stalin in 1953, the Soviet Union made overtures to the West for cultural exchange. Two years later, Emil Gilels, David Oistrakh, and Leonid Kogan made historic appearances as the first Soviet artists to be heard in America in decades, and *Porgy and Bess* went to Leningrad, Moscow, and Stalingrad. The next year, Isaac Stern and Jan Peerce performed in Russia. In 1958, the Lacy-Zarubin Agreement, in line with President Eisenhower's policy of "People to People" exchange, was first signed. The Soviets grumbled that the United States had failed to invite their most prominent artists, hinting that they would be willing to send bass Ivan Petrov or baritone Pavel Lisitsian, or both, to the Met for the 1958–59 season. Lisitsian sang in a single *Aïda* on March 3, 1960; Galina Vishnevskaya played Aïda and Cio-Cio-San in fall 1961. The most consequential of the preperestroika breakthroughs came in the summer of 1975 when the Bolshoi brought six operas to New York and Washington. The authenticity of the performances, sung in the original by artists native to the culture, was a revelation. It was mezzo-soprano Elena Obraztsova who would have the most extensive Met career during the thaw; she sang thirty performances of Amneris, Dalila, Charlotte, Carmen, and Adalgisa from October 1976 through April 1979. Baritone Yuri

Mazurok sang Germont and Onegin in 1978–79. In early 1980, Washington suspended talks surrounding the renewal of the Lacy-Zarubin Agreement as one response to the Soviet invasion of Afghanistan. In Moscow, there was fury over the recent defection of Bolshoi dancers Alexander Godunov and Leonid and Valentina Kozlov (*Washington Post,* Jan. 29, 1980).[20]

Only six years later, in a speech to the Twenty-Seventh Congress of the Communist Party, Mikhail Gorbachev made perestroika a household word. It came to stand for the policy of economic, social, and political restructuring, as glasnost did for the opening to the outside, particularly to the West. Operaphiles would see in the breach of the Berlin Wall three years later, and in the collapse of Communism throughout Eastern Europe, "the most important development in the world of opera in the last several decades." Perestroika released a "deluge of Russian opera" (*Times,* June 26, 1994), and Czech as well, that has yet to subside.[21]

### Slavic Opera: 1990–2006

In the wake of the seismic geopolitical shifts of the late 1980s, the collaboration with the unstoppable Gergiev, and the tide of Eastern European singers, the map of the Met's repertoire was once again redrawn. During the sixteen years of the Volpe era, six Gatti bequests were revived in new productions (*The Queen of Spades, Eugene Onegin, Jenufa, Boris Godunov, The Bartered Bride, Le Rossignol*) along with *Khovanshchina,* the single Slavic novelty introduced in the more than half-century that separated Gatti from Volpe. Seven Slavic premieres were on Volpe's calendar: Janáček's *Kát'a Kabanová* and *The Makropulos Case* (in its first season given in English), Antonín Dvořák's *Rusalka,* Dmitri Shostakovich's *Lady Macbeth of Mtsensk,* Prokofiev's *The Gambler* and *War and Peace,* and Tchaikovsky's *Mazeppa.* The Slavic project reached the impressive total of fourteen Russian and Czech works, and two more through 2012–13 under Peter Gelb, Janáček's *From the House of the Dead* and Shostakovich's *The Nose,* with more to come.

Mussorgsky's *Boris Godunov,* in the repertoire since its 1913 premiere and revived in 1990–91 in the Everding/Lee production, was the portal to the newly opened Eastern Europe. The first to step through was *Kát'a Kabanová.* With the Janáček work, Czech took its place among the company's languages. The beleaguered Kát'a, tormented by her provincial existence and by guilt over her adulterous desire, was Gabriela Beňačková, whose success in the operas of her native country had eased their way into the world's theaters. She

| Season | Title | Revival | New Production | Met Premiere | Conductor |
|---|---|---|---|---|---|
| 1990–91 | *Boris Godunov* | X | | | Emil Tchakarov |
| | *Kát'a Kabanová* | | | X | Charles Mackerras |
| 1991–92 | — | | | | |
| 1992–93 | *Eugene Onegin* | X | | | Seiji Ozawa |
| | *Jenůfa* | X | | | James Conlon |
| 1993–94 | *Rusalka* | | | X | John Fiore |
| 1994–95 | *Lady Macbeth of Mtsensk* | | | X | James Conlon |
| 1995–96 | *The Queen of Spades* | | X | | Valery Gergiev |
| | *The Makropulos Case* | | | X | David Robertson |
| 1996–97 | *Rusalka* | X | | | John Fiore |
| | *Eugene Onegin* | | X | | Antonio Pappano |
| 1997–98 | *Boris Godunov* | X | | | Valery Gergiev |
| | *The Bartered Bride* | X | | | James Levine |
| | *The Makropulos Case* | X | | | Charles Mackerras |
| 1998–99 | *Kát'a Kabanová* | X | | | Charles Mackerras |
| | *The Queen of Spades* | X | | | Valery Gergiev |
| | *Khovanshchina* | X | | | Valery Gergiev |
| 1999– 2000 | *Lady Macbeth of Mtsensk* | X | | | Valery Gergiev |
| 2000–01 | *The Makropulos Case* | X | | | Charles Mackerras |
| | *The Gambler* | | | X | Valery Gergiev |
| 2001–02 | *Eugene Onegin* | X | | | Vladimir Jurowski |
| | *War and Peace* | | | X | Valery Gergiev |
| 2002–03 | *Jenůfa* | | X | | Vladimir Jurowski |
| 2003–04 | *Rusalka* | X | | | Andrew Davis |
| | *The Queen of Spades* | X | | | Vladimir Jurowski |
| | *Stravinsky Triple Bill* | X | | | Valery Gergiev |
| 2004–05 | *Kát'a Kabanová* | X | | | Jirí Belohlávek |
| 2005–06 | *Mazeppa* | | | X | Valery Gergiev |
| 2006–07 | *Eugene Onegin* | X | | | Valery Gergiev |
| | *Jenůfa* | X | | | Jirí Belohlávek |
| 2007–08 | *The Gambler* | X | | | Valery Gergiev |
| | *War and Peace* | X | | | Valery Gergiev |
| 2008–09 | *Eugene Onegin* | X | | | Jirí Belohlávek |
| | *Rusalka* | X | | | Jirí Belohlávek |
| | *The Queen of Spades* | X | | | Seiji Ozawa |
| 2009–10 | *From the House of the Dead* | | | X | Esa-Pekka Salonen |
| | *The Nose* | | | X | Valery Gergiev |
| 2010–11 | *Boris Godunov* | | X | | Valery Gergiev |
| | *The Queen of Spades* | X | | | Andris Nelsons |
| 2011–12 | *Khovanshchina* | X | | | Kirill Petrenko |
| | *The Makropulos Case* | X | | | Jirí Belohlávek |
| 2012–13 | — | | | | |
| 2013–14 | *Eugene Onegin* | | X | | Valery Gergiev |
| | *Prince Igor* | | X | | Valery Gergiev |
| | *The Nose* | X | | | Valery Gergiev |
| | *Rusalka* | X | | | Yannick Nézet-Séguin |

had made her US debut as Kát'a in 1979 with the Opera Orchestra of New York in Carnegie Hall, and in the decade that followed she played the eponymous leads of Smetana's *Libuše,* of *Rusalka,* and of *Jenůfa* with the same group. At her Met debut, the *Wall Street Journal* went out on a long limb: "This is the most ravishing voice in the world." Beňačková held the stage against the formidable Leonie Rysanek in the role of the monstrous mother-in-law, Kabanicha. Charles Mackerras, an influential proponent of Janáček, was in the pit. The team of director Jonathan Miller and designer Robert Israel set the piece in vaguely surreal exteriors that respected the modernity of the composer's idiom without violating the nineteenth-century origins of the subject. Their sober concept came as a relief: "This relatively modest new production . . . reminds us of something so often smothered here by miles of drapes, overdressed extras and acres of sets. Music matters." In its first run and two revivals, the public failed to give *Kat'a Kabanová* the following it deserves. *Rusalka* did decidedly better. Beňačková won all hearts with the water sprite's apostrophe to the moon, by then familiar as a favorite show-piece of lyric sopranos. Schneider-Siemssen's wooded glen and shimmering pond were marvels of illusion. By whetting the public's appetite with few performances in any one season, and by capitalizing on Renée Fleming's affection for the title part, the Met saw scalpers hawking tickets outside its doors in 1996–97; attendance held up well in 2003–04.[22]

In December 1992, Beňačková and Rysanek squared off once more in the first Czech-language iteration of the 1974 *Jenůfa.* Just two weeks earlier, the 1957 *Eugene Onegin,* revived for the sixth go in its original language, was conducted by Seiji Ozawa in one of his two Met assignments; the other would be *The Queen of Spades. Lady Macbeth of Mtsensk* introduced Met audiences to a third Russian manner, not Mussorgsky's "national music dramas" nor Tchaikovsky's "lyric scenes," but Shostakovich's biting, broadly comic, and racy social comment. The Graham Vick/Paul Brown production was a circus of theatrical effects, among them the delivery of a double bed by means of a forklift, a crushed red automobile that served as a coffin for the murdered husband, an airborne set of mourners, and a disco ball revolving over a wedding party, all in sync with the violent momentum of the score. *Lady Macbeth of Mtsensk* carried with it the notoriety of its birth and infancy. The opera had had an enormous succès de scandale at its 1934 Leningrad premiere. It soon racked up an impressive total of outings in the Soviet Union and elsewhere. Drawn by publicity that exploited its blatant sexuality, in February 1935 New Yorkers filled the rented Met for Artur Rodzinski and his Cleveland

Orchestra staging. Stalin first saw the work at the Bolshoi the following year—and two days later a *Pravda* editorial, damning what it called the decadence of music and subject, effectively banned any further performances in the Soviet Union. A somewhat expurgated *Lady Macbeth of Mtsensk* resurfaced in Moscow in 1963 and made the rounds with the title *Katerina Ismailova*. The Met went back to Shostakovich's original score and libretto.

Valery Gergiev led the Met's 1995 new production of *The Queen of Spades*. On the recommendation of Domingo, he had made his debut in *Otello* in spring 1994. That same year, the agreement between his company, St. Petersburg's Kirov, and New York's Metropolitan was sealed: Volpe would give or lend the Kirov old productions, mostly Italian, and the Kirov would give the Met elements of its Russian shows in return. By then, Gergiev was a celebrity and he and Volpe had joined forces. Born in Moscow in 1953, Gergiev was raised in the Caucasus, within the borders of Georgia. He studied conducting at the St. Petersburg Conservatory, and at twenty-three was the winner of the Karajan Competition. At twenty-five, as assistant conductor at the Kirov, Gergiev made his debut in *War and Peace*. A decade later, in 1988, he was appointed chief conductor and artistic director of the company and set about the task of introducing original versions of Russian operas redacted or outlawed by the Soviets. He signed a recording contract with Philips in 1989, a move designed to promote Russian opera and the Kirov worldwide and to rake in hard currency. In summer 1992, the Kirov Opera came to New York and played at the Met for the first time, presented by Satra Arts International. *Boris Godunov, The Queen of Spades,* and Prokofiev's *The Fiery Angel* met with unusual excitement. And Gergiev returned to Russia with the dollars that would help fund his ambitious program. For the Metropolitan's *The Queen of Spades,* Gergiev had an outstanding cast headed by Ben Heppner. Karita Mattila was Lisa; her top notes shone in an aura reminiscent of the young Rysanek, who here played the old Countess to terrifying effect. In his debut as Yeletsky, Dmitri Hvorostovsky staked out his place as one of the company's stars with silken tone, long-breathed legato, and handsome presence. Mark Thompson's St. Petersburg was the site of entrapment and hallucination, framed by an unsettling canted interior proscenium. Elijah Moshinsky captured the work's feverish pulse most memorably in the act 1 sexual encounter of Lisa and Gherman and in the Grand Guignol materialization of the Countess's ghost in act 3.

The 1995–96 season also saw the Met premiere of *The Makropolus Case,* the last Slavic work to be introduced in English. The January 5 opening had hardly begun when it was halted by an event that blurred the divide between art and life. As the curtain rose on the set of a 1920s office, its filing cabinets reaching the full height of the stage, tenor Richard Versalle, playing the clerk Vitek and standing on a ladder to retrieve a document, sang the line "You can only live so long," and then plunged ten feet to the floor, victim of a fatal heart attack. Destiny continued to plague *The Makropulos Case* when a blizzard caused the cancellation of the rescheduled opening a few days later. At last, on January 11, the public followed the protagonist, an eternally young 337-year-old diva, to the end of her spiritual journey. Jessye Norman had just the voice—pure, immense, deep—and the diva persona to sound the near-timelessness of Emilia Marty. Two monumental representations took the measure of the character: a sphinx that served as her throne in act 2 and, as backdrop to much of the action, her portrait, consumed by flames at the climax. The opera has taken root in three revivals in the original Czech, the latest in 2011–12.

When, at long last, the Met replaced its forty-year-old *Eugene Onegin* (March 13, 1997), the conductor was Antonio Pappano, soon to be named music director of Covent Garden. The *Times* was not alone in bashing the Robert Carsen/Michael Levine production: "So difficult was it to hear and see, one can only assume that a strategy of concealment was at work." It was left to three revivals that featured Thomas Hampson and Solveig Kringelborn (2001), Dmitri Hvorostovsky and Renée Fleming (2007), and Hampson and Mattila (2009) to establish that this refitting was not a "concealment," but a revelation. The 2007 telecast, led by Gergiev, is among the most warmly remembered of the HD series. Three undecorated walls confine the playing space. The action unfolds within minimalist borders, chairs and tables arranged in a square for the provincial cotillion, richer seating to distinguish the gathering of cosmopolitan society. During the "Letter Scene," Tatiana, whose bedroom is delimited by no more than the outline of a swept floor, bursts forth from the implied interior of the chamber to express ecstatic longings in the sea of surrounding foliage. Carsen elides the intermission between the duel and the grand Petersburg ball of some years later: Tchaikovsky's famous polonaise is heard, but not danced, while the stationary, world-weary Onegin is attended by a bevy of servants who dress him, buff his nails, and perfume his gloves. In the final scene, on a stage bare but for a single chair, Fleming and Hvorostovsky, both at their peak, sum up the drama in one anguished moment of connection before separating forever.[23]

While Gergiev was in New York preparing and performing the 1995–96 *The Queen of Spades,* the Mariinsky's chief administrator and its choreographer were detained on charges of bribery, a situation the conductor was apparently expected to handle long-distance through his well-known political connections. The next year, 1996, Boris Yeltsin, President of the Russian Federation, turned complete control of the Mariinsky opera and ballet over to Gergiev. The close association of Gergiev with the regime was founded on his friendship with Vladimir Putin dating from 1992, when Putin was first deputy mayor of St. Petersburg. A critic for the London *Times* ventured, "I don't know of any case in musical history, except maybe for Wagner and mad King Ludwig of Bavaria, where a musician has been that close to a powerful ruler." In reply to those who groused that he had devolved from musician to businessman and politician, Gergiev retorted, "There are artists who do not care who is in the government. A society like America, they don't even have to know the name of the president if they are working in Hollywood.... If you run the Mariinsky and say you don't care what is happening in the government, you are a liar." Here is a sequel to the story. In summer 2013, on the heels of Russia's new law criminalizing "propaganda on non-traditional sexual relations," blowback from the sort of defense Gergiev made in 2009, and more specifically from his support of Putin's 2012 reelection, brushed up against the Met. Gergiev would not comment on the homophobic statute. To calls that the Met dedicate to Russia's LGBT community the 2013 opening night *Eugene Onegin,* with Gergiev in the pit and Anna Netrebko, also in the Putin camp, as Tatiana, Gelb responded, "We ... stand behind all of our artists, regardless of whether or not they wish to publicly express their political opinions. As an institution, the Met deplores the suppression of equal rights here or abroad. But since our mission is artistic, it is not appropriate for our performances to be used by us for political purposes, no matter how noble or right the cause."[24]

Volpe and Levine held their second joint press conference in more than twenty years in September 1996; their secretive MO had long been a sore point with reporters. The event was staged to present a united front in announcing that Gergiev had been appointed the first principal guest conductor in Met history, a post created expressly for him, and that he was committed to eight productions in five years, including two premieres. "I'm in heaven," Volpe enthused, "just to think what can be accomplished with everything Jim and I have tried to do, and now with Valery coming on and adding what he can do" (*Times,* Sept. 16, 1997). Behind the decision was, no doubt, the expectation, first, that the extroverted Gergiev would serve as backup—and antidote—to the very private Levine, and, second, that he would continue to expand the repertoire in the Slavic direction peripheral to Levine's interests. In fact, the only Slavic opera Levine conducted in this period was his well-oiled *The Bartered Bride*. Volpe returned to his old refrain: "People claim that James Levine is hogging everything, but that is just not true. . . . In bringing Valery to the Met, we are really beginning to get the world's premier conductors into the house" (*Times*, Dec. 19, 1997). Reminiscent of his nod to Dexter was Levine's "We have the most marvelous interaction" (*Times*, Dec. 15, 1997). Gergiev's appointment raised eyebrows in New York and hackles at home. A government official chided, "Gergiev must not take unilateral steps and sign foreign contracts without informing the Russian government of this and coordinating the matter with it." While denying that Gergiev's growing influence implied that Levine might soon be leaving, Volpe acknowledged that in that event, "Gergiev is the man he would go after." Meanwhile, despite his many remunerative and exhausting distractions, Levine kept up his Metropolitan schedule. In 1999–00, for example, he conducted sixty-five performances, very close to his habitual quota of 25 percent of the season's total.[25]

In May-June 1998, the Met assumed the risks, and ultimately reaped the rewards, of bringing the Kirov to New York under its own aegis. On the esoteric program were Prokofiev's *Betrothal in a Monastery*, Tchaikovsky's *Mazeppa*, Borodin's *Prince Igor*, and Glinka's *Ruslan and Lyudmila*. Sarah Billinghurst spoke warmly of the growing relationship: not only had the Met gained a first-flight conductor for extended periods, but through his good offices the company would have the opportunity to bring its partner troupe to New York every four or five years, exchange productions, and engage the Kirov's best singers. This was, she suggested, an extraordinary win-win proposition. The very next year, Gergiev was no longer "the man [Volpe] would go after" in the case, for whatever reason, of a Levine withdrawal. He was categorical in answering a sticky question put to him by Johanna Fiedler: "[Gergiev] won't be Jimmy's successor, because, as long as I'm here, Jimmy will be here. . . . You can say he'll become music director over my dead body." Besides, it had been widely reported that Gergiev had increasingly "tense relations with the Met musicians and choristers . . . [who were] dismayed by what they consider his idiosyncratic technique, lack of focus and penchant for showing up late to rehearsals." Gergiev was on a souped-up treadmill of conducting at home and abroad, touring with the Kirov, administering an opera and ballet company, directing the White Nights Festival, fund-raising, and much more.[26]

*War and Peace,* February 14, 2002.  In March and April 1999, Gergiev was busy with Met revivals of *The Queen of Spades* and *Khovanshchina;* in 2003–

04, he would take on the Stravinsky triple bill. His imprint is best measured by the Kirov/Met coproductions, *The Gambler, War and Peace,* and *Mazeppa.* Prokofiev's reading of Tolstoy's epic novel was by far the most newsworthy of the three. Coverage of *War and Peace* at the Metropolitan had begun in the early 1940s, the time in which the Soviet Union and the United States were World War II allies. Even before the opera's 1944 Moscow concert premiere, the Met had opened negotiations for a copy of the score. Correspondence that extends from July 1943 to November 1946 includes letters from the Met general manager, the board, the State Department, the US embassy in Moscow, agencies of cultural cooperation, and the New York clearing house for the rights to Soviet music. In February 1948, Edward Johnson wrote to Eleanor Belmont that, pending receipt of a usable score and an adequate translation, he would be in a position to assure an Opera Guild–sponsored concert presentation in English that fall. The very month of Johnson's letter, the composer and opera were censured by the Soviet government, and that was that. Prokofiev did not live to see his full version performed. NBC transmitted a little more than half of *War and Peace* to American television screens in 1957; Sarah Caldwell put it on in Boston in 1974; the Bolshoi presented it during its 1975 US tour; the English National Opera's production came to New York in 1984.[27]

The Kirov and the Met were hell-bent on producing the most complete and spectacular *War and Peace* ever. At a cost estimated between $3 and $4 million (much of it charged against Alberto Vilar's pledge), with fifty-two soloists, 227 supers, 120 choristers, forty-one dancers, a horse, a dog, and a goat, the show promised to live up to its ambition. Film director Andrei Konchalovsky handled the throngs of haughty aristocrats, oppressed peasants, and Russian and French soldiers; George Tsypin provided a design whose central feature was a perilously tilted, revolving dome. Just minutes before the curtain fell on the first performance, a super, one of the Grenadiers, slipped and rolled toward the pit, saved only by a provident net at the lip of the stage. The *Times* complained, "The set is terribly distracting for the audience. How can you be swept away by the operatic drama when you are worried about the singers' safety?" The *New Yorker* was effusive: "the most visually compelling opera production that I have seen in New York in many years," many of its scenes echoing "some of the great tours de force of the Russian cinema." Anna Netrebko, the Natasha, in her company debut, would make a meteoric ascent to enormous popularity. *War and Peace* was near the top of the box-office chart that season. A year earlier, the composer's *The Gambler*

FIGURE 39. *War and Peace,* part 2, scene 4, 2002 (Winnie Klotz; courtesy Metropolitan Opera Archives)

had done better than anticipated. In adapting Dostoyevsky's short story, Prokofiev was intent on defying convention—there were no arias to speak of, no ensembles, nothing much in the way of melody. The text was all. One reviewer observed that "a conscientious patron was ... forced to read [the titles] first, to watch and listen second." Tsypin and director Yuri Alexandrov contrived overdetermined, postmodern décors for *Mazeppa:* projected images of a Nazi death camp, an array of white statues displaced and dismembered through the course of the opera, a platform whose variable rake, as in *War and Peace,* occasionally threatened to send the artists sprawling. Gergiev traced a sure path through the changing landscape of Tchaikovsky's score, from the romantic yearnings of the young Maria for her far-too-mature god-father, the traitorous Mazeppa, to martial orchestral passages and nationalistic choruses, and finally to the lullaby the unhinged heroine sings to her dead past. Another high-profile Russian conductor, director of the Glyndebourne Festival, Vladimir Jurowski, led a new staging of *Jenufa,* still a hard sell, despite Mattila, definitive in the title role, and Deborah Polaski, a fearsome Kostelnicka. The spare production took its focus from two walls receding on the bias. There were objections to the ever-present rocks, in particular to the huge boulder that sat in the middle of the act 2 farmhouse.[28]

TABLE 19  Metropolitan Opera Premieres, 1990–91 to 2005–06

| Composer and Title | Met Premiere (*World Premiere) | Most Recent Met Performance | No. of Seasons in Met Repertoire | No. of Met Productions | No. of Met Performances, 1883–2013 | World Premiere | Director/Designer |
|---|---|---|---|---|---|---|---|
| Leoš Janáček, *Kát'a Kabanová* | Feb. 25, 1991 | Jan. 1, 2005 | 3 | 1 | 19 | Nov. 23, 1921, Brno, National | Jonathan Miller / Robert Israel |
| John Corigliano, *The Ghosts of Versailles* | Dec. 19, 1991* | Apr. 21, 1995 | 2 | 1 | 13 | | Colin Graham / John Conklin |
| Philip Glass, *The Voyage* | Oct. 12, 1992* | Apr. 11, 1996 | 2 | 1 | 12 | | David Pountney / Robert Israel |
| Giuseppe Verdi, *Stiffelio* | Oct. 21, 1993 | Jan. 30, 2010 | 3 | 1 | 23 | Nov. 16, 1850, Trieste, Grande | Giancarlo Del Monaco / Michael Scott |
| Antonín Dvořák, *Rusalka* | Nov. 11, 1993 | Mar. 21, 2009 | 4 | 1 | 20 | Mar. 31, 1901, Prague, National | Otto Schenk / Gunther Schneider-Siemssen |
| Giuseppe Verdi, *I Lombardi* | Dec. 2, 1993 | May 13, 1994 | 1 | 1 | 11 | Feb. 11, 1843, Milan, La Scala | Mark Lamos / John Conklin |
| Dmitri Shostakovich, *Lady Macbeth of Mtsensk* | Nov. 10, 1994 | Mar. 30, 2000 | 2 | 1 | 15 | Jan. 22, 1934, Leningrad, Maly | Graham Vick / Paul Brown |
| Leoš Janáček, *The Makropulos Case* (in English) | Jan. 11, 1996 | May 11, 2012 | 4 | 1 | 18 | Dec. 18, 1926, Brno, National | Elijah Moshinsky / Anthony Ward |
| Benjamin Britten, *A Midsummer Night's Dream* | Nov. 25, 1996 | May 10, 2002 | 3 | 1 | 13 | June 11, 1960, Aldeburgh | Tim Albery / Anthony McDonald |
| Giaochino Rossini, *La Cenerentola* | Oct. 16, 1997 | May 9, 2009 | 5 | 1 | 32 | Jan. 25, 1817, Rome, Valle | Cesare Lievi / Maurizio Balò |

| Work | | | | Premiere | | Director / Designer |
|---|---|---|---|---|---|---|
| Richard Strauss, *Capriccio* | Jan. 9, 1998 | Apr. 23, 2011 | 2 | 1 | Oct. 28, 1942, Munich, Nationaltheater | 13 | John Cox / Mauro Pagano |
| Arnold Schoenberg, *Moses und Aron* | Feb. 8, 1999 | Dec. 23, 2003 | 3 | 1 | *In concert:* Mar. 12, 1954, Hamburg, Northwest German Radio; *Staged:* June 6, 1957, Zurich, Stadttheater | 12 | Graham Vick / Paul Brown |
| Carlisle Floyd, *Susannah* | Mar. 31, 1999 | Apr. 22, 1999 | 1 | 1 | Feb. 24, 1955, Ruby Diamond Auditorium, Tallahassee, FL | 7 | Robert Falls / Michael Yeargan |
| John Harbison, *The Great Gatsby* | Dec. 20, 1999* | May 11, 2002 | 2 | 1 | | 12 | Mark Lamos / Michael Yeargan |
| Franz Lehár, *The Merry Widow (Die lustige Witwe,* in English) | Feb. 17, 2000 | Jan. 17, 2004 | 3 | 1 | Dec. 30, 1905, Vienna, an der Wien | 26 | Tim Albery / Antony McDonald |
| Ferruccio Busoni, *Doktor Faust* | Jan. 8, 2001 | Jan. 29, 2001 | 1 | 1 | May 21, 1925, Dresden, Sächsiches Staatstheater | 6 | Peter Mussbach / Erich Wonder |
| Sergei Prokofiev, *The Gambler* | Mar. 19, 2001 | Apr. 12, 2008 | 2 | 1 | Apr. 29, 1929, Brussels, La Monnaie (in French) | 11 | Temur Chkheidze / George Tsypin |
| Sergei Prokofiev, *War and Peace* | Feb. 14, 2002 | Jan. 3, 2008 | 2 | 1 | *In concert:* Oct. 16, 1944, Moscow, Writer's Club; *staged:* June 12, 1946, Leningrad, Maly | 18 | Andrei Konchalovsky / George Tsypin |
| Ermanno Wolf-Ferrari, *Sly* | Apr. 1, 2002 | May 4, 2002 | 1 | 1 | Dec. 29, 1927, Milan, La Scala | 9 | Marta Domingo / Michael Scott |

*(continued)*

TABLE 19 (continued)

| Composer and Title | Met Premiere (*World Premiere) | Most Recent Met Performance | No. of Seasons in Met Repertoire | No. of Met Productions | No. of Met Performances, 1883–2013 | World Premiere | Director/Designer |
|---|---|---|---|---|---|---|---|
| Vincenzo Bellini, Il Pirata | Oct. 21, 2002 | Feb. 8, 2003 | 1 | 1 | 9 | Oct. 27, 1827, Milan, La Scala | John Copley/John Conklin |
| Michael Bolcom, A View from the Bridge | Dec. 5, 2002 | Dec. 28, 2002 | 1 | 1 | 7 | Oct. 9, 1999, Chicago, Lyric | Frank Galati, Santo Loquasto |
| Hector Berlioz, Benvenuto Cellini | Dec. 4, 2003 | Jan. 1, 2004 | 1 | 1 | 8 | Sept. 10, 1838, Paris, Opéra | Andrei Serban / George Tsypin |
| George Frideric Handel, Rodelinda | Dec. 2, 2004 | Dec. 10, 2011 | 3 | 1 | 22 | Feb. 13, 1725, London, Haymarket | Stephen Wadsworth / Thomas Lynch |
| Franco Alfano, Cyrano de Bergerac | May 13, 2005 | Mar. 16, 2006 | 2 | 1 | 9 | Jan. 22, 1936, Rome, Reale | Francesca Zambello / Peter Davison |
| Tobias Picker, An American Tragedy | Dec. 2, 2005* | Dec. 28, 2005 | 1 | 1 | 8 | | Francesca Zambello / Adrianne Lobel |
| Peter Ilyich Tchaikovsky, Mazeppa | Mar. 6, 2006 | Mar. 30, 2006 | 1 | 1 | 8 | Feb. 15, 1884, Moscow, Bolshoi | Yuri Alexandrov / George Tsypin |

Peter Gelb extended the Slavic wing with two stunning premieres: Patrice Chéreau's Spartan *From the House of the Dead,* already seen in Vienna, Amsterdam, and Aix-en-Provence, and William Kentridge's kaleidoscopic *The Nose.* Richard Peduzzi's baleful yard for the Janáček piece glossed Chéreau's explicit intention: to evoke "all the prisons in the world . . . at once the Gulag and all the camps of the 20th century, a place that can become almost abstract." Esa-Pekka Salonen, in his debut, led the ensemble cast through ninety relentless minutes. There was no less enthusiasm for the collage of effects Kentridge arranged for the strident, farcical *The Nose:* "the Met found the perfect match for Shostakovich's sensibility in William Kentridge . . . the biggest cheers at the curtain call went to him and the rest of his design team." Gogol's Czarist 1830s became the Soviet 1920s, crammed with Constructivist bits of newspaper, poster art, words, projected images, and film clips that included stop-action animation and the composer at the piano. Gelb demonstrated the power of crafty marketing by coordinating the run of *The Nose* with the Museum of Modern Art's Kentridge show. *The Nose* was a hot ticket.[29]

OTHER STAGINGS

## Rereadings

The company mined the same voguish vein in its ongoing exploration of the nineteenth- and twentieth-century Western European repertoire as it had for its Slavic survey. And with that, the Met moved squarely to the center of the debate that continues to dominate discourse on operatic practice. The polemic was joined early in the Bing era, swelled first under Dexter and Levine, then under Volpe and Levine, and crested with the installation of Peter Gelb in 2006. At one extreme are direction and design that propose—many would say, impose—radical rereadings of familiar and sometimes unfamiliar titles. Of the nearly 170 new productions mounted in the forty years between the beginning of Bing's era in 1950 and the start of Volpe's in 1990, we count only nine as rereadings. The first two—the much scorned, updated *Cavalleria rusticana* and the somewhat surreal *Pagliacci* of Bing's inaugural season—came just as avant-garde productions were taking hold at the reopened Bayreuth Festspielhaus. But the *Regietheater* (director's opera) that would soon become the norm in Germany and elsewhere in Europe remained exceptional at the stubbornly retro Metropolitan. In a defamiliarizing reinvention, Tyrone Guthrie rid *Carmen* of many of its tired trappings. Peter Brook's *Faust* dumped Gothic Germany for Gounod's own nineteenth century. With the move to Lincoln Center, Bing took a chance on a *Lohengrin* in the abstract style of Wieland Wagner. A decade would go by before Dexter unveiled his Brechtian take on Meyerbeer's *Le Prophète*. The 1982 *Macbeth* reclaimed the apparatus of Romantic melodrama. The cartoonish 1979 *Der Fliegende Holländer* was strapped into the straitjacket of the Steersman's nightmare; in 1989, Salome did her number in a basement of a decadent modern city.[30]

This brings us to the late 1990s. *Moses und Aron* (Feb. 8, 1999), Arnold Schoenberg's magnum opus, was a peak that a world-class house would sooner or later have to scale. Shunning Hollywood-Biblical iconography, Graham Vick and Paul Brown turned the children of Israel into modern Jews, the "Golden Calf" bacchanal into a paparazzi shoot. Levine, the cast, and the stage machinery combined to pull off Schoenberg's "impossible snarl of religion, politics, and musical aesthetics." Thomas Hampson repeated his tour de force in the *Doktor Faust* that had originated at the 1999 Salzburg Festival. Time and place were transposed once more. The doublets and capes of medieval Wittenberg became shabby overcoats, dark against a wintry landscape. In this version of Ferruccio Busoni's thorny work, the action unfolded in the protagonist's "daydream . . . a journey inside his head." The intriguing anachronisms and abstractions of *A Midsummer Night's Dream* were edgy, emphatically "anti-pretty." In the Britten opera, the midsummer dream was "a dream by classical Athenians about a life that hasn't happened yet because it's happening in the 20th century." The directors' arcane conceit no doubt eluded many in the audience.[31]

Jonathan Miller hatched illuminating rereadings of *Pelléas et Mélisande* (March 25, 1995) and *The Rake's Progress* (Nov. 20, 1997). Debussy's enigmatic characters had hitherto been swathed in impenetrable mists, and Stravinsky's Tom Rakewell and Anne Trulove reduced to the single dimension of their names. John Conklin replaced the medieval castle of *Pelléas* with an immense revolving nineteenth-century manor whose shifting public and private spaces implicated the audience in the disturbing voyeurism that permeates the libretto. For *The Rake,* Miller took on "the brave task of humanizing an opera that may be more about style than people." Updated from Hogarth's eighteenth century to 1920s England, Stravinsky's neoclassical pastiche delivered an unexpected emotional punch. In a time shift that recalled the updating of *Moses und Aron* to the decadent twentieth century, Jürgen Flimm propelled the Biblical Judea of *Salome* (March 15, 2004) into the contemporary Middle East, Herod's court revels into a jet-set orgy, the daughter of Herodias into a teenaged lush. As sensational as Mattila's full frontal nudity at the climax of

"The Dance of the Seven Veils" was her fearless confrontation with the role. Designer and director Herbert Wernicke, who projected his Marxist vision of *Die Frau ohne Schatten* (Dec. 13, 2001) inside a dazzling mirrored box, disparaged the opera's 1966 landmark production: "With all those set changes and props, I'm sure the audience didn't get what the story was all about." Wernicke was liable to his own criticism: even among New Yorkers, many would not "get" this "parable of New York" in which the "lofty Central Park West" spirit world was dialectically opposed to the "underworld of poor people."[32]

Just a handful of the rereadings of the Volpe era fell to the dominant Romantic corpus. When *La Cenerentola* finally came to the Met, Rossini's infectious opera buffa was chosen to exercise the hyperkinetic Cecilia Bartoli. Thanks to her extraordinary technique and industrious publicists, Bartoli had recently become an international celebrity. She dispatched an irrepressible Angelina with coloratura of military precision. The venerable fairy tale was retold in a surrealist lexicon borrowed from Magritte. For *Lohengrin* (March 9, 1998), Robert Wilson banished representation altogether: the banks of the River Scheldt, the castle, and the bridal chamber were nowhere to be seen. The singers were confined to slow, ritualized movement. Some operagoers were bewildered by the absence of narrative signposts, others infuriated. But for others still, Wagner's score glowed through Wilson's abstract light show. Booed on the first night, Wilson drew bravos when the opera returned in October. For *La Juive* (Nov. 6, 2003), Günter Krämer came up with the reductive scheme of dramatizing religious conflict in fifteenth-century Constance by splitting the stage horizontally. The Christians, mostly in white period costumes, occupied the steeply raked, larger, brightly lit upper level; the Jews, in mid-twentieth-century black, huddled in the claustrophobic den below. The contrast was numbingly simplistic. Neil Shicoff, the guiding spirit of the project, justified the Holocaust analogue during his overwhelming voicing of Eléazar's great aria as he removed his coat and shoes in a gripping figuration of the gas chambers.[33]

The two truly grievous rereadings of the period were inflicted on *Lucia di Lammermoor* (Nov. 19, 1992) and *Il Trovatore* (Dec. 7, 2000). In yet another iteration of the dream/nightmare/hallucination frame, John Conklin's skewed ruins, projections of Lucia's crumbling mind, mirrored the psychological space in which the action transpired. Gone were the Scottish lairds and ladies in Francesca Zambello's construction of solipsistic dementia. June Anderson sang the heroine's runs to herself while balancing precariously on a pile of coffins. The company swallowed its pride, and the loss; it endured this version of Donizetti's opera for a slim two seasons. As for *Il Trovatore,* the

FIGURE 40. *Lucia di Lammermoor* "Mad Scene," June Anderson as Lucia, 1992 (Winnie Klotz; courtesy Metropolitan Opera Archives)

irony that Vick and Brown visited on Schoenberg and Shostakovich was misplaced on Verdi. The evening was strewn with unintentionally comic touches: an oversized hoop skirt for the soprano, identical beards, mustaches, and pasty white lookalike makeup for the tenor and baritone, unsuspecting to the end that they are long-lost brothers. The loudest guffaws came in the convent scene: as if to illustrate that Manrico had actually descended from heaven to rescue his beloved Leonora ("sei tu dal ciel disceso"), a slender ramp, in the form of an inverted cross, dropped noisily to the stage, bearing the anxious hero. Volpe took the blame for the absurd production, much modified as early as the second performance. *Il Trovatore* came back two seasons later, minus the names of the director and designer, and then never again.[34]

## Refittings

Among the premieres out to renew rather than reinterpret was *Capriccio*, displaced from the late eighteenth century to the early twentieth, and filled with beguiling fashions and furnishings that flattered Kiri Te Kanawa, the star for which it was mounted. To compensate for the weak libretto of *Benvenuto Cellini,* another company first, director Andrei Serban dished up endless stage business: the ironic miming of a commedia dell'arte troupe; two nearly nude male models, stand-ins for the sculptor's statues; a stand-in for Berlioz himself, scribbling away as he roamed the stage. The décor, a semicircular colonnade surrounded by two curved staircases, at times moving singly and at others revolving together, defined the playing space. Berlioz's fascinating though flawed work died after one season. In the interest of realism, Stephen Wadsworth's staging of *Rodelinda* swept away the stock poses inseparable from the Baroque da capo aria since time immemorial. Thomas Lynch rolled out contiguous spaces that mimicked the flow of cinematic continuity. The "off-camera" courtyard replaced the "on-camera" apartment, only to be replaced in turn by the stable, and then back again. Surrounded by representations of the quotidian—a washbasin, an unmade bed, shelves filled with books—the characters passed from one environment to another in a simulation of real time. Renée Fleming, Stephanie Blythe, John Relyea, and Bejun Mehta enacted the narrative with fervor and sang with astounding technique. David Daniels, who had done so much to accustom the public to the exquisite timbre of that relative newcomer to the operatic stage, the countertenor, was remarkable as the heroic Bertarido. Handel sold out the Met.

The ham-fisted *Fidelio* of Jürgen Flimm (Oct. 28, 2000) embedded Beethoven's meanings in a present-day banana republic cluttered with khaki uniforms, assault rifles, and bare bulbs. Symptomatic of the overall blunder was the mob lynching of the sadistic Pizarro, a violation of the triumphantly humanistic act 2 finale that celebrates Leonore's virtue and courage. In the October 28 telecast, Mattila is a youthful and intrepid protagonist; René Pape turns Rocco into a star vehicle. The other refittings of German revivals and those of Mozart's Italian operas evinced taste and occasional originality. The cherished 1984 *Die Meistersinger* was replaced by an equally *gemütlich* Nuremberg (Jan. 14, 1993). Dieter Dorn's restrained staging of *Tristan und Isolde* (Nov. 22, 1999) accommodated the limited mobility of the weighty Jane Eaglen; none but the hidebound estate of Sybil Harrington would find Jürgen Rose's spare, geometric designs controversial. Elektra's rage had its correlative in the broken statue of a mammoth horse beneath Mycenae's walls (*Elektra,* March 26, 1992). The canny tiered set of *Ariadne auf Naxos* (March 11, 1993) stacked a grand mansion above the grubby backstage of its private theater. Looming shadows conveyed the burden of existence that destroys the downtrodden, *untermensch* protagonists of Berg's *Wozzeck* (Feb. 10, 1997).

Julie Taymor's puppets and masks for *Die Zauberflöte* (Oct. 8, 2004), shades of her Broadway *The Lion King,* were just the ticket for Mozart's singspiel. An earthy kitchen for Despina distinguished this *Così fan tutte* (Feb. 8, 1996) from its elegant predecessors. Bartoli, a Rossini specialist, had her many New York fans scratching their heads at the choice of the undemanding role of the meddling maid for her debut. But even without recourse to her bravura technique, from the moment she entered, grinning mischievously, pulling an entire house at the end of a rope, she stole the show. When it came to *Le Nozze di Figaro* (Oct. 29, 1998), Bartoli turned the tables: this time the role was not virtuosic enough. For three of her seven performances, she prevailed on Levine to substitute two florid arias for Susanna's more lyric "Venite inginocchiatevi" and "Deh vieni non tardar." Director Jonathan Miller took his irritation public; he has not since returned to the Met. Nor has Bartoli, for reasons not altogether clear. With the exception of *Ariadne auf Naxos,* Levine led the revivals of each of these conductor's operas.[35]

The Italian and French refittings were, by contrast, of uneven quality. We sample here just a few from a large group. The vigor of *Nabucco* (March 8, 2001) reverberated in a series of bold images, the most arresting the appearance of the Children of Israel on a revolving stage piled high with rough-hewn stone blocks, an apposite rostrum for the choral lament, "Va pensiero," inevitably encored to sold-out houses. Allusions to Renaissance astronomy that idealized the erotic attraction of the "star-cross'd lovers" of Gounod's *Roméo et Juliette* (Nov. 14, 2005), their marriage bed floating in the Empyrean, were among the best of the period's directorial inventions. Zeffirelli's were among the worst. In his second *La Traviata* (Nov. 23, 1998), he paid no more mind to the opera's intimate scale than he had in his first: Violetta was made to drag herself from her consumptive bedroom down a flight of stairs to breathe her last in her party-girl ballroom. *Don Pasquale* (March 31, 2006) sacrificed wit to gags. Donizetti's comedy was a romp for the acrobatic Anna Netrebko. Her mugging and flouncing, presumably blessed by director Otto Schenk, unleashed justifiably outraged notices: "the most self-serving performance this writer has ever witnessed"; "a caricature of a tough Italian whore." Volpe's bel canto bona fides were better served by the exhumation of *Semiramide* (Nov. 30, 1990), primarily for Horne, and the Met premiere of *Il Pirata,* a vehicle for Fleming. For disparate reasons, among them Levine's indifference, the Met was very late in programming the lesser-known Rossini, Donizetti, and Bellini pieces that, for decades, Sutherland, Horne, and Caballé had sung the world over. While the company refitted chestnuts such as *Lucia* for Sutherland and *Il Barbiere di Siviglia* for Horne, and dusted off *I Puritani* and *L'Italiana in Algeri*, other theaters presented the likes of *Anna Bolena* and *Maria Stuarda*, titles in the Met's future.[36]

## CLOSING THE BOOKS

Volpe had two announcements for the board meeting of February 2004: that Levine's title would revert to music director and that he himself would relinquish his position as general manager at the expiration of his contract, August 2006: "This is a young man's job. I live a block away; I'm here night and day. The job is the focus of your life. No matter where you are, there's always some problem" (*Times*, Feb. 10, 2004). The lame-duck thirty months to come worried the critics. One suggested that Levine had "left Mr. Volpe in the curious position of being the de facto artistic director, a job that he has no doubt coveted but for which he is perhaps less than ideally suited. . . . Can he plan repertory and oversee casting and productions with the requisite, insightful sophistication and taste?" Others suspected that not much would change, that it had been an entire decade since Levine had been fully engaged in "the overall artistic profile of the company." The outlook was further troubled by the worsening balance sheet. The Met had lost $10 million in each of the two preceding seasons. Donations had dropped significantly; audience capacity, at 91 percent prior to 9/11, had fallen to 82 percent in 2001–02 and 80 percent in 2003–04. And "with empty seats [came] renewed questions not just about Mr. Volpe's policies, but also about his methods, and especially his combative personality. Within the company more people are probably barked at by the general manager than is absolutely necessary; it's hard to give your best when you're constantly demeaned." Most damning was the "persistent criticism . . . that he [had] fostered a creative climate . . . dominated more by fiscal than by artistic priorities." At the same time, there was fulsome recognition of Volpe's managerial genius: he would leave behind an extraordinarily efficient operation, durable labor peace, Met Titles, reconfigured subscription packages, a beefed-up international touring schedule, a longer season, and an impressive record of fund-raising. Nonetheless, the consensus painted Volpe as musically oafish, intrusive, bullying, and consumed with the bottom line.[37]

When all is said and done, Volpe's legacy rests on the rigorous policy of repertoire remapping he pursued together with Levine. Nearly a third of their seventy-three new productions was allocated to American, Slavic, and twentieth-century European works, and of these, the great majority were company premieres. Whereas Bing had tagged the Met a repertory theater frozen in the nineteenth century, a proud "museum," Levine and then Levine and Volpe, despite pushback along the way, oversaw a house of expansive and expanding repertory. The flag of staging reform, waved briefly by Bing, and then strenuously by Dexter, fluttered repeatedly over Volpe's Met when Jonathan Miller, Elijah Moshinsky, Tim Albery, Robert Carsen, and Robert Wilson were in residence. New repertoire and the prestigious stratum of the core were the particular beneficiaries of their determination. Zeffirelli, Schenk, Schneider-Siemssen, and other pictorialists had to make do with a smaller share of the pie.

As for Volpe's rosters, they broadcast that the stock of stars capable of arousing the infectious passion of operaphiles was not what it had been at Bing's house of singers. For new productions, the solo bow before the encore curtain had given way to a short run to the center of the final set, and then a few steps forward from the line of principals. If cheering was sometimes lusty, it was invariably brief. Only rarely did a bouquet sail across the pit or bits of paper rain down from the family circle. The more egalitarian ritual acknowledged the entire cast, including chorus and dancers. That said, in the course of Volpe's sixteen seasons, individual performances were among the best by any standard. To name only a few: for Mozart, the Pamina of Kathleen Battle and the Sarastro of Kurt Moll, the Countess of Renée Fleming and of Anja Harteros, Dorothea Röschmann's Donna Elvira, Bryn Terfel's Figaro; for Wagner, Mattila's Eva and Elsa, Heppner's Walter von Stolzing and Lohengrin, James Morris's Hans Sachs, René Pape's King Marke, Waltraud Meier's Kundry; for Strauss, Natalie Dessay as Zerbinetta, Deborah Voigt as Ariadne, Gwyneth Jones as Elektra; the Natasha and Andrei of *War and Peace* of Anna Netrebko and Dmitri Hvorostovsky, the Abigaille of *Nabucco* of Andrea Gruber, the Didon of *Les Troyens* of Lorraine Hunt Lieberson, Stephanie Blythe and David Daniels in *Giulio Cesare,* Olga Borodina and Juan Diego Flórez in *L'Italiana in Algeri,* the Billy Budd of Dwayne Croft and of Thomas Hampson. At Volpe's farewell gala, May 20, 2006, Plácido Domingo was in the pit to accompany tenors Roberto Alagna and Ramón Vargas. When he took the stage, nearly forty years after his debut at Bing's 39th Street Met, the audience thrilled to his familiar burnished tone.

# In the Age of New Media, 2006–2013

## PASSING IT ON

EIGHT MONTHS OF SPECULATION on the succession followed Joe Volpe's announcement of his retirement. Among the ten or so names floated were those of six general managers of opera houses in the United States and Europe, two symphony orchestra and ballet company directors, and the head of a national performing arts center: David Gockley, Houston Grand Opera; William Mason, Lyric Opera of Chicago; Plácido Domingo, Washington Opera; Sir Peter Jonas, Bavarian State Opera; Pierre Audi, Netherlands Opera; Gérard Mortier, formerly of Salzburg, later to take over in Paris; Deborah Borda, Los Angeles Philharmonic; Lesley Koenig, San Francisco Ballet; and Michael M. Kaiser, president of the Kennedy Center. Only Peter Gelb had run neither a performing arts company nor an arts complex.

It was Beverly Sills, chair of the board from 2002 to 2005, who prevailed on her colleagues to interview Gelb. Within forty-eight hours, the agreement was sealed and delivered. The appointment on October 29, 2004, took everyone by surprise. Gelb would join the Met in August 2005, spend 2005–06 preparing to take over from Volpe, and assume the title of general manager on August 1, 2006. Board president William Morris later pointed to "knowledge of marketing" and "youthful vigor" as the two qualities of "particular interest" to his colleagues. Typical of the response of Met watchers at large was the initial reaction of Mercedes Bass, whose $25 million came as one regime was handing the reins to the next: "I thought, Oh, there's a man who doesn't have a clue about how to run an opera company!" She went on, "But then Beverly Sills, bless her heart, said, 'Mercedes, don't worry, you will love him.' And I must say she was right. . . . The first impression was that he had so much vision, and we were not used to so much vision." As Gelb remarked later, "My pitch to [the search committee] was that the Met was an organization that had a great history and past, but that was completely disconnected from contemporary culture and society. I was very straight with them. I told them what I really believed, which is that it had disengaged itself and that it needed to be re-engaged."[1]

## Peter Gelb

The general manager–elect first set foot in the Met in 1967. With his father, Arthur, then metropolitan editor and later managing editor at the *New York Times,* fourteen-year-old Peter sat in Rudolf Bing's box for a performance of *Carmen.* His mother, Barbara, niece of violinist Jascha Heifetz and step-daughter of playwright S. N. Behrman, is a biographer of Eugene O'Neill (with her husband) and of John Reed and Louise Bryant, and the author of other works of nonfiction. By his own admission, Gelb concluded early on that "access was more important than wealth," and indeed, given his aspirations, this youthful judgment proved correct. While in school, Gelb took a turn as usher at the Met and worked in Sol Hurok's mailroom, and then again for Hurok for a year before enrolling grudgingly at Yale, leaving after just one semester to launch his career as a publicist with an artist management firm. In 1978, he was director of promotions for the Boston Symphony; there he oversaw the first tour of an American orchestra to China after the thaw in relations with the West. In 1980, he shepherded Vladimir Horowitz's return to the stage, and for the next decade he was manager to the great pianist. In 1982, back in New York, Gelb went to work for Ronald Wilford, chairman and CEO of Columbia Artists Management Inc. (CAMI). As he remembered it, Wilford gave him "an office and a salary, and said, 'You decide what to do and create your own job.' And out of that, CAMI Video was born" (*Times,* Nov. 6, 2004). Between 1988 and 1992, while at CAMI, Gelb was executive producer of the Met's media department with responsibility for "The Metropolitan Opera Presents," a series of twenty-five telecasts that included the 1990 "Ring." Working with the Maysles brothers, vérité documentary filmmakers, he also produced and "occasionally directed" more than fifty television events around Horowitz, Karajan, Rostropovich, and Battle, among other artists. In 1993, when his division was bought from Wilford, Gelb followed CAMI Video to Sony Music Entertainment. "He didn't leave," the "Black Knight of 57th Street" was quoted as quipping, "I sold him."[2]

As head of Sony Classical U.S.A., then in 1995 of Sony Classical internationally, Gelb was finally positioned to redefine the marketing of music and musicians. He first rescinded recording projects in the standard repertoire. He then went about resetting the boundaries of classical music by presenting cellist Yo-Yo Ma in multimedia Bach and in trio with folk virtuoso fiddler and composer Mark O'Connor and bass player Edgar Meyer; he released pop musician Joe Jackson's *Symphony No. 1*. Turning to the big screen, Gelb recorded John Corigliano's score for *The Red Violin* and Tan Dun's for *Crouching Tiger, Hidden Dragon*. The road from the concert hall to the movie palace was well traveled: in 1908, Camille Saint-Saëns was recruited for the silent *L'Assassinat du duc de Guise* and, in 1938, Sergei Prokofiev for Sergei Eisenstein's *Alexander Nevsky*. What was new—and dubious—was Gelb's contention that "anything written for film is classical music." That premise led to the reassignment of movie soundtrack CDs to the classical bins, John Williams's themes for *Star Wars*, James Horner's for *Titanic*. But then, *Titanic* sold an astounding twenty-nine million copies worldwide. In the course of his career in media, Gelb collected a Grammy and six Emmys.[3]

All this no doubt dazzled the Met directors, as it had Mercedes Bass. But those who had heard Renée Fleming in duet with Michael Bolton in their bizarre "O soave fanciulla" must have been at least somewhat conflicted. Would the Met stage have to make room for a pop singer's yen to play Rodolfo against the Mimì of its star diva? "Popera" was the specter the vituperative Norman Lebrecht raised online. Volpe warned, "Pop singers are definitely not the answer. . . . Pop singers brought in for one act of an opera to attract an audience detracts from the aesthetic you're presenting." The more serious question surrounding the Gelb appointment was this: did he have the resumé of a legitimate Metropolitan GM? From his vantage, the many parts of his working life taken together produced a sum that credentialed his claim to the position. He cited his sole lyric theater credit, the *Oepidus Rex* he organized in Japan for Seiji Ozawa's festival, and added, "between projects like that and being executive producer of *Fantasia 2000* [conducted by Levine], and running a record label, I've had a wide variety of experience dealing with artistic temperament, production deadlines, and budgets. And through my experience at Sony, I've learned the fiscal responsibility of running a for-profit company" (*Times,* Oct. 30, 2004). If both supporters and skeptics were uncertain how to define him (publicist? artist manager? media executive?), Gelb was glad to set them straight: "a producer . . . is what I consider myself to be" and, later, "I am a marketer. I'm not ashamed to be a marketer."[4]

In truth, very few of Gelb's fifteen predecessors throughout 123 years of Met history brought with them a textbook curriculum vitae. In the context of that history, the board's choice was not all that exceptional. Henry Abbey and Maurice Grau were theatrical and concert impresarios; Leopold Damrosch was primarily a symphony conductor; Edmond Stanton, a son of New York's aristocracy, had been secretary to the board without particular métier; Heinrich Conried was an actor-director-manager in theater and operetta; after heading a conservatory, bass Herbert Witherspoon had been the one-year artistic director of the Chicago Civic Opera when it shut its doors; Edward Johnson was a tenor, Schuyler Chapin a media executive; Anthony Bliss and Bruce Crawford were businessmen and members of the board; and Hugh Southern dealt in arts management. Only three came with records to match the job: Rudolf Bing had been general manager at Glyndbourne, though a festival and not an opera company; Goeran Gentele had run the relatively small Swedish National Opera; Joseph Volpe had risen from carpenter to assistant general manager at the Met. And only one, Giulio Gatti-Casazza, came with an impeccable pedigree: he had been intendant at La Scala for a decade.

### Preparatory Season: 2005–2006

From September 2005 to May 2006, Volpe and Gelb reported monthly to the board's executive committee, and from time to time to the full board. In general, Volpe was responsible for keeping the directors up to date on labor talks, on the "horribly" limp box office, on cuts to offset the drop in ticket sales ascribed primarily to the contraction of tristate patronage. Gelb had the more grateful role. He kept the trustees abreast of changes in staffing (tellingly, the first were new directors of marketing, communications and editorial comment, and development), of repertoire and casting plans, and of media initiatives designed to "reach out to a broader audience and give the Met a new exciting high exposure." At the annual meeting of May 25, 2006, board president Morris cited audience capacity as the single greatest challenge facing the organization: it had fallen below 77 percent in the season just concluded. Gelb, he said, had evolved a seven-part strategy to reverse the downward slide: he would increase the number of new productions from four to six, commit the biggest stars to more performances each season, program contemporary works each year, market through new media, introduce family entertainments at holiday time (*Hänsel und Gretel* and an abridged *Die*

*Zauberflöte* [both in English]), forge relationships with visual artists, and open the doors wider to the public. (The meeting was interrupted by the unexpected arrival of Levine. He had wanted to assure the board that his shoulder was on the mend after his fall on the stage of Boston's Symphony Hall and to express his delight at the prospect of working closely with the new leadership.) Volpe took the floor to report on the season loss of $2.2 million, noting pointedly that the general manager transition had come to approximately $2.5 million. The good news was that, over many months, he and Gelb had reached five-year agreements with the Met's three largest unions, that the musicians had accepted terms for media rights, and that negotiations for these rights were ongoing with the other locals. Gelb zeroed in on his signature innovation: he would "make the Met's performances available in every possible media format, including the internet, with digital downloading and satellite radio. If the unions give us the rights, we will start many of these media initiatives next year, including transmitting into movie theatres around the country the Saturday matinee performances in high definition, so people will be able to go to their local cinemas to see a Met performance live in surround sound." In place of the crushing up-front fee per product released, labor would share in the revenues.[5]

## GELB'S "NEW MET": 2006–2007

"What fuels me," Gelb told *CNN Money* in 2011, "is the fear of the art form not surviving. To think that an art form or an institution like this is immune to the possibility of extinction would be a big mistake. . . . How can we possibly keep this thing going when the audience at the Met was literally dying of old age?"—a question driven by the findings of the 2005–06 survey that put the average age of regular patrons at sixty-six. Gelb was convinced that behind the alarming number lay a failing endemic to the classical music business. Prophesying its consequences had been his mission for more than a decade and a half: "There is a danger whether you are running a record label or an orchestra or an opera house, of not understanding who the public is. It doesn't mean you should pander to the public, but you should understand that there is a public. You can't operate an opera house in a vacuum, and I think more often than not that is how opera houses operate." Each of the seven points of Gelb's agenda spoke to this "vacuum"; all were designed to appeal to the sensibilities of a more demographically diverse clientele.

Thanks to an expanded, increasingly heterogeneous pool, the Met's share of the cultural market of New York and beyond would grow, saving the company from stagnation, even "extinction," and securing a vigorous artistic and financial future. The trick would be to hold on to the largely conservative converted while proselytizing among the flock in thrall to contemporary media.[6]

However modestly, publicizing the Met began with its founding. In 1883, Abbey joined other New York impresarios in listing his weekly programs and casts in small inserts in the theater sections of the city's newspapers. It was not until the mid-1970s that the company began taking out sizable independent ads splashed with blurbs and photos, a practice neighboring playhouses had adopted decades earlier. Anthony Bliss had had to press hard for this break with discretion, arguing that the path to financial stability on the heels of the debilitating 1969 strike and the mid-1970s fiscal crisis was through growth, and that growth depended on publicity. On his watch, the Met chanced the full-page "You are invited to strike a blow for civilization" ad some found impossibly déclassé, set up a marketing department, and multiplied the advertising budget more than tenfold to $400,000 in one year. All the same, the perception persisted into the twenty-first century that "the Metropolitan Opera has wrinkled its elegant nose at advertising campaigns, preferring discreet sales tactics like direct mail and phone solicitations." By early 2006, big changes were on the way. On January 16, months before Gelb was to take official charge, Thomas Michel, the new director of marketing, was ready to report to the board on a sweeping campaign: his office would produce brochures targeted at distinctly different audiences, and it would place ads not only in *New York Magazine,* in *Time Out New York,* in the *New York Observer,* and in the *New York Sun,* but also, in an effort to reach a younger crowd, through e-mail services such as *TheaterMania, Playbill,* and *DailyCandy* and, for tourists, on *Expedia* and *Travelocity.* The Met would no longer be identified by its imposing façade and opulent chandeliers; it would be branded instead through signs of theatricality and stardom. In April, Gelb gave the directors a preview of a fall Saks Fifth Avenue window dressed in Cio-Cio-San's wedding kimono for the new opening night *Madama Butterfly.* By early September, the Met's $500,000 campaign burst onto New York streets; posters were plastered everywhere, on telephone booths, at subway stations and bus stops, on the sides of the buses themselves, and on the roofs of taxi cabs. Business woman and Met managing director Agnes Varis picked up the tab.[7]

## Radio

No sooner was Gelb installed than the stately Saturday afternoon radio ritual mushroomed into a 24/7 groaning board for opera lovers. Since 2006, via satellite radio, he has offered SiriusXM subscribers broadcasts culled from an archive fifteen hundred recordings strong and, in season, three live performances weekly. In addition, the Internet has provided streaming audio and, for a fee, a library of sound and video transcriptions accessible on computer, smartphone, and other receiving devices. What has lately become available can be counted a giant step in the long journey begun in defeat on January 12, 1910, when, alas, the first two transmissions from 39th Street were doomed by an inadequate apparatus. Fremstad's Tosca, Destinn's Santuzza, and Caruso's Canio were barely audible to the handful of listeners who held telephone receivers to their ears. Two decades would elapse before general manager Gatti-Casazza could be persuaded that microphones and amplifiers had met the fidelity demands of grand opera. In 1931, the Met began inveigling its way into millions of homes across the country, advancing the elusive ambition of naturalizing the stubbornly European art form. Almost from the start, announcer Milton Cross was the unmistakable voice of the Met. In orotund tones and purple prose, he told the stories of the operas, described the sets and costumes, and added his own enthusiastic observations to the applause. Regular intermission features were "Opera News on the Air," often devoted to the musical analyses of conductor-educator-impresario Boris Goldovsky, and "Opera Quiz," a jocular precursor of Trivial Pursuit (in which opera does the mezzo-soprano sing an aria about her cat?) and questions that called for longer answers from the knowledgeable contestants. Later came singers' roundtables and reminiscences about the stars of the past. In 1940, Texaco took over the prestigious sponsorship; its sixty-three years remain the longest run in radio history. Cross's more than four-decade streak ended with his death in 1975. He was succeeded by Peter Allen and, on Allen's retirement in 2004, by the current host, Margaret Juntwait. For more than eighty years, Met broadcasts have generated a pool of opera consumers readily and repeatedly tapped for often sorely needed revenue. Radio was key to the Depression "Save the Met" campaign as it was in 1940 to acquiring the house from the Metropolitan Opera and Real Estate Company.

## Recorded Sound

The opera house and the technology of sound reproduction first found each other at the dawn of the twentieth century; without commercial intent,

Lionel Mapleson, the company's librarian, captured excerpts from performances between 1901 and 1903. At that very moment, Caruso cut his first records, launching his phenomenal career as a phonograph artist. The fame and prestige of the Metropolitan spread with the sound of the tenor's voice and of those of his colleagues, acoustically recorded on Victor, Columbia, and other labels. Beginning in the mid-1920s, opera singers benefited from the higher fidelity achieved through electronic recording processes. But it was not until 1947 that the Met produced its own albums with Columbia Records. In the mid-1950s, there was a flurry of twenty titles, most abridged, the result of a collaboration with the Book-of-the-Month Club. Transcriptions of historic broadcasts were offered as premiums to contributors to the Metropolitan Opera Fund beginning in the 1970s. And in 1990, the company began recording for CBS, Sony, Philips, and Deutsche Grammophon, an arrangement that flourished until DVD spelled the end of opera produced expressly for the audio format of the compact disc. In 2011, and in partnership with Sony Classical, the Metropolitan began to release CDs of its vast archive of broadcasts. Among these are some of the company's most cherished portrayals—Melchior and Flagstad as Tristan and Isolde, Björling and Sayão as Roméo and Juliette, Caballé as Luisa Miller, Vickers as Florestan, Price and Corelli in Il *Trovatore*.

## Television

Of Gelb's multiple electronic incursions—from satellite radio to ring tones— "The Met: Live in HD" has left the deepest and broadest imprint on the cultural atlas. The potential of pay TV was tested twice by Bing through closed-circuit transmissions to movie theaters, and then by Volpe with the cable transmission of the 1991 opening night gala. But the story of the Metropolitan Opera on television, free to anyone within broadcast radius, began with the birth of commercial TV just before the entry of the United States into the Second World War.

In 1940, W2XBS, the New York NBC channel, was on the air for a few hours a day from Wednesday through Sunday, mostly for sports, news, and movies. On March 10, the several thousand equipped households were invited to watch an hour-long program of arias and an abridged act 1 of *Pagliacci* emanating from a studio in Rockefeller Center, simulcast on radio station WJZ. Among the artists featured were Licia Albanese, just a month after her New York debut, and the young Leonard Warren. Edward Johnson seized on the occasion to solicit contributions to the Metropolitan Opera Fund. Soon after the lifting of the World War II suspension of commercial television, the company was back in the game: *Otello*, opening night, November 29, 1948, was the first live telecast of a complete stage production in the history of the medium. Ramon Vinay and veteran TV hands Albanese and Warren led the cast. The auditorium had been wired for DC; alternating current had to be brought in to power cameras cooled by dry ice. The image was compromised by stage lighting often far dimmer than that specified for the lenses, by scenes too crowded for the small screens then current, by decrepit scenery, and by sweeping gestures calibrated to the expanse of the house. Although *Variety* screeched, "preem fizzles," the broad critical consensus was positive: "The view ... that came into one's living room frequently was more detailed and more revealing than that obtained from a seat 'down front' in the Metropolitan auditorium"; "a stirring experience, about five times as stirring, I should say off-hand, as *Otello* by radio alone." Live opera had taken to the medium. Two successive opening nights followed, *Der Rosenkavalier* and Bing's inaugural *Don Carlo*, before Texaco, balking at the cost, withdrew its support.[8]

Failing to secure commercial sponsorship, Bing tried closed-circuit theater television, the home of championship prize fights. The December 11, 1952, *Carmen* made its way to movie screens in twenty-seven cities. Despite uneven aural and visual quality, the results were encouraging enough to schedule a closed-circuit presentation of opening night 1954, acts from three operas chosen to show off the company. Sound and image had made notable strides, staging better accommodated the camera. Warren, in mufti, wearing television's obligatory blue shirt, sang the *Pagliacci* "prologo" to an estimated sixty thousand to seventy thousand spectators, some in formal dress, at giant movie palaces and small art cinemas, again across twenty-seven cities. But neither the artistic nor the financial rewards justified the continuation of the project. Bing would not give up. Capitalizing on the high profile opera enjoyed in the press, a gift from Maria Callas, he again turned to commercial network television and this time secured a contract for a series of spots on Ed Sullivan's popular "Toast of the Town," starting in November 1956. The variety show allotted an astonishingly generous sixteen minutes to Callas and George London for the act 2 duel-to-the-death of Tosca and Scarpia. Despite unflattering closeups and wretched sound, the video preserves the crackling encounter of these two singing-actors, as compelling today as they were more than a half-century ago. Yet the majority of Sullivan's immense audience, accustomed to a hodgepodge vaudeville lineup of acrobats, comics, and pop singers, reported switching to Steve Allen to hear Gene Autry instead, or to the tail end of Ted Mack's Original Amateur Hour. The Met's spots were cut back from five to four; on March 10, 1957, Sullivan reassured his public that the final segment, Tebaldi and Tucker in the act 4 *Andrea Chénier* duet, would last only four minutes. As it turned out, their splendid voices took up five minutes of Sullivan's airtime, just a bit longer than the ventriloquist Señor Wences and his dummy.[9]

On March 15, 1977, public television carried a performance of *La Bohème,* the first in the "Live from the Met" series. PBS was the right network; the medium was now capable of transmitting satisfactory images to large home screens; the sonics, particularly in FM stereo simulcast, did justice to Luciano Pavarotti, in peak form, as Rodolfo, and to the subtle inflections of Renata Scotto's Mimì. Starting in the mid-1980s, as a consequence of a long-sought agreement with its unions, the company could market these performances, first as videocassettes and Laserdiscs, and then as DVDs. Soon after, Peter Gelb, as the company's executive producer, had his first hands-on experience in filming the Met. The offerings, generally three a season, sometimes five or six, included *Carmen, Il Trovatore,* and *Don Giovanni,* but also rarities such as *Rise and Fall of the City of Mahagonny, Lulu, Idomeneo,* and *Francesca da Rimini.* PBS surrendered to falling ratings by scheduling only two telecasts between December 2001 and Volpe's farewell gala of May 2006. The times and technologies were ripe for reinvention.

In short order, Gelb sold "The Met: Live in HD" to a spectrum of stakeholders—board members, labor unions, and artists. His formula was this: transmissions would be "live," that is, simulcast in high-definition image and sound from the Met stage on Saturday afternoons via satellite to movie theaters and art centers across the United States and beyond. Ticket prices would be kept affordable; the series would be sustained through aggressive publicity. Exhibitors took some convincing:"From the start we told the theatres that we were not looking to attract movie audiences but opera audiences. . . . We urged them to think of it more as a live sporting event or a reality show, as a reality operatic show." On December 30, 2006, the first of six simulcasts, *Die Zauberflöte,* went out to ninety-eight screens and to an aggregate audience of twenty-one thousand; the second, *I Puritani,* to 123 screens; *The First Emperor* to 176; *Eugene Onegin* to 208. *Il Barbiere di Siviglia* was on view in 275 locations, and grossed $850,000, an average of more than $3,000 per screen; the average capacity reached 77 percent; Rossini would have been

FIGURE 41. *Madama Butterfly* simulcast on screen outside the Met, September 25, 2006 (courtesy Corbis)

eighteenth in *Billboard*'s weekly movie rankings. Each telecast cost between $850,000 and $1 million; at 50 percent of the receipts, the Met was due about $3 million from the 2006–07 series. Sponsors, donations, and $1 million from the company's coffers made up the difference. Despite the loss, by spring 2007, the existence of a significant niche audience for HD performances was indisputable. Opera would be a force in "alternative content," cheek by jowl with athletes and rock bands. *Variety* concluded, "After years on the ropes, high art is battling back. And it's the august Metropolitan Opera leading the way, cribbing moves from the pop culture playbook by wooing talent from other fields, adopting hip marketing strategies, exploiting ancillary revenue streams and otherwise throwing off elitist mantles." High art had met high tech in the person of the general manager moonlighting as executive producer. On simulcast Saturdays, Gelb could be found in the satellite truck whose controls monitor the thirteen cameras that capture the more than one thousand shots of each telecast.[10]

Seven countries, the United States aside, constituted the 2006–07 "The Met: Live in HD" network: Canada, Denmark, Germany, Japan, Norway, Sweden, and the United Kingdom. The next year saw the inclusion of

FIGURE 42. Peter Gelb, right, in production truck, simulcast of *Aïda,* Dec. 15, 2012 (© Marty Sohl)

Australia, Austria, Belgium, the Czech Republic, and the Netherlands. Venues at home and abroad grew each season until screens in spring 2013 numbered nineteen hundred spread over sixty-four countries on six continents; from the Homer Theatre in Homer, Alaska, to the Shanghai Grand in Shanghai, China, the Walter Reade only spitting distance from the Metropolitan itself, the Cairo Opera House, the Icaria in Barcelona, Spain, the CMAX in Devonport, Tasmania, the Teatro Nescafe de las Artes, Santiago, Chile, and the Roxy in Missoula, Montana. Gelb had signed exclusivity agreements with optimal venues everywhere, "preventing other opera companies from relaying their work on the same screens—hardly a collegiate move," the *Guardian* observed wryly. Gelb's response? "We don't force movie theatres to take our movies; we don't hold a gun to their heads. They could take the Royal Opera if they wanted to." David Gockley was philosophical: "I think Peter, with his media background with Sony and some of the colleagues he worked with saw the light before any of the rest of us did." Rival top-tier opera houses and festivals that attempted to get into the telecast act—La Scala, Covent Garden, and Salzburg, among others—settled principally for the transmission of previously recorded performances. Together with fellow newcomers to alternative content, ballet and theater, their product, often edgier than that of the Met, proved profitable to exhibitors on days and times otherwise fallow. And such became the popularity of the Met Saturday afternoon transmissions that many movie houses began to repeat the Met simulcasts as weekday "Encores."

The new medium provided the opera novice intimate contact with the forbidding art form, extracted from its inaccessible habitat, magnified, and subtitled, its ceremonial demystified by intermission interviews and shots of stagehands striking one set, erecting another. Satellite television preserved operagoing as a communal venture, collecting audiences to share the real time of performance in the Met's red and gold hall. By the same token, shots of the in-house spectators, most of whom had spent five to ten times the price of a HD admission for their seat, made the sociological divide between the two audiences emphatically clear, one observed surrounded by patrician splendor, the other left to its observation in ordinary surroundings. Still, it was not uncommon for attendees miles and time zones distant from New York to applaud, to shout "bravo" along with the privileged few thousand at Lincoln Center.

The telecasts were not without warts. There were those who objected to the sacrifice of the full stage to close-ups that exposed the more hapless singers as they strained for high notes and high volume. Some were disconcerted by the abrupt transition from the enchantment of the stage to the frenzy of backstage interviews. There were vagaries of sound and image reproduction, occasional interruptions or distortions in the satellite transmission, and the unwelcome smell of popcorn. The irremediable grief was the amplified acoustic, the electronic mediation between singers trained to project their voices without intervention and listeners frustrated at the interference of sound engineers. On the technologically leveled playing field, performers swamped by the orchestra in the house came through loud and clear at the multiplex. Without question, "Live in HD" was not the same as being there, as the host of each telecast was duty bound to insist. Gelb himself made the point: "It's like watching 'Monday Night Football.' You're getting extra information and commentary, but there is still no replacement for the visceral thrill, excitement, and sound of being at the actual opera house."[11]

## Stagings

The new productions of 2006–07 continued the drift away from the pictorialism ubiquitous in the years prior to the Volpe/Levine regime. Only *Il*

*Trittico* (April 20, 2007) could be counted, as Gelb described it, a "wedding-cake production." The general manager shoehorned a *Madama Butterfly* of his own choosing into his first opening night (Sept. 25, 2006), reviving the Bing tradition of kicking off the season with a new production. This *Butterfly* could not have been more unlike its 1994 investiture. Michael Scott's detailed Japanese house, leafy garden, and honest-to-goodness pond gave way to Michael Levine's unadorned box, its high-polished floor sloping upstage, a mirror slanted above to reflect the action. Sliding screens defined and redefined the spaces, minimal props were brought in as needed. As critical as the décor was the staging of Anthony Minghella, Oscar-winning director of *The English Patient,* in his opera debut. Minghella and his wife and collaborator, choreographer Carolyn Choa, brushed an already stylized mise-en-scène with borrowings from Bunraku theater. Their most wondrous invention was Trouble, Butterfly's son, a puppet artfully manipulated by three veiled puppeteers garbed in black. The patently artificial effigy of a Japanese-American boy in a sailor suit, fondled by his mother first in love and pride and then in grief, was infinitely more affecting than the flesh-and-blood prop conventionally carted about by Cio-Cio-San and her faithful Suzuki. Other details remain indelible: the entrance of Butterfly in a line of geishas appearing from below; the love duet in a garden of lanterns and bamboo stalks wielded by actor-dancers; the mimed opening of act 2, Pinkerton vanishing in the time it took for a screen to cover his exit, leaving behind an empty chair as a sign of his absence. Viewers would have been hard put to recall a more moving presentation of the opera or a more gorgeous series of stage pictures. With this sortie, Gelb kept his tricky promise: the Minghella/Levine *Butterfly* challenged the audience while shielding it from the "unpleasant artistic experiences" of regietheater commonly dubbed "Eurotrash." As Alex Ross wrote joyfully of the coproduction with the English National Opera and the Lithuanian National Opera, "for the duration of the gala, there was no more fabulous place on earth, which is as it should be."[12]

From the second night of the 2006–07 season to the start of 2009–10, the extent of Gelb's responsibility either for new productions or for the selection of repertoire, directors, designers, and casts, necessarily made years in advance, is difficult to calculate. Tan Dun's *The First Emperor* (Dec. 21, 2006) was a world premiere, and Richard Strauss's *Die Ägyptische Helena* had last been heard at the Met in 1928. Fan Yue's unit set for *The First Emperor,* a stage-filling staircase, bore the weight of Qin's resolve to unify China. Film director Zhang Yimou was left minimal downstage space to block the sketchy

FIGURE 43. Cristina Gallardo-Domâs as Cio-Cio-San with "Trouble" and puppeteer in *Madama Butterfly*, September 11, 2006 (© Ken Howard, 2006)

personal drama. The score called for the chant of a Beijing opera singer, the twang of the *zheng* (a Chinese zither), the thud and clank of various percussive surfaces, Tibetan singing bowls, and a giant bell stationed at the foot of the proscenium. Musical interest waned when the composer looked to the West: "The lyrical set pieces in *The First Emperor* are couched in a sickly sweet Americana idiom that sounds rather like watered-down Copland or Bernstein with a dash of Hollywood banality." Sixty-seven-year-old Domingo, his middle range still warm and secure, had nothing to fear from a role tailored to his bari-tenorial register. Despite Tan Dun's negative notices, spurred by Domingo's stardom *The First Emperor* did very well at the box office through its two-season run. *Die Ägyptische Helena* (March 15, 2007) was a vehicle for Deborah Voigt. The soprano had lost some of the gleam and thrust that had made her an authoritative Straussian. But even in prime vocal form, she would have strained to win an audience for the opera's riff on marriage and adultery, encumbered as it is by a ludicrous scenario. Director and designer David Fielding set the action (again!) "in a dream landscape . . . in the head of Aithra [the sorceress]. . . . It's as if the opera is driven by her own psychosis or psychoanalysis." Fielding's surrealist take—skewed walls, crooked doors, a flat etched with the silhouette of a man running, Helena's giant bed, the clash of business suits and classical gowns—was preferable to the exhausted alternative of cramming an irrational libretto into an ersatz depiction of an ancient civilization.[13]

It was Gelb who brought in Bartlett Sher, fresh from his Tony-nominated *A Light in the Piazza,* for *Il Barbiere di Siviglia* (Nov. 10, 2006). Sher's nimble staging of Rossini's opera buffa put Michael Yeargan's portable barbershop, moveable doors and orange trees, and floating balcony and staircase through their paces. The director and designer came up with an ingenious ramp that circled the pit, creating the intimacy wanted by comedy. Peter Mattei, Juan Diego Flórez, Diana Damrau, and the rest of the cast enacted the madcap goings-on with wit, and tossed off the fioritura with ease. For *Il Trittico* (April 20, 2007), Volpe had contracted Broadway heavy hitter and three-time Tony winner Jack O'Brien. But it was Gelb, heralding the advent of his era once again, who introduced O'Brien to the board on June 25, 2006. O'Brien bounced the ruses of *Gianni Schicchi* from thirteenth-century Italy to the Italian boom years of the 1950s, a perfect fit for the greedy tricksters tricked. Each of Douglas W. Schmidt's realistic sets drew applause: the bedchamber of *Gianni Schicchi* that sank below stage, giving way to a sunny terrace overlooking Florence; the barge of *Il Tabarro* jutting downstage, framed by a row of factory buildings and the high arch of a bridge; the cobblestoned convent courtyard of *Suor Angelica.* Two stands of rotating risers replaced the routine of crumbling Grecian columns in the *Orfeo ed Euridice* (May 2, 2007) of director Mark Morris and set designer Allen Moyers. Orfeo's pleated tunic gave way to couturier Isaac Mizrahi's modish black, the winged Amore flew earthward in sneakers and spangled shirt, the dancers were turned out like twenty-somethings on a gambol in the park. Stacked in the bleachers were choristers costumed as Cleopatra, Shakespeare, Garbo, Honest Abe, Jackie O., Princess Di, and on and on, witness to the timelessness of the Orpheus myth. Morris's playful choreography made its strongest effect in the happy finale. The run was dedicated to mezzo-soprano Lorraine Hunt Lieberson who had been scheduled to play the lead. At her death in July 2006, the role passed to countertenor David Daniels.[14]

That first exciting year, along with HD simulcasts that projected the newly reerected Great Wall of China, the reconceived Sevillian farrago, and the restored Puccini triptych onto movie screens, Gelb programmed video transmissions of *Die Zauberflöte* and *Eugene Onegin,* among the most conspicuous stagings of the Volpe era, and for Anna Netrebko, the Met's newest star, *I Puritani.*

## Star Vehicles

At the board meeting of January 19, 2006, Gelb announced that he had assurances of two productions per season, on average, from Renée Fleming, Marcello Giordani, Susan Graham, Karita Mattila, Anna Netrebko, René Pape, and Bryn Terfel, and further, that these top draws would sing longer into each run. As never before, in promoting itself the company would promote its most bankable assets. In 2006 an anonymous geisha was displayed on the sides of Metropolitan Transit Authority buses; in 2007 millions of New Yorkers and Big Apple tourists gaped from the sidewalks at Natalie Dessay as Lucia ("You'd Be Mad to Miss It"), in 2008 at Fleming as Thaïs, in 2009 at Mattila as Tosca, in 2010 at Terfel as Wotan, in 2011 at Netrebko as Anna Bolena, in 2012 at Jonas Kaufmann as Parsifal.

Within a few months, visual media in its various expressions had come to define Met stardom. True, it had been decades since a voice, if great enough, was all it took and a diva could brush off the director with impunity, as Zinka Milanov had Margaret Webster. Equally true was that the history of the Met was replete with wonderful singers who were also charismatic actors, among them Jean de Reszke, Emma Calvé, and Antonio Scotti in the Gilded Age, Olive Fremstad, Geraldine Farrar, and Fyodor Chaliapin in the early 1900s, Maria Jeritza and Lawrence Tibbett, who made their debuts in the 1920s, Regina Resnik, Risë Stevens, Astrid Varnay, Licia Albanese, and Ljuba Welitsch in the 1940s, and since then Hildegard Behrens, Maria Callas, Leonie Rysanek, Renata Scotto, Teresa Stratas, Shirley Verrett, and Jon Vickers. As far back as the 1890s, with the end of the German seasons, critic W. J. Henderson had issued this warning: "The Italian singer is always a singer, and he conceives it to be his divine right to face the footlights, sing directly to the audience, and dwell on all his high notes. . . . This style of thing, however, is dead in New York" (*Times*, March 22, 1891). To stand and sing, as Henderson had formulated it, or "park and bark," as Gelb and others delighted in calling "this style of thing," was not at all dead at the end of the nineteenth century. It would soon be outmoded to oppose the wooden Verdian to the thespian Wagnerian, a vanishing breed once the resurrected star system displaced the ensemble. At about the same time, Edmund Stanton protested that the audience would "not tolerate the old-fashioned style of operatic art, in which every illusion of the stage is sacrificed to the display of the voice." For decades, audiences did more than tolerate it; in the main, they lived with it quite happily.[15]

The lineup Gelb promised the board in 2006 affirmed that, under his producer's eye, the whole star package, image and acting, voice and technique, would be the rule, not the exception. Voigt's journey served as an object lesson: fired in 2004 from a Covent Garden *Ariadne auf Naxos,* ostensibly because the little black dress the director had in mind would have fit incongruously on her large frame, Voigt risked gastric bypass surgery and reset the trajectory of her career. Together with Renée Fleming, Natalie Dessay, Susan Graham, Patricia Racette, and Sondra Radvanovsky, she not only has starred in several simulcasts, but has been the presenter of many of the Saturday intermission features.

As early as 2004, Gelb had determined to hoist one name to the top of his A-list. Sometime after his appointment, he flew to Vienna to meet with Anna Netrebko; over lunch, he proposed to make the young Russian soprano "the star of the Met," a postmodern *prima donna assoluta.* By the end of 2012–13, she was tied with Fleming, twelve years her senior, for the HD lead; each had chalked up eight telecasts. Fleming had long been marketed as a beautiful woman with "The Beautiful Voice," the title of one of her best-selling CDs, and not as an exceptional actress. What the audience took away from her opening night gala (Sept. 22, 2008), the first to honor a single artist, was the sound of her velvety timbre and the sight of her as Violetta, Manon, and *Capriccio*'s Madeleine in well-publicized costumes created for the occasion by a trio of high-fashion designers. Netrebko, by contrast, was acknowledged as "a natural actress blessed with sensational looks," "a true stage animal," labels rarely affixed to opera singers. And when they are, for better or for worse, it is in consequence of some memorable bit of stage business. Geraldine Farrar, for example, captured the sweetness of *Königskinder*'s heroine by tending a gaggle of geese; Maria Jeritza will forever be associated with Tosca by her "Vissi d'arte" delivered face down on the floor; the place of Marjorie Lawrence in Met lore was assured by her equestrian ride into the flames of Siegfried's funeral pyre. Netrebko's moment was recorded in her first telecast, *I Puritani* (Jan. 6, 2007). In a gesture some dismissed as grandstanding and others found breathtaking, near the climax of Elvira's mad scene, the soprano ran to the lip of the stage and then lay on her back, as if in the throes of desire for her absent lover, her long hair dangling into the orchestra pit. As she explained with her customary bluntness, "Was crazy, no? But felt good. Yes, was my idea. I agree to sing this opera, then open score and don't like, it's crap, I want to cancel. And Met production was so dull, stage director no help. I had to do something, so I get on floor."[16]

Of greater import than Netrebko's coup de théâtre was the whole of the performance. Her dissing of one of Bellini's richest works notwithstanding, she stayed in character throughout, inhabiting the deranged world of the febrile English damsel with palpable sincerity. Movie audiences enjoyed at least one advantage over those at the Met that afternoon: they were privy to the emotions inflected on Netrebko's face and in her smallest movements. She showed no concern for the next coloratura hurdle, played not to the audience but to her colleagues on stage, and avoided stock postures and the exaggerated expressions that close-ups often render irritating to the telepublic. During a *Puritani* intermission, the star made plain that she was as much a screen as a stage animal; she was acutely aware of the camera and gauged her attitudes accordingly. Netrebko is in top form for the telecasts of the 2011–12 season, sensitive to the many moods of Manon (April 7) and to the regal dignity of Anna Bolena (Oct. 15). Massenet's transgressive protagonist emerges in all her complexity: naïve, pensive, conflicted, ironic, seductive, forlorn. And for *Bolena,* in what is certainly her most moving HD performance, Netrebko revisits the on-again, off-again lunacy of Elvira and Lucia, but on the tragic plane befitting a queen facing the executioner's block with the defiance born of pride.

It was another singing actress, Natalie Dessay, who reaped the extraordinary exposure of three new bel canto productions in just two seasons, 2007 to 2009. Chicago-based director Mary Zimmerman signed *Lucia di Lammermoor* (Sept. 24, 2007), a title that had long awaited a passable staging. What it got in the end was no better than a mixed bag. Zimmerman piled on distracting inventions: the ghost of a murdered girl (to dramatize Lucia's act 1 narrative), a wedding photographer (to shoot the stasis of the sextet), a physician (to administer a hypodermic to the unhinged protagonist), and the ghost of Lucia herself (to assist in Edgardo's suicide). More successful was the mad scene staged on Daniel Ostling's skeletal staircase and balcony, the site of Lucia's anguished entry into the bridal chamber, and then of her precipitous descent into insanity. The press received the director's efforts with greater warmth than did Dessay, openly critical of Zimmerman's inexperience.

By the time of *La Sonnambula* (March 2, 2009), director and diva were on the same page. Neither was disposed to take seriously the story of an innocent maiden who walks in her sleep; the victim of ignorance and prejudice, a vessel of pathos, became the target of their derision. Dessay had admonished early on, "whatever you do, don't set it in a Swiss village," and Zimmerman had obliged with a contemporary New York rehearsal studio. She turned Amina into a hip soprano, armed with cell phone and shades, winking along with her stage coconspirators both at the character she plays and, more generally, at Romantic sensibility. Here and there, she resorted to low comedy, a register discordant with the elegiac score. The heavy hand of her ironic rereading came close to annihilating Bellini. Thankfully, the director rose to the two sleepwalking scenes: in the first, the spotlighted somnambulist wandered down a long aisle of the Met's orchestra floor; in the second, she teetered on the ledge outside the windows of the rehearsal space. The third of the Dessay vehicles, *La Fille du régiment* (April 21, 2008), directed by Laurent Pelly, was, on the other hand, ideally suited to low comedy. In dingy undershirt and trousers, sprouting a Raggedy-Ann braid, the French soprano reveled in the slapstick, all the while sharing tender moments with bel canto paragon Juan Diego Flórez who was regularly called to encore his nine high Cs. An endless clothesline hung with the regiment's underwear, sleepy servants dusting to a slow waltz, and a tank coming to the rescue at the climax were just a few of Pelly's hilarious sight gags. Donizetti's opéra-bouffe was everyone's delight, a virtual sellout.[17]

## Other Stagings

In what has become a commonplace of reinvestiture, the fourth-century Hellenic Egypt of *Thaïs* (Dec. 28, 2008) was updated to something like the 1890s—when the work was first heard—to the detriment of the outcome. The opera's libretto instructs the lubricious courtesan to strike poses still thought daring in 1907 when Mary Garden stood admiringly before her mirror at Hammerstein's Manhattan Opera House. One hundred years later, neither Fleming's beauty nor her seductive song could prevent early-twentieth-century scandal from devolving into twenty-first-century camp. Like *Thaïs, La Rondine* (Dec. 31, 2008) was a well-traveled retro production created for a specific diva, Angela Gheorghiu, who would sing it in multiple venues. The eight remaining new productions of 2007–09 bore the mark of contemporary practice. None could be mistaken for the decorative shows that were Met specialties only a decade or so earlier. The black-and-white *Macbeth* (Oct. 22, 2007), in which the witches sported the pocketbooks and bobby socks of 1950s bag ladies, dripped with blood; the gritty, Goyaesque *Trovatore* (Feb. 16, 2009) bristled with violence and eroticism, its revolving set riot with camp followers and buffed blacksmiths naked to the waist. The nightmarish *Hänsel und Gretel* (Dec. 24, 2007) was hell-bent on terrifying children far in excess of the tale's demands. The tormented protagonist of *Peter Grimes* (Feb. 28, 2008) found himself oppressed throughout by a wall of weather-beaten boards as threatening as the community they represented.[18]

*Iphigénie en Tauride* (Nov. 27, 2007) had been given in 1916–17 in German, in a version by Richard Strauss; *La Damnation de Faust* (Nov. 7, 2008), it too effectively a company premiere, had stopped at the Met in concert performances in 1896 and in a 1906 staging for Farrar early in her debut season. On Thomas Lynch's rough-hewn unit set for the Temple of Diana, Stephen Wadsworth's mise-en-scène for *Iphigénie* infused graphic realism into the classical subject. Oreste was the thirty-seventh Met role appropriated by Domingo, only his second in an eighteenth-century opera. *La Damnation de Faust,* conceived for the concert hall, is a series of arias, ensembles, and bravura pieces for orchestra. For his initial Met assignment, Robert Lepage devised startling stage pictures: acrobats striding horizontally from floor to ceiling and then ceiling to floor (a nod to the director's collaboration with the Cirque du Soleil), soldiers marching backward, sylphs swimming under water, and replicated silhouettes of Faust and Méphistophélès on their ride to Hell, all framed in tiers of stacked boxes. New technologies connected projections of virtual scenery to the music through microphones and motion sensors. Lepage's gadgetry made an intriguing, occasionally forceful case for staging a work meant to appeal to the mind's eye. That said, his visuals eclipsed the protagonists: "All these devices remain external to the drama itself. Like a painting with brilliantly executed background and accessories but blank faces, the production often treats the three principals as supporting players."[19]

The Gluck and the Berlioz, as well as the company inaugurals of Philip Glass's *Satyagraha* and John Adams's *Doctor Atomic* , made good on the old pledge of repertory expansion. *Satyagraha* abstains from conventional narration. The subject is Gandhi's awakening to nonviolent resistance. The Sanskrit text, drawn from the Bhagavad-Gita, tells the story not of the Mahatma's political struggle as enacted on the stage, but of his spiritual journey. Director Phelim McDermott and designer Julian Crouch contrived their staggering production from homely materials consonant with Gandhi's message of love and hope for the downtrodden: newsprint, corrugated metal—and tape. As Anne Midgette describes it: "In the final act, singers crossed the stage with rolls of packing tape, unrolling them at all different heights, until the whole space was filled with dozens of shimmering

FIGURE 44. *Satyagraha,* act 2, 2008 (© Beth Bergman 2008, NYC)

bands, vibrating like the music around them; this whole construct was eventually crumpled into a small ball, showing visuals as ephemeral as the passing notes." Glass's musical patterns and the cast's ritualized movements led inexorably to the sublime logic of the final scene: singing a repeated rising phrase, Gandhi stands at the foot of a podium upon which Martin Luther King Jr., facing upstage, preaches in silence. Penny Woolcock set much of *Doctor Atomic* against tiers of portals, a structure reminiscent of the stacked boxes of *La Damnation de Faust,* and the walls of *Peter Grimes* and *Satyagraha.* Led masterfully by Alan Gilbert, the drama of anxiety over the horrific effects of the atom bomb is played out between government officials and researchers at Los Alamos, and privately in the bedroom and soul of the project chief. The silken tone and the barely contained intensity of Gerald Finley's J. Robert Oppenheimer kept the balance between the lover of poetry and the conflicted scientist.[20]

RECESSION: 2009–2011

In the first two years of Gelb's stewardship, the Met's budget had grown more than 16 percent from the $221.7 million of fiscal year 2006, the last of the

Volpe era, to $258.2 million in fiscal year 2008. Whether the path Gelb had charted was sustainable was open to mounting question. Gelb responded that he had anticipated losses in years one, two, and three. In 2008–09, the operating budget surged again, this time to approximately $282 million, roughly quadruple that of San Francisco, the next largest opera company in the hemisphere. Ballooning expenditures, the explanation went, were due to the increased number of new productions and to costly media initiatives. At the same time, there were signs that validated Gelb's high-wire mantra— you have to spend money to make money. Following six years of declines, capacity in 2006–07 climbed to nearly 84 percent from the dispiriting 77 percent of 2005–06; revenues, too, were higher. The next year, the annual report put capacity at a heartening 88.1 percent.[21]

The onset of the Great Recession in fall 2008 came just as Gelb was set to announce plans for 2009–10, the first season entirely under his purview. He spelled out the Metropolitan's plight in a January 2009 interview: The endowment was down by a third from $300 million, donations were off by $10 million, ticket sales were expected to miss goals by several million more. Gelb said he had taken a 10 percent cut, a step that did little to quell grumbling over his $1.5 million in salary, benefits, pension, and expense account; 10 percent cuts in pay for the rest of the staff would take effect at the end of the fiscal year; he would seek concessions from the Met's many unions— shades of the draconian actions taken by Gatti-Casazza in the early 1930s and the dire measures threatened in 1975 by Anthony Bliss. Four revivals were scheduled for the season to come, 2009–10: *The Ghosts of Versailles* and *Benvenuto Cellini*, both expensive shows, would be replaced with familiar works, and *Lady Macbeth of Mtsensk* and *Die Frau ohne Schatten* with the less costly *Ariadne auf Naxos* and *Elektra*. Plans to raise ticket prices would be shelved.[22]

The gravity of the situation came home to the public in March 2009 with the news that the Met had put up its Chagall murals as collateral on a $35 million loan, "a decision of last resort," according to one board member. The bank had judged the shriveled nest egg inadequate guarantee on its note. The endowment had been drawn down by more than 8 percent in 2008–09 and would be again in 2009–10, amounts in perilous excess of the 5 percent sanctioned for not-for-profits. The following spring, Gelb owned that even the $30 million unrestricted donation of board member Ann Ziff, the largest in Met history, was "not enough to save us" (*Times,* Mar. 27, 2010). When the last word was in on 2009–10, the Met's operating budget of $289.8 million had surpassed that of any other arts organization in the city. And the deficit had spiraled upward to $47 million. Dependency on donations, and especially on the purses of managing directors, had reached the point that half the budget rested on the shoulders of development; for every dollar spent, something less than one dollar had to be raised. In fiscal 2009, contributions accounted for 45.3 percent, up from 38 percent in 2005, ticket sales for only 33.1 percent. In 2010–11, contributions grew again by an astonishing 50 percent to $182 million. Still, the debt, the endowment (in three years, $61.5 million had been redirected to operating expenses), and the underfinanced pension accounts continued to be enormously worrisome, especially in the face of the $325 million operating budget and further declines in capacity: from the 87.9 percent of 2008–09 to 83.2 percent in 2009–10 and then to 79.2 percent in 2010–11, only two percentage points above Volpe's nadir. If the depth of the recession had sent the Met staggering, it had dealt a deathblow to many other performing arts organizations, driving the New York City Opera out of Lincoln Center (and eventually out of business) and shutting down Baltimore Opera, Connecticut Opera, and Opera Boston, among others.[23]

Gelb claimed one bit of good news: the average age of the audience had fallen to sixty-two or sixty-three, presumably from the earlier estimate of sixty-six. More impressive was the success of the HD simulcasts. In fiscal 2011, profits reached $11 million, after, as Gelb explained, "we've covered all of the incremental production costs including cameras and satellite, and payments to artists and unions." He forecast the sale of three million tickets globally in 2011–12; the ten-millionth ticket would be issued in that season. As the sixth simulcast year was just underway, he "acknowledged for the first time" what so many had maintained from the outset, "that competition from the HD transmissions may have cannibalized [a term Gelb later repeated and ultimately regretted] box office sales, particularly from people in nearby cities like Boston, who might have traveled to New York before." Gelb would test this and related hypotheses through a summer 2012 survey circulated to Met members via e-mail. Among the queries related to the impact of HD on house attendance was this: "Overall, since attending Live in HD has your attendance at Met Opera House performances increased significantly, increased slightly, not changed, decreased slightly, decreased significantly?" Several questions touched on productions—are they "consistently excellent"? "highly innovative"? is "production quality slipping"? The Met's press office has declined to make the survey results available. At one point, Gelb did admit that data showed that opera was, generally speaking, not new to the

HD public, which seemingly means that the telecasts had not, by and large, created a new public for opera. In late 2012, with the first bond sale in the Met's by now nearly 130-year history, company finances drew press attention once again. In the context of the slow recovery and growing operating expenses and losses, management looked to raise $100 million; $63.2 million would go to repay loans extended by Bank of America, the balance toward operating expenses and renovations. As Moody's reported in assigning the bonds its seventh highest rating, A3, if the Met's "uncommonly high amount of donor support" was a strength, the company's "high reliance on gift revenue" was a "challenge."[24]

## Stagings

Eight new productions would be on the calendar for 2009–10 and seven more for 2010–11, a number unparalleled in eighty years. However painful the belt-tightening exacted by the recession, it would not interfere with Gelb's program of repertoire renewal. The first season totally of Gelb's devising opened with a new *Tosca* (Sept. 21, 2009), a collaboration between Swiss director Luc Bondy and French designer Richard Peduzzi. There was no escaping the two Puccini comparisons that would either buoy or sink this *Tosca*'s reception, one with the fascinating 2006 *Madama Butterfly,* the other with the 1985 Zeffirelli *Tosca* Gelb had vowed to replace. As it turned out, the Bondy/Peduzzi effort got the worst of both matchups. It drowned in an ocean of boos that reverberated in furious notices: "The Met's New Twist on *Tosca?* It's the Audience That Gets the Knife"; "an uneven, muddled, weirdly dull production that interferes fatally with the working of Puccini's perfect contraption"; "puny and halfhearted." The *Times* called it "A Kinky Take on a Classic," and faulted Bondy for turning "the twisted, complex Scarpia into a cartoonish lecher." When the production reached the Bavarian State Opera in 2010, a Vienna paper shouted "Schweinerei" (trash); when it got to La Scala in 2012, a Milanese headline sputtered, "Volgare verismo." One or two European publications found some good in the New York performances. A Zurich correspondent was taken with the staging's "refreshingly blasphemous edge," and *Opera Britannia* with the "life and relevance" the production lent the work. But for once, the favorable views from abroad were not attributable to the American-European divide over regietheater. This *Tosca* was no rereading of a beloved title rejected by unreconstructed conservatives; it was, in essence, nothing more than an extreme refitting.

For its part, the Bondy/Peduzzi production made no pretense to a radical reinterpretation of the text, let alone to an ideological subtext. Instead, the artistic team lodged its claim to originality in drastic mutations of the scenario. In act 1, a huge painting of the bare-breasted Magdalene hung on the otherwise unadorned brick walls of an inauthentic Sant'Andrea della Valle as it waited to be slashed by a jealous Floria Tosca. Not to be outdone, a statue of the Virgin waited to be kissed on the lips by a sex-crazed Scarpia. In act 2, red divans provided a garish setting for three prostitutes invented to minister to Scarpia's every pleasure. To the puzzlement of the audience, Bondy discarded the time-honored stage business wherein Tosca sets candlesticks by the body of the freshly murdered police chief, throws a crucifix onto his chest, and stealthily makes her exit. In its place, he had Tosca climb to a window, contemplate suicide, think better of it, and then repair to one of the divans to fan herself as she gathered her wits until the curtain finally fell. At the end of act 3, a Tosca double attached to a wire leaped from the parapet of the Castel Sant'Angelo and hung in midair, affecting a pointless freeze-frame.[25]

In numbers too great to be ignored, the crowd in the orchestra, the galleries, and even on the plaza staring at the giant screen exercised the prerogative of booing that—though common to other arenas of spectatorship, theatrical and sporting—is the signature privilege of opera. The history of this tradition has its own three acts: the first targeted the composer, the second, particularly popular at Bing's Met, the singer. The third, the booing of productions, is a phenomenon of recent vintage, that is, since designers and directors have had the freedom to ignore convention as they put their own stamp on décor and staging. Booing greeted the 1979 *Fliegende Holländer,* whose action, from start to finish, took place in the dream of the Steersman; the 1982 *Macbeth,* a Halloween-fest complete with witches flying about on broomsticks; the 1992 *Lucia,* whose heroine had to enact her mad scene all by herself; the 2000 comic book *Trovatore;* and most recently the contemptuous 2009 *Sonnambula.* Gelb's response to the noisy *Tosca* controversy? Subscribing to the timeless maxim that it is preferable to be spoken of ill than not to be spoken of at all, he was gratified at so much attention from the media, only much later conceding that *Tosca* had been a "fiasco." Zeffirelli's take? That Bondy was "not second rate. He's third rate" (*Post,* Sept. 23, 2009). Bondy rebutted, "I'm a third-rate director, and he is a second assistant of Visconti" (*Times,* Sept. 23, 2009).[26]

Unlike *Tosca,* the other refittings of the period, *Carmen* (Dec. 31, 2009) and *Boris Godunov* (Oct. 11, 2010) originating at the Met, and Ambroise Thomas's *Hamlet* (March 16, 2010) and *Don Carlo* (Nov. 22, 2010) coming from Barcelona and London, were standard productions at their core. They shared largely positive notices. It made little difference that Bizet's opera was fast-forwarded by almost a century to the Spanish Civil War. What mattered more was the extensively retouched portrait of Carmen herself, no longer the hip-swinging gypsy, but a woman so confident in her alluring individuality that she carried off the "Habanera" seated, casually washing her smock and then her feet in a bucket of water. Carmen (Elina Garanča) and Don José (Roberto Alagna) kept their wrenching appointment with fate, brilliantly staged by British director Richard Eyre, beneath the threatening overhang of the Plaza de Toros, one of Rob Howell's four superb sets. Known to New York for her elegant Rossini, Garanča applied musical rectitude and her creamy, equalized voice to the passionate protagonist. Yannick Nézet-Séguin, soon to be named music director of the Philadelphia Orchestra, made an auspicious debut. But alas, this edition of *Carmen* succumbed, as did many Met productions, to the apparently irresistible temptation to mime the purely orchestral passages of the score. Well before Gelb, overtures and preludes had been taken as invitations to enact what composers intended to be heard and not seen. Such passages were sometimes funny (Sher's for *Il Barbiere di Siviglia* and *Le Comte Ory*), sometimes arresting (Decker's for *La Traviata*), often no more than distracting. The *Carmen* inserts were among the most egregious. For the preludes to act 1 and act 3, Christopher Wheeldon choreographed smoldering pas de deux so explicitly erotic that the music receded into mere accompaniment to the dance. And Eyre took the false step of cutting away from what should have been the opera's final image, the distraught lover cradling the inert body of the woman he has just stabbed. The stage revolved to disclose the interior of the bull ring, spectators in the stands, the toreador Escamillo, his sword pointed at the slain bull. Unforgettable, yes, but better forgotten. The searing climax of Bizet's masterpiece had turned into a tacky coup de théâtre.

The refittings of *Hamlet, Boris Godunov,* and *Don Carlo,* all comparatively uncontroversial, shared a stripped-down aesthetic that permitted the free and rapid movement of singers and sets. Unadorned walls rearranged in full view of the audience, or lowered from above, redefined locales. The focus fell on text and interpretation, and on the music, of course. *Hamlet*'s principals, led by Simon Keenlyside's melancholy Dane, carried off the melodrama with panache, and no one more than Marlis Petersen, the Ophélie, called in after the final dress rehearsal to replace the indisposed Dessay. In the withering, twenty-minute-long mad scene, the score's best pages, she rendered the pain of derangement in high notes that bordered on hysteria, and in a display of grizzly self-mutilation that covered her breast, arms, and white nightgown in blood. At the conclusion, Ophélie lay prone on the ground, blanketed by flowers, in a chilling simulation of drowning. René Pape, the preeminent bass of his generation, was at once an imperious Boris and a czar of human dimension, most poignantly in the scenes with his children. The sum of the many excellent parts of this production might well have been greater had Stephen Wadsworth not been saddled with sets conceived for the famed German director Peter Stein. Stein had withdrawn from the assignment the previous July, citing rude treatment from the consular bureaucrat responsible for processing his work visa and his distaste for Gelb and the Met: "I'm not used to working in a factory" (*Times*, Sept. 4, 2010). Nicholas Hytner's *Don Carlo* respected the work's majesty, made sense of its complex mesh of love and politics, and found something of a solution for the opera's problematic ending. The libretto stipulates that a friar, actually the ghost of Emperor Charles V, drag Don Carlo into the tomb. Here, instead, Carlo duels with the king's guard, is mortally wounded, and dies in the arms of his beloved Elisabetta as the ghost appears.[27]

Three high-concept rereadings unveiled between the winters of 2009 and 2010, *Les Contes d'Hoffmann* (Dec. 3, 2009), *Attila* (Feb. 23, 2010), and *La Traviata* (Dec. 31, 2010), fueled the debate around stagings. Broadway's Sher and Yeargan returned for Offenbach. The concept was that E. T. A. Hoffmann, an analogue for Franz Kafka, was, like the Prague-born novelist and the Cologne-born composer, a Jew, an outsider. But Hoffmann as Kafka failed to emerge with purpose from a flood of disordered detail. To the derby hats of 1920s Mittel-Europa, Sher added Federico Fellini grotesques, clowns, and prostitutes. The director granted that he had not had "enough time to . . . get [it] right." He had been pressured by a company strapped for money and time enough to mount a whopping eight new productions in one season. And the cast was less lustrous than promised. Rolando Villazón, felled by a vocal crisis, was replaced by the affecting Joseph Calleja. Anna Netrebko , contracted for the poet's four loves, bowed out of two, retaining only Antonia, the consumptive singer, and the mimed role of Stella. René Pape decided to forgo the four villains altogether. If the reception of *Les Contes d'Hoffmann* was poor, worse still were the notices for the lustily booed *Attila* at its company premiere. The audience was accustomed to stagings of Verdi's early works that cleaved to the letter of the scenario. Here, the high-fashion costumes of Miuccia Prada and the décor of hip architects Jacques Herzog and Pierre de Meuron smothered the narrative. The team's "post-Apocalyptic" construction of "political instability," of the "contrasts between the old and new world and the clash of religions," took a backseat to the look of the production: a magnificently arranged pile of rubble and tremendous wall of foliage. Director Pierre Audi was left with little space to play out the drama. The principals, dressed in Prada's outlandish leather and fur, had nowhere to go, no option, save to "park and bark," pace Gelb. The *Wall Street Journal* called the "stage picture . . . all concept and no theater—a monumental and bizarre creation in which the singers interacted with neither the set nor each other." Only that paragon of Verdi conductors, Riccardo Muti (in his Met debut), came off with distinction.[28]

Willy Decker's *La Traviata* trailed the prestige of the full-blown regie-theater production that was the darling of critics and public at its 2005 Salzburg premiere. Many at the Met saw this *Traviata* as a Eurotrash challenge to the performance practice of the third-most-frequently-programmed opera in the repertoire. The director emptied the stage of whatever might distract from his concept: that the protagonist is stalked by two implacable forces, her illness and the patriarchal society that engulfs her. Banished were the picturesque mock-ups of nineteenth-century France indulged in previous editions, notably in Zeffirelli's two extravagant antecedents; the luxurious ballroom, the charming country hideaway, the splendid gambling house, and the dying woman's bedroom were jettisoned in favor of a bare, curved wall, a bench, a few boxy modern sofas, and a giant clock. Violetta exchanged her long gowns for a short red dress and white slip. The dumb show enacted at the start prefigured the end. As the conductor gave the downbeat, Violetta entered, staggered slowly across the stage, doubled over in pain, and then collapsed into the arms of her aged doctor, an incarnation of death whose recurring presence would haunt the action. When the final notes of the mournful prelude faded away, the chorus of menacing merrymakers, males and females dressed alike as men in dark business suits, was propelled by the feverish rhythm toward the lone, frightened woman in red. A moment later, she morphed into the dissolute party girl. As one critic wrote, even if some of the director's "reconceptions . . . are as heavy-handed as the melodramatic clichés he abhors in traditional productions," this was "an involving and theatrically daring production that belongs at the Met." *La Traviata* became a high-profile addition to the company's slim stock of illuminating rereadings.[29]

FIGURE 45. Natalie Dessay as Violetta in act 1, *La Traviata,* March 30, 2012 (© Marty Sohl)

Lastly, from 2009 to 2011, the Met fielded five company premieres. We discussed in chapter 9 Janáček's *From the House of the Dead* and Shostakovich's *The Nose,* continuations of the Slavic project. Two more were entries in the bel canto expansion, Rossini's *Armida* and *Le Comte Ory,* and one was American, Adams's *Nixon in China.* For *Armida,* apparently still unpersuaded that music, words, Met Titles, program notes, and above all the imagination of the audience could be trusted, Zimmerman once again reached for cue cards. This time it took "Ballo" to tell us that a ballet was about to begin, and "Fine" to alert us that the final curtain was falling, echos of her enervating use of the blackboard in *La Sonnambula. Opera News* saw "the thumbprint of her staging [as] a busyness that trivializes music Rossini intended to be noble and mocks music he intended to be fantastical." Zimmerman's condescension to the material was seconded by Richard Hudson's jocular design for the gates of Jerusalem; his pleasure palace and garden were barren, uninviting places of purported enchantment. The flamboyantly arduous Armida that had given Fleming a hand up as she rose to international stardom in 1993 now obliged the soprano to a degree of caution that compromised Rossini's incisive line. The composer got all he asked from Lawrence Brownlee and several other of the six bel canto tenors the opera prescribes. The Met premiere of *Le Comte Ory,* it too originating at Lincoln Center, recalled once again Sher and

Yeargan, the team that had restored the fizz to *Il Barbiere di Siviglia*. Their version of Rossini's French bedroom farce was witty and well paced. A crotchety prompter, kin to the sleepy servant Ambrogio much in evidence in *Il Barbiere,* presided over a nineteenth-century theater where birds flew, castles materialized, and storms raged through tricks as transparent as the nun's habit donned by the raunchy count. Direction and music coalesced uproariously—and sublimely—in the trio for Ory, his young aide Isolier, and the Countess Adèle, object of the passionate affections of both master and page. Flórez, Joyce DiDonato, and Diana Damrau executed the intricate threesome choreographed for Adèle's bed, all the while carrying off the filigree of Rossini's fioritura.[30]

Peter Sellars's staging of *Nixon in China,* imported from the English National Opera, re-created its 1987 Houston world premiere. Sellars was joined at the Met by his original collaborators, designer Adrianne Lobel, choreographer Mark Morris, John Adams, conducting his own score, and James Maddalena, who had been the first to play the thirty-seventh president. The sets bore the imprint of photographs of the 1972 encounter of Nixon and Henry Kissinger with Mao Tse-tung and Chou En-lai. In Sellars's blocking of the final scene, the world leaders and their wives, on beds lined up side by side, meditate on the intersections of their private lives and clashing cultures. By 2010, *Nixon in China* had shaken off the hostility it had first aroused. It now wore the patina of an indigenous classic.

## POWER AND PERFORMANCE: 2011–2013

We bracket the initial half-dozen years of Gelb's regime with two pieces by Alex Ross, one of October 9, 2006, "Metamorphosis," and the other of May 23, 2012, "Crack-up at the Met." The first flattered Gelb with a comparison to the visionary Otto Kahn, and continued, "For time out of mind, the Met has been a stately and secretive place, impenetrable yet strangely predictable, where stars have sung in plush productions of standard operas, to the accompaniment of minimum publicity. . . . The old behemoth is suddenly . . . flying by night in high style." Six years later, referring to Gelb's clumsy move to silence *Opera News* criticism of Met performances, Ross suggested that "America's leading opera company was cracking up in public." In the interim, Gelb had consolidated the power he had become famous for exerting over the many facets of the company's operations. He emerged not only as the Met's CEO, producer, marketer, and executive producer of HD simulcasts, but also as its director of productions. To Anthony Tommasini's suggestion that he bring in a stage professional in the manner of John Dexter, Gelb replied, "I am the director of productions. I hope you will accept that" (*Times*, April 4, 2012).[31]

Levine's consuming commitment to the Metropolitan was no longer beyond question. In 2004, with his appointment as music director of the Boston Symphony Orchestra, he had relinquished his post as artistic director to reassume the lighter cloak of music director. A series of medical crises conspired to limit his presence at Lincoln Center further. In March 2006, there was the tear of his rotator cuff caused by the fall in Boston. In 2008, a malignant cyst required the removal of a kidney. At this point, Levine had taken to conducting seated at the podium. Three back surgeries followed, occasioning frequent cancellations and, in 2011, his resignation from the BSO. Its management and the orchestra, not to mention the Boston press and public, were undisposed to the patience shown by his own profoundly indebted Metropolitan community. A more calamitous fall in August 2011 resulted in a severe spinal injury. Levine had no alternative but to cancel all performances for 2011–12. Fabio Luisi, guest conductor since spring 2010, was appointed principal conductor. However much respected by the orchestra and admired by the audience, Luisi had little clout. In late 2011, responding to a comment that "from the outside, it's hard to say who's directing the musical operation," he confided, "it's not easy to understand from the inside either," adding almost bemused, "sometimes the administration invites me to sit in on auditions." Levine's health kept him from the Met podium for a second season, 2012–13. In an unusually forthright interview in fall 2012, he spoke of his inability to walk and "acknowledged what many had suspected for a while," that since 1994 he had had "a nonprogressive condition related to Parkinson's disease that causes hand tremors, which his doctors called 'benign Parkinsonism.'" He would lead the Metropolitan orchestra in Carnegie Hall in May 2013 (which he did to a dithyrambic reception) and was scheduled for *Wozzeck, Così fan tutte,* and a new production of *Falstaff* in 2013–14.[32]

Speculation was rife that Gelb was just as happy to be at some remove from Levine's powerful sway, particularly as it affected the stage. There had been talk from the outset that the artistic director, "a dramaturgical traditionalist," and the general manager were likely to collide over reinterpretations of the standard rep. Levine had been openly dismissive of the shift away from the preeminence of singer and conductor in this directors' era that Gelb saw as key to the salvation of the genre. In an uncharacteristically biting moment, Levine complained, "For some people, you keep redefining the cutting edge—and then you are a conservative if you are not on it," and, "There is a degree to which some aspects of the operatic repertoire cannot be reinvented." Levine's shuttling back and forth to Boston and absences for reasons of health left the field to Gelb. His iron grip has been extended to 2022, the expiration date of his most recent contract.[33]

### Stagings

*Anna Bolena* (Sept. 26, 2011), *L'Elisir d'amore* (Sept. 24, 2012), *Maria Stuarda* (Dec. 31, 2012), and *Don Giovanni* (Oct. 13, 2011) were unsurprising refittings typical of the company's approach to bel canto and Mozart. *Manon* (March 26, 2012), *Un Ballo in maschera* (Nov. 8, 2012), and *Rigoletto* (Jan. 28, 2013) were provocative refittings bent on enlivening the nineteenth-century repertoire. The genuine rereadings of *Faust* (Nov. 29, 2011), *Parsifal* (Feb. 15, 2013), and *Giulio Cesare* (April 4, 2013) were relatively tame intrusions of regietheater. *The Enchanted Island* (Dec. 31, 2011) and *The Tempest* (Oct. 23, 2012), a world and a company premiere, escape categorization.

Opening night 2011 paraded the sixteenth-century royals of *Anna Bolena* in splendor modeled on Holbein's Tudor portraits. A diagonal wall marked out corridors and rooms, exteriors and interiors that favored the public/private schism at the court of Henry VIII. It also favored the HD audience. Those seated some distance from the center of the Met auditorium were out of luck: they would see little if anything of key moments staged on the "wrong" side of the wall. *L'Elisir d'amore,* the second consecutive opening night for Netrebko and for Donizetti, was a "big, old-fashioned-looking show." The soprano's star turn was marred by what critics agreed was a sound no longer suited to the score's leggero requirements. Sher's attempt to inject Risorgimento violence into a bucolic romantic comedy was bound to result in a "dramatic mishmash." *Maria Stuarda* was clothed in trappings of no particular distinction, "hardly a bold take" on an opera that, nonetheless, provided a stunning vehicle for the glowing tone and irresistible fervor of DiDonato in the title role. And nothing about the new *Don Giovanni* gave off the excitement director Michael Grandage (a Tony for *Red,* a Laurence Olivier for *Caligula*) generated in the legitimate theater. The moveable curved walls pierced by doors and windows were all too familiar. To complaints of timidity such as "this *Don Giovanni* almost makes you yearn for those new stagings where the creative team is booed on opening night" (*Times,* Oct. 15), Gelb shot back, "Don't get me started on that.... I feel damned if I do, damned if I don't" (*Guardian* [London], Dec. 9, 2011). Maurice Grau, Heinrich Conried, and Giulio Gatti-Casazza, chided in the press for putting on the same-old, same-old and then blasted for departing from the beaten path, would have said "amen." In their time, it was contemporary repertoire, not contemporary staging, that made them liable to critical double jeopardy.[34]

The premiere of the new *Manon* ended in triumph for Netrebko and Piotr Beczala, and in isolated bravos, half-hearted applause, and a smattering of boos for Laurent Pelly's production. Two of Chantal Thomas's sets were variants on conventional designs: a love nest atop a staircase open to the tangled comings and goings of the plot; for Manon's death, a barren road lined with street lights receding in forced perspective. Moved forward from the eighteenth century, the queen of the Belle Époque demimonde found herself surrounded not by sinuous Art Nouveau décors true to the transposed action, but vamping about a gaming establishment one reviewer compared to a "maximum-security facility." The libretto does indeed specify that Manon seduce Des Grieux in Saint-Sulpice, that the Chevalier fall into her arms, and that the two run off together at the scene's conclusion. But frenzied love-making on a cot unaccountably placed within the sanctified perimeter of the church was a very different proposition: the crass enactment of blasphemy managed to subvert the erotic charge of music and text. In the end, the director succeeded in giving the work a shove strong enough to set it back on its heels, and not so strong as to lay it flat. Both *Un Ballo in maschera* and *Rigoletto* were robust enough to survive similar pushback. An American director with long experience in European avant-garde production, David Alden, dropped *Ballo* into a near-abstract Sweden of the 1920s. A giant image of Icarus hovered over the stage, presumably to presage that the ambition of King Gustav III would, like the hubris of the young Athenian, lead to his downfall. The conceit was irrelevant and ultimately grating. Altogether riveting was Alden's direction of the actors. Michael Mayer chose to transplant *Rigoletto* from elegant, decadent sixteenth-century Mantua to the amoral Las Vegas of the 1960s in all its vulgarity. Mayer took his metamorphosis one step further: not only did il Duca became the crooner Duke, but Duke became a stand-in for Frank Sinatra, Rigoletto for comedian Don Rickles, and the courtiers for the Rat Pack. The fit was generally, if not always, plausible. But much of the opera's emotional complexity was lost under the glare of Vegas neon. At best, "This rejiggered *Rigoletto* offers no great revelations or insights, nor is it likely to stand the test of time, but it makes for an enjoyable alternate spin on a familiar work."[35]

Des McAnuff's regietheater rereading of *Faust,* a London import, wielded shock and currency in a desperate effort to bring the favored opera of the Gilded Age into the twenty-first century. The production telegraphed an unequivocal pacifist message. The jaded philosopher was here a scientist horrified at the fallout of his work on the atom bomb; a photographer's flash sent a traumatized veteran into fits of hysteria; the Walpurgis Night was a hellish banquet for disfigured survivors of Hiroshima. But like so many rereadings, the high-concept enunciated from the start acknowledged the score and subject only sporadically. The love story that is, after all, at the heart of the opera moved uneasily among metal staircases and railings discordant with the familiar lilting melodies. The most offensive of the inventions had Marguerite give birth onstage and then drown her baby in a baptismal font. *Opera News* called the new *Faust* "contrarian yet predictable"; for the *Times,* "the grimness and irony ... felt imposed on Gounod's opera, not drawn from it." François Girard's *Parsifal* had its detractors as well, but they were outnumbered by those who thought the production "perfectly suited to the music" and replete with "arresting, consistently absorbing stage pictures." In the place of Klingsor's magic garden was an immense pool of blood, a referent for Amfortas's unstanchable wound; the blighted realm of the knights was bisected by the bed of a stream, sometimes dry. The opening moments established a strong bridge to present-day operagoers, many of them disturbed by the ideology Wagner embedded in the chivalric romance. During the prelude, a group of men removed their jackets and shoes in silence. They played their parts in stripped-down contemporary garb for the six hours of music that followed. These were the Grail knights, formerly in quest of Christian redemption and now modern seekers of meaning and healing. The three principal male singers, Jonas Kaufmann (Parsifal), René Pape (Gurnemanz), and Peter Mattei (Amfortas), gave listeners a taste of a Wagnerian golden age long past. If the stars of *Giulio Cesare,* David Daniels (Cesare) and Natalie Dessay (Cleopatra), fell short of consistent vocal distinction, they offered a compelling mix of sometimes remarkable singing and always astonishing acting and dancing. McVicar's anachronistic production had originated at Glyndebourne in 2005 and was known through the DVD recording and subsequent presentations elsewhere. Gelb's decision to bring the show to the Met was a rare feather in his 2012–13 cap: "so stuffed full of treats and surprises that even if some are not to your taste, you're likely to enjoy what you find in the next slice," "all the theatrical ideas worked, and their arc captured the opera's potent mix of wit and pathos." Handel, the British Raj, and Bollywood commingled smartly in the challenge march/dance of Cesare and Tolomeo (the acrobatic Christophe Dumaux), in Cleopatra's seductive gyrations during "V'adoro, pupille" ("I adore you, eyes"), and in many more of the director's ploys. Production, cast, and the virtuosic leadership of conductor Harry Bicket proved that a long evening of da capo aria and recitative, in the right hands, has immense appeal to modern audiences.[36]

The previous season, the Met had paid homage to the Baroque with *The Enchanted Island*. George Frideric Handel, Antonio Vivaldi, Jean-Philippe Rameau, André Campra, Jean-Marie Leclair, Henry Purcell, Jean-Féry Rebel, and Giovanni Battista Ferrandini were credited with the posthumous collaboration. Gelb had tapped Jeremy Sams to fashion a libretto for this pasticcio, a form of musical anthology dating back to the seventeenth century. Sams mixed *The Tempest* with *A Midsummer Night's Dream,* adding Caliban's mother, a female antagonist for Prospero, to the brew. The production and performance were better received than was the musical compilation. For some, it was a question of quantity. There was just too much of Handel et al. Others objected to the bland rhymed couplets awkwardly set to the music. But there was general delight over the cast headed by DiDonato and Daniels, and the conducting of Baroque specialist William Christie. Domingo's appearance as Neptune surrounded by his aquatic court, four mermaids dangling above his throne, was applauded wildly, as were the direction and the sets. Prospero's island returned, absent its "midsummer night" contingent, in Thomas Adès's *The Tempest*. Apart from complaints about Meredith Oakes's trite verse, the work, "magical in every respect," was welcomed for its musical sophistication, for expert performances, and most particularly for the production itself. Robert Lepage's riff on theatricality situated Shakespeare's scenario inside Milan's La Scala, with a different perspective on stage and auditorium for each of the three acts. Among the many extraordinary images were the tempest itself, Ariel twirling madly on a chandelier above a rippling cloth, and the enraptured Miranda and Ferdinand in silhouette on a moonlit beach.[37]

## "The Machine": 2010–2012

"There's nothing that defines an opera house more than new productions. There's no new production that's more significant or more important than

TABLE 20  Metropolitan Opera Premieres, 2006–07 to 2012–13

| Composer and Title | Met Premiere (*World Premiere) | Most Recent Met Performance | No. of Seasons in Met Repertoire | No. of Met Performances, 1883–2013 | World Premiere | Director/Designer |
|---|---|---|---|---|---|---|
| Tan Dun, *The First Emperor* | *Dec. 21, 2006 | May 17, 2008 | 2 | 12 | | Zhang Yimou / Fan Yue |
| Philip Glass, *Satyagraha* | Apr. 11, 2008 | Dec. 1, 2011 | 2 | 14 | Sept. 5, 1980, Rotterdam, Stadsschouwburg | Phelim McDermott / Julian Crouch |
| John Adams, *Doctor Atomic* | Oct. 13, 2008 | Nov. 13, 2008 | 1 | 9 | Oct. 1, 2005, San Francisco, War Memorial | Penny Woolcock / Julian Crouch |
| Leoš Janáček, *From the House of the Dead* | Nov. 12, 2009 | Dec. 5, 2009 | 1 | 7 | Apr. 12, 1930, Brno, National | Patrice Chéreau / Richard Peduzzi |
| Giuseppe Verdi, *Attila* | Feb. 23, 2010 | Mar. 27, 2010 | 1 | 10 | Mar. 17, 1846, Venice, La Fenice | Pierre Audi / Jacques Herzog and Pierre de Meuron |
| Dmitri Shostakovich, *The Nose* | Mar. 5, 2010 | Mar. 25, 2010 | 1 | 6 | Jan. 18, 1930, Leningrad, Maly | William Kentridge / William Kentridge |
| Gioachino Rossini, *Armida* | Apr. 12, 2010 | Mar. 5, 2011 | 2 | 15 | Nov. 11, 1817, Naples, San Carlo | Mary Zimmerman / Richard Hudson |
| John Adams, *Nixon in China* | Feb. 2, 2011 | Feb. 19, 2011 | 1 | 6 | Oct. 22, 1987, Houston, Grand Opera | Peter Sellars / Adrianne Lobel |
| Gioachino Rossini, *Le Comte Ory* | Mar. 24, 2011 | Feb. 5, 2013 | 2 | 14 | Aug. 20, 1828, Paris, Opéra | Bartlett Sher / Michael Yeargan |
| Gaetano Donizetti, *Anna Bolena* | Sept. 26, 2011 | Feb. 4, 2012 | 1 | 12 | Dec. 26, 1830, Milan, Carcano | David McVicar / Robert Jones |
| George Frideric Handel et al., *The Enchanted Island* | Dec. 31, 2011* | Jan. 30, 2012 | 1 | 10 | | Phelim McDermott / Julian Crouch |
| Thomas Adès, *The Tempest* | Oct. 23, 2012 | Nov. 17, 2012 | 1 | 8 | Feb. 10, 2004, London, Covent Garden | Robert Lepage / Jasmine Catudal |
| Gaetano Donizetti, *Maria Stuarda* | Dec. 31, 2012 | Jan. 26, 2013 | 1 | 8 | Dec. 30, 1835, Milan, La Scala | David McVicar / John Macfarlane |

the 'Ring' cycle," Peter Gelb asserts in the documentary he commissioned, Susan Froemke's *Wagner's Dream* (2012). The scale of "Der Ring des Nibelungen" tested the limits of his ambition. Each part of the tetralogy lays down its own gauntlet: the three swimming nixies of *Das Rheingold,* the seven equestrian warrior maidens of *Die Walküre, Siegfried*'s dragon, and the final conflagration of *Götterdämmerung.* Gelb turned to Lepage and Fillion who had brought off the floating sylphs and the ride to Hell of *La Damnation de Faust.* The team came up with a "tectonic" set, as Lepage called it, a beam almost as long as the width of the stage, supporting twenty-four massive planks that moved separately and together, rotated and tilted, functioned as floor, wall, and ceiling. Developed, constructed, and rehearsed over the span of two years in the director's Québec studio, carrying a price tag of $16 million, give or take, the set was hyped as no other Met production since Conried's 1903 *Parsifal.* The immense "Machine" would reconfigure itself to represent river, forest, and mountaintop, and to reflect computerized projections of the imagery issuing from music and text. If Wagner was moved to build his Festspielhaus to the measure of his creation, and Conried to rebuild the 39th Street stage for his grandiose *Parsifal,* Gelb saw to buttressing the Lincoln Center stage for the ninety-thousand-pound apparatus to which he had given his repeated blessing.[38]

The playbill of the first "Ring" opera heard at the Met, *Die Walküre,* triumph of Leopold Damrosch's 1884–85 season, reassured the public that "the stage settings, by Herr Wilhelm Hock, are after the original at Bayreuth." Slavishly devoted to the Master's blueprint, cognoscenti took exception to the slightest deviation ventured by the three subsequent reinvestitures through 1913–14—a curtain in place of a door, the scarcity or excess of foliage. Apart from a refitting of *Die Walküre* in 1935 attacked for minor infractions of the rule, the 1913–14 sets were trotted out for more than three decades. Lee Simonson's perspectives of the Hudson Palisades in 1948 rankled purists. When Karajan and Schneider-Siemssen unveiled the first installment of their "Ring" in 1967, what little could be made out in the dimly lit décor proposed a reading that would have been legible to charter Wagnerites of the 1880s. And these same apostles would have been thrilled at the reverence paid to Wagner's dictates in the late 1980s by Schenk and Schneider-Siemssen. Thanks to their edition, the Met became a Mecca for traditionalists infuriated by the heresies of regietheater.

The opening minutes of *Das Rheingold* (Sept. 27, 2010) promised a raft of imaginative applications of Lepage's technology. The tops of the planks

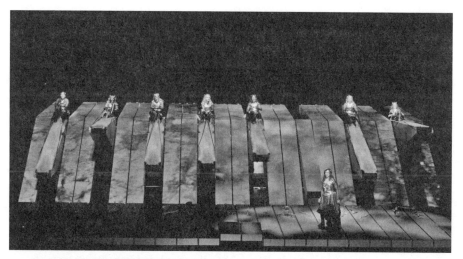

FIGURE 46. *Die Walküre,* act 3, "The Ride of the Valkyries," 2011 (© Beth Bergman 2011, NYC)

undulated in imitation of the river; the Rhinemaidens rose from what had the appearance of bubbly depths. But then the "water" settled into a surface on which the mermaids were made to perch far too long. So it continued, unevenly: stunning and apposite effects—the god of fire walking backward up an incline, the acutely angled descent of Wotan and Loge into the Nibelheim on a twisted stairway—and dramatically inert stretches with the principals stranded on a narrow platform for the length of two entire scenes. A few prudent reviewers withheld judgment. Most took up sides, for ("worth its weight in gold," "audience ... spellbound") and against ("[Lepage was just] playing with toys"). *Opera News* touched a painful nerve: "The current conventional wisdom is that the Met has abandoned the 'park and bark' school for operatic performance, but this *Rheingold* often seemed like its very embodiment."[39]

Die Walküre (April 22, 2011), *Siegfried* (Oct. 27, 2011), and *Götterdämmerung* (Jan. 27, 2012), unlike *Das Rheingold,* seesawed between felicitous and wrongheaded solutions. In a simulation of galloping steeds, the bobbing planks made surprisingly apt conveyances for the always problematic "Ride of the Valkyries." The natural world came alive in projections of cascading streams and tangles of flora and fauna; through 3D animation, the Forest Bird, heretofore invisible, could at last flit among the branches. Lepage erred nowhere more glaringly than at the climax of *Walküre* where he chose to sacrifice the emotional crescendo of the farewell to yet more trickery. The sorrowful Wotan led Brünnhilde offstage only to reappear on high and lower her body double upside-down against the tilted rock. By the finale of *Götterdämmerung,* the director seemed to have run out of ideas. The "Machine" and video illusions would, one might think, have been made to order for Siegfried's funeral pyre, Brünnhilde's immolation, the collapse of the hall of the Gibechungs, the river's flood, the triumph of the Rhinemaidens, the drowning of Hagen, and the distant vision of Valhalla in flames. Lepage offered only a metal hobbyhorse for Grane, Brünnhilde's brave mount, and toppling statues to mark the fall of the gods, gestures inadequate to the gigantic musical and dramatic conclusion of the composer's sixteen-hour opus. Gelb could not have forgotten the stupendous cataclysm engineered with more conventional means by Schenk and Schneider-Siemssen. He had been executive producer for that 1990 unforgettable telecast.

Since the early 1950s, Wagner had had to subsist on a shallow pool of *hochdramatisch* sopranos and heldentenors. Given the times, Deborah Voigt was an adequate Brünnhilde. The originally scheduled Ben Heppner withdrew nearly a year before the premiere of *Siegfried* and was replaced by Gary Lehman, who withdrew, in turn, only days before the opening. It was up to Lehman's cover, Jay Hunter Morris, to save the show. He assumed the role with aplomb and energy, and minus the heroic voice Wagner had in mind. The "Ring" standouts were Jonas Kaufmann, a lyric Siegmund; Bryn Terfel, a Wotan inhibited in *Rheingold* but towering in *Walküre* and *Siegfried;* Eric Owens, a wrathful yet vulnerable Alberich; and Stephanie Blythe, a Fricka tender beneath her moral outrage. The virtuoso orchestra, led first by Levine, and then by Luisi when the music director was obliged to cancel, was by itself worth the inflated ticket price.

Lepage argued that he had purged "layers and layers of socio-political stances," had peeled away "all of that from the 20th century and [gone] back to the 19th century," to the "poetical world, the mythological world" as they were first staged by Wagner himself in 1876 (*Times,* April 22, 2012). Gelb boasted, "Lepage may be the first director to execute what Wagner actually wanted to see onstage" (*Times,* April 4, 2012). It could be argued that in producing a computer-generated translation of Wagner's intentions, Lepage had advanced a true version of the "Ring." But the noisy hulk was more often hostile than friendly to poetry. The other claim, that Lepage had swept away tired high concept, whether Marxist, "Green," abstract, archaic, or futuristic, foundered, as had poetry and mythology, under the weight of the immense set. The "Machine" itself was the concept, the tectonic object the message. Décor and staging had wrestled narrative and character to the ground: theatricality, Gelb's watchword, had swallowed drama. Having rejected pictorialism, and then concept as normally defined, this particular third way was unlikely to serve as template for future operatic design and direction.

The culminating episode of the "Ring" saga reached the readership of the *New York Times* on May 21, 2012, when the paper, whose masthead had long carried the Gelb family name, ran a story under the headline "Latest Met Aria: Bad Opera News is No News." The "Ring" had made the rare and in this instance embarrassing leap from the Arts and Leisure section to the front page. F. Paul Driscoll, editor in chief of *Opera News,* had announced the previous day that with the June issue the publication would no longer review Met performances, "a policy prompted by the Met's dissatisfaction over negative critiques." Its coverage of other companies would continue. The previous month, *Opera News* had panned *Götterdämmerung* as "less an interpretation of the opera than a desultory series of tactics for dealing with its daunting challenges." Asked by the *Times* to comment on the decision, Gelb pulled out this blistering sentence from a piece by features editor Brian Kellow in the May issue: "The public is becoming more dispirited each season by the pretentious and woefully misguided, misdirected productions foisted on them." Gelb might as easily have pointed to pans of *Tosca* or *Armida* or *Faust.* To his mind, such acid criticism crossed the line between *Opera News* and its publisher, the Metropolitan Opera Guild, and by extension between the Guild and its parent Metropolitan Opera Company, a boundary Gelb had lately blurred by appointing one of his assistant general managers to the Guild directorship and by moving Guild education programs to the Met itself.[40]

Founded in 1936 and circulated year round to upward of one hundred thousand, among them Met contributors, *Opera News* had reviewed company performances since 1971–72, Bing's final season. On May 22, in the wake of outrage that clotted the operatic internet and threats from subscribers to discontinue their memberships and halt their contributions, Gelb reversed himself on what he had first termed a determination made in concert with the magazine. The world perceived his action as censorship. Gelb did not. As late as March 2013, he argued, "My point was that the guild should stop publishing reviews of the Met altogether, which was not an act of censorship but what seemed to me like common sense under the circumstances. Why should the Met pay for a publication that's writing negative reviews of Met productions?" His defense only compounded the fracture. It is hard to know whether the spring 2012 contretemps colored commentary in *Opera News* in 2012–13. Volume 77 was nothing if not judicious.[41]

As to the "Machine," it was dismantled in May 2013. Its parts were carted off to warehouses in New Jersey and upstate New York. First announced for revival in 2016 or 2017, the Lepage production, according to Gelb, would , in all likelihood, return in 2018–19, the postponement caused by "a certain amount of 'Ring' fatigue."[42]

In 2012–13, attendance was down to 79 percent of capacity. The management put the onus on Sandy, the hurricane of October 2012, and on jacked-up ticket prices (*Times*, Feb. 27, 2013, Jan. 29, 2014). The Met announced that the increases would be rolled back by roughly 10 percent in 2013–14. The greater number of tickets sold would make up for the price cuts; "at least it better" was the way Gelb put it. The hard fact was that due, in part, to the hike in prices, in 2012–13, box office had yielded only 69 percent of its potential, over 10 percent less than in most of the previous decade. In late spring, the Met dissolved the last vestige of its resident ballet troupe; in the future, dancers would be hired show by show. The brunt of the blame for the company's woes continued to fall on the number and kind of new productions, each costing $2 to $3 million, and the "Ring" much more. Extreme reinvestitures were subject to particular scrutiny, as they had been under Volpe. But their greater number under Gelb altered the equation. In the last four years of the previous administration, of sixteen new productions, only *Jenufa*, *La Juive*, *Mazeppa*, and *Salome* challenged the expected. In the first four years fairly ascribed entirely to Gelb, 2009–13, there were seven rereadings among his twenty-three new productions. And among these were the indisputably core *Les Contes d'Hoffmann*, *La Traviata*, *Faust*, *Rigoletto*, and *Parsifal*. It was not only the number of radical restagings that separated Gelb from Volpe; it was that Gelb's rejection of convention tampered with operas well known and best loved. To this calculus we should also include the in-your-face refittings of *Tosca*, *Un Ballo in maschera*, and *Manon*.

Whatever many Met faithful may have felt about the results, Gelb had kept his promise to breathe new life into the repertoire. To the question of whether high-concept productions of core titles were systematically rebuffed by the musical press, the answer is no: its response ranged from high praise for *La Traviata*, to mild enthusiasm for *Faust* and *Manon*, to thumbs down for *Les Contes d'Hoffmann*. The attitude of the public, though probably more generally negative than that of the critics, cannot be assessed without access to box-office figures. To the question of whether reviewers were tougher on directors with only marginal opera experience than on opera professionals, the answer is again, no. They handled veterans Bondy and Audi no more gingerly than Zimmerman, Lepage, and Grandage. Did they find less to like

FIGURE 47. West 72nd Street, New York City, September 2013

in productions incubated at the Met than in productions that debuted else-where? Here, yes. Of the sixteen Met offspring from 2009–10 through 2012–13 (counting the "Ring" as one), only *The Enchanted Island* and *The Tempest* drew raves, and *Carmen* strongly positive notices. A poor reflection on Gelb? Yes and no. He did, after all, have the decisive say in cosponsoring or importing productions first mounted elsewhere.

## POSTSCRIPT

The owners of the original seventy boxes, the Vanderbilts, the Astors, and the rest, would doubtless have been gratified that fifteen of the twenty operas presented in Henry Abbey's inaugural 1883 season are still among the offerings of the early twenty-first century. And only a handful of the titles on the calendar at the approximate midpoint of the Met's history, the decade of the 1950s, are missing from today's lists. In fact, all of the slices of the repertoire to which we devote our chapters—bel canto, French opera, Puccini, Wagner, Verdi, American opera, twentieth-century European opera, Baroque and Slavic opera—retain a strong presence. Crucial to the vitality of the institution, contemporary works in growing number have established themselves through the approbation of critics and public. Most astonishing to the Met's founders would be the company's sphere of influence. Abbey's universe was circumscribed by the stops on his tour; Gelb projects his singers larger-than-life on satellite beams around the planet. It is no longer a matter of making an essentially nineteenth-century European art form at home in the New World. It is a question of globalizing what has been, almost from the beginning, an international enterprise, purported to speak a universal language as well as multiple national tongues. Through the intermediary of an American opera company, arguably preeminent in the world, America, or better New York, has become the imperial capital of opera.

# NOTES

## CHAPTER ONE

1. "a few ultra": cited in *Life* (Nov. 1, 1883): 224. We refer the reader to www.measuringworth.com for relative dollar values. The $5 balcony ticket for the 1883 opening night was roughly equivalent to $116 in today's dollars.

2. In 1883, the location of the Met marked the northern boundary of the theater district. With the development of Long Acre Square (Times Square after 1904 and the completion of the Times Building), it became the southern boundary of the theatre/movie district.

3. The Opéra in Paris, an exception, did not have separate access to the top gallery.

4. "loomed up against": Nov. 1, 224.

5. "elegance": "The Metropolitan Opera House," *Harper's New Monthly Magazine,* (Nov. 1883): 889. "Architecturally it is": M. G. Van Rensselaer, *American Architect and Building News* (Feb. 23, 1884): 86.

6. "a republic of": *Harper's New Monthly Magazine* (Nov. 1883): 883.

7. "An unalterable and": *The Age of Innocence* (London: Electric Book Company, 2001), 15. As in the instance of opéra comique, musical terms that may be foreign to the reader are defined in the text following their first use, and in the index. "Mme. Nilsson and": *Critic,* Oct. 27.

8. A specialist in French roles, Christine Nilsson also created Ophélie in Ambroise Thomas's *Hamlet* at the Opéra in 1868. The composer's *Mignon* was the vehicle of her New York operatic debut.

9. For a précis of music journalism during the early decades of Met history, see Robert Tuggle, *The Golden Age of Opera* (New York: Holt, Rinehart and Winston, 1983), 9–12. "[her Violetta] surpasses [Patti's] in sympathy": *Critic* (Nov. 10, 1883): 90. Sembrich had at least one detractor: "The prima donna has been accorded no place in the hearts of her listeners, and she will be allowed to go hence, if we are not much mistaken, without profound regret." The writer found a "want of sympathetic quality in her voice" and a "lack of personal magnetism and distinction as an actress" (*Times,* Jan. 20, 1884).

10. For the effect of acoustic recording on the reproduction of voices, see J. B. Steane, *The Grand Tradition: Seventy Years of Singing on Record* (New York: Charles Scribner's Sons, 1974), 7.

11. "this famous soprano": W. J. Henderson, *The Art of Singing* (New York: Dial Press, 1938), 460.

12. For the Erie Canal celebration, see Edwin G. Burrows and Mike Wallace, *Gotham: A History of New York City to 1898* (New York: Oxford University Press, 1999), 430.

13. For the Astor Place riot, see Karen Ahlquist, *Democracy at the Opera: Music, Theater, and Culture in New York City, 1815–60* (Urbana: University of Illinois Press, 1997), 139–42; John Dizikes, *Opera in America: A Cultural History* (New Haven: Yale University Press, 1993), 160–63; and Burrows and Wallace, *Gotham,* 761–65.

14. "populists who disdained": Ahlquist, *Democracy at the Opera,* 67.

15. For descriptions of the Academy of Music, see *Tribune,* Oct. 2, 1854; *Times,* Oct. 3, 1854; *Harper's New Monthly Magazine* (Dec. 1854): 123. For the seating capacity of the Academy of Music in 1883, see *Pictorial Diagrams of New York Theatres,* www.daviscrossfield.com/academy.html.

16. "when our air": Henry James, *A Small Boy and Others* (New York: Charles Scribner's Sons, 1913), 240–41.

17. "But it was": *Harper's New Monthly Magazine* (Feb. 1882): 468.

18. Henry Edward Krehbiel, *Chapters of Opera* (New York: Henry Holt, 1908), 85–276, offers an extensive account of the establishment of the Met and the rivalry between Abbey and Mapleson. For Patti's fees and the Gerster-Patti feud, see John Frederick Cone, *Oscar Hammerstein's Manhattan Opera Company* (Norman: University of Oklahoma Press, 1965), 11, 54–55. For the Metropolitan budget and box office, see Martin Mayer, *The Met: One Hundred Years of Grand Opera* (New York: Simon and Schuster, 1983), 44. The *Times,* Feb. 16, 1884, estimated the Met's weekly nut at the much higher $35,000.

19. Callas recorded *Lucia* and *I Puritani* in 1953, *Norma* and *Il Turco in Italia* in 1954, and *La Sonnambula* in 1957. In 1955, the Chicago Lyric put on *I Puritani* for Callas, a rarity at the time. After the December 8, 1956, *Lucia* broadcast, baritone Enzo Sordello was fired, officially for insubordination toward conductor Fausto Cleva, unofficially for having held the last note of the act 2 duet longer than Callas (Edward Downes, *Times,* Dec. 15, 1956).

20. Rossini, Donizetti, and Bellini composed a total of nearly 120 operas, of which twenty-two have been performed at the Met through the 2013–14 season. Rossini's *Guillaume Tell* and *Le Comte Ory* and Donizetti's *La Favorite* and *La Fille du régiment* were composed to French librettos, *Guillaume Tell* and *La Favorite* in a style that attenuates the embellishments of bel canto. *Le Comte Ory* and *La Fille du régiment,* examples of French opéra comique, demand the full arsenal of bel canto technique. *Crispino e la comare* (1850), by the Ricci Brothers, Luigi and Federico, had four performances in the 1918–19 season. Saverio Mercadante and Giovanni Pacini have never been heard at the Met.

## CHAPTER TWO

1. The New York Symphony Society and the Philharmonic-Symphony Society merged in 1928 to form what is still today the New York Philharmonic. The terms under discussion at the board's August 8, 1884, meeting differed somewhat from those proposed by Damrosch: the average cost per performance rose to $4,000; Damrosch's salary would be $1,000 weekly. For ticket prices in the Met's early seasons, see George Martin, *The Damrosch Dynasty: America's First Family of Music* (Boston: Houghton Mifflin, 1983), 74; and Joseph Horowitz, *Wagner Nights: An American History* (Berkeley: University of California Press, 1994), 76.

2. For German-American demographics, see Martin, *The Damrosch Dynasty*, 27, 41, 74; Edwin G. Burrows and Mike Wallace, *Gotham: A History of New York City to 1898* (New York: Oxford University Press, 1999), 739, 745, 995. For the history of German-American theatrical troupes, see John Koegel, *Music in German Immigrant Theater* (Rochester: University of Rochester Press, 2009).

3. "were vast, political": Jessica C. E. Gienow-Hecht, "Trumpeting Down the Walls of Jericho: The Politics of Art, Music and Emotion in German-American Relations, 1870–1920," *Journal of Social History* 36, no. 3 (2003): 586, 606.

4. Where titles have conventionally acceptable variants, such as *William Tell* or *Guillaume Tell,* we have followed the lead of the Met online archives. Gluck's *Orfeo ed Euridice* was performed only once, in Boston. Boieldieu's *La Dame blanche* was given only in Chicago and Boston.

5. "Something in the": Louis Auchincloss, *The Vanderbilt Era: Profiles of the Gilded Age* (New York: Charles Scribner's Sons, 1989), 147.

6. "impulse dominated reflection": Henry Finck, *Anton Seidl: A Memorial by His Friends* (New York: Charles Scribner's Sons, 1899), 136, 168.

7. "old favorite operas": "The Opera" (Feb. 1892): 210. "could no more": ibid., 211. "prohibiting the production": ibid., 215.

8. Of the fourteen operas programmed for 1884–85, only three were by Wagner, and two more were German. Box-office records for the German seasons are not known to be extant. The information we provide was published by Krehbiel in the *Tribune* and repeated in Henry Edward Krehbiel, *Chapters of Opera* (New York: Henry Holt, 1908), 212.

9. "continual warfare": cited in Krehbiel, *Chapters of Opera,* 211. "many complaints having": board minutes, Jan. 15, 1891.

10. "What she did": Frances Alda, *Men, Women and Tenors* (1937; Freeport, NY: Books for Libraries Press, 1970), 110. Mrs. Astor, née Caroline Webster Schermerhorn, was the wife of William Backhouse Astor Jr., grandson of John Jacob Astor. "The 400" invited to her annual ball defined "le tout New York." Quaintance Eaton asserts, "Nowhere else in American history is there recorded an instance of equal social power in the hands of one woman." Eaton, *The Miracle of the Met* (Westport, CT: Greenwood Press, 1976), 21. For Mrs. Astor at the Patriarch or Assembly ball, see Lucy Kavaler, *The Astors: A Family Chronicle of Pomp and Power* (Lincoln, NE: An Authors Guild Backinprint.com edition, 2000), 118.

11. "occasional and curious": *Harper's New Monthly Magazine* (April 1885): 807. For the salaries of German artists, see *Musical Courier,* Jan. 30, 1889.

12. "revolt . . . against": Auchincloss, *The Vanderbilt Era,* 149. Nellie Melba did not appear at the Metropolitan until 1893.

13. Krehbiel's notice of *Asrael* read in part, "[Franchetti] was a young Italian (or, rather, Italianized Hebrew), a member of one of the branches of the Rothschilds. . . . He was very wealthy, having a purse as large as his artistic ambition, and was not disinclined, when a work of his composition was accepted for performance, to care for its sumptuous production by paying for the stage decorations out of his own pocket. He resembled Meyerbeer in being a Jew" *(Tribune).*

14. In a 1904 recording, the sixty-two-year-old Marianne Brandt is still a trenchant Fidès. She was a student of Pauline Viardot, the first Fidès and sister of Maria Malibran.

15. Patti's Almaviva was Italo Campanini, who returned briefly to the Met after eight years. Fittingly, the final Met appearance of the company's first Faust took place two years later in that very role when he replaced the ailing Jean de Reszke.

16. The board minutes of Oct. 3, 1894, reflect approval for the coming season of the de Reszkes, the Italian tenor Francesco Tamagno, the French baritone Victor Maurel, and the sopranos Nellie Melba and Sibyl Sanderson, one Australian and the other American. See Martin Mayer, *The Met: One Hundred Years of Grand Opera* (New York: Simon and Schuster, 1983), 66, for a précis of the refinancing of the organization; for the redistribution of boxes, see Frank Merkling, John W. Freeman, and Gerald Fitzgerald, *The Golden Horseshoe: The Life and Times of the Metropolitan Opera House* (New York: Viking, 1965), 46. The Abbey-Schoeffel-Grau contract served as a template for the next fifty years: "The term was five years. The lessees took the house for an annual rental of $52,000, and pledged themselves to give opera four times a week for thirteen weeks in the winter and spring. The lessors paid back to the lessees the $52,000 for their box privileges." Krehbiel, *Chapters of Opera,* 228–30. For the rights that devolved to the board, see ibid., 229.

17. *Faust* and *Roméo et Juliette* opened the season seven out of eight times between 1891 and 1900. *Tannhäuser* was chosen for 1898–99. Calvé's 137 *Carmen*s, followed by Risë Stevens's 124, is a company record. "the most sensational": Krehbiel, *Chapters of Opera,* 233.

18. Herman Bemberg wrote the incidental music for Oscar Wilde's *Salome.* Tamagno performed his signature Otello and several other roles from the Met stage in March and April 1890, in a supplementary Patti-Tamagno season organized by Abbey and Grau. On November 21, 1894, at his company debut in *William Tell* (in Italian), Tamagno was involved in an unforgettable contretemps. Libia Drog, the hapless Mathilde, a role new to her, lost her way in her act 2 aria, and then stopped singing altogether. Glaring at the conductor, she appealed for help but "he seemed to have lost his head as completely as the lady had her memory." Krehbiel, *Chapters of Opera,* 242. There followed much walking off the stage and back on in a series of farcical comings and goings.

19. From 1883 to 1895–96, the company performed on Monday, Wednesday, and Friday evenings, and on Saturday afternoons.

20. During 1897–98, the Damrosch-Ellis Grand Opera presented a short season during which Lillian Nordica sang the three Brünnhildes.

21. For the neglect of stage sets during the Grau regime, see Rose Heylbut, *Backstage at the Opera* (New York: Thomas Y. Crowell, 1899), 24. In 1891–92, Jean's fee was $20,000 a month for two performances each week. In addition, he was due 25 percent of the gross in excess of $5,000; Edouard was due 10 percent. The de Reszkes are the only singers in Met history whose contracts called for a share of the box office. For de Reszke's fees, see Clara Leiser, *Jean de Reszke and the Great Days of Opera* (1934; Westport, CT: Greenwood Press, 1970), 114. With regard to the exorbitant fees paid to principal artists during the Grau regime, Mayer notes as follows: "In 1899–1900, for example, after paying $80,500 to Calvé, $61,000 to Sembrich, $49,660 to Edouard de Reszke, $39,000 to Nordica, $39,000 to the Wagnerian tenor Ernest Van Dyck, $37,250 to Eames, and $25,700 to Plançon—Grau had split a profit of $103,510 fifty-fifty with his shareholders. This meant that the Real Estate Company received a $12,050 dividend, a 46 per cent return on investment in a single year.... The entire orchestra received only $100,000, the chorus $36,000, the ballet $13,000 for the whole season. Each of the seven highest-priced singers was paid more than the entire conducting staff." Mayer, *The Met,* 75. "No one has": cited in Irving Kolodin, *The Metropolitan Opera, 1883–1966: A Candid History* (New York: Alfred A. Knopf, 1966), 157.

22. For the Melba/Sembrich rivalry, see Stephen Herx, "Marcella Sembrich and Three Great Events at the Metropolitan," *Opera Quarterly* (Winter 1999): 57.


CHAPTER THREE


1. James A. Roosevelt, the first president of the Metropolitan board, was also associated with the Metropolitan Museum of Art; William C. Whitney was active in the early years of the New York Zoological Society and the American Museum of Natural History, established in 1877; George G. Haven, later president of the Metropolitan Opera and Real Estate Company and managing director of the board, was also identified with the Museum of Natural History; William K. Vanderbilt was president of the short-lived New Theatre; Adrian Iselin was aligned with the Museum of Natural History and the Metropolitan Museum of Art.

2. "New York plutocrats": Quaintance Eaton, *The Miracle of the Met* (Westport, CT: Greenwood Press, 1976), 141–42.

3. A new gold curtain rose for the first time in 1905.

4. The credit for bringing Caruso to the Met belongs to both Grau and Conried. Grau's contract with Caruso was void on Grau's retirement; Conried re-signed him, but for fewer performances. For the chorus's demands for a raise in pay, see Martin Mayer, *The Met: One Hundred Years of Grand Opera* (New York: Simon and Schuster, 1983), 94.

5. For Louise Homer's miscarriage, see Anne Homer, *Louise Homer and the Golden Age of Opera* (New York: William Morrow, 1974), 255–56. A full analysis of

documents relative to the Central Park incident is provided by Ruth Bauerle, "Caruso's Sin in the Fiendish Park: 'The Possible Was the Improbable and the Improbable the Inevitable' (FW 110.11–12)," *James Joyce Quarterly* (Fall 2000–Winter 2001): 157–81. In the concluding section of her essay, Bauerle tracks the many allusions to the Caruso scandal in *Ulysses* and *Finnegan's Wake*.

6. For the appeal to the Kaiser, see Irving Kolodin, *The Metropolitan Opera, 1883–1966: A Candid History* (New York: Alfred A. Knopf, 1966), 161. The European copyright on *Parsifal* was not due to expire until February 1913. Conried ascribed the objections of his German peers to their resentment that Americans would have first crack at Wagner's last masterpiece. Conried's response to his opponents is reproduced in full in Montrose Moses, *The Life of Heinrich Conried* (New York: Thomas Y. Crowell, 1916), 233–43. His arguments were rejected by many New York critics; Krehbiel called his appropriation of *Parsifal* "the rape of the work." Henry Edward Krehbiel, *Chapters of Opera* (New York: Henry Holt, 1908), 331. For an account of concert presentations of *Parsifal* in New York prior to the opera's staged premiere in 1903, see Jeffrey S. McMillan, "Grail Crazy," *Opera News* (March 2013): 16–17.

7. For a description of Conried's renovation of the Opera House, the dividends paid by *Parsifal* profits, and the refunded tickets, see Rose Heylbut, *Backstage at the Opera* (New York: Thomas Y. Crowell, 1937), 46, 43–44. Jean de Reske offered to come out of retirement for *Parsifal*, a role he had never sung; Conried was unwilling to pay the tenor's high fee. Mayer, *The Met,* 90. For the immediate *Parsifal* spin-offs, see Joseph Horowitz, *Wagner Nights: An American History* (Berkeley: University of California Press, 1994), 266. Conried's high-profile success persuaded conductor and impresario Henry Savage to take the opera on the road throughout the United States and Canada with his English Grand Opera Company; well before Berlin and Paris, New Orleans and Montreal could boast a fully staged *Parsifal,* albeit in English translation; Thomas Edison filmed scenes from the opera; a Yiddish translation was performed on the Lower East Side; at the Lee Avenue Theatre in Brooklyn, among other venues, it was given as a play in blank verse with orchestra and chorus.

8. For correspondence from Conried to Strauss, Moses, *Life of Heinrich Conried,* 293–96. "more than a": *Times,* Jan. 23, 1907. In Germany in 1908 alone, *Salome* registered 217 performances (*Times,* Jan. 29, 1909).

9. "as though to": Mayer, *The Met,* 92.

10. "kisse[d] the bloody": Krehbiel, *Chapters of Opera,* 352.

11. "moving spirit and": Pierre Van Rensselaer Key, "The Only Opera Octopus," *Cosmopolitan Magazine* (April 1910): 545. Jean Strouse, *Morgan, American Financier* (New York: Random House, 1999), 561, notes that the Morgan papers make no mention of J. P. Morgan's leadership role in the *Salome* affair. Herbert L. Satterlee, the husband of Morgan's daughter Louisa, an earlier biographer, makes no reference to *Salome* in *J. Pierpont Morgan, an Intimate Portrait* (New York: Macmillan, 1939). Architect Stanford White was murdered in a crime of passion by Harry Thaw on June 25, 1906, at the Madison Square Roof Garden.

12. A Feb. 8, 1907, letter from the Conried Opera Company to the board of the Metropolitan Opera and Real Estate Company describes the losses Conried incurred over *Salome*.

13. The remonstrations in New York against the Manhattan Opera Company's *Salome* in 1909 were mild by comparison with the outcries in Philadelphia and Chicago. The Boston performances were canceled.

14. "lust for revenge": cited in John Kobler, *Otto the Magnificent: The Life of Otto Kahn* (New York: Charles Scribner's Sons, 1988), 73.

15. "an artist of": Jan. 3, 1922, Feb. 14, 1922. "the most refulgent": W. J. Henderson, *Sun*. Rarely cast in Wagnerian roles (only once on 39th Street), Lily Djanel, the Met's Salome of the early 1940s, was also its principal Carmen. For Strauss's wish that Salome be sung by a youthful voice: "Strauss suddenly said that he thought she [Elisabeth Schumann] should sing Salome. When Elisabeth protested that she was a lyric soprano and could not sing such a dramatic role Strauss replied that the youthfulness of her voice, the silvery quality, was exactly what he wanted in the character of Salome." Strauss offered to alter the orchestration and transpose sections for Schumann; she refused: Gerd Puritz, *Elisabeth Schumann, a Biography,* ed. and trans. Joy Puritz (London: A. Deutsch, 1993), 77.

16. For audiences at the Metropolitan and the Manhattan on Jan. 2, 1907, see Mayer, *The Met,* 93.

17. For the enmity between Conried and Hammerstein, see ibid., 94. Hammerstein's theater on 34th Street between Eighth and Ninth avenues is now the Manhattan Center.

18. For the enticements that contributed to Melba's defection, see Therese Radic, *Melba, the Voice of Australia* (South Melbourne: MMB Music, 1986), 116.

19. "with a contemptuous": Giulio Gatti-Casazza, *Memories of the Opera* (New York: Scribner, 1941), 168. For Hammerstein's stars and their salaries, see Kolodin, *The Metropolitan Opera,* 179. For the Manhattan's skyrocketing subscriptions, see John Frederick Cone, *First Rival of the Metropolitan Opera* (New York: Columbia University Press, 1983), 122.

20. For New York's population explosion at the turn of the century, see Kolodin, *The Metropolitan Opera,* 184–85. On losses during the second opera war: "The 1907–1908 season, for example, ended for the Met with a loss of $84,039.... [At the conclusion of that same season], Hammerstein commented: 'My season was successful inasmuch as I lost only $50,000, whereas I expected to lose $75,000.'" Kobler, *Otto the Magnificent,* 71.

21. For a discussion of "verismo" as applied to opera, see Alan Mallach, *The Autumn of Italian Opera: From Verismo to Modernism, 1890–1915* (Boston: Northeastern University Press, 2007), 42–46.

22. For Puccini on *Manon Lescaut* and *Madama Butterfly* at the Met, see letters to Tito Ricordi, Feb. 18, Feb. 19, 1907, in *Carteggi pucciniani,* ed. Eugenio Gara (Milan: Ricordi, 1958), 339–41.

23. "most sensational fiasco": Krehbiel, *Chapters of Opera,* 320, 324, 325.

24. Kahn letter to Conried cited in Mayer, *The Met,* 95.

25. "public [that] was opera-mad": Krehbiel, *Chapters of Opera,* 326.

## CHAPTER FOUR

1. "very important person": Giulio Gatti-Casazza, *Memories of the Opera* (New York: Scribner, 1941), 142–48.

2. The *Times* headline ran, "Appointment of Gatti-Casazza and Andreas Dippel to Succeed Conried Confirmed" (Feb. 12, 1908). "Mr. Dippel's appointment": Henry Edward Krehbiel, *More Chapters of Opera: Being Historical and Critical Observations and Records Concerning the Lyric Drama in New York from 1908 to 1918* (New York: Henry Holt, 1919), 24.

3. For a discussion of the letter in support of Dippel, see Martin Mayer, *The Met: One Hundred Years of Grand Opera* (New York: Simon and Schuster, 1983), 104–6.

4. The text of the Kahn announcement following the February 11, 1908, meeting was published in the *Times* of the next day. For Gatti and casting, see Frances Alda, *Men, Women and Tenors* (1937; Freeport, NY: Books for Libraries Press, 1970), 116.

5. "Perhaps his love:" John Kobler, *Otto the Magnificent: The Life of Otto Kahn* (New York: Charles Scribner's Sons, 1988), 51. Kahn was at least as devoted to the company of sopranos as he was to that of "grandees"; he had affairs with Maria Jeritza and Grace Moore (ibid., 166–71).

6. "Six and three-quarter": Feb. 21, 1925, 9–10. "I wondered at": Alda, *Men, Women and Tenors*, 73.

7. "The theatre is": Gatti-Casazza, *Memories of the Opera*, 68–69.

8. "The Maestro . . . was": Geraldine Farrar, *Such Sweet Compulsion* (New York: Greystone Press, 1938), 116.

9. Toscanini became principal conductor at Milan's La Scala in 1898 at the age of thirty-one; Mahler became artistic director at Vienna's Hofoper in 1897 at thirty-seven. Mahler's letter to Dippel, cited in Joseph Horowitz, *Understanding Toscanini, How He Became an American Culture-God and Helped Create a New Audience for Old Music* (New York: Alfred A. Knopf, 1987), 55.

10. The Met's activities at the New Theatre were administered by Dippel, another sign that Gatti had taken control of the home base. Widely considered a fatal flaw in 1909, the New Theatre's uptown address was a stone's throw from the Met's present site at Lincoln Center. For a full discussion of the New Theatre, see Mary Jane Matz, *The Many Lives of Otto Kahn* (New York: Pendragon Press, 1963), 68–78.

11. For a detailed account of the Met's Paris tour, see Quaintance Eaton, *Opera Caravan: Adventures of the Metropolitan on Tour, 1883–1956* (New York: Metropolitan Opera Guild, 1957), 152–56.

12. In 1909–10, the Met also presented twenty-five ballet programs. The growing importance of ballet is signaled by the debuts of Anna Pavlova and Mikail Mordkin. When the Met acquired the Philadelphia Opera House, it was renamed the Metropolitan Opera House. The company performed there regularly until 1920. The building, on Broad and Poplar streets, now houses the Holy Ghost Headquarters Revival Center at the Met. The Academy of Music is home to Opera Philadelphia and to the Pennsylvania Ballet. A hefty share of the $1.25 million was contributed by

a Met patron who saw in the payoff a chance to banish Lina Cavalieri, one of Hammerstein's divas; this extravagance put an end to the involvement of Cavalieri, billed as "the most beautiful woman in the world," with the gentleman's son. Cavalieri had been exiled from the Met in 1908 following her marriage to one of the Astor clan. For Hammerstein's buyout, see Mayer, *The Met*, 112.

13. "staged a coup": John Dizikes, *Opera in America: A Cultural History* (New Haven: Yale University Press, 1993), 316–17. "The *Girl* may": Puccini to Giulio Ricordi, n.d., in *The Letters of Giacomo Puccini,* ed. Giuseppe Adami, translated from the Italian and edited for the English edition by Ena Makin (New York: Vienna House, 1973), 176.

14. The *Sun* account of the *Fanciulla del West* rehearsal is cited in Robert Tuggle, *The Golden Age of Opera* (New York: Holt, Rinehart and Winston, 1983), 65–71.

15. "the great composers": John C. Freund, "First Production of Puccini's Opera," *Musical America* (Dec. 1910): 1–4. *Königskinder* had been scheduled for the previous season, but the composer had failed to complete the score in time.

16. For Belasco on Destinn, Caruso, and staging *La Fanciulla del West,* see David Belasco, *The Theatre through Its Stage Door* (New York: Harper & Brothers, 1919), 103.

17. For Puccini's reaction to the *Fanciulla* cast, letter to Carlo Clausetti, Jan. 1, 1911, in *Carteggi pucciniani,* ed. Eugenio Gara (Milan: Ricordi, 1958), 383. Had it not been for the veto of Tito Ricordi, who had again accompanied Puccini to New York, we might have had an aural shard of the first *Fanciulla* cast. Ricordi had made himself a nuisance at rehearsals and, most grievous, had barred all recordings in a greedy effort to protect sales of the published score. Soon after the premiere, Casa Ricordi began marketing *Fanciulla* through, of all things, a piano roll. For Ricordi's prohibition of *Fanciulla* recordings, see Tuggle, *The Golden Age of Opera,* 71.

18. For the incidents surrounding *Un Ballo in maschera* and *Carmen,* see Johanna Fiedler, *Molto Agitato* (New York: Doubleday, 2001), 20. "General Musik Director": Mayer, *The Met*, 134.

19. Gatti on ocean travel during World War I: "We docked in New York a day before German submarines sank several ships within the vicinity of the city. All the passengers had been worried. Caruso was with us on the boat. . . . We finished the trip, travelling in a zigzag manner." Gatti, *Memories of the Opera,* 179–83. "lest Germany should": *Sun,* Sept. 15, 1917, cited in Fiedler, *Molto Agitato,* 22. The company's last German-language performance was the April 28, 1917, Atlanta *Siegfried,* with Gadski as Brünnhilde; the first following the four-year suspension was the US premiere of *Die Tote Stadt,* on November 19, 1921, Maria Jeritza's debut.

20. Goritz parody cited in *Musical America* (April 21, 1917): 1–2.

21. The *Times* (Nov. 3, 1917) reported, "In the last few weeks a new turn of affairs appeared to have taken place." Melanie Kurt, Hermann Weil, Margarete Ober, and Johannes Sembach were not reengaged. Sembach returned in 1920 to sing *Tristan* in English. German had long been the lingua franca of US symphony orchestras; in 1918, the New York Philharmonic dropped "konzertmeister" in favor of "concertmaster"; see George Martin, *The Damrosch Dynasty: America's First Family of Music* (Boston: Houghton Mifflin, 1983), 251.

22. "made no definite": Ziegler to subscribers, Nov. 13, 1917.

23. Met singers on the covers of *Time*: Melba (April 18, 1927), Farrar (Dec. 5, 1927), Jeritza (Nov. 12, 1928), Bori (June 30, 1930). Also on the covers of *Time*: Toscanini (Jan. 25, 1926) and Gatti twice (Nov. 5, 1923, and Nov. 1, 1926).

24. For Caruso's fees, see Michael Scott, *The Great Caruso* (New York: A. A. Knopf, 1988), 181; and Irving Kolodin, *The Metropolitan Opera, 1883–1966: A Candid History* (New York: Alfred A. Knopf 1966), 298.

25. For the terms of the agreement between the Met and Victor, see C. G. Child, Victor Recording Machine Co., to Ziegler, March 6, 1917.

26. In 1919, Farrar was briefly the head of her own production company, Diva Pictures, associated with Samuel Goldwyn. For the account of the "rough" Farrar/ Caruso *Carmen*, see Alda, *Men, Women and Tenors*, 214–15.

27. For Farrar's witty barbs directed at colleagues at once tempted and reluctant to engage with the movies, see Henry Finck, *My Adventures in the Golden Age of Music* (New York: Funk & Wagnalls Company, 1926) 331–32. For Caruso's movie career, see Scott, *The Great Caruso*, 160–61.

28. "perhaps the most," cited in Mary Jane Phillips-Matz, *Puccini: A Biography* (Boston: Northeastern University Press, 2002), 256, 279. "From my seat": Farrar, *Such Sweet Compulsion*, 139.

29. Jeritza boosted *Die Ägyptische Helena* above the season's average box office. Between 1929–30 and the end of his regime, 1934–35, Gatti introduced eight more twentieth-century operas: Strauss's *Elektra*, Felice Lattuada's *Le Preziose ridicule*, Jaromir Weinberger's *Schwanda the Bagpiper*, Italo Montemezzi's *La Notte di Zoraima*, Howard Hanson's *Merry Mount*, and the world premieres of Deems Taylor's *Peter Ibbetson*, Louis Gruenberg's *The Emperor Jones*, and John Laurence Seymour's *In the Pasha's Garden*.

30. The Met sold the *Turandot* production to the Chicago Opera in 1933 for $3,000. It had cost more than $60,000 (Met online archives).

31. "the afternoon off": W. J. Henderson, *Sun*, March 11, 1928.


CHAPTER FIVE


1. "Calvary": Giulio Gatti-Casazza to Bruno Zirato, cited in Martin Mayer, *The Met: One Hundred Years of Grand Opera* (New York: Simon and Schuster, 1983), 185.

2. Ironically, on the day of Olin Downes's review of opening night, a front-page story led off with this headline: "Architects Picked to Plan Rockefeller Centre Which May Have Opera House as a Nucleus."

3. Kahn, *The Metropolitan Opera*, statement, 20–21. "A considerable number": Kahn to Real Estate Board, Jan. 5, 1926, attached to the Minutes of the Metropolitan Opera Company, Jan. 4, 1926. Real Estate Board response to Kahn on April 12, 1927 and Dec. 21, 1927, cited in Mayer, *The Met*, 163. The Parc Vendome apartments built on Kahn's site are extant. Kahn's architect for the opera house, Joseph Urban,

designed the International Magazine Building commissioned by Hearst in 1926, completed in 1928, to house the twelve magazines Hearst owned. The Hearst Building, reconceived by Norman Foster, was completed in 2006.

4. For finances during the Depression, see Mayer, *The Met,* 170–79.

5. The opera house was to be positioned where the RCA building now stands. It, too, was to face an ice skating rink.

6. When the Met signed its contract with NBC in 1931, live classical music was already heard regularly on nationwide radio: the Chicago Civic Opera, retransmissions from Dresden, Covent Garden, and Salzburg, and NBC's own National Grand Opera Company, as well as the New York Philharmonic, the Boston Symphony, and the Philadelphia Orchestra. For the NBC/Metropolitan agreement relative to negotiating with Metropolitan artists for performances outside the Met, see Paul Jackson, *Saturday Afternoons at the Old Met: The Metropolitan Opera Broadcasts, 1931–1950* (Portland, OR: Amadeus Press, 1992), 14.

7. "the deluge": Giulio Gatti-Casazza, *Memories of the Opera* (New York: Scribner, 1941), 313.

8. For the early history of opera on the radio, see C.J. Luten, "Golden Age of Opera," *Opera News* (Dec. 18, 1976): 54–58. For the Met broadcasts in 1931–32 and 1932–33, see Jackson, *Saturday Afternoons,* 23.

9. For the formation of the Metropolitan Opera Association, Inc., see Mayer, *The Met,* 175. "organized for educational": minutes, May 14, 1932. "It is this": Downes, *Times,* May 22, 1932.

10. For Gatti's salary, see Irving Kolodin, *The Metropolitan Opera, 1883–1966: A Candid History* (New York: Alfred A. Knopf, 1966), 24. Even with reductions, Gatti was well compensated during the Depression seasons. His salary had risen to $67,057 in 1930–31, fell to $59,169 in 1931–32, $57,736 in 1932–33, and $43,108 in 1933–34. For management's role in the open letter censuring Gigli, see ibid., 24. Correspondence regarding the termination of Jeritza's contract, April 30, May 9, July 14, 1932. Jeritza returned to the Met stage on November 8, 1932, under the aegis of the Musicians' Symphony Orchestra. Led by Fritz Reiner, she sang excerpts from *Salome* in a concert version prepared by Strauss.

11. "Under the management": Kahn, *The Metropolitan Opera,* statement, 7–8.

12. "*Peter Ibbetson* made": Ruby Mercer, *The Tenor of His Time: Edward Johnson of the Met* [discography by J. B. McPherson, W. R. Moran] (Toronto and Vancouver: Clarke, Irwin & Company Limited, 1976), 148. *Peter Ibbetson* is based on George Du Maurier's eponymous novel published in 1891 and its dramatization in 1917 by Constance Collier as a vehicle for herself, John Barrymore, and Lionel Barrymore. The apotheosis of Peter and Mary echoed Broadway's spectral romances of the late 1920s: *Outward Bound, The Dybbuk, Berkeley Square,* and *Death Takes a Holiday.* "a tremendous argument": Leonard Liebling, *American.* "rather negligible": Oscar Thompson, *Post.* "oddly featureless": Edward Cushing, *Brooklyn Eagle.* "Strong men actually": Downes, *Times.*

13. "Our present form": cited in Jackson, *Saturday Afternoons,* 29–30.

14. August Belmont Sr. né Schönberg, born Jewish, curator of the Rothschild interests, married the daughter of Commodore Matthew Perry.

15. For the radio appeals, see Mayer, *The Met*, 179. For the position taken by Cornelius Vanderbilt, IV, see Quaintance Eaton, *The Miracle of the Met* (Westport, CT: Greenwood Press, 1976), 249.

16. Individual salaries are listed in the Metropolitan paybooks. For Depression salaries, see Mayer, *The Met*, 186.

17. "cultivation of vocal": www.Operaclub.org. "that the people": cited in Mayer, *The Met*, 193, from the *American*, Jan. 8, 1934. "the democratization of": Eleanor Robson Belmont, *The Fabric of Memory* (New York: Farrar, Straus and Cudahy, 1957), 266.

18. "could assemble a": Witherspoon to Stephens, March 12, 1933. "if an appeal": Stephens to Cravath, March 16, 1933. "Shifting the opera": Cravath to Stephens, March 17, 1933. "The Juilliard backing": Stephens to Witherspoon, March 21, 1933. Witherspoon to Erskine, see Mayer, *The Met*, 202.

19. "I've just dumped": cited in Eaton, *The Miracle of the Met*, 252–53. Two years before the Juilliard agreement, in a letter of Dec. 5, 1933, Cravath had urged Gatti to introduce a popularly priced supplementary spring season.

20. "in a desperate": *Time* (March 18, 1935): 58. Two Juilliard trustees were already Metropolitan directors, Frederick A. Juilliard, the nephew of Augustus, and Allen Wardwell, lawyer for the Real Estate Company.

21. Five years later, Gatti died in Ferrara at the age of seventy.

22. "responsible for the": *Chord and Discord* (Dec. 1935), cited in Kolodin, *The Metropolitan Opera*, 361.

23. The Met should have had doubts about Konetzni. Reviewing her in Vienna, the *Times* found her "superb" voice "imperfectly schooled . . . while to the temperamental, dramatic and intellectual demands of Isolde the singer is woefully unequal" (Herbert F. Peyser, May 20, 1934). The *Herald Tribune* was even more cutting after her December 26, 1934, New York debut as Brünnhilde: "Of dramatic illusion there was little, while the voice itself was pale and tones none too steady." Ziegler wrote his brutal assessment to agent Erich Simon: "The press were almost uniformly severe. . . . We are convinced that the New York public, with its memories of the great Isoldes, would scarcely have found Konetzni to their liking. Her face is singularly without expression, and is unfortunately, very round" (Jan. 4, 1935).

24. For Flagstad's audition and rehearsal, see Mayer, *The Met*, 195. "Today we are": cited in Howard Vogt, *Flagstad: Singer of the Century* (London: Secker & Warburg, 1987), 111–12.

25. For Gatti's losses, see Mayer, *The Met*, 185–86. Witherspoon's 1935–36 repertoire included *Pelléas et Melisande, Martha, L'Africaine, Boris Godunov, Les Contes d'Hoffmann, La Gioconda,* and *Il Barbiere di Siviglia;* Johnson added *Gianni Schicchi, La Juive,* and *La Rondine.*

26. "has lost a": Witherspoon to Cravath, April 1, 1935. "the outstanding success": Cravath to Witherspoon, April 12, 1935.

27. "Beneath the surface": Mercer, *The Tenor of His Time*, 64.

28. "vocal gold": James Huneker, *Times*.

29. Talley's concert fees were estimated by her former agent, F. C. Coppicus.

30. For an exhaustive account of Tibbett's career, see Hertzel Weinstat and Bert Wechsler, *Dear Rogue: A Biography of the American Baritone Lawrence Tibbett* (Portland, OR: Amadeus Press, 1966), 65–70.

31. "has as yet": Eleanor Steber, with Marcia Slota, *Eleanor Steber: An Autobiography* (Ridgewood, NJ: Wordsworth, 1992), 77.

32. The broadcast of a singing competition had been successfully tested by the Atwater Kent Foundation radio auditions beginning in 1930.

33. Beginning in the 1940s and through the 1970s, a vigorous regional opera movement spread from coast to coast. By 1980, each of the cities cited in the *Variety* article, and many more not mentioned, could claim their own opera company. The Connecticut Opera and the Greater Miami Opera were founded in 1942; in 1945, it was the turn of the Fort Lauderdale Opera Guild Incorporated. The 1950s saw the birth of the Dallas Opera and the Omaha Civic Opera Society; the 1960s, of the Seattle Opera, the Minneapolis Opera, and the New Jersey State Opera; the 1970s, of the Atlanta Opera, the Michigan Opera Theatre, the Cleveland Opera, and the Des Moines Metro Opera. "to mean it": Texaco to Johnson, April 18, 1941.

34. "to avert unemployment": Belmont, *The Fabric of Memory*, 265. "to develop and": document of incorporation.

35. For the Opera Guild's activities, see annual report, 1936–37, in *Opera News* (March 22, 1937).

36. Rudolf Bing had his troubles with the unruly behavior of young audiences. He complained that BB shots had rained down on the orchestra and its instruments and that students had spent their time smoking in the lounges during the student performance of *Rigoletto* on March 2, 1956.

37. "big stars": Earle R. Lewis survey, May 21, 1937.

38. Ziegler pitched *Gianni Schicchi* in English in a June 6, 1933, letter to Gatti; Gatti replied on June 28, 1933. The English-language versions of *The Bartered Bride* and *Mârouf* were introduced during the spring seasons. *The Bartered Bride* proved popular enough for inclusion in the regular season.

39. For contributions to the Metropolitan Opera Fund, see Kolodin, *The Metropolitan Opera*, 37.

40. For Tibbett's veto of Warren for the role of Ford, see Weinstat and Wechsler, *Dear Rogue*, 64.

41. "a great triumph": Ziegler to Flagstad, May 22, 1935. Flagstad sang Handel's *Rodelinda* in Göteborg in 1932. We have no way of knowing how much fioritura was retained in this performance. For Flagstad's preparations for *Norma*, see Vogt, *Flagstad, Singer of the Century*, 124–26..

42. A snippet of Flagstad's warrior-maid is preserved in the movie *The Big Broadcast* of 1938. Paul Jackson counts twenty-seven preserved broadcasts of Wagner operas between 1933 and 1940. Since the publication of his *Saturday Afternoons at the Met*, other performances have surfaced. "the enormous range": Jackson, *Saturday Afternoons at the Met*, 105.

43. Flagstad's other Tristans were Carl Hartmann (twice) and Paul Althouse (once).

44. In a memorandum of February 25, 1940, Ziegler lays out Flagstad's maneuvers against Leinsdorf. "Since Mr. Leinsdorf": *Time* (Feb. 5, 1940): 57.

45. The first two of Wagner's thirteen operas, *Die Feen* and *Das Liebesverbot,* are not likely ever to play the Met, and the third, *Rienzi,* was presented only by Stanton.


CHAPTER SIX

1. "was practically trembling": cited in Ruby Mercer, *The Tenor of His Time: Edward Johnson of the Met* [discography by J. B. McPherson, W. R. Moran] (Toronto and Vancouver: Clarke, Irwin & Company Limited 1976), 202.

2. "in the first": "Bruno Walter Talks of Liberty," *Opera News* (Feb. 17, 1941): 21.

3. "At the end": Astrid Varnay, with Donald Arthur, *Fifty-Five years in Five Acts: My Life in Opera* (Boston: Northeastern University Press, 2000), 160.

4. "after terrible times": Simon to Villa, May 27, 1933.

5. The contractual obligations of Italian artists at the Metropolitan is the subject of communications from Gaetano Vecchioti to Johnson, May 2, 1940, and from Johnson to Bori, February 7, 1940. For Schipa and Fascism, see Tito Schipa Jr., *Tito Schipa* (1993; Dallas: Baskerville Publishers, 1996), 137–41.

6. "I should indeed": Johnson deposition in support of Pinza, March 1942.

7. "aliens who are": Public Law 831, 81st Congress.

8. For Belmont on Flagstad, see Eleanor Robson Belmont, *The Fabric of Memory* (New York: Farrar, Straus and Cudahy, 1957), 275. For the story of Flagstad's return to the United States, see Robert Tuggle, "Clouds of War," *Opera News* (July 1995): 17; and Martin Mayer, *The Met: One Hundred Years of Grand Opera* (New York: Simon and Schuster, 1983), 227–28. Flagstad sang in opera in Chicago in 1947 and in San Francisco in 1949 and 1950.

9. For detailed accounts of the Met's fiscal operations during the decade of the 1940s, see Irving Kolodin, *The Metropolitan Opera, 1883–1966: A Candid History* (New York: Alfred A. Knopf 1966), 436, 442, 448–49, 454, 461–62, 468, 476–77, 483; and Mayer, *The Met,* 219, 223–25.

10. The minutes of December 11, 1941, reflect the language policy at the Met during World War II: "It was felt that until the public served by the association indicated its dissatisfaction with the management policy with respect to opera that no change should be made." In a twist of narrative fate, between 1943 and 1945, while *Butterfly* was banished from the Metropolitan, the Puccini work was unusually popular in Italy. As reported in the *Herald Tribune* of January 20, 1946, worried Italian parents saw it as a cautionary tale for daughters susceptible to the attractions of the US forces.

11. "somebody might yell": Howard Taubman, "Boss of the Opera," *Collier's* (Dec. 6, 1941), cited in Mercer, *The Tenor of His Time,* 226. "associate itself with": Wise to Johnson, Dec. 18, 1942.

12. Feodor Chaliapin (1921–29) and Alexander Kipnis (1943) sang in Russian in the Italian performances of *Boris Godunov*.

13. "I cannot accept": Walter to Zirato, Aug. 27, 1942. Walter made known his refusal of *Carmen* in a September 22, 1941, letter to Johnson. In a memorandum of January 25, 1944, Johnson records a luncheon conversation with Walter in which the conductor refused *Norma* and *Entführung* and expressed his reluctance to be known exclusively for Mozart.

14. For Szell and the Met orchestra, see Mayer, *The Met*, 220.

15. "conductor's opera": Oscar Thompson, *Sun*, August 30, 1941. "monuments of operatic": Johnson's report to board after 1941–42 season.

16. "Men and events": notes from Walter to Belmont on the occasion of Marjorie Lawrence's return to the Metropolitan, cited in Belmont, *Fabric of Memory*, 278.

17. *Otello* fell below the box-office average in 1939–40, 1941–42, and 1946–47.

18. "the Baroque atmosphere": *Opera News* (Nov. 20, 1950): 22.

19. "variety and movement": *Opera News* (Jan. 13, 1947): 22.

20. Minutes of February 20, 1947, reflect the decision to engage Toscanini for *Falstaff*. "his transfiguration of": *Musical America* (March 1949): 5.

21. For Johnson's troubles with the board in the late 1940s, see Mayer, *The Met*, 237.

22. "The day is": Report of general manager to board for fiscal year ending May 31, 1942. The long-anticipated postwar arrival of European artists proved to be not a new wave but a passing ripple. Renée Mazella, Hjördis Schymberg, Elen Dosia, and Erna Schlüter ran up a grand total of sixteen Met appearances and were promptly forgotten. The phenomenal Tagliavini, Elmo, and Welitsch came and made memorable impressions, only to leave after a handful of seasons. A decade later, Rudolf Bing, Johnson's successor, would publish an article titled "American Export: Opera Stars" (*Times*, Dec. 26, 1954) in which he names Met American artists appearing in European theaters at roughly the moment of his writing: Astrid Varnay, Eleanor Steber, and Regina Resnik at Bayreuth; Risë Stevens at La Scala; Lucine Amara at Glyndebourne; and Blanche Thebom, Leonard Warren, George London, Martha Lipton, and Jerome Hines elsewhere. Americans based in Europe in the postwar era were Maria Callas, Teresa Stich-Randall, Lucille Udovich, Dorothy Dow, Keith Engen, Jess Walters, Nan Merriman, and Claire Watson.

23. "the frequency with": Mayer, *The Met*, 225. "the wisdom of": Kolodin, *The Metropolitan Opera*, 495.


CHAPTER SEVEN


1. There has been no full-length biography of Rudolf Bing. "How would you": Rudolf Bing, *5000 Nights at the Opera* (Garden City, NY: Doubleday, 1972), 9. Although there were aspirants for Johnson's position, there were no formal candidates. Aside from Frank St. Leger, the following were mentioned: Lawrence Tibbett, Lauritz Melchior, John Brownlee, Richard Bonelli, and Charles Kullman, all

singers, and Laszlo Halasz, general manager of the New York City Opera. Looking back, Bing wrote, "Supporters of Lawrence Tibbett, I was told later, had actually established a campaign headquarters with a desk and a telephone in an office." Bing, *5000 Nights*, 11. For Belmont's report to the Met executive committee, see Martin Mayer, *The Met: One Hundred Years of Grand Opera* (New York: Simon and Schuster, 1983), 238. "socially acceptable": Mayer, *The Met*, 237.

2. For Bing's initial contract negotiations, see Bing, *5000 Nights*, 13. "For the first": John Erskine, *My Life in Music* (New York: William Morrow, 1950), 236, 237. "ladies": Belmont's review of *My Life in Music*, *Opera News* (Nov. 27, 1950): 26–28.

3. It is generally acknowledged that Bing, an avowed Catholic, obscured his Jewish birth. In Howard Taubman's early profile, we have as direct a reference as Bing made to his origins: "He made clear that he had every personal reason to despise Nazism. When the Nazis came into power in Germany he had to leave, and his family and friends were victimized by them" ("The Curtain Rises on Rudolf Bing," *Times*, March 5, 1950). In newspaper accounts of Bing's appointment, he is mistakenly credited with having directed the Darmstadt and Charlottenburg operas two decades or so earlier. A month after the announcement, on July 3, 1949, a letter from Carl Ebert correcting the record was published in the *Times*. Ebert's inference was that Bing had embellished his resumé. On the day Ebert's letter appeared, Bing wrote to the *Times*, subscribing for the most part to Ebert's correction, all the while protesting that the error had been made by the Metropolitan's press office.

4. For Johnson's objections to the press conference, see Quaintance Eaton, *The Miracle of the Met* (Westport, CT: Greenwood Press, 1976), 304. Bing later wrote that he had heard Melchior on a visit to New York in 1939 "looking like a moving couch covered in red plush (though he sounded fine)." Bing, *5000 Nights*, 9.

5. Bing's message to Tibbett is dated March 8, 1950. For the Warren dispute, see Mary Jane Phillips-Matz, *Leonard Warren, American Baritone* (Portland, OR: Amadeus Press, 2000), 181–82. The Associated Press published a photo of Traubel holding the score of *Die Walküre* together with the sheet music of the "Saint Louis Blues" (Sept. 28, 1953). "Miss Traubel used": Bing to G. Wendell Hawkins, Oct. 9, 1953.

6. "he is a": Bing to Kleiber, Nov. 25, 1950. The exchange between Ruth Kleiber and Bing is dated Dec. 17, 1950, and Dec. 28, 1950.

7. "conductor-personality": Bing to Belmont, Sept. 18, 1951. "After all we": Bing to Belmont, March 2, 1953. Some years later, Leinsdorf took this swipe at Bing: "With ex-Nazis he [Bing] took diverse attitudes according to the artistic interests of the Met. Those whom the opera needed had not been tainted, and all those who were suspect the Met did not need." Erich Leinsdorf, *Cadenza: a Musical Career* (Boston: Houghton Mifflin, 1976), 177.

8. "to open the": Margaret Webster, *Don't Put Your Daughter on the Stage* (New York: Alfred A. Knopf, 1972), 204. For the height of the *Don Carlo* sets, see Rolf Gérard, cited in Lilian E. Forester, "Don Carlo: Duet for Director and Designer," *Opera News* (Nov. 6, 1950): 4.

9. "not the best": Martin Dickstein, *Brooklyn Eagle*. "singularly powerful if": Olin Downes, *Times*.

10. In his January 18, 1950, letter to Bing concerning Tebaldi and Rigal, Erede suggests Mario Del Monaco as a possible Don Carlo and, for roles in other operas, Victoria de los Angeles and Maria Callas, the last "a very good Aïda and Norma, Leonora but a step back [from] Rigal and Tebaldi." Bing navigated the choppy waters of the McCarran Act with characteristic sarcasm. Having given up on Christoff, he quipped, "I have now engaged Siepi who was in Switzerland during the war, so I hope he may be all right; but I have just discovered that in Milan he lives in the via Moscova [the river that flows through Moscow] which strikes me highly suspicious!" Bing to Alfred Diez [agent], Oct. 10, 1950. Fedora Barbieri was detained at Ellis Island. The reason given was her affirmative response when asked whether she had attended a Fascist school. Like all Italians of her generation, she had, of course, gone to school under Fascism. Stignani, whose forty-seven years and dumpy mien kept her from the Met, sang with the San Francisco Opera before and after the War, and in Chicago as Azucena in 1955. "a new standard": Bing to Del Monaco, Aug. 1951, informing the tenor that his presence at rehearsals was expected.

11. "The whole present-day": Mordecai Gorelik, *Times,* Dec. 5, 1954. "When the curtain": Robert Sabin, *Musical America* (Dec. 15, 1950): 15. On Welitsch in *Der Fliegende Holländer,* Bing to Diez, Jan. 6, 1951: "We agreed jointly that she [Welitsch] should not do Senta after all because I felt in the condition in which she now finds herself she might have risked a severe set-back with press and public and I thought it was imperative, not only in our own but in her interest, to avoid that. . . . [I] would never have done *Hollander* without Welitsch. *Hollander* is an unpopular work, but last year's success of Welitsch made me feel that I could risk it. This year nobody cares about Welitsch at all; nobody asks at the boxoffice for her because she had one or two bad notices and has no doubt disappointed her audience. The cruelty and speed with which the New York public forgets is extraordinary, and, as I said, in this case I think quite unjustifiable." Only Jeritza and Schorr, in 1931, had drawn large audiences to *Der Fliegende Holländer.* In the late 1930s, not even Flagstad and Schorr could turn a profit for the opera.

12. "Fleder-Mice": Johnson in *Cleveland Press,* cited in Irving Kolodin, *The Metropolitan Opera, 1883–1966: A Candid History* (New York: Alfred A. Knopf, 1966), 492.

13. "Mr. Bing should": Rudolf to Bing, Aug. 21, 1950. The Met principals who sang their roles in the Columbia recording were Welitsch (Rosalinda), Tucker (Alfred), and Kullman (Eisenstein). The Met's Adele, Patrice Munsel, and its Orlovsky, Risë Stevens, sang in the RCA recording. Neither of RCA's tenors, Jan Peerce (Alfred) and James Melton (Eisenstein), would ever sing in a Met *Fledermaus.* In fact, Melton was no longer on the company's roster. RCA, with its starrier galaxy, eventually came out ahead in its rivalry with Columbia. In 1950, it released *Rigoletto* with Warren, Berger, and Peerce, in 1951 the Reiner-Stevens *Carmen,* in 1952 the resplendent *Trovatore* with Milanov, Björling, Barbieri, and Warren.

14. "If it could": John Chapman, *Daily News.* "With it Rudolf": Miles Kastendieck, *Journal-American.* Second-string coloratura to Pons's Lucia and Gilda since her 1943 debut, Munsel had at last found her repertoire and became the company's star

soubrette. *Fledermaus* propelled her onto the covers of *Time* (Dec. 3, 1951) and *Life* (March 3, 1952).

15. "laughing hysterically and": cited in Nigel Douglas, *More Legendary Voices* (New York: Limelight Editions, 1995), 126.

16. For Broadway, Armistead designed Menotti's *The Telephone, The Medium,* and *The Consul,* and Marc Blitzstein's *Regina.* "meaningless detail": *Opera News* (Feb. 26, 1951), 6. For Walter on *Cav/Pag,* see Bing, *5000 Nights,* 277. "a bargain-basement": cited in Mayer, *The Met,* 245. "find symbols to": cited in "Lightning in Calabria," *Opera News* (Feb. 26, 1951), 7.

17. "The aftermath of": Mayer, *The Met,* 245. "Critics have the": Bing, cited in "New Settings," *Theatre Arts* (Nov. 1951): 90.

18. For an account of finances early in Bing's tenure and his conflict with the board, see Mayer, *The Met,* 254–55.

19. In a May 2, 1952, communication to Joseph Rosenstock, Bing outlined his objections to the New York City Opera repertoire. "It is just": Bing to Rosenstock, May 25, 1953. "unfriendly": Bing to Sloan, Dec. 11, 1954. "Not very long": Feb. 6, 1953.

20. "the familiar Bing": Paul Jackson, *Sign-Off for the Old Met: The Metropolitan Opera Broadcasts, 1950–1966* (Portland, OR: Amadeus Press, 1997), 331. Bing wrote to Rudolf on June 28, 1953, regarding the Berlin offer.

21. "professional . . . amateurs": Tibor Kozma, "Ave Atque Vale—Fritz Reiner," *Opera News* (April 6, 1953): 5–6. Downes, *10 Operatic Masterpieces* (New York: Scribner, 1952). "No smallest item": "Worlds of Opera," *Opera News* (April 6, 1953): 22.

22. Bing's Nov. 14, 1953 memorandum advises his staff to deny tickets to the chief claqueur.

23. "I think the": Bing to Reginald Tonry and Lincoln Lauterstein, Nov. 16, 1954. "standing room problem": Tonry to Bing, Feb. 24, 1955.

24. An undated "Memorandum of Events Leading Up to Cancellation and Reinstatement of Season 1956–57" is a diary of the negotiations between the Met and AGMA in July 1956.

25. For the intersection of the Civil Rights movement and the 1961 strike threat, see Mayer, *The Met,* 303.

26. "Negro singers": Met Online Annals, see Rudolf Bing.

27. "Mr. Ziegler is": Gatti-Casazza to Kahn, April 20, 1927. "It almost didn't": Joe Nash, "Pioneers in Negro Concert Dance: 1931–1937," in *American Dance Festival* (Durham, NC, 1988), 11.

28. "Dusky Harlemites, high": *Time* (July 31, 1933): 28. "see itself clear": White to Cravath, Aug. 17, 1932. For the auditions of Rahn and Brice, see Allan Keiler, *Marian Anderson: A Singer's Journey* (New York: Scribner, 2000), 270.

29. In 1962, seven years after Anderson's debut, Elinor Harper became the first African-American chorister contracted by the Metropolitan.

30. "Only recently have": Ziegler to Arnold Hodas. "Nobody can admire," April 20, 1950, cited in Allan Morrison, "Who Will Be the First to Crack Met Opera?," *Negro Digest* (Sept. 1950): 54.

31. In the Met version of *Ballo* broadcast on December 10, 1955, the line "Ulrica, dell immondo sangue dei negri [Ulrica, of unclean Negro blood]" became "Ulrica, del futuro divinatrice [Ulrica, seer into the future]."

32. "Miss Anderson's voice": Winthrop Sargeant, *New Yorker* (Jan. 15, 1955): 94.

33. For the story of McFerrin's success in the Met auditions, see *The Encyclopedia of Arkansas History and Culture,* www.encyclopediaofarkansas.net/encyclopedia/. "The SCLC regrets": *Atlanta Journal,* May 6, 1961. The "color line" was coined by W. E. B. Dubois in 1903. "Leontyne Price at": Bing to Bliss, May 21, 1963.

34. For Bing's favorite operas, see *Times,* March 5, 1950.

35. For Webster on staging *Don Carlo* and *Aïda* at the Met, see Webster, *Don't Put Your Daughter on the Stage,* 202–24. Elena Nikolaidi (Amneris) and George London (Amonasro) made successful debuts in the opening night *Aïda.*

36. The 1951 *Rigoletto* was directed by Graf and designed by Eugene Berman.

37. "special . . . found it": *New Yorker* (Nov. 22, 1952): 106. "as it now": Stiedry, "*La Forza* from the Podium," *Opera News* (Nov. 24, 1952): 6. The 1952 *La Forza del destino* was directed by Graf.

38. Warren was furious at Mitropoulos over fast tempos. His publicist, Edgar Vincent, reported that the baritone confronted the conductor: "If you don't conduct this as we rehearsed it, I'll walk right off the stage and you can sing the opera yourself." Phillips-Matz, *Leonard Warren,* 234. The 1956 *Ernani* was directed by Dino Yannopoulos and designed by Esteban Frances. The 1957 *La Traviata* was directed by Tyrone Guthrie. "magnificent": Paul Henry Lang, *Herald Tribune.* "stole the show": Kastendieck, *Journal-American.* "sends sparks across": Robert Coleman, *Mirror.* "reached the highest": Armando Romano, *Il Progresso Italo-Americano.*

39. For the "Brava Callas" incident, see Bing, *5000 Nights,* 245.

40. For the pro-Italian cabal, see Phillips-Matz, *Leonard Warren,* 273. The 1959 new production of *Il Trovatore* was directed by Graf and designed by Motley.

41. "fussily arty and": *New Yorker* (Nov. 5, 1960): 215–16.

42. Like the previous production (1940), the 1962 *Ballo,* directed by Günther Rennert, was set in Sweden, as the composer and his librettist specified, rather than in the Colonial Boston mandated by the Roman censors in 1859. "rather self-conscious": *New Yorker* (Feb. 3, 1962): 97–98. The production committee minutes of Nov. 17, 1961 reflect that Del Monaco was originally slated for *Otello,* with McCracken contracted for a few performances.

43. After Bing, the repertoire was opened to early and twentieth-century opera. Schuyler Chapin presented five such novelties in three seasons; Anthony Bliss, Bruce Crawford, and Hugh Southern, fourteen in sixteen seasons; Joseph Volpe, twenty-five in sixteen seasons; Peter Gelb, fourteen in his first eight seasons.

44. "deemed it not": Ziegler to Leslie Reggel, Dec. 23, 1941. "I would like": Gutman to Bing, Nov. 21, 1955. "blandly representational and": *Saturday Review* (March 21, 1959): 32. The house had to be heavily papered for the benefit premiere of *Wozzeck.*

45. "at sixty-nine": Lang, *Herald Tribune.*

46. "Immensely supple, the": Jackson, *Sign-Off for the Old Met*, 122. For Nilsson and *Ariadne auf Naxos*, see Bing, *A Knight at the Opera* (New York: G. P. Putnam's Sons, 1981), 149.

47. Bing made plain his preference for Munsel in a Nov. 29, 1955 memo to Ritchard. "one of the": Kolodin, *Saturday Review* (Jan. 5, 1957): 29. Arias of *La Périchole* available in recordings in 1955 were sung by the low-voiced Jennie Tourel and Gladys Swarthout. Among the second-string singers and comprimarios cast as leads in Metropolitan Record Club recordings were Albert da Costa as Canio, Jon Crain as Hoffmann, Heidi Krall as Rosalinde, Mary Curtis-Verna as Maddalena, and Charles Anthony as Ernesto.

48. "run the risk": Gian Carlo Menotti, "I Am the Savage," *Opera News* (Feb. 8, 1964): 12.

49. "that for reasons": Bing to Stravinsky, Jan. 16, 1952.

50. "Mr. Barber's mastery": Lang, *Herald Tribune*. "American masterpiece": *Newsweek,* Jan. 27, 1958. "capable of holding": Sargeant, *New Yorker* (Jan. 25, 1958): 108–10. Bing mentions Jurinac's breakdown in a letter to Roberto Bauer, Nov. 30, 1957. In the same letter, Bing inquires about the availability of American soprano Margherita Roberti for the part of Vanessa.

51. The 1952 *La Bohème* was designed by Gérard. Eugene Berman designed the 1954 *Il Barbiere di Siviglia*. Rolf Gérard designed the 1955 *Les Contes d'Hoffmann*. Oliver Messel designed *Le Nozze di Figaro*.

52. "romantic trappings": "Tyrone Guthrie Finds Squalor in Seville," *Opera News* (Feb. 11, 1952): 6. "totally conventional realistic": memo to Reginald Allen and staff, June 3, 1957. "restraint and delicacy": *Time,* March 3.

53. "One wonders why": Lang, *Herald Tribune*. Ita Maximovna designed the 1963 *Manon*. Attilio Colonello designed the 1964 *Lucia di Lammermoor*.

54. "an opera man": *Herald Tribune,* Nov. 1, 1957. "first pseudo-revolving": Jackson, *Sign-Off for the Old Met,* 158. "sample of operatic": *Saturday Review* (Oct. 17, 1964): 39. George Szell returned to the Met to conduct the 1953 new production of *Tannhäuser*. The revered leader of the Cleveland Orchestra was so demanding in his negotiations for a future *Salome* that the general manager withdrew the offer. In response, Szell wrote an open letter to the *Herald Tribune* (Jan. 14, 1954), criticizing "present conditions at the Metropolitan Opera" and announcing the cancellation of his remaining performances. Bing vented his anger to George Sloan: "I feel he [Szell] has behaved like a cad and I will under no circumstances repeat my mistake of inviting Mr. Szell again wherever I may work to the end of my days" (Jan. 20, 1954). Later, to the assertion that Szell was his own worst enemy, Bing retorted, "Not while I am alive." Cited in Mayer, *The Met,* 250. Bing rehearsed his feud with Szell in a January 18, 1954, letter to Bruno Zirato.

55. "a stately bore": Harold C. Schonberg, *Times,* Dec. 16, 1960. "To hear her": Kastendieck, *Christian Science Monitor,* Feb. 26, 1963. The 1963 *Adriana Lecouvreur* was directed by Nathaniel Merrill and designed by Camillo Parravicini.

56. Valletti sang in concert in New York through the 1960s. In a June 4, 1962 memo to Bing, Herman notes Valletti's refusal to return to the Met. "My voice is": *Time* (Nov. 17, 1958): 53.

## CHAPTER EIGHT

1. Most critics agreed with the *Journal-American* reviewer that "Falla's struggles with the score took the edge off his inspiration" and that his disciple's effort to complete the work "does not sound like a major contribution." The *Times* described *Atlantida* as "a strange mixture of paganism and Christianity that moves from Hercules and the mythical continent of Atlantis to the discovery of America by Columbus."

2. For a complete account of the move to Lincoln Center, see Martin Mayer, *The Met: One Hundred Years of Grand Opera* (New York: Simon and Schuster, 1983), 263–72.

3. "Stupidity has triumphed": Bing to Herman, June 25, 1966.

4. "actual physical plant": Bing to staff, Oct. 24, 1955. "must be radically": Rudolf to Bing, Nov. 11, 1955. Gutman memo to Bing, Nov. 17, 1955. "Personally, I am": Bing to staff, Oct. 24, 1955.

5. By way of comparison, the seating capacity of the Civic Opera House in Chicago is 3,563, the War Memorial Opera House in San Francisco 3,146, Teatro alla Scala in Milan 2800, Opéra Bastille in Paris 2,723, and the Royal Opera House in London 2,256.

6. "The new Metropolitan": Leinsdorf to Bing and Kravitz, Nov. 5, 1959. "In an opera": cited in Josh Greenfeld, *Times,* Aug. 21, 1966.

7. For the story of the turntable, see Joseph Volpe with Charles Michener, *The Toughest Show on Earth: My Rise and Reign at the Metropolitan Opera* (New York: Alfred A. Knopf, 2006), 47. "The fault was": Bing, *5000 Nights at the Opera* (Garden City, NY: Doubleday, 1972), 307.

8. "favorite": Schippers interview, *Opera News* (Sept. 17, 1966): 35. "Almost everything about": Harold C. Schonberg, *Times.* "Appallingly pretentious, appallingly": Winthrop Sargeant, *New Yorker* (Sept. 24, 1966): 123. "a disaster": *Newsweek* (Sept. 26, 1966): 96. "a severe blow": Alan Rich, *World Journal Tribune,* Oct. 2, 1966.

9. *The Metropolitan Opera: A Statement by Otto H. Kahn,* Oct. 5, 1925.

10. Giannini's *The Scarlet Letter* premiered in German in Hamburg in 1938, Tamkin's *The Dybbuk* at the New York City Opera in 1951. In a January 19, 1939, letter to Ziegler, Downes made his case for the three American operas. At the end of the 1941–42 season, Johnson made a written report (undated) to the board about the Carnegie Foundation grant.

11. On March 2, 1956, Bing wrote to Gutman to express his preference for *Vanessa* over *The Alcestiad.* "If it finally": Gutman to Bing and Bliss, June 10, 1959, and Feb. 2, 1960.

12. For a detailed account of the Metropolitan Opera National Company, see Mayer, *The Met,* 312–15. In its first season, 1965–66, the National Company presented *Madama Butterfly, La Cenerentola,* and *Carmen* in addition to *Susannah;* in its second and final season, *Le Nozze di Figaro, La Traviata, La Bohème,* and *The Rape of Lucretia.* For the personal reasons that contributed to Bliss's resignation, his

divorce from Jo Ann Sayres and his marriage to the Met ballerina Sally Brayley, see Johanna Fiedler, *Molto Agitato* (New York: Doubleday, 2001), 74.

13. "outstanding successes": Bing's annual report to the board, April 10, 1967. Margherita Wallmann directed the 1966 *La Gioconda*. Graf staged the 1966 *Elektra*. Rennert directed the 1967 *Die Zauberflöte*. "On the whole": Schonberg, *Times*.

14. For the first Lincoln Center season shortfalls, see Mayer, *The Met*, 310.

15. "They'd Never Strike": Alan Rich (Sept. 1, 1969): 50.

16. "to get authorization": Bing, *5000 Nights at the Opera*, 302.

17. "In terms of": Martin Bernheimer, *Los Angeles Times,* Sept. 21, 1967. The 1967 *Roméo et Juliette* was directed by Paul-Emile Deiber and designed by Gérard. The 1967 *Carmen* was directed by Jean-Louis Barrault and designed by Jacques Dupont. "ridiculous . . . awkward": Sargeant, *New Yorker* (Dec. 23, 1967): 54. The 1971 *Werther* was directed by Deiber and designed by Rudolf Heinrich. The 1968 *Tosca* was directed by Otto Schenk and designed by Heinrich. The 1971 *Der Freischütz* was directed and designed by Heinrich. The 1968 *Luisa Miller* and the 1969 *Il Trovatore* were directed by Merrill. "entirely conventional": Sargeant, *New Yorker* (Oct. 9, 1971): 132. "full of dated": Schonberg, *Times,* Sept. 30, 1971. "hideous": Rich, *New York* (Oct. 11, 1971): 65. "[The onstage spectators]": Schonberg, *Times*. "a cavelike collection": Raymond Ericson, *Times*.

18. August Everding directed the 1971 *Tristan und Isolde*. "The sets [were]": Harriett Johnson. Schenk directed the 1970 *Fidelio*.

19. "ominously magnificent throughout": Harriet Johnson, *Post*.

20. Karajan's oversight of eight lighting rehearsals in Vienna prompted Bing to quip, "I could have got it that dark with one" (Bing, *5000 Nights*, 320). Although absent from New York, the credits designate Karajan as "director" of the 1974 *Götterdämmerung;* Wolfgang Weber was credited with its staging.

21. Fiedler reports that Bliss was the sole trustee to vote "no" on the renewal of Bing's contract to 1972. Fiedler, *Molto Agitato*, 74. "The Metropolitan Opera": *New York* (Dec. 15, 1969): 66–67.

22. "Nine out of": *Cue* (Feb. 21, 1970). "operated on the": Schonberg, *Times,* April 16, 1972. "It would be": *New York* (April 17, 1972): 82–83.

23. "What the Met": Hubert Saal (May 18, 1970): 109. The critical consensus was that *Don Carlo, L'Elisir d'amore, Eugene Onegin, Falstaff, Fidelio, Die Frau ohne Schatten, Die Meistersinger, Otello, Parsifal, Rigoletto,* and *Tristan und Isolde* were Bing's successful new productions. We agree, and would add *Il Barbiere di Siviglia, Carmen, Così fan tutte, Fledermaus, La Forza del destino, Madama Butterfly, Mourning Becomes Electra, Peter Grimes, Der Rosenkavalier, Samson et Dalila,* and *Vanessa* at the very least.

24. "I am solely"; "I don't see": *Cue* (Feb. 21, 1970).

25. Stephen E. Rubin "Changing the Guard at the Met," *Stereo Review* (April 1972): 61–66. "Strong-minded conductors": Schonberg, *Times,* April 16, 1972.

26. For the salaries of Met stars, see Donal Henahan, *Times,* Sept. 17, 1972.

27. For Bing's thoughts on the succession, see Bing, *A Knight at the Opera*, 26–38.

28. "the Metropolitan sweepstakes": Jane P. Boutwell, *Times,* Sept. 12, 1971.

29. "From my point": Gentele to Kubelik, Oct. 11, 1971. Gutman was convinced that Chapin's appointment had everything to do with his relationship with Bernstein, with whom he had made two films, one of the Verdi "Requiem" and the other about Beethoven: "Schuyler's appointment obviously lies exclusively in the realm of what you call science fiction. . . . As long as Chapin will help Mr. Moore in making all those millions through electronics, it is, no doubt, a very useful appointment. You may be quite sure that Schuyler has no intention to bother with such minor matters as the ones which, so far, have been handled by Bob Herman, quite apart from the fact that he is utterly unqualified" (Gutman to Bing, July 26, 1971).

30. Elisabeth would have been Marilyn Horne's first Wagner role at the Met and Tannhäuser McCracken's first Wagner lead. In a November 17, 1971, letter to Moore, Gentele explained his decision to direct *Carmen*.

31. "Deeply shocked tragic"; "Appreciate greatly your": Schuyler Chapin, *Musical Chairs* (New York: G. P. Putnam Sons, 1978), 277–78. "Up to this": ibid.

32. For Gentele's work on *Carmen,* see Harvey E. Phillips, *The Carmen Chronicle: The Making of an Opera* (New York: Stein and Day, 1973), 36, 129, 161, 198. For Leonard Bernstein and the Met orchestra, see ibid., 124. "a level of": Rich, *New York* (Oct. 2, 1972): 66.

33. "the soprano poured": Louis Snyder, *Christian Science Monitor* (Nov. 22, 1972). Once again, although absent from New York, the credits designate Karajan as "director" of the 1972 *Siegfried;* Wolfgang Weber was credited with its staging. "smaller productions and": minutes, Sept. 17, 1987. The minutes of Jan. 16, March 20, and Sept. 18, 1997, reflect discussions of a small theater at Lincoln Center.

34. "disturbed by the": minutes, Jan. 11, 1973. The Met had put on a concert version of *I Vespri Siciliani* in Newport, Rhode Island, in 1967.

35. "close to hysteria"; "You and I": Chapin to Kubelik, June 20, 1973. In a September 23, 1974, interview, Chapin observed, "We were able to effect some small economies last year—about $.25 million—but other sources of income must be found" (*Christian Science Monitor* [Sept. 23, 1974]).

36. Merrill directed the 1973 *Les Troyens.* "The fact is": *Newsweek* (Oct. 1, 1973): 74. "the sets and": Michael Steinberg, *Boston Evening Globe,* Nov. 11, 1973. The 1973 *Les Contes d'Hoffmann* was directed by Bliss Herbert and designed by Allen Charles Klein.

37. The three tenors in the December 28, 1959, *Tristan und Isolde* were, in order of appearance, Ramon Vinay, Karl Liebl, and Albert Da Costa. Aside from their single *Tristan und Isolde,* the only Wagner opera shared by Nilsson and Vickers was *Die Walküre.* "One would have": Donal Henahan, *Times,* Feb. 2, 1974.

38. For the advice Levine sought from Wilford, see Fiedler, *Molto Agitato,* 102. "tried in vain": cited in Chapin, *Musical Chairs,* 370.

39. The 1974 *Gianni Schicchi* was directed by Fabrizio Melano and designed by David Reppa.

40. "A tall, slender": Volpe, *The Toughest Show on Earth,* 77.

41. Previous to her house debut, Sills sang only once with the company: at Lewisohn Stadium in the summer of 1966, she played Donna Anna in a concert

presentation of *Don Giovanni*. "to re-create": Manuela Hoelterhoff, *Wall Street Journal*.

42. For Marilyn Horne's advocacy of Magda Olivero, see Marilyn Horne with Jane Scovell, *Marilyn Horne: The Song Continues* (Fort Worth: Baskerville Publishers, 2004), 194–95.

43. For Wilford's delay in renegotiating Levine's contract, see Kolodin, *Saturday Review* (June 1980): 22.

44. The *Saturday Review* article and its title are drawn from Chapin, *Musical Chairs*. For approaches made to Callas and Bongianckino, see ibid., 318–23.

CHAPTER NINE

1. "a European-style": Michael Walsh, "Maestro of the Met," *Time* (Jan. 17, 1983): 58. "Jim has to": Robert C. Marsh, *Dialogues and Discoveries, James Levine: His Life and His Music* (New York: Scribner, 1998), 20. "stayed with their": Johanna Fiedler, *Molto Agitato* (New York: Doubleday, 2001), 95. For a biography of James Levine, see Marsh, *Dialogues and Discoveries,* 17–60. "I've always been": cited in Martin Kettle, "Staying Power," *Guardian,* Nov. 17, 2000.

2. "the company situation": John Dexter, *The Honourable Beast: A Posthumous Autobiography* (London: Nick Hern, 1993), 81.

3. "not a single": Fiedler, *Molto Agitato,* 120.

4. "She led a": Manuela Hoelterhoff, *Wall Street Journal,* Jan. 21, 1976. "Her conducting ... was": Schonberg, *Times,* Jan. 15, 1976. Caldwell led ten more performances of *La Traviata* in 1976 and five of *L'Elisir d'amore* in 1978. Simone Young, the second of the two women to conduct at the Met to date, led the orchestra between 1996 and 1998 in thirty-five performances of *La Bohème, Cavalleria rusticana, Pagliacci, Il Trovatore,* and *Les Contes d'Hoffmann.*

5. For accounts of marketing and development initiatives in this period, see Martin Mayer, *The Met: One Hundred Years of Grand Opera* (New York: Simon and Schuster, 1983), 336–40; Fiedler, *Molto Agitato,* 111–12; and Susie Gilbert and Jay Shir, *A Tale of Four Houses* (London: HarperCollins, 2003), 509–10.

6. There were two network telecasts from the Met stage during Bing's tenure: the first was his inaugural *Don Carlo* in 1950; the second excerpts from his gala farewell of 1972, transmitted a week after the event. "This recording embodies": CD booklet cited in Marsh, *Dialogues and Discoveries,* 39.

7. "There is an": Mayer, *The Met,* 344. "has allowed his": *Saturday Review* (June 1980): 22–27. For Bernstein's reaction to Levine's *Parsifal,* see Hillenbrand, *Time* (Jan. 17, 1983).

8. "a troublesome colleague": cited in Gilbert and Shir, *A Tale of Four Houses,* 518. "being under some": Dexter, *The Honourable Beast,* 170. "If there is": letter to James Dolan, cited in Dexter, *The Honourable Beast,* 110–11. "When Dexter entered": Joseph Volpe with Charles Michener, *The Toughest Show on Earth: My Rise and Reign at the Metropolitan Opera* (New York: Alfred A. Knopf, 2006), 69.

9. Reppa designed the 1976 *Aïda*. "What Mr. Dexter": Andrew Porter, *New Yorker* (Feb. 7, 1977): 98. The three *Prophète* principals can be heard in a recording made just months before the Met revival. "with the virtuosity": *Time* (Jan. 31, 1977).

10. For Dexter on *Dialogues des Carmélites,* see Dexter, *The Honourable Beast,* 108–19. "sensitively direct, lovingly": Porter, *New Yorker* (March 12, 1979): 125.

11. "seemed almost incompetent": Porter, *New Yorker* (Nov. 21, 1977): 175.

12. "the Lucifer-like": Andrew Porter, *The Observer,* June 4, 1995. "the work [did]": *Wall Street Journal,* Nov. 30, 1979. "It is a": *Times,* Nov. 17, 1979.

13. "disaster . . . horrid travesty": *New Yorker* (Nov. 13, 1978): 234.

14. The 1978 *Thaïs* was directed by Tito Capobianco and designed by Carl Toms. The 1978 *La Favorita* was directed by Patrick Tavernia and designed by Ming Cho Lee.

15. The 1975 *Le Nozze di Figaro* was directed by Rennert and designed by O'Hearn. The 1980 *Manon Lescaut* was designed by Desmond Heeley. The 1977 *La Bohème* was directed by Melano. "to indulge in": Dexter, *The Honourable Beast,* 175. "finest hour": Bill Zakariasen, *Daily News.* "a 20th-century": *New Yorker* (Jan. 9, 1978): 77.

16. "If we don't": Volpe, *The Toughest Show,* 87.

17. Audience interest in *Parade* fell to 79.2 percent of capacity in 1982–83 and to 64.6 percent in 1985–86. "Every so often": Donal Henahan, Feb. 22, 1981.

18. "jerk": *Opera News* (March 13, 1982): 26.

19. "Leave it to": Dexter, *The Honourable Beast,* 182. The 1982 *Così fan tutte* was directed by Colin Graham.

20. "The worst new": Henahan. "serious-minded, ambitious": *New Yorker* (Dec. 13, 1982): 179.

21. "it is clear": Walsh, *Time* (Jan. 17, 1983): 61. For Bliss's oversight of Levine's spending, see Fiedler, *Molto Agitato,* 189.

22. The afternoon concert of the Centennial Gala was transmitted to Europe.

23. "'seen' the music": Porter, *New Yorker* (Dec. 12, 1983): 166. The Met premiere of Mascagni's *Il Piccolo Marat,* announced in 1980 for Freni, fell victim to the disruptions of the delayed 1980–81 season. "the evening stretched": Henahan. "third-rate music": Porter (March 26, 1984): 92.

24. *Phoebus and Pan* (Jan. 15, 1942) was not an opera, but a stage adaptation of a Bach cantata.

25. "because Jimmy Levine's": Volpe *The Toughest Show,* 156. "the Met was": ibid., 104–5.

26. "the separation of": Mayer, *The Met,* 353. "Either engage me": Will Crutchfield, *Times,* Sept. 22, 1985.

27. "My job is": *Times,* Sept. 22, 1985. "We must": Bliss to Levine, July 15, 1983. "conservative swing": *Times,* Sept. 22, 1985. Cecile Zilkha joined the board in 1978, and became a managing director in 1982, vice president in 1993, vice chairman in 1999. For more on Zilkha, see Fiedler, *Molto Agitato,* 207–8.

28. Levine on the state of singing in the mid-1980s: "I can't imagine a world without marvelous performances of *Aïda.* Clearly, we can't do it with the consistency

we once could" (*Times,* Sept. 22). "a shambles": Thor Eckert Jr., May 15. "so depressing that": Hoelterhoff, May 29. "not in most": Crutchfield, *Times,* Jan. 11, 1987.

29. The moveable dungeon of Zeffirelli's *Tosca* was dropped in later performances.

30. "short list of": *New Yorker* (April 7, 1986): 75. "only a little": Henahan, *Times.* "a manic-depressive," Hoelterhoff, *Wall Street Journal,* March 19. "an object lesson," Eckert, *Christian Science Monitor,* April 28. Otto Kahn had urged Gershwin, Irving Berlin, and Jerome Kern to compose an opera. Berlin was an implausible choice; Kern, on the other hand, given the sweep of his *Show Boat,* was a lost opportunity. "less than convincing": Porter, *New Yorker* (Feb. 25, 1985): 95.

31. For an exhaustive history of Met tours, see Quaintance Eaton, *Opera Caravan: Adventures of the Metropolitan on Tour, 1883–1956* (New York: Metropolitan Opera Guild, 1957).

32. "The tour is": Bing to Liduino Bonardi, Sept. 27, 1955.

33. "If you had": Frank Taplin diary, May 5, 1984, cited in Gilbert and Shir, *A Tale of Four Houses,* 642.

34. "Serious opera fans": Bernard Holland.

35. "For box-office": Henahan, *Times,* March 8, 1987. "The general manager": Rockwell, *Times,* May 27, 1987.

36. "about halfway through": Henahan, *Times,* Dec. 5, 1986.

37. "lost in the": John Freeman, July 1987. "elephantine": Porter, *New Yorker* (March 2, 1987): 104.

38. "John Pascoe's sets": Henahan, *Times,* Sept. 29, 1988.

39. "all very chic": *Los Angeles Times,* Jan. 18, 1989.

40. "has to be": Kettle, *Guardian,* Nov. 17, 2000.

41. "even to be": ibid. "widespread resentment among": Rockwell.

42. "I rarely saw": Volpe, *The Toughest Show,* 112.

43. For the exclusion of Levine in the Southern appointment and Bliss's reaction, see Volpe, *The Toughest Show,* 260.

44. "passivity...failure to": Rockwell, *Times,* June 27, 1990. "During Southern's seven": Volpe, *The Toughest Show,* 115.


CHAPTER TEN

1. "Although Jimmy and": Joseph Volpe with Charles Michener, *The Toughest Show on Earth: My Rise and Reign at the Metropolitan Opera* (New York: Alfred A. Knopf, 2006), 113. "The translation—'Not": ibid., 115. "the triumvirate model": ibid., 5.

2. For the story of the Ouija board, see ibid., 4.

3. "rugged ship": ibid., 122. "I knew that": ibid. 126.

4. "Jimmy Levine was": ibid., 129.

5. The conception and gestation of *The Ghosts of Versailles* is recounted by Corigliano in Michael C. Nott, "The Long Road to Versailles," *Opera News* (Jan. 4,

1992): 9–11, 49; Hoffman in Lanford Wilson, "Ghost Writer," *Opera News* (Jan. 4, 1992): 16, 18–20, 48–49; and Matthew Gurewitsch in "Revolutionary Strains," *Atlantic Monthly* (Dec. 1991): 112–17.

6. "considerable achievement": Alex Ross (Jan. 10, 2000): 88–90.

7. In the most recent directory of Opera America, *Susannah* is third in the list of North American operas, after *Amahl and the Night Visitors* and *Porgy and Bess*. Opera America, founded in 1970, is a national organization devoted "to supporting the creation, presentation and enjoyment of opera" (www.operaamerica.org). The organization maintains a database of opera performances in North America. "modern-day Mascagni": Anthony Tommasini, *Times,* Dec. 7, 2002.

8. After his recovery, Carreras sang only once at the Met, a single act of *Carmen* at a gala in May 2000. For Levine's tours and fees, see Johanna Fiedler, *Molto Agitato* (New York: Doubleday, 2001), 324. For "The Three Tenors" and the diffusion of opera, see James R. Oestreich, *Times,* April 28, 1997. For opera attendance, see *1997 Survey of Public Participation in the Arts: Research Division Report #39, December 1998,* National Endowment for the Arts, Washington, DC. The percentages had declined to 3.2 by 2002 and 2.2 by 2008.

9. The 1996 production of *Andrea Chénier* was staged by Nicolas Joël and designed by Hubert Montloup. "He . . . spent a": Martin Bernheimer, *Los Angeles Times,* April 18, 1996.

10. For Volpe's economies on *La Forza del destino,* see Barry Singer, "Mission Accomplished," *Opera News* (Jan. 2006): 14. *Samson et Dalila* was directed by Moshinsky and designed by Richard Hudson.

11. *Cyrano de Bergerac* was staged by Francesca Zambello and designed by Peter J. Davison. "especially good": Tommasini, *Times,* May 16, 2005. "fifty works that": Ross, *New Yorker* (May 30, 2005): 95. The Beppe De Tomasi/Ferruccio Villagrossi production of *Fedora* originated at Barcelona's Gran Teatre de Liceu. "allusions to old": Bernard Holland, *Times,* Feb. 19, 2000.

12. For Volpe's firing of Kathleen Battle, see Volpe, *The Toughest Show,* 219–23. "Bing will be": Manuela Hoelterhoff, *Cinderella & Company: Backstage at the Opera with Cecilia Bartoli* (New York, Alfred A. Knopf, 1998), 53. Volpe later regretted his handling of the Battle affair: "I find myself thinking maybe there was something I could have done. Maybe I could have prevented it. But I wasn't able to. In one way, let's say that I failed to keep it together." *Opera News* (Jan. 2006), 14. "not banning them": Tommasini, *Times,* April 4, 1998.

13. "When Plácido Domingo": Volpe, *The Toughest Show,* 164. For Crawford on Met Titles, see "The Met Looks to the Future," *Opera News* (Sept. 1993): 66. "Jimmy and I": *Times,* Feb. 7, 1994. "it is much": Edward Rothstein, *Times,* April 9, 1995.

14. "false alternative": Rupert Christiansen, *The Telegraph* (London), Dec. 13, 1997. "The Met continues": Holland, *Times,* May 2, 1999.

15. "I don't understand": interview, Aug. 1999, in Fiedler, *Molto Agitato,* 337. "The Met has": interview, Dec. 17, 2000, in ibid., 339. Peter Gelb, too, has a copy of a Met chandelier in his Manhattan apartment: Chip Brown, *Times,* March 24, 2013. "manipulate opera world": Allan Kozinn, *Times,* Oct. 8, 2000.

16. "to get nervous"; "Some board members": Volpe, *The Toughest Show,* 258. For a detailed account of the Vilar story, see James B. Stewart, "The Opera Lover: Onward and Upward With the Arts," *New Yorker* (Feb. 13. 2006): 108–22.

17. "the most difficult": minutes, May 23, 2002. "to underwrite traditional": *Times,* July 24, 2003.

18. "By 2005–2006": minutes, Sept. 18, 2001. Robert Whitehead, also rewarded with membership in the Golden Horseshoe Program, although for a far smaller donation, $50,000, was charged with grand larceny and securities fraud and convicted in 2001.

19. Five of the thirteen operas of Gatti's Slavic project have not returned to date: *The Polish Jew, Snegurochka, Sadko, The Fair at Sorochintzy,* and *Schwanda.* A sixth, *Prince Igor,* returned in the 2013–14 season.

20. For the Lacy/Zarubin agreements and US/Soviet cultural exchanges, see Yale Richmond, *Cultural Exchange and the Cold War: Raising the Iron Curtain* (University Park: Pennsylvania State University, 2003), 10, 15. For the Soviet pique, see "Russians Hurt by Met Failure to Invite Their Leading Singers," *Times,* May 21, 1958. Obraztsova returned to the Met between 1987 and 2002 for *Il Trovatore, Un Ballo in maschera,* and, in Russian at last, *The Gambler* and *War and Peace.*

21. "the most important": John Rockwell.

22. Beňačková, who was first scheduled for Eva in *Die Meistersinger* on October 13, 1976, did not make her debut until 1991 in *Kát'a Kabanová.* The Met had also offered her Micaela, a role she judged inadequate for her debut. In 1988, the *Times* commented disapprovingly that "she was told that Micaela was the only part in which the casting department felt she could be useful to the Metropolitan. This from a company that has recently had in the repertory such Slavic works as *Khovanshchina* and *Jenufa*" (Donal Henahan, Nov. 27). "This is the"; "This relatively modest": Manuela Hoelterhoff, *Wall Street Journal,* March 4, 1991.

23. "So difficult was": Holland, March 15, 1997.

24. "I don't know": Richard Morrison, cited in *Times,* Mar. 15, 2009. Netrebko, Austrian since 2006, was circumspect; her statement made reference neither to Russia nor to the controversy: "As an artist, it is my great joy to collaborate with all of my wonderful colleagues—regardless of their race, ethnicity, religion, gender, or sexual orientation. I have never and will never discriminate against anyone."

25. "Gergiev must not": Igor Shabdrasulov, cited in John Ardoin, *Valery Gergiev and the Kirov: A Story of Survival* (Portland, OR: Amadeus Press, 2001), 252. "Gergiev is the": Matthew Gurewitsch, *Times,* April 19, 1998.

26. For Billinghurst on the Met's relationship to the Kirov, see Ardoin, *Valery Gergiev,* 256. "[Gergiev] won't be": Fiedler, *Molto Agitato,* 322. The Kirov returned in July 2003, copresented by the Metropolitan, with *Semyon Kotko, Khovanshchina, Eugene Onegin, Macbeth, The Demon* (in concert), and *The Invisible City of Kitezh.* "tense relations with": Tommasini, *Times,* Aug. 21, 2003.

27. For an account of the negotiations to secure *War and Peace* for the Met in the 1940s, see Peter Clark, "Early Attempts to Stage *War and Peace* at the Met," Met Online Annals.

28. "The set is": Tommasini. "the most visually": Ross (March 4, 2002): 86–87. "a conscientious patron": Bernheimer, *Opera* (June 2001). Olivier Tambosi directed and Frank Philipp Schlössmann designed *Jenůfa*.

29. "all the prisons": cited in Geoffrey O'Brien, "Sparks of God," *New York Review of Books* (Jan. 14, 2010). "the Met found": Mike Silverman, *Associated Press,* March 6, 2010.

30. See chapter 5 for the George Balanchine/Pavel Tchelitchev *Orfeo ed Euridice,* the only true pre-1950 experimental rereading.

31. "impossible snarl of": Ross, *New Yorker* (March 8, 1999): 84, 86. "daydream . . . a journey": Peter Mossbach in John W. Freeman, "Doktor Faust's Lab Partners," *Opera News* (Jan. 2001): 26. "anti-pretty"; "a dream by": Tim Albery in Matt Wolf, "Dream Team," *Opera News* (Dec. 14, 1996): 26.

32. Peter J. Davison designed the 1997 *The Rake's Progress.* "the brave task": Holland, *Times,* Nov. 22, 1997. Santo Loquasto designed the 2004 *Salome.* "With all those": *Opera News* (Jan. 2002): 47.

33. Gottfried Pilz designed the 2003 *La Juive.*

34. A dream/nightmare/hallucination had previously framed *Der Fliegende Holländer, Doktor Faust,* and *A Midsummer Night's Dream.* For Volpe on *Il Trovatore,* see *Times,* Nov. 7, 2004.

35. Schenk directed and Schneider-Siemssen designed the 1993 *Die Meistersinger.* Schenk directed and Rose designed the 1992 *Elektra.* Moshinsky directed and Yeargan designed the 1993 *Ariadne auf Naxos.* Mark Lamos directed and Robert Israel designed the 1997 *Wozzeck.* George Tsypin designed the 2004 *Die Zauberflöte.* Lesley Koenig directed and Yeargan designed the 1996 *Così fan tutte.* Davison designed the 1998 *Le Nozze di Figaro.*

36. Moshinsky directed and John Napier designed the 2001 *Nabucco.* Guy Joosten directed and Johannes Leiacker designed the 2001 *Roméo et Juliette.* "the most self-serving": Marion Lignana Rosenberg, *Newsday,* April 4, 2006. "a caricature of": Heidi Waleson, *Wall Street Journal,* April 5, 2006. Langenfass designed the 2006 *Don Pasquale.* Copley directed and Conklin designed the 1990 *Semiramide* and the 2002 *Il Pirata.*

37. "left Mr. Volpe": Robin Pogrebin, *Times,* Feb. 10, 2004. "the overall artistic": Tommasini, *Times,* Nov. 1, 2004. "with empty seats": Rockwell, *Times,* Feb. 10, 2004. "persistent criticism . . . that": Singer, "Mission Accomplished," *Opera News* (Jan. 2006): 14.


CHAPTER ELEVEN

1. For biographical information on Peter Gelb, see Rebecca Mead, "Man behind the Curtain," *New Yorker* (Oct. 22, 2007): 138–49; and Nina Munk, "The Met's Grand Gamble," *Vanity Fair* (May 2010). "knowledge of marketing": Mead, *New Yorker* (Oct. 22, 2007): 141. "I thought, Oh": ibid., 148. "My pitch to": Munk, *Vanity Fair.*

2. "access was more": Mead, *New Yorker* (Oct. 22, 2007): 144. Volpe is said to have cast a jaundiced eye on Gelb's work at the Met from the start. In 1992, he replaced Gelb's executive producer position with a radio network producer and a television producer: "I didn't need an executive producer. Guess why? I was the executive producer." In 2006, Gelb created the position of director of media and presentations, to which he appointed Mia Bongiovanni. "occasionally directed": "Peter Gelb, General Manager," www.metoperafamily.org. "He didn't leave": Ralph Blumenthal, *Times,* May 23, 1995.

3. "anything written for": Allan Kozinn, *Times,* Nov. 7, 2004.

4. "Popera": *The Lebrecht Weekly,* Nov. 11, 2004. "Pop singers are": Barry Singer, "Mission," *Opera News* (Jan. 2006), 16. "a producer . . . is": Mead, *New Yorker* (Oct. 22, 2007): 141. "I am a": Munk, *Vanity Fair* (April 2010).

5. "horribly": Volpe to executive committee, Oct. 20, 2005. In 2005–06, subscribers accounted for 50 percent of attendance; in Bing's day, they had accounted for 75 percent. Joseph Volpe with Charles Michener, *The Toughest Show on Earth: My Rise and Reign at the Metropolitan Opera* (New York: Alfred A. Knopf, 2006), 250–51. "reach out to": Gelb to executive committee, Oct. 20, 2005. A comparison of the first seasons for which Gelb felt fully responsible, 2009–12, with Volpe's last three seasons shows no meaningful change in either the commitment of the stars to an increased number of productions annually or to a greater number of performances of each production. What Gelb had in mind were "paintings or sculptures based on their [the artists'] impressions of operas and opera characters in next season's repertoire at no cost to the Met": Gelb to board, Jan. 19, 2006. A gallery for this purpose was carved out of the south lobby. In the midst of negotiations on the media project, there was an embarrassing demonstration on Lincoln Center Plaza by non-unionized workers employed by a firm to which the Met had outsourced its food services. "to make the": Gelb to board, May 25, 2006.

6. "What fuels me": interview with Shelley DuBois, Dec. 6, 2011. "There is a": Hamburg speech, 1997, cited in Mead, *New Yorker* (Oct. 22, 2007): 147.

7. "the Metropolitan Opera": Julie Bosman, *Times,* August 29, 2006. For *Madama Butterfly* and the Saks Fifth Avenue display, see *Times,* April 13. It was Varis who underwrote a program to further another of Gelb's ambitions: to open the doors of the house to a wider public. Two hundred rush tickets in the orchestra were reserved for weekday performances (later extended to the weekend as well) at $20. On her death in 2011, the program was sustained by board members and a subsidy from the Met.

8. "preem fizzles": Arthur Bronson, Dec. 1. "The view . . . that": Jack Gould, *Times.* "a stirring experience": John Crosby, *Herald Tribune.*

9. Risë Stevens's low-cut Carmen costume drew "audible gasps from the big-screen patrons": *Variety,* Dec. 17, 1952.

10. "From the start": Wilborn Hampton, "Peter Gelb on HD Live, His Controversial Gamble at the Met," *Huffington Post,* Oct. 11, 2012. For an accounting of the first season of "Live in HD," see Daniel J. Wakin, *Times,* May 17, 2007. For *Billboard* rankings, see Dade Hayes, "Pop Goes to the Opera," *Variety,* April 2–April 8, 2007.

For Gelb in the TV satellite truck, see Munk, *Vanity Fair* (May 2010). Neubauer Family Foundation sponsorship of the HD telecasts began with the 2007–08 season; Bloomberg began with the 2009–10 season. The telecasts carry this acknowledgment: "'The Met: Live in HD' series is made possible by a generous grant from its founding sponsor, The Neubauer Family Foundation. Global corporate sponsorship of 'The Met: Live in HD' is provided by Bloomberg."

11. "It's like watching": Lawrence Johnson, *Musical America Worldwide* (Dec. 16, 2008).

12. "unpleasant artistic experiences": *Seattle Post-Intelligencer,* Feb. 13, 2006. "for the duration": *New Yorker* (Oct. 9, 2006): 89–90.

13. "the lyrical set": Peter G. Davis, *New York* (Jan. 8, 2007). "in a dream": Matt Wolf, "Unconventional Means," *Opera News* (March 2007): 28.

14. For Gelb's engagement of Sher, see Helen Sheehy, "Sher Touch," *Opera News* (Nov. 2006): 27. In "Resisting Rossini, or Marlon Brando Plays Figaro," *Opera Quarterly* (Spring-Summer 2011): 153–78, Mary Ann Smart examines Sher's production in her analysis of artifice and naturalism in operatic staging.

15. "not tolerate the": "The Opera," *North American Review* (Feb. 1892): 215.

16. "the star of": Zachary Woolfe, *Times,* Sep. 23, 2011. "a natural actress": Mike Silverman, *Associated Press,* Dec. 6, 2006. "a true stage": Anne Midgette, *Times,* Dec. 27, 2006. "Was crazy, no": *Observer* (England), Sept. 7, 2007.

17. For Dessay's criticisms of Zimmerman, see the television interview with Charlie Rose, Oct. 9, 2007, Youtube. "whatever you do": Rebecca Mead, "The Actress," *New Yorker* (March 2, 2009): 58. Ostling designed the 2009 *La Sonnambula.* Chantal Thomas designed the 2008 *La Fille du régiment.*

18. John Cox directed the 2008 *Thaïs;* no designer is credited in the Met annals. The Nicolas Joël production of the 2008 *La Rondine* was directed by Stephen Barlow and designed by Ezio Frigerio. Adrian Noble directed and Mark Thompson designed the 2007 *Macbeth.* David McVicar directed and Charles Edwards designed the 2009 *Il Trovatore.* Richard Jones directed and John Mcfarlane designed the 2007 *Hänsel und Gretel.* John Doyle directed and Scott Pask designed the 2008 *Peter Grimes.*

19. "All these devices": David J. Baker, *Opera News* (Feb. 2009): 52.

20. "In the final": Midgette, *Washington Post,* April 14, 2008.

21. For Gelb's expectation of losses in the first three years of his tenure, see Judith H. Dobrzynski, "A Knight at the Opera: Big Plans—Large Bills," *Wall Street Journal (Online),* April 24, 2008. Volpe responded to Gelb's agenda with skepticism: "Mr. Volpe said he had concerns about how the house would pay for Mr. Gelb's ambitious plans. 'Hopefully it will be financed and it will be funded,' he said. 'If it's not, then Peter will have to reconsider.'" Wakin, *Times,* Feb. 14, 2006. For annual reports for the years 2007–08 and 2008–09, and for Form 990 of the Met's Federal Income Tax return for 2010–11, see www.metopera.org. Erica Munk remarks that the Met has been unforthcoming in releasing financial information. See Munk, "The Met's Grand Gamble," *Vanity Fair* (May 2010). Her piece is based on the twelve years of data she "managed to gather." We rely on her analysis.

22. For Gelb on the fiscal crisis, see Wakin, *Times,* Jan. 16, 2009. The endowment was $336 million in fiscal 2007 and $247 million in fiscal 2009.

23. "a decision of": Erica Orden, *New York Magazine* (Feb. 27, 2009). For the depletion of the Met endowment, see Munk, *Vanity Fair* (May 2010). For the Met budget for 2009–10, see Rebecca Olles, *Crain's New York Business,* Oct. 9, 2011. In March 2013, Ziff family contributions were reported to have exceeded $53 million, see Chip Brown, *Times,* March 24, 2013.

24. For the average age of the Met audience, see Charlotte Higgins, *Guardian* (London), Dec. 9, 2011. "we've covered all": Warrick Thompson, "Star Manager Gelb's Live Broadcasts Make 11 Million for Met," *Bloomberg.net,* March 4, 2012. "acknowledged for the": Wakin and Kevin Flynn, *Times,* Oct. 10, 2011. "that competition from": Anthony Tommasini, *Times,* March 15, 2013. Early on, in 2007–08, Opera America and the Metropolitan, working with Shugoll Research, conducted a survey to "analyze the impact of the Met's HD transmissions." See *Opera America* (Fall 2008): 38–44. Given the infancy of the project, the findings were few and tentative. They included the following: the core audience comprised primarily frequent operagoers; the majority of respondents professed to derive equal enjoyment from live opera and simulcasts; most of those who had not been at a live performance in two years agreed that they were likely to attend one in the near future, implying that "HD transmissions may serve to reintroduce these recent non-attendees to opera." But the big question was, and remains, "What has been the impact of HD on opera house attendance?" The research team's tentative conclusion was that "the transmissions may truly be creating a new audience for opera." About Gelb and the HD public, see Tommasini, *Times,* March 15, 2013. "uncommonly high amount": cited in Philip Boroff, "Met Opera to Sell $1 Million in Bonds as Revenue Drops," *Bloomberg,* Dec. 11, 2012.

25. For Gelb on Zeffirelli's *Tosca:* "I promised the Met subscribers when I first came on board—well, I didn't promise anything, but I did say that there were two iconic Zeffirelli productions, *Bohème* and *Turandot,* and that the other Zeffirelli productions are going to be replaced. A lot of these things are just sitting there like lead weights, so there is a lot of catching up to do." Mead, *New Yorker* (Oct. 22, 2007): 143–44. "The Met's New": Midgette, *Washington Post*, Sept. 22, 2009. "An uneven, muddled": Ross, *New Yorker* (Oct. 5, 2009): 84. "puny and halfhearted": F. Paul Driscoll, *Opera News* (Dec. 2009): 53. "A Kinky Take": Tommasini, Sept. 23, 2009. "Schweinerei": Walter Dobner, *Die Presse,* June 30, 2010. "Volgare verismo": Paolo Isotta, *Corriere della Sera,* April 24, 2012. "Refreshingly blasphemous edge": Andrea Kohler, *Neue Zürcher Zeitung,* Sept. 3, 2009. "life and relevance": Adam Margulies, *Opera Britannia,* Oct. 1, 2009.

26. For the booing of *Tosca,* see Charles Affron and Mirella Jona Affron, *Times,* Sept. 27, 2009. "fiasco": Brown, *Times,* March 24, 2013.

27. Patrice Caurier and Moshe Leiser directed and Christian Fenouillat designed the 2010 *Hamlet.* Ferdinand Wögerbauer designed the 2010 *Boris Godunov.* Bob Crowley designed the 2010 *Don Carlo.*

28. Offenbach's posthumous score has often been rearranged; the 2009–10 version contained much music never before heard at the Met. Levine was criticized for

not adopting musicologist Michael Kaye's recent scholarly edition. For Sher on Hoff-mann's character: "I think Offenbach had that sense of anxiety and outsiderness that comes with being Jewish. I think it was his core." Barry Singer, "Bartlett's Quotations," *Opera News* (Dec. 2009): 28. "enough time to": Munk, *Vanity Fair* (May 2010). "political instability": Anna Battista, "Prada at the Opera," www.dazeddigital.com, Feb. 23, 2010. "stage picture . . . all": Heidi Waleson, *Wall Street Journal*, March 4, 2010.

29. "reconceptions . . . are as": Tommasini, *Times*, Jan. 3, 2011. Wolfgang Guss-mann designed the 2010 *La Traviata*.

30. "the thumbprint of": William R. Braun (July 2010): 43.

31. Ross, "Metamorphosis," *New Yorker*, 89–90. Ross, "Crack-up at the Met," May 23, 2012, www.newyorker.com.

32. "from the outside": Justin Davidson, *New York* (Dec. 12, 2011). "acknowl-edged what many": Wakin, *Times*, Oct. 11, 2012.

33. "a dramaturgical traditionalist": Matt Dobkin, *New York* (Jan. 8, 2006). "For some people": Munk, *Vanity Fair* (May 2010). Luisi appears to share Levine's view of trendy restagings: "He avoids working with directors who stage radical reinterpreta-tions of opera story lines. Instead, the conductor looks for meaning in the score, which he calls his 'codex.'" Jennifer Maloney, *Wall Street Journal*, April 7, 2012.

34. "big, old-fashioned-looking": Waleson, *Wall Street Journal (Online)*, Sept. 25, 2012. "dramatic mishmash": Martin Bernheimer, *Financial Times*, Sept. 26, 2012. "hardly a bold": Tommasini, *Times*, Jan. 2, 2013. "this *Don Giovanni*": Tom-masini, *Times*, Oct. 15, 2011.

35. "maximum-security facility": Rupert Christiansen, *Daily Telegraph* (Lon-don), June 24, 2010. "This rejiggered *Rigoletto*": Eric Myers, *Daily Variety*, Feb. 1, 2013. *Un Ballo in maschera* was designed by Paul Steinberg. *Rigoletto* was designed by Christine Jones.

36. "contrarian yet predictable": Baker (Feb. 2012): 50. "the grimness and": Tom-masini, Dec. 1, 2011. Robert Brill designed the 2011 *Faust*. "perfectly suited to": Waleson, *Wall Street Journal (Online)*, Feb. 19, 2013. "so stuffed full": Silverman, *Associated Press*, April 5, 2013. "all the theatrical": Waleson, *Wall Street Journal (Online)*, April 8, 2013. *Parsifal* was designed by Michael Levine. *Giulio Cesare* was designed by Robert Jones.

37. "magical in every respect": Waleson, *Wall Street Journal (Online)*, Oct. 24, 2012.

38. "tectonic," Lepage in *Wagner's Dream*.

39. "worth its weight": Silverman, *Associated Press*, Sept. 28, 2010. "audience . . . spellbound": Claire Prentice, *Daily Telegraph* (London), Sept. 29, 2010. "playing with toys": Bernheimer, *Financial Times*, Sept. 29, 2010. "The current conventional": Fred Cohn, *Opera News* (Dec. 2010): 59.

40. "a policy prompted": Wakin. "less an interpretation": *Opera News* (April 2012): 54. "The public is": Ibid. (May 2012): 80. For other instances of Gelb's attempts to suppress criticism of his regime, see *Times*, May 21, 2012.

41. "My point was": Brown, *Times*, March 24, 2013.

42. "a certain amount": *Times*, May 17, 2013.

# INDEX OF NAMES, TITLES, AND FOREIGN-LANGUAGE MUSICAL TERMS

*In addition to proper names and titles of works, the index includes opera houses and companies with their locations, as well as the first instance of the use of foreign-language musical terms, which are defined in parentheses. Page numbers for illustrations are in italic, followed by* fig *for figures and* tab *for tables. Years listed in subentries are given in* **boldface**.

Beczala, Piotr, 382
Beecham, Sir Thomas, 129, 167, 170–72, 178, 192
Beethoven, Ludwig van, 54, 157–58
Behrens, Hildegard, 295, 301, 303, 365
Belasco Theatre (New York), 88
Belasco, David, 86–89, *87fig,* 401n16
Bel Geddes, Norman, 197
Bellini, Vincenzo, 9, 11–13, 20–22, 346, 394n20
Belmont, August, 13, 123
Belmont, Eleanor (Mrs. August, Jr.), 123, 126–27, 141, 143, 162, 182–83, 197–98, 199, 229, 328, 336
Belohlávek, Jirí, *330tab*
Beňačková, Gabriela, 329, 331, 420n22
Bennett, James Gordon, 39
Bennett, John, 201
Bennett, Max, 201
Benois, Alexander, *97tab*
Benois, Nicola, *267tab*
*Benvenuto Cellini* (Berlioz), 371; **2003–04,** 345
Berg, Alban, 215
Berger, Erna, 162, 290
Berghart & Co., *74tab, 95–97tab*
Berglund, Joel, 145
Bergman, Gustav, 159
Bergman, Ingmar, 254–55
Bergonzi, Carlo, 210, 212–13, 298, 303
Berkowitz, Phoebe, 284
Berlioz, Hector, 345
Berman, Eugene, 211, 213
Bernardi, Mario, 292
Bernhardt, Sarah, 6, 14, 47, 72
Bernheimer, Martin, 251, 302
Bernstein, Leonard, 188, 214, 229–30, 251, 253, 256, 258, 275, 305, 363
Berry, Walter, 244
*Betrothal in a Monastery* (Prokofiev), 335
Bianco, Pieretto, *98tab, 106tab*
Billinghurst, Sarah, 311, 335
*Billy Budd* (Britten): **1978–79,** 279
Bing, Rudolf, 73, 168, 182–210, *185fig, 208fig,* 210, 212, 214–18, 220–27, 229–31, 234, 236–38, 240–41, 243, 245–51, 253–56, 259, 266, 271, 274, 298, 308, 310–11, 317, 320, 328, 341–42, 348, 352, 356–57, 362, 374, 389
Bizet, Georges, 19
Björling, Jussi, 149, 157, 190, 356

Blech, Leo, *96tab*
Bledsoe, Jules, 205–6
Blegen, Judith, 284
Bliss, Anthony, 204, 229, 243, 253, 259, 264–66, 270–74, 276, 283–84, 288–89, 292, 294, 297, 306, 307, 311, 352, 354, 371
Bliss, Cornelius N., 124, 129, 147–48, 264
Blitzstein, Mark, 194, 240
Bloch, Max, 92
Blomdahl, Karl-Birger, 254
Bloomberg, 422n10
*Bluebeard's Castle* (Bartók): **1973–74,** 260, 263; **1988–89,** 299, 302
*Blue Bird, The [L'Oiseau Bleu]* (Wolff), *106tab*
Blythe, Stephanie, 302, 345, 348, 388
*Boccaccio* (von Suppé): **1930–31,** 120
Bodanya, Natalie, 146
Bodanzky, Artur, 67, 118–19, 131, 133, 137, 151, 153–54, 173, 187
Bogianckino, Massimo, 253, 268
*Bohème, La* (Puccini), 69, 82, 87, 111, 143, 168; **1900–01,** 47, 71, 297; **1909–10,** 68, 84; **1936–37,** 151; **1952–53,** 220, 285; **1965–66,** 223; **1968–69,** 315; **1976–77,** 273, 281, 358; **1980–81,** 285–86, *286fig,* 295, 300–301; recording) 165
Böhm, Karl, 183, 215–16, 244
Bohnen, Michael, 205
Boieldieu, François-Adrien, *29tab,* 395n4
Boito, Arrigo, 16
Bolcom, Michael, 314–15
*Bolivar* (Milhaud), 166
Bolm, Adolph, *98tab*
Bolshoi Opera (Moscow), 328–29, 332, 336
Bolton, Michael, 351
Bonaparte, Joseph, 11
Bonci, Alessandro, 68, 201
Bondy, Luc, 373–74, 390
Bongiovanni, Mia, 422n2
Bonnefous, Jean-Pierre, 287
Bonynge, Richard, 251, 300
Boosey & Hawkes, 216
Booth, Edwin, 6
Borda, Deborah, 349
Bori, Lucrezia, 84, 99, 111–12, 119, 122–24, 126, 129, 134, 161, 179
*Boris Godunov,* 91, 147, 171, 332; **1912–13,** 327–28; **1921–22,** 327; **1943–44,** 166; **1990–91,** 329; **2010–11,** 375–76
Borodin, Alexander, 327, 335

Novak, Joseph, 170
Novotna, Jarmila, 160, 174, 175, 176, 77
*Nozze di Figaro, Le* (Mozart), 134, 170, 172,
    177; **1893–94**, 44; **1939–40**, 151, 174;
    **1943–44**, 174–75; **1959–60**, 220; **1965–**
    **66**, 226; **1975–76**, 281; **1985–86**, 320;
    **1998–99**, 325, 346

Oakes, Meredith, 384
Ober, Margarete, 92
*Oberon* (Weber): **1918–19**, 135
Obraztsova, Elena, 328, 420n20
O'Brien, Jack, 364
O'Brien, Timothy, 296
O'Connor, Mark, 351
Odéon, Théâtre de (Paris), 226
*Oedipus Rex* (Stravinsky), 351; **1981–82**, 287
Oenslager, Donald, 178, 280
Offenbach, Jacques, 216
Ohana, Maurice, 259
O'Hearn, Robert, 213, 223, 244, 247–48
Ohms, Elisabeth, 152
Oistrakh, David, 328
Olivero, Magda, 266
Olszewska, Maria, 152
O'Neill, Eugene, 130, 191, 221
Opéra, Théâtre de l' (Paris), 3, 84, 253, 284,
    349, 393n3
Opera Boston (Massachusetts), 372
*Opera News,* 145, 198–199, 379, 388–89
opéra-bouffe (genre of French comic opera
    associated with Offenbach), 216
opéra-comique (genre of French opera with
    spoken dialogue), 6
Opéra-Comique (Paris), 84
*Oracolo, L'* (Leoni), 91
Ordynski, Richard, *98tab, 107tab*
*Orfeo ed Euridice* (Gluck), 170, 172, 307;
    **1893–94**, 44; **1935–36**, 146; **1938–49**, 173;
    **1939–40**, 173; **1941–42**, 173; **2006–07**,
    364
Ormandy, Eugene, 192
Ostling, Daniel, 367
*Otello* (Verdi), 129, 173; **1891–92**, 40, 297;
    **1909–10**, 84; **1937–38**, 149, 173; **1939–40**,
    173; **1945–46**, 174; **1946–47**, 173; **1948–**
    **49**, 357; **1957–58**, 298; **1962–63**, 213;
    **1979–80**, 274; **1993–94**, 318, 332; **1995–**
    **96**, 321; film (Zeffirelli), 316
Otto, Teo, *219tab*

Ötvös, Gabor, 251, 261
Owens, Eric, 388
Ozawa, Seiji, 270, 306, 331, 351

Pacini, Giovanni, 394n20
Paderewski, Ignacy, 51
Pagano, Mauro, *339tab*
*Pagliacci* (Leoncavallo), 71, 82, 102, 356;
    **1893–94**, 44; **1909–10**, 84, 355; **1934–35**,
    131; **1950–51**, 194–96, 341; **1958–59**, 221;
    **1969–70**, 248; **1974–75**, 272; **1977–78**,
    273; **1994–95**, 315
Palmo, Ferdinand, 11, 25
Palmo's Opera House (New York), 11–12
Panizza, Ettore, 151, 174, 176, 187
Pape, René, 345, 348, 365, 376, 383
Pappano, Antonio, 333
Paquereau, Paul, *95–96tab*
*Parade* (Satie; Ravel; Poulenc): **1980–81**, 285
Parker, Horatio, *96tab*
Parravicini, Angelo, *95tab*
Parravicini, Camillo, *121tab*
Parry, William, *48–50tab*
*Parsifal* (Wagner), 32, 91, 94, 134, 155; **1903–**
    **04**, 56–59, 60, 62, 69, 70, 73, 197, 386;
    **1934–35**, 131; **1970–71**, 248; **1978–79**,
    275; **1990–91**, 318; **2012–13**, 365, 381, 383,
    390
Pascoe, John, 302
Pavarotti, Luciano, 259, 280, 281, 284, 287,
    290–91, 315–17, *316fig*, 318, 358
Pears, Peter, 263, 279
*Pêcheurs de perles, Les* (Bizet), 269; **1895–96**,
    44
Peduzzi, Richard, 341, 373
Peel, "Colonel," 297
Peel, Mrs., 297
Peerce, Jan, 192, 328
*Pelléas et Mélisande* (Debussy), 52, 69, 82, 86,
    170, 173; **1924–25**, 108; **1934–35**, 135;
    **1943–44**, 177; **1944–45**, 177; **1994–95**,
    342
Pelly, Laurent, 368, 382
Pergolesi, Giovanni Battista, 130
*Périchole, La* (Offenbach): **1956–57**, 215–17,
    220; recording, 217
Perry, John M., 129
*Peter Grimes* (Britten): **1947–48**, 167, 171,
    179; **1966–67**, 243–44; **1972–73**, 259;
    **1983–84**, 299; **2007–08**, 369–70